Stress Management and Prevention

"This third edition has evolved into a more 'mindfulness' approach to stress management within a positive psychology framework. The student centered explanations to the neuroscience underlying the concepts are presented at a level of complexity that is appreciated by science majors, but reasonably comprehensible to the non-science major as well. The video-based activities and the 'Reflection' exercises provide self-assessment of individual stress levels, which enhances active student engagement. Text content addresses multiple individual and interpersonal health belief models, thus successfully linking theory to practice."—**Ellen Lee, RN, MS, Ed.D., CHES**, adjunct faculty, Department of Health Science, California State University, Fullerton

"An excellent book from which all students of stress management will benefit. From clearly presented theories and concepts to vivid, real-world examples, the information provided by Dr. Chen is stimulating and thought-provoking. Dr. Chen takes more of a positive psychological perspective when presenting stress management topics, not leaving out cultural differences that may exist. The highlighted Reflection boxes are especially helpful in allowing students time to ponder over the information recently read and applying it to their everyday life experiences."—**Dr. Steven J. Radlo, PhD**, associate professor of stress management and sport & exercise psychology, Western Illinois University

"*Stress Management and Prevention: Applications to Daily Life* is a well-organized and remarkable tool for teaching stress management. Students will find the material interesting to read and the exercises throughout the text useful and impactful. Dr. Chen's book delivers scientific research about the effects of stress, along with holistic modalities designed to help students increase their coping skills and the quality of their lives."—**Karen Fazio, MSG, HHP**, gerontologist, holistic health practitioner, health science and gerontology instructor, California State University, Fullerton

"*Stress Management and Prevention* by Dr. Chen is both insightful and comprehensive, while being understandable and straightforward. He has written a book that anyone can digest, regardless of their stress management knowledge. The real-life examples are immediately applicable, allowing for instant absorption. A fantastic piece of work."—**Gina Harmston, MS**, Department of Kinesiology, Department of Health Science, California State University, Fullerton

Gain a critical understanding of the nature of stress from a positive psychology framework that allows you to look beyond a simple pathology of stress-related symptoms. This new edition of *Stress Management and Prevention* integrates Eastern and Western concepts of stress while emphasizing an experiential approach to learning through the use of exercises, activities, and self-reflection. This student-friendly text contains chapters on conflict resolution, mindfulness meditation, time management, prevention of health risks, and cognitive restructuring. Included throughout are an emphasis on mindfulness and the neuroscience behind it, more theories, and new techniques for stress reduction and time management. An updated companion website includes even more video-based activities so students can see techniques in practice.

David D. Chen, PhD, is a professor of kinesiology at California State University, Fullerton.

Stress Management and Prevention
Applications to Daily Life

Third Edition

DAVID D. CHEN

Routledge
Taylor & Francis Group

NEW YORK AND LONDON

Third edition published 2017
by Routledge
711 Third Avenue, New York, NY 10017

and by Routledge
2 Park Square, Milton Park, Abingdon, Oxon, OX14 4RN

Routledge is an imprint of the Taylor & Francis Group, an informa business

First edition published by Brooks Cole 2007

Second edition published by Routledge 2011

Library of Congress Cataloging in Publication Data
Names: Chen, David D.
Title: Stress management and prevention : applications to daily life / David D. Chen.
Description: Third edition. | New York, NY : Routledge, 2017. | Previous edition: Stress management and
prevention : applications to everyday life /Jeffrey A. Kottler and David D. Chen.
Includes bibliographical references and index.
Identifiers: LCCN 2015047129| ISBN 9781138906280 (alk. paper) | ISBN 9781315695594 (alk. paper)
Subjects: LCSH: Stress management--Textbooks.
Classification:
LCC RA785 .K68 2017
DDC 616.9/8--dc23
LC record available at http://lccn.loc.gov/2015047129

ISBN: 978-1-138-90628-0 (pbk)
ISBN: 978-1-315-69559-4 (ebk)

Typeset in Times New Roman
by Servis Filmsetting Ltd, Stockport, Cheshire

Visit the companion website for this title: www.routledge.com/cw/chen

Brief Contents

Contents

Part II: Strategies of Stress Management and Prevention   145

A Personal Introduction
From the Author to the Students

Welcome to the journey of stress management and prevention! I feel that I must be one of the luckiest guys in the world I know. Ironically, it all has to do with being stressed out during the earlier part of my career (you will get the story later in this introduction). The usual approach to the subject of stress is that it is altogether a bad thing that must be "managed," if not eliminated, at all costs. However, when you take a class on stress management, learning such stress reduction techniques as deep breathing, mindfulness meditation, progressive muscle relaxation, yoga, tai chi, journaling, time management, and visualization, to mention a few of the options, you will find out how much it will transform your life for the better. Like many of my students, they may regret not having taken it at an earlier time. But I have to give you a sobering fact, namely, learning and practicing stress management and prevention skills requires lots of self-discipline, significant time, energy, and commitment in order to make the changes last over time.

The reality is that most people don't stick with diets, exercise programs, or stress-reduction plans for very long. That is one reason why there is always a new best-selling book on the market that promises immediate, dramatic results—with little effort. That is also why, a few years after you graduate from college, little that you learned will stick with you. One reason for this is a lack of relevance of the content to your personal interests and goals. Another is that the material may not have been introduced to you in a way that was compelling or interesting.

KEY QUESTIONS

- What are the reasons that you have not maintained important changes in your life, especially those related to your health?

- In which classes have you learned the most? What contributed to that learning remaining a permanent part of your life?

- What have been the most critical incidents that have occurred in your life and how have they impacted on the choices you have made, as well as those you are considering in the future?

- After reading the personal story of the author, what might you expect from what will follow?

You may *never* have a learning experience that is more directly related to your success and satisfaction in life than this class on stress management and prevention. My goal is to assist your instructor so that this experience will not only teach you some new skills to reduce the stress in your life in the present and the future, but also to help you approach the inevitable pressures in life in such a way that you can perform at peak levels—whether in school, on the job, or in the relationships that mean the most to you.

You already know, from previous experience, what it takes not only to learn something, but to make it part of who you are and the ways you function characteristically. In order for the methods in this class to become a permanent part of your repertoire, several factors must be operating:

1. *You must actively engage with the content.* You can't just read about the subject, or listen to lectures about it; you must think critically about the material and try it out for yourself.

2. *You must personalize and adapt the learning to your particular needs.* With anything that you read it is legitimate for you to ask yourself what this has to do with your life. You are the one who must figure out ways to take these ideas and apply them in ways that mean the most to you.

3. *Practice and rehearsal are a necessary part of any systematic learning program.* At first, new skills seem awkward and time-consuming. Over time, with diligence and effort, they become as easy for you as driving a car (which once seemed awkward and frustrating). In order for you to be willing to devote the time and energy into practicing new skills, without increasing your stress levels, you'll need to feel as if the effort is worth the outcome.

4. *Finally, you need a support system to reinforce your efforts.* It may be fairly difficult for you to undertake new behaviors unless you are surrounded by those who support what you are doing. That is one distinct advantage of having classmates who are part of this same journey.

With these cautions in mind, I invite you to keep an open mind to the ideas that will be presented to you, as well as to think critically and realistically about what you are prepared to do in your life, and what you are not. You certainly have enough stressful circumstances that you don't need additional burdens, or commitments, unless they can be demonstrated to lighten your load significantly. I aim to show you how to do that—not just from solid theory and research, but also based on your own experiences.

A textbook such as this not only involves presentations of content, but also engages you in a process. This is, after all, a very personal subject: I am talking about those times when you are most vulnerable and most helpless. If I expect you to reflect honestly on those instances when you feel most flooded by anxiety (as well as what you can do about it), then I must be willing to do the same to earn your trust and respect. My expertise in the areas of kinesiology, sport psychology, cognitive psychology, pedagogy, health science, and stress, tai chi, and qigong is informed not only by my research, teaching, and practice, but also by my personal history.

I first felt attracted to the subject of stress management because I experienced so much stress in my life. At age 23, I came to pursue my graduate studies in America with very limited financial resources and no relatives here. I left behind my family and my wife whom I had married just a few weeks prior to boarding the plane. I was totally alone and utterly unsure about my future.

After several days spent recuperating from jet lag and adjusting to my new home in rural Florida, a new semester immediately started. I was scheduled to take four graduate classes that were intense and demanding. I worked my heart out for these courses, each of which required a huge term paper (in English rather than Mandarin!). I spent seven consecutive sleepless nights cranking out those papers. Although I was pleased to receive excellent grades, I also began to experience chest pains, as well as difficulty breathing. I medicated myself with aspirin and tried to take it easy, and noticed some relief of symptoms. Later, I began jogging regularly and playing basketball, which helped immensely.

My stress started to build again about the time I completed my graduate studies. First, we found out that my wife was pregnant with our first child. Second, I began my first teaching job and had to prepare four conference presentations simultaneously. On the inside, I felt almost paralyzed with stress, but I behaved as if I had everything under control.

During this time, I stopped exercising and began eating junk food because it was cheap and convenient. I recognized the same symptoms of breathlessness that I had experienced earlier. After strolling for a few minutes, I started to feel light-headed and experienced increasing chest pains. I fell to the ground, clutching my chest, in the throes of what I believed was a massive heart attack.

I recovered that evening, figuring it had been a false alarm. When the symptoms returned the following morning, my wife drove me immediately to the hospital. We had no health insurance and very little money, so the thought of paying the hospital bill only added to my sense of impending doom. By the time the doctor came in to see me, I burst out sobbing. I cried so hard that I couldn't speak. After consulting with several specialists, I eventually learned that my heart-attack-like symptoms were induced by severe stress. Until I learned to control these symptoms, I would remain vulnerable to both stomach ailments as well as other distressing feelings.

This experience got my attention like nothing else could. I began to examine the ways I conducted my life, especially my tendency to procrastinate and put things off until the last minute. I had been a competitive athlete in China, but had virtually given up exercise after arriving in America because I was so driven to succeed academically. Within days after the hospital visit, I started practicing tai chi, a form of moving meditation I will teach you later in this book.

I wish I could tell you that I lived happily ever after—that upon embarking on this plan to manage the pressures in my life, I have been stress-free ever since. However, life stressors seemed to arise in proportion to the speed I learned to adapt.

Playing basketball or practicing tai chi didn't seem to put a dent in the pressure that had now migrated from my chest down to my stomach. I began experiencing severe stomach problems. Rather than surrendering, however, I decided to apply what I had been learning all these years about health. I knew that, in order to deal with severe stress like this, I had to take care of my body, my mind, *and* my soul. I learned that physical fitness is just one component of well-being. In order to be healed and healthy, I must enhance the other parts of my life including work productivity, interpersonal communication, and spirituality. Most of what you will read in this book I have tested personally and have applied to my own life.

One of my great opportunities came when I was assigned to teach stress management, a general education class on our campus. My skills and knowledge about stress

management and prevention began to expand and deepen with teaching. Imagine that my students only hear me teach the concepts and skills of stress reduction once while I have heard myself countless times to the point that these great ideas find their way into my feelings and actions. Another important skill I learned to manage my stress is counting blessings and showing gratitude. So, let me sincerely show my gratitude to my mentor and collaborator Dr. Jeffrey Kottler who generously let me take over the book. I am grateful to my wife and children whose love and support sustained my motivation during the revision of this edition.

FOR REFLECTION

Note: This is the first of many reflective exercises and activities that you will be asked to complete throughout this book, as well as the accompanying workbook. They are intended to help you put into practice the principles associated with lasting change. In other words, if you want the things you learn in this class to stick with you over your lifetime, rather than merely memorize and forget them after the semester is over, then it is critical for you to apply the ideas to your own life. This means taking an active part in reflecting on the content and making it relevant to your particular situation. Personalizing the concepts and applying the principles to your daily life will help you make changes in your own life.

In the personal story of your author, I disclosed a few of the critical incidents of my life that have most shaped who I am, including career and personal lifestyle choices. Note below several of *your* most significant life experiences that influenced you, for better or worse.

1.

2.

3.

4.

How have these particular incidents continued to influence and affect you?

SUMMARY

In this personal introduction to the text, I have tried to be honest and realistic regarding what lies ahead. I can't imagine that there is any class you could ever take that could be more valuable and transformative than one that teaches you to prevent and manage stress. Such skills will not only help you to be more productive and perform at higher levels in all areas of your life but, just as importantly, will help you to find greater enjoyment in what you are doing and how you are living.

My personal introduction was intended to demonstrate that although I have some expertise in the area of stress, conducting research in this area and teaching the class for many years, I am also a work in progress. I so enjoy studying this area because I find it so personally relevant. I hope my own story intrigues and inspires you enough to trust that what I have to offer has been tested not only by research in the field, but by my own experiences. As much as possible, I try to practice what I will teach you.

No matter what you view as your own strengths or weaknesses, no matter what your personality is like, or your life experiences, or what you have endured or suffered, or how you feel vulnerable, you *can* make great strides in your personal functioning. This study of stress management will teach you what you need to know to function more effectively in every aspect of your life.

About the Author

David D. Chen is professor of kinesiology at California State University, Fullerton. He has authored and co-authored more than 20 research articles in the areas of motor learning, sport psychology, stress reduction, and tai chi. His research interests include mindfulness practices, human performance under stress, feedback strategies in motor skill learning, and self-regulated learning. He has taught or is teaching stress management, motor control and motor dysfunction, motor control and learning, advanced studies in teaching human movement, motor development, sport psychology, and tai chi. He has been a consultant of stress reduction for corporations and organizations and is an adjunct professor for an institute of oriental medicine in Los Angeles.

Understanding the Nature of Stress

1

The Meaning of Stress

It is Monday morning and the sun is just beginning to peek over the horizon, casting a dim shadow through the slats of the window blinds. In the mostly darkened room you can see the barest outline of a body sitting at a desk with his head cradled in his arms, resting near a laptop. The surface of the desk is littered with papers, cups half-filled with coffee, crushed cans of caffeinated energy drinks, and the remnants of pizza crust. If you look closer you can see that the person, although half-dead to the world, is not quite sleeping: his eyes are barely open, red, and blurry. It has been a long night without sleep and Blaine has been prepping for an exam scheduled that morning, as well as a paper due in the afternoon.

Somehow, someway, Blaine has *got* to regain some energy to get through the day, stay awake through his classes, and then show up for his part-time job. It's been especially tough lately with money so tight and getting worse. He can't afford to miss a day of work or he'll risk lowering his main source of income. With problems of their own, his parents are in no position to help him much.

To make matters even more challenging, Blaine and his girlfriend have been fighting lately. She complains that they never seem to have much time to be together anymore—and when they do hang out, he is so tired that all he wants to do is watch TV or play computer games. In addition, he just hasn't been feeling well lately. Headaches have been occurring with greater frequency. He isn't sleeping well—when he finds the time to sleep at all. His grades are slipping because he can't find the time to study as much as he'd like. About the only thing that gives Blaine some relief is drinking beer with friends, but then he has trouble waking up the next morning to make his early class. He wonders how he will ever dig himself out of this hole.

Although this scenario is not exactly uncommon among college students, I hope that it isn't too familiar to you. Unlike some people you may know whom stress has buried beyond recovery, Blaine actually made significant progress in regaining control of his life. A friend had recommended that he take a stress management class so they could coordinate their schedules. As it happened, Blaine agreed, mostly because it was offered at a convenient time and seemed like an easy grade. But once he began learning about the cumulative effects of stress on his body and well-being, Blaine began experimenting with some of the methods introduced in class and his text. More than anything else, it was the social support he felt from others in the class that encouraged him to incorporate the new stress reduction strategies into his life.

Regardless of your particular age, gender, socioeconomic background, major, family situation, and the college you are attending, managing stress effectively is perhaps the single most important skill to get the most from your experience and perform at the highest level. Among "nontraditional" adult students, who represent one-third of college enrollment, there are added challenges to balance school with jobs, family, and personal responsibilities (Giancola, Grawitch, & Borchert, 2009). According to a number of surveys of college students conducted by the Associated Press (2009), the American College Health Association (2009), and the *Chronicle of Higher Education* (2008), 85% report that stress is a major problem and the single greatest obstacle to success. Apart from actual performance in classes and grades achieved, excessive stress affects almost every aspect of life satisfaction. In recent times, economic problems have led to cutbacks in classes, staff, faculty, and services on campus. Scholarships have been reduced during a time when three-quarters of all students graduate with debt (Berg-Gross & Green, 2010).

Stress means different things to different people. To some, it represents a complete breakdown in their lives; to others, it means a minor annoyance that is best ignored, or tolerated; and in some circumstances, stress means an opportunity to rise to new levels of performance in a variety of areas. Some people tolerate stress reasonably well, some fall apart, and others hardly seem to notice the pressure in the first place.

KEY QUESTIONS IN THE CHAPTER

- What are the different ways that stress can be defined and conceptualized?

- What are the different ways that people respond to adversity in their lives?

- How can you assess the signs and symptoms of stress as they occur in yourself and others?

- Stress is ordinarily thought of as a fairly negative state, something to be avoided whenever possible. But how can stress be highly functional and operate as a survival mechanism?

- What is the general adaptation syndrome (GAS) and how does it function during times of stress?

- What is the primary goal of stress management? Can such a program completely eliminate stress?

- What are major sources of stress and how are they recognized?

- How do you interpret the following statement: "Stress is not what exists on the outside, but how you perceive a situation on the inside"?

- How does the dynamical systems theory interpret stress and stress coping? What are the six key concepts of the dynamical systems theory?

What *Is* Stress Anyway?

This may seem like a rather obvious question. *Everyone* knows what stress is or, at the very least, knows when they are experiencing it firsthand or witnessing its effects on someone close to them.

Stress is that feeling when you can't seem to sit still, when your thoughts are racing and you feel out of control. Your body feels tense, as if tied into a knot. You feel revved up but can't figure out where to direct your energy. Time pressures weigh down on you. Concentration seems difficult.

Intense pressure: you feel it in your neck, in your back, in your belly. You notice your jaw muscles are clenched. There is, perhaps, a throbbing in your head. Your heart rate has increased, and your hands feel clammy.

This is stress, or at least some of the symptoms. As you will learn, there are many others that you will learn to recognize, and understand how they develop. There are also different kinds of stress, some of which break down your body and mind while others actually help you perform at peak levels.

One definition of **stress** is that it represents both a psychological and a physiological reaction to a real or perceived threat that requires some action or resolution. It is a response that operates on cognitive, behavioral, and biological levels that, when sustained and chronic, results in significant negative health effects (Linden, 2005). Stress is, therefore, what happens when life exerts pressure on us, but also the way it makes us feel. According to landmark brain researcher Bruce McEwen (McEwen, 2002; McEwen & Wingfield, 2010), it is both a stimulus *and* a response.

A more humorous (and perhaps accurate) description of stress is offered by Elkin (1999, p. 24) as the condition created when "your mind overrides the body's basic desire to choke the living daylights out of some idiot who desperately deserves it." (Note: There is a high likelihood that your friends and family are going to ask what you are learning in "that stress class you are taking." Please offer them the first definition rather than the second one.)

Stress is actually a survival mechanism, programmed a long time ago, to increase internal awareness of danger and transform all the body's resources to a heightened state of readiness. It is, essentially, the experience of *perceived* attack. It doesn't matter whether the threat is real or not; the **autonomic nervous system** (think "automatic") is activated. This system works well only when it turns itself on and off within a reasonable period of time so as to not wear out its welcome (and deplete your energy). Unfortunately, half of all Americans report significant stress in their lives. Even more disturbingly, according to a recent survey, most people don't intend to do anything about it (Schuler, 2006).

There is a fairly good possibility that you are experiencing some degree of stress in your life right now, perhaps this very minute. How do you know when you are stressed? Stress responses have some common symptoms and signs, but they are also highly individualized, impacting your body, your internal thoughts, your emotional reactions, and your behavior (see Table 1.2 later in the chapter).

Stress symptoms are the body's way of getting your attention to tell you: *Look, you've got to get your act together. I'm a little tired of you running me ragged. I'm going to annoy you until you do something about this situation. And if you don't pay attention to me, well then, I'll just have to figure out more ways to get to you.*

If your body could talk to you, it might communicate this message. The problem is that stress symptoms are not always obvious and direct; sometimes they can become disguised or rather subtle and their messages somewhat clouded.

Meanings of Stress

Trey thought he had things under control. He was well organized and intentional in almost everything he did. He had a plan for his life and clear ideas about just how he wanted to reach his goals.

In addition to his college courses, Trey had a good job and was well respected at work. There were opportunities for advancement within the company and almost no limit to how far he could rise, especially after he completed his degree. He was involved in a long-term relationship with Mia, whom he had been seeing since they were both 16.

Trey was doing well in school, enjoyed a good social life with friends, and was getting along well with his family. He was in good health, exercised regularly, and—except for a fondness for Hawaiian pizza with extra ham—monitored his diet.

So it was all the more surprising, given how well everything seemed to be going in his life, that he suddenly (or maybe it was gradually—he couldn't remember) started to lose control. First the headaches started, and this was highly unusual for him; he was almost never sick. He tried to ignore them and, when that didn't work, starting consuming up to a dozen aspirin a day to reduce the throbbing.

Eventually, Trey decided to visit his doctor, but after a thorough physical exam, no physiological cause was found. His blood pressure was a little high, as was his cholesterol, but otherwise he was in reasonably good shape.

"They seem to be stress headaches," the doctor suggested to him. "Are you under a lot of pressure lately?"

Trey shrugged. "Not really," he replied. "Everything is going pretty well in my life. I've got everything under control." These were the mantras of his life, his trademark responses every time anyone asked him how things were going. Indeed, Trey was much admired by friends and family alike for his calm, controlled demeanor and ability to keep things under control.

Here is the key question: what is the particular *meaning* of Trey's stress symptoms? Later, when he was asked this question by a friend who had taken a stress management class, all Trey could do was shake his head in frustration.

It turned out that Trey's strengths were also his weaknesses. He was absolutely relentless in his desire to maintain control and keep everything on course to follow his plan. He would be graduating in two years (19 months to be exact). He and his girlfriend would then get married and have four children, two of each gender. By then he would be a regional manager for the company. They'd own a home in a particular neighborhood that appealed to him. He even knew what kind of car he wanted once he had achieved his success.

So, what's the problem? And why would a stress response like headaches emerge just when things seemed to be so under control? What was the meaning of stress in Trey's life? How were these symptoms trying to get his attention to look at something he was ignoring? (See For Reflection 1.1.)

Avoiding the situation did not work for Trey, nor did medicating himself first with aspirin and later with increasing quantities of beer. The headaches worsened. Then other symptoms developed, including a skin rash.

It took some time before Trey confronted what was going on in his life. He realized eventually that he so over-structured and controlled his life that he didn't ever have to think about where he was headed and whether, in fact, he actually wanted to reach the goals that he had declared. As it turned out, he was very fond of his girlfriend but he didn't love her, and he certainly didn't want to spend the rest of his life with her. But for years he hadn't wanted to hurt her feelings. He wanted to do the right thing, so that meant continuing to live a lie.

And this great job he had, and bright future with the company? He never really wanted to be in business. That was the influence of his father, who was so proud of him. Now that he realized it, Trey had no idea what he wanted to do with his life because it had never seemed like he had a choice.

Now that the headaches had forced him to stop doing what he was doing, Trey had the opportunity to actually consider where he was headed and whether he really wanted to go there. Once he discovered the particular meaning of stress in his life, the headaches went away (although the skin rash stuck around for almost a year afterwards, a residual reminder to follow through on his new commitments). Finding meaning in stress is thus not just an academic exercise but often is absolutely necessary to put life challenges in perspective and allow you to restore feelings of well-being after experiencing disappointment or trauma (Fontana & Rosenheck, 2005).

What's in a Name?

Stress is the name given to the pressure that cracks bridges or the force that places strain on an object or body. It is synonymous with tension, fatigue, failure, trauma, or difficulty. The word is derived from the Middle English *stresse*, meaning "hardship," and the Old French *estrece*, meaning "oppression." More often than not, the subject of stress is thought of in the most negative terms possible—it is something to be managed, or at least tolerated, but rarely understood.

The term has cropped up in medicine since the seventeenth century, recognized by physicians as the cause of physical illnesses that might result from social pressure. It came into common usage during the 1950s when a Canadian biologist, Hans Selye, first published a book that adapted the concept of strain on physical structures from engineering to describe what happens to the human body during times of crisis. In retrospect, Selye didn't much like the term after it became popular—much preferring "strain"—but by then it was too late (you can't exactly issue a word recall).

FOR REFLECTION 1.1

What ideas might you have as to what stress could mean in Trey's life? What might he be ignoring that needs attention? What are the principal repeating themes in this narrative?

Given that control and (over)planning are such an ingrained part of Trey's life, is it any wonder that this might suppress other desires and dreams that he does not allow himself to think about?

There are several important questions that are useful in identifying the meaning of disguised or subtle stress. Consider each of them in response to Trey's situation.

1. What does Trey need to look at that he might be ignoring?

2. How are the stress symptoms capturing Trey's attention?

3. What might the symptoms be communicating to him?

4. What would it be like if he tried doing something else, or followed another path?

Think of a situation in your own life in which you feel perplexed by chronic symptoms of distress that won't go away no matter what you do. Ask yourself some of the same questions that you applied to Trey's case: what particular meaning does the problem have in the larger context of your life? In other words, what function might it be serving to get you to examine something important that you might be ignoring?

The seventeenth century of Rousseau, Descartes, and Locke was called the "Age of Reason"; poet and essayist W. H. Auden announced in his Pulitzer Prize-winning verse of the same name that the twentieth century was the "Age of Anxiety." This catchphrase soon became popular, resulting in dozens of books about how to find the balanced life during a time with so much daily pressure. In 1983, the cover of *Time* magazine proclaimed that we now live in an "Age of Stress." Our lives are "consumed by demands for our resources and threats to our well-being" (Hobfoll, 1998).

Judging by the hundreds of books and thousands of articles published each year on the subject, stress has become the obsession of our time. Doctors warn about the epidemic of health problems that result from excessive stress. Employers worry about the effects on absenteeism and work productivity. Relationship experts cite stress as a main factor in divorce and other interpersonal conflicts.

The problem of stress has become so pervasive that people flock to courses on stress management, meditation, and yoga. Individuals hire personal trainers and join health clubs, while businesses hire consultants to reduce stress in the workplace. Stress has become the universal challenge of our time, the condition that can suck the fun out of life and kill us just as surely as any plague we faced in ancient times.

How Is Stress a Problem?

It has been estimated that 75% to 90% of all visits to a primary care physician are because of stress-related disorders (Rosch, 1991). These include stomach ailments, tension headaches, high blood pressure, addictions, and almost any other disease you can think of. Stress is linked to the six leading causes of death in North America (see For Reflection 1.2). The American Institute of Stress (2015) estimates that job stress costs US industry over $300 billion annually. The main sources of work-related stress include accidents, absenteeism, employee turnover, diminished productivity, and direct medical, legal, and insurance costs.

FOR REFLECTION 1.2

What *are* the six leading causes of death in North America? See if you can name them:

1.

2.

3.

4.

5.

6.

Answers are at the end of the chapter.

Nine out of ten adults report that they have experienced serious stress at some time in their lives; almost half of these people say that their symptoms were serious enough to disrupt their lives. Some people experience stress to the point where they cannot function well on a daily basis, cannot enjoy a decent night's sleep, and feel ravaged by the effects in such a way that their relationships are impaired and their productivity compromised.

Consider yourself fortunate if you are managing to cope reasonably well with the stresses you face in your life. Rest assured that there will come a time in the near future when you will be tested in ways you never imagined. Preparation is the key to preventing serious problems; hence, the purpose of this text is to equip you with those skills you will find so helpful during times of crisis.

Stress as a Stimulus or Response

In both the physical and psychological worlds, stress implies a judgment that something is damaged as a result of extreme pressure. For our purposes, in talking about stress in relation to human functioning, it is most often thought of as either a **stimulus** or a **response**. In the first case, stress is the description we give for someone or something that is putting pressure on us to do something that feels beyond comfortable limits. It is an external pressure ("Could you help me write this paper?"), event (earthquake), or incident (car accident) that produces a response.

In the second case, with stress as a response, it represents the *result* of internal or external pressure. Regardless of what happened in the outside world, the internal mechanisms of the body and mind activate stressful reactions.

In both instances, you can see a clear linkage between something that happens in the world and how the person responds afterwards. **Stressors** are those stimuli in the environment or daily life that result in *perceived* pressure. Perception is a key factor in this definition because people respond in such different ways to exactly the same stimuli. For instance, imagine the following: Your instructor announces that she has changed the requirements of the course and now expects you and all your classmates to come up in front of the room and tell a story about the time you each felt most stressed in your life. We're willing to bet that some people might respond to this invitation with abject terror ("Oh my gosh! I can't do that!"). And yet, there are a few others who would rub their hands together with glee, thinking to themselves: "What fun! That sounds *so* interesting."

There are some stressors that would likely produce anxiety in almost anyone (death of a loved one, catastrophic illness, divorce in the family, loss of a job, failing a class) and others that depend on a number of factors including a person's prior experiences and history, personality style, resources available, and resilience. Regardless of these variables, research consistently finds that certain life events act as stressors to produce extreme emotional reactions that include anxiety, depression, and other negative emotions.

TABLE 1.1 Stress as a stimulus or a response

Stimulus	Response
• She's stressing me out with her demands.	• I am so stressed after the exam.
• The deadline is putting stress on me.	• I feel the stress in my shoulders and my neck.
• This class is so stressful the way the instructor organizes things.	• When you said that, you made me so upset afterwards.

A Selected History of Stress Research

It is only relatively recently in human history that stress has become a major issue of discussion—in the previous centuries people usually died before the ravages of stress-related illnesses could take a toll. Yet stress has been with us since the first humans dealt with the life-threatening challenges of hunting—and avoiding being the hunted.

Ancient Contributions

Our ancestors developed coping mechanisms to handle the stressors specific to their times. In a Chinese medical classic, *Yellow Emperor's Classic on Internal Medicine,* written more than 2,000 years ago, the principles of moderation and balance in living were presented. Just as adherence to these guidelines would promote health, their violation was believed to cause sickness.

On the other side of the world, at about the same time, the Greek physician and father of modern medicine Hippocrates (460–377 BC) observed that the experience of disease offers some benefits in that the *pathos* (suffering) is always followed by the response of the body and the *ponos* (the toil of being sick). Hippocrates was also among the first to observe that emotional stress might put pregnant women at risk for miscarriages and so cautioned them to remain as calm as possible.

Modern Era

Advances in medical knowledge during the past 150 years have made it possible to track the ways that stress affects body systems.

Claude Bernard (1813–1878), who lived in the age of steam engines and other mechanical inventions, used a metaphor for understanding the workings of the human body. He noticed a remarkable similarity between a steam engine and a living organism in that both require the process of converting stored energy through a combustion process in order to move some mechanical parts to generate motion. To explain how a living organism could move itself without any external assistance, he developed the concept of **internal environment** that caused the step-by-step processes living organisms employ in moving themselves.

Bernard believed that complex living organisms depend on both the external environment *and* the internal environment. Based on his thinking, one major function of the internal environment was to keep the body constant in the face of the changing external environment through various chemical and physical responses. This concept of **homeostasis** states that all the physiological systems work in unison to keep the internal environment stable and balanced. If the body's core temperature, for example, should move beyond relatively small established limits, then immediate efforts are made to lower the temperature through sweating, or raise it through shivering. Likewise, if the body should become activated during an emergency, it will attempt to stabilize itself after the emergency has passed.

About the same time that Bernard was exploring the nature of balance within the body, Charles Darwin was sailing around the Galapagos Islands in South America, charting the nature of evolution. Based on his years of study—first of the ways that animals developed adaptive responses to their environment, and later applying these observations to humans—Darwin was among the first to theorize that fear and stress are useful or otherwise they would have extinguished themselves a long time ago. According to evolutionary theory, fear responses are passed on from one generation to the next because they serve as a survival mechanism. Darwin further noted that humans could display a range of stress/fear emotional responses, describing the behavioral changes that take place, including facial expressions and physiological changes.

A few decades later, into the twentieth century, Sigmund Freud presented the most coherent theory of emotions, making a clear distinction between fear and anxiety. The former could very well be part of what Darwin considered adaptive stress, while "neurotic anxiety" is a chronic condition of permanent apprehension. Freud eventually developed a whole theory of psychological disturbance based on the conscious and unconscious fears that motivate behavior.

A contemporary of Freud's, Walter Cannon (1932), was the first physiologist to begin talking about stress in the context of emotional responses. He worked with the homeostasis concept developed by Bernard, that humans develop coping mechanisms to keep the internal environment constant and secure the integrity of the cells and organs inside.

Cannon's contributions went far beyond the mechanisms of how the nervous and endocrine systems regulate internal stability. He believed that psychological disturbances and emotional distress can compromise the system in such a way that it fails to respond appropriately and can compromise health. He also gave a name for the stress response that becomes activated during perceived threats: the **fight-or-flight reaction**. This will be discussed in detail a little later in the chapter.

General Adaptation Syndrome

Hans Selye, an endocrinologist (someone who studies the glandular system) from Canada, built on the work of Cannon and others to give the area of stress research greater legitimacy. Selye is recognized as one of the parents of stress research, a title that he earned through the most serendipitous of circumstances.

In the early stages of his career, Selye was investigating hormonal processes by injecting rats with various chemical substances. Alas, he may have had a brilliant mind but less than nimble dexterity. He was terribly inept at injecting his rats, at times mishandling them, even dropping them accidentally, and then chasing them around the lab. Once he relocated his subjects, he discovered that they had suffered a number of physiological changes that were different from those that had not been terrorized: their immune systems malfunctioned and they developed ulcers. Much to his surprise, Selye learned that psychological trauma could actually stress the body to the point that it makes rats (and humans) sick.

Selye experimented with placing the rats under various challenging environmental conditions. He subjected some to Sahara Desert-like conditions, and others to a simulated Arctic environment. He introduced toxins into their cages and tried isolation, and then extreme crowding. Eventually, a consistent pattern of bodily changes emerged. The rats' adrenal glands became enlarged from overwork. Other organs such as the thymus, spleen, and lymph nodes changed dramatically. Selye called this consistent pattern of changes in response to demands in the external environment the **general adaptation syndrome (GAS)**. This means that when someone is stressed by a crisis, perceived danger, or threat, the brain activates more than 1,000 different chemical responses to deal with the situation (see Figure 1.1).

FIGURE 1.1 General adaptation syndrome.

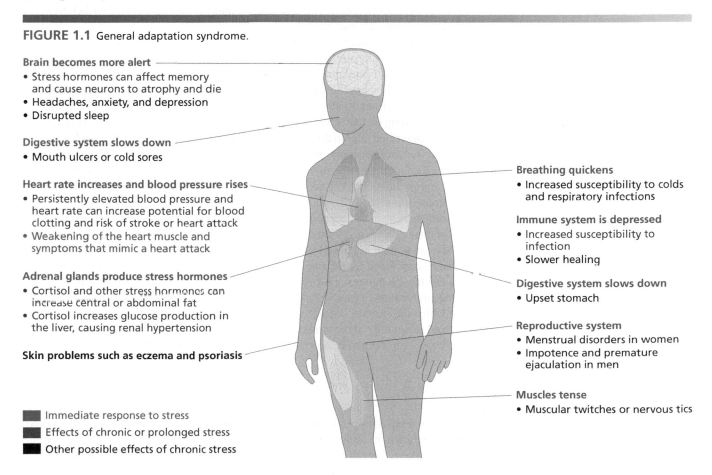

Brain becomes more alert
- Stress hormones can affect memory and cause neurons to atrophy and die
- Headaches, anxiety, and depression
- Disrupted sleep

Digestive system slows down
- Mouth ulcers or cold sores

Heart rate increases and blood pressure rises
- Persistently elevated blood pressure and heart rate can increase potential for blood clotting and risk of stroke or heart attack
- Weakening of the heart muscle and symptoms that mimic a heart attack

Adrenal glands produce stress hormones
- Cortisol and other stress hormones can increase central or abdominal fat
- Cortisol increases glucose production in the liver, causing renal hypertension

Skin problems such as eczema and psoriasis

Breathing quickens
- Increased susceptibility to colds and respiratory infections

Immune system is depressed
- Increased susceptibility to infection
- Slower healing

Digestive system slows down
- Upset stomach

Reproductive system
- Menstrual disorders in women
- Impotence and premature ejaculation in men

Muscles tense
- Muscular twitches or nervous tics

■ Immediate response to stress
■ Effects of chronic or prolonged stress
■ Other possible effects of chronic stress

TABLE 1.2 Stages in the general adaptation syndrome

Phase 1: Alarm reaction
The body's first exposure to the stressor that disrupts its homeostasis starts a series of physiological reactions through the autonomic and endocrine systems. The endocrine system will produce corticosteroids that will supply the body with resources to fight or flee. Unfortunately, these corticosteroids may weaken the immune system.

Phase 2: Resistance
The continued presence of the stressor will activate the stage of resistance during which the purpose is to sustain life and make necessary adaptations as long as the required fuel and biochemical material are available. It is like a gun that keeps firing over and over until it runs out of ammunition, or the shooter's finger cramps to the point it can no longer function.

Phase 3: Exhaustion
If the stressor remains present (or is *believed* to be present), the body will deplete its stored energy to the point that it is no longer capable of mounting any resistance. Mental and physical energy are on empty. Exhaustion sets in. Permanent damage will result, leading to illness or even death.

The general adaptation syndrome (see Table 1.2) goes through three phases, if necessary, each one activated if the previous stage fails to be adequate. The first phase signals an alarm reaction—the fight-or-flight response described earlier. This is a short-term, quickly mobilized system to deal with threats as quickly as possible. The second phase is initiated once the body realizes that this will not be a sprint, but a marathon. Long-term reactions are launched to try to keep the system functioning in the face of enduring assaults. At this juncture, either homeostasis is restored or the third phase begins. Finally, exhaustion sets in with the body systems depleted. This explains, in part, why people subjected to long-term stress develop various illnesses and chronic problems: their defenses have been breached.

The result of Hans Selye's research was not all bad news. He also discovered that an animal's ability to handle stress could be enhanced if it was repeatedly exposed to mild or moderate challenges presented at incrementally higher levels. This is *exactly* the strategy that is now used by psychologists to treat phobias using **systematic desensitization**. Someone who is irrationally afraid of mice, for example, would be gradually exposed to tiny, non-threatening cartoon character mice, perhaps even Mickey Mouse. Using relaxation training (described later in this book), the subject is taught to stay calm while increasing tolerance for progressively more stressful stimuli. This could include a photograph of a mouse, then a movie of a mouse, then a mouse in a cage at the far end of the room, and then a mouse being held by someone else, until such time as the person can actually hold the mouse himself.

We can strengthen our capacity to deal with stressors in the future by preparing and training for them. This is just what coaches and performance experts try to do with athletes so that they can remain in Phase 1 of their GAS without suffering lingering side-effects.

It can be concluded from Selye's findings, and subsequent research, that exposure to stressors can have long-term consequences, which are harmful and even life-threatening or in some circumstances can be beneficial. Other investigators have since found that the extent to which the stressor impacts the body for better or worse depends not only on the intensity and magnitude of the stressor, but also on how we perceive the stressor and our ability to cope with it (Ganzel, Morris, & Wethington, 2010).

Allostasis

The concept of homeostasis developed by Cannon implies that once the balance is restored, the body will return to its static and unchanged pre-stress state. Selye pointed out that chronic stress brings certain costs to the organism when its resources for coping are depleted.

Noting the cost of achieving this homeostatic balance in the face of stressors, Sterling and Eyer (1988) coined the term **allostasis** to mean the combined physiological and psychological adaptation to the experience of threats or adversities. In other words, the body will experience wear and tear and decreased capability to cope with future stressors as long as the threats continue and the need to maintain homeostasis still exists.

Bruce McEwen, a renowned neuroendocrinologist, expanded the idea of allostasis by creating the concept of **allostatic load** to describe what happens when the same adaptive (GAS) system that was designed to protect us actually tears us apart (McEwen & Stellar, 1993; McEwen & Wingfield, 2010). The allostatic load comes out of balance when there is a systemic malfunction that occurs either by repeated exposure to perceived threat, or poor health and lifestyle choices on the part of an individual. This would be like someone constantly revving the engine of a car to the highest revolutions per minute (RPM), overheating the engine, and never changing the oil or adding lubrication.

McEwen (2002) cites the example of spawning salmon as an extreme case of what can happen when the allostatic load becomes excessive. Chinook salmon of Alaska will swim up to 60 miles per day, upriver, against the current, even jumping *up* waterfalls, in order to lay and fertilize their eggs. During this heroic and improbable journey, the salmon rely on every possible reserve of hormones and energy to complete their task. In the end, the constant stress on their system, plus the draining of their reserves, kills them. They literally die of overstress.

This phenomenon of death from overstress occurs within our own species as well, mostly in the form of suicide. Some of our most creative geniuses imploded as a result of internal and external pressures that pushed them over the limit of what they could stand. In studies of such lives (Jamison, 1993; Kottler, 2006), of innovators in art (Mark Rothko, Vincent van Gogh, Arshile Gorky), literature (Sylvia Plath, Virginia Woolf, Ernest Hemingway), and music (Pyotr Tchaikovsky, Kurt Cobain), it can be found that consistent exposure to chronic stress, combined with feelings of perfectionism, often leads talented people to drain their reserves like salmon.

The concept of allostasis has further enriched our understanding of adaptive mechanisms in the face of life's threats or traumas. It emphasizes that even minimal stressors can cause long-term damage to your health when they endure, demanding ongoing coping responses from the body.

TABLE 1.3 Evolution of concepts of stress

Stage 1: Claude Bernard: Disruption to the ability to maintain a constant fluid environment bathing cells of the body–the internal environment.

Stage 2: Walter Cannon (1929, 1939): Threats to homeostasis evoke activation of the sympathoadrenal system as a functional unit. The concept of homeostasis suggests that regaining balance only requires local changes in the body.

Stage 3: Hans Selye (1946): Stress as a state characterized by a uniform response pattern, regardless of the particular stressor, that could lead to long-term pathologic changes.

Stage 4: Sterling and Eyer (1988): Process of achieving stability through physiological or behavioral change with the assumption that no single ideal set of steady-state conditions in life exists and setpoints and other response criteria change continuously. Allostasis suggests that adaptation to a stressor involves all the process in the body.

Source: Goldstein & Kopin (2007)

Responses to Stress

There are a number of ways that people respond to stressful situations in their lives, depending on their personalities, their cognitive style (characteristic thinking patterns), their background and prior experiences, their gender and ethnicity, and a host of other factors. These responses may be grouped according to physiological reactions (covered in Chapter 2), emotional reactions (reviewed in Chapters 3 and 4), cognitive reactions (discussed in Chapter 6), and systemic reactions (presented in Chapter 12). Stress responses occur on multiple levels, and within many systems, in the body and mind (see Table 1.4).

TABLE 1.4 Major responses to stress

Physiological	Cognitive	Emotional	Behavioral
Heart palpitations	Impaired memory	Fear	Crying
Sweating	Disorientation	Worry	Rage
Dry mouth	Unrealistic demands	Panic	Withdrawal
Fatigue	Disasterizing	Guilt	Substance abuse
Insomnia	Illogical thinking	Anger	Self-medication
Nausea	Externalized blame	Denial	Impulsiveness
Dizziness	Obsessiveness	Hopelessness	Phobias
Loss of appetite	Loss of humor	Numbness	Hyperactivity
High blood pressure	Suicidal ideation	Depression	Lethargy
Personality traits	Surrender	Despair	Aggression
Weight loss or gain	Excessive fantasies	Impatience	Rambling

FOR REFLECTION 1.3

How Do You Know When *You* Are Stressed?

Everyone reacts to stress in different ways, even if there are some common signs and symptoms. Some people have difficulty sleeping or lose their appetites, while others sleep too much and go on eating binges. Some people have thoughts of doom and gloom, imagining the worst, and others keep an upbeat state of mind.

Review Table 1.3, and then consider how you characteristically respond to stress in your life, in the past as well as the present.

What are your typical reactions?

Where do you feel stress in your body?

What is the usual way that you think when first confronted with a crisis or stressful situation?

How do you respond emotionally to stress? Which feelings are dominant?

How do you typically behave when confronted with stress? If you are inclined to "act out," or respond dysfunctionally in some way, what does that look like?

Biologist Robert Sapolsky (2004) talks about the uniquely human response to danger as compared with herd animals. Whereas zebras become stressed only during times of immediate threat from a predator, we are the only species that gets upset over the future. We spend more time worrying about things we can't control than we do actually preparing to meet the challenges. Imagine a zebra, or a penguin for that matter, thinking about where she is going to vacation during spring break, and how she's going to pay for it. You get the point: animals do experience stress when they are subjected to life-threatening situations but we are the only species that literally kills ourselves out of imagined fears.

FIGURE 1.2 Contemporary human beings retain the same physiological responses to stress that were present in our Stone Age ancestors.

Fight-or-Flight Response

There you are stalking your prey. Outfitted in your recently acquired skins made from a mammoth you killed the previous week (with others from your clan), you are hot on the trail of a woolly rhino that had been spotted by scouts. You are fleet on your feet and an excellent spear-thrower. At 19, you are rather experienced and old compared with others among your people, where the average life expectancy is in the early twenties.

Like any self-respecting member of the Paleolithic Era, you are rather hairy and squat (but good news: so is your spouse). You are hiding behind a huge boulder, club in hand, ready to attack any animal that might come through your ambush spot. Your senses are heightened, especially your senses of smell and sight and hearing. Because of this state of hyperarousal, you hear the soft rustling of foliage on a cliff above your head. Your heart begins pounding in your chest but you force yourself to remain still and calm. You slowly turn your head and glance upward. Your worst fear has been confirmed: a saber-toothed tiger appears to be stalking you, ready to pounce. In your last conscious thought, you notice that one of the cat's eight-inch-long teeth is chipped at the end, not that this observation will do you much good.

If we could freeze this moment, and glimpse inside the body of this hunter from 20,000 years ago, we would observe a number of changes taking place. Within the span of a few seconds, the hunter (let's call her Pela) has a decision to make: she has one of two choices in order to save herself—to run or to fight. Whatever Pela chooses—and her life depends on making the right choice—her body is preparing itself for either option. And it turns out that this fight-or-flight response is going to give her every advantage possible under the circumstances either to escape the danger or to win this battle.

Now, if you could manually customize the systems of Pela's body (or anyone else's under similar circumstances), what might you do to give her the best chances of survival? (See Table 1.5.)

She is going to need maximum sensory acuity. The eyes dilate to better perceive danger, increase night vision, and judge distances. The blood pressure increases, along with the heart rate, to deliver more nutrients to the muscles that will be needed during a sprint or a battle (that is why her heart is pounding in her chest). Muscles tense in preparation for a quick movement, to either dodge an attack or get out of the way. Pela starts breathing heavily, pumping as much oxygen into the blood supply as possible. The body begins to perspire freely, cooling off the skin and core body temperature so that things don't overheat with all the fuel that is being burned. The endocrine system kicks in and provides a surge of adrenaline that will augment strength. And finally, serum glucose levels spike to supply sugar, a fast energy source. This is supplemented with a release of free fatty acids that help sustain endurance.

TABLE 1.5 Summary of major fight-or-flight responses

1. Eye dilation
2. Increased blood pressure
3. Increased heart rate
4. Muscle tension
5. Heavy breathing
6. Sweating
7. Adrenaline surge
8. Increased serum glucose
9. Release of free fatty acids
10. Vasodilation of arteries in arms and legs
11. Digestive system shuts down
12. Inhibition of sexual desire and reproductive capability
13. Immune system shuts down
14. Blood coagulation

As if it is not amazing enough that the body can turn on these systems when needed, Pela's body also shuts down those systems that won't be needed during the next few critical minutes, saving energy and increasing endurance. Arteries restrict to prevent excessive bleeding if Pela should be wounded. The digestive system shuts down since she is not planning on a snack or bowel movement during the next few minutes. Likewise hormones related to sex and reproduction are inhibited, since sex is the *last* thing on her mind at this moment. The immune system will not be needed either during this temporary emergency. Lastly, the blood thickens so as to provide maximum coagulation in the event of a wound.

It turns out that this was a false alarm. Much to Pela's relief, the long-toothed cat had already eaten a meal earlier in the day, so rather than pouncing he had been more interested in finding a nice spot in the sun to take a nap.

Pela sighs with relief and then an interesting phenomenon takes place: once given the "danger over" signal, all the body's systems begin to return to normal. This homeostasis will take time to complete but eventually things will return to previous levels.

As Pela backs slowly away, her breathing returns to normal and the danger signals shut down. She does notice, however, that her palms are so sweaty she can barely grip her club. Her legs and arms are shaking from the surge of adrenaline still coursing through her arteries. Her stomach feels queasy from having been shut down.

Does any of this sound familiar? It is *exactly* what happens during an encounter with stress. Picture approaching an attractive classmate you like. Imagine that the instructor announces a pop quiz for which you are minimally prepared. Recall walking in the dark and being startled by a weird sound. In each case, your body receives a danger signal from the hypothalamus, that part of your brain that alerts the appropriate systems to prepare for a potential threat.

The only problem is that most of the time in contemporary life we get false alarms. We aren't really facing life-threatening dangers, even if it sometimes feels that way. Our culture has evolved over thousands of years but our neurological systems are essentially the same as they were during Pela's time. They still see saber-toothed tigers and woolly rhinos behind every rock. I mentioned earlier how Walter Cannon described this survival response almost a hundred years ago by observing the ways that animals respond to perceived threat. All the bodily systems just described become activated in response to a danger signal (a human scream, the sight of a predator, the smell of fire burning, the taste of poison), and they remain engaged until such time that they are given the "all clear" signal. However, it doesn't matter to the body whether the danger is real or just seems that way. It could be an actual threat, or a hallucination of one: the body reacts the same way.

Twenty thousand or more years later, our culture has evolved significantly. Our lifespan has increased from 23 years to nearly 85. We have moved from caves into condos. Now about the only danger of predators we face is from our own kind in certain parts of the city that are to be avoided if possible.

Recall what happens when the brain turns on the danger signal that sets in motion all the physiological changes needed to fight or flee. What happens if this system, designed for brief flashes, stays on almost all the time? More specifically, what happens if your immune system is suppressed for long periods of time while you fight imaginary battles during a sleepless night of worry? What are the effects of straining the body's system in ways for which it was never designed? The answer is that you can become sick.

Types of Stress: The Good, the Bad, and the Ugly

Like most phenomena that have been identified and studied, stress comes in different flavors. There is **short-term stress**—the kind activated by a sudden threat or danger. Imagine, for example, that you are driving in traffic and another car swerves into your lane, or a situation in which you are asked to make an impromptu presentation in front of a large audience. Under such circumstances, you will no doubt feel the familiar surge of a **stress-hormone** response, activating the fight-or-flight system described earlier. This is usually followed by deactivation producing a **relaxation response**, at which point you begin to calm down and all systems return to normal. Short-term arousal like this does not usually create problems; if anything, it keeps the system in working order, so to speak.

Long-term stress is another story altogether. This is when the system is turned on at high volume, and then remains that way even when the initial danger has passed. There is the sort of wear and tear on the body and mind you would expect when a mechanism that was designed for "sprints" is told that it has to run a "marathon." Invariably, parts start to break down and the system fails. This is a different sort of marathon than practiced by those who use running as one of many ways to manage their stress, burning off excess energy, distracting them from worries, and better conditioning their bodies (see Voice of Stress Management 1.1).

One of the best ways to study long-term stress is using the Daily Hassles Scale (Lazarus & Folkman, 1984), which quantifies cumulative hassles, such as dealing with demanding customers and difficulty finding parking on a university campus. Prolonged stress affects the body in a number of predictable ways that can be deduced from your prior understanding of what happens during arousal of the fight-or-flight reflex.

Over time, without sufficient time for recovery, marathon runners suffer a host of depletion-related injuries: stress fractures, tendonitis, shin splints, muscle strains, joint problems, and nutritional imbalances.

1. Muscles tense to prepare for battle or flight. Over time this can lead to muscle fatigue, cramps, and chronic back pain.

2. Digestion shuts down since it won't be needed. Over time, the system can develop ulcers, colitis, spastic colon, irritable bowel syndrome, and acid reflux.

3. Increased blood and oxygen flow brings more nutrients and hormones that can be mobilized. This can create high blood pressure over time.

4. Blood vessels constrict to prevent bleeding in the event of injury. In a chronic state, a person can experience dizziness, blackouts, headaches, and skin lesions.

5. The liver produces and distributes sugar and nutrients in order to provide energy to combat the perceived danger. Over time, hypoglycemia or diabetes can result.

VOICE OF STRESS MANAGEMENT 1.1

Note: Throughout the text there are a number of "voices" that speak about struggles with stress, as well as ways that people manage the challenges they face.

Thirty-year-old female teacher

I would say that I am a bit insecure. I am often concerned with how others see me and feel that they may judge me. I get nervous really easily. I have been successful in coping with the stress in my life, but I used to let it rule my life. After getting divorced a few years ago, I felt lost and lonely. I joined a group for people coping with divorce. It really helped to talk about what I was going through and hear that others had similar problems. I also took up running. It was a wonderful way for me to focus my attention on something other than all the things that I worry about. When I run, I look at my surroundings and simply enjoy being out and active. It's a great way for me to release my tension. I even started running marathons!

My insecurities are still there but I am just able to escape them with more frequency. I run six days per week and feel exhilarated each time. I have a new circle of friends with similar interests. It is wonderful to have others with whom to share my sport. Many of my fellow runners find that it is a great way to relieve the stress caused by their hectic lifestyles. Of all the things I have done to relieve stress, running has really been the most rewarding for me. Besides the exercise, most of all it is a mental break.

Hans Selye coined a number of specific terms to distinguish between "good" stress and "bad" stress. Like most things in life, too much is not particularly healthy. The term **hyperstress** means an excessive amount that overloads the system, while **hypostress** is not enough to keep the body tuned and ready for action.

There are three additional kinds of stress that Selye identified in an effort to cover the range of possible meanings:

- *Distress:* Pop quiz for which you are unprepared

- *Neustress:* Poor economic news

- *Eustress:* Supportive friends cheer you on during a game

Distress is what you usually associate with the word "stress." This is the destructive and harmful sort that means trouble, especially if it moves beyond acute arousal to a chronic condition. Distress occurs when our ability to cope with stressors is insufficient. Distress causes anxiety and confusion and decreases your performance in daily activities. Distress is often associated with stressful events that occur unexpectedly. Even when good news strikes too suddenly, it may shock the recipient and cause stress. Distress also may occur when you try to manage too many things simultaneously and lose control of the situation. The degree to which you feel you can control your life influences the valence of stress. Earlier researchers like Holmes and Rahe (1967) believed change per se was associated with health status and stress while later researchers found that undesirable events are more predictive of health problems than positive events.

Neustress is, just like it sounds, rather neutral. It has little impact, or lasting effects, one way or the other. It might be upsetting for others, in another location or context, but has little measurable effect on your life. Alternatively, you might find yourself in a performance situation in which the added presence of an audience is below your radar because you are concentrating so hard on your job.

Eustress is the kind of stress that inspires or motivates you to go beyond present levels of functioning. This is what happens with the so-called "clutch" hitter in baseball, or the "pressure player" in other sports: the presence of an audience, combined with high stakes on the line, motivates the athlete to unparalleled performance. The same could be true for artists, actors, writers, and others who are required to perform under pressure.

Eustress stimulates the systems of the body to function at peak levels; this can even be the case for the kind of growth that can take place for some people after a crisis or trauma (Orloff, 2009). It should therefore make sense that although moderate doses of stress can be good for you in creating excitement, enhanced attention, improved performance, or healthy competitive instincts, the other side of the coin—boredom—is almost never desirable. At the very least, stress signifies intense engagement with life and what you are doing whereas boredom means you don't find meaning or purpose in activities or daily life (Oz, 2010).

Sources of Stress

Another way to categorize stress is based on the source. Typically, stress can be activated by (1) an external source, (2) an internal source, or (3) the interaction of internal and external sources. In addition, stress can be manifested as a physical sensation (pounding heart), a psychological experience (feelings of panic), as well as biochemical and other processes.

Physical stress occurs when the human body is affected by sleep deprivation, overworking, excessive physical exertion, physical injury or trauma, viral or bacterial infections, inflammation, physical disease, or chronic pain. It is under such circumstances that the body begins to lose functioning and to break down.

Psychological stress is often used synonymously with mental stress or emotional stress because they share many common features. Psychological stressors are related to how we interpret the events in our life; they are determined by our values, beliefs, attitudes, and philosophies of life. Given the same situation, different people may react very differently due to their outlooks on life. Emotional reactions such as anger, fear, low self-esteem, and hostility are also influenced by our beliefs. The good news is that you can change your thoughts (Chapter 6), thereby changing your reactions to the events in your life. The bad news is that some thought patterns have been deeply engrained in your psyche and they require a consistent effort to be modified.

Psychosocial stress arises from interactions with people and the society in which you live. Individuals must make constant adjustments to the demands imposed on them by the environment and culture, especially during times of economic, environmental, political, and social challenges. Think about how the effects of a recession, natural disaster, crowding, trauma, war, poverty, abuse, family conflict, neglect, or other factors can create tremendous stress.

In addition to these sources of stress, there are *biochemical triggers* that result from excessive use of substances such as sugar, nicotine, caffeine, or alcohol, as well as food preservatives. Stress reactions can also be activated from exposure to substances in the environment such as mold, dust, allergens, industrial pollutants, environmental toxins, pesticides, and automobile exhausts. We can suffer chemical stress from using contaminated foods, such as tuna that contains mercury or shellfish that is laden with cadmium.

It is important to be able to identify the sources of stress in your life, and their origins, before you can develop a plan to prevent and manage the negative effects. This is easier said than done considering that there are often complex interactions among all the sources. Sometimes a significant addition to the already stressed-out person can trigger a major anxiety attack as a straw could crush a camel if the camel was dead tired as the idiom suggests. Please read the section on the dynamical systems theory to further understand the dynamical interactions among sources of stressors at the end of this chapter.

Self-Assessment of Stress

This book emphasizes *prevention* as well as treatment of the stress problem. It is far preferable to minimize risk for the future rather than waiting until it is too late.

FOR REFLECTION 1.4

Self-assessment of Stressors

Identify the top five stressors in your life. Describe how you have coped with them. Rank how effective you've been in dealing with these situations (1 = least effective; 5 = most effective).

Stressors in my life	Coping strategies	Ranking
1.		
2.		
3.		
4.		
5.		

As a general rule, the earlier you can detect signs of danger, the more likely you can do something to avoid it. If you have advance warning that there is a traffic pile-up on the highway ahead of you, you can begin to reduce your speed and prepare for a sudden stop. If you know that that you are going to be asked to make a toast at a wedding, you can think about what you want to say, rehearse your speech, and visualize things you want to remember. Early warnings can be just as helpful in stress prevention. If you can learn to recognize some of the earliest signs of chronic stress, then you are in a far better position to take remedial steps to make needed changes in your thinking, behavior, or lifestyle. What are the sorts of things you might look for? The answer depends, in part, on what is normal for you.

The Dynamical Systems Perspective of Stress Management and Prevention

Up till now, you have learned about various aspects about the nature of stress, i.e., evolution of the concepts of stress, sources of stress, types of stressors, etc. You will now learn a new theoretical tool that will help you tie up all the loose ends together. It is called the **dynamical systems theory** (DST). In a nutshell, the DST views reality including psychological and physiological phenomena in terms of self-organizing and coevolving patterns of relationships among the elements of the systems rather than in terms of static and isolated factors. I hope that the DST will help you better understand all the major concepts in this text and apply what you learn to your daily life. Next I will outline six key concepts of the DST and their implications for stress management and prevention.

Concept 1: Complexity and Nonlinearity of Dynamical Systems

A dynamic system is an open and changing entity that consists of multiple input and output channels as well as mechanisms of processing the input. For example, we are complex dynamical systems that take in information through sensory and cognitive processes that result in perceptions and ideas. With motor processes, we produce speech and movements that interact with other human beings in our surroundings. A dynamic system is capable of regaining equilibrium once its stability is lost, and this notion is consistent with homeostasis (Cannon, 1932) and allostasis (Sterling & Eyer, 1988). The process of a dynamical system regaining balance can take on various pathways.

In a complex dynamic system, the pathway of the movement of the system is nonlinear, which means the input into the system is not proportional to the output. A small change can trigger a big result and a huge change produces nominal results. The human brain is a nonlinear system with the brain possessing about 100 billion neurons and each neuron has tens of thousands of synaptic connections with other neurons.

Concept 2: Mutual Causality

Mutual causality describes the behavior of certain dynamical systems whose states evolve over time. The mutual causality principle states that a result is a function of interaction between multiple factors in a person's life; no one result is any more important than another result. Translated into stress terms, stress results from the interactions of multiple factors, e.g., internal and external. Internal processes include genetics, beliefs, values, philosophies, knowledge, experience, hopes, and dreams. External processes are your surroundings, social support, weather, etc. When stress happens, it is not due to one factor, but results from the interactions of multiple internal and external factors.

Concept 3: Sensitivity to Initial Conditions of the System

This concept suggests that any small change you initiate in your life can cause a significant end result for better or worse. This concept can be illustrated by the butterfly effect popularized by Dr. Edward Lorenz, the famous meteorologist from the Massachusetts Institute of Technology (MIT). The metaphor used by Dr. Lorenz was that a butterfly flapping its wings was the cause of a tornado in Texas, suggesting an insignificant amount of input diverges and contributes to a significant result. Stress reactions can occur in the same way. Sometimes a seemingly small annoyance can trigger a major psychological or physiological crisis in an individual's life. However, with mindfulness and mindfulness training (Chapters 4, 6, 7, 8, 12), you will become aware of these triggers of stress and keep your poise and equanimity in your communication with yourself or others, and even turn stressors into useful energy.

Somtimes a clear solution emerges out of a chaotic self-organization.

Concept 4: Self-Organization and Emergence

Self-organization can be defined as a process in which the internal organization of an open and dynamic system changes automatically without being guided or managed by an external script. **Emergence** refers to the appearance of new properties that have not existed before as a result of self-organization, suggesting that the whole sometimes is greater than the sum of the parts. Self-organization and emergence are characteristics of stress reactions and coping. For instance, Chapter 13 covers the concept of post-traumatic growth, i.e., the positive changes in a person as a result of exposure to a trauma in life.

Concept 5: Attractors

Attractors describe a steady, stable state of mind or body. Habits, beliefs, and addictive behaviors are examples of attractors. In Chapters 4 and 5, you will learn about maladaptive behaviors and stress-prone personalities, which exemplify negative attractor states. In Chapters 13 and 14, you will learn about positive attractors such as signature strengths, and positive emotions. In Chapter 6, you will learn ways to challenging stressful thinking, which is a skill or a new attractor state that you have yet to learn.

Concept 6: Bifurcation

To understand this key concept, you will have to apply the five aforementioned concepts. The idea of bifurcation suggests that a qualitative change in an attractor's structure, as a control parameter is varied. Bifurcation basically means that one becomes two and two becomes four. Human beings are dynamical and open systems and are constantly on the verge of bifurcating and changing. In the face of stressors, we either become rigid and maladaptive (Chapters 4 and 5), or we become enlightened, being transformed into someone bigger and more resilient (Chapters 13 and 14). With mind–body skills of stress coping presented in Chapters 7, 8, and 9 (e.g., rational emotive behavioral therapy, tai chi, meditation, yoga), you can choose to transcend your stressful life and turn stressors into fuel for vigor and health as shown in empirical research. Choosing a transcendental pathway allows the person to reach a new equilibrium that is much more balanced and healthy, while also allowing that person to evolve and become more complex. Complexification defines whether or not an individual becomes more complex and flexible (Chapters 6 and 14).

In summary, one advantage about the DST is that it is a process theory, meaning that it is suited to describe any complex and dynamical systems or phenomena; however, its use still calls for the support of existing empirical research evidence. Recent findings in neuroscience either support or are grounded in dynamical systems principles (Cozolino, 2006; Schore & Schore, 2008; Siegel, 1999, 2007). Also, stress researchers are advocating unifying multiple bodies of research findings in the context of the DST (e.g., Keenan, 2010).

Overview of Stress Management and Prevention

Understanding the nature and meaning of stress is an important part of implementing a comprehensive program of stress management and prevention. You have learned already that stress is a dynamic process that consists of a stressor and stress response. You have also learned that a stressor can be any severe challenge, real or imaginary, that disrupts normal functioning. This can be anything from a flat tire to traveling to a foreign land.

Management of stress involves neutralizing or reducing the magnitude of your responses to stressors, while prevention focuses on shaping, modifying, or eliminating stressors in the first place. The first part of the text is devoted to understanding the nature of stress while the second and third parts will be devoted to interventions.

The model of stress management and prevention presented in this text (see Figure 1.2) is based on the research of many professionals, all of whom conclude that multiple and varied techniques are required that address all facets of the problem. Our model depicts a four-stage process of stress development. Before each stage of stress development occurs, you have the power either to prevent its occurrence in the first place or, at the very least, to reduce its momentum. The best scenario is when you can prevent a full-blown stress episode by stopping it in its embryonic stage. The second-best situation occurs when you have developed sufficient coping mechanisms that the demand for change can be easily met. Once the perceived threat is met, the body's alarm will be turned off and homeostasis will be restored.

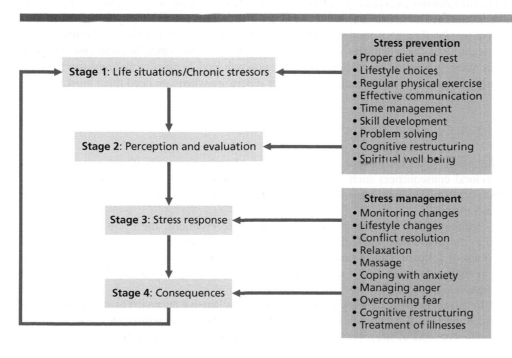

FIGURE 1.2
The four-stage model of stress management and prevention.

Stage 1: Life Situations/Chronic Stressors

Before a major event disrupts your life, you need to do everything you can to prevent the formation of a stressor. You may have heard the saying, "Discipline weighs ounces while regret weighs tons." An exam is a major stressor for those who are unprepared and for whom it may have a serious consequence, while it may be a minor annoyance, or even a fun challenge, for those who are prepared.

No matter how hard you try, certain adversities and traumatic events will inevitably occur in your life. In most cases, you will not have a choice about whether you are subjected to the stressors but you can choose, to some extent, how you respond to them. Obviously, a pleasant stressful situation such as getting married (eustress) will be handled with more ease than a negative stressor like a divorce (distress).

In this first stage it is critical that you have an accurate and comprehensive view of the stressors in your life, as well as the characteristic ways you respond to them. It is important to know where and how you are most vulnerable.

Stage 2: Perception and Evaluation

As mentioned earlier, people will perceive the same stressor in a variety of ways and, therefore, react to it differently. An event will be overwhelming to one person and exhilarating to another. For some people, the fear of speaking in front of a group is greater than that of death. Others live to get up on stage in front of a crowd.

Your perception of a situation or a chronic stressor also depends on your personality type, your resilience, life experience, health status, and mental and emotional resources. In general, healthy, competent, and optimistic people will cope with stress more successfully than those who tend toward pessimism and negativity (Brooks & Goldstein, 2003).

In this second stage, it is critical for you to have a solid background in the theory, research, and mechanisms of stress so that you can better prepare yourself for what lies ahead.

Stage 3: Stress Response

This stage will demonstrate an individual's emotional, psychological, and physiological responses to the perception of the stressor. The magnitude of the responses from the endocrine and autonomic nervous systems depends on the perception of the response. Your major task, in the face of stress, is to reduce pressure and release excessive physical and psychological tension through a number of options (such as meditation, exercise, and other relaxation techniques described later in the book). It is not enough to merely know how to apply stress management and prevention strategies; you will have to practice and rehearse them on a daily basis so they will become part of your repertoire when you need them most.

Stage 4: Consequences

At this stage, you experience the frequent results of stress responses. These can range from behavioral consequences such as accidents to physiological consequences such as a heart attack or ulcer. The final stage of stress development feeds back to the first stage and then repeats the cycle.

Without proper prevention and management interventions, the cycle will perpetuate itself to the point where you feel like one of those Chinook salmon swimming upstream until the point of collapse. Unlike this fish, however, you have choices along the way that allow you to change direction, take a snooze onshore, or take a boat, or even decide you don't feel like spawning after all.

In this textbook I advocate a holistic and comprehensive approach to stress prevention and management. What does this mean? The following principles will allow you to learn and apply the concepts of stress prevention and management more effectively.

Situations that are anxiety provoking for some are extremely enjoyable for others. Many politicians, comedians, and public speakers absolutely love to appear on stage in front of huge crowds. The familiar stress responses only arouse them to perform at a higher level. If they are successful in their work and healthy, then they have learned to quickly restore a level of relaxation as soon as the event is over.

1. *Prevention is more effective than management.* Prevention is a more proactive approach since you start to change your living habits before you have serious health issues. Prevention is also cheaper than treatment, as it is well known how expensive it is to treat a serious disease. Once stressors strike, manage your reactions to them and tap all your resources to deal with them; don't allow them to become a chronic condition that wreaks havoc on your body.

2. *Small changes can lead to big effects.* A small discipline exercised in your life may engender multiple benefits, a notion consistent with the key concepts in the DST. If you apply this idea to stress prevention and management, a small change in your lifestyle may have a long-term benefit to your longevity and well-being. Since many of your health habits are deeply engrained, it can take considerable effort to initiate and maintain changes. But starting small will eventually lead to a fundamental change.

3. *Don't count on a magic solution for solving all your stress problems.* Good health and well-being characterized by abundance of energy and low stress

come from the interactions of all the body systems and a harmonious relationship between you and your environment. There is no single panacea that, once learned, will make all the difference. It takes discipline to make systemic changes in every aspect of your life. This course offers a comprehensive way to prevent and manage your stress that is designed to keep you healthy throughout your lifetime.

4. *Tailor a program to your own schedule and means.* You hear people tell you all the time that you should do what they're doing, but often such advice is not particularly helpful. Everyone is unique and you must adapt any program, no matter how successful, to your particular lifestyle, values, interests, strengths, and resources.

5. *Develop a comprehensive plan for stress prevention and management.* Since the sources of stress come from within as well as from without, it is essential that you have a plan to change your thinking, modify your diet, improve relationships, and acquire new skills throughout the lifespan. Like a good mechanic who possesses a variety of tools for different jobs, you also need to develop all kinds of skills for stress prevention and management. You may use one or more techniques more frequently, but being open to different skills offers you more flexibility and resources. Also, you should consider short-term improvements as well as those for the long term. It is always good to have multiple options, depending on your mood, circumstances, and needs.

SUMMARY

Stress represents a psychological and physiological reaction to a perceived threat, whether it is the result of fantasy, exaggeration, or actual danger. In situations where the threat cannot be eliminated or significantly reduced, there are dire consequences for people in terms of physical, psychological, emotional, interpersonal, and spiritual functioning.

There are three elements in the definition of stress: the stressor, the response, and the person experiencing the condition. The stressor can be a real physical threat or an imaginary or symbolic one. The same stressor can be good for one person and bad for another, depending on how capable the person is in coping with the situation.

Over the past hundred years, our understanding of the stress response has evolved thanks to the contributions of scientists such as Cannon, Selye, Sterling, Eyer, and McEwen. In the homeostatic view of stress, the stress response is initiated once the body is perturbed by a stressor. Under optimal circumstances, the body returns to a relaxed state once the threat has passed.

The allostatic view suggests that the stress response can trigger a series of body-wide changes to bring the organism back to a resting condition. This idea also implies that even small, consistent episodes of wear and tear carry long-term consequences for the body.

The dynamical systems theory serves as a good unifying theme for this book – albeit requiring more empirical support in the future – in that it has the necessary process-based concepts suited to describe such complex phenomena as stress coping and maladaptive behaviors and such dynamical systems as nervous systems and endocrine systems as well as their interactions.

The stress response varies from person to person. The consequences of a stress response represent the composite effects of the individual characteristics such as personality, health status, and the nature of the stressor. A comprehensive stress management program proposed in this text cannot realistically eliminate all stress in your life. To do so, even if possible, would make for a very dull and dreary existence. Stress can be the scourge of your life, but also the lifeblood for everything you find stimulating and exciting.

QUESTIONS FOR REVIEW

1. Define and discuss the concept of stress from different perspectives.
2. Explain when stress becomes a problem.
3. Analyze the different sources of stress in your own life.
4. Differentiate between homeostasis and allostasis. Define the term "allostatic overload."
5. Describe the general adaptation syndrome developed by Hans Selye and the fight-or-flight response.
6. What is the primary goal of stress management? Can we eliminate stress?
7. Describe how the concepts of stress evolved over the years.
8. Describe the four-stage model of stress management and prevention proposed in this chapter.
9. Why did Hans Selye define stress as a "nonspecific response to any demand placed upon the body"? Explain the meaning of "nonspecific." Do you handle eustress and distress similarly in life?
10. Describe the dynamical systems theory and its six key concepts. Explain how these concepts will help you understand stress management and prevention.

SELECTED ANSWERS

Answers to FOR REFLECTION 1.2
The six leading causes of death, in order, are: 1) heart disease, 2) cancer, 3) stroke, 4) chronic lower respiratory diseases, 5) accidents, 6) diabetes (Xu, Murphy, Kochanek, & Bastian, 2016).

REVIEW ACTIVITIES

Review Activity 1.1: Understanding the Meaning of Stress
Directions: The following statements are not accurate. State why they are false by using evidence cited in the text, or examples from your life, to refute them.

1. Stress is the same for everybody.

2. The relationship between stress and the incidence of illness is simple and straightforward.

3. Stress is always bad for you.

4. Stress is everywhere, so you can't do anything about it.

5. Whenever someone experiences a stressor, he/she will inevitably experience physiological arousal or emotional anxiety.

6. If someone does not display symptoms, it means that he/she has no stress.

7. Only major stressors cause damage to your health.

8. Your goal in stress management class is to completely eliminate stress.

Review Activity 1.2: Sentence Completion Exercises

Directions: In these exercises, complete the sentences as many times as you can with different endings.

1. I feel most stressed out when

2. I feel most relaxed when

3. When I feel stress, I would normally (talk about how you feel, behave, and think)

4. If I had known more about the harm of excessive stress to my health, I would have

REFERENCES AND RESOURCES

American College Health Association (2009). *Reference group executive summary for Fall, 2008.* Baltimore, MD: ACHA.

American Institute of Stress (2015). *Workplace stress.* Retrieved on October 12, 2015 from http://www.stress.org/workplace-stress/.

Associated Press (2009). *Financial worries, stress and depression on college campus: A survey.* May 21. Retrieved from http://surveys.ap.org.

Berg-Gross, L., & Green, R. (2010). The impact of the recession on college students. *Journal of College Student Psychotherapy, 24,* 2–16.

Brooks, R., & Goldstein, S. (2003). *The power of resilience: Achieving balance, confidence, and personal strength in your life.* Chicago, IL: Contemporary Books.

Cannon, W. B. (1929). *Bodily changes in pain, hunger, fear, and rage.* New York, NY: Appleton.

Cannon, W. B. (1932). *The wisdom of the body.* New York, NY: Norton.

Chronicle of Higher Education (2008). This year's freshmen at 4-year colleges: A statistical profile. *Chronicle of Higher Education, 54*(21), 23.

Colbert, D. (2005). *Stress less.* Lake Mary, FL: Siloam.

Cozolino, L. (2006). *The neuroscience of human relationships: Attachment and the developing brain.* New York, NY: W. W. Norton.

Csikszentmihalyi, M. (1990). *Flow: The psychology of optimal experience.* New York, NY: Harper and Row.

Elkin, A. (1999). *Stress management for dummies.* Foster City, CA: IDG Books.

Fontana, A., & Rosenheck, R. (2005). The role of loss of meaning in the pursuit of treatment for posttraumatic stress disorder. *Journal of Traumatic Stress, 18*(2), 133–136.

Ganzel, B. L., Morris, P., & Wethington, E. (2010). Allostasis and the human brain: Integrating models of stress from the social and life sciences. *Psychological Review, 117*(1), 134–174.

Giancola, J. K., Grawitch, M. J., & Borchert, D. (2009). Dealing with stress in college: A model for adult students. *Adult Education Quarterly, 59*(3), 246–263.

Goldstein, D. S., & Kopin, I. J. (2007). Evolution of concepts of stress. *Stress: The International Journal on the Biology of Stress, 10*(2), 109–120.

Hobfoll, S. E. (1998). *Stress, culture, and community: The psychology and philosophy of stress.* New York, NY: Plenum.

Holmes, T. H., & Rahe, R. H. (1967). The social readjustment rating scale. *Journal of Psychosomatic Research, 11,* 213–218.

Hutchinson, J. G., & Williams, P. J. (2006). Neuroticism, daily hassles, and depressive symptoms: An examination of moderating and mediating effects. *Personality and Individual Differences, 42,* 1,367–1,378.

Jamison, K. R. (1993). *Touched with fire: Manic-depressive illness and the artistic temperament.* New York, NY: Simon & Schuster.

Keenan, E. (2010). Seeing the forest and the trees: Using dynamical systems theory to understand "stress and coping" and "trauma and resilience." *Journal of Human Behavior in the Social Environment, 20*(8), 1,038–1,060.

Kottler, J. A. (2006). *Divine madness.* San Francisco, CA: Jossey-Bass.

Lavee, Y., & Ben-Ari, A. (2008). The association of daily hassles and uplifts with family and life satisfaction: Does cultural orientation make a difference? *American Journal of Community Psychology, 41,* 89–98.

Lazarus, R. S. (1984). Puzzles in the study of daily hassles. *Journal of Behavioral Medicine, 7,* 375–389.

Lazarus, R. S., & Folkman, S. (1984). *Stress, appraisal, and coping.* New York, NY: Springer.

Linden, W. (2005). *Stress management: From basic science to better practice.* Thousand Oaks, CA: Sage.

Maslow, A. H. (1968). *Toward a psychology of being.* New York, NY: Van Nostrand.

McEwen, B. (2002). *The end of stress as we know it.* Washington, DC: The Dana Press.

McEwen, B. S., & Stellar, E. (1993). Stress and the individual: Mechanisms leading to disease. *Archives of Internal Medicine, 153,* 2,093–2,101.

McEwen, B. S., & Wingfield, J. C. (2010). What is in a name? Integrating homeostasis, allostasis and stress. *Hormones and Behavior, 57,* 105–111.

Orloff, J. (2009). *Emotional freedom.* New York, NY: Harmony.

Oz, M. (2010, February). The lighting round. *Esquire,* p. 34.

Rosch, P. (1991, May). Job stress: America's leading adult health problem. *USA Today,* pp. 42–44.

Sapolsky, R. M. (2004). *Why zebras don't get ulcers* (3rd ed.). New York, NY: Henry Holt.

Schore, J. R., & Schore, A. N. (2008). Modern attachment theory: The central role of affect regulation in development and treatment. *Clinical Social Work Journal, 36*(1), 9–20.

Schuler, K. (2006, February 23). Only half of worried Americans try to manage their stress. *USA Today*, p. 13B.

Selye, H. (1946). The general adaptation syndrome and the diseases of adaptation. *Journal of Clinical Endocrinology & Metabolism, 6*, 117–230.

Selye, H. (1974). *Stress without distress*. New York, NY: Lippincott.

Selye, H. (1976). *The stress of life*. New York, NY: McGraw-Hill.

Siegel, D. J. (1999). *The developing mind: How relationships and the brain interact to shape who we are*. New York, NY: Guilford.

Siegel, D. J. (2007). *The mindful brain: Reflection and attunement in the cultivation of well-being*. New York, NY: W. W. Norton.

Sterling, P. & Eyer, J. (1988). Allostasis: A new paradigm to explain arousal pathology. In S. Fisher, & J. Reason (Eds.), *Handbook of life stress, cognition and health* (pp. 629–649). New York, NY: Wiley.

Wolff, H. G. (1953). *Stress and disease*. Springfield, IL: C.C. Thomas.

Xu, J., Murphy, S. L., Kochanek, K. D., & Bastian, B. A. (2016, February). Deaths: Final data for 2013. *National Vital Statistics Report, 64*(2).

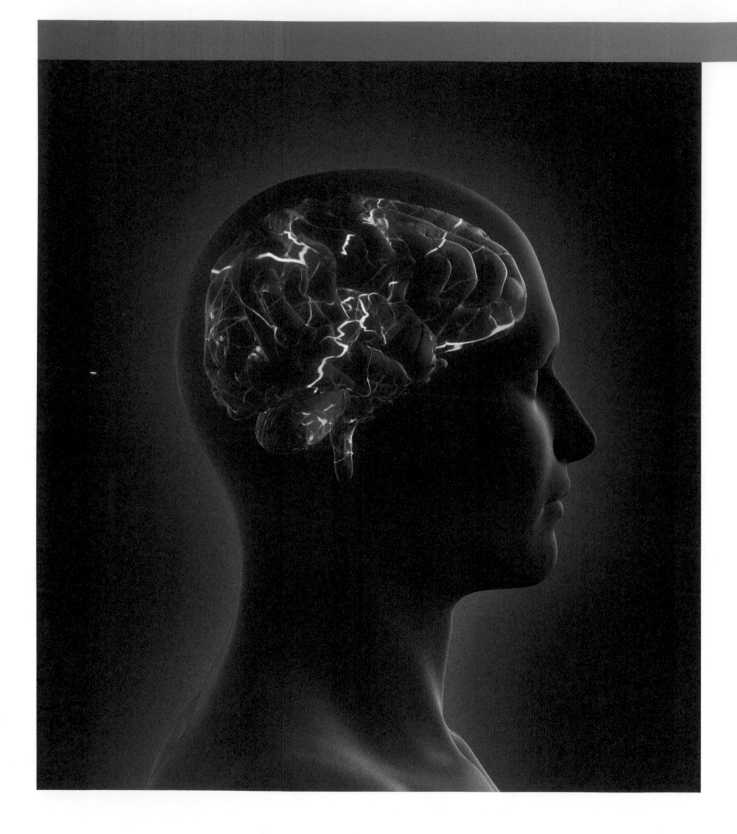

The Body's Reactions to Stress

This course is one of the few you will ever take that integrates many different disciplines—psychology, physiology, biology, health, sociology, and even the humanities. Unless you are a science major, it is probably not absolutely necessary for you to have perfect understanding of all the material presented in this chapter. I am more concerned that you grasp the broad strokes. With that goal in mind, the first time you read this chapter work toward comprehension of main ideas contained in each section, most of which come down to the main idea that prolonged stress wreaks havoc in almost every part of the body.

KEY QUESTIONS IN THE CHAPTER

- Why is it important to study the physiological basis of stress responses?

- How can you apply what you learned in this chapter to understand better why people struggle so much in their lives?

- How can studying the physiology of stress assist you in making sense of your own stress reactions, as well as those you witness in others?

- How do chronic stress and anxiety affect the various systems in the body?

- How do the nervous and endocrine systems work together to coordinate the body's responses to stress?

- How do the sympathetic and parasympathetic nervous systems work in concert to control physiological stress responses?

- What are the body's sequential steps in responding to perceived threats?

- How is the immune system affected by chronic stress?

- What are the risk factors associated with heart disease and other chronic health conditions?

- How is sexual functioning affected by chronic or acute stress?

- What are some ways that stress is helpful?

The Battle Within

A soldier who just returned from the battlefield in Iraq was experiencing a number of distressing feelings. This is what he reported:

I just felt so weak, like I couldn't lift my arms or make my legs move. We were under fire, guys getting hit all around me. I knew I needed to move, to get the hell out of there, but I just couldn't get going. My sergeant was yelling at me—at least I think he was yelling—but I couldn't hear anything except the sound of rushing water in my head.

The really strange thing about the whole experience is that my heart was pounding so hard inside my chest I thought I was going to have a heart attack. I couldn't seem to catch my breath either. I was starting to get dizzy to the point of almost passing out.

I must have been wounded, I figured at first. I was terrified that I'd been paralyzed, taken shrapnel in my spine or something. I just felt so sick and nauseated. My hands felt so tingly I couldn't even hold my weapon. All I could do was just lie there, and hug the ground. Then I passed out.

Called **battle fatigue**, shell shock, or combat stress by the military, or traumatic stress by mental health professionals, this soldier is describing exactly what happens to the body during maximum activation of the sympathetic nervous system.

If he is not able to recover from the episode, or if he is continually subjected to additional combat danger without time and resources to pull himself back together, this traumatic stress will become *post*traumatic stress—chronic problems that may become even worse over time. Without treatment, he could suffer flashbacks, nightmares, headaches, memory deficits, depression, relationship problems, inability to hold a job, even a psychotic break.

In case you breathe a sigh of relief thinking you intend to avoid such combat as much as possible, you should know that it isn't necessary to actually be in a war to suffer similar symptoms. Those who have suffered sexual abuse, physical abuse, or survived catastrophes may exhibit comparable disabling symptoms.

Based on what you learned in the previous chapter about the general adaptation syndrome and the fight-or-flight reflex, you already have some idea of what was going on, physiologically, in this soldier's disturbing responses. His autonomic nervous system, especially the sympathetic division, was working at peak volume. It would be reasonable to surmise, based on his emotional collapse, that he has been repeatedly overexposed to combat stressors for some time.

Unfortunately, once this solider is removed from the battle scene, he may have permanent damage that will continue to affect him in the future. It is entirely possible that he will overreact to stressors once he reenters civilian life. His sleep might be disrupted. He will be far more likely to engage in substance abuse to self-medicate his discomfort. His immune system may be weakened. He may be at greater risk for heart disease and a host of other physical illnesses (Nutt, 2006).

Battle fatigue is one kind of extreme stress reaction that results from an overload of perceived danger and nervous arousal. Failure to recover from the experience can result in posttraumatic stress reactions that produce a number of severe symptoms including insomnia, recurrent nightmares and flashbacks, a sense of helplessness, and debilitating depression.

Not only are soldiers and trauma victims subject to the deleterious effects of extreme stress, but studies have indicated that people living relatively ordinary lives experience debilitating anxiety that makes them up to five times more likely to suffer cardiac death (Goble & Le Grande, 2008; Kawachi, Sparrow, Vokonas, & Weiss, 1994; Shively, Musselman, & Willard, 2009). Their physiological systems are strained to the point that they begin to break down, resulting in much higher death rates than in those who have effective coping strategies (Childre & Rozman, 2005).

It is no wonder that stress has become such a focal point of interest considering that it so impairs performance, clear thinking, and decision making. In one study, rats subjected to continual stress became stuck in habitual and ineffective patterns, making it difficult for them to get their basic needs met; once the stressors (shocks, unpredictable events) were removed, the rats were able to regain sufficient concentration and clarity to function at a much higher level (Dias-Ferreira et al., 2009).

Any time you are subjected to extreme stress, whether sudden or chronic, you may very well freeze up and feel unable to respond effectively. This instinctual reaction once served an important survival function in that loud noises or surprises (potential attacks) result in programmed startle-freeze responses, thus camouflaging your presence with predators around: as long as you remain quiet and perfectly still, you are less likely to be detected. The part of the brain responsible for speech (Broca's area) actually shuts down. The problem, however, is that freezing on a test, giving a speech, or in a social situation is not very useful even though your brain misinterprets such situations as life-threatening.

The body reacts to stressors in a number of ways. These effects can be most logically described according to the specialized systems that serve different functions. The major body systems include the following:

1. The **nervous system** provides overall "executive management" of other systems and communicates orders to coordinate activities.

2. The **endocrine system** works in partnership with the nervous system to control functions through secreting hormones.

3. The **circulatory** and **cardiovascular systems** are concerned with transporting nutrients, waste, and other chemical messengers within and out of the body.

4. The **respiratory system** provides oxygen and nourishment to the body's cells.

5. The **immune system** does exactly what it sounds like: provides defense against invaders.

6. The **musculoskeletal system** (including **skin**) provides support and movement for the body.

7. The **digestive system** processes food sources, converting them into usable energy.

8. The **reproductive system** is concerned with sexual functions and reproduction.

A few of these specialty areas are more involved with, and affected by, stress responses than others. We will look most carefully at the nervous and endocrine systems, and then at how stress affects the heart, digestion, muscles, skin, and other organs. Because this chapter introduces so many medical terms related to anatomy and physiology, I have been selective about which ones are highlighted in bold and inserted in the glossary of key terms at the end of the book. Your instructor may wish you to learn others; if so, he or she will advise you as to which ones are most important.

Nervous System

Stress experience often begins in the brain, even though the stressor often appears in the external environment or outside world. The senses connected to the brain make it possible

FIGURE 2.1
The central nervous system.

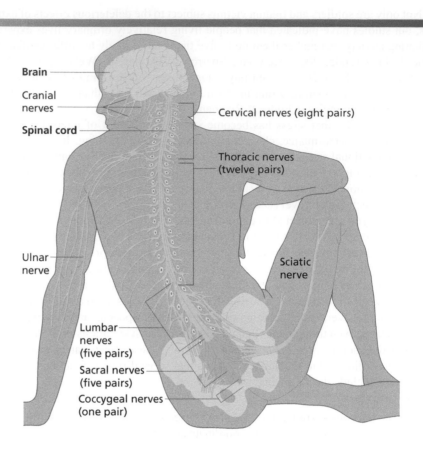

Brain

Cranial nerves

Cervical nerves (eight pairs)

Spinal cord

Thoracic nerves (twelve pairs)

Ulnar nerve

Sciatic nerve

Lumbar nerves (five pairs)

Sacral nerves (five pairs)

Coccygeal nerves (one pair)

for you to know what is happening around you, and within you. Your hearing, sight, smell, touch, and perhaps intuition signal that danger is near.

The human nervous system is organized into several different subsystems. First, there is a **central nervous system**, which is exactly like it sounds—centrally located and housing the brain and spinal cord (see Figure 2.1). The average adult human brain weighs about three pounds and contains 100 billion nerve cells (neurons) in addition to trillions of "support cells" called glia. The spinal cord is located within the vertebrate column that receives messages from, and sends motor commands to, the **peripheral nervous system**.

The peripheral nervous system is divided into two major parts: the **somatic nervous system** and the autonomic nervous system. The somatic nervous system consists of peripheral nerve fibers that receive information from the sensory organs and send information to the central nervous system and motor nerve fibers that communicate with skeletal muscles.

The autonomic nervous system is so named because it operates on "automatic," meaning beyond your conscious awareness and control. It handles many of the regulatory functions that keep you alive—your breathing, blood flow, digestion, and so on. The autonomic system branches off into three other divisions, each with specialized functions: the **sympathetic nervous system**, the **parasympathetic nervous system**, and the **enteric nervous system**. They are all designed to control your various internal organs and glands. In fact, the autonomic nervous system can be regulated by the central nervous system. Just thinking about your inability to pay this month's bill causes your heart rate to go up, and that is evidence that your cerebral cortex plays an important role in autonomic regulation.

We move next to the diencephalon, which houses the **hypothalamus** and the **thalamus** (remember these in particular as they will be referred to a lot). If you are following this on the figure, we are now at the point where the spine connects into the skull. The hypothalamus, about the size of a grape or olive, plays a disproportionate regulatory role considering its small size. It controls body temperature, as well as regulating emotions, hunger, thirst, and sleep rhythms. It is also the part of the brain that is most involved

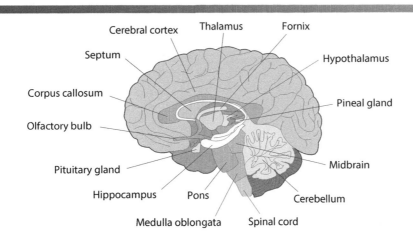

FIGURE 2.2
The major components of the limbic system.

in responding to stress by controlling the pituitary and autonomic nervous system. The thalamus receives sensory information and relays this information to the cerebral cortex and also is involved in motor action planning. The cerebral cortex also sends information to the thalamus, which then transmits this information to other areas of the brain and spinal cord.

The **limbic system** consists of such structures as the **amygdala**, the hippocampus, mammillary bodies, and cingulate gyrus. These areas are important for controlling the emotional response to a given situation. The amygdala is located at the base of the temporal lobe and controls anger, fear, and aggressive behavior. The **hippocampus** is important for formation of new memories and memory retrieval.

Initiation and Control of the Stress Response

You learned in the previous chapter that the function of a stress response is to secure the safety of the organism. A stressor can be any stimulus, real or imaginary, that is perceived to threaten the existence of the organism. The body follows a predictable sequence of reactions in the face of a stressor.

Step 1. The brain *perceives* danger. It doesn't matter whether the threat is real or a figment of the imagination; the senses bring in distressing information that is interpreted as potentially harmful. Naturally there are false alarms, but the brain is programmed to react defensively. It sends out warnings to all systems to activate emergency conditions (the fight-or-flight response). The Greek word for messenger is **hormone**—chemical signals that are launched from the thymus, pituitary, thyroid, and adrenal glands. They are the scouts, like Paul Revere and his compatriots who were sent out all over the countryside during the British invasion to warn of impending attack in the American Revolutionary War. The chemical agents are launched through three separate pathways, making certain to mobilize maximum response to the threat.

Step 2. The first pathway is directed to the muscles, resulting in immediate tension that might be useful for actions such as sprinting, ducking, kicking, punching, biting, and screaming. When the brain perceives a threat, this information comes through the thalamus to the hypothalamus, which in turn activates the autonomic nervous system. For the immediate reaction, the sympathetic nervous system carries signals to the adrenal medulla (i.e., the SAM complex) that secretes **epinephrine** (better known as **adrenaline**) and **norepinephrine** into the bloodstream to be circulated to target organs. These hormones increase the heart rate, raise the blood pressure, accelerate the rate of respiration, dilate bronchial tubes, and inhibit digestive activities. This is the alarm phase, according to Selye, and it involves the autonomic nervous system.

Step 3. If the threat continues beyond a few minutes, the hypothalamus triggers a series of events to prepare the body for the second phase of the stress response that involves more pervasive activation of the bodily functions. At this point, the body realizes

FIGURE 2.3
The HPA process.

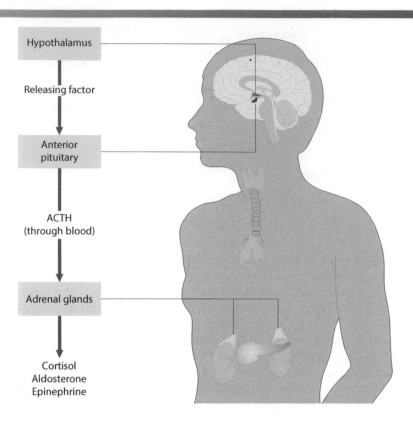

that what seemed, at first, to be a short skirmish is now turning out to be a prolonged battle. This second pathway goes to the immune system, preparing for possible wounds.

The anterior (front) hypothalamus releases a hormone called **CRF** (corticotrophin releasing factor), which then stimulates the pituitary gland to secrete **ACTH** (adrenocorticotropic hormone). ACTH then stimulates the cortex of the adrenal glands to produce cortisol (a **glucocorticoid**) and aldosterone (a **mineralocorticoid**). When you put this chain reaction of chemical responses together, what you end up with is a control pathway called the **HPA** (hypothalamus–pituitary–adrenal) **axis**. This is the central core of the body's reaction to stress. It is the resistance phase in Selye's general adaptation syndrome in which the body is engaged in a prolonged battle with the stressor.

As in all high-functioning organisms and machines, redundancy is built into the system to protect against missed cues. Since this system evolved to protect against life-threatening situations in which survival was at stake, it is not a waste of energy to send out triple signals in case something is lost in translation. This third pathway jump-starts the sympathetic nervous system, kicking in gear all the various systems that were described in the previous chapter. Meanwhile, back in the hypothalamus of the brain, orders are being directed to send reinforcements where they will be most needed.

The way the system was designed to operate, the fight-or-flight response is turned off once the physical threat is no longer perceived. This gives the system time to recover and recalibrate itself before the next sign of danger. The only problem is that this capability decreases with chronic exposure to stressors. It is like an engine system that has been revved into the red zone once too often.

The Brain and Stress

The brain is the most important feature in the stress response, directing every other process. It controls the endocrine system and regulates the rate of metabolism. It directs the activity of the cardiovascular system by influencing the autonomic nervous system. The immune system is also under its direct stimulation by nerves or indirect influence

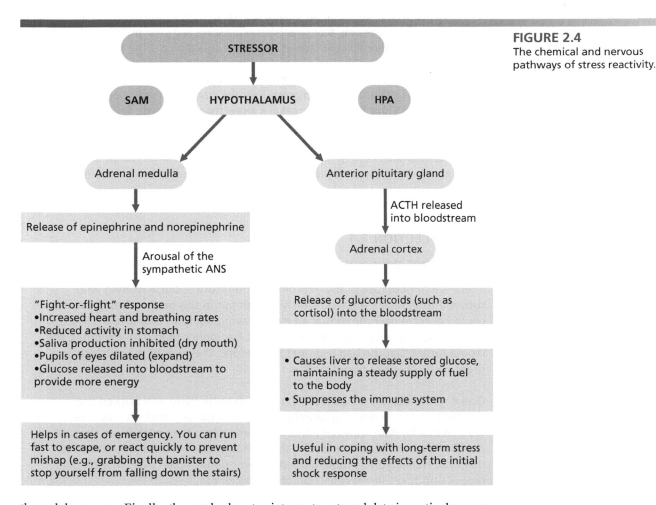

FIGURE 2.4
The chemical and nervous pathways of stress reactivity.

through hormones. Finally, the cerebral cortex interprets external data in particular ways, making almost instantaneous decisions about the most appropriate response.

You have learned how your perception of an experience determines whether it is experienced as stressful or enjoyable. When encountering a similar situation such as the breakup of a relationship, two different people will often have different interpretations, thereby creating different physiological and psychological consequences. One may feel devastated while the other may feel relieved. This is due to your brain making different choices and interpretations.

Despite all the above influences the brain exerts over other bodily systems, it also suffers the consequences of the stress produced by psychological and physiological arousal. The brain areas most susceptible to these effects happen to be the same systems that are activated for the fight-or-flight response, such as the HPA axis and the SAM complex (Bremner, 2005).

The areas of the brain responsible for memory include the hippocampus and amygdala. People who are experiencing severe stress, such as test anxiety, distracting worries, or lingering trauma, tend to make more errors in tasks that require concentration. They have difficulty making decisions. They are more prone to accidents, more inclined toward addiction, and experience a host of physical and psychological complications (Bambling, 2006; Hyman, 2009).

The amygdala is the first structure to be activated during fear responses. It functions to avoid and detect danger and is also involved in forming emotional memories related to fear and social situations. It evaluates threats unconsciously, at lightning speed, before conscious thoughts have time to get into the act.

The amygdala receives input directly from the thalamus before the cortex processes the information, producing a series of bodily responses. For instance, you are walking alone in a dark alley at night and see what you think is a snake crawling toward you, ready to strike. Before you have the chance to consider the improbability of this scenario in an urban area, you already feel your heart rate racing and your muscles tense. As you approach closer you see that the "snake" is really a coiled pipe. Your heart rate begins to slow and your muscles relax.

This quick thalamus–amygdala pathway gives you extra time in resolving a potentially harmful situation. It also overgeneralizes the threat, or, in the words of an ancient Chinese saying, "Once bitten by a snake, a straw rope will startle you ten years later." This means that the amygdala is essentially an impulsive reactor, setting off a fear response before there is a moment to consider what might really be going on. It would rather overreact than hesitate and end up dying with the rest of you in the throes of a python attack. By contrast, the cerebral cortex processes the threat more slowly—and accurately.

FOR REFLECTION 2.1

Two Different Memory Systems (adapted from Joseph LeDoux)

There is a famous case in the neurological literature about a woman who suffered from severe amnesia. The hippocampus in this patient was impaired and could not form new contextual memory, leaving her with only a few minutes of conscious memory. When her doctor left her longer than a few minutes, she would forget that she had ever met him before. They would shake hands and greet each other like two strangers.

One day, the doctor carried a pin in the palm of his hand and pricked the woman's hand when they greeted each other in the accustomed way. The woman quickly withdrew her hand. Next time when they introduced themselves, she didn't remember ever meeting the doctor, yet her hand didn't extend to meet his. Her amygdala remembered the emotions of pain even though her hippocampus lost any recollection of that incident!

Another important structure responsible for fear, anxiety, or emotional memory is the **prefrontal lobe**. It forms a partnership with the amygdala, which is the first-response organ. Among humans, the frontal lobes of the brain are the latest in our evolutionary development and unique to our species: they are the source of reflective thought. This is both a benefit and a burden: on the plus side, the frontal lobes of the cortex permit us to scrutinize our surroundings systematically, consider possible threats that might develop in the future, predict the consequences of certain actions we might take, and plan particular courses of action. This is all very well, but such capacity for imagination and forethought also results in our sometimes engaging in improbable and irrational fantasies about things that could happen (Restak, 2004). The frontal lobes are thus our greatest gift when it comes to anticipating and avoiding danger, but also our greatest liability when they become overstimulated.

Scientists have been attempting to unravel the mysteries of the prefrontal lobes for some time, mostly by examining the effects of having this area inadvertently or surgically destroyed. When lesions are formed in this part of the brain, for instance, people are unable to process certain memories effectively.

In the 1950s, Dr. Wilder Penfield (1975) used electrical stimulation to map the cortex of conscious human patients who were about to be operated on. One day, he probed the cortex of a patient and the man raised his arm. Surprised by this reaction, Penfield asked the man what he was doing. The patient shrugged (as best he could under the circumstances) and reported that he just felt the urge to do so. He didn't know why exactly. Penfield instructed the man to restrain himself next time and touched the same portion of the brain. Again he got the same reaction, even when the man deliberately tried to hold himself back. From this experiment, Penfield learned that the motor portion of the prefrontal lobe has the capability to override the signals sent from other systems. It also explains how, even with the best of intentions, you might feel helpless to control certain impulses that are overridden by another source of power.

FOR REFLECTION 2.2

Emotional and Cognitive Functions of the Cerebral Cortex

Phineas Gage was a construction worker who was supervising a railroad crew laying tracks in a rural part of Vermont in 1848. Dynamite was used frequently to drill holes in the bedrock. Gage was in the process of setting the charge when he was momentarily distracted. An iron rod that was used to press down the powder was launched like a missile through his cheek, skewering his eye and exiting through the top of his skull.

The force of the explosion knocked the poor fellow off his feet and he briefly lost consciousness. Although most of the left side of his cerebral cortex was obliterated, Gage regained consciousness a few minutes later. His memory remained intact and he could describe in perfect detail what had happened.

A few months later, Gage felt well enough to resume his work. He was still physically strong and highly motivated. Unfortunately, one outcome of his accident was that his personality completely changed. Previously he had been seen as dedicated, hardworking, shrewd, and polite—a good man to have on your side. But since the brain damage he was hard to be around. He swore a lot (which he had never done before) and was seen as impulsive and unpredictable. To his friends and coworkers, he was no longer the same person.

Gage's transformation became a landmark case for understanding the mechanisms of the brain and how the frontal lobes of the cerebral cortex not only house thinking processes, but also influence emotions and the structure of the personality.

Naturally, it is easier to keep your fears in check before they develop into full-blown phobias. Research has demonstrated that it is very hard to wipe out fear memories completely even with an intact prefrontal lobe. That is why a simple treatment process is not very effective with phobias. It also explains why certain inborn fears, such as of snakes, spiders, and falling, are hard-wired into our brains, as throughout the evolution of our species they are the most likely ways that we might become grievously injured. Avoiding each of these dangers requires instant action without conscious thought.

When subjected to prolonged or extreme stress, nerve cells begin to degrade over time. When volunteers are given synthetic cortisol, the hormone most prevalent during stress responses, their memories became seriously impaired (Marieke, Tollenaar, Elzinga, & Walter, 2009; Wolkowitz, Reuss, & Weingartner, 1990). Imagine that you have prepared to give a talk on a particular subject and suddenly the circumstances have radically changed. Instead of facing a half dozen of your classmates in an informal setting, you have been asked to give a formal speech in an auditorium housing 600! Furthermore, you are told that the presentation begins in five minutes. You are led on stage to find there is no lectern; you have no choice but to leave your notes behind. While it is possible you might rise to the occasion, it is far more likely that the rush of stress chemicals in your brain might slow down your thinking a bit, not to mention impair your ability to recall the talk that you had so carefully prepared.

As if memory impairment is not bad enough, excessive glucocorticoids in the system have been shown to actually kill off parts of your brain, taking little bites at a time (Porter & Landfield, 1998). The hippocampus, the region of the brain that controls much of learning and memory, is particularly vulnerable to deterioration. It is a specialist in imprinting new memories: you might recognize as a symptom of Alzheimer's disease that older people can remember the more distant past as if it happened yesterday, but have no distinct memories of what actually happened yesterday. This is devastating, but consider that a reduction in the size of the hippocampus is also associated with severe depression and mental illness (to be discussed in Chapter 4).

Sapolsky (2004) summarizes some of the major effects of hippocampus atrophy that occur with sustained stress.

1.   It can create severe depression, the kind that doesn't go away after a short period of time, but reappears unrelated to any stressor. It is considered endogenous; that is, biologically based, as opposed to triggered by grief or loss.

2.   Soldiers or abused children who experience posttraumatic stress have been found to have smaller hippocampus tissue than those who have not experienced it. The more devastating the trauma or crisis, the more deterioration takes place.

3.   Cushing's Syndrome is a form of cancer that excretes excess quantities of glucocorticoids, affecting all the usual suspects: memory, blood pressure, sexual functioning, the immune system.

4.   There is higher risk of permanent impairment after a stroke. Brain adaptability and healing become compromised when the hippocampus limps along at less than full strength.

The Autonomic Nervous System and Stress

As previously explained, the autonomic nervous system (ANS) regulates all the organs and tissues not controlled by the central nervous system. It innervates the actions of glands, the smooth muscles of hollow organs and vessels, and the heart muscle.

The ANS is divided into two major branches, namely, the sympathetic and parasympathetic nervous systems. The sympathetic system (so named because the Greek physician and writer Galen believed that the brain worked in sympathy with the visceral organs) operates as an "on" switch. Its partner is the parasympathetic system, the "off" switch, which turns down the energy expenditure when it is no longer needed.

The sympathetic system becomes aroused mostly under four conditions. These have been memorized by generations of medical students as the "Four Fs." The first two are easy since you already learned them: **F**ight and **F**light. The third F refers to the accompanying **F**right. So, that leaves a certain four-letter word, beginning with F, that is used both as a swear word and as description of copulation. (Well, you can remember *that* one.)

While the sympathetic system accelerates energy expenditure and promotes the stress response, the parasympathetic system slows energy expenditure by promoting energy storage and cell reparation. For example, sympathetic arousal increases heart rate while parasympathetic activation reduces it (see Table 2.1). The sympathetic system is for fight or flight and the parasympathetic system is for "rest and digest." In most cases, the two systems are antagonistic, meaning opposing, in that when one is high in activity the other is low.

The sympathetic system also inhibits other systems not immediately involved in the stress response, such as the urinary, digestive, and reproductive systems. You may have noticed that you have trouble swallowing food before you take an important exam for which you are not quite ready. Your mouth is dry. The parasympathetic system promotes the activity of the digestive tract, constricts blood vessels, and stimulates the formation of urine. When you are relaxed, saliva abounds in your mouth and your appetite is enhanced.

The Endocrine System

As I have mentioned, the endocrine system and nervous system control and coordinate all the other systems in the body. The nervous system controls rapid activity such as

FIGURE 2.5 The effects of sympathetic and parasympathetic nervous system activation on various organs and body systems.

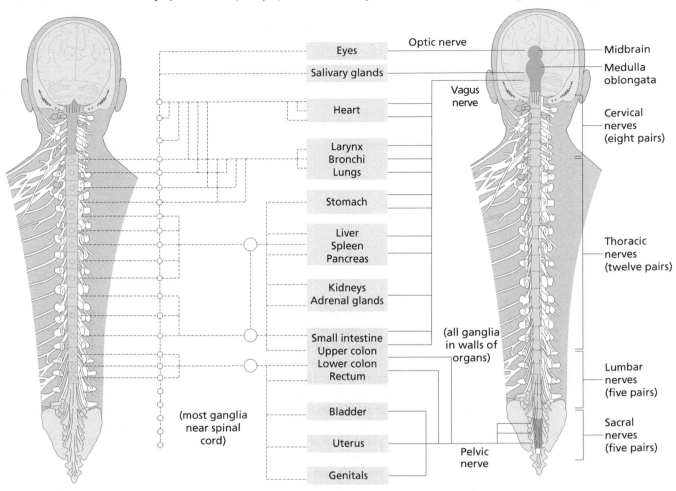

A Sympathetic outflow from spinal cord

B Parasympathetic outflow from the spinal cord and brain

Examples of responses
Heart rate increases
Pupils of eyes dilate (widen: let in more light)
Glandular secretions decrease in airways to lungs
Salivary gland secretions thicken
Stomach and intestinal movements slow down
Sphincters (rings of muscles) contract

Examples of responses
Heart rate decreases
Pupils of eyes constrict (keep more light out)
Glandular secretions increase in airways to lungs
Salivary gland secretions become dilute
Stomach and intestinal movements increase
Sphincters (rings of muscles) relax

voluntary muscle action and intestinal activity through electrical and chemical signals. The endocrine system exerts its control by means of chemical signals whose effects on the body are initiated more slowly and last longer.

The endocrine system produces those potent biochemical substances called hormones via a group of glands. They are carried in the bloodstream to control specific organs. These hormones only affect certain target tissues or organs where specialized receptors are found. This structure is not unlike the communication system of a modern home in which there are telephone wires, cell phone signals, cables, and electrical wires that are all designed for specific functions to control different systems.

The glands that are most relevant to the stress response are the **pituitary, thyroid,** and **adrenal glands** (see Figure 2.6). The pituitary plays an important role in stress responses

TABLE 2.1 Effects of the sympathetic and parasympathetic systems on selected organs

Effector	Sympathetic system	Parasympathetic system
Pupils of eye	Dilation	Constriction
Sweat glands	Stimulation	None
Digestive glands	Inhibition	Stimulation
Heart	Increased rate and strength of beat	Decreased rate and strength of beat
Bronchi of lungs	Dilation	Constriction
Muscles of digestive system	Decreased contraction	Increased contraction
Kidneys	Decreased activity	None
Urinary bladder	Relaxation	Contraction and emptying
Liver	Increased release of glucose	None
Adrenal medulla	Stimulation	None
Blood vessels to:		
skeletal muscles	Dilation	Constriction
skin	Constriction	None
respiratory system	Dilation	Constriction
digestive organs	Constriction	Dilation

because it secretes several hormones into the bloodstream that stimulate the adrenal cortex, the thyroid gland, the gonads (testes and ovaries), and other tissues of the body. However, the pituitary is controlled by the hypothalamus, which in turn is influenced by other higher brain centers. The adrenal glands are very important officers in this operation—specialists, so to speak, in stress response. They consist of two small glands located above the kidneys. Each gland has two parts, an inner area called the medulla, and an outer portion called the cortex. The thyroid gland is an endocrine gland located in the base of the neck producing thyroxine that can have significant effects on the metabolism of the body.

The adrenal gland is involved in two parallel response pathways during the stress response. The first is the SAM complex discussed earlier, and the other is the adreno-cortical pathway, which is part of the HPA axis regulated by the hypothalamus and the pituitary. Each of these takes a different route to sound the alarm, just in case one of the "scouts" doesn't make it through.

Cortisol is among the most important hormones involved in stress responses. It has several different functions. First, it increases the supply of blood glucose to the body and the brain that can be used as "fuel" for fighting or fleeing. It also turns off all bodily systems not immediately required to deal with a threat. For instance, cortisol turns off insulin so that the liver releases more glucose, thus creating a temporary homeostatic imbalance. It also shuts down reproductive functions and inhibits the immune system. Unfortunately, this extra cortisol in the bloodstream is also associated with increased incidence of hypertension and coronary heart disease because it channels excessive cho-lesterol into the blood and leads to plaque buildup along the walls of arteries. When endo-crine glands become depleted through overproduction of hormones (such as adrenaline), this can lead to medical conditions such as reactive hypoglycemia that can eventually lead

---

FOR REFLECTION 2.3

Based on what you already learned about the way that epinephrine (adrenaline) is released into the blood at 20 times the normal rate under conditions of stress, why do you suppose that immediately after a crisis has passed you feel a need to urinate?

Answer at the end of the chapter.

FIGURE 2.6 The endocrine system.

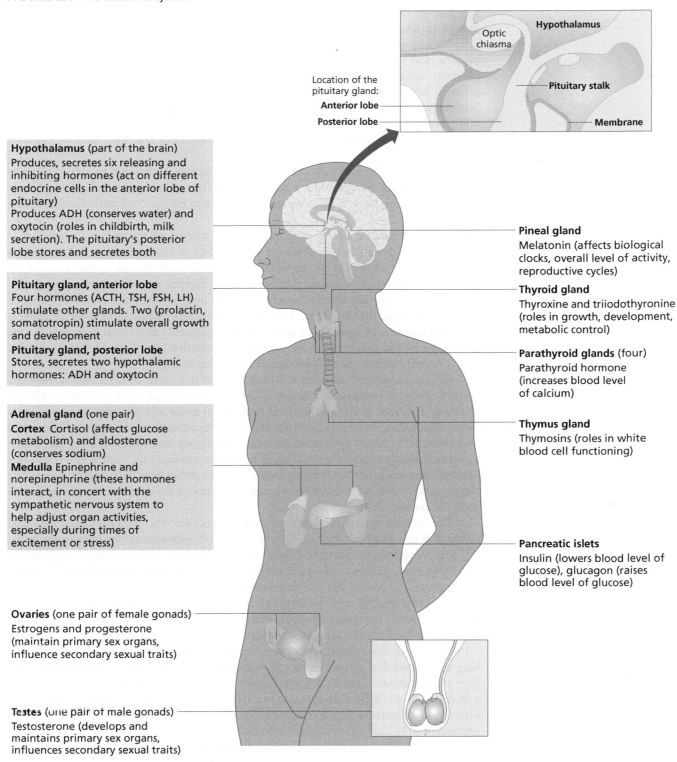

Location of the pituitary gland:
Anterior lobe
Posterior lobe

Optic chiasma
Hypothalamus
Pituitary stalk
Membrane

Hypothalamus (part of the brain)
Produces, secretes six releasing and inhibiting hormones (act on different endocrine cells in the anterior lobe of pituitary)
Produces ADH (conserves water) and oxytocin (roles in childbirth, milk secretion). The pituitary's posterior lobe stores and secretes both

Pituitary gland, anterior lobe
Four hormones (ACTH, TSH, FSH, LH) stimulate other glands. Two (prolactin, somatotropin) stimulate overall growth and development
Pituitary gland, posterior lobe
Stores, secretes two hypothalamic hormones: ADH and oxytocin

Adrenal gland (one pair)
Cortex Cortisol (affects glucose metabolism) and aldosterone (conserves sodium)
Medulla Epinephrine and norepinephrine (these hormones interact, in concert with the sympathetic nervous system to help adjust organ activities, especially during times of excitement or stress)

Ovaries (one pair of female gonads)
Estrogens and progesterone (maintain primary sex organs, influence secondary sexual traits)

Testes (one pair of male gonads)
Testosterone (develops and maintains primary sex organs, influences secondary sexual traits)

Pineal gland
Melatonin (affects biological clocks, overall level of activity, reproductive cycles)

Thyroid gland
Thyroxine and triiodothyronine (roles in growth, development, metabolic control)

Parathyroid glands (four)
Parathyroid hormone (increases blood level of calcium)

Thymus gland
Thymosins (roles in white blood cell functioning)

Pancreatic islets
Insulin (lowers blood level of glucose), glucagon (raises blood level of glucose)

to diabetes. On the other hand, if the endocrine system overfunctions, remaining stuck in the "on" position and flooding the body with cortisol, bad things can also happen. When cortisol-based drugs (cortisol is a steroid) are prescribed for diseases such as cancer, arthritis, and asthma, common side-effects include intestinal bleeding and ulcers, as toxic levels begin to eat away at the stomach lining. The endocrine system maintains a very delicate balance in which too little, or too much, cortisol can prove destructive.

The Immune System

Just like the Department of Homeland Security, the immune system is designed to stop foreign invaders. Rather than identifying human terrorists, the body's immune system is calibrated to recognize and respond to invading agents such as fungi, parasites, bacteria, and viruses. In addition to defending against attacks, the immune system also conducts surveillance activity in order to prepare for any future assaults. In this way it seeks to destroy any suspicious-looking cells before they mutate to cancer. Based on intelligence gathered during previous attacks, it also initiates immunity systems that will protect against similar infections in the future. In other words, it has a memory that keeps track throughout your lifetime of all those invaders that have tried to colonize your body.

The first barriers to the invasion of infectious agents are the skin and mucous membranes. The intact skin prevents many microbes from entering the body. The mucous membranes lining body cavities secrete substances to entrap small particles like spider webs.

Once the harmful agents penetrate the first barriers of the immune system, it is necessary to activate other mechanisms to neutralize or kill them. The challenging job of the immune system is to tell the difference between cells that are normal parts of the body and those that are invading microbes. These immune responses are made possible by circulating white blood cells (lymphocytes and phagocytes) that develop in the bone marrow and in the thymus gland. There are three categories of lymphocytes: T cells, B cells, and natural killer cells (NK), each of which operates to assist cells in trouble. As the name implies, NK cells are the most aggressive—your first line of defense against mutant and virus-infected cells or diseases that threaten your health.

During an immune reaction, the body mounts two types of reactions: *nonspecific* and *specific*. One nonspecific reaction is familiar to you in the form of inflammation or swelling. This is an acute physiological response to tissue injury caused by such factors as chemicals, heat, trauma, or bacterial invasion. The damaged tissue secretes substances that increase the blood circulation and make capillaries leak fluids, causing the region to become swollen and inflamed. This is not unlike climbing the highest hill (or in this case building one) and then lighting a signal flare to attract help. These secretions attract phagocytes to destroy the invading microbes and remove the dead tissue from the breakdown of the body cells.

The immune system produces two types of specific reaction: chemically mediated (through B cells) and cell-mediated (through T cells). When a microbe invades the body, it is first recognized by macrophages and if they cannot dispatch the culprit, they call for T cells to assist. This puts out a general alarm that leads to the production of NK cells, which attack and destroy the invading agent.

The other strategy employed through chemical means is to call on B cells to produce antibodies, which are specific proteins that don't much like the invaders. They mobilize to target the foreign cells, searching and destroying until given the all-clear sign.

So, what is the connection between stress and the immune system? Research has long established that chronic stress can weaken the immune system and all the things it does to protect you. Specifically, chronically high levels of cortisol are associated with a decrease in the body's natural immune response, a decrease in DNA repair mechanisms, and an increase in autoimmune mechanisms (Stojanovich, 2010; Stojanovich & Marisavljevich, 2009). To understand the mechanisms of stress influence on diseases, we will examine the interconnections among the brain, immune system, endocrine system, and illnesses.

Immunity and Stress

In the past, scientists focused on the investigation of the immune system in relative isolation, as if it were a discrete system that functioned independently and autonomously. It was not until the 1980s that the connections between the immune and nervous systems were gradually clarified. The study of the interactions between the immune system, the endocrine system, the nervous system, and behavior is called **psychoneuroimmunology (PNI)**, also known as **psychoneuroimmunoendocrinology (PNIE)**. It was formed as a discipline because unless endocrinologists, neurologists, and psychobiologists began collaborating, they were likely to miss a large piece of the puzzle (Ader, Cohen, & Felten, 1995; Kendall-Tackett, 2010; Leonard & Myint, 2009).

In an earlier section, you learned about the communication between the nervous system and the endocrine system through neurotransmitters and hormones that have to be combined with receptors of cell membranes of target tissues or organs. You may wonder how the immune system communicates with the endocrine and nervous systems so effectively. In fact, the chemical messengers of the immune system are cytokines, large proteins that are secreted by immune cells and glial cells of the brain. The cytokines activate specific receptors on immune, endocrine, or neural cells. Cytokines can either increase or decrease inflammation.

Inflammation is a double-edged sword. The good function is the body's way to fight against infection, irritation, toxins, and foreign molecules. White blood cells and cytokines are unleashed to protect your body in a rapid immune response. However, when the immune system is under chronic stress, it will rev up the process of sending more and more proinflammatory cytokines into the systems and causing all kinds of diseases. You have learned that stress can be real or imaginary; therefore, even imaginary stressors can cause inflammation in your body through the release of proinflammatory cytokines (Zachariae, 2009). Recent research shows that many diseases—heart disease, diabetes, depression, multiple sclerosis, Alzheimer's, and autoimmune disorders—are strongly associated with inflammation (Jaremka, Lindgren, & Kiecolt-Glaser, 2013; Kiecolt-Glaser et al., 2007; Leonard & Myint, 2009; Pace, Hu, & Miller, 2007).

VOICE OF STRESS 2.1

Twenty-Three-Year-Old College Senior

At age 15 when I was starting high school I was overwhelmed with transferring from an average classroom setting to honors classes. I didn't deal with this transition very well. I started to get terrible stomach aches that were eventually diagnosed as colitis. The doctor said it was totally from nerves.

For about a year I felt so sick I could barely go to school at all. I couldn't even leave the house sometimes because I was afraid I'd throw up or have to use the bathroom. I stopped eating much and lost a lot of weight.

Then I started to get more stressed because my family didn't believe that my pain was real. They thought I was just making it up so I didn't have to go to school.

I learned after that I would have to be very careful with stress in my life or my body would act up again. I felt really proud about how I recovered but ever since that time I have to guard against things building up too much or I'll get stomach aches again.

The major question to consider is, how is the immune system actually suppressed in the face of a chronic stressor? In the earliest years of stress research, Selye noticed that the thymus gland atrophied among rats that underwent chronic stress (Selye, 1946). It was found that stress suppresses the formation of new lymphocytes and their release into the bloodstream. This inhibits the production of new antibodies. Chronic and uncontrollable stress leads to the secretion of excessive blood cortisol, hypertension, and increased inflammatory changes in the HPA axis. Also, chronic stress produces so many changes in the SAM system that unhealthy metabolic changes will occur including diabetes, obesity, and hypertension.

If stress takes a toll on the immune system and wears it out, what are the consequences for the host body? **Autoimmune diseases** are those in which the body actually attacks itself. The sensors that detect foreign invaders become confused, signal false alarms, and worse of all lose the ability to distinguish genuine enemies from friendly forces. Rheumatoid arthritis is one such disease in which the immune system, depleted and exhausted by stress, begins attacking the connective tissue. This results in inflammation and extreme pain in the joints and other parts of the body.

Autoimmune diseases can affect all the systems of the body, especially the nervous system (multiple sclerosis), muscular system (lupus), gastrointestinal system (colitis), **circulatory system** (Behcet's disease), endocrine systems (Graves' disease), and skin (psoriasis). In each case, the effects of stress have so disoriented and exhausted the immune system that it loses the ability to locate appropriate targets.

Another variation of immune dysfunction occurs when rather than attacking the body itself, the immune system overreacts to relatively benign stimuli. For example, allergies form when the body perceives dust, pollen, and mold as serious enemies. Stress exacerbates conditions such as asthma and inflammatory disorders.

The immune system is concerned not only with warding off enemies but with acting as all-round guardian of maximum longevity. It is perhaps not all that surprising that stress reduces your lifespan in measurable ways. In one study conducted with women who were suffering prolonged stress, it was found that the parts of their immune cells that are devoted to reproducing themselves (the ends of chromosomes) were significantly deteriorated. This is considered one way that scientists measure aging. This condition not only increases the risk of contracting physical diseases but also signals significantly reduced lifespan, by as much as ten years (Nautiyal, DeRisi, & Blackburn, 2002).

VOICE OF STRESS 2.2

A Twenty-Four-Year-Old Waitress and College Student

My boyfriend and I just broke up and it's been unbearable. Not only did I lose the love of my life, but I had to find a new place to live. And fast! Well, while dealing with the move, the breakup, and having to change schools, I started to notice that I wasn't sleeping well. The next thing I knew I could see my hair was getting thinner. I would wake up on my friend's couch, and find clumps of hair on my pillow!

I absolutely freaked out—I could see bald patches on my head! I went to see a doctor and she ran every test in the book. She sent me to a specialist. It turns out that my body had a bad reaction to the stress that I had been going through. They said the stress triggered the alopecia. Imagine that, a bad enough reaction to stress that I start to go bald! I had to have 20 cortisone shots in my skull, plus some relaxation training, before my hair started to grow back.

The Cardiovascular System

The cardiovascular system delivers oxygen, hormones, nutrients, and white blood cells throughout the body by circulating blood. The heart, a fist-sized series of muscles that is nothing more than a pump, powers everything. As I alerted you in the previous chapter, just like any mechanical device, the heart has a finite lifespan—80 years, more or less, which is pretty good for any pump. Depending on how hard and how fast it is required to run, under what conditions it is forced to operate, and how it is cared for, it can last significantly shorter or longer than its advertised specifications. Unlike most other pumps, the heart is subject to both automatic and manual operation. It can be speeded up or slowed down at will, just by thinking about an image of a South Pacific beach, an impending deadline, or an attractive classmate. The heart is also capable of independent action as it continues to beat steadily, thumping away when you are awake or asleep.

As you learned earlier, one immediate response to a stressor is accelerated heart rate and increased blood pressure. To accelerate the cardiovascular system, the body cranks up the sympathetic nervous system to release epinephrine and norepinephrine and causes the adrenal glands to secrete more glucocorticoids and mineralocorticoids. In addition, the thyroid gland gets into the act, teaming up to help increase blood pressure and heart rate. At the same time, the kidneys decrease urine production, thereby increasing the blood volume. During stress reactions, blood thickens and clots tend to form more easily, resulting in increased likelihood of strokes.

When the stressful situation is over, the parasympathetic system is activated to bring the metabolic rate down through lowering the heart rate, dilating blood vessels, and returning more blood to the gut. Yet, when you experience chronic stress, the cardio-vascular system is kept working overtime without regular breaks, creating a condition of **hypertension**, or chronically elevated blood pressure. It is estimated that 15% to 20% of the adult population is faced with this disease.

Elevated blood pressure is harmful to the heart and the blood vessels in a number of ways. When blood is returning to your heart with greater force, it makes a stronger landing on the muscle, causing a thickening and enlargement over time. Once this occurs, the heart requires more blood than the coronary arteries can supply.

The connecting places where large vessels branch into smaller vessels bear the brunt of the increased blood pressure. Repeated crushing against these spots causes wear and tear, eventually leading to tissue damage. Once the smooth lining of the vessel begins to form little craters of damage, inflammation results. These craters become a gathering site for circulating platelets, fats, cholesterol, glucose, and other material in the body. Over time, the blood vessels will become fragile and clotted, leading to **arteriosclerosis** (heart disease). As the vessels become further infused with plaque, calcium, and other fatty acids, they harden and lose elasticity. Coronary events (as heart attacks are called) may soon follow.

High blood pressure combined with arteriosclerosis (plaque/cholesterol) is very dangerous. Greater force is pushing blood through pipes that are on the verge of rupture. When the rupture occurs in the brain, it is a cerebral hemorrhage leading to a stroke or apoplexy. When a coronary artery ruptures, a heart attack or a myocardial infarction occurs, because a part of the heart dies from lack of oxygen. Scientists have learned that many factors contribute to the development of arteriosclerosis and hypertension. High saturated fats in diet provide a significant source of bad cholesterol. Lack of exercise, and little time for relaxation, further increase the allostatic load on the body. Other con-tributing factors include smoking, heredity, and diabetes. Yet more than anything else it is often psychological factors that predispose some people to have fatal heart attacks: half of all such victims did not have elevated cholesterol but rather manifested certain behavioral and attitudinal traits that are associated with chronic stress (Underwood, 2005).

Let's review to this point: the heart is a pump; the arteries and veins are pipes. Stress increases the fluid pressure within this circulatory system, over and over, straining the walls, the valves and seals. Stressed blood is thicker with platelets that are needed to provide emergency clotting and with fatty nutrients needed for energy. This leaves behind deposits (called plaque) in its wake, creating weakening in the linings, inflammation, and higher concentrations of cholesterol. Where does all this lead? Stress increases the risk of heart disease, stroke, and high blood pressure. No matter how much you control your diet or take drugs, stress leaves behind a combination of chemicals that clog your arteries and slowly restrict the functioning of the pipe system. That means your heart now has to work even harder to deliver the necessary oxygen and nutrients to other areas. And what do you think *that* does to its longevity?

Perhaps you recognize that this is all very much like a sump pump located in the basement of a building. The pump is activated only when the water level rises to a prede-termined level, and then it whirrs into operation until the level is brought down, returning to a resting state. When such a pump malfunctions, or when the water keeps flooding in faster than the pump can operate, the mechanical parts wear out—stress fractures its weakest parts. This is what happens to your heart during prolonged stress.

The Gastrointestinal System

The gastrointestinal (GI) system is a biological mechanism that breaks down foods into their chemical components. This makes it easier for the body to create energy and form muscle, bone, blood, skin, or other tissue. The first stage of digestion takes place in the mouth, where solid food is chewed and crushed by the teeth while saliva enters the mouth from three glands on each side of the face. Saliva is rich in an enzyme that starts the conversion of starches into simple sugars and assists the swallowing of the food.

The now mashed substance is further compressed and liquefied as it makes its way through the esophagus to the stomach. More squeezing takes place while the nutrients are absorbed into the system as needed. At the very bottom of the esophagus is a ring of muscle called the sphincter. This valve opens to release food into the stomach and then shuts again, preventing food from backing up as sometimes happens when a garbage disposal breaks down.

The stomach serves as a storage tank for swallowed food while it continues to break down the material into even smaller parts. These secretions include hydrochloric acid and pepsin, a chief protein-splitting enzyme. The food substances then pass into the small intestine where secretions of juices will assist with a more complete breakdown of these proteins, fats, and carbohydrates and the absorption of the usable parts. The unused and undigested parts will be pushed into the large intestine and moved by muscle contractions into their final destination out of the body through the anus.

Like most other systems in the body, this whole nutritional process of metabolizing food sources is controlled in the brain, particularly in the hypothalamus which signals hunger responses. You can therefore appreciate that the GI system would also be affected by the stress response.

Let's return to the stage where food first enters your mouth. Have you ever had difficulty swallowing food, especially when you were feeling nervous about something? As you learned before, the fight-or-flight reflex shuts downs all nonessential systems, including digestion, since it would be too late to create new sources of energy quick enough to be useful. This is why saliva secretion drastically decreases and your mouth feels dry.

Emotional stress also causes stomach cramps as a result of contractions that take place when the digestive process is suddenly halted (see Voice of Stress 2.3). During conditions of chronic or repeated interruptions, all the stomach acids that are useful for breaking down solid foods begin to eat away at the linings of the digestive tract. This can lead to ulcers and other stomach problems.

VOICE OF STRESS 2.3

A Student in His Mid-Twenties

I get real moody when I'm stressed. But when I'm dealing with something really serious, like financial problems or a relationship problem, I literally cramp up! I mean I get abdominal cramps that are so painful that I can't even function. Sometimes it gets so bad I have even had to pull my car over to the side of the road for fear of crashing. Then I get diarrhea that turns me into a complete wreck.

I've been through every type of medical test possible. I even had a probe inserted to examine my insides. All the doctors say is that I have to keep my stress level down. I realize that but it just feels out of my control sometimes. When I get in a fight with my wife, or it comes time to pay my tuition for college, or finals are coming up, I just feel the cramps coming on.

Disruption of digestion breaks up the rhythm of the operation. Once repeatedly halted and restarted, the assembly line can move too quickly, providing insufficient time for the food substance to dry out through water absorption. The result: diarrhea.

Alternatively, the system can move too slowly and the material dries out so much that constipation takes place.

Of course during stress situations the last thing in the world your body is thinking about is eating a meal or going to the toilet. You've got more pressing business to take care of—like a snake attached to the heel of your foot or an enemy with a weapon in your face. Right after the perceived danger is over, you may find yourself voraciously hungry to replenish the energy depleted, especially with fast foods that have plenty of starch and fat to provide quick nutrient sources. That is one reason why stress can lead to obesity: donuts, chocolate, ice cream, and pancakes are called "comfort foods" because they literally reduce the stress that is still circulating in the body from the activation of perceived threat.

You are waiting nervously for a boyfriend or girlfriend to call, afraid that something has gone wrong; maybe the relationship is over. You pace back and forth, anxious, stressed, jumping at the sound of any noise that might signal the phone ringing. You stare at the phone over and over willing it to ring. But it remains silent. What could have gone wrong? It's clear he/she probably doesn't love you after all. Surely you can recognize that this is a fully fledged stress response even in the complete absence of any direct threat; it is all in the mind. It will come as no surprise, however, that the chosen coping strategy is to go for the double chocolate ice cream in the freezer. This craving is actually the body's signal that it needs more immediate energy sources if this stress battle is going to become a long siege.

Once the all-clear sign is given, the gastric juices rush back to work, behind in their jobs as if they missed a whole week's work. A host of gastrointestinal disorders are caused by stress. In its mildest form you may feel a queasy stomach, the result of hormonal flooding, or perhaps temporary diarrhea. During prolonged bouts of stress, the consequences become far more serious and chronic: irritable bowel syndrome and hypoglycemia to mention a few, most of them the result of excessive stress hormones that remain in the system long past the point they are doing you any good.

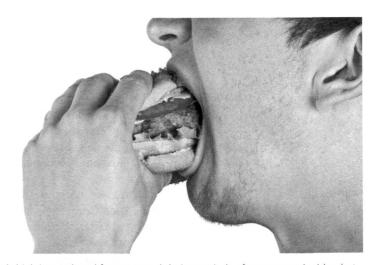

Foods high in starch and fat are craved during periods of stress to replenish what the body believes is an emergency. These foods quickly enter the bloodstream, producing surges in blood sugar that the body believed were crucial to fight or run. If such an energy binge is not actually needed, then the excess sugar becomes converted into fat.

The Musculoskeletal and Skin Systems

The skeletal system makes up the framework of the body and allows us to move when our muscles contract. It stores minerals (such as calcium and phosphorus) and releases them into the body when they are needed. The skeletal system also protects internal organs and produces blood cells. Different types of muscle enable motion, generate heat to maintain body temperature, move food through the digestive tract, and contract the heart. In total, the human body has more than 600 such muscles.

Muscles have just two states: contraction and relaxation. Under normal circumstances, that works out fine. But when you are under chronic stress, the nervous system issues faulty commands to contract muscles that really are not needed. It is as if you are in a trench on a battlefield, ready to charge. Every few minutes you get an order to prepare yourself to jump out and run. False alarm. You relax for a moment and gather your breath. But then there it is again, that damn alarm signal, telling you to prepare for immediate attack. You keep getting the signal over and over again, relentlessly, never sure whether it is a real alert or just your imagination.

What happens to your muscles under such conditions? They fatigue, begin to ache, and become tight like coiled wires. Pain and discomfort ensue. In fact, this is the surest way to know whether you are feeling stress in the first place, when you can feel the tension in your muscles, especially those in your neck, face, shoulders, and back.

Most of the time this is all going on without your awareness. You don't realize that your muscles are tight. Perhaps only later do you feel a headache coming on or notice that your hands are sweaty. Most of all you feel soreness in your neck and back. This unnecessary muscular contraction is called **bracing**.

The skin is a part of the immune system (keeping bad things out of the body), and it joins forces with muscles and bones to provide support. Skin actually forms the largest organ of the body and provides the body with the first barrier that protects you from invading microbes and loss of water from the moist internal tissues. It helps control the body's temperature and excretes some wastes, and serves as a major sensory organ, registering pressure, pain, and temperature.

The stress response is manifested through the skin system in numerous ways. As you have no doubt noticed, under conditions of stress you start to sweat. Your armpits feel wet. You can feel droplets falling down your back. Your brow and palms collect moisture. The skin is doing all it can to cool what it believes is an overheated body while running or fighting. The increased moisture also improves electrical conductance which can be measured by a galvanometer (a lie detector).

The Reproductive System

As if stress does not wreak enough havoc within other body systems you hold dear, sexual functioning and fertility are also strongly impacted. Sexual dysfunctions are most commonly classified as psychological in origin (estimated at 90–95%), especially those that have to do with "performance." In the case of a man, this is related to attaining and maintaining an erection, as well as continuing the sex act long enough to satisfy one's partner.

There are sexual dysfunctions that have an organic cause; that is, they result from neurological diseases or side-effects of medications. Most problems, however, are caused by psychological factors such as stress, lifestyle, and relationship issues. That is one reason why sexual dysfunctions such as premature ejaculation and erectile dysfunctions in men, and orgasmic dysfunctions in women, are almost always treated within the context of the couple's relationship. After all, when a man can't have an erection with his partner (but he can with others or during masturbation), he is communicating a message. Likewise, if the woman can't have an orgasm with her partner, or a man has an orgasm too quickly, there are certain messages associated with those behaviors as well.

When you consider how much of sexual arousal and performance is regulated by the endocrine system, limbic system, sympathetic (stimulates orgasm) and parasympathetic (stimulates arousal) nervous systems, as well as desire as created in the cerebral cortex, it is easy to see why sexual activity would be affected so profoundly by physiological stress. Unbalanced hormone levels affect sexual interest and arousal. High blood pressure jeopardizes vascular functioning (useful during erections). High blood sugar (associated with chronic stress syndrome) reduces testosterone levels.

Then, given how much of sexual experience is mentally based, meaning the thoughts and feelings that accompany the physical act, it is nearly impossible to attain/maintain an erection or enjoy an orgasm if the whole time your head is filled with anxious thoughts like: "Oh my God, what if I don't get hard?" or "I've got to come. What if I don't come? Does that mean there's something wrong with me?"

Even if, with all the obstacles just described, a couple does manage to complete a sex act to a satisfactory conclusion, that still may not end the ordeal. Both menstruation and ovulation cycles are affected by stress, as are the frequency of miscarriages, and preterm labor. A laundry list of stress-related factors can sabotage reproductive functioning: lack of hormones (progesterone), too much of a hormone (prolactin), impaired blood flow, flooded corticols affecting glands (ovaries, testes), and the loss of **libido** or sexual desire, the most common sexual disorder of all. It is sad but true that many contemporary couples report that they are just too busy, too tired, and too stressed to have sex.

Not All Doom and Gloom

You learned in the previous chapter that stress, in itself, is neither a problem nor a health hazard; it is chronic, unremitting stress that presents a severe health hazard with all the terrible things that happen to various body systems previously described (and summarized in Table 2.2). You will learn more in Chapters 13 and 14 about how performance can be actually *enhanced* by moderate levels of stress in certain circumstances. For now, I would like to tell you some good news: the positive changes and adaptations that take place within the body.

Let's start with the most obvious: stress is often fun. Why else would you ever take any risks to deliberately stoke up your adrenaline levels and heart rate? Why would you ever voluntarily get on a roller coaster? Why would you drive fast and increase the probability of an accident? Why would you sometimes do stupid or dangerous things (that you *know* are misguided at the time)? Why would anyone ingest drugs like amphetamines or cocaine that specialize in activating hormonal overload?

The brain creates pleasure and pain. Glucocorticoids, those same chemicals that can create havoc in excess, can also stir up **dopamine**, another hormone that greases the skids of the pleasure pathways in the brain. When dopamine is activated in moderate, brief intervals (like during the ride on a roller coaster), it is experienced as pleasurable. When it becomes sustained and repetitive, chronic anxiety can result. It's another case of too much of a good thing.

TABLE 2.2 Diseases and medical conditions affected or exacerbated by stress	
Asthma	Allergies
Diabetes	Heart disease
Stroke	Ulcers
High blood pressure	Hypertension
Multiple sclerosis	Infertility
High cholesterol	Obesity
Cancer	Depression
Alzheimer's disease	Addison's disease
Constipation	Irritable bowel syndrome
Hypoglycemia	Fibromyalgia
Common cold	Menstrual irregularity
Eczema/Psoriasis	Hives
Sexual dysfunction	Premature aging
Chronic fatigue syndrome	Chronic pain
Colitis	Arthritis
AIDS	Epstein–Barr disease
Miscarriage	Dwarfism
Anorexia	Canker sores/herpes

Stress in moderate doses can act as a motivator to get things done. It heightens awareness to the point that performance can increase. It helps you assess and respond to potential threats. All these conditions are seen as positive if your system can return to normal functioning within a reasonable period of time (Muller, Kohn, & Stein, 2005). Note that short-term stressors may actually boost the immune system while long-term stressors weaken it, making you more susceptible to chronic diseases (Segerstrom & Miller, 2004). Recent research in psychoneuroimmunology has examined the beneficial effects of acute stressors on health. It has been found that acute stressors can activate innate immunity through increasing trafficking of immune cells to the site of challenge and by inducing long-lasting changes in immunological memory (Campisi & Fleshner, 2003; Viswanathan, Daugherty, & Dhabhar, 2005). Edwards et al. (2006) showed that acute physical and mental stress increased antibody responsiveness in women before influenza vaccination.

At regular intervals, a healthy dose of stress activation keeps the body, and all its systems, well tuned. That is one reason why we enjoy stimulation in our lives, and why boredom can kill us as easily as too much excitement. The same sort of conditioning that prepares an athlete for a competitive race also helps you to stay in shape for any real dangers you might face. You've got to keep all systems operating at peak functioning, and that's not going to happen during a sedentary, sheltered life in which you avoid all possible dangers or risks. The key, again, is moderation.

There are basically four conditions that separate "good" stress (eustress) from "bad" stress (distress) (Lazarus, 1993; Levine, Baade, & Ursin, 1978), as follows:

1. *Extent of uncertainty*. Too many unknown factors increase stress levels. That is why people like to travel to places that are novel and different, but not *so* different that they seem completely out of the realm of experience. Wandering around a strange city is enjoyable if it is within the limits of your uncertainty tolerance; becoming hopelessly lost goes a step too far.

2. *Amount of relevant information available.* Data, preparation, homework, and rehearsal are crucial not only to performing well but also to enjoying the experience. When you are called upon to perform in challenging circumstances, you attempt to reduce the stress associated with uncertainty by arming yourself with as much information as you can, but not so much that you take away all element of surprise. You might, for example, study maps and guidebooks about a place you intend to visit but you wouldn't want to watch a three-hour video that shows everything you are about to see.

3. *Amount of control.* Too much control over a situation means no surprises and no delights except through the satisfaction of predicting the inevitable. At some stages of life, and levels of functioning, children (and impaired adults) will engage in repetitive activities over and over, reveling in the sameness of things, providing a semblance of order to an otherwise chaotic inner world. To most people, however, control already rules too much of our lives—work schedules, study schedules, family obligations. This can be a good thing in that it keeps you organized and on track, thereby reducing the stress of uncertainty. But there are also times when you love to surrender control and let yourself go not completely, but enough that you feel greater freedom.

4. *Interpersonal conflict.* I include a whole chapter on this subject because it is so often a source of stress in people's lives. In one sense, such relationship difficulties also result from uncertainty, lack of reliable information, and loss of control. Ask people to describe their biggest problems in this area and they will often point to friendships, family, and love relationships in which they feel misunderstood or disrespected.

FOR REFLECTION 2.4

Complete this exercise either on your own or in small groups.

What is the common factor in all of the elements just described that distinguish good stress—the kind that is enjoyable and stimulating—from the kind that is destructive and painful? Look at each of the factors separately and then try to determine a common denominator. Try to come to a consensus in your group, or form your own conclusion if you are doing this on your own.

The answer is at the end of the chapter.

In later chapters I will talk in greater detail about ways that you can prevent the bad kind of stress and manage it when avoidance is not possible. Already you can see from this overview that the best strategy is one in which you attempt to exercise as much control as possible over situations that you might find stress-inducing. This is more easily said than done, especially when such control involves the unpredictable environment and other people's behavior.

SUMMARY

The stress response, in all its various manifestations within the body, is essentially feedback. The nervous system, and all its components, exists to help the organism protect itself against harm. All of its alarm functions are designed, then, to get us to alter our behavior in such a way that we reduce threats. When those danger signals are ignored, then the nervous and endocrine systems mobilize recruits from all over the body to turn up the heat—whatever it takes to get your attention and get you to stop doing what you are doing that is not working very well, or to start doing something else. In the words of one writer, "Stress doesn't kill us—but it makes everything that does kill us much worse" (Lehrer, 2010, p. 132).

I have reviewed each of the major systems of the body and discussed how they operate and how they are affected by stress. While you may be feeling a bit anxious yourself about all the complex physiology and anatomy terms that have been introduced, as well as the dense material packed into a relatively small space, you have just learned the foundation for much of what you need to understand about how stress operates in the body. I urge you to study this material with more than the usual level of attention and dedication. I promise that these concepts will come up again in the chapters that follow.

FOR REFLECTION 2.5

Time to Take a Deep Breath

The content of this chapter was particularly dense and challenging. A lot of terms and many physiological concepts were introduced that require years of study in order to understand well. Don't sweat the small stuff or get caught up in the details. Think about the big picture regarding what happens to your body during stress reactions.

Clear your mind for a moment.

Take a deep breath.

Now, write down what you remember from this chapter that strikes you as most important and useful.

QUESTIONS FOR REVIEW

1. How do the nervous and endocrine systems work together to coordinate the body's responses to perceived dangers?
2. Explain why chronic stress has such devastating effects on the various body systems.
3. How do the amygdala and prefrontal lobes of the cerebral cortex function differently in their assessments of potential threats?
4. Diagram how the body operates during the fight-or-flight response.
5. What process, when affected by stress, can cause diarrhea or constipation? Explain the underlying mechanisms.
6. What are the ways that stress can be helpful and enhance performance and enjoyment of activities?

SELECTED ANSWERS

Answer to For Reflection 2.3

Epinephrine is released into the blood by the adrenal glands to ignite the fight-or-flight response. The effects typically last one to two minutes, after which the hormones are immediately converted into waste products that are expelled from the body through urination. The initial inhibitions of urination and defecation that take place during stress are suspended immediately afterwards—hence the expressions "he was so scared he pooped in his pants" or "peed in his pants." Those urges would actually come afterwards.

Answer to For Reflection 2.4

During your discussion, or reflections, you may have found several different possibilities that capture the common feature(s) of all the factors that separate good stress from bad stress. Certainly one big theme has to do with helplessness. Even during caveperson days, the problem was *not* in facing predators, but in encountering one without adequate means to defend yourself. So it is with bad stress situations that you are facing: (1) great uncertainty, (2) lack of useful information about the situation, (3) little control over matters, and perhaps (4) some type of conflict. If you feel some degree of control over matters, then stress may be neustress or eustress rather than distress.

REVIEW ACTIVITIES

Review Activity 2.1: Physiological Basis of Stress

Directions: Test your understanding of the following concepts by matching the neural structures with the clues.

	Neural structure		Clue
1	Nervous system	A	Consisting of organs that process food sources, converting them into usable energy
2	Endocrine system	B	Allowing us to move when our muscles contract
3	Cardiovascular system	C	Collective name for all of the neurons in the body
4	Respiratory system	D	Consisting of the sympathetic and parasympathetic nervous systems
5	Immune system	E	Increasing the bodily metabolism and energy expenditure
6	Musculoskeletal system	F	Producing hormones and emptying them into the bloodstream
7	Digestive system	G	Delivering oxygen, hormones, nutrients, and white blood cells to the body
8	Reproductive system	H	The adrenal cortex hormones that affect metabolism of fats and carbohydrates
9	Autonomic nervous system	I	The endocrine gland under the hypothalamus that secretes hormones that control other glands
10	Sympathetic nervous system	J	An adrenal cortical steroid hormone that regulates mineral metabolism and fluid balance
11	Parasympathetic nervous system	K	Also known as "sensory relay center"
12	Hypothalamus	L	Playing an important role in memory, spatial navigation, and stress termination
13	Thalamus	M	An abbreviation for corticotrophin-releasing factor
14	Limbic system	N	An abbreviation for adrenocorticotropic hormone
15	Hippocampus	O	The endocrine glands on top of each kidney that secrete stress hormones
16	CRF	P	The endocrine gland in the neck that secretes the hormone thyroxin
17	ACTH	Q	Providing defense against foreign invaders
18	Glucocorticoids	R	Also known as the "seat of emotions"
19	Mineralocorticoids	S	Processing emotions and activating the fight-or-flight response
20	Pituitary gland	T	Dedicated to the production of offspring
21	Thyroid gland	U	Providing oxygen and nourishment to the body's cells
22	Adrenal gland	V	Reducing the bodily metabolism and energy expenditure

See p. 59 for the answer key.

Review Activity 2.2: Understanding the Sympathetic and Parasympathetic Systems
Directions: Fill in the spaces provided to indicate the effects of the autonomic nervous systems on these target organs.

Effects of the Sympathetic and Parasympathetic Systems on Selected Organs		
Effector	**Sympathetic system**	**Parasympathetic system**
Pupils of eye		
Sweat glands		
Digestive glands		
Heart		
Bronchi of lungs		
Muscles of digestive system		
Kidneys		
Urinary bladder		
Liver		
Adrenal medulla		
Blood vessels to: *skeletal muscles* *skin* *respiratory system* *digestive organs*		

REFERENCES AND RESOURCES

Ader, R., Cohen, N., & Felten, D. (1995). Psychoneuroimmunology: Interactions between the nervous system and the immune system. *Lancet*, January, 99–103.

Bambling, M. (2006). Mind, body, and heart: Psychotherapy and the relationship between mental and physical health. *Psychotherapy in Australia, 12*(2), 52–60.

Bremner, D. (2005). *Does stress damage the brain? Understanding trauma-related disorders from a mind–body perspective.* New York, NY: Norton.

Campisi, J., & Fleshner, M. (2003). The role of extracellular HSP72 in acute stress-induced potentiation of innate immunity in physically active rats. *Journal of Applied Physiology, 94*, 43–52.

Childre, D., & Rozman, D. (2005). *Transforming stress.* Oakland, CA: New Harbinger.

Dhabhar, F. S. (2007). Immune function, stress-induced enhancement. In G. F. Fink (Ed.), *Encyclopedia of stress* (2nd ed., Vol. 2, pp. 455–461). San Diego, CA: Academic Press.

Dhabhar, F. S., & Viswanathan, K. (2005). Short-term stress experienced at time of immunization induces a long-lasting increase in immunologic memory. *American Journal of Physiology— Regulatory, Integrative and Comparative Physiology, 289*, R738–R744.

Dias-Ferreira, E., Sousa, J. C., Melo, I., Morgado, P., Mesquita, A. R., Cerqueira, J. J., et al. (2009). Chronic stress causes frontostriatal reorganization and affects decision making. *Science, 325*, 621–625.

Edwards, K. M., Burns, V. E., Reynolds, T., Carroll, D., Drayson, M., & Ring, C. (2006). Acute stress exposure prior to influenza vaccination enhances antibody response in women. *Brain, Behavior, and Immunity, 20*, 159–168.

Goble, A., & Le Grande, M. (2008). Do chronic psychological stressors accelerate the progress of cardiovascular disease? *Stress and Health, 24*, 203–212.

Hyman, M. (2009). *The UltraMind solution: The simple way to defeat depression, overcome anxiety, and sharpen your mind.* New York, NY: Scribner.

Jaremka, L., Lindgren, M., & Kiecolt-Glaser, J. (2013). Synergistic relationships among stress, depression, and troubled relationships: Insights from psychoneuroimmunology. *Depression and Anxiety, 30*(4), 288–296.

Kawachi, I. Sparrow, D., Vokonas, P. S., & Weiss, S. (1994). Symptoms of anxiety and risk of coronary heart disease. *Circulation, 90*(5), 2,225–2,229.

Kendall-Tackett, K. A. (2010). Treatments for depression that lower inflammation: Additional support for an inflammatory etiology of depression. In K. A. Kendall-Tackett (Ed.), *The psychoneuroimmunology of chronic disease: Exploring the links between inflammation, stress, and illness.* (113–131) Washington, DC: American Psychological Association.

Kiecolt-Glaser, J. K., Belury, M. A., Porter, K., Beversdoft, D., Lemeshow, S., & Glaser, R. (2007). Depressive symptoms, omega-6: omega-3 fatty acids, and inflammation in older adults. *Psychosomatic Medicine, 69*, 217–224.

Lazarus, R. S. (1993). From psychological stress to the emotions: A history of changing outlooks. *Annual Review of Psychology, 44*, 1–21.

Lehrer, J. (2010). Under pressure. *Wired*, August, 130–137.

Leonard, B. E., & Myint, A. (2009). The psychoneuroimmunology of depression. *Human Psychopharmacology: Clinical and Experimental, 24*, 165–175.

Levine, S., Baade, E., & Ursin, H. (1978). *The psychobiology of stress.* New York, NY: Science and Technology Books.

Marieke, S., Tollenaar, B. M., Elzinga, P. S., & Walter, E. (2009). Immediate and prolonged effects of cortisol, but not propranolol, on memory retrieval in healthy young men. *Neurobiology of Learning and Memory, 91*(1), 23–31.

McCance, K., Forshee, B., & Shelby, J. (2006). Stress and disease. In K. L. McCance, & S. E. Huether (Eds.), *Pathophysiology: The biologic basis for disease in adults and children* (5th ed., pp. 311–332). St Louis, MO: Mosby.

Muller, J., Kohn, L., & Stein, D. (2005). Anxiety and medical disorders. *Current Psychiatry Reports, 7*(4), 245–251.

Nautiyal, S., DeRisi, J. L., & Blackburn, E. H. (2002). The genome-wide expression response to telomerase deletion in *Saccharomyces cerevisiae. Proceedings of the National Academy of Sciences of the United States of America, 99*(14), 9,316–9,321.

NDCHealth (2003). *PharmaTrends: 2002 year in review—U.S. market.* New York, NY: NDCHealth.

Nutt, D. J. (2006). *Post-traumatic stress disorder: Diagnosis, management, and treatment.* New York, NY: Taylor & Francis.

Pace, T. W., Hu, F., & Miller, A. H. (2007). Cytokine-effects on glucocorticoid receptor function: Relevance to glucocorticoid resistance and the pathophysicology and treatment of major depression. *Brain, Behavior, and Immunity, 21*, 9–19.

Penfield, W. (1975). *The mystery of the mind: A critical study of consciousness and the human brain.* Princeton, NJ: Princeton University Press.

Porter, N. M., & Landfield, P. W. (1998). Stress hormones and brain aging: Adding injury to insult? *Nature Neuroscience, 1*, 3–4.

Restak, R. (2004). *Poe's heart and the mountain climber: Exploring the effect of anxiety on our brains and our culture.* New York, NY: Harmony.

Sapolsky, R. M. (2004). *Why zebras don't get ulcers* (3rd ed.). New York, NY: Henry Holt.

Segerstrom, S. C., & Miller, G. E. (2004). Psychological stress and human immune system: A meta-analytic study of 30 years of inquiry. *Psychological Bulletin, 130*, 601–630.

Selye, H. (1946). The general adaptation syndrome and the disease of adaptation. *Journal of Clinical Endocrinology, 6*, 117–230.

Shively, C. A., Musselman, D. L., & Willard, S. L. (2009). Stress, depression, and coronary artery disease: Modeling comorbidity in female primates. *Neuroscience & Biobehavioral Reviews, 33*(2), 133–144.

Stojanovich, L. (2010). Stress and autoimmunity. *Autoimmunity Reviews, 9*, A271–A276.

Stojanovich, L., & Marisavljevich, D. (2009). Stress as a trigger of autoimmune disease. *Autoimmunity Reviews, 7*, 209–213.

Underwood, A. (2005, October 3). The good heart. *Newsweek*, pp. 49–53.

Viswanathan, K., Daugherty, C., & Dhabhar, F. S. (2005). Stress as an endogenous adjuvant: Augmentation of the immunization phase of cell-mediated immunity. *International Immunology, 17*, 1,059–1,069.

Willenberg, H. S., Bornstein, S. R., & Chrousos, G. P. (2007). In G. F. Fink (Ed.), *Encyclopedia of stress* (2nd ed., Vol. 1, pp. 709–713). San Diego, CA: Academic Press.

Wolkowitz, O., Reuss, V., & Weingartner, H. (1990). Glucocorticoids disrupt memory in healthy humans. *American Journal of Psychiatry, 147*, 1,297–1,310.

Zachariae, R. (2009). Psychoneuroimmunology: A bio-psycho-social approach to health and disease. *Scandinavian Journal of Psychology, 50*, 645–651.

Review Activity 2.1: answer key	
1	C
2	F
3	G
4	U
5	Q
6	B
7	A
8	T
9	D
10	E
11	V
12	S
13	K
14	R
15	L
16	M
17	N
18	H
19	J
20	I
21	P
22	O

3

Sources of Stress across the Lifespan

So far I have been talking about stress in the most general terms. I have discussed the ways the body responds to stress, described how neurological and endocrine systems function, and outlined the mechanisms of the fight-or-flight reflex. Each of these descriptions refers to how people (or organs) behave, without reference to particular differences in the individual. Yet you know that not everyone acts the same way in given circumstances, nor do their bodies react identically.

What determines the differences in individual responses to stress? One reason is variations in the ways each of us is built; not all mechanisms in the body are constructed exactly the same way. The heart and accompanying coronary connections are located in the chest, usually a bit off center to the left; but in truth, there are exceptions to this rule where particular organs end up a few inches in one direction or the other. Personality is another variable that influences stress responses, as are your background, gender, ethnicity, religion, and culture.

KEY QUESTIONS IN THE CHAPTER

- How is human development reflected in a series of sequential stages?
- What are the "developmental tasks" of childhood? Adolescence? Young and middle adulthood? Later maturity?
- What is the theory of fetal origins of adult disease?
- How do primary and secondary appraisals of stress affect a person's emotional responses?
- What are the major sources of stress throughout the lifespan?
- What are the most reliable indicators of serious suicidal intent among those who are overstressed?
- How are drugs and alcohol used as forms of self-medication?
- How does stress impair sexual functioning?
- What is the "family life cycle" and how does it influence the individual's stress reactions?

The next several chapters look at some of the differences in the ways that people react to stress. I begin with one of the most obvious factors: the person's age. Throughout the lifespan, from birth until old age, stressors take a different form, just as the capacity to respond to these stimuli changes as you mature. What concerns you most at this point in your life is quite different than what got under your skin a few years ago, or when you were in elementary school, or an infant.

Stress is prevalent all through life and, as you have seen, this is not altogether a bad thing. Every phase of human growth benefits from the presence of a reasonable amount of stress. Without the pressure of gravity, for instance, your skeletal system would lose calcium and become very brittle. If you did not experience resistance, you would never develop muscular strength and endurance. Likewise, without transcending adversity, you would never mature intellectually, emotionally, and spiritually. It is precisely the same challenges in life that create stress that help you to build resilience and personal resources.

Developmental Tasks

As you age, you go through a series of rather predictable stages. These changes are physical, but also involve emotional and cognitive functioning. In the first month of life, the newborn will already respond to stressful overstimulation by emotional bursts of tears to signal distress. By the second month, the baby learns to cry to get needs met. During the third month of life, the baby can determine cause–effect relationships, and by the fourth month she starts exploring the world by putting anything and everything in her mouth to taste it (the most highly developed sense at that point).

One theorist, Robert Havighurst (1953), collected ideas from all the developmental models of his day and conceived of the notion of **developmental tasks**. These are specific challenges that are supposed to arise at a particular stage in life. If the person does not manage to master this task, then he is going to suffer and experience problems later in life. If you follow the progression of locomotion, for instance, scooting is a developmental task in infants that leads to crawling, then standing, walking, and running.

Havighurst compared life to climbing a mountain. The climber may have easy and level terrain for a period of time, when minimal effort and skill are required. When obstacles are encountered such as steep walls, overhanging rocks, few handholds, or unstable surfaces, no further progress can be made until the climber masters the set of skills required to overcome the challenges. Likewise, at various times in your life, you may encounter difficulties that require mastery of new tasks. For instance, until you understand the physiology of stress in Chapter 2, and the developmental aspects in this chapter, it is going to be difficult for you to truly comprehend the concepts that follow; the chapters in this book follow a developmental series of increasingly complex tasks, each of which builds on the previous steps.

The developmental-task theory emphasizes the importance of lifespan education that requires the individual to be engaged in formal or informal learning for the sake of resolving life's most stressful challenges. The theory also puts forth the concept of "teachable moments"; that is, that people have a certain readiness to deal with challenges that they would not be able to do during an earlier stage. You can't force a kid to walk or talk, or learn calculus, until such time as she has developed the necessary cognitive and physical skills. Keep in mind, however, that developmental tasks are derived not only from biological maturation, but also from the expectations of your culture, peer group, and personal goals. In some settings, surfing or playing video games might be the major developmental tasks of a typical ten-year-old in Huntington Beach, California, whereas hunting springboks might be crucial in the Kalahari Desert in Namibia.

Rock climbing is much like the developmental tasks we face in life. Each new obstacle requires a set of skills that build on those that came previously. Unless you master the intricacies of scrambling, it's very difficult to do belaying and rappelling. And these tasks must be mastered before you can ever hope to do free climbing.

Developmental Stages and Major Stressors

A number of other theorists have developed stage models to explain the evolution of gender, spirituality, cultural identity, moral reasoning, or career choices. In each case, theorists have described the ways that people at various ages and stages most often function—what they are able to do at that age and what tasks they must complete before they can move on to the next stage. All of these developmental theories follow similar assumptions that growth is progressive, incremental, and becomes increasingly complex.

Most prominent among the theorists of human development was Erik Erikson (1963), whose psychosocial theory of development has made a great contribution to our understanding of the stages of human development throughout the lifespan. He was the first developmental theorist to seriously consider development beyond adolescence. His stages of development are based on the need to develop mastery and personal identity through a series of challenges that occur at different points in one's life cycle.

Each of the developmental theories organizes certain developmental tasks according to certain stages. In Table 3.1 I summarize the developmental stages, including the major stressors that are likely to take place at each point. The particular age divisions in Table 3.1 are a bit arbitrary (for example, young adulthood as 24–38 years). I separated them in this way based on approximate times when life transitions take place. For instance, most college-age students (those who are not adult learners) are in early adulthood, in which the major developmental tasks include finding a life mate and planning for a career. While these tasks might be accomplished during your college years, it is also entirely possible that you will not be ready or have the opportunity to connect with a partner until you are well into your thirties or forties. This does not mean that you have "failed" this stage; it merely means that these stages are somewhat flexible and fluid. They give you a rough template of what to expect when considering the major stressors at various points in

TABLE 3.1 Overview of developmental stages and major stressors

Stage	Age	Developmental tasks	Major stressors
Infancy	Birth to 2 years	Learning to trust, master physical tasks of feeding, communicating, movement, talking, crawling, walking	Helpless to meet needs, body control, environmental obstacles
Early childhood	3–5 years	Getting along with age-mates, social skills and roles, developing independence, control own behavior, gender role, learning right from wrong	Manage frustration, first conflicts, guilt, self-restraint
School age	6–12 years	Develop sense of competence, basic values, learning to read, develop social circle, adapt to siblings, learn abstract reasoning	Feeling inferior, school and sports performance, emotional control, delay gratification
Adolescence	13–18 years	Identity development, plan for future work, organizing time, sexual orientation, peer roles	Social pressures, drugs, emotional volatility, hormonal changes
Early adulthood	19–23 years	Developing intimacy, education and apprenticeship, career plans, learning to love, friendships	Loneliness, sexuality, career confusion, financial independence
Young adulthood	24–38 years	Marriage/Partnership, launch career, commitment to life goals, creativity and productivity	Moving away from home, forming own family, parenting
Mid-life transition	39–50 years	Productive years, social and civic responsibilities, taking leadership roles	Promotions and advancement at work, family conflicts, economic pressure
Later maturity	51–65 years	Mentoring next generation, using authority for others' welfare, grandparenting	Loss of parents, empty nest, declining health and functioning
Old age	66 to death	Retirement, coping with death and illness, reduced physical functioning, increased leisure time, coming to terms with life's meaning and worth	Dealing with losses, adjusting to changes in health, being marginalized

the lifespan. So, at age 20, you might not be prepared or interested in connecting with someone in a love relationship, but that does not mean that you do not feel pressure from peers, parents, and yourself to do so.

Models such as those depicted in Table 3.1 give the impression that development proceeds in a linear, incremental, and highly organized manner. Yet transitions between changes can be chaotic and stressful times that do not at all seem to follow a logical progression. Much depends on exactly what kind of developmental transition you are experiencing. For each of the transitions described in Table 3.1, think of a time in your life in which you experienced this stress and how you dealt with it. Some transitions can either be initiated or not (such as divorce or ending a relationship), while others can occur suddenly or gradually beyond your awareness (such as weight gain). Stress is most likely to occur in those situations in which you feel the least control.

Transactional Model of Stress

As you have experienced yourself at times, developmental transitions involve changes that can be quite stressful. You may be reasonably satisfied in the role of student, in which

---

FOR REFLECTION 3.1

The stress of change

Make a list of three of the most significant changes you have made in your life during the past few years. Consider those that took place in the domain of family, friendships, love, health, work, living situation, finances, or other personal decisions.

1.

2.

3.

What was it about each of these personal changes that produced the most stress for you?

All changes require work and adjustment of some sort—learning new skills, relearning old habits, dealing with new challenges, facing the unknown. Among all the factors that determine whether a lifestyle change is experienced as "stressful" or "challenging" is your *cognitive appraisal*. In the transactional model of stress, this simply means how you choose to think about your situation and how you internally interpret an external event.

In looking at the stress events you listed above, consider the internal thoughts that went through your mind as you faced each of these life transitions. Think about a few of them that could be considered negative, discouraging, and pessimistic ("I'll probably never be able to handle this") versus those that were far more upbeat and encouraging ("This is going to be a fun challenge").

Note the difference between those situations in which your assessment of potential threat was relatively dire and bleak versus those in which you thought to yourself that you could handle whatever came up.

your primary responsibility is learning as well as preparing for the future. Your "job" in life is to read, study, write about what you are learning, have interesting conversations with people about new ideas, and generally to soak up as much knowledge as you can. You are also working to qualify yourself for some opportunities you'd like to pursue in the future. Yet just when you figure out what is going on and develop an effective system for success, you get thrown out (graduate) after a few years. Now you must master a whole different set of rules, behaviors, and developmental tasks in order to succeed in a different environment.

Stress can become most intense during transitions in which you move from one stage to the next one. Think of **puberty** as a dramatic example when, seemingly abruptly, a person experiences major physiological, psychological, and social stressors associated with the move from childhood to adulthood. Coping strategies that worked well during earlier stages (crying, pouting, throwing temper tantrums) are not nearly as effective later in life.

Transitions occur not just within each individual, but within the larger society. In 1900, 40% of Americans lived in urban areas, and today that number has doubled to 80%. The crowding, noise, pollution, and threats of crime and terrorism associated with urban living add extra stress to people's lives. The increasing pace of life, plus the advent of new technologies, put more pressure on people to adapt to transitions for which they were unprepared.

The **transactional model of stress** developed by psychologist Richard Lazarus (1991) helps to shed light on the mechanisms through which changes in life may be converted into either subjective stress or a source of euphoria. Lazarus places great emphasis on the importance of cognitive appraisal in the stress response (more on cognitive approaches will be discussed in Chapter 6). This means that stress is the result of a "transaction" between an external event and an internal event. The mediator between the two is the cognitive appraisal or interpretation.

This theory helps explain why a similar event, say the loss of $100, can trigger very different emotional and physiological responses for two different people; it all depends on their **cognitive appraisal**. For someone who is broke, this loss can make him sick to his stomach while, to a millionaire, the loss can represent an insignificant nuisance.

In order for the stress response to be evoked, there are two separate but related cognitive events: the **primary appraisal** and the **secondary appraisal**. The primary appraisal will identify the nature of the environmental demand on the person, or the relationship between the event and one's personal goals. This initial perception of the event can be plotted along a continuum, depending on the extent to which the situation is viewed as dangerous or benign (Lazarus, 1991, 2006; Lazarus & Folkman, 1984).

If the primary appraisal looks at the situation or object to assess its potential as a threat, the secondary appraisal considers your own resources to meet the challenge. In this second stage, the severity and immediacy of the threat are considered, as well as whether you are in a position to deal with it effectively.

The secondary appraisal determines the severity of a problem and the degree of stress reactivity. A millionaire perceives the loss of $100 as a minor event because she is "resourceful," while to an economically disadvantaged person this loss of money represents a catastrophe. Another example of this secondary appraisal could occur if you recently discovered that you would never become a great gymnast, but this did not particularly upset you because it was in no way related to your goals.

The transactional model of stress includes three major developmental stages (Figure 3.1):

1. An individual faces a challenging event or potentially threatening task.

2. The person determines first the nature of demand (primary appraisal), as well as the resources and skills available to cope with the demand (secondary appraisal).

FIGURE 3.1 Transactional model of stress.

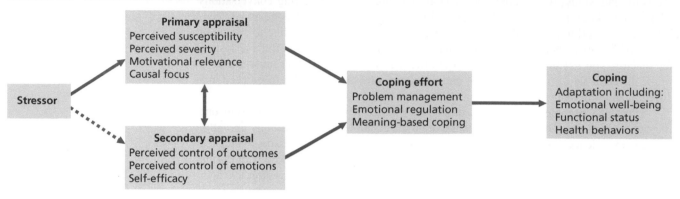

3. Based on the previous appraisals, the person initiates a strategy to cope with the situation in the most effective way possible.

When the situation is resolved successfully, the person is able to move on to the next series of tasks without lingering effects. If, however, the demands of the situation exceed the capabilities of the person, physical and psychological damage can result. This could impede future coping with new developmental tasks for all the reasons you have learned previously, including ongoing health and self-esteem difficulties.

The transactional model, as well as the other developmental theories just reviewed, provides a foundation for understanding the ways that stress is experienced and metabolized throughout the various stages in life. This leads to a helpful question to ask yourself whenever you or someone else seems stuck repeating unsuccessful coping strategies during a stressful encounter: what developmental tasks are you facing that require skills or resources that are not immediately at your disposal?

For each of the various stages of life, beginning at birth (or even before then), and continuing to later maturity, I will review the particular stress challenges that people face and how they attempt to resolve these difficulties.

Stress in Childhood

Today's children mature much earlier than those who lived several generations ago. They are faced with a much faster pace of life, more complex moral and behavioral decisions to make, and more information to digest and sort through. In addition, children are not afforded the same opportunities as adults in dealing with the problems they face. They can't easily walk away from situations with the same freedom that grown-ups have. They can't openly display anger and get away with it. They can't directly gain access to prescription or illicit drugs, nor can they seek counseling without parental permission. In many cases, children would be punished for exactly the same coping strategies that are frequently employed by adults.

Prenatal and Infant Stress

It may strike you as a bit odd, if not improbable, that even fetuses experience stress. In one study in which the birth records in Sweden were examined after the assassination of their prime minister (murder is quite rare in Scandinavia), it was found that there was a disproportionately low birth weight of babies (Catalano & Hartig, 2001). The same held true in an examination of the birth records in Estonia after the trauma of a sinking ferry that killed many citizens. In a study of Quebec women who were pregnant during a severe ice storm, the level of objective stress experienced by the pregnant mother was associated with lower scores on the Bayley Scales and lower language abilities in their two-year-old toddlers (Laplante et al., 2004). The work of David Barker and his colleagues indicates that events during fetal life may program lifelong aspects of bodily function (Barker, 1997; Barker & Osmond, 1986), which morphed into the theoretical framework known as the **fetal origins of adult disease** (FOAD). The main idea of FOAD is that intrauterine environmental exposures and events affect the fetus' development, and thereby increase the risk of specific diseases in adult life such as coronary artery disease, hypertension, obesity, and insulin resistance heart disease (Calkins & Devaskar, 2011).

How does a mother's exposure to a national trauma or personal ordeal affect the fetus' health? Remember from Chapter 2 the impact of corticosteroids on the system. Apparently, these stress hormones act to force an early delivery of the baby before it is fully developed. This is explained, from an evolutionary perspective, as the body's way of getting rid of potentially weak links in the gene pool by expelling a fetus that has been exposed to unhealthy stress. Another theory is that increased stress in the mother weakens her immune system, precipitating infections and early delivery.

Even quite early in fetus development, the HPA (hypothalamic–pituitary–adrenal) axis begins operating, making it particularly vulnerable to the same kinds of high cortisol levels that affect adults. This can lead to the death of brain cells and perhaps lead to later memory problems and childhood emotional disorders (Andersson et al., 2006; Graham, Heim, Goodman, Miller, & Nemeroff, 1999; Levine, Oandasan, Primeau, & Berenson, 2003).

In addition to the ways that the mother's stress flows into the developing nervous system of the fetus, the internal environment itself is not nearly as quiet and placid as you might have imagined. The womb is actually a pretty noisy, chaotic place. Imagine trying to get some sleep hunched over in that uncomfortable position, constantly being jostled around, hearing the continuous thumping of a heart nearby, the gurgling sounds of stomach upsets and the sudden noises from the environment. Pregnant mothers know all this intuitively (and from experience), which is why they make continual adjustments in their positioning, posture, and environment to not upset the finicky baby who will kick back if disturbed (Aldwin, 1994).

Once evicted from the womb—perhaps the most stressful event in life—newborns immediately resort to self-soothing sucking as a means to cope with stress. Whenever they are overstimulated, infants will rely on crying as a means to work off excess energy. They can also cope with stress by falling asleep, closing their eyes, and changing positions. As I mentioned earlier in reference to Erikson's theory, this is a time in which we learn the basic components of trust, assuming we are provided with consistent and stable care.

Stress in Elementary-School-Age Children

At just about the time children begin preschool (one of the major stressful transitions of life), they have learned the capacity for coping with troubles by expressing themselves emotionally in a variety of ways. You will even notice young children practicing making facial expressions in the mirror to hone their skills in emotional communication.

Sigmund Freud was the first to plot the emergence of **defense mechanisms** that come into play at this age (Freud, 1961). These are coping strategies in which threatening or uncomfortable events are dealt with in such a way as to protect the person against harm for which he does not feel prepared. If you observe a child of this age (three to five years) you will notice examples of defensive coping strategies such as **regression**, when a child reverts to earlier coping behavior such as thumb sucking, or **displacement**, when diverting anger from one source (a parent or sibling) to another (a doll or toy).

VOICE OF STRESS 3.1

Eleven-year-old female, finishing fifth grade

Sometimes it's hard to keep doing all of the stuff I am supposed to do. My mom wants me to keep doing tap dancing and softball and basketball when softball is over. I also have to go to special reading classes. And my mom tells me I'm fat and I have to lose weight. But I can't help it because I get nervous sometimes and then I guess I eat stuff that I shouldn't.

I get teased a lot, but I am used to it now. At my dad's we eat all of the time. My dad is really, really big, and my mom is kind of big too. I just think that I am going to always be fat because both my parents are big. I like to eat. I eat everything; I'm not picky at all. And, whenever I win a game, or score a point, I get to pick whatever I want for dinner and for desert! And when I am happy I eat. I eat when I am bored too, like when all there is to do is watch TV.

Sometimes I feel sad, like when I get teased a lot, or someone tells me they won't be my friend. Sometimes my one friend will tell me that I can't talk to someone and if I do, then she won't be my friend. It is mean, but I just have to decide if I want to be her friend that day. Besides, I have a good friend who lives two houses away who never teases me and is my friend no matter how fat I am.

As you grow older, your defense mechanisms against stress become far more sophisticated, such as the use of **rationalization** to justify yourself in situations in which your behavior does not match your stated intentions.

It is about the time when children start elementary school that they develop a variety of other coping strategies to address the added stress they face on the playground, in the neighborhood, the classroom, and at home. They now have adequate command of language and emotional expression to confide in others, solicit support, and express distress. They can work off anxieties through physical play, strenuous exercise, fantasy, and various social outlets.

As with most problems, the earlier symptoms are diagnosed, the more likely it is that intervention is going to be successful to alleviate stress. Typically children exhibit a number of warning signs that can act as cries for help before things get out of control or behaviors become chronic. These include such behaviors as bedwetting, weight gain or loss, withdrawal or isolation, frequent emotional outbursts, reckless behavior, unexplained physical problems, insomnia, and sudden fears. It isn't surprising that children would be more vulnerable to problems, especially considering that child abuse "may be our number one public health issue" (Wylie, 2010, p. 20).

How Children Cope with Stress

Just like adults, children attempt to cope with stress by doing the best they can. With fewer options, less freedom and autonomy, and increased powerlessness, they often resort to more indirect coping strategies that are perceived by adults as acting-out behaviors. In some cases, their attention-seeking may be interpreted as a cry for help—one that is often ignored. Even though less than 3% of parents report that their children have stress-related problems, 20% of children worry excessively about school, friends, and family finances. They most often exhibit symptoms of stomach aches, headaches, and sleeplessness (American Counseling Association, 2010).

In childhood, the two most common coping strategies are avoidance or problem-focused. You will recall that the infant's options are somewhat limited—when confronted by stressors in the environment she has no option except to block out the stimuli or cry for help. But as children age, they develop the capacity to sort out those situations in which they are powerless (the weather, the choice to go to school) versus those that they can handle themselves. Now, in addition to being able to avoid some situations they find upsetting, they can also distract themselves, as well as resolve the difficulties using their own resources. This is what Erikson called developing a sense of competence.

In the same ways that infants use thumb-sucking as a form of self-soothing when anxious or upset, children seek ways to deal with their pent-up frustrations. As you know, stress interferes with attention span and brain functioning, so poor school performance will be a red flag. Overstressed children will also act out, become discipline problems, and engage in aggressive or violent behavior.

When children have a stable family system and a solid group of friends, they are more likely to talk through their troubles and find more socially acceptable solutions to their problems. It also helps when they are provided with opportunities to learn more effective ways to manage and prevent stress.

Children learn from the youngest age to deal with stress-related problems through the use of medication or other external cures. The implicit message they get growing up is that all pain is bad and should never be tolerated. This contributes to low frustration tolerance later in life, as well a lack of internalized coping skills.

Children learn to self-medicate their stress, in large part, from the media and their parents. Television, radio, web, and print advertisements bombard us with promises of quick fixes for whatever ails us. This is especially true with respect to any pain whatsoever, which is not to be tolerated under any circumstances.

One disturbing trend in recent years is how the medical establishment colludes with parents to prescribe what are perceived as instant "cures" for any child's complaint of distress. In a period of five years from 1991 to 1995, the number of prescriptions for antidepressants doubled. As for the prescription of methylphenidate and other stimulants for attention deficit disorders, the number of children who were given these chemical crutches nearly tripled (Zito et al., 2000). The five-fold increase in Ritalin production suggests that it has been overprescribed and overused in violation of common sense and good practice of medicine (Bromfield, 2010). And this is largely for a population of preschoolers! Imagine what happens as they get older and encounter continued stressors in life. The message they learn is that whenever you face a difficult situation in life, or any stressful situation, reach for the medicine cabinet (or the alcohol).

Stress in Adolescence

Puberty brings about many physiological changes and generates a potent impact on the cognitive, emotional, and social development of young adolescents. Physical changes start to appear in late childhood and early adolescence. In boys, these changes include enlargement of the testes, growth of auxiliary hair, deepening of the voice, and the ability to ejaculate semen. Girls will experience the first menstrual period, a slight lowering of the voice, and enlargement and development of the breasts. By the end of puberty, adolescent bodies are fully developed and capable of reproduction, yet many adolescents are not ready to carry out sexual activities with others and to bear the consequences of their sexual behaviors. The obvious discrepancy between their physiological maturity and psychosocial immaturity poses a significant source of stress for teenagers.

Adolescence is often considered the most challenging stage of life because of the sheer number, intensity, and rapid pace of simultaneous changes that take place.

Larson and Ham (1993) surveyed close to 500 fifth to ninth graders and their parents in order to understand the important changes that take place during the onset of puberty. They concluded that adolescents experience more changes related to family (e.g., not getting along well with parents), school (e.g., disciplinary action, changing schools), and relationships (e.g., breaking up with a girlfriend or boyfriend). Adolescents also reported significantly more negative emotional responses than their preadolescent counterparts. The researchers believe that higher rates of distress experienced by adolescents can be accounted for partially by the greater number of negative events in their lives.

Peer Relationships

The most important task of adolescence is the formation of identity, which occurs primarily in interactions with others. During this stage, the family becomes less influential while peer groups become more important. Adolescents spend more time with their friends than they did in childhood. They will try different friends and imitate some whom they view as "cool." This is a time of explorations and experimentation. Their personalities are being formed on the basis of their evaluations of different experiences and people they have come to know.

VOICE OF STRESS 3.2

Eleven-year-old, female fifth grader

I don't really know if I get so stressed, but I think it is like getting really frustrated or something. I do okay I think. I do get moody a lot. And, sometimes when I don't get what I want I get frustrated, and if I'm with my mom, I yell a lot. She asks me not to yell, but I told her that I yell because she does it too. She says that she is trying to yell less and that I should too. I guess she's right cause I get really upset when she yells at me. I feel sick inside.

When I don't feel good I like to play with my friends instead of doing homework, but I usually have to finish all of my work first. Sometimes when I don't understand my math I have to ask my mom for help. She usually tries to explain it and then tells me I have to do the rest myself. I get so frustrated sometimes. Once I even tore up the paper but then my mom grounded me. I wish I didn't get so frustrated and upset about things like this but I can't seem to control my feelings.

My mom told me to stop and think about what I am doing. She said that most things are not worth getting mad about. Like, when my one friends, Kimmy, said that she won't be my friend anymore because I was friends with Tricia. My mom said that Kimmy would come around in a couple of days, and she did! Now, we are all friends! So, some of the stuff my mom says is okay, but most of the time it seems like she is trying to tell me what to do and that's when I just plug my ears and try not to listen. My mom says it's a phase. Maybe it is. I'm just looking forward to horse camp this summer.

Early adolescents desire popularity and belonging to a same-sex group. They will become understandably distressed when their admittance is denied. Far more distressing is the estimated one-third of all children who have been victims of bullying in some significant way. Such interpersonal abuse does the most lingering damage when it leads to feelings of isolation (Newman, Holden, & Delville, 2005).

In middle adolescence, boys and girls begin to mix; romance occupies an important part of their life. Teenagers report stress during this stage when they are learning new skills to establish romantic relationships. They may also feel pressure to engage in sexual activity. Usually, adolescent relationships are transient and do not lead to enduring intimacy and unions, even though they may start with strong feelings.

Academics and School

The transitions from elementary school to middle school, and from middle school to high school, are yet other common stressors teenagers face. Most teenagers have mixed feelings of both anticipation and apprehension about these transitions. The physical environment of middle and high schools is a major change from elementary school, and academic demands and new psychosocial expectations also challenge the skills of teenagers of this age. Everything looks larger physically. Assignments are more difficult and schedules are more complicated. Middle schools are more impersonal and require more independence and self-reliance as compared with elementary schools. Many middle-school students lack a sufficient repertoire of self-management skills to deal with the new challenges and may experience heightened stress in the beginning. However, this is also an age of rapid cognitive and emotional development. With enhanced cognitive and metacognitive skills, teenagers develop better coping mechanisms.

When adolescents reach high school, they confront more challenges of juggling attractive extracurricular activities with the demand for better grades. All of a sudden, academic performance "counts" in ways that it never has before. Any kid who even thinks about attending college will now feel the competition increase dramatically. Teachers and parents put tremendous pressure on high school students to do well on achievement tests. And then there is all the exaggerated activity related to taking the SAT exams and filling out college applications.

The sum total of all this stress in a teenager's life—at home, in school, in sports and extracurricular activities, in religious school, in a part-time job, among friends, with a boyfriend or girlfriend, preparing for the future, dealing with major physical changes— is that many seek quick cures for the tension in the form of drinking, drugs, sexual activity, and gangs.

Unusual Stressors

Unfortunately, a minority of adolescents will have a greater share of stressors in this stage of life than most of their peers. These stressors can be categorized into three types: family, social, and individual problems. Examples of family problems include parents with medical and mental illnesses, parental alcohol abuse, and parental marital conflict and divorce. In some cases, teenagers may experience some traumatic event such as sudden loss of a parent. Increasingly, teenagers are exposed to violence, in both their schools and their neighborhoods.

Individual problems some teens face are pregnancy, serious illness, or school failure. Teenage girls who get pregnant are less prepared than their adult counterparts in raising children. Forty percent choose abortion, 45% choose to keep their child, and the other 15% either miscarry or choose adoption. About 5–10% of children suffer from a serious illness and have to deal with many stress-related issues. Finally, 10–15% of teenagers drop out of school. They will find it difficult to get employed because of lack of skills and knowledge, and face more stressors than their educated peers.

How Teenagers Cope with Stressors

Adolescents develop better coping strategies as they mature. Those with adequate cognitive abilities, emotional maturity, and supportive families appear better able to cope with stress than those who have experienced multiple stressors, or have little social support. One recent study of 2,000 middle-class adolescents in six countries showed that they used negotiating and support-seeking to cope with relationship stress more often than using emotional outlet or withdrawal (Seiffge-Krenke et al., 2013), a sign of mature development. Younger adolescents tend to become more egocentric and isolated when dealing with stress (Dwan, 2009). There is also a tendency to use coping strategies such as drugs, alcohol, tobacco, and sexual activities that have maladaptive side-effects (Aldwin, 1994; Elkind, 2001; Finkelstein, Kubzansky, & Goodman, 2006).

In one survey of high school students it was found that 40% of them, including 30% of eighth graders, used marijuana. Among high school seniors, over a third use marijuana on a regular basis to deal with stress. In spite of nagging on the part of their parents and public service announcements, adolescents realize they have discovered temporary numbing of their stress in much the same way that adults resort to alcohol and prescription drugs.

FOR REFLECTION 3.2

Going Back into Time

It has been said that adolescence is by far the most stressful period of life, fraught with so many simultaneous stressors related to biological changes, social pressures, identity development, struggles with love, sex, peer acceptance, parental authority, school pressures, family conflicts, drugs, and so on. Go back in time to your own high school years and recall the most difficult challenges you faced. Write down a few of those that still make you shiver with apprehension.

What might have helped you to cope better with these stressors?

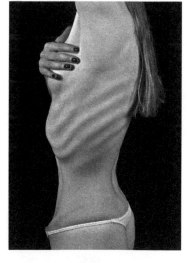

Social pressures and internal stress can lead someone to become so stressed that they literally die of starvation. Anorexia (starving) and bulimia (bingeing and purging) are most common among girls in high school and college who attempt to cope with stress by becoming obsessed with the physical appearance of their bodies. They feel helpless in many areas of their lives and so try to exert control over their eating. Unfortunately, they also hold a distorted body image that leads them to see fat where none exists.

Eating disorders are becoming increasingly common among young people, especially among adolescent girls. **Binge eating disorder**, in which the person eats a large amount of food in one sitting, often as a form of self-punishment or self-medication for stress, is one of several kinds of coping mechanism that can produce life-threatening side-effects. **Anorexia nervosa** (systematic self-starvation) and **bulimia nervosa** (bingeing and then purging through vomiting or laxatives) are becoming increasingly prevalent.

Eating disorders are one of many dysfunctional coping mechanisms (to be covered in the next chapter) that provide temporary relief at the cost of long-term negative health hazards. In the case of anorexia, up to 20% of the victims actually starve themselves to death, even with attempted medical intervention. Those with less severe symptoms still wreak havoc in their bodies.

Stress in Young Adulthood

Young adults are faced with the task of selecting a course for their lives that may include a career, marriage, children, and social activities. It is an exciting stage of life as well as full of challenges. In order to succeed in these developmental tasks, young adults must acquire particular skills and knowledge to fulfill their dreams and realize their goals.

Friendships and Tribal Affiliations

The major developmental issue during this stage is finding intimacy versus isolation. Intimacy involves the formation of healthy and satisfying relationships with others of both genders, while isolation is an inability to form such connections. Those who manage to create or join close relationships with peers, mentors, friends, and like-minded people feel a degree of support that helps insulate them against some life stressors.

Our species has always been tribal. For tens of thousands of years, we have functioned as part of close interpersonal networks that were designed to maximize success in hunting and food-gathering activities. Just imagine the challenges of trying to bring down a large animal by yourself, armed with only a spear. During these early days of our history, a person alone was easy prey for predators and unable to survive in the harsh environment. Tribal affiliations permitted cooperation among members, as well as specialization in those activities for which you were most suited.

Even though in today's world it is possible to operate much more independently, we still retain strong instincts to form cooperative, tribal units. Often these social networks can be formed based on one significant feature—ethnicity, religion, college major, sexual orientation, hobbies, interests—but just as often they can represent a complex melding of many such variables.

FOR REFLECTION 3.3

Consider Your Yribe

Your "tribal affiliations" are often the result of choices you make based on common values and interests, as well as similarities in ethnicity, religion, and professional goals.

Who are the members of your "tribe"? Make a list of the people with whom you share the closest friendships.

On what basis is your particular social group(s) drawn together? What is it that you all have in common that ties you together?

Your friendship groups serve a number of constructive purposes that help reduce stress. Certainly there are others available with whom you can talk and share your experiences. But there are also many exchanges you provide for one another: trading favors, watching one another's backs, helping one another out in time of greatest need. Imagine, for example, you are on your way to an important appointment when you encounter car trouble. The more loyal members of your tribe you have listed in your address book, the more likely you can recruit someone to rescue you in this time of need.

Selecting a Life Partner

One of the most important developmental tasks of young adulthood is selection of a life partner. Although this process can continue well into one's thirties or forties, in most societies the selection is either arranged or completed during adolescence or early adulthood.

Mate selection can be a tremendous source of stress because the stakes appear to be so high. Nobody goes into a marriage or cohabitation thinking that it will be a temporary experiment; this sort of commitment implies ongoing plans for the future. And things can get quite messy if the relationship should begin unraveling.

There are fears about making the wrong choice, or basing the decision on factors that might not endure over time (such as physical attractiveness alone). Whereas, in our culture, mutual attraction (love) is cited by both men and women as the single most important ingredient in choosing a partner, this is not universal. Among the Zulu of South Africa, or the Chinese, mutual attraction would rank behind emotional stability, maturity, a pleasing disposition, or earning power. Many Chinese men, for instance, would consider the partner's health, child-bearing potential, and virginity before other considerations.

FOR REFLECTION 3.4

Choosing a Life Partner

Rank the list of characteristics according to how important they are to you in selecting a mate who you would intend to spend your life with. Try to be as honest as you can about your most desired values.

Characteristic	Rank
Ambition and goals in life	
Social skills	
Honesty and integrity	
Family background	
Sense of humor	
Similar religious background	
Financial prospects	
Educational level	
Ethnicity	
Health	
Physical attractiveness	
Intelligence	
Dependability	
Compatible political convictions	

The selection of a mate implies that there is an endless source of possible candidates from which you are lucky enough to choose your favorite. For most people, however, considerable stress is associated with finding likely options with whom you would enjoy spending a few evenings, much less a lifetime. All the anxiety around meeting new people, making favorable impressions, engaging in small talk, and dating can feel over-whelming. That is one reason why there is the temptation to isolate and protect yourself versus reaching out to others and risking hurt and rejection.

College and Stress

As you might readily testify, the first year of college is considered among the most stressful developmental transitions. This is especially the case for students who move away from home for the first time and must deal with dramatic changes in their sleep and eating habits, plus take on new responsibilities and social pressures.

In one study of stress among college students, the most frequent challenges cited include conflicts with roommates, class workload, trouble with parents, financial difficulties, and changes in social activities (Ross, Niebling, & Heckert, 1999). For many years, relationship problems were cited by college students as the most frequent source of stress—and this makes perfect sense when you keep in mind the developmental tasks of this age (intimacy). But more recently, anxiety has been mentioned as the most frequent problem among college-age students. Relationship problems are still there, but they are now coped with in different ways. Forty percent of women have an eating disorder at some time during their college years (Marano, 2004).

In other studies of the most stressful problems of college students (Feldman, 2003), some differences were found among male versus female students (see Table 3.2).

TABLE 3.2 Most stressful problems of college students

Men	Women
1. Grades in school	1. Concerns about the future
2. Maintaining a good social life	2. Developing relationships
3. Vocational decisions	3. Pressure from too much work
4. Concerns about the future	4. Grades in school
5. Sexual relationships	5. Adjust to life at school
6. Friendships and peer relationships	6. Gaining independence

When Stress Leads to Suicide

High school and college-age young adults are particularly prone to mood swings, anxiety, and depression. Among those in the 15–24-year-old range, the three leading causes of death are accidents, homicide, and suicide. Self-destruction is certainly one option for those under so much stress that they can't imagine a satisfactory way out.

People who are serious about killing themselves believe no one cares about them, so the single most important thing that you can do is to show your concern. Be as supportive as you can. Try to get the person to make you a promise to not do anything rash. Most importantly, get the person some professional help. If all else fails, or you sense that the person really might be serious, notify the authorities immediately. There is a risk to this in that you could lose a friend who feels betrayed or embarrassed by your getting others involved, but the alternative is to do nothing and have to live with this choice for the rest of your life.

Assuming that one of your friends or family members is showing symptoms of severe anxiety or depression and may be at risk of a suicide attempt, what are the most reliable signs of risk? The first thing you should know is that predicting serious intent is a very inexact science. No matter which variables are closely associated with successful suicides, there are many cases in which individuals did not fit this profile at all. Nevertheless, when intervening with someone who seems bent on self-destruction, consider the following.

- *Talk about suicidal intentions with the person.* Contrary to popular belief, you do not increase the risk by asking someone to talk about her feelings.

- *Listen for allusions to suicidal thoughts*. Examples include "I wish I were dead" or "Maybe I won't be around much longer." Often people signal their intentions by reaching out for help by dropping hints about their intentions.

- *Find out if there is a plan*. When someone has an elaborate and detailed plan for self-harm, there is considerably more risk than if someone hadn't given the specifics much thought.

- *Check out the ability to carry out the plan*. Even more disturbing than having a plan is having the means to carry it out. Consider access to a gun, dangerous drugs, or other means.

- *Observe whether the person has made arrangements*. Notice if the person begins giving away prized possessions.

- *Note signs of serious depression*. The more hopeless, despondent, agitated, and severely depressed the person is, the greater the risk.

- *Note obsessive thinking*. Recurring fantasies about death or self-destruction may signal impending self-harm.

In addition to these factors, professionals consider two other areas that best predict whether someone will harm herself. The first is a family history of suicide in which parents or other family members killed themselves. The second is whether the person has made previous attempts. In fact, the best single predictor of suicidal risk is whether the person has tried before. Once again, keep in mind that even with these warning signs, it is very difficult to know for sure what someone intends to do. When in doubt, get professionals involved.

FOR REFLECTION 3.5

Going Forward in Time

Project yourself ten years in the future, to the next stage in life development in which you are reasonably settled into your life and work. Given your personality, history, aspiration, and goals, what do you anticipate will be the greatest stressors you will face?

How do you intend to prepare for them?

Sex, Drugs, Rock and Roll

What are the most common ways that college students cope with stress? The answer is rarely given much space in texts like this: sex, drugs, and music. These are the three most reliable ways to soothe oneself, or at least forget about your troubles for a little while.

Sex can mean a relationship with a partner, or, more often, it involves solitary sex in the form of masturbation. Even infants learn to stimulate themselves as a stress reliever, that is, until they are scolded and taught that such public displays are not appropriate.

Once puberty hits, masturbation becomes a private activity, one that is still often filled with shame and guilt even though there are a number of distinct benefits. There is almost nothing in life more pleasurable than an orgasm, but masturbation also increases your sexual awareness, which is useful in teaching a partner how to pleasure you. It reduces wet dreams in men, and menstrual cramps in women. It helps relieve insomnia and generally reduces stress. Things that masturbation does *not* do are cause blindness or insanity. On the contrary, learning to appreciate and pleasure your own body can often help you feel much clearer and saner.

At least as effective as sex for coping with stress (in the short run) are drugs and alcohol. No longer merely a form of social stimulation, alcohol, marijuana, cocaine, ecstasy, methamphetamines, and other illicit substances provide almost instantaneous relief. If you were to ask anyone who regularly drinks or uses drugs why they do it, the immediate answer you are likely to get is "It feels good." And it does.

The main problem, as you know, is the side-effects. Illicit drugs (those not prescribed by doctors) and alcohol are actually pretty lousy antidotes for stress, at least in the long term. They not only have very short-acting effects, but have very serious long-term consequences (collegedrinkingprevention.gov, 2010).

- 1,825 college students die each year from alcohol-related injuries.

- 599,000 students are injured, directly or indirectly, because of alcohol.

- 696,000 students are assaulted by someone who is intoxicated.

- Another 97,000 students are raped or sexually assaulted by someone who had been drinking.

- 3,360,000 students drove their cars while drinking.

- 400,000 students have unprotected sex and more than 100,000 students report having been too intoxicated to know if they consented to having sex.

- 25% of students who drink frequently report having serious academic problems in school.

- Almost one-third of all college students qualify for a diagnosis of alcohol abuse.

- 50% of male students and 39% of females have engaged in binge drinking (five or more drinks in one sitting) within the previous two weeks.

It is because alcohol and drugs are temporarily so effective as stress relievers that they are so difficult to curtail. They are also so prevalent in our culture that it is virtually impossible to escape the temptations. Just look around at all the adults smoking, drinking caffeine, drinking alcohol, and using prescription anti-anxiety medications, all to deal with their own stresses. Unfortunately, these substances have significant negative side-effects that are not present in the stress management and prevention techniques you are learning in this course.

As for music as a stress reliever, I have nothing but the most positive things to say. Throughout the ages, playing or listening to music has proven effective in reducing anxiety and depression. There are still strong remnants of this tradition among indigenous people around the world, whether in Africa, South America, Asia, the South Pacific, or among Native Americans. Whenever someone within the tribe experiences personal difficulties or interpersonal conflicts, the community is called together—not so much to talk about the problems but rather to play music and dance. Drums call forth the ancestral spirits to provide additional support, as well as to provide a beat. A chorus sings chants, prayers, and melodic harmonies. Whenever the spirit moves a particular person, he jumps into the circle to dance troubles away. Within our own contemporary culture, music is also used by children, adolescents, and adults to soothe aching spirits and relieve the pressures of daily life.

TABLE 3.3 Side-effects of alcohol as a stress reliever

Nausea, dehydration	Difficulty concentrating and studying
Missing classes	Impaired judgment
Brain damage	Liver damage
Sleep disruption	Physiological addiction/dependence
Infertility	Impotence or erectile problems
Fatigue and energy depletion	Irritability and mood swings
Depression	Diminished motivation
Birth defects	Gastritis and ulcers
Nutritional deficiencies	Dysfunctional peer group

VOICE OF STRESS MANAGEMENT 3.1

Nineteen-Year-Old College Sophomore

The freeways are often so clogged with traffic that I can be stuck in traffic for hours on the way to work or school. It's not just that sometimes I'm late for a class, or my boss gets upset because I missed a meeting we're supposed to have, but it's all the damn waste of time. I sit there pounding the wheel and screaming in frustration. It drives me crazy when I'm in the wrong lane—which seems to be whichever lane I pick—and I watch a line of cars whizz by me. Then, as soon as I switch lanes, I'm stuck again. Sometimes it feels like my chest is going to explode.

But then I remember to put in one of my favorite CDs (listening to the radio with all those ads makes me feel even more frantic). I stoke up the volume about as high as it goes without blowing a speaker out. And then I just chill. I can feel the tension just drain away as I feel the tunes wash through me. It might not get me to my destination any quicker, but at least it helps me to keep my sanity.

Career Selection and Stress

The stated purpose of the apprenticeship years, whether they involve formal education or job training, is to prepare for your life's work. Whereas once upon a time young adults were guided into a career (usually the same one as their same-sex parent) and could expect to remain in this job throughout their lifetime, options have changed considerably in modern times. In your grandparents' generation, it was not uncommon for someone to join a company (or work the farm) and stay with it until retirement. Likewise, sons went into their fathers' businesses and daughters followed the template established by their mothers before them. In the early days of our species, women would become the gatherers while men would become the hunters. Such specializations continued right up until the middle of the twentieth century.

No longer is it expected that you will choose one career, or stay in one job throughout your life. In fact, the average college student changes her major four times prior to graduation. That is the average! That means that for every student who comes to the university absolutely committed to engineering or teaching or business, and stays the course all the way to completion, another student might change fields five, six, or even more times.

Once you graduate from school, finally settled on a career path, it is highly likely that you will change directions a number of times, perhaps as often as every decade or so. This means that you could have as many as half a dozen or more distinctly different careers in your lifetime. I mention this reality in order to reduce the potential stress you might be feeling to make the "right" or "correct" decision regarding your future.

It is your primary job in life as a college student, and the primary developmental task of young adulthood, to settle into a career path. But keep in mind that it is just a "pathway" to the next stage along the road.

Stress during Middle Adulthood

Adults in their late thirties, forties, and fifties face new and different challenges, but the good news is that stress levels tend to decrease as you grow older. After age 50 there is a marked drop in reported stress and significant increase in life satisfaction (Stone, Schwartz, Broderick, & Deaton, 2010). On the one hand, adults in the prime of life strive to provide emotional and financial support to their children, their communities, as well as their aging parents. On the other hand, they need to handle job pressures, financial difficulties, and marriage problems. In a career, they may be committed to a line of work and may have even established themselves, but rising competition from the global economy forces them to work extra hours in order to stay afloat in the business. This may be the most challenging stage of life in one sense.

This could be a time of prosperity in which people are settled in a career and doing well. They may own a home and be making progress on their mortgage. If they are fortunate, they are still in the prime of health. Their children are growing and, basically, things feel reasonably under control. Yet for a growing number of adults, there is a period of reassessment regarding one's career and life path. This could be brought on by economic hardship, loss of a job, or new life goals that become possible with aging. Regardless of the reason, the number of adult students is growing. While they bring maturity, experience, and a certain wisdom to the campus, they also struggle with juggling multiple responsibilities to their families, social and civic obligations, and jobs at the same time they are trying to keep up with their studies and adapt to a college environment that was designed for those much younger. This creates a different set of stressors that are no less difficult to negotiate.

Middle adulthood presents its own forms of stress that are somewhat different from the stages that preceded it. Perhaps you are no longer having to prove yourself as much, but it may be a time of trying hard to hold onto what you have. This involves not only a degree of success and security that might have been attained, but also greater responsibility for others. Parenting adolescent children is particularly worrisome and stressful, putting extra strain on the marriage and family structure. It takes a delicate balance to provide the limits that are often needed, but also allow the freedom that adolescents yearn for the most. This involves the transition of launching children to go off on their own (see Table 3.5).

Len Deighton, a novelist who wrote a number of spy books many years ago, made a wise statement that summarized the essence of the stresses faced by middle-aged couples. "If parents and children did not fight," he said, "then the children would never leave home. And then the world would end." In other words, conflict in families with middle-aged parents and adolescent children is not only inevitable but necessary in order to promote independence and autonomy. Still, knowing this does not make the time significantly less stressful.

Middle-aged people have different worries than those you probably think about now. In a survey conducted by *USA Weekend* newspaper in 1997, these were the most frequently mentioned things about which readers were "very afraid":

1. being in a car crash;

2. having cancer;

3. inadequate retirement;

4. food poisoning from meat;

5. getting Alzheimer's disease;

For Reflection 3.6

Think about the ways that you might have challenged your parents and other adult authorities during adolescence (and during young adulthood) as a way to assert your independence. College is even intended as a transitional environment for leaving home, a place to experiment with new ways of being away from the close supervision of your parents.

Consider what this separation has been like, from your parents' point of view. What have they gone through and suffered during this time of learning to live without you in their immediate domain of influence? In what ways have you observed that your parents have suffered stress as a result of this transitional period in the life of your family?

6. pesticides on food;

7. being a victim of violence;

8. inability to pay debts;

9. exposure to a foreign virus;

10. getting AIDS.

Do you see a pattern here that gives you clues as to what the primary stressors are in middle adulthood?

Middle-aged individuals, at least the upper-middle-class readership of *USA Weekend*, feel stressed most often about health concerns and economic security. Most of all, they are afraid of losing what they have.

This is a time when people are beginning to feel their own mortality, in more than abstract terms. By this stage, you recognize that you have just about passed the halfway mark in your lifespan; perhaps you are closer to death than your birth. You begin noticing subtle but significant changes in your body. It is harder to maintain your weight. It is difficult to get through the night without having to get up to urinate. Men notice hair loss. Women notice the ways their bodies are changing.

This is a stage when it is necessary to accept some of the limits of what is possible; many goals of your youth now seem out of reach. Work may have become routine, or predictable, but it feels riskier at this stage of life to make voluntary changes. As is evident from the survey above, people are concerned with staving off illnesses and economic disaster. They see early signs of winter and want to store nuts for the hard times that are coming.

The Family Life Cycle

Among his many contributions to the field of family therapy, Jay Haley (1987) developed a model of the family life cycle that was later expanded by others (Carter & McGoldrick, 2005; Ivey, Ivey, Myers, & Sweeney, 2005). Although the developmental stages of family life can be plotted from the time of young adulthood, when a person first finds a mate and forms a family, many of the developmental tasks related to separation and attachment occur during the middle stages of life. This era presents a host of new stressors that are quite different from those that emerged earlier in life (see Table 3.4).

As mentioned during the "leaving home" stage of the family life cycle, middle-aged individuals are struggling with parallel challenges that are occurring at work and home. Not only is the family being restructured in light of children becoming independent and

TABLE 3.4 The family life cycle

Stage	Developmental tasks	Variations
Young adulthood	Separation from parents and family of origin; increasing importance of friends; finding and selecting a life partner	Early pregnancy brings adult child back home
Marriage	Establishing a home; joining partner's family; adjusting to shared life; further separation from family of origin; making new friends	Gay partnership; cohabitation without marriage
Childbirth/ Childrearing	Attachment to infant; effects of newborn on couple relationship—loss of sleep and sex; building of family with new member; parenting; balancing work with child's needs	Adoption; childlessness; difficulty conceiving
Leaving home	Separation from child who leaves home for work or school; renegotiated relationship without child (or children) present; financial pressures of paying for college education; increased freedom and independence	Most common time for divorce; child moves back home
Middle marriage	Taking care of aging parents; enjoying prosperity; nurture relationship through a time of life reassessment; new role as grandparents	Parents move in for care; children return home
Retirement	Ending of careers; increased leisure time that is shared; major role as grandparents; negotiated relationship with adult children; feelings of being marginalized by society	Health concerns; financial problems; worries over children and grandchildren
Old age	Death of lifelong friends and peers; loss of health and peak physical functioning; dependent on children for care; grandparenting	Loss of spouse; major health problems; alienation from family

Source: Adapted from Haley (1987), Ivey et al. (2005)

being launched in the world, but new stresses likely emerge at work. It is still not too late to make another career change, or job adjustment, based on experience that has been accumulated. People typically yearn for more responsibility and new challenges that provide additional stimulation and growth. It is depressing to think that you might be doing basically the same thing for another 20 years until you retire.

You may have heard the saying: "Be careful what you wish for, because you might get it." If you do get what you are asking for—a job promotion or change that challenges you in new ways—the price you pay for this wish is additional pressure. This puts even more strain on the marriage that might already be reeling from the family conflicts that result from children leaving home. All in all, this is a time of great productivity that comes with a price.

Stress in Later Adulthood

Our society has witnessed a tremendous increase in the number of people who live to be older than 85 years. If you are under 25 years of age, there is a very strong likelihood that you could live to be close to 100. That means that so-called "middle age" may not actually begin until you are well into your fifties or sixties and supposed "old age" not until your eighties.

Aging is no longer associated with disease and loss of physical and mental capacity. **Ageism**, which is a pervasive negative view about advancing age, is being gradually replaced with the view that all people can maintain an active lifestyle and can contribute meaningfully to their families and society. Yet no one can deny the fact that aging brings about many changes that challenge all of us who will, sooner or later, be faced with it.

In Erikson's model of psychosocial development, the major developmental task of old age is maintaining integrity in the face of despair. Older adults have to face the prospect of impending death. They begin to examine how they have lived their lives, evaluating their successes and defeats. Those who believe that they have lived a worthwhile life will more likely look forward to future challenges with optimism, while others who regret having wasted their lives may lack the moral courage to face the challenges aging brings them and become depressed. In reality, the picture is more complicated than what I describe here.

FOR REFLECTION 3.7

Project yourself into the future during a time when you are retired. Just close your eyes for a few moments and try to see yourself as an elderly person no longer actively working. Picture what you look like, where you are living, who you are living with, and how you spend a typical day.

What was it like for you to imagine yourself at this stage of life?

Talk to several family members, neighbors, or acquaintances who are now retired. Tell them you are doing research for a project in school about how the elderly cope with stress. Ask them about the greatest sources of stress in their lives and how things are different from when they were your age.

Adjustments to Retirement

Retirement often refers to the end of full-time employment, and represents a major milestone in the lives of many people. There are those who work hard their whole lives, saving and preparing for the days when they can pursue leisure activities as a full-time "job," completely disengaging from their previous professions. There are others who never completely retire, only reducing their commitments gradually over time. The particular choices and style depend a lot on available economic resources. For those who are forced to retire against their will and lack sufficient savings, retirement presents a different set of challenges than for those who can maintain their previous standard of living and who actually choose to let go of work.

Regardless of the circumstances, retirement is not quite as relaxing and stress-free as it is made out to be. You may picture someone sleeping until noon, spending all their time fishing and puttering around the house. But imagine how challenging it can be for someone who has spent his whole life being productive, feeling needed, and then all of a sudden, that stage abruptly ends. You may not only feel marginalized and insignificant, but be treated that way.

Retirement does change the way you look at yourself, as well as how others see you (Blonna, 2005). Interestingly, western society is one of the few cultures in which the aged experience lowered status instead of heightened respect as wise elders. In most societies around the world, the elderly are considered sacred and are afforded special privileges as a result of their accumulated life experience and accomplishments. By contrast, the elderly in our culture are often treated as annoying refuse. They are warehoused in special facilities, waiting to die.

Even among those elderly who do retain their health and family support, there are stressors associated with their reduced income and status. For the first time since childhood, they feel dependent. In addition, their free time that, at first, seems like a gift can become its own kind of prison after all. It is not easy to structure your days in such a way that they become as fulfilling, interesting, and stimulating as they were during the height of your life's work.

Health Changes

Age-related physiological changes present stressors in the lives of older adults. Older adults experience decreased sensory acuities, as well as some limitations on physical stamina. Their vision will decline, especially the ability to identify objects clearly. The senses of hearing, smell, and taste diminish with age. Older adults tend to have significantly slower reaction times when responding to unexpected stimuli, thus making certain daily activities such as driving more challenging and stressful. Memory also declines, but the extent and rate depend on the amount of physical and mental exercise the person maintains.

Contrary to some beliefs, the elderly are often able to maintain a vigorous and active lifestyle after retirement. Unlike in most cultures around the world in which the aged take on the role of wise mentors and community leaders, it is up to each individual to negotiate productive pursuits as part of daily life.

As you have already learned, if an individual has experienced chronic stress throughout the lifetime then it is not unusual that the immune system would be significantly compromised and that premature aging would result. In Chapter 2 you were familiarized with how the long-term circulation of glucocorticoids can produce breakdowns in a number of systems, especially damage to the hippocampus portion of the brain. This means that early and consistent exposure to stress can predispose you to problems later in life.

After age 75, people experience more frequent health problems. The number of individuals with chronic health problems is expected to have increased from 100 million in 1985 to over 135 million individuals by the year 2020 (Goodheart, Marganoff, & Ricketts, 1997). Conditions such as cancer, arthritis, Alzheimer's disease, multiple sclerosis, diabetes, and Parkinson's disease all take a huge toll—not only on the elderly

TABLE 3.5 Myths of aging

Myth	Reality
Most old people suffer memory problems that interfere with their ability to recall basic information.	Memory does decline, but not to the point that most elderly people are dysfunctional; many such problems are compensated for by experience.
It is more difficult to cope with stressful events with age.	Much depends on your economic and personal resources, as well as social support; life experience makes up for deficiencies in other areas.
Older people decline in physical functioning to the point where they must become dependent on others.	Through improved nutrition, exercise, and healthcare, most elderly people remain vibrant and independent, able to take care of themselves (and others).
There is a universal deterioration in cognitive functioning and creativity.	Some of the most important contributions to a career have been made during later maturity; most elderly do not suffer extreme deterioration but only minor changes.
Older people feel powerless and controlled by circumstances beyond their control.	Self-esteem and a sense of personal power do not change much with age; much depends on one's personal resources.

patient, but also on the family and caregivers. In fact, it is not at all uncommon that people who take care of a chronically ill family member develop a number of stress-related problems themselves, many of which can lead to their own permanent health consequences (Woodrow, 2005).

Psychiatric conditions such as depression can develop in response to somatic illnesses. Those who enjoy relatively good health can still develop stress problems because of excessive preoccupation with one's bodily functions, thereby exaggerating the normal aches and pains associated with aging.

On the other hand, there are a number of myths about aging (Schulz & Salthouse, 1999) that make this stage in life far more stressful than it needs to be (see Table 3.5).

Death

Death has to be the biggest stressor of all. We all know we are going to die someday—eventually. But that time seems so far off, so remote and in the future, that we can easily forget about our mortality. What happens, however, when you are 70, 80, or 90 years of age and must confront the reality that death is lurking around the corner?

For those who have experienced serious health problems, or significant reduction in daily functioning, impending death is an even higher probability. This is no longer an abstract concept but a daily concern that your days on this earth are not only finite, but also quite few.

This is a time to assess one's life, to make sense of a life's work and contributions. It is also a time to come to terms with disappointments and unfinished business. Many of your own friends are now gone at this age, and that presents a whole other set of stressors to deal with. Imagine reviewing the obituaries, and seeing the names of your lifelong friends and acquaintances. Imagine further what it is like to be alone after 30, 40, or even 50 years with a life partner who has passed on. Even if you wanted to ignore your own impending death, that would be difficult.

Interestingly, Robert Neimeyer (2001; Neimeyer, Winokuer, Harris, & Thornton, 2011) has conceived of a different perspective on the experience of loss based on his work with grieving clients in therapy. He has found that the grief process is far more individualized than once imagined. He cites older models that say that time is supposed to heal all wounds, but this isn't quite true: some people become even more incapacitated over time. His research, however, says that it isn't what time does for the grieving person that is important, but rather what she does with her time.

Ordinarily, when people are going through the grief process, we say something to them like, "I am sorry for your loss." Neimeyer's point is that when someone dies you don't actually "lose" him. Instead you "renegotiate" a different kind of relationship. After all, you continue to have conversations with the person in your head, just as the person still talks to you. You still retain vivid images of your time together. The person still "lives" in your heart, in your memories, in your stories, so they are not really "gone" at all. The goal of grieving is thus not to let go, but rather to find a way to hold on with much less pain.

SUMMARY

Each stage in life, from birth to death, presents its own set of challenges to be negotiated. Stress associated with these obstacles is not only inevitable, but often leads to increased growth and development as you learn new skills and add to your resources. In other cases, non-mastery of these developmental tasks can lead to life dissatisfaction, as well as all the accumulated damage to your body from chronic stress.

Familiarizing yourself with the stressors and developmental tasks of each stage in life better prepares you for facing these challenges and taking them in your stride.

Knowing, for example, that conflict is normal and can be constructive in families going through major transitions (such as birth of a first child, last child leaving home, divorce) can help to reduce stress levels and increase your tolerance for frustration. If you know that, in the short run, couples who are breaking up need to dislike each other for a period of time in order to separate from one another and get on with their lives, then you will feel less distressed by this normal developmental process.

Understanding stress within a developmental context helps you to cope with predictable life events as they arise, without putting even more pressure on yourself. For example, you are *supposed* to feel disoriented your first year in college, just as most students feel both excited and frightened by the prospect of graduation. In fact, all transitions involve a degree of adaptation that, temporarily, produces feelings of apprehension, as well as new levels of growth.

QUESTIONS FOR REVIEW

1. Discuss the developmental tasks that need to be achieved at each stage of life.

2. Differentiate between primary appraisal and secondary appraisal in the transactional model of stress developed by Lazarus.

3. What factors have caused the length of childhood to be reduced in modern times? Discuss the "hurried child" phenomenon.

4. Discuss the theory of fetal origins of adult disease and how it may influence your plan to become a parent.

5. Describe strategies that can most effectively reduce childhood stress.

6. Discuss the variables that give rise to stress for adolescents.

7. Why is it that middle age could be the most challenging and most productive time? Identify certain risks people face during this stage of life.

8. Describe the stressors associated with old age.

9. Consider how knowing a person's age and stage in life can help you predict which stressors are likely to be most present.

REVIEW ACTIVITIES

Directions: Complete the following exercises by interviewing people of different age groups.

1. Interview an elementary school student (using only first name and age). Describe his/her stressors and challenges in daily activities. Also mention their resources in coping with their challenges.
2. Interview a junior high school student (using only first name and age). Describe his/her stressors and challenges in daily activities. Also mention their resources in coping with their challenges.
3. Interview a high school student (using only first name and age). Describe his/her stressors and challenges in daily activities. Also mention their resources in coping with their challenges.

4. Interview a middle-aged adult (using only first name and age), such as one of your parents or relatives. Describe his/her stressors and challenges in daily activities. Also mention their resources in coping with their challenges.

5. Interview a senior citizen 65 years or older (using only first name and age). Describe his/her stressors and challenges in daily activities. Also mention their resources in coping with their challenges.

6. Based on your interviews and previous experience, analyze your past life in terms of its stressors and challenges and how you have dealt with them. Also, project into the future as to the kinds of stressors you might confront when you reach that age. Describe how you plan to deal with some of these adversities.

REFERENCES AND RESOURCES

Aldwin, C. M. (1994). *Stress, coping, and development: An integrative perspective*. New York, NY: Guilford.

American Counseling Association (2010, March). Stress and kids. *Counseling Today*, p. 4.

Andersson, L., Sundström-Poromaa, I., Wulff, M., Aström, M., & Bixo, M. (2006). Depression and anxiety during pregnancy and six months postpartum: A follow-up study. *Acta Obstetricia et Gynecologica Scandinavica, 85*, 937–944.

Barker, D. J. P. (1997). Fetal nutrition and cardiovascular disease in later life. *British Medical Bulletin, 53*, 96–108.

Barker, D. J. P., & Osmond, C. (1986). Infant mortality, childhood nutrition, and ischaemic heart disease in England and Wales. *The Lancet, 327*, 1,077–1,081.

Blonna, R. (2005). *Coping with stress in a changing world* (3rd ed.). Boston, MA: McGraw-Hill.

Bromfield, R. (2010). Is Ritalin overprescribed? Yes. Retrieved on August 15, 2010 from http://school.familyeducation.com.

Brown, S., Teufel, J., Birch, D., & Kancherla, V. (2006). Gender, age and behavior differences in early adolescent worry. *Journal of School Health, 76*, 430–437.

Calkins, K., & Devaskar, S. (2011). Fetal origins of adult disease. *Current Problems in Pediatric and Adolescent Health Care, 41*(6), 158–176.

Carter, B., & McGoldrick, M. (2005). *The expanded family life cycle: Individual, family, and social perspectives*. Boston, MA: Allyn & Bacon.

Catalano, R., & Hartig, T. (2001). Communal bereavement and the incidence of very low birthweight in Sweden. *Journal of Health and Social Behavior, 42*, 333–341.

Collegedrinkingprevention.gov (2010). *A snapshot of annual high-risk college drinking consequences*. Retrieved on July 27, 2010 from www.collegedrinkingprevention.gov.

Collins, L. (2005, October). Attention getter. *Outside*, p. 28.

Dwan, T. (2009). Psychological stress and anxiety in middle to late childhood and early adolescence: Manifestations and management. *Journal of Pediatric Nursing, 24*, 302–313.

Elkind, D. (2001). *The hurried child: Growing up too fast too soon* (3rd ed.). New York, NY: Addison-Wesley.

Erikson, E. H. (1963). *Childhood and society* (2nd ed.). New York, NY: Norton.

Feldman, R. S. (2003). *Development across the lifespan* (3rd ed.). Upper Saddle River, NJ: Prentice Hall.

Finkelstein, D. M., Kubzansky, L. D., & Goodman, E. (2006). Social status, stress, and adolescent smoking. *Journal of Adolescent Health, 39*, 678–685.

Freud, S. (1961). The ego and the id (J. Strachey, Trans.). In J. Strachey (Ed.), *The standard edition of the complete psychological works of Sigmund Freud* (Vol. 19, pp. 12–66). London: Hogarth Press. (Original work published 1923)

Goodheart, C. D., Marganoff, P., & Ricketts, K. S. (1997). Integrated disease management: Psychology and medicine. *Behavioral Health Management, 17*(4), 16–21.

Goodman, E., McEwen, B. S., Dolan, L. M., Schafer-Kalkhoff, T., & Adler, N. E. (2005). Social disadvantage and adolescent stress. *Journal of Adolescent Health, 37*, 484–492.

Graham, Y. P., Heim, C., Goodman, S. H., Miller, A. H., & Nemeroff, C. B. (1999). The effects of neonatal stress on brain development: Implications for psychopathology. *Development and Psychopathology, 11*, 545–565.

Haley, J. (1987). *Problem solving therapy* (2nd ed.). San Francisco, CA: Jossey-Bass.

Havighurst, R. J. (1953). Developmental tasks and education. New York, NY: Longmans, Green, & Co.

Humphrey, J. H. (2004). *Childhood stress in contemporary society*. New York, NY: Haworth Press.

Ivey, A., Ivey, M., Myers, J., & Sweeney, T. (2005). *Developmental counseling and therapy: Promoting wellness over the lifespan*. Boston, MA: Houghton Mifflin.

Kottler, J. A. (2006). *Divine madness*. San Francisco, CA: Jossey-Bass.

Kupetz, L. A. (1993). Reducing stress in your child's life. *PTA Today, 18,* 307–313.

Laplante, D. P., Barr, R. G., Brunet, A., Galbaud du Fort, G., Meaney, M. L., Saucier, J. F., et al. (2004). Stress during pregnancy affects general intellectual and language functioning in human toddlers. *Pediatric Research, 56,* 400–410.

Larson, R., & Ham, M. (1993). Stress and "storm and stress" in early adolescence: The relationship of negative events with dysphoric affect. *Developmental Psychology, 29,* 130–140.

Lazarus, R. S. (1991). *Emotion and adaptation*. New York, NY: Oxford University Press.

Lazarus, R. S. (2006). *Stress and emotion: A new synthesis.* New York, NY: Springer.

Lazarus, R. S., & Folkman, S. (1984). *Stress, appraisal and coping*. New York, NY: Springer.

Lefrancois, G. R. (1996). *The lifespan* (6th ed.). Belmont, CA: Wadsworth.

Levine, R. E., Oandasan, A. P., Primeau, L. A., & Berenson, A. B. (2003). Anxiety disorders during pregnancy and postpartum. *American Journal of Perinatology, 20,* 239–248.

Marano, H. E. (2004). A nation of wimps. *Psychology Today*, Nov./Dec.

Neimeyer, R. A. (2001). *Meaning reconstruction and the experience of loss*. Washington, DC: American Psychological Association.

Neimeyer, R. A., Winokuer, H. R., Harris, D. L., & Thornton, G. F. (Eds.) (2011). *Grief and bereavement in contemporary society: Bridging research and practice.* New York, NY: Routledge.

Newman, M. L., Holden, G. W., & Delville, Y. (2005). Isolation and the stress of being bullied. *Journal of Adolescence, 28*(3), 343–357.

Ross, S. E., Niebling, B. C., & Heckert, T. M. (1999). Sources of stress among college students. *College Student Journal, 33*(2), 312.

Sandberg, S. (2000). Childhood stress. In G. F. Fink (Ed.), *Encyclopedia of stress* (Vol. 1, pp. 442–449). San Diego, CA: Academic Press.

Schulz, R., & Salthouse, T. (1999). *Adult development and aging: Myths and emerging realities*. Englewood Cliffs, NJ: Prentice Hall.

Seiffge-Krenke, I., Persike, M., Karaman, N. G., Cok, F., Herrera, D., Rohail, I., Macek, P., & Hyeyoun, H. (2013). Stress with parents and peers: How adolescents from six nations cope with relationship stress. *Journal of Research on Adolescence, 23*(1), 103–117.

Stone, A. A., Schwartz, J. E., Broderick, J. E., & Deaton, A. (2010). A snapshot of the age distribution of psychological well-being in the United States. *Proceedings of the National Academy of Sciences of the United States of America, 107*(22), 9,985–9,990.

Swanson, G. N. (2000). Adolescence. In G. F. Fink (Ed.), *Encyclopedia of stress* (Vol. 1, pp. 32–41). San Diego, CA: Academic Press.

U.S. Department of Health and Human Services, Administration on Children, Youth, and Families (2001). *Child maltreatment,* 1999. Washington, DC: U.S. Government Printing Office.

Woodrow, P. (2005). Recognizing and managing stress. *Nursing Older People, 17*(7), 31–38.

Wylie, M. S. (2010). The long shadow of trauma. *Psychotherapy Networker*, March/April, 20–27.

Zito, J. M., Safer, D. J., dosReis, S., Gardner, J. F., Boles, M., & Lynch, F. (2000). Trends in prescribing of psychotropic medications to preschoolers. *Journal of the American Medical Association, 283,* 1,025–1,030.

4

Adaptive and Maladaptive Behavior

You learned in the previous chapter about how throughout the lifespan you are faced with certain developmental tasks and stressors that must be negotiated successfully or else additional problems will persist. You also had a glimpse into some of the more functional strategies, as well as those that were maladaptive, meaning that they produce negative side-effects. In this chapter I will concentrate more specifically on how humans adapt well, or poorly, to stressors they face. I will also look at the consequences of certain dysfunctional behaviors.

Key Questions in the Chapter

- How do your unresolved issues from the past influence your stress and coping in the present?

- Why do we often make the same mistakes and adopt maladaptive behaviors?

- When faced with stressors, which perspective do you take on: looking into the future or dwelling on the analysis of the past? Running away or facing reality and trying to solve the problem?

- Which perspective posits that maladaptive behaviors result from mindlessness characterized by reflexive and habitual patterns of cognitive and emotional reactions?

- If you accept the fact that stress can never be eliminated, what kinds of resources are available for you to cope with life challenges?

- What are the differences between the two notions of mindfulness espoused by Kabat-Zinn and Langer? What commonalities do they share?

- How do your thoughts and beliefs affect the way you cope with stress?

- What are some predictors of maladaptive behaviors under stress?

- What are some consequences of maladaptive behaviors and how do they affect every aspect of your life?

- Have you ever analyzed the way you live? Do you know that everything in your life, including the environment you live in and the relationships you are engaged in, is related to your stress experience?

Theoretical Models of Coping and Adaptation

Adaptive behavior is a constructive adjustment in thinking and behavior to a stressor experienced by an individual, which allows him or her to exert more control over certain aspects of life. On the other hand, a maladaptive behavior is an adjustment of thinking and behavior that may temporarily reduce symptoms of stress but carries negative long-term consequences.

There is an assortment of explanations as to why and how some people cope reasonably well with stress in their lives, and others fall apart. This section provides a brief survey of some popular models. Table 4.1 summarizes the main theories I will review.

Psychoanalytic Model

I have already touched on some of the main ideas of the theory that was originally developed by Sigmund Freud and some of his followers such as Carl Jung and Alfred Adler. Although there are now many variations of this approach to understanding stress, some placing more emphasis on some factors than on others, I will review a few of the basic ideas.

According to Freud's theory, stress results from internal conflicts as well as those initiated in the outside world. Freud theorized that we spend our life trying to reconcile instinctual drives (**id**) with our conscience (**superego**). The **ego** acts as the negotiator and mediator of these two often conflicting forces, constantly attempting to find compromises that allow us to pursue pleasure without doing harm to ourselves and others.

As mentioned previously, another key part of this theory has to do with unconscious desires that operate beyond our awareness to motivate behavior. When people suffer trauma, or experience stressful events early in life that are too difficult to deal with at the time, defense mechanisms such as repression bury these memories so that they are no

TABLE 4.1 Theoretical models of coping and adaptation to stress

Theory	Goals	Philosophy
Psychoanalytic Sigmund Freud Carl Jung Alfred Adler	Resolve conflicts from the past; change character; promote insight; strengthen ego	Past influences the present; basic drives; role of the unconscious; developmental history
Humanistic Carl Rogers Rollo May Victor Frankl	Create authentic relationships; increase awareness; express feelings; development of self; explore core issues that give life meaning; address barriers to freedom and responsibility	Humans as growth-oriented; increased awareness of self and others to improve self-esteem and personal functioning; search for underlying meaning
Behavioral B. F. Skinner Joseph Wolpe Albert Bandura	Identify target behaviors; modify dysfunctional behaviors; learn adaptive responses	People shaped by environment and experience; all behavior is learned and reinforced
Cognitive Aaron Beck Albert Ellis Richard Lazarus	Increase awareness of cognitive activity; identify and challenge irrational beliefs; teach adaptive behavior	People learn maladaptive patterns; thinking precedes feeling and action; problems stem from core beliefs
Mindfulness Jon Kabat-Zinn, Ellen Langer	Bring one's attention and awareness to the present moment with an attitude of non-judgmental acceptance; enhance openness to novel information; increase awareness of multiple perspectives	Maladaptive patterns of thoughts and behavior result from mindlessness characterized by reflexive and habitual patterns of cognitive and emotional reactions

longer felt as threatening. Although this can act as an adaptive mechanism initially, eventually such hidden material can become toxic, leading to a host of maladaptive behaviors.

Freud and his colleagues are credited with highlighting that sometimes self-defeating behaviors occur because of unresolved conflicts from the past that continue to weigh on your mind, even if this is not within your conscious awareness. For example, Micah struggled for years to lose weight but found every diet to be less than helpful. What she eventually discovered was that remaining heavy was a way to stay less attractive and thus prevent intimacy; this became a defense to protect herself against the risks of loss and rejection. Such phenomena can occur without your awareness of what is going on; all you know is that you feel stuck and powerless.

Various defense mechanisms, such as those reviewed in the previous chapter, act to protect you from potential harm, but sometimes become overzealous. **Denial**, for example, can help you to forget painful memories, but it can also lead to gross distortions of reality in that you do not face up to things that are clearly getting in your way. In one study, men who had survived heart surgery, but who underreported their fears, distress, and anger, were found to be significantly more likely to suffer heart attacks or early death than those who acknowledged and discussed their fears (Mahr & Goldberg, 2000).

Likewise, **rationalization** is useful in that it allows you to justify a situation by making up a reasonable explanation for it, but it can also encourage excuse-making that allows you to continue to engage in self-destructive behavior.

According to the psychoanalytic perspective, coping with stress is best facilitated by respecting unconscious desires and strengthening your ego to the point that you can ward off potential threats. The defense mechanisms profiled in Table 4.2 provide a

TABLE 4.2 How defense mechanisms respond to stressors

Defense mechanism	Description	Example
Rationalization	Justifying a situation through faulty logic	You cheat on an exam but tell yourself that this is okay because the teacher didn't provide enough preparation
Denial	Pretending that something unpleasant didn't really happen	Even though a love relationship has recently ended, you continue to make plans for marriage
Intellectualization	Distancing yourself from painful feelings by presenting overly rational explanations	Saying that it is all for the best that you didn't get the job you really wanted because it will help you to become more resilient
Projection	Perceiving that others hold those undesirable qualities that you find most unacceptable in yourself	Believing that your instructor doesn't respect or like you when that is how you really feel toward her
Repression	Burying painful memories into the unconscious	Forgetting a time in your childhood when you were beaten
Sublimation	Converting unacceptable impulses or desires into more socially acceptable outlets	You feel a loss of control or order in your life that you channel into stamp collecting
Fantasy	Distracting yourself from unpleasant situations by escaping	Sitting in a class you find too difficult and lapsing into a seduction scenario of someone you find attractive
Regression	Reverting to coping strategies of an earlier time in development	When under stress, you start biting your nails (oral stage)
Reaction formation	Behaving in exactly the opposite way to how you really feel in order to ward off threatening material	Going out of your way to be nice to someone that you really despise
Minimization	Trivializing behavior in order to avoid responsibility	Saying that it was no big deal that you did poorly on an exam since you don't like the class anyway
Displacement	Converting negative feelings from one person or object to another that is more acceptable	Getting into an argument with your father and later yelling at your younger sibling

You might often wonder why people engage in behavior that is so obviously harmful. Sometimes there are unconscious motives at work—those beyond awareness—that protect the person against threatening and stressful situations. Overeating can be not only a means of self-medication, but also a way to stay unattractive and inaccessible to others—and thereby avoid greater intimacy.

certain protection, but often at the expense of sabotaging more responsible, fully functioning behavior.

This means developing deeper understanding into the reasons why you behave the way you do, looking at consistent patterns that are getting in your way, and seeking to uncover **repressed memories** that have long been buried. In other words, your response to current stressors is influenced, to some extent, by unresolved issues in the past. Until you deal with such previous intrapsychic conflicts, you can easily repeat the same mistakes and maladaptive behaviors over and over again.

Humanistic Model

Each of the models presented in Table 4.1 offers different reasons for adaptive and maladaptive coping strategies. In direct contrast to the fatalistic Freudian approach that looks at the past and instinctual drives as the primary factors that influence behavior, the humanistic approach remains in the present. One of its founders, Carl Rogers, advocated stress reduction primarily through the establishment of trusting relationships with others—the kind that permit you to honestly and genuinely talk about how you feel, in a context of acceptance and respect.

Like the psychoanalytic approach to coping with stress, the humanistic model shares the belief that **catharsis**, or expression of pent-up feelings, is important to resolve life's difficulties. Taking a far more optimistic rather than fatalistic approach to life, humanists see people as basically growth-oriented. The times you are most likely to experience stress are when you are either not aware that tension is building inside you or when you do feel this pressure but are not inclined to express yourself in healthy, authentic ways.

One subgroup within humanistic thought consists of the existentialists, who see maladaptive lifestyles developing as a result of a lack of meaning in life. They are less concerned with eliminating stress than with helping people to live with the normal anxieties that are part of being fully alive.

The following are some important existential ideas:

1. *Living in the present moment.* Being fully alive means being totally focused and aware of what is happening in the here and now. It is when people get stuck in the past, when they avoid full engagement with what is going on, that they deaden themselves. People who are stressed spend too much time thinking about what has already happened, or what might happen in the future, and not nearly enough time appreciating the precious moments of the present. Some of the stress reduction methods such as tai chi, yoga, and muscle relaxation are intended to help one focus more on the here and now.

2. *Accepting anxiety as part of life.* The term **angst** is used to describe the normal dread that is part of life. Rather than escaping or denying the stress that we sometimes feel, it is sometimes healthier to accept it as part of life. This is especially useful when it involves things you cannot change, such as fears associated with an uncertain future or the prospect of death.

3. *Accepting responsibility.* Stress can result as often from avoiding responsibility as from taking on too much of a burden. Many people do not want to make their own choices; neither do they want the responsibility that comes with choice.

Yet to the existentialist, true freedom means living with our decisions, as well as their consequences, without complaint.

4. *Making contact with others.* Each of us is born alone, and we will die alone. What we do between these two points is make the best effort we can to have intimate relationships with others. Stress arises from conflicts with others, but even more from isolation.

5. *Finding personal meaning.* This is the most important theme of all. Pain, discomfort, annoyances, even tragedies, are an inevitable part of life. There is no way to avoid getting hurt as long as you take risks, as long as you allow yourself to love others, as long as you engage with life. The key to coping with such stressors, however, is creating some purpose and meaning to the experience.

FOR REFLECTION 4.1

What is it that gives *your* life the most meaning?

Think of some suffering, discomforts, pain, or even tragedies you have suffered. What did you learn from these experiences that helped you to grow?

What are some ways that you have tried to take responsibility—or, conversely, *avoided* responsibility—for the disappointments and stress you have encountered most recently?

Behavioral Model

During the 1920s, John Watson designed an experiment to test his hypothesis that anxiety, and especially **phobias**—anxious reactions to specific situations or stimuli—are essentially learned behaviors. Ivan Pavlov had demonstrated classical conditioning several years earlier when he taught dogs to salivate in response to the sound of dinner bells ringing prior to the presentation of any food. Watson saw this as a useful model to explain how maladaptive behaviors such as phobias develop in response to stressors.

Albert, an 11-month-old baby, was shown a white rat. Just prior to its appearance, Watson banged a hammer against a metal pipe, startling Albert into tears. After a few rounds of this, the baby learned to become terrified not only of the rat, but of anything that even resembled it. Thus the behaviorists showed, experimentally, how phobias and fears can develop.

In **classical conditioning**, demonstrated in the story of Albert, fears or stressors become paired with other stimuli in the environment that will then evoke similar reactions in the future. Another example of this might be a particular food that you now dislike because of previous associations with a negative experience.

In **operant conditioning**, later highlighted by the work of B. F. Skinner, instead of stimuli evoking a maladaptive response (**stimulus–response learning**), a particular overreaction to stress is reinforced by a stimulus (**response–stimulus learning**). A good example of this might be when a certain self-defeating behavior was either inadvertently or deliberately rewarded (reinforced) earlier in life, eventually developing into a habit. This is one way that addictions begin.

This shows rather simply the behaviorist position with respect to maladaptive coping responses—they believe that, like all behavior, it is learned.

FOR REFLECTION 4.2

What are some of the things that you fear the most? Common fears include fear of the dark, fear of being left alone, fear of snakes, and fear of falling. If you think about it, all of these anxieties make perfect sense and would be highly adaptive, at least in our ancestral environment. In other words, being afraid of all the things mentioned above has been important for survival; they have been programmed into our systems—hard-wired, so to speak. But there are other fears that do not have as logical a base: fears of public speaking, going to the dentist, public toilets, flying, getting fat, and taking exams, to mention a few.

What are some of *your* fears that are not based on age-old survival mechanisms?

How did you learn to fear those particular things?

Cognitive Model

In Chapter 3 I covered one version of a cognitive approach championed by Richard Lazarus. Lazarus believed that stress coping involves processes that combine features of behavioral and cognitive action. After becoming aware that a stressor exists in the environment, you make some internal assessments about its degree of threat, as well as your resources to deal with the situation. He called this **self-efficacy**, which represents all your internal capacities for managing stress that might arise. This includes prior experience, self-confidence, skills and abilities, creativity, optimism, faith, persistence, resilience, and self-discipline.

Another model of cognitive coping shares the belief that your interpretations of the world determine your perception of stress, as well as how you manage it. Rather than arising from a theory of emotions, however, **cognitive behavioral therapy** (CBT) and **rational emotive behavior therapy** (REBT) were developed by Aaron Beck and Albert Ellis respectively as schools of psychotherapy. Chapter 6 will take up these approaches in sufficient detail to allow you to learn how to apply their concepts to reduce stress through cognitive restructuring methods.

All of the cognitive methods share the premise of behavioral theory that poor responses to stress are learned behaviors or, rather, learned irrational beliefs. The essence of the theory is that all feelings (except instinctual fears that are routed through the amygdala) are preceded by thoughts. If you are overreacting to a situation in your life, this occurs because of the way you are *choosing* to interpret the situation. Emotional disturbance takes place during those times when you exaggerate threats or overgeneralize from limited information. An example of this is the variety of ways in which people respond to the same situation. If your instructor announces in class that there will be a pop quiz on the material in this chapter, there is not necessarily an automatic response. If we could listen in on the thinking of three different classmates, this is what we might hear.

1. "Oh my God! Now what am I going to do? I didn't read the chapter, only skimmed it a little. I don't understand this stuff anyway. I just *know* I'm going to fail the quiz. This sort of thing *always* happens to me. This *proves* that I'm not cut out to be a student. I'll *never* do well enough to succeed." You will note the emphasized words in this thinking imply generalizations and predictions that don't seem to be based on much evidence. They are also exaggerations. Given what he is thinking, it is no wonder this person can barely function and will most likely fulfill his prophecy of doing poorly.

2. "This is great. I am *so* ready for this quiz. I read the chapter twice, studied it more. I'm pumped!" Given the preparation and attitude of this person, she is actually delighted with the same situation that has allowed her classmate to put himself into an advanced state of panic.

3. "This is surprising. I hadn't really expected a quiz, nor had I particularly studied for one. I wonder how well I know the material? It will be interesting to find out." The third student represents a more moderate cognitive approach, halfway between the other two. She is neither unduly anxious nor excited about the prospect of showing what she learned—simply a dispassionate observer of the situation.

Mindfulness Model

In the last 10 to 15 years there has been a significant amount of growth in research about the effectiveness of mindfulness and mindfulness-based training in reducing stress and alleviating associated health problems (Creswell & Lindsay, 2014). Ellen Langer and Jon Kabat-Zinn, two pioneers of mindfulness science, have contributed greatly to our understanding of the mindfulness model that is being used to elucidate the nature of stress and suffering. Kabat-Zinn conceptualized **mindfulness** as nonjudgmental and purposeful attention to and awareness of the present moment experience with an attitude of acceptance and compassion (Kabat-Zinn, 2003). He developed the mindfulness-based stress reduction program that has demonstrated efficacy in the treatment of chronic pain (Kabat-Zinn, 1982; Kabat-Zinn, Lipworth, & Burney, 1985), and subsequently in various clinical disorders, including major depression (Teasdale et al., 2000), anxiety (Kabat-Zinn et al., 1992), and substance abuse (e.g., Bowen et al., 2006; Brewer et al., 2009). Mindfulness as described by Langer (1989, 1997, 2000) includes the following elements: 1) openness to novelty; 2) alertness to distinction; 3) sensitivity to different contexts; 4) awareness of multiple perspectives; and 5) orientation in the present. These two approaches of mindfulness have the following predictions about maladaptive behaviors:

1. Maladaptive patterns of thoughts and behavior result from mindlessness, characterized by reflexive and habitual patterns of cognitive and emotional reactions.

2. Automatic thoughts and judgments, which lead to stereotypes and schemas and conserve our energy for the time being, will blind us to new opportunities and nuances of a situation.

3. Reflexive emotional reactions to perceptions of fear cause people to behave irrationally and result in unwholesome health and personal consequences. Mindlessness underlies major stress-related health issues such as mental depression and addiction as well as interpersonal conflicts.

4. Remedies for treating the health issues and alleviating suffering can be found in mindfulness practices including mindfulness meditation.

Emotional Responses to Stress

In the models just described, you have been introduced to a number of ways that we can explain how and why people respond to stress in the ways they do. Some of these responses are highly functional and adaptive, while others consistently create problems—with yourself and with others.

Fears and Phobias

Fear can be described as the unpleasant, distressing feeling that is evoked by the perception of danger. As you have learned, it can be stimulated by actual threats to life and safety (a truck heading directly toward you in a head-on collision), or simply by the interpretation or misinterpretation that impending threats are present (the startle response from a honking horn). Whereas fear can be highly adaptive in terms of igniting the fight-or-flight response, phobias, or irrational terrors, arise way out of proportion to the actual threat. Washing your hands a few times per day can be useful in preventing infections and warding off germs, but doing so a dozen or more times a day, scrubbing the skin with brushes until the skins bleeds, is more than a little eccentric.

You learned in Chapters 1 and 2 that fear evolved as a protective mechanism to signal immediate mobilization of all the body's resources to deal with a perceived threat. You may recognize the following fear-related behaviors which begin as highly adaptive instincts but can become self-defeating (Marks, 1987):

- *Escape.* This is the flight response that is usually the first course of action. If you run into a predator or other creature that is potentially dangerous, the best option is to avoid the threat altogether. However, avoiding all conflicts, or anything remotely challenging, would be unhealthy and prevent significant growth and productivity.

- *Aggression.* This is the fighting alternative when escape is not advisable. If you feel backed into a corner, or feel unable to avoid a danger, the next best option is to fight back, perhaps preemptively to discourage an attack. When this strategy is misused, a person can become verbally or physically abusive towards others—a bully—who hurts others before she can become harmed.

- *Submission.* Observe animals in the wild, whether chimpanzees, moose, or lions, and you will see their rituals designed to establish a dominance hierarchy for priority in mating privileges—only the fittest are allowed to reproduce their genes, which preserves the strength of the group. Surrendering to a stronger foe is a sensible alternative to almost certain defeat and injury. However, some people become passive, submissive, and withdrawn in order to avoid rejection or threat of any kind.

- *Freezing.* When confronted with a sudden threat, such as a snake or predator, the most immediate reaction is to freeze. This gives you time to assess the level of threat, at the same time that you reduce the possibility of an attack. After all, many animals attack only in response to movement. What may once have served a useful purpose can still be found in the tendency of some people to become immobilized, or freeze, under pressure.

We evolved certain fears, and instinctual responses to them, based on life-threatening situations our ancestors faced in their daily lives (Neese, 1990). It makes perfect sense, for instance, that you would develop intense fears, or even phobias, of snakes or spiders since they could be quite dangerous. Likewise, it seems reasonable to develop into a **hypochondriac** (a person with an exaggerated fear of disease), or for children to develop separation anxiety, school phobia, or stranger anxiety, since all of them might involve increased threats from the environment. In other words, being cautious and vigilant when it comes to avoiding sick people or strangers, and sticking close to your parents, was probably a good idea.

Phobias represent overreactions to negative experiences. They are exaggerated responses to imagined threats (see Table 4.3 for some unusual examples, and Table 4.4 for some famous people who have suffered from phobias). As you have seen, some of them are based on actual dangers that once existed in the ancestral environment for which our nervous systems were designed. Even though the actual risk of encountering a poisonous snake or spider in urban areas is pretty remote, we still carry around the remnants of those embedded fears. From an adaptive point of view, it may make sense to overreact a bit to potential threats, especially when you consider the alternative of not reacting at all and getting snatched. Zebras, horses, and other herd animals start moving away from a potential threat at the slightest provocation.

How and why do we develop phobias in response to objects or situations that carry no immediate threats, such as eggs, roses, or bathwater? In some cases, these fears may have developed early in life when they were paired with another distasteful experience (classically conditioned), or reinforced (operant conditioned). You may avoid certain foods, for example, not because of their taste or appearance but because of unpleasant memories you associate with them. The same might be true for a child who was sexually molested in the bathtub and so may develop phobic reactions to bathwater in later life.

Recent research shows a strong physiological component to anxiety and phobias, particularly centered on a part of the prefrontal cerebral cortex which sends direct nerve connections to the amygdala (the fear center). Apparently, when rats or humans have an underdeveloped prefrontal cortex (PFC)—the center that suppresses fear responses in the amygdala when there are "false alarms"—they are more likely to develop crippling phobias and fears. In addition, those who develop posttraumatic stress disorder have abnormally small or inactive PFC centers, as seen on magnetic resonance imaging (MRI) (Kolassa & Elbert, 2007; Milad & Quirk, 2002).

TABLE 4.3 A partial list of unusual phobias you have probably never heard of

Fear of:	Phobia
Accidents	Dystychiphobia
Marriage	Gamophobia
Lightning	Astraphobia
Others' opinions	Allodoxaphobia
Inner conversations	Deipnophobia
Sex, or even talking about the subject	Erotophobia
Vegetables	Lachanophobia
Having a bad odor	Autodysomophobia
Becoming bald	Phalacrophobia
The number 666	Hexakosioihexekontahexaphobia
Being tickled by feathers	Pteronophobia
Being chased around a kitchen table on newly waxed floors in your socks by timber wolves (from Gary Larson cartoon)	Luposlipophobia
Developing one of these, or other phobias	Fearophobia

TABLE 4.4 Famous people and their phobias

Here is a partial list of well-known historical and contemporary figures who developed phobias or irrational fears as a result of stress in their lives:

- Howard Hughes, perhaps the most famous eccentric of all, was so crippled by his phobias and fears that he became a recluse. He was particularly afraid of germs (mysophobia).
- Donald Trump, industrialist and real estate baron, also fears germs, but limits his maladaptive behavior to avoiding handshakes.
- Edgar Allan Poe, the writer of stories of terror, lived with his own nightmare of claustrophobia—the fear of closed-in spaces.
- Adolf Hitler also suffered from claustrophobia, an ironic condition for a man who spent his last days hiding in a bunker.
- Anne Rice, author of *The Vampire Chronicles*, has an intense fear of the dark.
- Natalie Wood, an actress most active in the 1960s and 1970s, had an intense fear of the water. She drowned after falling off a boat.
- Alfred Hitchcock, esteemed director of many films, had a fear of eggs.
- Queen Elizabeth I had an extreme fear of roses.
- Napoleon Bonaparte, who conquered most of Europe, feared cats.
- Frederick the Great had such a fear of touching water that he even refused to bathe with it.

Phobias respond well to behaviorally oriented exposure therapy in which the person is helped to face the fear in incremental doses until such time as the stress arousal is extinguished. The person is first taught a method of relaxation and deep breathing that permits self-regulated reduction in anxiety. After a relatively minimal level of stress is present, the person reaches a point where that level of stress is acceptable, and then moves on to the next level.

Anxiety and Panic Disorders

It is estimated that over 13% of Americans currently suffer from anxiety disorders and as many as 25% will experience severe symptoms at some time in their lives (Preston, O'Neal, & Talaga, 2002). Large population surveys show that up to 33.7% of the population are affected by an anxiety disorder during their lifetime (Bandelow & Michaelis, 2015). This qualifies anxiety disorders as the most common group of mental disorders, including subgroups of phobias mentioned earlier, obsessive-compulsive disorder, panic disorder, generalized anxiety, and adjustment disorder with anxious mood. The cost of these disabling symptoms, in terms of lost work and productivity, would average about $1,500 per American per year (Szegedy-Maszak, 2004).

One reason that anxiety disorders are so debilitating is that the symptoms often involve physical sensations—you feel like you are about to faint, or have a heart attack or a stroke. It doesn't feel like it is "just in your head," because it isn't! Rapid heartbeat, racing pulse, sweating, lightheadedness, fluttery stomach—these are all indicators of stress arousal and can easily be mistaken for terrifying physical conditions. This is one reason that victims of these disorders so often end up in a doctor's office or hospital, absolutely convinced they are dying.

Panic disorder is a particularly insidious and severe form of anxiety in which a person suddenly feels a rush of dread, fear, and terror, often without warning. It feels like the world is closing in on you. In addition to the usual anxiety symptoms just described, the person may also experience nausea, numbness, shortness of breath, chills, and trembling.

VOICE OF STRESS 4.1

Businessman in His Forties

I was shopping at the market, just picking up a few things I needed, when all of a sudden I could feel my heart beating so hard I thought I was having a heart attack. Maybe that made things worse—I don't know—but the next thing I know I thought I was feeling chest pains. I was so dizzy I could barely stand up, so I sat down on the floor and leaned against these cans of Campbell's soup. It's weird that I can remember that so clearly.

They called an ambulance for me and rushed me to the emergency room. I was terrified, convinced I was dying. It sure felt that way. I was sweating like a pig. My vision was blurry and I just felt totally sick. When they stuck me in the back of that ambulance, things seemed to close in more and I couldn't catch my breath. They had to give me oxygen.

Well, it shocked the hell out of me after they ran a bunch of tests and told me that there was nothing wrong with me, nothing physical anyway. So they referred me to a shrink and that's how I found out it was a panic attack.

Rather than arising from learned responses, there is increasing evidence that panic disorder has strong biological origins. There tends to be a clear family history of this problem, since a sufferer is four to eight times more likely to have a parent or sibling with the same problem (Foreman, 2004). Even more compelling evidence is how well the symptoms respond to medications called selective serotonin reuptake inhibitors (SSRIs), which improve the efficiency of serotonin (a neurotransmitter) to facilitate better brain functioning. It has been found that SSRIs are about 90% effective in treating this disorder, especially when combined with cognitive therapy (described in Chapter 6).

Posttraumatic stress disorder (PTSD) is not merely an exaggerated response to trauma, but rather produces physiological changes in the output of cortisol (which impairs the stress response), increased sympathetic nervous system arousal, increased adrenaline, and increased blood flow to the amygdala (Restak, 2004). I mentioned earlier that it is most often precipitated by a severe trauma such as the sort that might occur in combat, natural disasters, or physical or sexual abuse. It is not unusual that the victim would experience depression in addition to the anxiety symptoms.

While this diagnosis is a relatively new addition to the diagnostic manual of mental health professionals, and has been found to be useful in helping people give a name to their disturbing symptoms that may follow trauma, there is also some danger in pathologizing what could be viewed as normal and useful coping strategies (Burstow, 2005). It is perfectly appropriate to feel somewhat out of control after experiencing a major disaster or stressor, although lingering effects that last more than several months may indeed require some medical or psychological intervention.

Anxiety symptoms are often elicited by stressors in daily life but they can also result from medical conditions such as hypoglycemia, hyperthyroidism, cardiac diseases, and premenstrual syndrome. Certain drugs, especially amphetamines, caffeine, steroids, asthma medications, appetite suppressants, and any other stimulant can also produce anxiety-like symptoms. For this reason, it is important to monitor not only stressors in your life, but also any underlying medical conditions and lifestyle factors that could be causing or exacerbating the problem.

Interventions for this disorder often involve a variety of strategies that begin with giving the person an opportunity to talk openly about the experience, followed by increased exposure to the incident by reliving it under safe, controlled conditions until the memories lose their haunting power (Nutt, 2006). Group therapy or support groups often prove useful as well, giving participants opportunities to share their common experiences and develop a sense of universality (Yalom & Leszcz, 2005). This may be combined with medications that are designed to help rebalance serotonin levels in the nervous system.

Existential Angst

If so-called "simple stress" is a temporary response to perceived danger, then the condition of angst is something else altogether: it is a relatively permanent feeling of dread that is part of being alive—at least for those who are reasonably self-conscious. Angst is the inevitable, constant anxiety that always lies just beneath the surface, but rears its head most often whenever you consider the "big" questions of life: Why am I alive? What is the meaning of my life? Is there a God? What happens after I die?

Any time you read a novel, or see a movie, in which the main character is struggling with issues related to finding meaning, breaking free from feelings of alienation, dealing with the consequences of freedom, or expressing terror at the prospect of impending death, this is angst in action. It is a kind of stress that we have to live with as part of the package that comes with being alive.

FOR REFLECTION 4.3

Angst is a German word, difficult to translate literally into English. It means, roughly, a kind of dread or anguish. Want to know what angst feels like? You already know, even if you didn't have a word (until now) to describe it.

Look at the timeline below:

◀——————————————————————————————▶

Birth   Death

One end of the line represents your birth, the other end your eventual death. Place a mark on the line approximately where you are now in your lifespan.

First impression: seems like you have a long way to go, doesn't it?

Now, put your hand on your heart. Feel your heart beating in your chest. Feel it pumping blood throughout your body, keeping you alive.

The heart is only a muscle, and it is wearing out, this very moment. Feel your heart slowly wearing itself out, like any mechanical pump. It has a finite number of contractions allotted to it before it will stop beating altogether.

If you are fortunate enough to live to be 80 years old, the average human heart will beat approximately 3 billion times before it stops. Sounds like a lot, doesn't it? But then you've already used up hundreds of millions already. Even since you started reading this book, tens of thousands of heartbeats have been used up.

This is existential angst, the condition of considering, with honesty and clarity, your relatively brief, temporary residence on this planet. If that thought doesn't elicit a certain degree of stress, you haven't been paying attention—not to us, but to that voice in the back of your mind that is always reminding you to grab the most out of life that you possibly can—because your time here is ticking away, heartbeat by heartbeat.

Monitoring Anxiety

Most forms of anxiety produce both physical and emotional symptoms. Not surprisingly, the physical symptoms resemble "fight or flight" as I summarized previously:

- muscle tension and aches;
- fatigue and insomnia;

- headaches, dizziness;

- heart palpitations;

- stomach problems;

- sweating.

The emotional symptoms are also consistent with what you would expect in a hyper-aroused state. In other words, the body believes that imminent danger is lurking around the corner so this produces corresponding activation:

- jumpiness and irritation;

- sleep disruption during hypervigilance (being on constant guard);

- dread, despair, apprehension;

- impatience;

- difficulty concentrating;

- distressing images of impending disaster.

The key to diagnosing stress constructively, whether in yourself or others, is to recognize the symptoms *as they are occurring*. Some people live with tension so long, or have become so accustomed to their symptoms, that they don't notice anything unusual about their maladaptive behavior. They grind their teeth in their sleep. They break out in hives. They bite their nails. They go without sleep for long periods. They worry about things incessantly. They live with a short fuse, exploding at a moment's notice. They walk around like nervous wrecks. And yet they remain in denial.

Before you can ever hope to manage the stress in your own life, you will have to become much more aware and sensitive to the times when you are feeling pressure or strain. Keeping a stress journal is one way to increase this awareness (see Stress Management Technique 4.1). Another is to become more aware of the tension you carry inside your body.

For instance, as you are reading these words, notice the way your body is feeling. No matter how you are sitting, standing, or reclining as you read this, concentrate on the sensations in your muscles, starting with your neck and shoulders—the places where most people carry their stress. Change your posture for a moment and try to loosen the muscles in your back, just to feel the difference. Reach behind you and massage the muscles in your neck to stretch them as much as you can (or better yet, find someone else to do this for you). Feel the tightness there, and the tension.

I will be talking more about muscle relaxation in later chapters, but for now it is important to get into the habit of monitoring more carefully what is going on within your body. Sometimes you won't even notice you are under pressure until it is too late—the symptoms have advanced to the point where you can't reverse them very easily.

Depression

Depression and anxiety are often linked. People feel depressed because they are anxious and unable to reduce it no matter what they try to do; they also feel anxious because they are depressed. Moreover, it is possible to respond to a stressor by feeling extremely anxious, as well as saddened and isolated. Depression becomes a likely result of overwhelming stress when it activates a sense of helplessness and powerlessness.

There are many kinds of depression, each with a different meaning, cause, symptoms and responsiveness to treatment (see Table 4.5). Depression can be a short-term response to a stressor, particularly a loss, or it can be a chronic condition that worsens during periods of crisis.

STRESS MANAGEMENT TECHNIQUE 4.1

One way to get a handle on those situations that most often create difficulties for you is to start monitoring what you find most upsetting in daily life. You may think you already have a clear picture of this, and you probably are aware of the big things that get to you most consistently. But you experience other stressors every day that you gloss over. These could include getting upset when someone interrupts you, when you are stuck in traffic, or when someone does something you find annoying.

Keep a stress journal for at least one week. Carry around a notebook with you at all times. *Every* time you feel any stress about something, whether this results from something someone says or does, something that occurs in your world, or something that you encounter, make the following sort of entry:

Day/ Time	Place	Context	What happened?	Reactions	Thoughts
Monday 7:42 a.m.	In bed, staring at alarm clock	I am falling behind in class but promised myself to do better. I work late at night and have trouble waking up.	I overslept. Again. This is the third time this month. I'll be late for class and the teacher is going to be upset.	Difficulty breathing. Feel overwhelmed. Headache.	I'm an idiot. It seems hopeless to try to handle everything. Maybe I should just drop the class? I don't know what to do.
Monday 7:47 a.m.	Sitting on bathroom floor	Rushing into the bathroom, deciding to try to make my class even if late (even later after writing in this stupid journal)	I slipped on wet bathroom floor, rushing to take a shower and get dressed. Wrenched my back I think.	Laughter (covering up wanting to cry). Screaming: "Yeooowww!"	I'm doomed. Nothing I do seems to be going well right now. I guess I won't make class after all. Maybe I'll just take a hot bath and try to relax.

The humanists/existentialists mentioned earlier believe that a certain amount of depression can't be avoided in life with the usual disappointments, losses, and tragedies that we encounter, not to mention the prospect of eventual death. It can be depressing thinking about all the terrible things going on in the world—the violence, the wars, the injustices, poverty, crime, natural disasters. It is normal to feel helpless and powerless observing some of the cruel things we see all around us—how people can treat one another with neglect, dishonesty, manipulation, and hurtful behavior.

Still, there is a big difference between feeling occasionally saddened by events versus the kind of debilitating depression that leads one to seriously consider suicide. There are people who have given up all hope. They can't remember a time when they ever felt very good, and they can't imagine a time when things will ever get better.

You may know people like this. You may also have gone through your own depressive episodes at some time in your life. You may remember during these difficult periods that you felt so little energy and such poor motivation that you could barely deal with daily life, much less get your work done.

TABLE 4.5 Types of depressive disorder

- *Adjustment reaction with depressed mood*. This is a normal response to stressors or events that result in sadness. It is normal to feel depressed, for instance, after a disappointment or loss, if the feelings do not endure for more than a few months.
- *Prolonged grief reaction*. If the depression after a loss endures beyond a "reasonable" period of time, often arbitrarily set at six months, and if the person is significantly impaired, then this indicates a more serious emotional disturbance that may not run its course without intervention. Keep in mind that grief is highly individualized as well as culturally influenced.
- *Dysthymia*. This is chronic, low-grade depression that seems to be a part of the person's personality. People with this condition are often functional. They hold jobs. They are involved in relationships. Nevertheless, they always seem to be down and have a pessimistic attitude to life.
- *Major depression*. This is a severe form of depression that is mostly biologically based. Whereas the above forms of depression might all be treated with psychotherapy, major or **endogenous depression** often responds to medications that adjust the neurotransmitters in the nervous system.
- *Bipolar disorder*. You may know this as manic depression, in which periods of mania (extreme hyperarousal) alternate with incapacitating depression. This is a condition that is also biologically based. It is treated with medications but may be triggered or exacerbated by stress.

Fortunately, there are medications to help those with more severe and chronic forms of depression, the kind that are biologically based. Counseling is especially well suited as an adjunct to medication, and is often enough by itself to help people regain emotional control.

One way to tell the difference between normal sadness or grief and a serious depressive disorder is the presence of physiological signs that include the following:

1. sleep disruptions (early morning waking, frequent awakening, sleeping constantly);

2. appetite disturbances (significant weight loss or gain);

3. fatigue or general lack of energy;

4. impaired concentration and inability to make sound decisions;

5. lack of pleasure in daily activities;

6. decreased sex drive;

7. feeling especially bad in the morning on awakening (with the prospect of having to survive another day).

Biologically based depressions (those with the above symptoms) often result from chemical imbalances in the body caused by the absence or depletion of neurotransmitters (chemicals that facilitate the transmission of nerve impulses) such as serotonin and dopamine. Medications for depression are intended to help stabilize deficiencies that may be the source of the mood disorder and they often do so reasonably well. Problems are sometimes associated with these drugs in that they often take several weeks before their therapeutic effects become apparent. They also can produce undesirable side-effects that could include insomnia, weight gain, and apathy.

In addition to being biologically based, depression can be caused by certain medical conditions (Alzheimer's disease, hepatitis, arthritis, menopause, Parkinson's disease, diabetes, etc.). It may also be a side-effect of certain prescribed medications (for high blood pressure, anxiety, Parkinson's, and those with steroids such as cortisol) and drugs (alcohol). If the depression becomes severe, doesn't go away within a few weeks, disrupts sleep and eating, or is accompanied by suicidal thoughts, it is essential to seek the help of a professional.

For all kinds of depression, psychotherapy has proved extremely helpful in combating negative thoughts and learning ways to feel more empowered. People who feel depressed need support more than anything else. They also need a better understanding of the sources of stress in their lives and to learn ways to work through their difficulties without giving in to despair and pessimism.

VOICE OF STRESS 4.2

I am afraid. I am not solid, but hollow. I feel behind my eyes a numb, paralyzed cavern, a pit of hell, a mimicking nothingness. I never thought, I never wrote, I never suffered. I want to kill myself, to escape from responsibility, to crawl back abjectly into the womb. I do not know who I am, where I am going and I am the one who has to decide the answers to these hideous questions.
(Plath, 2000, p. 149)

This journal entry, written by the poet Sylvia Plath on November 3, 1952, describes the incredible despair and depression that she carried inside her most of her life. Whenever she encountered extraordinary stress, she was driven to the point of madness in which she attempted to put an end to the unrelenting pain. Finally, in 1963, after her husband abandoned her and their children for another woman, she could stand it no longer. Her chronic anxiety and depression became so severe that even the prescribed drugs she was taking could not calm her spirit. She calmly put her young children to bed, left food in their room in case they got hungry, and then went down into the kitchen where she turned on the gas oven and stuck her head inside. Her depression had become so unbearable that she chose to end her pain.

Sylvia Plath.

Anger and Aggressive Behavior

When under stress, or confronted by threat, humans react in one of a few principal ways: run, become submissive, or become aggressive. To some extent, such reactions are socially constructed, meaning they are prescribed by our culture depending on your gender, socio-economic status, ethnicity, religion, profession, and other factors. For instance, within the culture of hospitals, physicians, especially male doctors, are "allowed" to express anger overtly. Nurses, especially female staff members, are expected to deal with their stress in other ways, such as talking, venting, or crying. Within your own culture, ethnicity, family, and gender, you will notice ways that you have either been prohibited from or encouraged to express anger when you are feeling upset.

VOICES OF THE AUTHOR 4.1

Once I went shopping for a few items at a well-known grocery store where we live. I visited the store many times before and clerks were friendly and helpful. Quickly I found what I wanted and walked towards the checkout area. A young man with a beard was talking with a smile with a lady in front of me. When she was done, I put items on the counter. The young man did not say a word to me and his face seemed to have become sullen suddenly. After I paid for the grocery, he pushed the grocery bag to the corner of the counter. I was stunned at what had happened. Blood surged to my temples and I really wanted to scream at him. However, I controlled myself and walked away without a word. I went to the manager and complained about this rude clerk and felt a little better after that. Luckily my meditation practice allowed me to catch myself "doing anger" and began to realize that it was not the young man that made me angry, but I who allowed something on the outside to get angry.

Anger actually has a survival function in that it mobilizes all systems to prepare for maximum defense against perceived threats. As an emotional demonstration, it might also work well to frighten or ward off potential adversaries. If you can settle disputes or discourage an enemy solely by a display of rage, then you save yourself the trouble of risking mortal combat.

Anger is a stress coping response that often creates more problems than it is intended to fix. It might feel good for a few minutes to dump on someone, but this explosion comes at a cost. For one thing, such behavior does not often endear you to others. They usually feel resentful, hurt, and angry about how they have been treated. In some cases, they are inclined to retaliate, which only increases the level of conflict and tension.

Contrary to popular belief, anger does *not* ultimately lead to a release of stress. Freud and other theorists postulated that the process of catharsis would help people to purify themselves by emptying their emotional reservoir. This theory has not necessarily held up to research scrutiny. It turns out that releasing or expressing anger sometimes just leads to increased feelings of arousal. This is evident in the results of studies performed on particular personality styles associated with stress disorders and heart disease. Angry people carry more internal tension and stress. Their hostility not only tends to frighten and alienate others, but also eats away at their own tranquility. Feeling justified in a position of indignation is not a state of mind conducive to a stress-free existence.

FOR REFLECTION 4.4

Recall a time when someone in authority—a boss, teacher, or parent—censured you in the most angry manner imaginable. Whether you had done something to deserve a corrective response or not, remember how you *felt* when this person yelled at you, perhaps even embarrassed you in front of others. Did you feel grateful for their intervention? Did it seem like they were being particularly helpful to you?

The answer is almost always "no." When teachers or parents or supervisors engage in angry outbursts toward others, it is generally not to help the other person, but rather to help themselves deal with their own frustration. Such behavior may make them feel better in the short run, but the likely consequences were that you felt humiliated and not at all thankful for their concern on your behalf.

Keep in mind that whenever you explode emotionally, or angrily censure someone, you are doing it more for your own benefit than to teach the other person anything useful. When anyone feels attacked, they usually respond in one of two ways: either they shut down or they respond aggressively. In both cases, they are not in a receptive mood toward learning.

Anger Management

Since anger has the potential to cause tremendous harm to yourself and others, it is worthwhile to learn strategies to moderate the intensity and frequency of such outbursts. Here are several suggestions:

1. *Accept what is unchangeable.* Self-righteous people often get angry about things that are totally outside their control—the weather, a natural disaster, rush-hour traffic, or similar events. You may demand that the world treat you in a particular way that you consider just and fair, and then become irate when things don't go your way. Ranting and railing about a flat tire, snow storm, high interest

rates, or someone you believe slighted you not only doesn't make the situation any better, but gets you worked up to the point that the negative effects are magnified.

2. *Try to understand the deeper causes of your anger.* Since your erroneous beliefs can lead to anger, the choice of healthy thoughts may also help control and prevent unnecessary eruptions. Fear and lack of self-confidence may underlie your anger experience. Many angry people remain angry because they direct their energy at the wrong sources.

3. *Learn to be more empathic.* Anger is almost always a response of self-indulgence in which you are so focused on your own experience that you can't appreciate what others around you might be feeling. Getting mad at someone who cut you off on the freeway need last only as long as it takes you to realize that the act was unintentional. Feeling upset with a friend who you believe was rude to you is easily dissipated when you realize that he had just gotten some terrible news. I am not saying that you should allow people to walk all over you, or treat you disrespectfully; just that you can reduce the intensity of emotional responses by keeping things in better perspective.

4. *Realize that anger does not solve the problem.* Anger may have once served our ancestors well as they engaged in the fight-or-flight survival response to mobilize energy for warding off danger, but it is considerably less functional today. In many family and work situations anger and rage may initially intimidate others into surrender, but often with many negative side-effects (lingering resentment, retribution, injustice).

5. *Maintain realistic expectations.* Disappointment often comes from expecting things from life or from others that are not reasonable or realistic. Likewise, anger can arise from expecting people to behave in ways that they are not willing or able to do.

6. *Contemplate the consequences of anger.* Consider the price you pay for becoming angry. In the short run, you may enjoy some relief. But what happens in the long run to your health, your relationships, and your peace of mind?

7. *Use the "time-out" method.* When two people are angry with one another, it is highly unlikely that a mutually satisfactory resolution of the situation is going to occur. That is why professional mediators attempt to reduce the emotional arousal during negotiation sessions. It is difficult, if not impossible, to hear and respond to one another in respectful, caring ways when one or both parties are out of control. By definition, anger represents a loss of control.

8. *Express anger in more constructive ways.* During those times when you can't help yourself and you feel yourself becoming indignant or angry, try to find alternative ways to release that energy rather than taking it out on others. Physical activities are particularly well suited to working off the steam.

Every time you become aware that you are angry, carefully monitor the effects this intense emotional state is having on you, and on others around you. If you like the result, then by all means keep it up. But if you are unhappy with the accompanying side-effects, the feelings of being out of control, the residual stress, the ways you intimidate and push others away, then consider that you can choose alternative ways of dealing with the situation.

FOR REFLECTION 4.5

List three times in the past week or two that you have felt really angry about something:

1.

2.

3.

Looking back on these episodes, does it strike you that your rage or intense feelings of indignation were justified in light of what happened, the context of the situation, and the ultimate effects on your own stress level?

How could you have responded differently to these situations, applying one of the strategies I have described?

Maladaptive Behaviors

In addition to the acute signs of emotional disorders that I have just reviewed, there are other dysfunctional and self-defeating behaviors that can arise from excessive stress.

Eating Disorders

Largely a problem among adolescent girls and women, eating disorders represent a form of self-destructive, even potentially life-threatening, behavior in which distortions of body image and poor self-esteem lead to forms of self-starvation, unhealthy eating habits, chronic vomiting, and bingeing. Food is no longer experienced as a form of nutrition and pleasure, but rather as a struggle for self-control.

The two most common types of eating disorder are **anorexia** (nervosa) and **bulimia**. The former is based on an irrational fear of gaining weight that is made far worse by distortions in viewing one's body. An anorectic can look in the mirror at an emaciated, 80-pound-body, and still imagine that there is excessive fat in evidence. Under such conditions, she can literally starve to death if there is no intervention.

The most prominent feature of bulimia is binge eating (see Voice of Stress 4.3). People with this condition consume a large amount of food, then get rid of it quickly by vomiting or taking laxatives. This is commonly known as "binge and purge" behavior. A variation of this pattern, somewhat more common in males, is engaging in excessive exercise to maintain "normal" weight, which is viewed within a distorted body image. I am not talking about someone who is a habitual exerciser, or someone who has what is called a "positive addiction" to regular, healthful exercise; I am speaking about those who exercise to such an extreme that their bodies literally start to break down.

Persons with eating disorders and chronic over-exercisers often attempt to hide or disguise their behavior from others. They may pretend to eat something but actually hide the food, or just move it around on their plate. They will lie about what they've had to eat. They may politely excuse themselves from the table and then vomit secretly in the bathroom. Most disturbing of all, they will resist attempts to intervene on their behalf, denying that they have a problem.

What causes some people to respond to stress by starving themselves? Because it is primarily a disorder of adolescent girls and women, consider the ways our culture glorifies extreme thinness in women as the ideal of beauty. Almost all models are tall and slender, if not gaunt. The media is saturated with images of overly thin celebrities, accompanied with messages that being overweight makes one unpopular and undesirable.

VOICE OF STRESS 4.3

A Saleswoman in Her Thirties

I'm still in recovery now, and I've been going to OA [Overeaters Anonymous] meetings for years, but I used to have a terrible problem. Whenever I was feeling especially anxious or depressed about something—usually related to my boyfriend or parents—I'd go to KFC and order a big bucket of fried chicken, mashed potatoes, slaw, and biscuits—the whole deal. I'd have this ritual where I'd coat my stomach in the mashed potatoes first, kind of like to line it with something soft. Then I'd stuff myself with all that fatty food, all the while feeling like I was punishing myself for some weird crime that I thought I committed—usually it was just because I was mad at myself for letting other people walk all over me. The thing is: I never enjoyed the food. I never even really tasted it.

Then I'd go to the bathroom in the back of the restaurant and vomit my guts out, try to get all that crap out of my system. It was gross. And I was totally out of control. But I just couldn't seem to help myself. I would get these urges building and it didn't seem like there was anything I could do to stop them.

FOR REFLECTION 4.6

Unresolved Issues

It has been said that stress is caused, in part, not only by current circumstances that put you under pressure, but also by unresolved issues from the past that come up again and again. Examples of this might include such things as problems with authority figures, early child trauma, codependency in relationships, unstable parenting, lack of confidence due to early failures, and so on.

What are some of the issues or recurrent problems in your life that arise repeatedly in slightly different forms?

Eating disorders may also have a genetic component, since they tend to run in families and occur more commonly among identical twins (Baker et al., 2009; Klump, Suisman, Burt, McGue, & Iacono, 2009; Strober, Freeman, Lampert, Diamond, & Kaye, 2000). These problems are often treated with family counseling and behavior therapy. In extreme cases inpatient treatment may be required. Sometimes medications can be used as well to address underlying causes.

The damaging effects of eating disorders can be profound, with behavior that compromises healthy nutrition. It is not uncommon to damage the heart, liver, and kidneys. Victims develop anemia (red blood cell deficiency) and low blood pressure. Their hair tends to fall out and their fingernails break off. Those who engage in bulimic purging (vomiting) develop stomach problems from all the acid buildup. Sometimes stomach acids damage the enamel on their teeth. Eventually, as the disorder becomes chronic, death can result without drastic medical intervention.

Substance Abuse

In the previous chapter I talked about substance abuse and drinking as a favored coping style of college students. Reliance on intoxicants, prescription medications, alcohol, and other addictive behaviors are prevalent among people of all age groups, and all cultures, and reflect the universal human urge to seek relief of pain and the pursuit of pleasure. Some of the most common forms of addiction are (Milkman & Sunderwirth, 2010):

- alcohol abuse (8% of the population afflicted);

- drugs (20% of people become addicted at some time in their lives);

- tobacco (25% of adult population and the single most preventable form of death in the US);

- caffeine (90% of Americans experience mild stimulation);

- eating (bingeing, eating disorders, one-third of adults in the US are classified as obese);

- gambling (4% have a serious problem and online poker is an increasing problem among students);

- shopping (5% of population are prone to compulsive buying);

- sex (online porn is becoming increasingly common, represented in 25% of all search engine requests);

- internet (classified as an impulse disorder).

When someone experiences stress, or emotional pain, it is natural to want relief. Seeking medical or psychological care is not usually a first choice, but often a last resort, when everything else fails. Meanwhile, if a person has access to a substance that can provide temporary relief, intoxication can be an attractive option.

Stressed-out people "medicate" themselves in a number of ways. The principal goal is to numb the pain, or if that's not possible, at least to distract yourself long enough that you can find some enjoyment. In this regard, abusing drugs and alcohol is almost never about mere indulgence; it is as much an escape from something in your life as it is an attempt to seek pleasure.

Substance abuse will definitely create additional stressors such as relational conflicts, irresponsibility, impulsiveness, money problems, and health issues. It is as much a symptom of underlying problems as it is their cause. While it is important to get at these core issues, treatment for addictions is not usually effective unless it provides some form of social support (such as through a "12 Step Program" like Narcotics Anonymous or Alcoholics Anonymous), significant changes in lifestyle, alternative means of stress relief, and a hard look at your life and what you are seeking to escape.

FOR REFLECTION 4.7

When you are stressed, or feeling blue, what do you do to seek immediate relief?

Think of a time recently in which you were feeling overwhelmed with something going on in your life. This could have been a fight with someone you love. It could have been a major disappointment, or you might not be able to identify a particular thing at all—you were just feeling really down or upset and didn't know why. What did you do to soothe yourself? Consider the options I have reviewed, including uses of food, exercise, drugs, alcohol, sex, music, prayer, compulsions, and distractions.

My favorite self-medications:

Their helpful effects:

Their negative consequences:

How do you know if you have a drinking problem? There are a few key signals that are worth monitoring, as follows.

- Do you drink when you are alone?

- Do you drink when you feel sad or lonely or angry?

- Does your drinking ever make you late for class or work?

- Have family members or friends ever expressed concerns about how much or how often you drink?

- Do you ever have trouble remembering what you did while you were drinking?

- Do you ever start drinking even though you told yourself you wouldn't do so?

If you answered "yes" to any of these questions, you may have a serious alcohol problem that requires help. For those who wish to reduce their dependence on drinking as a coping strategy for stress, there are several strategies that may prove helpful.

1. Make a list of reasons why you want or need to cut down or stop your drinking. Include references to improved sleep, health, nutrition, job and school performance, and relationships.

2. Set a goal of how much you are going to drink and stick with it no matter what. If that doesn't work, or you can't stick to your goal, it is a sign that complete abstinence may be required.

3. Keep a record of how much you are drinking. For each day of the week, write down how many drinks you had, what type, and where you were at the time.

4. Don't keep alcohol accessible where you might be tempted to drink impulsively.

5. Drink slowly. Limit yourself to no more than one drink per hour.

6. Practice saying no when friends invite you to drink.

7. Experiment with taking a break from alcohol and see how you feel.

8. Get help from a support group if you find yourself unable to stay within your limits.

In some cases, if you can't manage to control excessive drinking on your own, and/or don't commit yourself to attending self-help groups such as Alcoholics Anonymous, outpatient or inpatient treatment may be required. Such programs work on different levels, providing education about the effects of the addiction, teaching alternative coping strategies for dealing with stress, and perhaps most importantly, helping the person to make lifestyle and peer group changes that will be more constructive and reinforce changes made.

Behavioral Addictions

Like addictions to drugs or alcohol, it is possible to become so habituated to particular behavioral patterns that you feel powerless to stop. Some addictions of this sort can be considered "positive" in the sense that they improve the quality of your life. Brushing your teeth is a positive habit in that it occurs without a conscious decision to do so or not; it is also good for your health. Exercise regimens can become positive habits in which you may feel restless and uneasy, and perhaps even have trouble sleeping at night if you skip more than a day or two. I have such an addiction, in that I *must* do tai chi each day or I don't feel centered.

Behavioral addictions can be harmful as well. In fact, *any* behavior can become self-defeating when it is taken to extremes. I will talk in the next section about workaholism as one example of this in which a person becomes so focused on one area of life that relationships and other domains are neglected. Compulsive shopping,

---

VOICE OF STRESS 4.4

Woman in Her Twenties

When I'm weirded out about something, I head to the mall. It's funny too, because when I get home and I see the stuff that I bought—things that I thought I absolutely *had* to have—I wonder what I could possibly have been thinking. You should see my closet. I have outfits and shoes in there that I've never even worn. Not once.

I'm embarrassed to tell you how high my credit card bills are. They keep raising my limit so I think, "What the heck, they must think I'm a good risk or that I can pay it off." But now I'm so over my head I don't know what I'll do.

I saw a counselor for a little while and he told me that I was a compulsive shopper—like an addict. I never went back, probably because I knew he was right. It's just when I get upset about something, like my parents' divorce, or I fight with my boyfriend, I just seem to feel better when I go shopping.

gambling, internet addictions, video games, and other such recreational activities can take over a person's life to the point that they become the sole focus of pleasure and satisfaction.

There is no real consensus about the causes of addictive behaviors. Some of them seem to run in families and are related to genetics; others are due to the acquisition of poor habits. In all their many forms, they represent a maladaptive way to cope with stress. They are effective in the sense that they help to distract the person from things they would rather forget, or they provide temporary relief, but they are expensive, time-consuming, and have side-effects that can be devastating for the individual, as well as for loved ones.

The proliferation of technology has created whole new categories of addiction, always characterized by a loss of control and interference with productivity and relationships. Many students (estimated to be at least one in ten) spend hours each day addicted to social network sites like Facebook, videogames, online porn, compulsive web surfing, poker, or videos (Block, 2008). In its various forms, internet addiction has been described by mental health professionals as becoming one of the most serious public health concerns, reaching epidemic proportions (Block, 2008; Watson, 2005). Online role-playing games such as *World of Warcraft*, *Second Life*, *RuneScape*, and *Habbo Hotel* are particularly seductive for college students, who may spend as many as 8–10 hours per day (or night) engaged in fantasy competition. "If you're not careful," confides one "Warcraft widow," "the game can take over your life" (Nash, 2008).

Behavioral addictions can take many different forms—compulsive gambling, shopping, porn, video games, internet communication—any activity that distracts the person from problems and provides temporary relief from stress. While such behaviors are effective in providing short-term relief, they often have costly side-effects and rarely help the person to resolve the underlying issues. In the case of internet addiction, they can lead to social isolation—at least in terms of face-to-face relationships.

Research on behavioral addictions indicates that activities like compulsive gambling produce the same kind of chemicals, such as serotonin and beta-endorphins, that are associated with drug states. People literally get a buzz from the addiction, at least for a little while. It's just like eating a piece of chocolate: you feel good for a little while, but then start to crave more.

All behavioral addictions have five main features (Earll, 2004), as follows:

1. *Fantasizing the behavior.* This means that you spend an inordinate amount of time thinking about the activity (shopping, gambling, gaming, etc.) even when you are involved in daily activities. The fantasies themselves become an escape.

2. *Medicating emotions.* There are certain feelings you experience that provide temporary relief from stress. This kind of euphoria acts as a temporary anesthesia that numbs the pain, or at least takes your mind away from whatever is troubling you—the emptiness of your life, the loneliness, the bleak future, the mundane daily existence, the frustrations, conflicts, and disappointments. Unfortunately, the effects never last long.

3. *False sense of control.* Instead of resorting to more healthy stress coping mechanisms, addicts hope to use their activities to relieve the stress and assume control. It may be that the only time the gambler or internet addict or compulsive shopper feels some semblance of control is when he is totally immersed in the activity. There is an illusion that everything will be fine.

4. *Self-nurturance.* Like a security blanket, behavioral addicts have found a way to soothe themselves at will. Whether through chronic masturbation, overeating, or playing computer games, there is instant access to a form of self-relief when the person feels overstressed. This false perception of freedom may bring temporary relief on demand, but at a steep price.

5. *Self-destructive behavior.* Addictions are, by definition, self-destructive. They have devastating costs in terms of relationships that are compromised and careers that are sidetracked. Embarrassed by their addictive behaviors, many addicts feel shame, guilt, and low self-esteem. These negative emotions will deepen their addictive behaviors and perpetuate the vicious cycle. All addictions have a strong component of self-destruction.

In summary, behaviors become addictive when they interfere with your relationships, your productivity, and become out of control. This can be assessed in a number of ways but some good clues usually involve: (1) lying to friends and family about what you are doing and how often; (2) school or work performance suffering as a result of the excessive activity.

Workaholism

One particular kind of behavioral addiction that is becoming increasingly common in our culture is **workaholism**—an addiction to overwork. When human beings lived primarily as hunter-gatherers in the savannahs of Africa, we worked only a few hours per day and spent the rest of the time resting and socializing. Even today, indigenous cultures in many parts of the world, such as the Bushmen of southern Africa, still work a few hours each day collecting or preparing food, and spend the rest of their time taking naps, hanging out, and gossiping. Lest you think that this luxury is only a remnant of the past, consider that in many European countries the number of work hours has fallen by 20% while in North America work weeks have increased by the same percentage. In France or Germany, a typical work week might comprise 35 hours, while in the United States it is common to work more than 45 hours in a normal week.

Even given the cultural emphasis on long work hours, there are still individuals who are so addicted to their work that they have totally lost control of their lives. Their families suffer. They have no time for friendships other than those that are cultivated at work to advance their ambitions. Their children know them as strangers, as remote figures who show up occasionally for ceremonial dinners or perhaps to tuck them into bed. They run themselves ragged, working 50, 60, even 70 hours each week. Furthermore, when others complain about their hectic schedules, they don't see what all the fuss is about. After all, they are admired for their dedication, commitment, and productivity.

Workaholism is not just about trying to accomplish a lot, or even make a lot of money and advance one's career: it is about hiding from life; it is a way to manage one kind of stress by immersing oneself in another variety. As long as they stay busy, in motion, workaholics don't have time to think about how dissatisfying their primary relationships might be or how terrified they are about the uncertainties of life. They feel control only in their own domain.

Because workaholics tend to be successful in their careers, they are actually reinforced for their behavior. Their families might not see them much, but they still enjoy the fruits of the excessive labor. They are on the fast track to further promotions. They are often held up as a model for other employees to become similarly overcommitted. And they often report considerable enjoyment and satisfaction from their work. So, what, then, is the problem? Many of these folks eventually seek therapy, complaining that they are isolated and misunderstood. Research shows that workaholism goes hand in hand with physical and emotional distress as well as with family conflict and communication difficulties (Levy, 2015; Piotrowski & Vodanovich, 2008). Their spouses and friends have abandoned them. They feel estranged from their children. They are experiencing major stress-related health problems, as would be expected from someone who neglects sound health habits and is exposed to chronic pressure. Perhaps what brought them to seek help at this time is that they experienced some major disappointment at work. That is one of the risks with any addiction: as long as you remain obsessed with only one aspect of life, you are bound to set yourself up for a fall.

FOR REFLECTION 4.8

How do you know if you have an addiction? Consider the following questions:

1. Are you constantly thinking about the activity to the point where it has become a major focus of your life?

2. Do you continue to engage in the activity even though you are aware it is hurting you and others in terms of physical problems, reduction in productivity, and relationship conflicts?

3. Do you engage in this activity over and over again and find that you are unable to stop? When you do cease the behavior, do you find yourself immediately planning when you can begin again?

4. Upon cessation of the activity, do you experience *withdrawal* symptoms? This means that you feel restless, depressed, irritable, and start craving the next time you can indulge yourself.

5. Do you experience a loss of control? In spite of any limits you set (to buy one pair of jeans, eat one cookie, or play one hour on the computer), you can't seem to stick with them?

6. Do you hide your problem? Addicts often lie about the frequency of their indulgence and deny they have a problem. They pretend they have everything under control when it is obvious that this is not the case.

You may know somebody who is a raging workaholic, someone who not only works long hours but remains single-mindedly devoted to only this one, satisfying area of his or her life. If you have wondered why someone might make this kind of choice, consider the following kinds of workaholism to see which one might fit (Posen, 1997):

- *Reluctant workaholics* work long hours out of necessity, not desire. Whether it's for money, to keep their job, in response to peer pressure, or to satisfy demanding clients, they feel they have no choice but to put in long hours. For them, it doesn't feel like a choice at all.

- *Pushover workaholics* work long hours because they can't set boundaries and limits and haven't learned to say no. They have trouble asserting themselves. They seek approval at any cost and they are willing to do almost anything to secure it, even to work themselves to death. They become vulnerable to manipulation by other people because they don't stand up for themselves.

- *Ambitious workaholics* try to move up the promotional ladder and are prepared to make sacrifices in order to do it. They are willing to put in long hours and hard work as the price for success. If this means that they won't have much time for families, friends, or leisure activities, so be it. They would rather operate in an environment where they enjoy feelings of control and competence.

- *Robot workaholics* slide into a pattern of long hours and an obsession about work without realizing what's happened. The pattern may begin out of necessity, or as a temporary plan, but then continues until they stop noticing how deeply enmeshed they've become.

- *Inefficient workaholics* are disorganized, or work slowly, and so need extra hours to get the job done. The problem is that working long hours creates fatigue, which increases inefficiency. The more inefficient they become, the more hours they need to get the job done, creating a vicious cycle.

- *Turtle workaholics* work long hours to hide from boredom or an unhappy relationship, or to avoid home responsibilities. Many workaholics of this type work long hours because they feel less tense and more appreciated at work than they do at home.

Regardless of the type of workaholism—or any behavioral addiction, for that matter—the first step is to recognize that there is a problem. People may have been telling the person for some time, in many different ways, that something is out of balance, but the workaholic doesn't listen. As with any addiction, it can be maintained only with denial.

SUMMARY

This chapter offers five theoretical perspectives with which you analyze the hidden mechanisms for those adaptive and maladaptive behaviors adopted in the midst of stress. People do the best they can when they feel under assault. It is common to resort to whatever coping strategies are readily available as a way of dealing with the situation that produces loss of control and feelings of apprehension, fear, isolation, and terror. During times of stress, certain maladaptive coping mechanisms are employed because they have worked in the past, regardless of their side-effects and negative consequences. It is only when things start to fall apart—when the coping strategy stops working or the price paid is too high—that people are confronted with the reality that they are going to have to get some help.

It is important to recognize signs of trouble in yourself and others. The most common symptoms include the various kinds of depression and anxiety which are often self-medicated with substances and self-defeating behaviors. Keep in mind, as well, that there are wide individual and cultural differences with regard to maladaptive and adaptive stress behaviors—a subject I will take up in the next chapter.

QUESTIONS FOR REVIEW

1. Describe the psychoanalytic model of stress coping in terms of its goals and philosophy. Identify the defense mechanisms in stress coping based on this model.
2. Apply the humanistic model of stress coping to solving a current problem in your life.
3. Differentiate between the psychoanalytic and the humanistic models in terms of how they approach understanding and working with stress.
4. Discuss some possible influences of the behavioral model and the cognitive model on stress coping and prevention.
5. How do you determine whether your behaviors are adaptive or maladaptive?

6. Discuss the impact of the mindfulness perspective on shedding light on the causes of maladaptive behaviors.
7. What are the different kinds of anxiety disorders and what are their particular symptoms and consequences?
8. What is posttraumatic stress disorder and what causes it?
9. Describe the different kinds of depression and discuss their relationship to stress and anxiety.
10. Explain what anger is and how it is generated. What are some methods to manage anger?
11. Why are behavioral addictions similar to chemical addictions? What are the common components of addictive behaviors?
12. What is workaholism and how does it affect people's lives?

REVIEW ACTIVITY

Review Activity 4.1: Explore Adaptive and Maladaptive Behaviors
Directions: Complete the following exercises and write a brief summary after they are completed.

1. Attend several different open meetings of Alcoholics Anonymous, Narcotics Anonymous, or some other self-help support group devoted to addictions. Write about what you learned from these experiences of observing lifelong addicts whose lives were destroyed from their substance abuse.

2. Describe a close friend or relative whose life was significantly changed as a result of drug/alcohol abuse. What impact did this behavior have on you and others who were close to him or her? What finally made a difference in helping him or her to stop?

3. Relive a time in your life when you "self-medicated" yourself for some sort of stress. This could have included the use of substances (alcohol, illicit or prescription drugs, coffee, cigarettes, etc.) or some other activity designed to provide escape (sleep, isolation, exercise, food, etc.). Describe the positive and negative impacts that experience had on your life. How did you decide to stop or cut down?

4. Describe a close friend or relative whose life was significantly changed as a result of drug/alcohol abuse. What impact did this behavior have on you and others who were close to him or her? What finally made a difference in helping him or her to stop?

REFERENCES AND RESOURCES

Baker, J. H., Maes, H. H., Lissner, L., Aggen, S. H., Lichtenstein, P., & Kendler, K. S. (2009). Genetic risk factors for disordered eating in adolescent males and females. *Journal of Abnormal Psychology, 118,* 576–586.

Bandelow, B., & Michaelis, S. (2015). Epidemiology of anxiety disorders in the 21st century. *Dialogues in Clinical Neuroscience, 17*(3), 327–335.

Block, J. J. (2008). Issues for DSM-V: Internet addiction. *American Journal of Psychiatry, 165,* 306–307.

Bowen, S., Witkiewitz, K., Dillworth, T. M., Blume, A. W., Chawla, N., Simpson, T. L., et al. (2006). Mindfulness meditation and substance use in an incarcerated population. *Psychology of Addictive Behaviors, 20,* 343–347.

Brewer, J. A., Sinha, R., Chen, J. A., Michalsen, R. N., Babuscio, T. A., Nich, C., et al. (2009). Mindfulness training and stress reactivity in substance abuse: Results from a randomized, controlled Stage I pilot study. *Substance Abuse, 30,* 306–317.

Burstow, B. (2005). A critique of posttraumatic stress disorder and the DSM. *Journal of Humanistic Psychology, 45*(4), 429–445.

Creswell, J., & Lindsay, E. (2014). How does mindfulness training affect health? A mindfulness stress buffering account. *Current Directions in Psychological Science, 23*(6), 401–407.

Earll, S. (2004). *Signs of trouble: Five criteria for addiction assessment.* Retrieved on April 3, 2005 from www.pureintimacy.org.

Engs, R. C. (1987). *Alcohol and other drugs: Self-responsibility.* Bloomington, IN: Tichenor.

Foreman, J. (2004, December 13). Biology of fear. *Los Angeles Times,* p. F3.

Kabat-Zinn, J. (2003). Mindfulness-based interventions in context: Past, present, and future. *Clinical Psychology: Science and Practice, 10*(2), 144–156.

Kabat-Zinn, J., Lipworth, L., & Burney, R. (1985). The clinical use of mindfulness meditation for the self-regulation of chronic pain. *Journal of Behavioral Medicine, 8*(2), 163–190.

Kabat-Zinn, J., Massion, A. O., Kristeller, J., Peterson, L. G., Fletcher, K. E., Pbert, L. et al. (1992). Effectiveness of a meditation-based stress reduction program in the treatment of anxiety disorders. *American Journal of Psychiatry, 149,* 936–943.

Klump, K. L., Suisman, J. L., Burt, S. A., McGue, M., & Iacono, W. G. (2009). Genetic and environmental influences on disordered eating: An adoption study. *Journal of Abnormal Psychology, 118,* 797–805.

Kolassa, I., & Elbert, T. (2007). Structural and functional neuroplasticity in relation to traumatic stress. *Current Directions in Psychological Science, 16,* 321–325.

Langer, E. (1989). *Mindfulness.* Cambridge, UK: Perseus Books.

Langer, E. J. (1997). *The Power of Mindful Learning.* Reading: Addison Wesley.

Langer, E., & Moldoveanu, M. (2000). The construct of mindfulness. *Journal of Social Issues, 56*(1), 1–9.

Levy, D. (2015). Workaholism and marital satisfaction among female professionals. *The Family Journal, 23*(4), 330–335.

Mahr, G., & Goldberg, A. D. (2000). Psychological factors affecting a medical condition: Ischemic coronary heart disease. *Journal of Psychosomatic Medicine, 48*(5), 357–367.

Marks, I. (1987). *Fears, phobias, and rituals: Panic, anxiety, and their disorders.* New York, NY: Oxford University Press.

Milad, M. R., & Quirk, G. J. (2002). Neurons in medial prefrontal cortex signal memory for fear extinction. *Nature, 420* (November 7), 70–74.

Milkman, H. B., & Sunderwirth, S. G. (2010). *Craving for ecstasy and natural highs.* Thousand Oaks, CA: Sage.

Nash, J. (2008). Help! World of Warcraft is ruining my relationship. *The Times.* Retrieved on October 7, 2010 from http://women.timesonline.co.uk.

Neese, R. M. (1990). *Evolutionary explanations of emotions in human nature.* New York, NY: Aldine de Gruyter.

Nutt, D. J. (2006). *Post-traumatic stress disorder: Diagnosis, management, and treatment.* New York, NY: Taylor & Francis.

Piotrowski, C., & Vodanovich, S. J. (2008). The workaholism syndrome: An emerging issue in the psychological literature. *Journal of Instructional Psychology, 35,* 103–105.

Plath, S. (2000). *The unabridged journals of Sylvia Plath* (K. Kukil, Ed.). New York, NY: Anchor Books.

Posen, D. B. (1997). *Always change a losing game! Playing at life to be the best you can be.* Toronto, Canada: Firefly.

Preston, J. D., O'Neal, J. H., & Talaga, M. C. (2002). *Handbook of clinical psychopharmacology for therapists* (3rd ed.). Oakland, CA: New Harbinger.

Restak, R. (2004). *Poe's heart and the mountain climber: Exploring the effect of anxiety on our brains and our culture*. New York, NY: Harmony.

Strober, M., Freeman, R., Lampert, C., Diamond, J., & Kaye, W. (2000). A controlled family study of anorexia nervosa and bulimia nervosa: Evidence of shared liability and transmission of partial syndromes. *American Journal of Psychiatry, 157*, 393–401.

Szegedy-Maszak, M. (2004, December 6). Conquering our phobias: The biological underpinnings of paralyzing fears. *U.S. News and World Report*, pp. 67–74.

Teasdale, J. D., Segal, Z. V., Williams, J. M. G., Ridgeway, V. A., Soulsby, J. M., & Lau, M. A. (2000). Prevention of relapse/recurrence in major depression by mindfulness-based cognitive therapy. *Journal of Consulting and Clinical Psychology, 8*, 615–623.

Watson, J. C. (2005). Internet addiction diagnosis and assessment: Implications for counselors. *Journal of Professional Counseling, 33*(2), 17–30.

Yalom, I., & Leszcz, M. (2005). *The theory and practice of group psychotherapy*. New York, NY: Basic Books.

5

Individual and Cultural Differences

So far, I have been discussing stress experiences by emphasizing certain universal features. I have talked about the mechanisms by which human bodies respond to stress. I have described physiological features, developmental processes, and concentrated on what people do to make themselves more miserable than they need to be. Yet in all these discussions, I have emphasized the common experiences of people without concern for the unique ways that individuals behave, depending on their personality, gender, cultural background, and particular life experiences.

KEY QUESTIONS IN THE CHAPTER

- Why are individuals dramatically different in response to stressors in life?

- Why is it that one person can cope with an enormous amount of stress while another succumbs to a much smaller amount?

- How can we understand gender differences in stress appraisal and reactivity?

- Are we predisposed to stress by our genetic heritage?

- How is socioeconomic status associated with stress and risk for disease?

- What impact does the cultural influence have on the way we cope with stressors in daily life?

- Can we predict the amount of stress and the type of stress experience we encounter in our lives?

Personality and Stress

Stress is a common human phenomenon yet it is experienced in so many different ways. Since each person is a different individual with a unique personality, genetic composition, social and cultural background, set of early experiences, and education, the stress response is also unique to each. Personality can be defined as a set of enduring and habitual psychological characteristics. It is the template, formed by both genetic and environmental influences, that guides your thoughts, beliefs, and behavior.

One can readily see, without much training, that even infants a few months old display unique personality styles in the ways they express themselves and get their needs met. Some babies are placid and easy-going while others are easily upset by the slightest disturbances. Some respond flexibly to changes in their schedules, or to different caregivers, while others break into fits if there are any alterations in established patterns related to sleeping, eating, or social interaction. These same characteristic styles of relating to the world develop into established personalities by the time a child enters elementary school.

Stress responses are the result not only of universal human physiological functioning, but also of individual traits and personalities. **Emotional intelligence**, for instance—a characteristic described and researched by Howard Gardner (1993), Daniel Goleman (2005), and others (Matthews, Zeidner, & Roberts, 2006)—refers to a person's ability to read and respond sensitively to interpersonal situations, and to manage feelings effectively. This allows you not only to deal with internal stress but also to prevent conflict with others. Some studies have found that those with high emotional intelligence—meaning that they are good at expressing, controlling, and responding emotionally—enjoyed better health and experienced less stress in their lives (Tsaousis & Nikolaou, 2005).

Just as particular personality traits such as emotional intelligence help to immunize people against stress, there are also particular stress-prone personalities that predispose certain people to sustained misery. There are thus individuals who are stress-resistant, as well as those who are prone to falling apart.

States versus Traits

Whereas there are circumstances, or states, in which most people would experience stress—loss of job or a loved one, for instance—individuals tend to respond to adversity according to a consistent style or set of traits known as a personality. You may have certain friends or family members who tend to be upbeat, optimistic, and try to look for the best in situations. You may know others who tend to be generally pessimistic and negative, no matter what situations they might face. This is the old adage about the glass of water being half full or half empty—or the optimist seeing a doughnut and the pessimist seeing only a hole.

You can imagine that people who present a more upbeat personality style are generally going to do better than those who see the worst in every circumstance. One exception might be that negatively oriented individuals protect themselves from disappointments by imagining the worst disaster imaginable; this way they feel prepared for things outside their control. You will already recognize in yourself to which end of the continuum you automatically gravitate.

Certain patterns of personality traits predispose individuals to stress-related illnesses and diseases. As we've mentioned, how a given individual responds to stress depends very much on how it is appraised. This is determined, in part, by (1) your previous experience in similar situations, (2) the ways you typically respond, (3) which coping skills are at your disposal, and (4) personality characteristics (Bambling, 2006). This helps explain why some people worry about things that don't even register on the radar screen of others. It also accounts for why some people return to a state of equilibrium rather quickly while others dwell on things endlessly.

In the sections that follow, I will review personalities including Type A, codependent, anxious neurotic, and the self-loather. I will also discuss learned helplessness. The stress-resistant personality types will be discussed in Chapter 13; many other factors such as coping skills and adaptive responses will also be presented in later chapters.

Type A Personality

In the late 1950s, two cardiologists who shared an office, Meyer Friedman and Ray Rosenman, noticed that one of the cushions on the couch in the waiting room showed significantly more wear than the others. This led them to pay closer attention to those patients who literally sat on the edge of their seats rather than those who reclined in a more relaxed posture. Based on a series of interviews, they were able to develop a psychological profile of individuals who exhibited characteristics that they labeled **Type A**:

- intense, sustained drive to be goal-directed;

- competitive attitude in almost every situation;

- strong desire for recognition;

- continuous involvement in multiple activities at the same time, all under the pressure of deadlines;

- always in a rush to finish tasks as quickly as possible;

- high level of mental and physical alertness.

You may be thinking that all these qualities sound pretty good; how do you get more of this yourself? Indeed these characteristics *are* associated with high achievement and success, but they are also consistent with extreme levels of stress. In fact, the researchers discovered that these Type A personalities paid a high price for their success and workaholism since they were more likely to suffer from coronary heart disease, elevated cholesterol, hypertension, and many other problems resulting from chronic stress arousal. Just consider the impact on your body of always rushing, talking rapidly, your mind racing, impatiently trying to do as much as you can, all the while watching the clock. No one ever gets this person's unlimited attention as he is trying to have a conversation with you at the same time he is talking on a cell phone, walking, eating, making notes, *plus* planning what he's going to do next. Does this kind of person get a lot done? Absolutely. But he is also eventually heading for a possible heart attack.

To add to their problems, Type A individuals are always looking for ways to get more done in a shorter period of time, often sacrificing quality along the way. Because they are operating at a deficit of sleep and rest, they often boost their energy with cigarettes and coffee, and use alcohol or other drugs to help themselves calm down. They

---

FOR REFLECTION 5.1

How Do You Know if You Are Type A?

Make a note of the questions to which you answer "yes."

✓ Do you interrupt people before they are finished talking?

✓ Are you always multitasking—doing several things at the same time, like eating, walking, texting, planning the next task?

✓ Do you find it difficult to relax and let go of all responsibilities without feeling guilty that you are being unproductive?

✓ When you are getting in an elevator do you press the "close door" button, believing this will save you some precious seconds of waiting?

✓ Do you stick with strict schedules so that you stay on task and don't "waste time"?

✓ Do you become unusually impatient, frustrated, and angry waiting in lines that can't be avoided?

✓ Do you easily lose your temper and become upset when others don't meet your exacting expectations?

✓ Do you find yourself trying to get things done as quickly as possible so you can immediately move on to the next task?

✓ Do you look at success only in terms of measurable rewards such as income, job prestige, promotions, and material possessions?

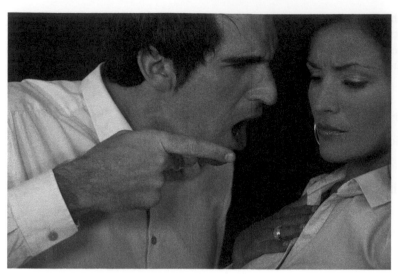

The Type A personality displays an assortment of characteristics that are associated with high productivity but at the cost of alienating others. Their constant impatience, low frustration tolerance, aggression, and overarousal predisposes them to coronary heart disease and other effects of chronic stress.

may be successful financially and professionally, but they are not much fun to be around. Type As exhibit the sort of aggression, hostility, and anger you might expect from someone who only cares about getting as much done as possible, in the shortest time possible, without regard for the consequences for themselves or others. They are short-tempered, impatient, and prone to explosive outbursts. To make matters worse, because they tend to chase others away, they find themselves isolated and alone during those times when they need support for the inevitable problems that will develop.

I don't mean to imply that *everyone* who exhibits strong ambition and high productivity is going to die prematurely of stress. There are certain aspects of Type A behavior—competitiveness and efficiency—that lead to significant achievements in science, art, business, and other fields. What seems to be the most toxic quality in this package is hostility. Explosive anger toward others leads to conflicts in most interpersonal relationships, but it is also the behavior that most stimulates maximum arousal of the stress response.

What would someone do if he exhibits Type A behavior and wants to reduce the risks associated with this way of dealing with life? The single best antidote is to s-l-o-w d-o-w-n. The pace of life is already so fast that most of us barely have time to catch our breath. The emails in your inbox, voicemails on your phone, and tasks that need to be completed seem to be present no matter how much you try to catch up. One physician (Dossey, 1982) called this "time sickness"—the belief that time is always getting away from us and the only way to catch up is to run faster.

FOR REFLECTION 5.2

Slowing Down

One reason people tend to overeat is that they don't actually taste what they are putting in their mouths. Eating has become automatic: your hand feeds your face as fast as it can without conscious thought. Yet you can enjoy food so much more, and eat so much less, if you slow down the pace of the process.

Try an experiment. For this, you will need the simplest of foods, perhaps a cracker. The object of this activity is to eat the cracker as s-l-o-w-l-y as you possibly can. We are going for quality of experience here, not quantity: you want this cracker experience to last as long as possible. Think of this as more than a mere nutritional–digestive process—this is a sensuous experience that involves all your senses.

Take at least five minutes to eat the single cracker. Make sure you spend time studying it, smelling it, looking at its colors and textures. Bring the cracker to your mouth as slowly as you can. Take tiny bites, one at a time, during which you replace the cracker on a plate in front of you after each bite. Make the experience last as long as you possibly can.

Now, imagine how you could slow down so many other things you do in life to a pace that allows you to focus with complete absorption and awareness of the experience.

In his book *In Praise of Slowness*, Honore (2004) tells the story of how he caught himself ordering a book of one-minute bedtime stories he could read to his children to save time. It was then that he had an epiphany: "In this media-drenched, data-rich, channel-surfing, computer-gaming age, we have lost the art of doing nothing, of shutting out the background noise and distractions, of slowing down and simply being alone with our thoughts" (p. 11).

The antidotes to Type A behavior are presented later in the book, when you are introduced to meditation, yoga, tai chi, and other methods that help you slow down the pace of your life. Going slowly means savoring every single minute, every second, of your life. It is about being calm, relaxed, and reflective. It is about intense awareness and consciousness of everything going on around you, and within you. It is about making deep connections to loved ones. It is about slowing down the pace of everything you do so that you emphasize quality rather than quantity.

Helpless and Hopeless Personality

Kyle and Kate have worked long and hard to accomplish a goal that was important to them: they were vying to be selected for an assignment that would give them valuable work experience and responsibilities related to a future career. There was a lot of competition for the job, but they had both been selected as finalists. After weeks of effort and preparation, each of them had just been told that he or she was not selected for this important assignment. This is what they each said to themselves immediately after hearing the disappointing news:

> Kyle: *It was just bad luck. I tried as hard as I could but there was nothing I could do. It's not fair! This sort of thing happens sometimes and all I can do is accept the situation and maybe look for another opportunity in the future. But it's so darn discouraging to be so disappointed after all the work I put into preparing for this job.*

> Kate: *There must have been something I could have done differently. I thought I had done all I could but, obviously, it wasn't quite enough this time. I need to find out what I can do to improve my chances next time. I don't believe the person they selected was any better qualified than I was; I've just got to figure out a better—or different—way to present myself the next time.*

FOR REFLECTION 5.3

What do you notice is the key difference in the characteristic ways that Kyle and Kate respond to the news that they were not selected?

Which one of them do you think is going to be more likely to feel depressed and anxious over the disappointing news?

Kyle blames the disappointment on a combination of bad luck, injustice, and circumstances beyond his control. Kate is more inclined to look at her own behavior and what she could have done differently to ensure a better outcome. Whereas Kate's reaction could lead to excessive self-blame and fault-finding, it is also indicative of someone who has an **internal locus of control** rather than an **external locus of control** (Rotter, 1966). This means that Kyle tends to be more passive, compliant, and helpless in situations that don't go his way. He would also be more inclined toward feeling hopelessness, despair, and depression in the face of situations that do not go as he anticipates.

Martin Seligman (1975, 1980) identified a personality trait called **learned helplessness** to describe Kyle's typical response to disappointment or adversity. Based on

In India, baby elephants are chained to trees during the early part of their training so as to prevent escape. Initially they try to break away, but eventually give up, even after the chain is disconnected. For the rest of their lives they believe themselves to be chained to a tree, unable to exert any free will, even though at any time they could simply walk away. This sort of learned helplessness is similar to what happens to overstressed and depressed humans who also believe themselves chained to the past.

experiments conducted with dogs that were repeatedly shocked, but believed they had no escape from the discomfort, Seligman observed that they later developed traits of helplessness in most other situations throughout their lives. It was the sense of not having control over one's fate that predisposed individuals toward maladaptive stress responses in the future. The person with the internalized personality trait of learned helplessness loses motivation and hope, and feels depressed because she does not believe that control over circumstances is possible (Seligman & Isaacowitz, 2000).

The concept of learned helplessness is useful in understanding human depression and posttraumatic stress disorder (PTSD). According to Seligman (1975), the learned helplessness phenomenon observed in dogs is very much like human depression in that they share such symptoms as emotional withdrawal, passivity, decreased motivation, and increased cognitive difficulty. This model, while helpful in some ways, also has some flaws.

First of all, not every dog or human being becomes helpless or depressed after experiencing stressful and uncontrollable events. While it is true that some people become discouraged and surrender to circumstances they believe are beyond their control, others draw on inner resources to become even more committed and motivated to persevere. One example is Senator John McCain, who spent many years in captivity as a prisoner of war. Even though the North Vietnamese did everything they could to break his spirit by reinforcing a sense of helplessness, this only made McCain more determined to fight back any way he could. After he was released, what he had learned as a prisoner of war (POW) made him more resilient in the world of politics.

A second flaw in the helpless personality model is that it is not specified whether the uncontrollable event is temporary and specific to an individual, or a permanent and universal event. For these reasons, Seligman and colleagues reformulated the theory by using the concept of **explanatory style** to describe how people make sense of stressful situations they face. The causes of stressful or disappointing events can be attributed to internal factors (Kate) or external factors (Kyle). They can represent either factors that are stable over time ("This always happens to me") or temporary situations ("I misjudged things this time"). Finally, the cause of the problem can be attributed to only one situation or generalized to all circumstances.

Suppose that you received what you consider a poor grade in your stress management class. How stressed you are over this predicament depends to a large extent on how you explain the grade. If you think that this grade is the fault of your instructor or the textbook, because you weren't provided with sufficient preparation to perform well, then you have a good excuse for the low grade, but you also feel helpless because you have to deal with similar resources in the future. In other words, by externalizing the blame you save yourself short-term responsibility for the problem at the expense of feeling any long-term competence to rectify matters on subsequent tests or assignments.

If, on the other hand, you attribute the grade to your own lack of preparation, then you have much more control and power to do better next time. If you also attribute the problem as situational ("Just because I did poorly on this one test does not mean I am a poor student") rather than universal, you are also better positioned to improve performance. A more optimistic, internally based explanatory style immunizes you against stress and depression that accompanies feelings of helplessness.

Repressive Personality

One of Freud's notable defense mechanisms for coping with perceived threats is called **repression**. This occurs when someone faces a trauma or situation that is so disturbing that it is submerged into the unconscious, as if it never happened. This is what makes it possible for people who were abused as children, or others who suffered horrible tragedies, to "forget" the trauma ever happened. The painful memories are repressed.

This repressive defense mechanism can also be adopted as a whole personality style. Certain people who feel particularly vulnerable to life's stressors try to organize their lives in such a way that they can prevent or minimize things that might upset their fragile world. These so-called **repressive personalities** have certain behavioral characteristics (Davidson, 1992; Davidson & Tomarken, 1989; Tomarken & Davidson, 1994). They are planners who are organized, rule-bound, and hate surprises. They resort to a well-tested pattern of behaviors that would bring them no unwanted attention. They want to keep the lowest profile possible and avoid conflict at all costs. Interestingly, psychological testing reveals that they are not necessarily depressed or anxious, yet they dread social disapproval and need social conformity.

In some ways, "repressors" are the exact opposite of the learned helplessness personality described in the previous section. Whereas the latter tend to exaggerate the external sources of control and blame, the former more often over-attribute results to their own efforts. In that sense, they hold overly optimistic expectations that are not based in reality. In such situations, someone would feel frustrated because someone else insists that everything will turn out all right, even though there is absolutely no evidence to support this prediction.

This sort of deluded personality style has certain advantages. It is adaptive in the sense that it reduces stress by minimizing perceived threats that might otherwise be extremely upsetting. Unfortunately, because this cognitive style is, by its very nature, distorting reality and ignoring possible dangers, it is likely to have significant negative consequences.

To complicate matters further, repressed personalities inhibit and restrict their emotional expression of any feelings that might be the least bit upsetting. They would be inclined to deny that they feel anything at all—fear, apprehension, anxiety, even attraction—so as to reduce the possible threats that could be associated with these risks. They simply don't recall things they might experience as unpleasant. The ultimate example of this type of repressed personality can be found in the comic-book or movie hero the Hulk. At the least sign of emotional arousal, he completely loses control. To avoid this, he maintains the most placid state he can, avoiding all stress.

Any benefits a repressed personality might imagine would likely be counteracted by the underlying physiological reactions that belie the surface calm. Measures taken of these individuals reveal that while they may appear to be in complete control and totally optimistic about whatever comes their way, their blood pressure and cortisol levels can be significantly elevated (Brown et al., 1996; King, Taylor, Albright, & Haskell, 1990; Tomarken & Davidson, 1994).

It turns out, not surprisingly, that inhibiting emotional responses takes a lot of energy. Repressors may develop impaired immune systems. There are some theories, not yet totally supported by research, that indicate that withholding all emotion in this way, and denying genuine adversity, can lead to cancer and other diseases.

Codependent Personality

One form of helplessness embedded in relationships is **codependency**. This is also a learned behavior, but one that is characterized by a one-sided, emotionally destructive/abusive relationship. Psychologists in the 1980s first discovered this in the process of treating alcoholism. They observed that one or more family members "enabled" the alcoholic's destructive behaviors—the same behaviors they complained about!

One clear example of this codependent phenomenon occurred with a couple who came for marital counseling. Among their many problems, the husband said that he was no longer interested in having sex with his wife because she was too fat. When the therapist asked the wife about this situation, she agreed that she had not always been so heavy and she was strongly motivated to do something about it. She wanted to lose weight not only for her husband's sake, but also for her own.

They developed a diet plan that worked pretty well for a few weeks until the woman reported in a session that she was frustrated because her husband kept buying the most tempting treats—potato chips, chocolate chip cookies, cashews—and leaving them around the house.

"How am I am supposed to lose weight," she asked, "when *he* keeps buying this crap and putting it in front of my nose all the time? He knows this was my downfall before." As she said this, she looked at her husband with a pleading look.

The therapist looked at him too, amazed that he would do such a thing knowing that his wife was doing everything in her power to please him and make herself more attractive as a partner. It was as if he was deliberately trying to sabotage exactly the behavior he said he wanted to change (see For Reflection 5.4).

"Well?" the therapist pressed the husband. He just sat there and shrugged.

"What?" he said innocently. "I should deprive myself of all the things that I love just because she can't control herself?"

FOR REFLECTION 5.4

Why do you imagine that the husband would deliberately sabotage exactly the outcome that he says he most wants—for his wife to lose weight?

Reason through what you think he might be "enjoying" as a result of her setback and what he would "suffer" if she were to succeed. This same process is useful in thinking through any situation in which you are puzzled as to why someone would do something that seems, at first, to be self-defeating.

Answer at the end of the chapter.

As incredible as this scenario might sound, it is a common one in relationships in which one partner is engaging in self-destructive behavior such as alcohol and drug abuse, overeating, eating disorders, and similar patterns. There exists a codependency between the "identified patient" (the one who appears to have the problem) and the "enabler" (the one who makes continued abuse possible through collusion, or conspiring unconsciously).

Over time, certain people are "trained" to be codependent personalities. They become used to having someone else take care of their needs and, as such, lose touch with the ability to take care of themselves. They might not suffer the stress of responsibility, but they experience a far worse kind of pressure that comes from being helpless and dependent on others.

Although codependents like the husband may have good intentions, the caretaking becomes compulsive and hurtful for both partners. The repeated rescue attempts allow the needy individual to continue on a destructive course and to become even more dependent on the unhealthy caretaking of the "benefactor." As this reliance increases, the codependent develops a sense of reward and satisfaction from "being needed." When the caretaking becomes compulsive, the codependent feels helpless and without choices in the relationship; he is unable to break away from the cycle of behavior that causes it. Codependents view themselves as victims and are attracted to relationships that allow them to re-create the same dysfunctional, dependent patterns over and over again. That is one reason why someone who finally manages to extricate herself from a destructive, abusive, codependent relationship might get involved in another one right afterward.

Typically, codependence develops in a dysfunctional home in which emotional needs are not met in healthy ways. There is often the presence of addictions in one or more family members. Abuse is often present as well, in the form of emotional, physical, or sexual behavior. In some cases, one member of the family suffers from chronic illness. In all of these situations, the children collude to take care of one another's needs, since they are not being addressed by their out-of-control parents. In codependent families, children grow up believing that their own needs don't matter; their self-worth is measured solely in terms of their caregiving role. Over time, codependent people lose touch with what their own needs or wants are.

Codependent persons develop emotional problems such as depression, anxiety, relationship dysfunctions, and cycling between hyperactivity and lethargy. Physical problems often result such as gastrointestinal disturbances, colitis, ulcers, migraine headaches, nonspecific rashes and skin problems, high blood pressure, insomnia, sleep disorders, and other stress-related physical illnesses.

FOR REFLECTION 5.5

Are *You* Codependent?

Check all that apply:
____ I have to be needed in a relationship in order to feel satisfied.
____ I feel a great sense of responsibility to take care of others in ways they couldn't do for themselves.
____ I often do more than my fair share.
____ I am involved in a relationship that I would do *anything* to hold onto.
____ I have feelings of panic at the prospect of being abandoned by a loved one.
____ I have great difficulty being alone for any prolonged period of time.
____ I feel guilty whenever I assert myself.
____ I have difficulty making decisions on my own without asking others for help.
____ I can't stand being with others who are in any pain and I feel like I *have* to do something to make their pain go away.
____ I feel like a failure when I disappoint significant others or don't meet all their expectations.
____ I sometimes agree with others just so they will like and approve of me.
____ I am very talented at guessing how others might be feeling and taking care of those needs even before they are aware of them.
____ I feel resentful when others won't let me help them.
____ I often neglect or put aside my own needs in order to take care of others.
____ Whatever I do for others, it never seems like enough; I could always do more.

There is no score to add up. But if you checked more than a few items, write some comments to yourself where about what you think that means in terms of the patterns of your relationships. Ultimately, *you* are the one who must decide if codependent patterns are a problem for you. If your own needs are often put aside, or if you are repeatedly involved in relationships that don't help you to reach your own goals, you may want to consider making some changes or seeking help.

Keep in mind that codependency is so rampant that if we add up all the alcoholics, illicit and prescription drug addicts, gambling and sex addicts, abusers, *plus* all their enablers, we will have included the vast majority of North Americans. Many Asian, African, Latino, and indigenous cultures do not view codependency as pathological but rather as sign of socially responsible behavior. The whole concept of meeting individual needs in a way that we might consider ambitious would be considered selfish and inappropriate within Chinese, Vietnamese, Korean, Aboriginal, Maori, Native Hawaiian, Mexican, or Puerto Rican cultures. Nevertheless, there is normative behavior within any cultural group in which extreme manifestations of taking care of others go beyond sanctioned standards and become destructive for all the parties involved.

Addressing Codependency Issues

Codependency is usually not an all-or-nothing phenomenon—it is not so much a matter of *whether* or not you are engaging in this sort of pattern, but rather *how often* you are doing so, and *with whom*. The first step in addressing these issues that may be needlessly creating stress in your life is to acknowledge that you have a problem. Codependency *can* become a type of addiction. As with any sort of addiction, there is often reluctance to own the problem in the first place. It is up to you to decide if certain relationships you are involved in have become codependent. If so, you will notice some of the symptoms I have covered. Feelings of resentment will also be present.

After acknowledging that you might have a problem in this area, there are several steps you can take to address codependency issues.

- *Get professional help*. A reputable therapist or a recovery group is an important resource for helping you to identify your own codependent behavior, as well as its impact on others. There is even a specialized support group, Codependents Anonymous (CODA), which holds meetings on a regular basis. Likewise, individual or couples therapists can assist you in the difficult process of making changes in longstanding patterns that have been with you since childhood.

- *Make recovery a first priority*. Like all addictions, codependency is insidious; you may recognize yourself in the symptoms but still deny their importance. You may recognize many chronic, self-defeating behaviors you know you need to change but still feel powerless to make those changes, or at least to make them last. In Chapter 14, I will address the subject of how you can make changes endure over time.

- *Seek support from others*. I am not talking about another form of codependency, but rather the importance of developing new resources to support your intended changes. One reason why it is so challenging to disengage from codependent patterns is that there are systems in place that try to maintain the status quo. Note what happened in the example mentioned earlier when the wife attempted to lose weight and the husband, even after urging the changes in the first place, tried to sabotage her efforts.

- *Develop alternative resources*. The only way that you can let go of one pattern, even if it has been detrimental, is to develop others that provide similar benefits without the negative side-effects. For those struggling to recover from codependency, it is crucial to develop a richer inner life as well as an extended support system. This could include such things as meditation and prayer, but could also involve secular spiritual activities that put you into closer contact with a Higher Power, with nature, or your own inner being.

- *Stop managing and controlling others*. This is a big challenge. It is, in fact, *the* challenge for someone who is codependent. There is power and a degree of control, as well as powerlessness, associated with codependency. As long as you are so totally devoted and immersed in someone else's life, you don't have to manage your own. Once you stop advising, fixing, and rescuing someone else, you are left to consider the emptiness and dissatisfaction of your own life. Look at a parent or spouse who is neurotically over-involved in their child's or partner's life and you will see someone who has a gaping hole to fill.

- *Become more self-sufficient.* There are cultural differences with respect to the parameters of healthy independence, but within every family, tribe, or ethnic context, there is a healthy balance between taking care of others versus taking care of yourself.

Gender and Stress

Gender refers to the attributes, behaviors, personality characteristics, and expectancies associated with a person's biological sex in a given culture. It may be based on biology or may be learned responses—usually it is a combination of the two. It represents the psychological process of being male or female, while "sex" refers to your biological characteristics.

Differences can be observed in how individuals respond to stress based not only on their personality styles, but also on their gender. In many areas of life, women and men can experience the world according to their unique psychological, biological, and cultural compositions. One study of gender-based hormonal differences found that sex roles and psychological environments were at least as important as any biological factors in the ways men and women responded to, and recovered from, life challenges (Lundberg, 2005). Certainly there are differences in people's endocrine systems and neurological pathways, based on individual and gender differences, but it seems that the ways that you structure and negotiate your life are even more critical in preventing stress and recovering from it afterward.

Gender Differences in Stress Responses

Since the pioneering work of Cannon and Selye on stress, it has been assumed that males and females have reacted similarly to a threat with a fight-or-flight response. After all, I have been talking about essentially biological reactions, and don't both men and women have much the same basic neurological response systems?

The work of Shelly Taylor and her colleagues (2000) has challenged this assumption. They suggest that the so-called fight-or-flight response may be an appropriate model to explain how men respond to challenges in life: when they are confronted by a threat, their first inclination is either to run or to do battle. But perhaps this scenario is *not* what happens with many women.

You may have noticed that most of the scientists who did the research on stress were men. Moreover, most of the subjects they studied were also men. Thus Taylor and her associates wondered whether these findings might perhaps not be as appropriate when applied more widely. Maybe if a more balanced sample had been used, or if women alone were studied, the results would be quite different.

Based on the data she collected, Taylor proposed an alternative theory to explain how females cope with stress that did not fit within a fight-or-flight paradigm but rather one that could be described as **tend-and-befriend**. What this means is that when females are under stressful conditions they may not feel pressure to fight or run away as much as they seek social contact and support from others. It is possible that, just as men have evolutionarily developed and been selected for their tendency to be aggressive and fierce, women have evolved a pattern of caregiving to protect themselves. When men are threatened, they might grab their spears, but women draw closer to their children and others of the tribe for mutual protection.

Different hormonal mechanisms would be elicited during a tend-and-befriend reaction than one in which fighting or running is on the immediate horizon. Instead of the catecholamines and glucocorticoids being mobilized for a fight-or-flight response, oxytocin, estrogen, and other female sex hormones appear to be involved in the tend-and-befriend response. Oxytocin, a hormone secreted in both men and women as a response to stress, has been shown to calm rats and humans, making them less anxious and more social. It is also found to encourage maternal behavior and greater affiliation. Male hormones seem to reduce the effect of oxytocin, while the female hormone estrogen augments it.

One way to notice these differences is to observe the typical ways in which a father and mother might react after having a stressful day at work. The father might be inclined toward fighting through verbal arguments or even physical aggression (fight), or to isolate himself (flight) through withdrawal by watching television, playing video games or escaping online. The mother, on the other hand, might deal with her stress by focusing on the children, talking with a friend on the phone, or taking care of other "community chores" around the house like cooking or cleaning.

These gender differences can easily be observed in the level of violence perpetrated by males as compared with females when both encounter stress in their lives. Our prisons are filled with a disproportionate number of men who have consistently resorted to aggression, anger, direct conflict, and violence when they felt cornered.

It should also be pointed out that while, historically, these gender differences have been more pronounced, in today's world, the gender roles are blending. Women attain greater equality in economic opportunities, and even approach men more closely in athletic prowess (times between men and women in marathon races are getting closer every decade). More and more men are choosing lifestyles that emphasize tend-and-befriend responses to stress while more and more women are operating in the aggressive theatres of politics, medicine, business, and law. Unfortunately, this transition for females is likely to become accompanied by the more fight-or-flight type stress activation that could take a significant toll on their greater longevity.

Gender Stereotypes and Gender Role Stressors

Within every known culture there are prescribed roles for each gender, evolved as part of the human tendency toward specialization based on different abilities. Because men are larger physically, with more highly developed large muscles, they were saddled with the primary responsibility for hunting and repelling invaders. Likewise, women, who have more highly developed communication and social skills, as well as eye–hand coordination, became specialized in food gathering and preparation tasks. This was the historical specialization of roles that has since evolved in our culture to a certain extent, but remains the dominant model within more isolated regions of the world such as sub-Saharan Africa, Amazonia, Aboriginal Australia, the Arctic, and the highlands of Papua New Guinea.

Male and female babies may start life with equal opportunities to develop skills, abilities, and thought patterns in a host of different areas, but they are quickly socialized into gender-specific roles—even with parents who attempt to counteract these rigid patterns. So-called "tomboys" or "sensitive boys" encounter tremendous peer pressure once they enter puberty to conform to standard gender roles. This involves not only specified patterns of behavior, but also ways of thinking and assessing stress situations.

Feminine Gender Role and Stressors

Understanding the typical feminine and masculine responses to stress explains much that is related to gender differences. There are generally five categories of common stressor specifically associated with the female gender (Gillespie & Eisler, 1992):

1.   fear of relationships devoid of emotional intimacy;

2.   concerns about being physically unattractive;

3. fear of becoming victimized;

4. apprehension about being involved in interpersonal conflicts that require assertiveness;

5. feeling like a failure in nurturing tasks.

Even though these five areas appear to be separate domains, they are all part of a general concept of interpersonal competence. Most of the sources of stress in the lives of girls and women tend to revolve around relationships with others, especially with regard to their own abilities to demonstrate tend-and-befriend behavior.

Subsequent research (Martz, Handley, & Eisler, 1995) indicated further that women who struggled with feelings of incompetence in one of these five dimensions were far more likely to develop health problems. For those women who join men in developing Type A characteristics, they also suffer the consequences of displaying more hostility in their behavior and being more prone to cardiovascular disease.

Males and females no longer have such clearly defined and prescribed gender roles. Women encounter tremendous stress from conflicting gender roles that are context-specific. Taking on traditionally male professions as surgeons, litigators, CEOs, and legislators, they are expected to demonstrate typically male, aggressive behavior to succeed. A woman is almost required to become a Type A personality to earn respect—not only from male colleagues but also other females. Yet once she comes home, her family expects her to display feminine characteristics that involve nurturance.

Male Gender Role and Stressors

Ask most women what they want in a man and they will describe such qualities as sensitive, caring, kind, emotionally expressive, communicative—and successful. Very few women would be satisfied with a nice guy who is unemployed or unsuccessful.

What does it take for a guy to be successful in most pursuits? Generally, it requires being competitive, aggressive, domineering, and emotionally restrictive. From early childhood males have been instilled with socially approved notions of masculinity that include toughness, independence, and task orientation. As just mentioned, these qualities are associated with success in those tasks that rely on aggression, but they also result in increased anxiety, depression, interpersonal intimacy problems, and fewer attempts to seek mental health services. These are exactly the opposite of what women say they want in a relationship. So men are caught in a paradoxical bind of being given mixed messages that they could never satisfy. How does a guy manage to be super-aggressive at work and then come home and turn off all that testosterone energy?

Of clients who seek help in therapy, 85% are women. This is not because women are more emotionally disturbed than men; quite the contrary, they are the ones who are designated to seek help on behalf of their families because many men feel too ashamed to admit weakness and seek help. This is one reason why in surveys women are far more likely to report significant stress than their male counterparts—not because they are more dysfunctional, but because they are more willing to talk about their worries whereas men would be inclined to deny or cover up their out-of-control feelings (Matud, 2004; Schuler, 2006).

It is a myth that men do not crave mutual support and nurturance in order to deal with stress. It is just that men express themselves emotionally in very different ways than women. Even when they cry, they do so for shorter periods of time and with fewer visible cues.

Why do you suppose that so few men go into therapy, even when they are on the edge of desperation? In order to answer this question, compare the abilities that are required to be a good therapy client versus those that are stereotypically male. Therapy requires a high degree of emotional expressiveness, vulnerability, and personal disclosure —exactly the opposite of the qualities reinforced in males, who have been taught to withhold feelings, never to allow oneself to be seen as weak, and who are not inclined to reveal things that could be used against them.

Gender Differences in Stress-Related Disorders and Coping Strategies

Men and women are prone to different stress-related health vulnerabilities. For instance, women suffer more from autoimmune illnesses while men are more prone to develop cardiac and infectious diseases. Women are more prone to develop psychiatric disorders such as anxiety, depression, and panic disorders, whereas men often show antisocial behavior, become substance abusers, and commit suicide.

Women are often reported to experience more stress than men, whether after a natural disaster or at work (Foley & Kirschbaum, 2010; Karanci, Alkan, Aksit, Sucuoglu, & Balta, 1999; Matud, 2004). As mentioned, one reason for this is that they are permitted to admit their suffering and talk about it more openly. Men are supposed to suffer silently, hold back their tears, and never admit that they have lost control.

In spite of women supposedly experiencing more stress than men, they live an average of seven years longer. This superior coping style could be the result of several factors. Women are more likely to ask for help when they are in need, so the residual symptoms would be addressed. By contrast, men would be more inclined to deny their pain and rely on alcohol or drugs as a coping strategy. Women are more likely to seek social support during times of trouble, one of the most effective means of resolving stress difficulties. However, Kirkwood (2010) argues that stress and good habits can't explain the superiority of women over men in longevity. His biological explanation suggests that women outlive men because men are more disposable and evolution favors women's role in reproduction over men's.

Culture and Stress

A culture is a group of people with shared values, characteristics, and interests. Ordinarily, you might think of this term in relation to ethnicity or race. Whether someone is Black, White, Latino, Japanese-American, or any other ethnicity, it actually encompasses a concept far more diverse that includes race, religion, gender, socioeconomic class, and even sexual orientation, disabilities, professions, hobbies, and neighborhoods. As a function of identification within a particular group, people tend to display common characteristics—and sometimes common responses to stress.

Whereas the experience of stress is universal, the way it is felt and expressed depends very much on the cultural context. Imagine how stress would be conceptualized and experienced differently if you were Buddhist (suffering is part of life) versus Catholic (your sins can be forgiven through confession), or living in prison versus a mansion. Thus religious and spiritual practices, life philosophy, cultural values, a collectivist versus individualistic society, all impact the experience (Wong, Wong, & Scott, 2006). In fact, culture can influence stress and coping in four distinct ways (Aldwin, 2000): the types of stressors experienced, the appraisal of these stressors, the choice of coping strategies, and the institutional mechanisms for coping with stress.

Culture and the Types of Stressors Experienced

Culture, as an organized set of norms and behavioral expectations, can serve to benefit people in a number of ways, as well as to limit their choices. As a means of adaptation, culture helps humans survive natural disasters and deal with illnesses and changes by providing structures to guide behavior. After the death of a loved one, for instance, a complex series of rituals and cultural norms come into play that tell you exactly what you are supposed to do and how to do it. Depending on your religion and culture, you will have prescribed "rules" for mourning, including where it takes place, for what period of time, and how people are to behave. These norms are intended to reduce the stress of the unknown by providing socially sanctioned procedures.

When individuals within a culture feel trapped or stifled by excessive cultural demands placed on them, additional stress results. People may feel a lack of freedom, a reduction of choices, and a fate that is not within their control. Consider, for instance, the limited choices that people in India have because of the caste they were born into. Within our own culture, being born into a lower **socioeconomic status** (SES) reduces freedom and increases stress in similar ways. Low SES is a predictor of higher stress levels, increased risk for various diseases, and shortened life expectancy (Adler & Snibbe, 2003; Bucholz, Ma, Normand, & Krumholz, 2015).

In more affluent countries, the culture of poverty creates a set of stressors to which more fortunate people are immune:

- greater exposure to violence, anger, and hostility in neighborhoods;

- greater incidence of crime including murder, rape, and assault;

- conditions of overcrowding and inadequate housing;

- unemployment and underemployment;

- increased chaos and disorder in daily life;

- lack of financial resources to secure basic needs;

- feelings of oppression and lack of perceived choices.

Being part of the "privileged caste," or upper middle class, does not immunize you against stress; it just produces a different set of culturally based challenges. With the reasonably affluent, tremendous pressure is associated with achieving material possessions that signify success and prosperity. Consider that a $15,000 Kia provides essentially the same transportation, at roughly the same speed, as a $100,000 Mercedes, yet people will go into debt, creating additional financial pressures, in order to own this symbol of success. It is also interesting to consider that no matter how much your car, watch, or house costs, there is still a strong motivation to move up to the next level: the guy with the expensive Mercedes daydreams about the time when he can afford a Rolls-Royce.

In Chapter 3, I mentioned that school-age children may experience stress related to academic performance. Since nations have different types of educational systems, the stressors placed on citizens can be very different. In China and other Asian countries such as Japan and Korea, elementary and secondary school students are faced with significant stress because of the rigorous course work and the pressure to succeed in entrance examinations. In places such as Singapore and Hong Kong, children are tracked into life paths by the time they are eight years of age! Their parents compete to sign their children up for the best preschools as soon as they discover they are pregnant. By the time their children are in third grade, they take competitive achievement tests that determine, once and for all, whether they will be tracked towards college preparatory education or a trade. Just imagine the kind of stress placed on young children and their parents.

Once they get to college, Asian students are more relaxed and academic demands are less rigorous. By contrast, because America offers more pathways to higher education, elementary and secondary school students in North America are less stressed than their Asian counterparts. However, college students in America often face more rigorous course work than elsewhere, and consequently experience more stress.

Culture and the Appraisal of Stressors

Just like the cliché about beauty being in the eye of the beholder, stressors vary through different cultural lenses. Yet another example of these cultural differences in the ways that stress is labeled, experienced, and described was evident in a series of interviews with Kenyan marathon runners who have so dominated their sport for the past decade. When asked how they are successful in managing the stress and pain associated with long-distance running, the Kenyans appeared surprised by the question: for them running is a joy, not an exercise in pain. They experience the so-called anguish of the marathon in a different way because they use different language and have different associations with the sensations that we might label excruciatingly painful.

Depending on the values enforced, particular behaviors could elicit considerable stress in one culture but not in another. Being overweight would likely be a huge source of anxiety in a Western culture where thinness is considered the major prototype for the female body. But among many South Pacific island nations, being obese is a sign of prosperity. Similarly, in Egypt a girl who has premarital sex risks exile, if not death. This same behavior in Tahiti might not cause no great concern.

In a country such as the United States that is made up of so many blended cultures, there are myriad possible stress reactions to the same stimulus. Western cultures have been labeled as individualistic, with people pursuing their own independence and attending to their own needs and satisfactions.

Asian cultures, by contrast, are described as collectivist in that individuals are expected to attend to others, gain interdependence, and fit into a group (Yee, 1992). Families are very much concerned with "saving face" and everything needs to be done to bring honor and glory to the family name.

Culture and the Choice of Coping Strategies

Each culture offers a unique repertoire of resources for dealing with stress, as well as a set of restraints. In affluent countries such as the United States and Great Britain, stress is considered a major problem. Individuals suffering from distress often resort to individual and group stress management techniques such as cognitive restructuring methods, time management, relaxation techniques such as yoga and tai chi, and autogenic training. For more serious problems, they may seek the services of physicians and psychotherapists.

Because the choice of coping strategies is mediated by cultural values, people in Asian countries would rely on a different set of coping options. In China, India, Korea, Vietnam, and many other parts of the world, seeing a professional therapist for stress relief would be relatively rare. Not only would the cost of such services be prohibitive, but it would be an inconceivable loss of face to admit to such a problem and ask a stranger for help. In most parts of the world, admitting to a problem like stress is tantamount to volunteering for ostracism. There is a stigma attached to such perceived loss of control.

In one study (Snyder, 2001), the stress coping and adjustment strategies of 45 Asian Americans and 45 Caucasian Americans were compared. Although these two groups of people displayed similarities in six of the eight strategy categories, the two exceptions revealed much about their differences. Compared with the Caucasian Americans, the Asian Americans reported more problem avoidance and social withdrawal. In other words, they chose to cope with the stress problem through disengagement rather than confronting the problem as those from the majority culture might be inclined to do. Another study shows that culture also moderates the effect of perceived emotional support on well-being and health (Uchida et al., 2008). For students and nonstudent adults with Euro-American cultural background the link between perceived emotional support and well-being was weak when self-esteem was controlled for, while this link was more direct among students with Asian backgrounds, suggesting that perceived emotional support affirms the ever-important sense of the self as interdependent and connected with others in the Asian culture.

Somatization of stress is also more common in cultures in which direct expression of feelings is not considered appropriate. In countries such as South Korea it would be highly unusual for someone to talk openly about the stress they are experiencing; they are more likely to report bodily symptoms that would be seen as a direct manifestation of their problems (Askew & Keyes, 2005).

Acculturation Stress

Acculturation stress refers to both the cultural and psychological changes that result from continuous contact between two or more cultural groups. It is often experienced by immigrants who are forced to deal with radical differences in language, customs, geography, values, and behavior (see Voice of Stress 5.1).

Even though there is much variability in the long-term acculturation process, most individuals caught in this process experience positive adaptation to the new cultural context based on several strategies (Berry, 2005). The first potential source of stress is related to the degree to which immigrants preserve their own cultural traditions versus adopting those of their new culture. This is a source of conflict within many immigrant families in which the parents may wish their children to speak their native language at home, but the kids feel strong peer pressure to speak the language of their new home.

VOICE OF STRESS 5.1

Thirty-Three-Year-Old Male Teacher and Part-Time Graduate Student

I remember when I first came to this country on a plane from Mexico City to Seattle. I had a window seat and there was this important-looking businessman on the aisle seat next to me who was working diligently on his laptop computer. I had to go to the toilet very badly but I didn't want to interrupt him. Besides, I had no words in English to explain that I needed to go; I wasn't even sure whether airplanes had toilets on them since I had never flown before.

It was a very long flight and I kept trying to hold control of myself as best I could. I was so afraid of making a bad impression on this American businessman. I didn't want him to know that I was so stupid and helpless that I couldn't even ask for what I wanted. I felt trapped in my seat with no way out. Finally, I could hold it no longer and I peed in my pants sitting in that window seat. I was totally humiliated but the rich businessman didn't even seem to notice—he just kept typing away.

This was my first introduction to America. I vowed during the rest of that flight, as I sat in my cold, wet pants, that I would speak this new language and I would do everything I could to fit in. Sure, it was a lot of pressure I put on myself. But look at me now: I am that guy with the laptop.

New immigrants not only experience the stress of acculturation, but also of oppression. They are often marginalized economically, socially, and politically. Whatever support and resources they had built over a lifetime are left behind; they are forced to start over again, but in a world in which they don't fully understand the rules.

A group of students taking a class on cultural differences were asked to examine the experiences of new immigrants. Since this was in Southern California, quite a number of the students identified themselves as such.

"How many of you can remember your first days in America?" the instructor asked them. Half the class signaled that they had clear recollections of their arrival in their new home. The instructor followed this question with another—he asked for volunteers to share some memorable incident that stood out for them during this difficult transition.

"I had the most confusing time trying to figure out what to do with shoes," Kira, a woman from Nepal, started the discussion. When we all looked puzzled, she continued her story. "You see the first thing that surprised me about this country was when I went to visit an American's home and I noticed that everyone wore their shoes inside. We would never do that at home because it is very unclean."

The class started to laugh, but Kira quickly interrupted. "No, I am serious. And I was also shocked that you allow animals inside your homes. I thought that this must indeed be a very rich country that you can afford to feed animals and have them live with you as family members. In my country, if we have animals we keep them only to eat."

Again the class started to laugh, at least until they fully appreciated what it must have been like for Kira to live in a place where poverty and starvation were so rampant. "So, when I went to an American's home I felt so nervous all the time. I wanted to fit in, but that would mean leaving my shoes on inside their homes. That would be disrespectful. So I would take my shoes off but that would make some of my friends look at me strangely."

"That is very interesting," another student, Rivkah, immediately jumped in. "I remember the first week I arrived in America from Israel. I had seen lots of American movies back at home, so I thought I knew how to behave here, but it didn't take long to figure out I was lost most of the time. What really got me was this shoe thing you were talking about, Kira."

"Shoe thing?" the instructor prompted.

"Yeah. The first time I went to an American home I noticed that everyone had taken off their shoes in the house and had them lined up by the door. So I figured that this must be an American custom—to take your shoes off inside. I thought this was kind of

FOR REFLECTION 5.7

Next time you are at a social gathering, engaged in the same predictable conversations about sports, politics, movies, or whatever, try taking things to a deeper level by asking people two key, open-ended questions. First, try answering them yourself. Then try them out with others whom you would like to know better.

1. What is your primary cultural identity? (You answered this in the earlier reflective exercise.)

2. What are the key features of your culture that I should know about and appreciate in order to understand you better?

weird because we don't do this in my country, and I had never seen this in an American movie. But I wanted to fit in with everyone else, so I took my shoes off. In fact, from then on, every time I visited an American, I always removed my shoes before entering their homes. I did this until, one day, I overheard a friend telling someone else that Israelis always remove their shoes before going inside. I looked at her like she was crazy— the only reason I had been doing this is because I thought this was what people did in America. Only later did I figure out that this whole misunderstanding began because that first American family had gotten new carpeting or something and I thought that everyone behaved in this way."

The class laughed uproariously at this alternative shoe story. Yet contained within these two different experiences are the seeds of acculturation stress. Both Kira and Rivkah wanted badly to fit into the norms of their new culture, yet they weren't sure what was considered appropriate behavior. It is difficult enough to navigate the trials of everyday life without the added stress of constantly feeling like an outsider.

Becoming sensitive to cultural differences is a major task for anyone who serves in a helping role for others. When you find yourself in conversation with someone from a different culture who is suffering the stresses of acculturation issues, the following suggestions might be helpful in your efforts to be supportive.

1. Monitor your biases and assumptions about this person based on your first impressions and past experiences with people who *appear* similar. The differences within a given culture are actually greater than those between cultures. What this means is that knowing someone is Mexican or Iranian or Samoan provides less information than you might imagine—there are as many differences among Mexicans as a people as there are between Mexicans and Iranians.

2. Ask open-ended questions to elicit information and help the person to tell his or her story. These are the sorts of queries that cannot be answered by "yes" or "no." Instead of asking someone, "Do you feel upset by that?" try asking, "How do you feel about that?" In all your communications with others you will find such questions encourage deeper exploration.

3. Ask the person to teach you what you need to know and understand. This is a handy approach favored by therapists. It isn't necessary for you to be an expert

on the culture of anyone you meet. Assume they are the experts on their own cultures. If you show genuine interest, most people are delighted to tell you about their worlds.

4. Make sure that you listen sensitively and respectfully, taking the posture of a curious investigator. Rather than peppering the person with a barrage of questions like an interrogator, try listening as much as possible, using subtle probes to encourage the person to elaborate further.

FOR REFLECTION 5.8

Team up with a partner. One of you will play the role of the person described below, or better yet, talk about your own cultural situation. The other partner will practice interviewing skills to explore this person's world by asking a few open-ended questions and then listening as carefully and sensitively as possible to get a grasp of this person's cultural world view.

The case: You are a 20-year-old college student. You and your family are immigrants from the Philippines, where your father still lives and works. You have been having problems with your boyfriend or girlfriend, a second-generation Peruvian-American. You fight a lot, especially over your families, each of whom disapproves of the relationship.

SUMMARY

Stress reactions not only are universally described as part of the human condition but are also highly individualized depending on your personality, gender, life experiences, and cultural background. You respond to some situations with relative tranquility, even though others might get upset when facing the same stimulus. Likewise, you tend to over-react to other situations, blowing things way out of proportion.

When you consider those circumstances that consistently cause you the most grief, it is important to get a handle on your characteristic reaction style in light of your upbringing, interpersonal patterns, and cultural identification. Whether you are a Catholic, Baptist, Muslim, or Jew; whether you are a student in engineering, health, psychology, or music; whether you are Black, White, Asian, Latino, or Middle Eastern; and whether you are in your twenties, thirties, or fifties, the ways you look at the world, the ways you process events that occur, and the ways you handle stress will be influenced by these variables.

This chapter concludes the section of the book that examines the mechanisms of stress, its physiological, psychological, and cultural features. We move next from understanding the phenomena to what you can do about them. The next series of chapters introduces you to a host of stress prevention and management strategies that will prove useful, no matter what sort of personality and cultural background you have.

QUESTIONS FOR REVIEW

1. What is personality? Describe the relationship between a personality state and a personality trait with regard to stress responsiveness.

2.   Identify the characteristics of Type A individuals. Which characteristic is most connected with coronary heart disease?
3.   Discuss several techniques to reverse Type A personality trends.
4.   What is learned helplessness? Why is the concept of learned helplessness conducive to the understanding of PTSD?
5.   "Don't judge people by their appearance!" What does this cliché have to do with the definition of a repressed personality?
6.   What characteristics does a codependent personality possess? What treatments can be useful for toning down the symptoms of codependency?
7.   Discuss how gender stereotypes and gender roles are related to how men and women cope with stressors. What advantages and disadvantages does each gender have in stress prevention and management?
8.   Discuss the distinct ways in which culture influences stress and coping. Provide examples from your own background.
9.   What can you do to help someone to cope with acculturation stress more easily?

SELECTED ANSWERS

Answer to FOR REFLECTION 5.4

There are a number of reasons why someone in a codependent relationship would unconsciously, or deliberately, sabotage the partner's attempts at progress. In this particular case, in spite of what the husband said, it is possible that: (1) he was threatened by the idea that his wife would become thin and more desirable to other men, (2) he was afraid of intimacy with his wife and once she lost weight he would no longer have an excuse for keeping his distance, (3) he would no longer be able to blame her for the problems between them, (4) he enjoyed the power he wielded knowing that her fate was in his hands (he felt powerless in many other areas of his life), (5) he had unconsciously cast her in a mold that was a reenactment of his parents' relationship.

REVIEW ACTIVITY

Review Activity 5.1: Assessing Type A Behavior

You learned in the chapter about a kind of personality style (Type A) that is far more prone than others to stressful reactions because of the compulsive, competitive, driven, overly motivated way in which such individuals function on a regular basis. You may be able to recognize some of these characteristics in others you know, if not in yourself. Select someone you know (or yourself if appropriate) who demonstrates Type A behavior. Write down (or discuss in groups) ways that the following qualities of this personality style significantly increase stress levels:

1.   being competitive;

2.   strong desire for recognition;

3.   impatience with self and others;

4.   multi-tasking;

5.   hostility and aggressive behavior.

REFERENCES AND RESOURCES

Adler, N. E., & Snibbe, A. C. (2003). The role of psychosocial processes in explaining the gradient between socioeconomic status and health. *Current Directions in Psychological Science, 12,* 119–123.

Aldwin, C. M. (2000). *Stress, coping, and development: An integrated approach.* New York, NY: Guilford.

Askew, R. A., & Keyes, C. (2005). *Stress and somatization: A sociocultural perspective.* Hauppauge, NY: Nova Biomedical Books.

Bambling, M. (2006). Mind, body, and heart: Psychotherapy and the relationship between mental and physical health. *Psychotherapy in Australia, 12*(2), 52–59.

Berry, J. W. (2005). Acculturation: Living successfully in two cultures. *International Journal of Intercultural Relations, 29,* 697–712.

Brown, L. L., Tomarken, A. J., Orth, D. N., Loosen, P. M., Davidson, R. J., & Kalin, N. (1996). Individual differences in repressive-defensiveness predict basal salivary cortisol levels. *Journal of Personality and Social Psychology, 70,* 362–371.

Bucholz, E., Ma, S., Normand, S., & Krumholz, H. (2015). Race, socioeconomic status, and life expectancy after acute myocardial infarction. *Circulation, 132*(14), 1,338–1,346.

Butler, K. (2006). Being there. *Psychotherapy Networker,* January/February, 61–64.

Davidson, R. J. (1992). Emotion and affective style: Hemispheric substrates. *Psychological Science, 3,* 39–43.

Davidson, R. J., & Tomarken, A. J. (1989). Laterality and emotion: An electrophysiological approach. In F. Boller & J. Grafman (Eds.), *Handbook of neuropsychology* (Vol. 3, pp. 419– 441). Amsterdam, The Netherlands: Elsevier.

Dossey, Larry (1982). *Space, time and medicine.* Boston, MA: Shambhala Publications.

Foley, P., & Kirschbaum, C. (2010). Human hypothalamus–pituitary–adrenal axis responses to acute psychosocial stress in laboratory settings. *Neuroscience and Biobehavioral Reviews, 35,* 91–96.

Friedman, M., & Rosenman, R. H. (1959). Association of specific overt behavior pattern with blood and cardiovascular findings. *Journal of the American Medical Association, 169,* 1,286–1,296.

Gardner, H. (1993). *Frames of mind: The theory of multiple intelligences* (rev. ed.). New York, NY: Basic Books.

Gillespie, B. L., & Eisler, R. M. (1992). Development of the feminine gender role stress scale: A cognitive-behavior measure of stress, appraisal, and coping for women. *Behavior Modification, 16,* 426–438.

Goleman, D. (2005). *Emotional intelligence* (rev. ed.). New York, NY: Bantam.

Helmers, K. F., Krantz, D. S., Howell, R. H., Klein, J., Bairey, C. N., & Rozanski, A. (1993). Evaluation by gender and ischemic index. *Psychosomatic Medicine, 50,* 29–36.

Honore, C. (2004). *In praise of slowness.* New York, NY: HarperCollins.

Karanci, N. A., Alkan, N., Aksit, B., Sucuoglu, H., & Balta, E. (1999). Gender differences in psychological distress, coping, social support and related variables following the 1995 Dinar (Turkey) earthquake. *North American Journal of Psychology*, *1*(2), 189–204.

King, A. C., Taylor, C. B., Albright, C. A., & Haskell, W. L. (1990). The relationship between repressive and defensive coping styles and blood pressure responses in healthy, middle-aged men and women. *Journal of Psychosomatic Research*, *34*, 461–471.

Kirkwood, T. (2010, November). Stress alone does not explain the longevity gap. *Scientific American*, *303*, 34–35.

Lundberg, U. (2005). Stress hormones in health and illness: The roles of work and gender. *Psychoneuroendocrinology*, *30*(10), 1,017–1,021.

Martz, D. M., Handley, K. B., & Eisler, R. M. (1995). The relationship between feminine gender role stress, body image, and eating disorders. *Psychology of Women Quarterly*, *19*, 493–508.

Matthews, G., Zeidner, M., & Roberts, R. (2006). *Science of emotional intelligence: Knowns and unknowns*. New York, NY: Oxford University Press.

Matud, M. P. (2004). Gender differences in stress and coping styles. *Personality and Individual Differences*, *37*, 1,401–1,415.

Rotter, J. (1966). Generalized expectancies for internal versus external control of reinforcements. *Psychological Monographs*, *80*, Whole No. 609.

Schuler, K. (2006, February 23). Only half of worried Americans try to manage their stress. *USA Today*, p. 13B.

Seligman, M. E. P. (1975). *Helplessness: Depression, development and death*. San Francisco, CA: Freeman.

Seligman, M. E. P. (1980). A learned helplessness point of view. In L. Rehm (Ed.), *Behavior therapy for depression* (pp. 123–142). New York, NY: Academic Press.

Seligman, M. E. P., & Isaacowitz, D. M. (2000). Learned helplessness. In G. Fink (Ed.), *Encyclopedia of stress*. San Diego, CA: Academic Press.

Snyder, C. R. (2001). *Coping with stress: Effective people and processes*. Oxford, UK: Oxford University Press.

Taylor, S. E. (1991). Asymmetrical effects of positive and negative events: The mobilization-minimization hypothesis. *Psychological Bulletin*, *110*, 67–85.

Taylor, S. E., Klein, L. C., Lewis, B. P., Gruenewald, T. L., Gurung, R. A. R., & Updegraff, J. A. (2000). Biobehavioral responses to stress in females: Tend-and-befriend, not fight-or-flight. *Psychological Review*, *107*, 441–429.

Tomarken, A. J., & Davidson, R. J. (1994). Frontal brain activation in repressors and nonrepressors. *Journal of Abnormal Psychology*, *103*, 339–349.

Tsaousis, I., & Nikolaou, L. (2005). Exploring the relationship of emotional intelligence with physical and psychological health functioning. *Stress and Health*, *21*(2), 77–86.

Uchida, Y., Kitayama, S., Mesquita, B., Reyes, J. A. S., & Morling, B. (2008). Is perceived emotional support beneficial? Well-being and health in independent and interdependent cultures. *Personality and Social Psychology Bulletin*, *34*, 741–754.

Wong, T. P., Wong, L. C. J., & Scott, C. (2006). Beyond stress and coping: The positive psychology of transformation. In P. T. Wong, & L. Wong (Eds.), *Handbook of multicultural perspectives on stress and coping* (pp. 1–25). New York, NY: Springer.

Yee, A. H. (1992). Asians as stereotypes and students: Misperceptions that persist. *Educational Psychology Review*, *4*, 95–132.

Strategies of Stress Management and Prevention

Challenging Stressful Thinking

Stress is a matter not just of circumstances but also of the ways you interpret them. In studies of people who have recurring heart attacks, or complications following a critical cardiac event, the majority were suffering major stress. Further, those who recovered most quickly from heart attacks were those who felt a sense of control over their thoughts and moods (Steward, Moser, & Thompson, 2004).

KEY QUESTIONS IN THE CHAPTER

- How is stress a self-inflicted misery rather than one imposed on you?

- What is the connection between stress mindsets and stress experiences?

- What are the five key components when considering the meaning of life according to Karen Wyatt?

- What are the most prevalent "toxic" or irrational thoughts that create or exacerbate stress?

- What's wrong with the statements: "It's not fair," "It's all my fault," and "This is terrible"?

- If it is not the events of your life that cause you to feel upset, what then determines this reaction?

- What is **"low frustration tolerance"** and how does it contribute to emotional problems?

- How would you initiate "self-talk" to counteract feelings of stress when facing an upcoming exam?

- What are the major strategies for **disputing irrational beliefs**?

- What's wrong with the statements "He made me so angry" or "The weather really bothers me"?

- What is "reframing" and how can it make solving problems much easier?

- How can "thought stopping" be used for someone who is stuck repeating himself, "I know I'll fail again"?

- What else could you do when challenging stressful thinking doesn't work?

Among all the stress reduction and management strategies, there is one that is most important and most universally applied. It is called **cognitive restructuring** and represents a way of changing how you experience and respond to stressful situations by changing how you view them. Cognitive restructuring methods are already within your repertoire, something you learned long ago during your childhood. Remember the rhyme you used to recite when other children teased you?

Sticks and stones may break my bones,
But names will never hurt me.

In essence, this is exactly what cognitive strategies are all about. With few exceptions, nobody or nothing outside yourself can harm you without your "permission." Stress is usually a self-inflicted misery that results from the particular ways that you interpret the world and the chosen manner in which you think about your circumstances.

Power of Mindsets and Cognitive Restructuring

Mindsets are implicit theories people hold about their traits such as intelligence and personality and the mindsets that they hold have significant impact on the quality of their lives. For instance, much research has revealed that people are less resilient and more frustrated when faced with difficulties if they hold a fixed mindset about their abilities. On the contrary, if people believe that their abilities can be improved with effort, they become more resourceful and more capable of solving problems (Dweck, 2012). What about people's mindsets about the effect of stress on their lives? According to Crum, Salovey, and Achor (2013), whether you believe stress will have enhancing or debilitating effects will make those expected effects more likely. In their study, 380 employees from an investment bank were assigned to three groups. One group watched a series of videos touting how stress can be enhancing, the second group watched a series of videos about how stress can be debilitating and the third was a control group who watched no videos. The final results indicated that the stress-is-enhancing group, as compared with the other two groups, had a significant reduction in stress-related physical symptoms and a significant improvement in a productivity assessment. So, what do you take away from this study? Probably you realize that this study is a demonstration of the self-fulfilling prophecy; that is, you get what you expect. Also, you may be impressed with how your mind can affect your stress experience and quality of life. The good news is that you can do something about your thinking patterns.

Imagine yourself about to speak in front of a large audience and panic setting in. Your brain locks up, sweat starts dripping down your back, and you feel like you're going to faint. Then, with a minute or so of **self-talk**, you immediately feel yourself become calm and centered.

Picture yourself at a party. You look across the room and see someone very interesting, someone attractive whom you would like to meet. As you consider even the possibility of weaving through the crowd to introduce yourself to this person, you start to engage the same **self-defeating thoughts** that have blocked such initiatives in the past. Then, with some concerted effort, you substitute some alternative thoughts along the lines of, "What's the worst that can happen?" Immediately, you feel a surge of resolve and courage that allows you to glide across the room with a grin on your face.

You are in class about to take an important exam. It not only determines your final grade, but you believe that if you do poorly it will effectively prevent you from pursuing your most cherished career goal. As you sit in your chair watching the instructor pass out the exam, you feel a familiar sense of impending doom. Even though you have studied long and hard, you can't help but think that all your best efforts were wasted. Before you even begin, you feel discouraged and overstressed, finding it difficult to concentrate. Then, with a few simple reminders that you have rehearsed ahead of time, you feel yourself regain confidence and focus. By the time the papers arrive at your desk, you can't wait to get started and show what you learned.

If all this sounds like fantasy or empty promises that could not possibly be delivered, let me assure you that I am absolutely serious about the potential content in this chapter. It is within your power to completely change your life—not just the ways you respond to stress, but the ways you *choose* to respond to anything that you face. Note that I have emphasized the word "choose," because a central feature of cognitive approaches is to recognize that the way you react to something depends, to a large extent, on how you decide to think about it. Such interpretations are about making some choices over others.

FOR REFLECTION 6.1

Think of a time recently in which you were really upset about something. Recall how out of control you felt, as well as how much stress you were experiencing. What have you noticed about the ways your negative feelings become better or worse, depending on what you think about and how you choose to interpret your situation?

During those times when you are most distressed, it is usually because you are imagining the worst scenarios, exaggerating the trouble, and feeling like you are being singled out for unjust treatment. Likewise, when you are feeling better about the situation it is often when you are working hard to keep things in realistic perspective.

I understand that you would be skeptical about what I have just offered. How is it possible that reading a chapter in a book could really change anyone's life? You've read so many chapters in so many different books; why would this one really be any different?

It won't—unless you are prepared not only to read the material, but to study and practice it. In order for the effects to last, however, it is essential to practice the strategies every day. You may get distracted and tire of the self-discipline that is required. You may forget why this was important in the first place. You might even decide that you don't like having the responsibility for such control—there will no longer be anyone else to blame for the times when you are feeling miserable.

If you practice these strategies in daily life, I can promise you a degree of self-control over the stress in your life that you have never imagined possible. Cognitive methods are not magical, but they might seem that way: they give you the power to change how you are thinking—and feeling—in any situation you might face.

Most Stress Is Self-Inflicted

It is a premise of cognitive approaches that stress results more from attitude than circumstances. The same situation that may seem stressful to one person feels exciting and challenging to someone else. For those who are suffering from extreme emotional upheaval, the problems persist in large part because of excessive ruminations and obsessions about factors or situations that are beyond your control. Likewise, those most likely to recover quickly from stressful situations are those who feel some degree of power to regulate their moods, change their thinking, and act constructively (Beckmann & Kellmann, 2004).

In studies done to compare those who performed well under pressure with those who folded, a strategy of "positive appraisal" seemed to be the decisive factor. That means that when taking a test or competing in an event, everyone experiences certain behavioral and physiological reactions in their bodies, but these can be interpreted in very different ways. When participants were told their fluttery stomachs, jittery hands, or pounding hearts would actually improve their performance, they believed the so-called nervousness was actually quite positive and functional (Jamieson, Mendes, Blackstock, & Schmader, 2010). So it all depends on how you choose to interpret so-called nervous reactions.

Cognitive restructuring, a term coined by psychologist Donald Meichenbaum (1977), refers to a particular coping style in which people inoculate themselves against stress by building up a reservoir of positive self-talk or internal dialogue to deal with life's challenges.

Two people get in their cars and prepare for the one hour commute to work. One person says the following to himself:

> *I hate this damn drive! The traffic is just about killing me. I'll probably have a heart attack one of these days, or choke on the pollution. Everyone is so rude. I swear sometimes they are trying deliberately to kill me, or at least run me off the road. There's nothing on the radio except the same old songs they play over and over again. What a colossal waste of time. It's like I'm in hell. Every day it's the same old thing. It drives me crazy. By the time I get to work I'm so anxious and stressed I can barely concentrate. Then I have to go through the whole thing all over again to get home.*

Now compare this internal dialogue to that of another person who has adopted quite a different attitude:

> *I actually look forward to the drive on the way to work and back. It gives me time to think about things, sort of get myself organized for the day. Then, on the way home, I review the day and what I've done, where I want to go next.*
>
> *Sometimes it seems like the hour drive is too short, if you can believe it. There is so much to do. I enjoy listening to music or catching up on news on the radio. Sometimes I listen to an audiobook on my iPod player that I wouldn't usually have the time to read.*
>
> *I don't mind doing absolutely nothing either, just putting my brain on automatic. I figure out alternative ways to get to work, seeing if I can beat my record. I watch the other people in the cars next to me, or ahead of me, and try to imagine who they are and what their lives are like. The drive really isn't so bad at all. I actually enjoy the time alone.*

One person becomes so stressed by the commute to work that he can barely function once he gets there, and the effects last all day. The other person, adopting a quite different mindset, not only doesn't feel perturbed by the drive but seems to enjoy it. Rather than feeling stressed, it helps her to relax and get herself organized for the day.

What is it that makes it possible for two people to react to identical situations in such different ways? The answer is found in their internal dialogue, the ways they cognitively construct their experiences. The first person feels stressed because of what he is telling himself inside his head. He is creating his own misery by dwelling on the most negative aspects of the commute. These **toxic thoughts** pollute the experience in such a way that the drive seems intolerable to him. His stress comes not so much from the two hours he spends in traffic each day, but rather from how he views his predicament.

To a large extent, what determines how you respond to any potential stressor or challenge is the self-talk going on inside your mind. In the example of the commuters above, you were offered a window into their internal dialogues. It is no wonder, therefore, that the first person would be so miserable while the second person took the situation in her stride.

Let's imagine another scenario in which someone returns home from work one day to find a note taped to the refrigerator door that reads:

> *I am sorry but I don't want to live with you anymore. I've had enough. So I took the Sony TV, and a few things and moved out. Have a nice life.*

How would this person respond to this rather sudden announcement? The answer depends very much on how she chooses to view the situation and the kind of self-talk they engage in. Again, here are two possible ways that someone might think to herself:

I can't believe I never saw this coming. Now I am so alone. I'll probably never find anyone to be with me again. Because he left me, nobody else will ever want to be with me. It's all my fault that this happened.

Understandably, this person could feel depressed, anxious, lonely, angry, or despondent, given the way she is interpreting what happened. Examining her internal dialogue, full of toxic thinking, what are the aspects that stand out as being most unreasonable and irrational?

1. *I can't believe I never saw this coming.* She is telling herself that she should have been able to predict what happened, without considering that maybe her partner was doing a good job of hiding intentions.

2. *Now I am so alone.* This is not true. She has other friends and family members who care deeply about her.

3. *I'll probably never find anyone to be with me again.* There is no basis for this assumption whatsoever. Where is the evidence that because this one relationship ended, all options for romance in the future are over?

4. *It's all my fault that this happened.* It is never solely any one person's fault when there is a misunderstanding or conflict in a relationship.

Now let's picture another person who arrives home from work to find the same note waiting, but reacts differently to the situation.

Gee, this is a bit unexpected, but it is not totally surprising. In some ways I am relieved that it is finally over. I'm feeling sad that we couldn't work things out, and I'm disappointed that he chose to end things in this particular way, but I also understand that we were building up to this for some time. Sure I'm upset about this, but I'm also excited that I can move on with my life.

This person is not denying the loss she feels at the ending of the relationship, but exhibits a more positive mindset towards the situation. She is looking more at the opportunities that open up for her rather than the losses. Notice that she is not blaming herself for what happened, nor is she looking at the worst aspects of the situation. Given her particular internal dialogue, the emotional result is that she feels sadness and disappointment, but does not feel overwhelmed or depressed.

FOR REFLECTION 6.2

Stopping the Little Annoyances

There are times when you consistently get upset about something that annoys you. You can't really do much to change other people's behavior, at least in the short run, yet you still allow these incidents to get underneath your skin over and over again. For each of the following common annoying situations, think of a way that you could talk to yourself inside your head so that you don't feel additional stress from these situations. I am not talking about what you say or do on the outside, but rather what you say to yourself on the inside.

A. Someone is speaking loudly on a cell phone in a public space.
B. A person on the freeway is driving slowly in the express lane, blocking you from driving faster.
C. Someone is standing in line in front of you, chatting to the cashier as if he has all the time in the world.
D. An instructor in one of your classes is giving a particularly boring lecture.

In both examples provided in this section, I have shown how people do not necessarily and automatically respond in the exact same ways to challenging situations in life. There are always options that depend very much on what you tell yourself about what happened, as well as what you think it means.

Creating Meaning

Very little of what you experience in life, stressful or otherwise, has meaning without your active construction of that perception. Throughout the ages, existential philosophers and theoreticians have wrestled with the difficult questions related to what gives life meaning. Some of the greatest thinkers, novelists, and playwrights have described the journey toward finding meaning in one's existence.

Stress, or for that matter, *any* kind of suffering, becomes intolerable when it seems to serve no purpose except to condemn one to misery. Yet individuals who have survived trauma may as often be led to positive transformations as they are to despair. What makes the difference is how survivors perceive their plight and how they restore meaning after experiencing loss (Fontana & Rosenheck, 2005).

Victor Frankl, a psychiatrist who was trapped in the Auschwitz concentration camp of Nazi Germany, watched most of his family and friends perish. Some succumbed to starvation and exposure to the elements, while others were outright murdered. What struck Frankl was those inmates who seemed to give up and die of despair. They abandoned all hope, and seemed to wither away. What saved Frankl, and others like him, was that somehow they were able to find some meaning for their suffering, even if it was to survive long enough to tell the world about what they witnessed.

In his book *Man's Search for Meaning*, regarded as one of the most important works of the twentieth century, Frankl described the core of **existential philosophy**:

> *We who lived in concentration camps can remember the men who walked through the huts comforting others, giving away their last piece of bread. They may have been few in number, but they offer sufficient proof that everything can be taken from a man but one thing: the last of the human freedoms—to choose one's attitude in any given set of circumstances, to choose one's own way.*
> *(Frankl, 1962, p. 104)*

Even in the most horrific of circumstances, human beings can still create meaning in their suffering and choose attitudes that will literally save their lives. Victor Frankl developed an existential approach to therapy that focused on the ways that people find meaning in their lives.

Compared to the stresses that most of us face in life, being interned in a death camp where the survival rate was less than 1% is surely a test of one's spirit. What Frankl sought to prove, however, was that even in the most horrific conditions imaginable, it is still possible for people to choose their attitude and find meaning in the experience.

While existential theory is rarely thought of as being part of cognitive therapies, it shares with these approaches a respect for the power of personal interpretation. Current research indicates that the presence of meaning in the life of an individual is positively associated with life satisfaction, happiness, and positive feelings (Park, Park, & Peterson, 2010).

Karen Wyatt (2015), a family physician and author, tells her readers that for most people the meaning of life is quite elusive until the last days of their lives. As a hospice medical director, she spends much of her time at the deathbeds of many patients pondering the meaning of life. She suggests that you consider five key components when you think about meaning: (1) perspective, (2) prioritization, (3) preparation, (4) practice, and (5) presence. To have perspective means acknowledging that your precious life is limited and will end someday. Prioritization comes after perspective because your life is limited, you must identify what matters most to you and invest your limited resources of time and energy in those things. As time progresses, your values change and you need to reprioritize, which takes effort and thought. Preparation means that you must plan for the changes that will come with time. Practice requires that you make effort to devote time to engage in mental, physical and spiritual disciplines on a daily basis such as journaling, prayer, meditation, and so on. These disciplines will enhance your peace of mind and enrich the sense of meaning. Last but not the least is presence. Meaning exists only in this moment and you must be able to bring your attention to this very moment in order to bring meaning to life. Before you proceed to the next section, I suggest that you take a moment to identify what you value most in your life, for example health, family, friends, education, career, spirituality/religion, by ranking them from 1 to 5 with 1 having the lowest value and 5 the highest value. Then make a decision to spend time and energy according to what matters to you most.

In the ideas that follow, I want you to keep in mind that the power remains within you to make your own choices about how you wish to respond to any adversity that might come your way.

Cognitive Theory in a Nutshell

Throughout the ages there have been thinkers who have been interested in the power of mental activity to influence one's mood and behavior. The Stoic philosophers of ancient Rome such as Marcus Aurelius, Epicurus, Seneca, and especially Epictetus were influential in the development of modern cognitive restructuring methods. In his classic treatise, Epictetus said: "Men are disturbed not by things, but by the view which they take of them." The essence of this idea, that emotional stress reactions are not caused by outside events but rather by internal perceptions, formed the basis of what have been known as the cognitive therapies.

Albert Ellis, a psychologist who practiced as a psychoanalyst in the 1950s and 1960s, was greatly challenged by the Stoic philosophers. Psychoanalysts encourage their patients to explore the past, as well as unconscious desires, to examine the ways that their early history affects current functioning. If you are unduly stressed in your life now, the psychoanalyst believes it is because you have unresolved issues that must be dealt with, many of which go back to early memories that you have repressed or conveniently "forgotten."

During the early stage of his career as a therapist, Ellis was crippled by self-doubt. He felt insecure, lacked confidence, and often felt crushed by disappointments and rejections. He began augmenting his psychoanalytic training by reading philosophy. He studied the emerging science of **behaviorism**, an approach that emphasized taking constructive action rather than simply developing insight as in psychoanalysis.

Ellis soon settled on a critical awareness of his own—that happiness in life was not based on what happened to you, but rather was related to your degree of self-acceptance and ability to tolerate frustration. If he could learn to be more accepting of himself, including his mistakes, weaknesses, and limitations, then he would be far better equipped to handle any challenge that came his way.

After first applying these ideas to himself, Ellis later experimented with methods that evolved into a system called **rational emotive behavior therapy (REBT)**. The goal of this approach is to teach people how to identify what they are doing to upset themselves and, in turn, to change the nature of their thinking in such a way as to produce a more desirable outcome. The seeds of this idea are contained in Ellis's **ABC theory of emotions**, which plots out, logically and sequentially, the mechanisms by which people become upset and how they might change negative feelings through certain thinking patterns that are deemed more rational and reality-based.

The ABC theory is so named because each letter stands for a stage in the process of emotional disturbance. The next two letters in the alphabet, D and E, lead to a different emotional response.

A: Activating Event

This is the situation that most people believe is *causing* the stressful difficulty. A flat tire, getting caught in congested traffic, receiving a low grade on an assignment, being yelled at by a supervisor, being ignored by a friend, or ending a relationship are all examples of events that *appear* to activate strong negative emotional responses. This is the initial event (A) that leads to a particular **emotional consequence** (C).

Let's take an example of how reading these chapters on stress is the **"activating event"** that is "causing" you to feel very upset.

A ————————————————————————————————▶ C
Activating event   Emotional consequence
Reading chapters in stress text   Anxiety, confusion, frustration, fear

C: Emotional Consequence

Most people believe that things outside of themselves, events or circumstances in the world, are what cause them to feel stressed and out of control. It feels like other people, weather, bad luck, a flat tire, or a reading assignment are the cause of the negative emotions. The clearest evidence for this is to listen to how you talk about things that happen to you. Often they involve externalized thinking, that is, the idea that feelings were *caused* by external events: "He made me so angry," or "The traffic really upset me," or "I got really stressed out by that party." In each of these cases, the person is attributing the emotional result to some particular event or stimulus that activated or caused it.

B: Irrational Belief

Between A and C is another letter—B, the belief that someone holds about what happened. The most significant contribution that Albert Ellis and other cognitive theorists made to the understanding of emotional disturbance was to recognize the kinds of interpretations and perceptions that take place inside someone's head. Their radical idea is simple and yet compelling, supported by decades of empirical research. Except for the fight-or-flight stress response that bypasses conscious thought altogether, emotional reactions almost always result from your beliefs about what happened to you rather than the events themselves. In summary, negative and positive feelings are not caused by what others say or do, nor by events you are subjected to; rather they are the result of your interpretations and individual perceptions of those circumstances.

Returning to Ellis's model of **irrational beliefs**, let's review my example of feeling stressed over the challenging material in the book chapters. In this new configuration, rather than the negative feelings (C) being caused by the antecedent event itself (A), you can see there is an important step in between that is missing (B).

What is it about these internal self-statements that makes them so irrational? Examine each one of them and consider how it might not reflect reality clearly or accurately.

Irrational beliefs are those that exaggerate or distort what is going on. They are considered dysfunctional or self-defeating because they tend to make unrealistic demands of yourself, others, or the world.

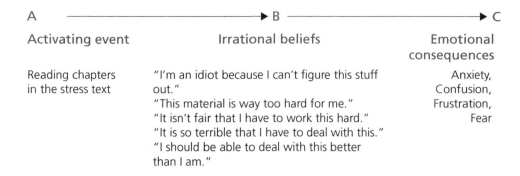

A	B	C
Activating event	Irrational beliefs	Emotional consequences
Reading chapters in the stress text	"I'm an idiot because I can't figure this stuff out." "This material is way too hard for me." "It isn't fair that I have to work this hard." "It is so terrible that I have to deal with this." "I should be able to deal with this better than I am."	Anxiety, Confusion, Frustration, Fear

---

FOR REFLECTION 6.3

Consider how the language you use reflects the underlying irrational beliefs at work. Do any of these expressions sound familiar?

- "He makes me so mad!"
- "The weather is so depressing."
- "It was just bad luck."
- "The damn election results just make me want to give up."
- "It really got to me. There was nothing I could do about it."
- "I can't help it. It's just the way I am."

What is wrong with these statements? In each case, they imply external control in which circumstances outside your mind are what make you upset. In truth, nothing outside of you can make you feel anything without your consent. All emotional responses result from your interpretations about what happened.

Ellis identified five major irrational themes. Most of these are represented in my case illustration.

1. Absolute Demands

One of the most common laments you hear whenever things don't go the preferred way is "That isn't fair." In fact, life is *not* fair. If it was, you wouldn't have to lock your doors. You wouldn't see people around you who have more than you even though they are not as smart or talented. You wouldn't have to take this course and study so hard. The world is not a fair place in which everyone gets what he deserves and you in particular get whatever you want. There are injustices all around you. People play by different rules and live by other values. It would be preferable if everyone else thought the exact same way that you do, and did just what you thought was best for them and for you, but that is just not going to happen most of the time.

Whenever you catch yourself believing that life should be fair, you are setting yourself up for increased disappointment, indignation, and frustration. So what can you substitute instead of this complaint? Try "Oh well. Isn't it annoying and disappointing that things are not going the way I prefer? I wish things were different, but they are not. So I might as well accept things as they are, work to change the things within my power, and stop dwelling on what is beyond my capability to change."

Instead of saying to yourself about the difficult reading assignment, "It's not fair that I'm expected to learn so much stuff in such a concentrated period of time," you could say instead, "I wish I had more time, and less material, but if these are the cards that I'm dealt, then I better try to make the best of them. Complaining and whining probably isn't going to get the job done."

2. Awfulizing

Awfulizing, or **catastrophizing**, describes a set of irrational beliefs represented by gross exaggerations of reality in which you think as if you have suffered the worst tragedy imaginable. Whenever you are subjected to an inconvenience, or an obstacle, if you are telling yourself that this situation is "awful," "terrible," or a "catastrophe," then you are going to react in proportion to this assessment. If, on the other hand, you treat the situation as a minor annoyance, a small disappointment, a temporary setback, you will feel much less stress and react emotionally in a much more appropriate way.

Examples of awfulizing in action include:

- "It is terrible that things worked out the way they did."
- "This is the worst thing that could have ever happened to me."
- "What a major disaster that I didn't get ..."

What makes statements like this irrational? For one thing, calling something awful or terrible implies that it is the absolute worst thing that could ever happen. After all, what is another term to describe something worse than "terrible"? Double terrible? Awfully terrible? Terribly awful?

No matter what happens to you, there is always something that could make it worse. If you are feeling stressed because you weren't promoted at work, and you think *that* is terrible, what would you say if you were fired from your job altogether? And if you were fired from your job, and you think *that* is an absolute disaster, then what would you call it if you not only lost your job but also all your savings? And if that should happen, then how would you label all that happening, plus being informed that you have a terminal disease? I am not implying that you should minimize life's difficulties, or deny their impact. There are indeed some situations that are extremely trying, if not terrible—rape, poverty, terminal disease, physical assault, and the loss of a loved one, to mention a few. But most of the things that you get stressed about in life are not nearly as serious or disruptive to your life as you think. And you would be surprised how little even supposedly catastrophic events affect many people's lives in the long term. In studies with people who suffer spinal cord injuries and become paralyzed as a result of an injury, most of them report feeling mostly positive about their situations within two months of the event. Eight out of ten consider their lives to be as good as, or better than, those of most other people (Seligman, 2002).

Awfulizing is best challenged by recognizing the extent to which you are exaggerating the importance of an event, or its ultimate effects on your life. You walk out of class, head out to the parking lot after a tough day, and discover that your car has a flat tire. You think to yourself, "What a disaster! I can't believe this sort of thing always happens to me! This whole day has just been a nightmare, one thing after another."

If you chose to counteract these irrational beliefs, then you might say to yourself instead: "Well, this is certainly annoying. It is disappointing that this will cost me some money I don't really have right now, but oh well, there's not much I can do about that now. I'd better get to work and get this tire changed."

In this second case, the person chooses to think something different about the situation. Rather than seeing this flat tire as a major disaster, the person instead treats it as an inconvenience. Presumably you can see how this alternative interpretation of the situation would produce a different emotional reaction—one in which stress is minimized.

3. Low Frustration Tolerance

A corollary of "This is awful" is "I can't stand it." It is bad enough that things didn't work out as you had hoped; even worse is to tell yourself that things are now intolerable because of this disappointment. What makes this belief so irrational is that, indeed, you can stand anything short of death.

Notice those times when you are feeling most upset and out of control. It is likely there is some cognitive activity occurring in which you are telling yourself that what is going on is beyond what you can handle. You would be amazed at what you can deal with if you are called upon to do so and if you have little choice in the matter.

Think about those times when you had to go to the bathroom really, really badly. You could hardly stand it. You thought to yourself that if you could not find a facility in one more minute you would explode, or perhaps embarrass yourself in public. Yet when is the last time that you couldn't make it to the bathroom and wet your pants? This might sound silly but it is an example of how you can go as far as you need to in order to get the job done. You see a toilet ahead and think to yourself, "Okay, this is it. I can't go one more step." Then you try the door and discover that the facility is out of service. Somehow you manage to run to the next available option. So it is with most situations in life—you can tolerate far more than you ever imagined you could.

What are the symptoms of **low frustration tolerance** that you should be on the lookout for?

- Demanding instant gratification of every desire and then whining and complaining about it when you don't get your way ("It isn't fair!").

- Thinking only about pleasures in the present rather than the implications for the future, such as how you will pay for what you want.

- Feeling impatient when things don't happen as quickly as you might prefer, or according to your most convenient schedule.

- Avoiding the self-discipline and hard work involved in giving up or avoiding habits and addictions that provide temporary relief but at long-term costs.

- Abandoning a planned program that could produce beneficial and desired goals because the work seems too hard, and the effort is considerable.

- Procrastinating rather than completing assignments or activities, and failing to deliver on your promises to yourself or others.

4. Musterbation

Musterbation refers to the demand that people or things be a particular way. Ellis (1962) called this a form of "self-abuse" because it implies that you are in some way special and deserving of special privileges not afforded to others. The universe does not care whether or not you get what you want. It is impartial and favors no one. The best way to diagnose what Aaron Beck refers to as **personalization** is to look for ways in which you exaggerate your belief that events in the world apply only to you and your sense of specialness; for example, "Every time I try to plan a picnic, it rains." Not only is this most likely not true (surely there was a time when it didn't rain), but it implies that the "weather gods" are only concerned with ruining your plans (as if they have nothing better to do—like disrupting others' lives with hurricanes, tornadoes, and such).

Ellis favored the term "musterbation" because it draws attention to the use of the "musts" and "shoulds" in our internal thinking and verbal speech. Consider the following statements as examples.

- "He *shouldn't* have behaved in that way." This means you are saying that because someone acted differently than you would, or lives by different rules than your own, he should be punished in some way.

- "I *must* go to my parents' house for dinner on Sunday." This demand implies that you must behave in a particular way or you are no good. There is a huge difference between telling yourself, "I *must* go to dinner" versus "I *choose* to go to dinner at my parents' house." It is all a matter of language, but words imply critical distinctions.

- "Either she's with me and does what she should do to help me, or she's against me and doesn't care at all." In reality, things are usually not so simple.

The use of musts or shoulds implies a degree of rigidity, as well as what Beck (1976) calls **dichotomous thinking**. This is the sort of irrational reasoning in which you force things into absolute categories: "Either I go to my parents' house like I should, and hate myself for it afterwards, or I don't go and then feel terribly guilty." A more measured assessment of this situation might recast it in such a way that whichever choice you make, you feel good rather than bad about it.

5. Absolute Judgments

Ellis called this the "tyranny of the I'ms," meaning the use of absolute self-descriptors that define who you are based on a limited sample of your behavior. The following are examples of **absolute judgments**.

- "I'm the type of person who doesn't do that sort of thing."

- "I'm not good in math."

- "I'm Italian. That's why I have a bad temper."

- "I'm shy. I've always been that way."

- "I'm incompetent because I didn't handle that situation well."

In each of these cases, the person is generalizing from one or more cases and defining herself in an absolute way. It is irrational to label yourself as shy just because you might behave that way in *some* situations; almost nobody is shy in *every* situation and context. Likewise, making a judgment about yourself as not good in math just because you haven't performed as well as you prefer thus far is to deny any possibility for improvement in the future.

Compare the statements above to alternatives that are carefully reworded to more accurately reflect reality.

- "I choose not to do that now, but I reserve the right to change my mind at some future time."

- "I don't do as well in math as I would like, but I hope to do better with practice and help."

- "Sometimes I lose control of my temper whereas at other times I am able to control myself quite well."

- "In certain social situations, such as being in a room full of strangers, I behave in shy ways. When I am with family or friends, however, I can be quite outgoing."

- "I didn't handle that situation as well as I would like. There are some areas I need to improve."

Note how this second set of self-statements is likely to result in a different kind of emotional response. Rather than feeling helpless and powerless (recall how these are correlated with stress), you are likely to feel positive and in control.

VOICE OF THE AUTHOR 6.1

For many years (even during my graduate years in the US), I lived a life of constant agony and "quiet desperation." I believe the incidental reading of one essay by Ralph Waldo Emerson in the book *Self-Reliance and Others* was a turning point in my life. I still recall the day when I seemed to be awakened by his poignant words and the images his words inspired in my heart. Probably the book started a journey for me to know more about myself and become a self-reliant person, responsible and with self-discipline. Once, my wife casually commented that she seemed to have married three different men. What she alluded to is that her husband has undergone major transformations over the years. The real change started when I was about 28 years of age. I used to complain all the time that my father "pushed" me into the sport of basketball about which I did not really feel passionate in the beginning and had to forgo my passion for science and math. I would attribute my lack of success in life to the decision made by my father. On the day I read *Self-Reliance*, I decided never to complain about my "fate" and made a commitment to ameliorating myself. I know it took a long time to change myself, but the thought of "self-reliance" was sown in my heart and I am eternally grateful to the inspiring words of Mr. Emerson.

FOR REFLECTION 6.4

Based on what you have already learned about examining beliefs, what is it about each of the statements in my example of the stressed student that strikes you as irrational?

"I'm an idiot because I can't figure this stuff out."

"This material is way too hard for me."

"It isn't fair that I have to work this hard."

"It is so terrible that I have to deal with this."

"I should be able to deal with this better than I am."

Answers at the end of the chapter.

Disputing the Irrational Beliefs

Based on your analysis of what is actually causing your emotional suffering, several insights are evident.

1. Emotional stress responses are a matter of choice rather than circumstances. You *choose*, consciously or unconsciously, to react in a particular way based on your beliefs about what happened and your interpretations of the meaning.

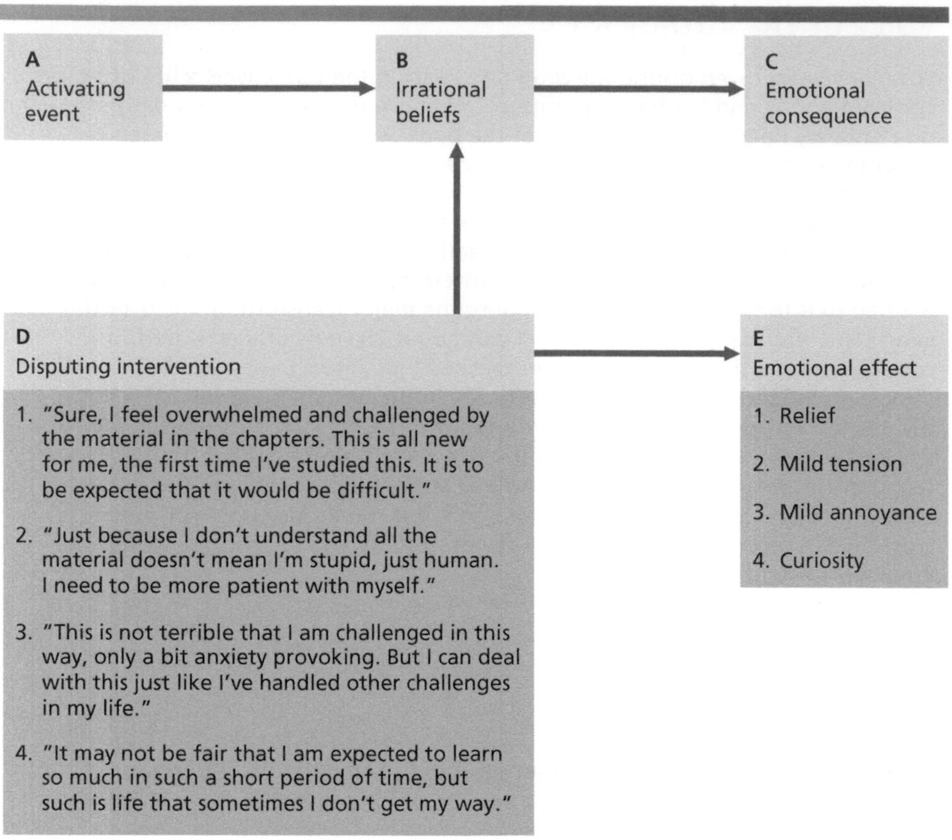

FIGURE 6.1
The ABCDE theory. Disputing (A) irrational beliefs (B) leads to different emotional consequences.

A Activating event	B Irrational beliefs	C Emotional consequence

D Disputing intervention	E Emotional effect

D — Disputing intervention

1. "Sure, I feel overwhelmed and challenged by the material in the chapters. This is all new for me, the first time I've studied this. It is to be expected that it would be difficult."

2. "Just because I don't understand all the material doesn't mean I'm stupid, just human. I need to be more patient with myself."

3. "This is not terrible that I am challenged in this way, only a bit anxiety provoking. But I can deal with this just like I've handled other challenges in my life."

4. "It may not be fair that I am expected to learn so much in such a short period of time, but such is life that sometimes I don't get my way."

E — Emotional effect

1. Relief
2. Mild tension
3. Mild annoyance
4. Curiosity

2. Other people or events do not disturb you; you do that to yourself based on the way you think and the way you talk to yourself about what happened.

3. You can change how you feel based on how you choose to think. This is not easy—it requires consistent use of the "three Ps": persistence, patience, and practice.

Once you understand that the way you are feeling is based on your chosen beliefs, many of which are irrational and self-defeating, the next step in the process is to dispute or counteract those interpretations. This means challenging some of your assumptions to determine the extent to which you might be exaggerating or distorting things, over-personalizing the situation, or overgeneralizing what is going on.

Disputing your beliefs is the most difficult part of this cognitive restructuring process. To review, you will have no difficulty identifying what set you off (A—the antecedent event). You will also find it easy to label your feelings (C—emotional consequences) as they have likely bubbled to the surface; they are what caught your attention in the first place. The irrational beliefs (B) take a little practice to label, but I have provided you a guide to make that task easier (Figure 6.1). Look for variations of the five themes I mentioned: (1) Life isn't fair, (2) It's awful, (3) I can't stand it, (4) I must get what I want, and (5) I'm incompetent.

Basically what you are trying to do is to force yourself to look logically, rationally, and systematically at your situation. Imagine that the events were recorded and you were watching the reenactment on a screen. What would you observe? What would the recorder capture in objective, accurate images?

There are three major questions to ask yourself when disputing your irrational beliefs, as follows:

1. *Where is the evidence that what you are experiencing is true?* I don't mean to invalidate the legitimacy of whatever you are thinking and feeling—you are perfectly entitled to any beliefs you want. But assuming that you don't like the

way you are feeling, and want to do something about it, then it is time to consider things more objectively. Ask yourself what a camera would record about this scene. Are things indeed as dire and disastrous as you think they are? Is this really the worst thing that ever happened to you? Is it true that you can't stand what is happening, that you will die as a result?

2. *Who says that things must be the way you think they are? You* do. You are the one who is demanding that things be a particular way. Examine your "shoulds" and "musts" that signify your rigidity, imposing your standards and values on the rest of the world. Look at your tendency toward perfectionism, holding expectations for yourself and others.

3. *Does your response seem logical and reasonable, given the situation?* Return to the task of watching yourself. How are you exaggerating things? How are you making invalid assumptions? How are you overgeneralizing based on limited cases? How are you overpersonalizing?

Table 6.1 Disputing questions for counteracting irrational beliefs

- Where is the evidence to support that you must . . .?
- Where is it written that you must . . .?
- Just because it is bad, how does that mean that it is the end of the world?
- If you continue to believe that, what will it do for you?
- What will be the consequences if you give up that idea?
- How is thinking that way getting you what you say you want?
- What will it mean if you don't get what you want?

In order to keep things in realistic perspective, it is often useful to remind yourself that what you are blowing up as so important now may not mean very much a few minutes, hours, days, weeks, or years in the future (see Voice of Stress Management 6.1). Who is going to care about this 100 years from now? In the grand scheme of things within the universe, how much does this really matter?

VOICE OF STRESS MANAGEMENT 6.1

Twenty-Two-Year-Old Student

I have been in recovery for three years. One of the things that I remember from my relapse prevention classes at the rehab center was the ABCs. This concept has really helped me make it through some rough times. I used to be an active alcoholic and drug addict. I used to jump to conclusions and was angry about everything. I would get high to avoid the pain of everyday life. I mean, I would think crazy thoughts. If my boss looked at me funny, I thought he had it in for me. If my girlfriend told me she had to work, I thought she was cheating on me. When I failed one class in high school, I dropped out after convincing myself that I was a loser and was going to fail all of my classes. It was nuts.

Looking back, it was like every one of my thoughts was out of proportion to what was actually happening. I just never took the time to really examine reality. What I learned was how to map it out. In class they taught us to A—look at the trigger that caused C—the emotional reaction. Then, B—the belief that I held that caused the emotional reaction ... Man, was it crazy to learn that I had control over C! I use to blame everything or everyone else. Or I would just consider myself a total screw-up and get high. It all changed for me when I learned how my emotions were controlled by my thoughts. It is still a struggle. I really have to remember to reappraise most situations, but it gets easier and easier as time goes on.

If you are intrigued by this approach enough to want to learn more about it, there are plenty of resources available that you might consult, including books by Ellis, Beck, and others.

The Power of Language

You have probably noticed that cognitive restructuring methods pay very close attention to the language that is used, both internally and in spoken words. This is not just making a big deal about little words. Language happens to be the best evidence of what you are thinking inside. If you are using **externalized language** like "He made me do it" or "I just had a bit of bad luck," then you are probably adopting toxic thoughts that minimize both your responsibility and your control.

People who are serious about adopting cognitive restructuring methods in their lives are precise about how they express themselves. Compare these two sets of expressions:

Externalized Language	Internalized Language
"He made me so angry." "It's not my fault. I can't help it." "The test made me so nervous." "That guy really gets underneath my skin." "The weather affects me like this."	"I made myself angry over what he did." "I chose to behave in this way." "I made myself nervous over the test." "I allow that guy to get underneath my skin." "I let the weather affect me like this."

In examining the two different ways that people responded to adversity, notice that the externalized versions blame outside factors for the trouble. This allows you to avoid responsibility for what is happening, but at the cost of surrendering control. On the other hand, the **internalized** responses use language in which the speaker/thinker believes that how he is feeling is a direct result of his own actions.

Keeping a Thought Journal

You can't change the way you think and feel unless you are aware of the cognitive activity going on inside you. One way to train yourself to monitor your irrational thinking more carefully is to keep a **thought journal** in which you note particular instances when you are experiencing undue stress and then identify the accompanying thoughts that are going on.

Purchase a notebook that you can keep with you at all times.

1. Divide your notebook into three columns, labeling each one as follows:

Situation	Feelings	Accompanying Thoughts

2. As soon as possible after you experience some distressing event, make the following notations in your thought journal. Start by noting either the situation that you find upsetting (A—the antecedent event) or the disturbing feelings you are experiencing (C—the emotional consequences).

3. Describe briefly what happened. Where were you? Who were you with? When did this happen? What happened exactly?

4. Label all the feelings that you were experiencing. Don't stop with just one or two. Often there are many different emotions going on within you. Try to generate at least a half dozen.

5. Go to the third column and fill in the thoughts that most likely preceded the feelings. These are the irrational beliefs that represent your interpretation of the situation and that led to the negative feelings (see example in Table 6.2).

Table 6.2 Example of a thought journal entry

Situation	Feelings	Automatic Thoughts
Context and setting	*One-word descriptors*	*What were you thinking just before and during the unpleasant experience?*
I received a paper back in a class with a grade of C−. I had been counting on a good grade and worked hard on this assignment. I don't know what I could have done differently. This is an important class that is required for my major. There's a lot at stake for me because I could risk losing financial aid.	Depressed	I'm in deep trouble now with no hope of pulling myself out.
	Humiliated	I might as well drop the class. Maybe I should think about quitting school.
	Angry	It isn't fair that this keeps happening to me over and over again. Why always me?
	Frustrated	This is just about the worst thing that could ever happen to me.
	Anxious	The instructor should have given us more direction and help on this.
	Discouraged	How am I supposed to read her mind about what she wants?

FOR REFLECTION 6.5

Albert Ellis originally described 13 different irrational beliefs that were eventually narrowed down to the five core themes mentioned earlier in the chapter. For each of these more detailed irrational beliefs, consider why it is irrational.

On your own, or in small groups, practice disputing each of these dysfunctional statements. We'll get you started by handling the first two. You do the rest.

- "Everyone must love and appreciate me all the time." This is irrational because it is impossible. You can't be loved and appreciated by everyone all the time. It is inevitable that some people will disapprove of what you do, no matter how hard you work to please them. The good news, however, is that you can love and approve of yourself no matter how you might behave in certain stressful circumstances.
- "I must be competent in everything that I do in order to feel okay about myself." Again this is impossible. You can't be competent in everything that you do. And even if this was possible, which it is not, why would your essential competence as a person be contingent on any single performance? Even the most skilled and talented individuals make mistakes at times. The best hitters in baseball fail to get hits 70% of the time.

Now it's your turn to do the rest of the exercises. Answers are at the end of the chapter.

- "Some people who are different from me are bad and should be punished."

- "It is terrible when I don't get what I want."

- "Other people and events cause me to be unhappy and I have little control over this situation."

- "If I keep dwelling on something awful, maybe I can prevent it from happening."

- "It is easier to avoid difficulties in life rather than having to face them."

- "I need someone stronger than I am to take care of me."

- "What has happened in the past determines how I must be in the future."

- "I should become upset over other people's problems."

- "There is a perfect solution to every problem and it's possible for me to figure out what it might be."

Reframing

A significant part of cognitive restructuring takes the form of recasting your situation or your problems in a different way, preferably one that is more self-enhancing. Stress-free living is not so much about what you do, or even how you do it, as it is about the ways you look at the world—your attitudes, beliefs, and interpretations. What can seem like an obstacle or annoyance to one person can be a challenge to someone else. It is all in the lens you choose to view the world through.

The problem is redefined in such a way that it can be more readily solved. This is called **reframing** and involves taking the problem out of its current context or "frame" and placing it in another one that makes it easier to deal with. So often, problems seem hopeless and intractable because they are perceived that way. Consider the following complaints:

- "My mother is always on my case. She's always bugging me, asking me questions, and trying to find out what I'm doing. She's so nosy."

- "My boyfriend is the problem. He is just lazy and inconsiderate."

- "My coworkers keep sabotaging my work and undermining me."

- "I'm shy and don't have any friends."

- "I'm getting poor grades because I am stupid."

FOR REFLECTION 6.6

Looking for Exceptions

Think of a problem you are experiencing in your life right now, one that is creating a fair degree of emotional disturbance. This should be an issue that you spend a lot of time thinking about. Perhaps your sleep is disrupted by this problem. At odd and often inconvenient times you find yourself obsessing about it over and over again, replaying conversations in your head, reviewing what you could have and should have said or done instead.

Now, instead of focusing on the times you have this problem, I want you instead to think about those times when you are *not* bothered by it. Surely there are moments, even several minutes or hours, when you manage to keep things under control. You might even forget you have the problem at such times. Or perhaps, in spite of the ways you feel disturbed much of the time, you still have found ways to function some of the time without giving in to this problem.

Perhaps you are now aware that much of the time, maybe even most of the time, this problem does not control your life, even if it sometimes feels that way. Instead of looking at the situations when the problem is there, focus on those times when it is not present.

During this search for exceptions, what is different about those times when the problem is not bothersome? What do you do differently to not permit the problem to take over your life?

Now, consider the preceding problem statements reframed in a more positive point of view.

- "My mother really loves and cares about me. She just shows her affection and concern in ways that I haven't appreciated."

- "I haven't been as effective as I could be in getting my needs met in this relationship."

- "My coworkers are trying to be helpful, but in a way that is different from what I prefer."

- "Sometimes I act shyly, but sometimes I don't. I would like to have more friends."

- "I'm getting poor grades because I haven't yet figured out how to study effectively."

In each case, these reframed problems take the edge off the emotional intensity of situations and make the problems easier to deal with. The life predicament is exactly the same—the only thing that has changed is the way things are interpreted. Remember, this is the essence of cognitive restructuring. You may not be able to control the world, or other people, but you can control how you respond by choosing certain attitudes over others.

Ceasing Disturbing Thoughts

All the methods I have presented so far involve active strategies in which you carefully monitor your thoughts, challenge your thinking, and work hard to construct alternative perceptions of your experience. Sometimes, however, the source of stress arises from too much thinking—you can't seem to shut your mind off. You obsess constantly about what is happening, or what could happen in the future. You ruminate about things that could go wrong. You struggle to find some meaning in life. You give yourself a headache, not to mention many sleepless nights and worry about things outside of your control. Or, in your most diligent efforts to master cognitive therapy methods, you constantly assess what you are thinking and how you are speaking. What started out as valuable skill can be taken too far.

It is indeed the case that worrying about things can better prepare you to face challenges in the future, but at a cost: worriers tend to die younger than those who avoid such behavior (Mroczek, Spiro, & Turiano, 2009). There is a magical belief that if you anticipate every possible negative scenario that might unfold, somehow you can better survive it. Yet focusing so extremely on potential disasters creates a level of chronic stress that becomes toxic.

Several other chapters in this book will teach you how to turn off your mind and put stressful thoughts aside—meditation, visualization, deep breathing, yoga, and tai chi are designed specifically for that purpose. So far I have been advocating that stress can be counteracted by thinking more rationally and logically, but sometimes the problem is made worse by thinking too much.

We are the only species that has the ability, and the inclination, to anticipate dangers. Rather than being grounded only in the here and now, we can imagine future possibilities, and we do this as routinely and naturally as breathing. One result of this remarkable talent is that stress activates thinking and internal fantasies that lead us to rehearse, over and over again, all the disastrous things that might happen or go wrong (Restak, 2004).

As originally intended, this future-oriented thinking helps us to prepare for possible threats that may be waiting around the corner: "Let's see, tomorrow when I go to the play I'm going to be parking in a bad neighborhood. Maybe I'll use the valet service at a nearby restaurant instead so I'd better make a reservation." Yet people who are overstressed have taken worst-case scenarios to their extreme. There are bestselling books on the subject that feed the public's anxiety about all the things that can go wrong. They give advice about where to sit on a plane in case the engines fail or fall off, how to jump off a moving train, or how to survive a herd of stampeding elephants. These sorts of worries are not rational by any means, especially if you consider the actual odds of being injured. According to Glassner's (1999) book *The Culture of Fear*, things we worry about such as shark attacks (one in a billion chance of occurring), being struck by lightning (one in four million), or being attacked by terrorists (several hundred victims each year), are actually quite rare. Our thinking in these matters is so irrational that we neglect far more legitimate threats like the danger of car or boating accidents, skin cancer, or electrical sockets. I mention these not to plant additional fears but just to remind you about all the needless worrying that takes place over things that not only will probably never happen, but over which you have absolutely no control.

Many Eastern stress observers wonder at the Western tendency to think so much about so many things that are beyond our direct influence. People read the paper in the morning, or watch the news, and then ruminate all day about the implications of the latest economic or political upheaval. You hear about a kidnapping or murder in some part of the world, and then spend an inordinate amount of time thinking about this person you have never met. You replay in your head a conversation you had earlier in the week, again and again, berating yourself for how you handled yourself. When you aren't worrying about these other things, you beat yourself over the head about another situation in which you did not perform absolutely perfectly. And these are only a few things that have already happened that you can't, or won't, let go of. Then there are all those things that *might* happen in the future—these provide an endless source of rumination and obsessions. Clearly, this is not very good for your health and well-being.

Some research on the subject of "not thinking too much" supports the idea that sometimes it may be better to deny or bury your worries. In one study of patients who experienced severe heart attacks, Karni Ginzburg and colleagues (2003) interviewed them about their coping styles after this traumatic health event. It seems that those patients who denied the risks they faced, and acted as if nothing much had happened, were far more relaxed and coped better than those who thought realistically about what they had faced. The repressed patients, even though they were denying reality to a certain extent, benefited from lower blood pressure and fewer stress symptoms. The lesson from this study: sometimes it is better to avoid thinking about certain things that are distressing.

One method for ceasing disturbing ideas is called **thought-stopping**. It is a device employed for people stuck in obsessive thinking patterns, or who can't seem to stop themselves from reviewing painful, stressful memories (see Voice of Stress Management 6.2). The method is quite simple:

1.   Place a thick rubber band around your wrist.

2.   Wait for the disturbing or distracting thought or image to come to mind.

3.   Reach over with the other hand and pull the rubber band to its stretched limit.

4.   Let the rubber band go.

5.   Notice that you are no longer thinking about the disturbing image.

Voice of Stress Management 6.2

Twenty-One-Year-Old Female Student and Retail Clerk

I feel like I am always freaking out about something. It never ends. I have bills, work, school, family, dating—it seems like there is just too much at once. I am always paranoid that I am going to fail out of school. And what if I get fired from my job? I'll be homeless! I absolutely can't go live with my parents! They are the worst, really strict and stuff. My boyfriend and I broke up a few weeks ago. He said that I was too stressed all of the time. He said that he couldn't handle my paranoia about him cheating and that I was not going to die of cancer (I have a thing about dying of cancer, I swear, I just know that I have cancer). I don't think that I will ever have another boyfriend. I think I'll just die alone, a spinster with ten cats!

I did start seeing a counselor at school recently. In the few weeks that I have been going, he has given me some good tips. He gave me this rubber band and told me to put it on my wrist and snap it when I start thinking about the cancer. It is supposed to help me stop my thoughts. Well, at first I thought that I might get cancer from the rubber on my wrist, but I tried it and it seems to work.

I mean, I will just snap it and it is like I am snapping myself out of it, out of the thought. So, the cancer thoughts are coming less and less, and sometimes I don't even have to snap the rubber band anymore, I will just remember the sting and stop the thought myself.

This may sound rather simplistic to you, but it works! This is a direct application of behavior modification in which you extinguish an undesirable behavior (in this case a disturbing thought) with punishment (snapped rubber band). This method is not so much designed to hurt yourself when you engage in dysfunctional thinking; it acts more as a reminder, a kind of memory anchor, that helps you remember to clear your mind and focus on the present.

Carolyn was absolutely despondent over the breakup of her relationship with her boyfriend. She worked as a nurse in the same hospital where her ex-boyfriend worked as an intern in medical school. In addition to the grief and loss Carolyn felt over their separation, she was immobilized by the prospect that she might accidentally run into him in the hallways of the hospital. This was not an unreasonable expectation, considering they both worked the same shifts.

Carolyn imagined the anticipated confrontation over and over again in her head, just like the loop of a scene in a movie that repeats itself endlessly. She saw herself turning a corner and then literally running into him. She stood there frozen, unable to speak, and pictured herself actually fainting in anxiety. Whenever she had this fantasy, which was frequently throughout the day, she could barely function and concentrate on her work.

Carolyn decided to "arm" herself with a thick rubber band. Every time the forbidden image came to mind, she snapped the rubber band discreetly. The effects didn't last very long, but the action gave her a measure of self-control: she did have the power to control her thoughts, even if for a few minutes.

When Carolyn finally did run into her ex-boyfriend (thankfully not literally), she managed to mutter a hello and hurry on her way. She drew some small satisfaction from the observation that he seemed to be even more uncomfortable about this meeting than she had been.

The point of this section on avoiding obsessive thinking is to remind you that too much of a good thing can also be harmful. I am a strong advocate of the power of cognitive restructuring, but if you find that you tend to become too involved in assessing your thoughts, then consider alternative ways of stress management to follow.

When Challenging Stressful Thoughts Doesn't Work

You have already learned that there are times when stress and anxiety actually serve important functions (eustress) to enhance performance, mental acuity, and physical capabilities during emergencies, competitions, or life-threatening situations. In general, in order for these normal reactions to operate effectively, there must be only a moderate degree of activation going on; otherwise you lose control. Yet there are also times when extreme stress and worry also serve useful purposes (see For Reflection 6.7).

FOR REFLECTION 6.7

The Functions of Worry and Stress

What comes to mind when you think about possible uses of worry and stress? What do they do for you, even in extreme degrees? What functions might they serve to help you in some way, even if they have negative side-effects?

Perhaps what immediately comes to mind is that worry and stress over the future give you some illusion of control: thinking obsessively about what might happen, you prepare yourself in some ways for dealing with frightening situations. To some extent, this really is useful in that you can think about problems and plan how you might deal with them. Sometimes, however, the worrying becomes excessive and counterproductive in that it goes far beyond mere problem-solving.

Other possible explanations as to why you might have trouble challenging negative thoughts include the following:

- You enjoy the attention and sympathy you get from others.

- You ward off fears by believing that you can somehow control the future by thinking about it so much.

- You prepare yourself for worst possible scenarios by thinking about them ahead of time.

- You have an excuse for not doing as well as you might like because you are "impaired."

- They create drama and excitement in your life.

- They can act as a motivation to get things done in order to protect yourself against further suffering.

- They help you to examine more closely unresolved issues that you have been avoiding.

All of these so-called "secondary gains" of worrisome thoughts actually prevent you from changing the pattern because they are serving some purpose, even if you aren't sure what that might be. In such cases, and others you might encounter, the cognitive methods of challenging irrational thoughts might not work as well as you would prefer. You might even find that trying so hard to make the negative thoughts go away only seems to make things worse.

In later chapters you will learn about "mindfulness" techniques such as those that are part of yoga, deep breathing, meditation, and visual imagery. The basic idea is that instead of trying to make thoughts go away, you simply "watch them" internally. You choose to entertain only the thoughts that are conducive to your health and well-being and replace or redirect those thoughts that are stressful. As an alternative to what you've learned in this chapter so far, there are certain therapeutic approaches that instruct people to develop a different relationship with their own stressful experiences—one in which instead of trying to change negative thoughts into something else, you concentrate on becoming more aware of what you are feeling (Hayes & Strosahl, 2010). There are several good sources that teach you how to do this by increasing your tolerance for emotional distress (Forsyth & Eifert, 2007; Lejeune, 2007). Instead of ignoring, denying, or wallowing in your pain, obsessing about what you can do to make it go away, you "spend time getting thoroughly acquainted with it instead" (Hayes, 2007, p. 50). In its simplest form you go deeply into your disturbing thoughts or feelings and then notice carefully what is happening in your body. Rather than struggling to escape from the feelings, you stay with them (this takes resolve and courage). Such an approach can sometimes help you to stop fighting a battle it seems you can never win and instead develop a greater awareness of the thoughts and sensations within both your mind and your body. In many cases you will feel the stranglehold relax.

With this approach, or any other I have presented, I offer no guarantees; I present a collection of alternatives that you have to try out for yourself and personalize in such a way that you find something that works best.

SUMMARY

In this chapter you learned the skills involved in systematic self-talk and cognitive restructuring that allow you to choose your reaction to almost any situation you might face. Negative feelings do not emerge out of thin air, nor are they caused by external events; they are the natural result of the ways you interpret events around you. You can change the way you are feeling, and thereby reduce significant stress, by changing the way you think.

Most self-defeating or irrational thought patterns arise from exaggerating reality, distorting what is going on, or holding unrealistic expectations for yourself or for others. These dysfunctional thoughts can be challenged by following several sequential steps:

1. Become aware that you are experiencing a negative emotion you would rather eliminate.

2. Label the particular stressor or event that you originally believed was causing the problem.

3. Identify the irrational beliefs that are the real source of your suffering.

4. Dispute and challenge these beliefs by forcing yourself to consider the evidence in a more systematic, logical manner.

5. Consider your tendencies to exaggerate, hold perfectionistic expectations, make demands of others they are unable or unwilling to meet, and imagine the worst possibilities.

6. Assess your new emotional reactions that result from using cognitive restructuring.

In some cases, you also learned that there is a point when cognitive activity gets out of control. It was suggested that an alternative to thinking more is to think less by staying more in the present moment. The chapters that follow present a number of stress prevention and management strategies that specialize in harnessing strengths other than cognitive functioning. These include the uses of movement, breathing, exercise, imagery, meditation, touch, diet, and lifestyle changes that lead to feelings of greater control and well-being.

REMINDERS ABOUT HOW TO TALK TO YOURSELF MORE CONSTRUCTIVELY

- Avoid the use of "shoulds" and "musts."
- Stop yourself from imagining the worst.
- Look for exceptions for when you are experiencing problems.
- Live in the present rather than dwelling in the past.
- Ask yourself, "Where is the evidence?"
- Keep expectations realistic to minimize disappointment.
- Monitor what you say.
- Take yourself off probation.
- Reframe problems to make them more manageable.
- Stop whining and complaining about things you can't control.
- Keep your sense of humor.
- Stop taking yourself so seriously.
- Watch your tendency to overgeneralize.
- Exchange optimism for pessimism.

QUESTIONS FOR REVIEW

1. Explain how and why most stress is self-inflicted.
2. Describe the connection between your mindsets about stress and stress reactions.
3. Discuss cognitive theory as it relates to stress management.

4. Describe the five key components when considering the meaning of life according to author Karen Wyatt.
5. Think of a specific incident in your current life that upsets you. Use the disputing method to talk yourself through the process and reduce your stress.
6. Describe how the language you use dictates how you subsequently think and feel.
7. Identify six irrational beliefs that have caused you stress and replace them with more empowering thoughts.
8. Identify three problems in your life and attempt to resolve them by using the reframing technique.
9. Explain what else you can do when challenging stressful thinking doesn't work.

SELECTED ANSWERS

Answer to FOR REFLECTION 6.4

- *"I'm an idiot because I can't figure this stuff out."* How does having trouble with this particular chapter necessarily lead to the conclusion that you are stupid? This absolute judgment is a kind of overgeneralization. Negative self-esteem often results from this sort of chronic, exaggerated thinking.

- *"This material is way too hard for me."* The material may, in fact, be difficult. But "way too hard" implies that learning the material is impossible rather than only challenging. This is an example of "awfulizing." With sufficient time, patience, energy, and even help, it is highly likely that at least some of the material could be learned. In order to do so, however, the student would need to work on his or her frustration tolerance.

- *"It isn't fair that I have to work this hard."* Since when is the world fair? There is a distortion of reality in making demands that the world (or one's teacher and textbook) make things easy for you and exactly fit your expectations. Telling yourself that you got a raw deal does not change the situation; it only increases your sense of victimhood.

- *"It is so terrible that I have to deal with this."* It may be annoying, disappointing, slightly frustrating, or inconvenient, but "terrible" is a rather strong label to describe this relatively small challenge in life. If this situation is terrible, then what would you say about a really serious matter that was life- or health-threatening?

- *"I should be able to deal with this better than I am."* The use of "shoulds" and "musts" signals **absolute demands** for yourself or others that things should be different than they are. This represents a lack of self-acceptance and often unrealistic expectations for what is reasonable and realistic.

Answer to FOR REFLECTION 6.5

- *"Some people who are different from me are bad and should be punished."* People are entitled to be any way they want, even if you don't like it. Of course, they have to suffer the consequences of their own choices but it is not your role in life to enforce compliance with your particular values. Demanding that others be a particular way is evidence of narcissism, rigidity, and authoritarianism.

- *"It is terrible when I don't get what I want."* It may be inconvenient or annoying or disappointing, but "terrible" is an extreme label for the worst possible thing that could ever happen.

- *"Other people and events cause me to be unhappy and I have little control over this situation."* Nobody or nothing outside of you causes your emotional disturbance and stress; you do that to yourself based on your beliefs and interpretations. You do, in fact, have control over your emotional reactions depending on how you choose to think about things.

- *"If I keep dwelling on something awful, maybe I can prevent it from happening."* This sort of magical thinking that leads to incessant worrying and obsessive ruminations has no impact on future events. It presents an illusion of control that is based on fallacious reasoning and fantasy.
- *"It is easier to avoid difficulties in life rather than having to face them."* You can avoid situations in the short run, but eventually you have to deal with conflicts.
- *"I need someone stronger than I am to take care of me."* As long as you believe that, it will be so. There is a certain comfort in not having to be responsible for your own welfare. You can blame others (like your protector) when things go wrong. You are absolved of responsibility. You can feel helpless, inviting others to do the hard work of taking care of you. You don't actually *need* anyone to take care of you, but you may enjoy some of the benefits, as well as the negative side-effects such as helplessness and lack of control.
- *"What has happened in the past determines how I must be in the future."* The past may certainly influence the present and future but does not necessarily *determine* what happens. It is up to you to decide how much you want past experiences to act as templates for how you behave in the future.
- *"I should become upset over other people's problems."* You can *choose* to respond this way if you want, but in doing so you have to examine what it is doing for you. Generally, as long as you focus on others' problems, you don't have to think about your own. The "should" in this statement is also evidence of absolute demands that can be rejected if you prefer.
- *"There is a perfect solution to every problem and it's possible for me to figure out what it might be."* If only this was true. Rarely in life do problems even have solutions, much less "perfect" ones that can be discovered and implemented. It is more often the case that problems have many possible responses, several of which might be useful. Rather than freezing yourself with inaction by trying to figure out the perfect option, you are far better off making the best decision you can under the circumstances, and then moving on to the next challenge.

REVIEW ACTIVITIES

Review Activity 6.1: Changing Your Negative Beliefs
Directions: In this exercise you will answer a few questions in order to help yourself change a negative thought.

1. Recall a recent event where an automatic negative thought occurred in your mind. Write down that negative thought. Comment on how much you believe this thought is true.

2. What is the evidence that this negative thought is true?

3.   What is the evidence that this negative thought is untrue?

4.   What is your core belief that generates your negative thought in the first place?

5.   What is the evidence for and against the core belief?

6.   What is an alternative thought, a more positive one that can replace the negative core belief?

Review Activity 6.2: Practicing the ABC Theory
In the chapter you learned how you can change stressful experiences by talking to yourself differently. This involves following a series of sequential steps you learned that constitute the "ABC theory." In Figure 6.2 you can review how your beliefs (B) determine the emotional consequences (C) that you experience. By disputing (D) these beliefs using the methods you learned in the chapter, you produce a different effect (E) and feeling (F).

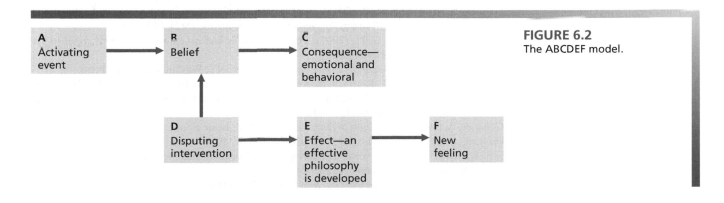

FIGURE 6.2
The ABCDEF model.

It was explained in the chapter that in order to make this system part of you so that you can naturally and routinely deal with stressors as they occur, you must practice these skills until they become second nature. In the space below, take an activating event (A) about which you are currently feeling upset. Follow the steps you learned to dispute your irrational beliefs (B) until you have been able to lower the intensity of the negative feelings. If you get stuck, consult with some other classmates or your instructor.

Review Activity 6.3: Externalized Language
You were introduced to the notion that language can be framed in terms of externalized or internalized control. The latter accepts responsibility for behavior while the former implies being a victim of circumstances outside of your control. In the examples below, substitute the externalized language with expressions that communicate greater personal power, choice, and responsibility.

Externalized Language	Internalized Language
"This job has really got me down."	
"I hate it when it is dreary outside like this."	
"I always get nervous when a paper is due."	
"She drives me crazy with her complaining."	
"He did this to me and it's all his fault."	

Compare your answers with those of classmates to make sure you understood the concepts.

REFERENCES AND RESOURCES

Beck, A. T. (1976). *Cognitive therapy and the emotional disorders*. London: Penguin Books.

Beckmann, J., & Kellmann, M. (2004). Self-regulation and recovery: Approaching an understanding of the process of recovery from stress. *Psychological Reports, 95*(3), 1,135–1,153.

Crum, A., Salovey, P., & Achor, S. (2013). Rethinking stress: The role of mindsets in determining the stress response. *Journal of Personality and Social Psychology, 104*(4), 716–733.

Dweck, C. (2012). Mindsets and human nature: Promoting change in the Middle East, the schoolyard, the racial divide, and willpower. *American Psychologist, 67*(8), 614–622.

Ellis, A. T. (1962). *Reason and emotion in psychotherapy*. New York: Lyle Stuart.

Fontana, A., & Rosenheck, R. (2005). The role of loss of meaning in the pursuit of treatment for posttraumatic stress disorder. *Journal of Traumatic Stress, 18*(2), 133–136.

Forsyth, J. P., & Eifert, G. H. (2007). *The mindfulness and acceptance workbook for anxiety*. Oakland, CA: New Harbinger.

Frankl, V. (1962). *Man's search for meaning*. New York, NY: Washington Square Press.

Ginzburg, K., Solomon, Z., Koifman, B., Keren, G., Roth, A., Kriwisky, M., et al. (2003). Trajectory of posttraumatic stress disorder following myocardial infarction: A prospective study. *Journal of Clinical Psychiatry, 64*, 1,217–1,223.

Glassner, B. (1999). *The culture of fear*. New York, NY: Basic Books.

Graham, J. E., Glaser, R., Loving, T. J., Malarkey, W. B., Stowell, J. R., & Kiecolt-Glaser, J. K. (2009). Cognitive word use during marital conflict and increases in proinflammatory cytokines. *Health Psychology, 28*, 621–630.

Haley, J. (1973). *Uncommon therapy*. New York, NY: Norton.

Haley, J. (1987). *Problem solving therapy*. San Francisco, CA: Jossey-Bass.

Hayes, S. (2007). Hello, darkness. *Psychotherapy Networker*, September/October, 46–52.

Hayes, S., & Strosahl, K. D. (Eds.) (2010). *A practical guide to acceptance and commitment therapy*. New York, NY: Springer.

Jamieson, J. P., Mendes, W. B., Blackstock, E., & Schmader, T. (2010). Turning the knots in your stomach into bows: Reappraising arousal improves performance. *Journal of Experimental Social Psychology*, *46*(1), 208–212.

Lejeune, C. (2007). *The worry trap*. Oakland, CA: New Harbinger.

Madanes, C. (1981). *Strategic family therapy*. San Franciso, CA: Jossey-Bass.

Meichenbaum, D. (1977). *Cognitive-behavior modification*. New York, NY: Plenum.

Mroczek, D. K., Spiro, A., & Turiano, N. A. (2009). Do health behaviors explain the effect of neuroticism on mortality? *Journal of Research in Personality*, *43*(4), 653–659.

O'Hanlon, W. H. (1993). *Solution-oriented therapy*. New York, NY: Norton.

Park, N., Park, M., & Peterson, C. (2010). When is the search for meaning related to life satisfaction? *Applied Psychology: Health and Well-Being*, *2*, 1–13.

Restak, R. (2004). *Poe's heart and the mountain climber: Exploring the effect of anxiety on our brains and our culture*. New York, NY: Harmony Books.

Reynolds, D. (1984). *Playing ball on running water*. New York, NY: William Morrow.

Seligman, M. E. P. (2002). *Authentic happiness*. New York, NY: Free Press.

Steward, S., Moser, D., & Thompson, D. R. (2004). *Caring for the heart failure patient*. New York, NY: Taylor & Francis.

Vowles, K. E., McCracken, L. M., & Eccleston, C. (2008). Patient functioning and catastrophizing in chronic pain: The mediating effects of acceptance. *Health Psychology*, *27*(2), S136–S143.

Wyatt, K. (2015). 5 keys to finding meaning in later life. Retrieved on October 12, 2015 from http://www.huffingtonpost.com/karen-m-wyatt-md/meaning-life_b_4219689.html.

7
Problem Solving and Time Management

S o much stress in daily life results from feeling overwhelmed by too much to do and not enough time to do it. Even without the pressure of limited time to accomplish all the things you need to do, you may feel trapped by a perceived lack of choices. Learning how to reduce stress by talking to yourself in constructive ways is a crucial skill, but not sufficient for dealing with the variety of challenges you face. There are also times when you have to think clearly to specify your most critical goals and cherished desires. Once these priorities have been identified, there is also the challenge of creating the time you need to accomplish what you think is most important.

KEY QUESTIONS IN THE CHAPTER

- What is the relationship between social problem solving and stress management?

- What are some of the differences between concern and worry?

- What are the major barriers that get in the way of effective problem solving?

- How does the way that you define a problem affect your ability to resolve the difficulty?

- What is the most important thing to manage in time management?

- What are the six principles of time management?

- What are the secondary gains of procrastination?

- What are the best strategies for managing your time on a daily basis?

- How can you determine which technique will work best for you?

Problems without Solutions

In some ways, I am reluctant to use the term "problem solving" when speaking about the challenges that you face. In truth, most of the things that perplex you in life don't have single, correct solutions; sometimes there are no resolutions at all!

Consider the whole notion of managing your time. No matter who you are, what you are doing, or where you are living, there can never be enough time to do all the things you want to do, or need to do. Not only is there insufficient time in a single day to complete everything you'd like to do, but there will never be enough opportunities in life to do everything you want before your time runs out.

Time management is a particular kind of problem-solving technique that will be covered later in the chapter; it is one that tries to match available resources with your goals. There are always people making demands on your time, and more tasks in any given day than you could possibly complete. No matter how many hours you study for an exam, you are never perfectly prepared; there are always more things you could do. The nature of life is that the clock is always ticking away the precious seconds, minutes, and hours of the time allotted to you. This is a tremendous source of stress.

One of the first things to understand about dealing with time-related stress, or problems that seem to be without easy solutions, is that this is a natural condition of life. No matter what you do, you are always going to feel behind schedule and struggle with thorny issues that perplex you. Rather than feeling unduly anxious and immobilized by this reality, there are several strategies you can employ to exert more control over the way you manage your life. That which cannot be "managed" can then be tolerated, or even embraced, as part of life's "gifts" in the sense that it teaches you important lessons.

Differences between Concern and Worry, and Why it Matters

In order to control stress you would have to surrender **incessant worrying** about things that are beyond your control. This is the type of chronic, persistent focus on things that can go wrong, on disasters that may befall you, and on even minor disruptions in your routine that may require greater flexibility and adaptation. It is a disease of "what if" (Leahy, 2005).

People worry about the weather. They worry about traffic. They worry about everything from catching a cold to contracting a terminal disease. There are aspects of such behavior that are, in fact, constructive in the sense that they lead you to take self-protective measures against possible threats or aggravations. But most of the time you tend to worry about things that seem to do nothing except waste your time and drive you to distraction.

There is a significant difference between **concern** and **worry**. It is one thing to be "concerned" about circumstances in which you might make intelligent plans. For instance, if you are *concerned* about traffic, then you might leave earlier than planned, or check current congestion patterns on the web. If you are *concerned* about catching the flu, you can get a flu shot to protect yourself. If you are *concerned* about doing poorly on an exam, then you will study more, get a tutor, or consult with the instructor.

Worry, on the other hand, involves persistent attention on matters that are beyond what you can manage on your own. Such behavior actually diverts you from taking constructive action. You engage in a kind of magical thinking that if you spend an inordinate amount of time worrying about some disaster that might befall you, then somehow this will prevent it. Or, at the very least, it is a kind of psychological preparation for the worst you can imagine. Interestingly, it is also a way to try to control other people.

Imagine, for example, that a roommate or family member tells you, just before you leave to go out for the night: "Please don't stay out late. You know I'll worry about you."

You may resent the heck out of this expression of concern that comes across as a feeble attempt at manipulation. But it also works some of the time. And even if this person is not successful in getting you to be more compliant with his or her wishes, then at least he or she is preparing for the worst should you somehow be waylaid or injured.

So, the question is: How do you let go of self-defeating worry that is getting in the way of your becoming more productive and effective in your life?

The first step is to become aware of what you are doing—that is, to identify the amount of worrying you actually do in your head. In Chapter 6 you already learned how important such self-monitoring can be before you can change a thought pattern.

FOR REFLECTION 7.1

Needless worry

What are some examples of things in your life that you spend time worrying about over and over, even though it appears to do little good?

What are some ways that this worrying behavior might be useful to you? Think in terms of its distractive value, the self-pity or sympathy you might enjoy, or even the magical belief that you might somehow prevent disaster through magical thinking.

The second thing to figure out is what the worrying is actually doing for you—how it is serving you?

- What are you distracting yourself from that you would rather not deal with? In other words, how does worry keep you from focusing on other things that might be even more frightening?

- How do you use worry to control other people? In what ways are you attempting to coerce family and friends to be more compliant with your wishes?

- How does worry help you protect yourself against disappointments and fears? If you worry about something, and it *does* occur as you feared, then you have the small satisfaction of having predicted the future.

- How does worry prevent you from taking action? Sometimes, this can be helpful since it can stop you from taking unnecessary risks.

- How does worry act to increase your attention to potential threats? This is one, solid constructive purpose of worry in that it does put you on hyper-alert status during times of perceived danger.

Assuming you are truly motivated to change the frequency of worry in your life (as opposed to constructive concern), there are several things you can do that involve taking action steps (see Table 7.1).

TABLE 7.1 A dozen ways to reduce needless worry

1. *Write your worries down.* It helps to give them a name and specific description.
2. *Pay attention to what you are worrying about.* Ask yourself what that means.
3. *Exaggerate the behavior.* Spend one uninterrupted hour worrying about anything and everything you can possibly think of. Then let them go.
4. *Keep things in perspective.* Ask yourself: How much of what you are worrying about will really matter a year from now?
5. *Imagine the worst thing that can happen.* Even if that came to pass you would still find a way to deal with it.
6. *Let go of what you can't control.* Turn your worries over to God, a Higher Power, or even fate since you can't do much to prevent many things from happening anyway.
7. *Realize that worry represents an obsession with the future.* Try to remain in the present as much as possible.
8. *Make a decision about something you can do.* Allow this to bring you some peace of mind.
9. *Don't sweat the small stuff.* Realize how trivial and insignificant most the things are that you spend so much time worrying about.
10. *Observe yourself when you worry.* Rather than pretending that something isn't bothering you (when it really is), instead devote conscious attention to the process going on inside you.
11. *Distract yourself.* Meditative-type activities are designed to keep you concentrating on the here and now. It is impossible to worry about anything if you are really fully engaged in what you are doing.
12. *Count your blessings.* Instead of focusing on what could go wrong, think about what is going right in your life. Reaffirm what you already have and how fortunate you are.

Problem Solving and Stress

There are not many people who actually enjoy confronting problems, except perhaps mathematicians. There can indeed be a certain amount of satisfaction, and even pleasure, from the *resolution* of problems, but once one is immersed in the throes of such uncertainty there is often accompanying stress. Nevertheless, it is the nature of life that every day you will face some challenges that test your patience, resolve, and skills. These can be framed either in terms of "challenges" to be dealt with, or experienced as "crises" that are beyond your ability to manage. Often the difference between whether a problem is seen as a puzzle or a scourge is based on your perception of whether you can manage it effectively or not.

A problem can be viewed as any situation in which there exists a gap between what you want versus what is actually occurring. You may want higher grades, a better living situation, a nicer car, more friends, or a better relationship with a loved one; if that is not happening as hoped and expected, a problem exists. With that problem usually comes a degree of stress.

Problem solving means closing the gap between your goals and the actual outcomes. Your ability to do this efficiently and effectively is, in fact, related to perceived life satisfaction. Those who can solve problems well are also able to manage their stress better (Chang, D'Zurilla, & Sanna, 2009; D'Zurilla & Nezu, 2007). Specifically, use of problem-solving skills helps individuals improve relationships (Sullivan, Pasch, Johnson, & Bradbury, 2010), as well as adjust better to daily stressors (Bell & D'Zurilla, 2009b), reduce symptoms of depression (Gellis & Kenaley, 2008). The good news is that regardless of your current ability to deal with problems you face, you can augment these skills the same way you would with any other area.

VOICE OF STRESS MANAGEMENT 7.1

Male Student in His Twenties

It would be safe to say that I'm a bit of a control freak. I like everything in its place and like to know exactly what to expect. Ordinarily, this works pretty well for me, but sometimes—like when I have to travel or go somewhere new—I kind of have a problem. I think my friends would say I have a really big problem.

Anyway, lately what I've been trying to do is to surrender as much as I can to things that are outside of my control. Like the other day I was supposed to visit a part of the city I'd never been to before. I miscalculated how much time it would take to get there. Traffic was terrible. I got lost. Everything went wrong. And I knew I was going to be late. Eventually, I realized that the directions I had were so bad that I couldn't even find the place at all.

Usually, I'd go crazy in a situation like this. My blood pressure would go up. I'd start screaming at myself—and anyone else in the vicinity. For someone who likes to be in control, I would totally lose it. But this time I tried to remind myself, over and over again, that there was nothing I could do about it. Rather than pouting, like I usually do, I decided to make the best of the situation. I found a coffee shop and just hung out, read the paper, relaxed a little. I tried to enjoy this unscheduled time.

Barriers to Effective Problem Solving

In learning problem solving, it is important to understand what most often gets in the way of becoming more effective. There are several common obstacles that hinder effective problem solving, most of which are related to your perceptions, beliefs, and interpretations about what is going on.

If you think of a problem that you are struggling with in your life right now, it is likely that you have already tried a number of strategies and solutions to resolve the difficulty, but without enduring success. Based on these previous attempts, there are several obstacles that have prevented you from being more effective. Some have to do with incapacitating emotional reactions that are both discouraging and immobilizing. Anxiety and depression can be paralyzing but so too can frustration and fear. It is fear—of the unknown, of making a mistake, of being wrong, and of taking risks—that can lead to feeling helpless to tackle problems. However, these problems only become worse from neglect.

Perceptual and cognitive barriers are related to the way you interpret and evaluate a situation. You learned in Chapter 6 the ways that stressors can be made far worse, depending on the ways that you view what is going on. For instance, most people in our culture have invested a lot of negative energy in the word "problem." The moment "problem" is mentioned, negative associations are conjured up and worrying thoughts emerge to stifle the creative process. By changing the way you think about problems, you reinterpret an annoying barrier as a stimulating challenge.

The ways you view your problems are based on the quality and quantity of information at your disposal. If all you know is that you will have an exam next Wednesday on the subject of stress, and you don't know the scope, content, or structure of what is expected, you are going to feel far more anxious than if you had a study guide that described the kind of test, what material would be covered, and so on. Thus one significant barrier to solving problems is a lack of relevant and useful information.

Inadequate or misleading information often results in misdiagnosis of the problem. If you don't have an accurate perception of what is plaguing you, it's going to be very difficult for you to address the issues. Imagine, for example, that you are faced with the problem of leading a discussion in a small group. After presenting the issues that you are to discuss, you observe complete silence from everyone else in the group—absolutely no response. Assuming you weren't clear enough in your instructions, you present the assignment again. Continued silence. So, *now* what do you do?

As with any problem you face, what you do depends on what is going on. In this case, you may have misread the situation, assuming that the silence was the result of the participants' lack of understanding. As such, you intervened by repeating the instructions. What if the silence meant something else? What if you misread the problem you were facing? What would you do in such a situation?

The correct answer, based on what you just read in the text, should be, "It depends." You have already learned that how you resolve any difficulty depends on the particular meaning of the situation.

Putting aside *what* you would do to deal with the prolonged and uncomfortable silence, consider the possible meanings of this behavior:

1. Perhaps the group members don't feel safe expressing themselves because of fear of criticism or looking stupid.

2. It is possible that they are being resistant due to resentment of being forced to do something they don't wish to do.

3. They *still* don't understand what you expect and don't wish to look foolish or disappoint you.

4. Maybe it isn't actually a nonproductive silence after all, but people are taking their time to reflect on what they want to say.

5. Perhaps the silence just *seems* unduly long to you because you are feeling the pressure to move things along.

As you can see, depending on how the situation is interpreted, and how the problem is defined, you might try any number of things to resolve the problem—give it more time, explain things in a different way, reduce the fear of criticism, build more trust, model what you want them to do, address the underlying resistance, or whatever. Likewise, in any situation you face, it is critical to fully understand what is going on before you attempt to intervene.

Keep in mind that if the only tool you own is a hammer, you will see all problems as nails. The more options you have in your toolbox, the more flexibility you can demonstrate and the more accurately you can diagnose what is going on. All of this is based on the premise that you are seeing the situation clearly and rationally.

Developing Problem-Solving Skills

Since our ability to solve problems is essential to reducing stress and building resilience, training individuals in problem-solving skills has been used as a means to cope with stressful situations. A training system called *social problem-solving therapy* has been developed to facilitate the process of developing these skills (Nezu, Nezu, & D'Zurilla, 2000). The term "social problem solving" refers to resolving challenges that occur in the natural environment (D'Zurilla & Nezu, 2007). Research indicates that individuals with adequate social problem-solving skills are more capable of coping with a variety of stressful life situations than those with inadequate problem-solving (Eskin et al., 2014). This system consists of two partially independent elements: (1) problem orientation and (2) problem-solving style, and has two major specific goals: (1) fostering the adoption of a positive problem orientation, and (2) facilitating the acquisition and real-life application of a rational problem-solving style.

Problem Orientation

Problem orientation is another term for describing the perceptual lens through which you view your situation. Individuals with a **positive problem orientation** are generally optimistic. They believe that not only are daily problems normal but, given sufficient time and effort, they can be reasonably resolved. Moreover, problems are regarded as possible opportunities for learning and growth rather than as inherently stressful. On the other hand, people with a **negative problem orientation** approach their situations with a degree of passivity and trepidation. They often feel helpless and exhibit pessimistic attitudes toward the eventual outcome. What is the use in even trying, they may reason, since nothing much will ever change?

The major differences between these two orientations are determined by people's early experiences, as well as their entrenched beliefs. Those with a negative orientation often approach problems in a careless or cavalier manner which only makes matters worse.

Problem-Solving Style

Problem-solving style refers to the cognitive and behavioral activities an individual uses to cope with stressful situations in life. The style can be adaptive, resulting in the resolution of a problem, or dysfunctional, leading to negative results. Dysfunctional problem-solving styles include both impulsivity/carelessness and avoidance/procrastination. I will focus on the adaptive style, the rational problem-solving style. A rational problem-solving style involves the deliberate and systematic application of four major problem-solving skills: (1) problem definition and formulation, (2) generation of alternative solutions, (3) decision making, and (4) solution implementation and verification (Bell & D'Zurilla, 2009a).

PROBLEM DEFINITION AND FORMULATION   The major focus of this problem-solving task is to better understand the nature of the problem and to set clearly defined and reasonable goals. One of the reasons that people struggle so much in trying to resolve their difficulties is that they choose goals that are too general to be of much use. What does it mean to say that you want to lose weight, or start exercising more, or make more friends, or do better in school? With such abstract goals, how would you ever know when you had reached them?

Whenever possible, problems, as well as their accompanying goals, should be defined as specifically as possible. This not only gives you a clear target to aim for, but also lets you know better when you've hit what you are aiming for.

Effectively set goals meet several criteria, as follows.

1. *Make the goals as specific as possible.* Rather than saying you want to study harder in school, you need to say how, when, where, and how often you are going to do this.

2. *Goals should be both realistic and attainable.* Set objectives that you know you can reach, no matter what. You must be absolutely certain that you are going to follow through on whatever you say you will do. If you are unrealistic, you will only create more pressure and stress for yourself. If you are facing a problem with respect to catching up on work, declare a goal that is modest and within your ability to accomplish. Leave yourself no room for excuses.

3. *Make the goal measurable.* It is important that you know whether you have reached your objective or not. Saying that you will try harder to make friends is laudable but how do you measure or observe whether you have, in fact, expended this effort? It is far more useful to state goals that can actually be assessed. In this example you might state you are going to make a minimum of three phone calls, twice per week, to ask acquaintances if they might like to get together.

4. *The goal should be clearly relevant to what you truly most want to achieve.* It does little good to focus on improving your test-taking skills if your ultimate goal is to improve your understanding of complex, theoretical material.

Since most problems you face are both complex and multifaceted, it is not easy to reduce their essence into a single problem definition or goal statement. If, for example, a person was struggling with poor body image there might very well be a number of variables related to this issue. Perhaps the person tends to overeat when stressed from

FOR REFLECTION 7.2

When attempting to resolve stressful problems, it is important to define objectives in ways that they can be more easily defined and addressed. The following steps are based on the criteria discussed previously.

Step 1: Describe the general problem. In one sentence describe one problem that has been an ongoing source of frustration and stress for you.

Step 2: Make the problem as specific as you can. Take one aspect of this general problem and focus in on one piece of it that seems more manageable to you. Define the problem again, but in a far more specific way. For example, instead of saying that you have a problem with (a) intimacy, (b) study habits, or (c) managing money, redefine as a problem with (a) getting close to one person in particular, (b) allocating time to prepare for an exam in a particular subject, or (c) stopping impulsive shopping that runs up your credit card bills. Write your more specific problem below.

Step 3: Define a goal for yourself that is highly specific. Just as you defined your problem in more detailed, specific terms, commit yourself to an objective that is equally precise.

Step 4: Develop your goal further by being realistic in what you are absolutely positive you can do. What *exactly* are you going to do?

How often are you going to do it?

When are you going to do this?

Where are you going to do this?

With whom are you going to do this? (if applicable)

What excuses might you use to avoid following through on what you say you are going to do?

overwork and problems with her boyfriend. In addition, she is taking a medication that has weight gain as a side-effect. Finally, the problem is mostly in her mind. Although she is a few pounds overweight, she is really within normal limits—it is not so much that she is grossly obese as that she feels that way.

When a presenting problem has so many interrelated features, it is hard to find the essential piece of the puzzle that most clearly needs to be addressed. In this case, would her goals focus on weight loss, self-image related to her perceptions, relationship issues with her boyfriend, getting off her medication, or reducing her workload that is creating the stress? The answer is that she might tackle each of these, one at a time. The important part is that she would feel less overwhelmed if she were able to deal with this overwhelming problem one small step at a time.

Problem solving often involves making the best possible choice based on the information available to you at the time. If this decision does not lead you where you want to go, you can learn from the mistake, forgive yourself, incorporate the feedback, and make a new choice based on prior experience.

GENERATION OF ALTERNATIVES   Stress is directly connected to a perceived lack of options. Ironically, it can also be the result of having too many options. If you are at a point in which you are supposed to declare a major, for example, and feel like there are too many options to consider—that no matter which major you choose, you will feel cheated by what you did *not* include—that is going to feel stressful. By contrast, if you are forced to choose a major and nothing seems especially appealing, that may also feel stressful. Like Goldilocks tasting the porridges, you want to find just the right options, not too cold and not too hot.

This stage of problem solving involves generating several possible solutions rather than narrowing them down. **Brainstorming** is a strategy to attempt to generate as many possibilities as you can without regard to their practicality. You want to turn off your critical voice and give yourself permission to be as creative as you possibly can. Your goal is to develop as many alternatives as you can. They don't have to make sense or lead to anything sensible, but sometimes silly ideas lead to practical solutions. There is also a sense of power and control that comes from feeling like you have dozens of different options, even if you are not interested in following most of them.

Nat, for example, feels trapped in a dead-end job. He hates his work, doesn't much like the people he works with, but can't figure out a way to get out and try something else. He earns a good wage, enjoys good benefits, and has seniority so he can't be fired. Unfortunately, he still feels miserable going to work each day. When pressed as to why he doesn't quit and try something else, he shrugs in frustration, saying only that he can't afford to quit. His expenses are too high and he could never find a job that pays this well. He feels trapped and understandably depressed.

With the prodding of a friend taking a stress management class, Nat is invited to try brainstorming alternatives. Here is his list below. As you can see, he started out thinking conventionally, but gradually loosened up and problem-solved more creatively.

- Renegotiate my schedule.
- Quit and go on unemployment.
- Borrow money and go to school full time.
- Ask to switch to another department.
- Request a change in job classification.
- Make some more friends at work.
- Cut my expenses so I can live on less.
- Change my wardrobe.
- Cover my office in plants so I feel like I'm helping things to grow.
- Take flute lessons as a distraction.
- Pretend I am living in a dream and that work is really an illusion.
- Join the circus.
- Sell everything I own and take a one-year sabbatical.

The point of this exercise, for Nat or for you, is not that this list will provide you with "The Answer"—the one, best solution to your problem—but rather that the process of doing this, of generating lots and lots of options, helps you to feel more freedom of choice. You are limited only by your imagination.

When brainstorming alternative solutions, either on your own or in small groups, follow these principles:

1. All ideas should be expressed and no idea is too wild to be listed. This **variety principle** encourages people to think of a wide range of possible solutions across various strategies or classes of approaches instead of focusing on only one or two narrow ideas.

2. Quantity is desired. Every idea that comes to mind should be expressed and listed (the **quantity principle**). The more ideas you generate, the more likely a reasonable solution will be found.

3. Combining ideas to improve solutions is highly desirable.

4. Criticism of any idea is discouraged as this inhibits the creative process.

DECISION MAKING   After a list of solutions has been proposed, the next step is to evaluate the potential for each solution to fulfill the goals. In the brainstorming exercise you generated (hopefully) around two dozen options and then circled those that struck you as most practical. These "finalists" are the ones that you want to give most serious consideration for implementation. Each one can be assessed according to its likelihood of meeting your desired goal(s). You would also want to consider how realistic it is for you to implement this plan: do you have the ability, resources, and skills that are needed?

As I mentioned earlier, sometimes it can be just as stressful selecting a best option among a number of choices as it is feeling like you have no choices at all. What if you make the wrong decision? What if you blow it and make a huge mistake? Of course both of these questions are based on the assumption that there is a "right" decision, and that it is possible to figure out what that is. All you can do is to collect all the information available, weigh the evidence as best you can, and then go for it. Eventually, you may discover that this was a good choice for you, or perhaps later learn that another course of action might have been preferable. A very important problem-solving skill is to make the best decision you can and then move on, regardless of the eventual outcome.

Micah found herself in the fortunate circumstance of having four different job offers upon graduating from college. While you might envy her situation, she was feeling absolutely terrified by her predicament. What if she made the wrong choice and picked a job that was not good for her?

FOR REFLECTION 7.3

Think of a problem that feels insurmountable to you now. This could be one that you declared in an earlier exercise, or one that comes to mind because you feel trapped and without many choices. Describe the problem below.

Brainstorming, list as many ways you could solve this problem as possible, without concern for whether they are sensible, logical, or useful. For now just concentrate on making a list that includes as many options as you can think of.

1.

2.

3.

4.

5.

6.

7.

8.

9.

10.

As an experiment, get together with a few classmates or friends, and try this exercise again. Tell them about your situation and ask them to brainstorm with you to generate creative solutions that could make a difference. Research has shown that groups are better able than individuals to come up with more possibilities and better ones. Add the ones from your group session below that were not developed during your individual session.

11.

12.

13.

14.

15.

16.

17.

18.

19.

20.

Now you have many choices you didn't have before. How does that feel? Even if most of the options are not something you would actually consider implementing, notice what a difference it makes to know that you do have alternatives other than those you had considered previously.

Go back over the lists above and circle the few alternatives that do strike you as potentially useful.

In order to help her to narrow her choices to the best option, she decided to quantify the alternatives in terms of her main priorities. She created a table that included her main values in a job and then examined each of the four jobs in terms of how likely they were to satisfy those values. Since not all the values were equally important, she weighted them according to whether they were important (+1) or extremely important (+2). You can see from her chart below that things like a high salary and flexible hours were not as important to her (ranked +1) as those that provided her with opportunities for growth, supervision, and challenges (+2).

After assigning weightings to each of the values most important to her, Micah next ranked each of the jobs on a 1 to 10 scale (10 being perfect, 1 being awful). She made these assessments based on considerable research she had done on the web, during her interviews, and in conversations she had with employees of each company.

TABLE 7.2

Job Value	Weight	Job 1	Job 2	Job 3	Job 4
High salary	1	8	5	1	3
Flexible hours	1	2	6	2	7
Opportunities for learning and growth	2	3	8	4	6
Good supervision	2	3	9	5	5
Desirable location	1	6	5	7	6
Short commute	1	2	4	6	3
Compatible coworkers	2	4	8	4	5
Challenging work	2	5	9	5	6
Opportunities for advancement	2	3	9	5	6

By glancing at the scores, you can see that Job 2 had the highest ratings in terms of the values that were most important to Micah. The salary was average, the location was only minimally convenient, and the hours were fairly strict and demanding, but in the things that mattered most to her, the scores were near perfection.

This is only one example of a way to help narrow your choices when confronting a problem. It is not so much the quantification of the process that is critical as your attempt to objectively assess the options after gathering as much information as you can. In most problem-solving situations you face, you will need to make adjustments by either increasing or decreasing the number of viable alternatives.

SOLUTION IMPLEMENTATION AND VERIFICATION It is one thing to develop a plan and quite another to put it into action. You can have all the best options in the world for solving problems but they don't do you much good if they remain sitting on the drawing board.

In the next section we will be moving from a discussion of solving problems to one related to managing time more effectively. This was exactly the situation that Felicity was facing. With considerable effort, she had defined her major problem in life in terms of an equation: tasks > time. In other words, the number of things she had to accomplish during any week far exceeded the amount of time she had available.

Using several of the above-mentioned strategies, Felicity generated a list of possible solutions that she had, in turn, narrowed down to those that seemed most practical. Here is what she came up with.

- Take public transportation to work and school. This would increase commuting time but she could use the travel time productively to read and study.

- Form a study group. Getting together with several classmates would allow her to study more efficiently and productively.

- Quit her volunteer work. She had been volunteering ten hours per week at a women's shelter. She enjoyed the work but it now seemed like a luxury she could not afford.

- Meet with her boss to cut down her hours at her paid job.

- Reduce the number of classes she was taking each semester.

- Use a weekly planner to schedule her time more efficiently.

- Sell the Sony PlayStation that was taking up so much of her discretionary time.

Note that none of the options are mutually exclusive. In reviewing the possibilities, Felicity had determined which ones she was willing to do and which ones she was not. She also combined several of them into a plan that would both reduce her commitments and increase her discretionary time. This would significantly reduce the stress in her life.

The key dimension will be actually following through on her commitment. It is easy to say what you intend to do, but quite another thing to do it—and do it every day thereafter.

FOR REFLECTION 7.4

Based on the problems you have been thinking about during the reading of this chapter, decide on one thing that you are prepared to do that gets you one step closer to your ultimate goal. If you want to lose weight, for example, say what you intend to do that is specific, attainable, and measurable. If you want to reduce stress in some way, declare how you intend to do that.

Write your commitment below.

It is one thing to make a private commitment of your intentions. It makes you even more accountable if you make a public declaration—with witnesses. You can do this in class, or in small groups, if your instructor provides an opportunity. Otherwise you can get together with family or friends and tell them about what you intend to do. You will find it a lot harder to make excuses, procrastinate, or fail to follow through when others are monitoring your progress.

Time Management and Stress

Time management is actually a form of life management. Controlling your life means controlling your time, and controlling your time means controlling the events in your life. Time is the most important resource for anyone alive, yet it can never be saved or stored.

Time management can be described as the act of organizing your schedule in such a way that you accomplish your desired goals efficiently and effectively. It is not about nervously watching the clock and obsessively calculating your efficiency—which would make you even more stressed—but about how to focus your energy on accomplishing the most valuable goals on a daily basis.

The Value of Time

If you think about it, time is all you really have. Nothing else really belongs to you. Even your tenure on this planet is temporary and fleeting, a mere blip in the grand scheme of things.

FOR REFLECTION 7.5

Before you can manage time, first you have to know how you spend it. Don't change any of the things you normally do, nor how and when you do them. Keep detailed track of all the things you do from the moment you awake until the moment you go to sleep. Carry a notebook with you at all times and record: (1) the time, (2) the activity, and (3) any quick thoughts or feelings about what you are doing, or not doing.

After spending three consecutive days keeping track of how you spend your time, write some notes to yourself about what you learned from this activity. Pay particular attention to some things that surprised you in terms of how much time you devote to certain activities. In particular, focus on aspects of your time that you would most like to change.

Example of entries in a time log:

Time	Activity	Reactions
7.18 AM	Woke up. Lounged in bed. Listened to the radio.	Guilt, indulgence
7.37 AM	Bathroom chores	In a fog
7.50 AM	Back to bed	Still tired
9.01 AM	Rushed to get dressed and out of apartment	Late again
10.04 AM	Sitting in class	Harried; still tired

You can spend your time doing practically whatever you want, within reason. You can feel happy or miserable, satisfied or frustrated. You can be productive or not. There is really no such thing as "wasting time" since you can choose to use it any way you want. One person might view being camped out in front of the television or computer as a complete squandering of time since she might prefer to be doing something more "active" or "useful." Another person might see spending time at work a total waste since it doesn't allow for much freedom. Regardless of what others think, time can be spent taking naps, talking on the phone, reading books, going for walks, traveling or staying still, working or playing. All of it has value in the sense that it does something for you, whether that be rest or stimulation. There are two key questions to consider.

- How do you want to spend *your* time?

- What is your time worth to you?

These two questions are actually linked. How much your time is worth may determine how you want to use it, as well as where and how. If you see time as something that is virtually endless, that can be squandered at will, that you have in great supply, then you probably won't be very careful in the decisions you make. This can depend on your age, your health, and your life situation.

FOR REFLECTION 7.6

Wasting Time

List five ways that you most often waste time engaged in behaviors or activities that don't seem productive or all that fun and satisfying.

1.

2.

3.

4.

5.

Cross out those items listed that you feel ready and prepared to eliminate and reclaim more time to do the things you really want to do.

Melody is 20 years old but feels like she has just started her life; she has nothing pressing that she is headed toward. Whether she spends time studying, hanging out with friends, or working in a part-time job, it is all the same to her. She's got plenty of time to make up her mind about what she wants to do with her life and has no wish to rush things.

Hanh, on the other hand, is the same age but he is in a great hurry. To him, it feels like time is running out; he doesn't want to waste a precious second. He knows just what he wants to do and how he wants to do it. He sees Melody standing outside class sometimes, chatting with people, talking on her phone, just staring out into space, and he shakes his head in wonderment. Hanh doesn't feel like he has a spare moment for such frivolous things: there are hundreds of tasks to take care of and never enough time to do them.

Both of these individuals are entitled to their individualized attitude about time. You can readily see that the particular view you have about time—whether it is precious or limitless, whether you have freedom or not to decide how it is spent—will guide how much it is worth to you and how you want to spend it.

Each of us walks through life with a view about what time is worth. Your particular opinion on this subject depends on several factors, most notably how much you want to do in the time allotted to you. Stress can develop from either not having enough time to accomplish everything you want to do or from not having enough meaningful, satisfying things to fill the available time. Before I present specific skills for managing time, I will present the following principles of time management. Don't be quickly turned off by these big words. These principles will prepare you for managing and cherishing the most valuable thing in your life—time.

VOICE OF THE AUTHOR 7.1

During my college years, I began to notice my patterns of procrastination. I often boasted of not studying for a particular exam until the last minute and still obtaining decent grades in front of my roommates. When I came to the United States to pursue my graduate degrees, I continued to practice procrastination until I started to suffer health issues such as stomach cramps and acid reflux. I wish I could relive those days with more self-discipline and time management skills I am writing about now. Looking back, I believe I was addicted to the rush of adrenalin, almost like a drug that I was unconsciously hooked on. How I wish I could have learned the danger of procrastination earlier and stopped procrastination before it cost a health toll.

FOR REFLECTION 7.7

How do you know if you are experiencing some degree of "time stress"? Ask yourself several questions suggested by Elkin (1999).

1. Do you have enough time to do the things that are most important to you, especially to spend quality time with friends and family?

2. Do you feel bored and restless much of the time, with little passion and excitement about your day's activities?

3. Are you constantly rushing to complete tasks and often doing things at the last minute?

4. Are you late for a lot of meetings and appointments?

5. Do you not have enough time to do the things that you enjoy the most?

6. Are you inclined to plan and prioritize the major things that you need to accomplish?

7. Are you able to say no to people who make demands of your time that are beyond what you can reasonably handle?

If you answered "No" to more than a few of these items, that is a good indication that you've got a problem with time-management issues.

Six Principles for Time Management

THE 80/20 RULE   The 80/20 Rule is also referred to as the "Pareto Principle," named after the Italian economist Vilfredo Pareto, who observed in 1906 that 80% of the land in Italy was owned by 20% of the population. This rule describes a surprising relationship between reward and effort in real life, because it suggests that 80% of what you do may contribute only 20% of what you achieve in life. This rule forces you to reallocate attention to those most valuable activities instead of spending time on the tasks that may bring you pleasure but no long-term rewards.

Do the following. List all the activities you did during a day and ask yourself which activities are very important and which can be completely ignored. You may be surprised at the discovery that 80% of the things you did were not very helpful to your productivity or personal happiness. This is what happens to most people. Remember that all tasks take time to do. Doing those trivial activities will not bring you pride and satisfaction and will often give you a false sense of achievement that you have finished a lot of activities.

To apply the 80/20 rule, make a list of the most important goals, projects, and tasks. Determine to spend more and more time concentrating on finishing those few areas that can really make a huge difference in your life and career, and less and less time on activities that produce little or no value.

Another application of the 80/20 rule is the observation that you usually complete 80% of a day's work in 20% of the time. Why is that you are so efficient during this 20% of the time? It is very likely that you do them during the time when you are most focused and alert. Everyone has a preferable time for work. For some, they enjoy working at night while others enjoy working during the morning hours. You are advised to find this period of time and get most of your work accomplished.

PARKINSON'S LAW   British historian C. Northcote Parkinson analyzed why large organizations including government agencies become less efficient and more bureaucratic with time, and developed the famous "Parkinson's Law" (Parkinson, 1957). The law states that "work expands so as to fill the time available for its completion." One piece of evidence to support the law comes from the observation that as Britain's overseas empire declined in importance, the number of employees at the Colonial Office increased. According to Parkinson, there is no or little relationship between the work to be done and the amount of resources allocated to it. Parkinson's Law could be made even more general, as: "The demand upon a resource always expands to fill the resource."

How can you apply this principle to managing your time? First of all, beware of this law. You are hoping that giving yourself more time is a sure way to secure the quality of your work. Based on my experience, that is not always true. The deadline for submitting term papers for my classes is often set for the Monday of the last week of the semester. I have noticed that most of the students have to finish their papers the night before the submission. One semester, I changed the deadline for a term paper from the fifteenth to the tenth week; once again, many of the students worked very hard the night before and completed the papers. I noticed two things. First, the quality of the papers was not dramatically worse for the earlier deadline group. Second, not many people had trouble completing their work once they learned the consequences of not being able to fulfill this assignment.

Here we need to differentiate between haste to finish the work and striving to complete a project under certain time pressure. Having too much time on hand often leads to low motivation and laziness. However, too little time will cause stress and sloppy work. While it is great to learn that masterpieces take time to write, it is important to learn when to stop. If Parkinson's Law suggests that people tend to be less efficient given too much time, the principle we'll discuss next will suggest that you'll be more efficient when time is scarce.

THE PRINCIPLE OF FORCED EFFICIENCY   The gist of this principle is that "There is never enough time to do everything, but there is always enough time to do the most important thing" (Tracy, 2004). In today's world, you must feel that you'll never have enough time to finish all the things you want to do. Don't worry! Everybody else has the same feeling and it will never change. Yet you and everyone else who is reading this book must have the following experience. A deadline for an important school project was quickly approaching. You realized that failing to finish this project would have painful consequences. After evaluating all the competing tasks, you decided to put them away for a short while, completely focusing on this major task. *Voila!* You did it successfully. The above scenario suggests that we always can find time to complete the most important task. The question is: Are you willing to make a decision about what is the most important thing to do right now?

The principle of forced efficiency is related to a theory of business management and improvement originally developed by Israeli business consultant Eliyahu M. Goldratt, who cowrote the best-selling book *The Goal* (Goldratt & Cox, 1992). This is called the theory of constraint (TOC). TOC suggests that like a chain that breaks at its weakest link, in a complex system (such as a corporation or a human being) at any time, there is often only one aspect that is limiting its ability to achieve more of its goal. For the system to attain any significant improvement, that constraint must be identified and the whole system must be managed with it in mind.

To apply TOC in time management, you need to identify the weakest link or the limiting factor in your life or career. Ask yourself this question: What can I and only I do that, if done well, will make a real difference in my life? Once you identify this limiting factor, spend most of your time on it until you make a breakthrough. Often, working on the major constraint in your life will help you achieve your major goals more quickly than scattering your time aimlessly on many different projects.

THE MOMENTUM PRINCIPLE   The momentum principle states that it takes tremendous energy to overcome the initial inertia and resistance to start a project, but once it is started, it takes much less energy to keep moving. It is said that when space shuttles are launched, 75% of the fuel is required to take the shuttle off the ground and out into the atmosphere. Once there, the remaining 25% of the fuel is sufficient to complete a mission. "Momentum" is a physics term; it refers to the quantity of motion that an object has. A sports team that is "on the move" has momentum. If an object is in motion ("on the move") then it has momentum. When you start a project, you start to generate momentum. No matter how small a piece of the project you start, it accumulates momentum. The "warm-up effect" refers to a phenomenon in sports when an athlete experiences loss of momentum after being replaced by a teammate. It will take a few minutes for that person to get into his/her most effective state of mind and body.

Here are three suggestions for applying this principle. First, become very clear about your most important goals in the long term and the short term. Break down your goals into doable projects. Start right away on a project. Since a project consists of several tasks, start on a task. Don't stop until you finish a task. Second, remember that the early part of your work is more demanding than the latter part since you have to overcome much psychic inertia. Stick to it until momentum develops. Finally, reevaluate your goals from time to time to make sure that what you are doing is aligned with your long-term goals. What you concentrate on will grow with each task. Your job becomes easier and easier with more and more practice.

THE CONCEPT OF PSYCHIC RAM   David Allen (2003), a well-known productivity and time management expert, observes that human beings, like computers, have a limited amount of RAM, or random access memory, which is what your computer uses to run its applications. Psychic RAM can be used to describe the mental working space that is used to run your life. When you clutter your psychic RAM to hold all the "woulds, coulds, shoulds, need-tos, ought-tos and might-want-tos," there is no space left for solving more important problems and creating new ideas. That is why Allen suggests that you write down all these self-commitments and unfinished projects and organize them on paper or in a document. Writing them down and reviewing them at a specified time may free up your mind, and allows you to focus single-mindedly on one task at a time.

Plutarch said that the "mind is not a vessel to be filled but a fire to be kindled." My PhD advisor Dr. Singer always puts down what he wants to do in his calendar or on

Post-it notes. Once he asked me to complete an assignment. Before I left, he asked me if I had written it down. I boasted that I had good memory. Later, events proved that my memory was not as good as I thought. Years later, I have learned the lesson that the shortest pencil is better than the most potent memory.

THE PRINCIPLE OF SUGGESTION: OUT OF SIGHT, OUT OF MIND This principle states good intentions to manage priorities based on your goals may be futile unless you always keep the goals and priorities "in mind and in sight." You may ask: How I can do that? To answer that question, you need to learn something from the TV advertisers. They are doing so well in reminding us of what benefits their products may bring us if you use them that many of you automatically get hooked on them without even knowing why you've bought them. In other words, you should advertise the important goals to your mind through your five senses. Since vision is the most dominant source of information, visual reminders can be most powerful.

I used this technique to earn tenure at my university. Since I got a slow start in publishing, my dean talked to me about the urgency of publishing more articles, and the number of articles I should publish before the deadline for submitting my promotion materials. I requested that she write down the number of articles for me to complete by the date. I laminated that hand-written note and posted it on the wall facing my desk. That note served as a spur for the three years before my tenure. As a result, I was more focused on doing research and submitting reports for publications. I ended up publishing more articles than was required of me.

So, to use this principle effectively, use the following ideas. First, figure out what you want to do and write it down. You can also draw a picture about what you plan to accomplish. Second, display that write-up or the picture in an obvious place for you to see every day. Third, ask your friends or relatives for help. Declare to them what you plan to do in the hope that this public announcement will bring some unintended supervision from them and help get your work done more quickly. Make sure that those people are supportive and positive. Sometimes the ridicule or criticism of your close relatives or friends is enough to dampen your enthusiasm for the goals you aim to achieve.

Procrastination

Do you find yourself waiting until the last minute to complete a task, get a job done, or finish your work? Procrastinating, or putting off what you can do today to tomorrow or

---

VOICE OF STRESS 7.1

Twenty-Three-Year-Old Female College Student, Living at Home

It seems that the more I have to do, the less I do. I will put off doing anything until the very last second. I can't help it. I'll drive myself crazy doing meaningless activities, such as surfing the net, downloading music, looking for guys on match. com. In reality, I have like two papers and a huge project due in a week. This procrastination thing I have going on is killing me! It's like I am just pushing myself to the edge, and just before I fall off, I take a tiny step back.

Right now I am supposed to be working on a project for school and I'm talking to you instead. I need to find a job. I have to register for summer school. I have a 15-page paper for my sociology class. Yet I spent this whole weekend either partying or sleeping. It drives my friends crazy. But I seem to thrive on the pressure that I produce for myself by putting everything off. It totally stresses me out when I realize just how much I have to do in a short period of time. Maybe I really don't want to do the work? I don't know. I always get my work done; sometimes I'll have to skip class because of it. I hate myself for doing it, but I can't stop!

the next day, is not a matter of being short of time, but rather is an inability to commit oneself to immediate action. It is *not* the same as being lazy, since the one in five people who struggle with this problem have the best of intentions but feel paralyzed to motivate themselves toward action (Szalavitz, 2003). Procrastinating is much worse among college students. According to Steel (2007), 80%–95% of college students procrastinate, with 75% of them considering themselves procrastinators. They tell themselves, for example, that they work better under pressure, or they minimize the importance of the goal being completed.

Procrastination is a self-perpetuating cycle of self-defeating behavior that keeps stress operating at high levels. People who engage in this pattern tell themselves that there is no reason to change since they've managed to survive this long without altering their inefficient patterns. There are also a number of "benefits" or **secondary gains** that they enjoy. These are hidden but self-reinforcing payoffs that make it difficult to change the behavior.

1. Procrastinators have a ready excuse for failure or poor performance. After all, if you get a grade lower than expected or do poorly on an assignment, you can always shrug and say, "What do you expect? I did it at the last minute."

2. They can enjoy the thrill of racing to meet a deadline. There is a sense of drama and excitement associated with trying to finish just under the wire. It is an artificial way to create excitement in one's life, to make a game out of seeing how close you can get to the edge without falling off.

3. You can exhibit a degree of control over tasks for which you feel reluctant or resentful. It is a way of saying that you do things on your own terms, even if it hurts you in the end.

4. By putting off things that you don't want to do, you can get attention. Sometimes you can even invite others to bail you out at the last minute.

5. You can drive other people crazy. Procrastination can give you a sense of power and manipulation when putting things off bothers other people more than it does you. It can represent a form of rebellion and acting-out toward authority figures.

6. It can distract you from other things going on in your life. Not only can you enjoy the "luxury" of avoiding things you don't want to do, but once you launch into the frenzy needed to complete the work you can also avoid how empty and unexciting other aspects of your life might be. It operates as a kind of diversion. Also, as long as you don't do the task you can keep thinking about it, which prevents you from having to think about other things you might wish to avoid.

7. You have a great excuse for not taking care of other responsibilities. When you are working under a tight time constraint, you can tell others that you have to neglect other chores because of a looming deadline.

People tend to procrastinate for a number of reasons, some of them good (avoiding tasks that are not meaningful or relevant) and some of them self-defeating. Often such behavior results from fear of failure, perfectionism, and benefits the person enjoys as a result of avoiding action.

With all of these tremendous "benefits" you might justifiably wonder why you would want to give procrastination up? After all, it provides so many apparently wonderful excuses and distractions.

Perhaps you're right. Maybe you don't need to change anything about the way you do things—as long as it keeps working for you. There are people who spend their whole lives working within a procrastinating lifestyle and still manage to get things done, more or less. Besides, there's little I can tell you that could change this pattern until such time that it no longer works for you. That's the thing about secondary gains: they keep you doing things that have destructive results because of their underlying reinforcing properties. It isn't until your system stops working for you that you will initiate other strategies.

FOR REFLECTION 7.8

Identify a task or job that you have been avoiding or putting off for some time—completing an assignment, cleaning a room, confronting someone, taking care of unfinished business. In spite of your best intentions, you can't seem to motivate yourself to complete this task; every time you get started, you find a reason to drop it and do something else. Meanwhile, it looms large in your mind. You *think* about doing it. You *want* to get it done. But you just can't seem to find the time—or the motivation.

What might be the secondary gains or benefits that you enjoy as a result of engaging in procrastination?

Based on this new awareness, what has changed for you in terms of how you think about this behavior?

Causes of Procrastination

There are many problems in life—and procrastination is one of them—in which knowing and understanding what is going on does not necessarily lead to change. Nevertheless, it is useful to have some grasp of the reasons why you might deliberately put off a task that will continue to weigh on your mind and increase the stress in your life. The most obvious explanation is that you don't find the particular activity to be very engaging, exciting, meaningful, or relevant. It is funny how you have no trouble finding the time, and the motivation to do the things that you most enjoy. It *is* hard to get motivated about completing something that is just plain boring.

You learned in the previous chapter about the ways that your cognitive activity (internal thoughts) strongly dictate how you feel about anything that you experience. If you are telling yourself things like "There is no sense in trying because I probably won't do well anyway," or "It won't help to get the work done ahead of time," then this is going to have a significant impact on procrastinating behavior. Under such circumstances, it feels futile to do anything any differently.

Perfectionistic attitudes also exacerbate procrastination. If you demand that you do something perfectly, then you are going to feel ambivalent about approaching an assignment. You will keep putting things off until you feel that you can do the most perfect job imaginable (which will never happen). It is important to make sure that the expectations you hold for your performance are realistic, and even desirable.

Distractions come into play with procrastination as well. If you operate in a noisy, chaotic environment, with lots of interruptions from phones, email, visitors, play activities, television, and the like, it would be hard to complete almost any task. Every time you think about getting back to work, you can always find something else you'd rather do more. Procrastination is on the rise today probably because there are more distractions (e.g., easier to access internet video games and email) and more tasks lack structure and require self-regulation.

Distractions can also be internally as well as externally based. If you are struggling with anxiety, depression, loneliness, or other strong negative emotions, you are going to find it hard to concentrate on anything for very long. It is difficult to remain focused, and when you do get going, momentum doesn't last long. By the time you start a task, you forget why it was so important in the first place. Or it doesn't seem to matter much anyway. When you are already distraught and anxious you might think to yourself that anything you do is futile.

FOR REFLECTION 7.9

Most of the time, you procrastinate about those things that are not a priority for you. They have been assigned by others, may involve tasks that are not of direct relevance to your life, or may seem like they are stupid or a waste of time. However, what about those times when you put off doing things that you know are really important to you? You may have told yourself, and others, a dozen times that you really wanted to complete the activity, yet you can't seem to find the time or energy to get it done. Why would you choose to hurt yourself, and prevent success, by not taking care of business that you say is important to you?

List some reasons why this might be the case for you.

Overcoming Procrastination

Let's assume that you do want to do something about your tendency to put things off, since it increases your stress and compromises your productivity and efficiency. The first step to overcoming a problem is to admit that you have one. Given that about 90% of college students engage in procrastination in some area of their lives, it may be that you are not prepared to do anything about it at this time. That's fine—as long as you are prepared to live with the consequences.

Assuming this is a behavior that you would like to change, it might be helpful to look at procrastination as a form of feedback. It is a way of telling you that you don't want to do something, even though you might say you do. If you keep putting something off, or can't manage to finish a task, maybe there is a good reason for this. The first step would be to determine whether you really want to take on this challenge.

Of course, procrastination has a way of significantly increasing your levels of stress. In some cases you may spend a lot more time avoiding a task than it would take to actually complete it. As you have learned, this can happen for a number of reasons, such as perfectionistic tendencies, unrealistic beliefs, and fears of letting yourself or others down (Knaus, 2002).

One way to take care of the problem is to take the unfinished task off your list of things to do. In other words, after a predetermined period of time, if you have not done what you said was so important, then it must not be that important after all—otherwise you would have done it!

It is also critical to look at the context for your procrastination: Is it a chronic style, or rather is it situational depending on certain activities? It is a different problem for one person who almost always puts things off until the last moment versus someone who usually gets things done except those that involve a particular person, or a certain class or job.

If one factor operating in your avoidance is a fear of failure (and often this operates below conscious awareness) then the problem is likely to persist until you address this issue. It is more than a little ironic that procrastination actually leads to what is most feared—that is, lowered performance—even if gives you a ready excuse afterwards ("Well, sure I got a C on that assignment, but I did it at the last minute").

Since procrastination is often a lifestyle issue, meaning that it is part of the way you characteristically function, you may have to make a major commitment to changing this pattern. And in order to do that you would have to be prepared for substantial changes in the way that you manage your life. This means clarifying your priorities and setting more realistic goals. It also means thinking of yourself in a completely new way (and teaching others to do so)—someone who gets things done on time (or early!) rather than waiting until the last minute.

The most obvious way to overcome procrastination is to follow the Nike slogan: just do it! It is one thing to talk about action, but another to follow through. Rather than worrying about where to start, or even how to start, just begin somewhere, anywhere, to get momentum going. Take, as one example, a resolution to begin a diet or regular exercise program. This may be something you've thought about for some time, maybe even started on several occasions but couldn't manage to sustain the commitment. If you want to break this cycle, all you have to do is begin, right now. Put down the book and go for a walk.

VOICE OF STRESS 7.2

Twenty-Three-Year-Old Male Student

I have so much to do that I'm stressed all of the time. Well, not when I'm partying or distracting myself. I guess you could say that I waste a lot of time, but it doesn't really feel like that. I like to work out, hang out with friends, listen to music, drink, or do whatever I can to avoid being stressed. When I am really feeling like I need a major break, I'll just check out. I might play an online video game for a few hours or check out a bunch of porn sites. Those are really distracting! My girlfriend gets pissed, but she doesn't understand; it's just my way to relieve the pressure. She can take a yoga class or something, I'm not into that. I take 12 credits. I'm a teaching assistant. Plus I have a job outside of school. My grades are okay, so I figure that I can do whatever I want to chill out in my spare time. Yeah, it can get out of hand sometimes. I've spent an entire night playing poker online and then missed class in the morning. And those porn sites—I get so many pop-ups on my computer now that I almost feel like giving them up. But that probably won't happen. I'm not hurting anyone and I'm totally relieving my stress, so I'm less likely to hurt anyone.

Strategies for Time Management

Once you know you have a problem matching the time available with all the things you've got to get done, what do you do about it?

If I provide you with a list of strategies to take greater control over time, would you actually use them? What if they involved making serious changes in the ways you conduct your life?

I ask these questions at the outset because merely providing you with tools will not do much good unless you are motivated to use them. If you are enjoying the benefits of procrastination and not suffering terribly as a result of your time irresponsibility, why would you want to initiate changes? You won't—you'll read over this material, nod your head that it all sounds like good ideas to you, but keep doing what you are doing. And that's fine if you are fine with your levels of productivity and satisfaction. But for those of you who would like to become (1) more efficient, (2) less harried and stressed, and (3) more productive, I present several helpful methods.

Differentiate between Important Tasks and Urgent Tasks

Author Stephen Covey classifies tasks according to whether they are important or urgent or both (Covey, Merrill, & Merrill, 1994) using the four-quadrant matrix of importance and urgency (see Table 7.3). This classification system recognizes that important tasks may not be urgent, and urgent tasks are not necessarily important. When people work on tasks in Quadrant 1 that are both important and urgent, they tend to be focused and may reap a focus dividend (Mullainathan & Shafir, 2013), since important tasks are associated with the achievement of one's own goals. Quadrant 2 lists the items that are non-urgent but important (see Table 7.4). These are the ones people tend to neglect and postpone. Putting off important but not urgent tasks is like borrowing a loan that you need to pay back in the future. Each day when you are in debt, you are paying interest for the loan. Economists Mullainathan and Shafir (2013) suggest that time scarcity like money scarcity impedes our cognitive faculty that could be devoted to more valuable tasks. In Chapter 6, you have learned how to create meaning by clarifying your values and reallocating your resources according to what matters to you most. Once you identify those most valuable tasks, prioritize your time and set goals to achieve them. Quadrant 3 lists tasks that are urgent but not important, for example, activities that demand immediate attention, and are often associated with the achievement of someone else's goals. Quadrant 4 deals with tasks that are neither important nor urgent. They are often used for tension relief from time-pressured and important activities. I encourage you to organize your tasks based on the Covey method.

TABLE 7.3 Importance vs. urgency task matrix

Importance\Urgency	Urgent	Not Urgent
Important	Quadrant 1: Urgent & Important	Quadrant 2: Not Urgent & Important
Not Important	Quadrant 3: Urgent & Not Important	Quadrant 4: Not Urgent & Not Important

Do Less, Not More

A major source of stress in modern life is the split and partial attention you give to every aspect of your life. Multitasking is the norm. Have you ever noticed yourself doing any of the following?

- You complete your homework or an assignment while watching television and talking on the phone.

- You talk to a dear friend or family member while grooming yourself and simultaneously thinking about something altogether different.

- You chat with a friend on the phone while cruising the web, texting, answering email, or playing video games.

- You eat a meal while reading the paper or a magazine, plus planning the day's activities.

Nobody or nothing in your life receives the full and complete attention and honor that he/she/it deserves. Not only does the quality of relationships, work, and enjoyment suffer, but this split attention is a major source of stress. Rather than getting more done during such frenzies of multiple activities, you end up compromising both the pleasure and the ultimate quality of the experience.

Just as an experiment, try altering your usual routines by doing only one thing at a time. This will be very difficult because of the habits you have established and the longstanding belief that you are getting more done by attending to so many things at the same time.

Monitor throughout the day how often you are splitting your attention between multiple tasks, doing none of them with particular relish. When you eat a meal, become mindful of just that activity. When you are involved in a conversation with someone, give him or her your full attention. If you reach a point of feeling bored, then end the conversation and do something else with your full attention.

Figure Out What's Getting in the Way

It's easy to say to yourself that you want to manage your time better. But what is getting in the way of you doing that? If you kept a time log for a few days as suggested earlier, you have some understanding of what is blocking your attempts to become more time-savvy. Some of the most common problems are as follows:

- *Reluctance or inability to delegate tasks to others.* You may have the feeling that you have to do everything yourself, that nobody else can do things as well as you can. Even if this were true (which it assuredly is not) you would run yourself ragged.

- *Unrealistic expectations and feelings of perfectionism.* This stems from the belief that you can never meet your exacting standards. You won't let go of a task because you are rarely satisfied with your performance.

- *Taking on too many tasks.* If you aren't good at estimating how long it will take to do things, and balancing that with how much discretionary time you have available, then you're going to feel overwhelmed.

- *Insufficient support.* You can't handle things alone. You've got to have a network of friends, peers, and colleagues who can help you out during times of stress.

- *Unhealthy lifestyle.* You may organize your life in such a way that you are doomed to always be running behind.

- *Failure to prioritize.* You might be spending too much time on things that don't matter much to you, which leaves relatively less time for the things that you say matter most.

- *Distractions and time wasters.* If you are constantly being interrupted, you'll find it hard to get anything done. There are more distractions than ever for people trying to concentrate on completing one important task. Messages come through on the internet. The cell phone is constantly ringing. It takes a lot of self-discipline to voluntarily cut yourself off from such distractions.

One example of what often gets in the way of college students is the prevalence of video games, computer games, and web-based games that eat up hours of time each day (not to mention additional time spent with Facebook, television, online porn, and the Internet). I don't mean spending an hour or two of mindless or stimulating entertainment to relax and decompress after a difficult day, but rather those who spend several hours, even 24-hour stretches, immersed in a virtual world. The problem has become so serious that mental health experts want to classify extreme gaming as an addiction, determined by the following symptoms: (1) playing more than three hours a day, (2) thinking about the game(s) continuously throughout the day, (3) losing sleep or neglecting work because of the gaming, (4) feeling a loss of control over how often games are played.

In order to become untethered from the virtual world, it is critical that you are honest with yourself about the amount of time you are spending (wasting?) immersed in technology. This means being more aware of what you are doing with your time and whether you are satisfied with the current situation or wish to make some changes.

Get a Calendar

Whether you use a digital scheduler (PDA), smartphone, daily planner, week-at-a-glance, or a paper pocket calendar, get in the habit of filling in all the deadlines that you have looming in the future. This can include when papers are due and when exams are scheduled, but also commitments you have made to friends and coworkers. Fill in as much detail as you can, not only about work assignments but also play dates and leisure activities. It is important to have a full grasp of anything that is likely to occupy your time.

VOICE OF STRESS MANAGEMENT 7.2

Twenty-Seven-Year-Old Male Technology Worker

I think I manage my stress level well. I am aware of what I need to get done and then plan accordingly. The day planner is an awesome tool. If I have a big project, I simply break it down into small projects that I'll do over a period of time. When I was an undergraduate I planned everything ahead of time and was always able to turn things in on time. When I had a big paper due, for example, I would make sure to work on it a little bit at a time. If it was going to be ten pages, I would write two pages per day. I played basketball too, so it was important to keep my grades up and have time to practice, study, and party!

I never got how anyone could just put things off until the last minute. That kind of stress would drive me crazy. My roommate spent more time sleeping and partying than anything else. He ended up dropping out in our senior year. Major bummer: he sells furniture now. I'm still a planner. I really don't let stress get to me. When something comes up that I didn't plan for, then whatever happens, happens! Stressing out about it won't get me anywhere.

Make a List and Check it Twice

Probably the single best way to take charge of the time in your life is to plan more wisely and systematically. Make a list of the major tasks that you want to get done during the day. Circle those items that are most important to you—those that are absolutely critical.

Check off the items as you get them done. As you cross the item off your list, note how good it feels.

Review the list at the end of the day. If there are items on there that you couldn't complete, consider revising the list for the next day so that the goals are more realistic.

Figure Out Where You Waste Time

If you have been monitoring your activities as suggested previously, you have a pretty good idea of where you waste time. Remember, this assessment is based on your own values related to what you consider important: *you* are the judge of what is considered wasteful, and what is not.

It is up to you to choose what is most meaningful and what is wasteful, but keep in mind that time is always limited so you have to make wise decisions about where and how you most want to expend your energy. Be especially careful of the ways that technology can become more a master of your life rather than a servant. The term "life hacking" was invented to describe ways that people are trying to reclaim their lives from their computers, digital assistants, and other electronic devices (Flynn, 2006).

Make the Best of "Down Time"

There are certain times of the day in which you may feel stuck doing nothing of consequence, perhaps during commutes in traffic or waiting for appointments. There is something to be said for reducing stress by avoiding too much multitasking and always having to feel productive, but there are still opportunities to use "down time" in more meaningful ways. This could involve listening to books on tape when in the car, or carrying around a novel to read at idle times when you want to relax. Time management is not only about being more productive, but about getting the most satisfaction and enjoyment out of your day.

Make Some Necessary Cuts

If you are finding it difficult to get everything done, and this happens consistently, then something is wrong: you are taking on more than you can do. It is time to make some cuts—to decide what has to go. I realize this could be painful, but you have made some poor decisions regarding what you could reasonably handle. Some possibilities: drop a class; work fewer hours; cut back on commitments and stop taking on new ones; learn to say "no."

Find Balance

Managing time is not just about getting work done, but about balancing your life in such a way that you are enjoying yourself and the things you do. When taking inventory of the different categories that take up your time, consider how much you would ideally like to allocate for the following activities.

- *School.* This involves not just attending class, but time spent reading, studying, preparing, and reflecting on subjects.

- *Work.* If you are working, part time or full time, a job takes priority to take care of economic needs.

- *Commuting.* Depending on where you live, and your transportation options, time spent in the car or on public transport can take a big chunk out of your day. This is an example of time that can be structured for relaxation or entertainment (listening to music), self-improvement (listening to a book on tape), conducting business or socializing (on the phone), or just turning your brain off.

- *Family time.* Spending time with your parents, siblings, children, and extended family is far more than obligation—these are the relationships that can sustain you.

FOR REFLECTION 7.10

Do More of What You Value the Most

Make a list of the ten things you absolutely love to do the most.

Things I love to do	Rank order	How often	More or less
1.			
2.			
3.			
4.			
5.			
6.			
7.			
8.			
9.			
10.			

In the column "Rank order," put the things that you love to do in order according to what is most important to you, and next most important, and so on. Place a "1" next to the item that is ranked highest, all the way through to 10.

In the column "How often" put down the number of times you have engaged in this activity in the past three days.

In the column "More or less" put down whether you wish you were doing this particular activity more often (+), less often (–), or whether you are happy with the current frequency (=).

Based on this review of your most cherished and valued activities in life, what do you conclude about the ways you prioritize your time?

(Source: Adapted from Simon, Howe, & Kirschenbaum, 1991)

- *Socializing.* Spending time with friends is among the most important use of your time. This is where you recharge your batteries, debrief after a stressful day, and let yourself go. Whether you enjoy going to parties, playing sports, going to movies or concerts, or just hanging out, it is crucial that you allow guilt-free opportunities to enjoy yourself with those you feel close to.

- *Love life.* If you have a partner, spouse, or girlfriend/boyfriend, you know that this relationship takes commitment if it is to flourish.

- *Leisure activities.* You likely have several outside interests, hobbies, or activities that are important to you. They also take time and devotion if you are to maintain your interest.

- *"Down time."* This includes those unscheduled transitions that occur between other activities when nothing whatsoever is scheduled. You require these cushions to gather your thoughts, recharge your batteries, and prepare for the next task.

Stop Complaining

You only make things worse when you whine and complain about not having enough time, or not allocating it wisely. Nobody really cares, or wants to hear your troubles; they've got enough of their own. Either do something constructive about getting your time more under control or just accept that this is going to be the way your life is—and get used to it.

SUMMARY

In this chapter, you've learned some important concepts about problem solving and time management. Since all the stressors can be regarded as problems, a thorough understanding of the problem-solving process is deemed essential to managing your stress.

Time management is another kind of problem-solving skill simply because you will never have enough time to do all the things you want to do. That's why the essence of time management is about identifying the priorities of life and devoting major segments of time to accomplish those. Several important topics of time management have been dealt with in this chapter, such as overcoming procrastination and inertia, learning to become a more effective problem solver, and making more efficient use of your time. Many of the strategies described in this chapter would require you to make a major commitment to altering your lifestyle and the way you conduct you daily business. This might sound wonderful on the pages of this text but involves considerable initiative on your part to implement the changes on a permanent basis.

QUESTIONS FOR REVIEW

1. Discuss the essence of problem solving and why problem-solving skills can be great stress–distress moderators.
2. Identify some of the barriers to effective problem solving.
3. List all the major components of a problem-solving approach.
4. Describe the major tasks during the problem-orientation stage of problem solving.

5. Describe the different ways you can look at a problem. Discuss what are the major goals during the stage of problem definition and formulation.
6. Discuss the principles of brainstorming for alternatives to solve a problem. Provide examples of barriers to the search for alternatives.
7. What may prevent individuals from taking action once solutions have been identified?
8. Discuss why some people don't manage their time effectively. What are the potential hidden barriers to their good use of time?
9. Describe the six principles of time management and discuss how they can help you manage your time more effectively.
10. Identify the major causes of procrastination.
11. Describe the Covey importance-urgency task matrix and develop a plan to use in organizing your daily tasks.
12. Discuss strategies you find most useful to reduce your stress and increase your productivity.

REFERENCES AND RESOURCES

Allen, D. (2003). *Ready for anything: 52 productivity principles for work and life*. New York, NY: Viking.

Bell, A. C., & D'Zurilla, T. J. (2009a). Problem-solving therapy for depression: A meta-analysis. *Clinical Psychology Review, 29*, 348–353.

Bell, A. C., & D'Zurilla, T. J. (2009b). The influence of social problem-solving ability on the relationship between daily stress and adjustment. *Cognitive Therapy Research, 33*, 439–448.

Chang, E. C., D'Zurilla, T. J., & Sanna, L. J. (2009). Social problem solving as a mediator of the link between stress and psychological well-being in middle-adulthood. *Cognitive Therapy Research, 33*, 33–49.

Covey, S., Merrill, A. R., & Merrill, R. R. (1994). *First things first: To live, to love, to learn, to leave a legacy*. New York, NY: Simon & Schuster.

D'Zurilla, T. J., & Nezu, A. M. (2007). *Problem-solving therapy: A positive approach to clinical intervention* (3rd ed.). New York, NY: Springer.

Elkin, A. (1999). *Stress management for dummies*. New York, NY: Wiley.

Eskin, M., Şavk, E., Uslu, M., & Küçükaydoğan, N. (2014). Social problem-solving, perceived stress, negative life events, depression and life satisfaction in psoriasis. *Journal of the European Academy of Dermatology and Venereology, 28*(11), 1,553–1,559.

Flynn, M. K. (2006, January 2). Pull the plug on tech distractions. *U.S. News and World Report*, p. 66.

Gellis, Z. D., & Kenaley, B. (2008). Problem-solving therapy for depression in adults: A systematic review. *Research on Social Work Practice, 18*(2), 117–131.

Goldratt, E. M., & Cox, J. (1992). *The goal: A process of ongoing improvement* (2nd ed.). Great Barrington, MA: North River Press.

Knaus, W. (2002). *Procrastination workbook*. Oakland, CA: New Harbinger.

Lazarus, R. S., & Folkman, S. (1984). *Stress, appraisal, and coping*. New York, NY: Springer.

Leahy, R. L. (2005). *The worry cure*. Toronto, Canada: Harmony.

Mullainathan, S., & Shafir, E. (2013). Scarcity: *Why having too little means so much*. New York, NY: Henry Holt.

Nezu, A. M., Nezu, C. M., & D'Zurilla, T. J. (2000). Problem-solving skills training. In G. F. Fink (Ed.), *Encyclopedia of stress* (Vol. 31, pp. 252–256). San Diego, CA: Academic Press.

Parkinson, C. N. (1957). *Parkinson's Law and other studies in administration*. Boston: Houghton Mifflin.

Simon, S., Howe, L., & Kirschenbaum, H. (1991). *Values clarification: A handbook of practical strategies for teachers and students*. New York, NY: Hart.

Steel, P. (2007). The nature of procrastination: A meta-analytic and theoretical review of quintessential self-regulatory failure. *Psychological Bulletin, 133*(1), 65–94.

Steel, P., & König, C. J. (2006). Integrating theories of motivation. *Academy of Management Review, 31*, 889–913.

Sullivan, K. T., Pasch, L. A., Johnson, M. D., & Bradbury, T. N. (2010). Social support, problem solving, and the longitudinal course of newlywed marriage. *Journal of Personality and Social Psychology, 98*(4), 631–644.

Szalavitz, M. (2003). Stand and deliver: Many procrastinators believe they work better under pressure. *Psychology Today*, July/August.

Tracy, B. (2004). *Time power: A proven system for getting more done in less time than you ever thought possible*. New York, NY: American Management Association.

Psychological and Spiritual Relaxation Methods

The mind has an amazing ability to control the processes of the body. Relaxation methods have been effective in helping people stay calm when they feel anxious, reduce tension, and even enhance performance in difficult circumstances. Whether in the context of mindfulness meditation, prayer, guided imagery, relaxation training, or self-hypnosis, all of the methods are best applied in a relatively quiet environment—one without too many distractions, in which you can feel both comfortable and focused. You will want to experiment with a number of these strategies in order to determine which ones work best for you.

Teachers from both ancient and modern times have admonished us to beware of our thoughts, since they can have profound effects on our well-being. As you learned in Chapter 6, we tend to become what we think about; what we think about often grows and expands with time. In this chapter, we will explore the impact of mental activities on the state of our subjective well-being. These include not only contributions from medicine and psychology, such as mindfulness meditation, thought control, imagery, muscle relaxation, and hypnosis, but also spiritual means that include mindfulness and prayer.

KEY QUESTIONS IN THE CHAPTER

- What do all psychological relaxation techniques share in common?

- What are altered states of consciousness and what forms do they take?

- What are some similarities and differences between the various imagery-based relaxation methods discussed in this chapter?

- What is the relationship between mindfulness and mindfulness meditation?

- What are some characteristics of mindfulness meditation as described by Hölzel and associates?

- What does research say about the benefits of mindfulness meditation? In particular, what are some functional and structural changes to the brain as a result of mindfulness meditation practice?

- How is imagery used to deal with chronic pain?

- What is autogenic training?

- What is the scientific basis for the benefits of prayer?

Prevention, Treatment, and Coping with Stress

"Relaxation" is a word we use so often that it may become ambiguous or even meaningless. What does it mean when you say that you are relaxed? Does it mean you feel calm, lazy, temporarily without stress, focused, or just sleepy? Do you mean your body is relaxed, or your mind?

Everyone yearns for the ability to feel relaxed at will, but very few individuals have the power to make this happen. If you wanted to relax yourself right now, how would you go about doing this?

Previous chapters have discussed some of the more common options that people report in helping themselves to relax, whether that involves taking a hot bath, going for a walk, chatting with friends, watching television, drinking a beer, or playing video games. Some of these methods work well on a consistent basis, with few negative side-effects; others provide relief only temporarily, with few enduring effects. In this chapter I review some of the major psychologically and spiritually based relaxation methods that have lasting results.

The understanding of relaxation has evolved over the years from a simple focus on muscle relaxation, or mere elimination of disturbing thoughts, to a more comprehensive notion of mental peacefulness characterized by the absence of stressful and unpleasant thoughts and decreased muscular tension (Payne, 2003). The good news is that the sensations of relaxation can be released by either a psychological approach, such as producing positive images in the mind, or a physiological approach, such as reducing the tension in muscles. Because many modern diseases such as hypertension and insomnia are related to stress, regular practices of relaxation techniques, either psychological or physiological, can achieve several objectives. First, relaxation techniques serve as preventative measures against any extra wear and tear brought about by modern-day stressors that bombard your body. Second, relaxation techniques may be used as effective ways of treatment of psychosomatic illnesses. Third, they can be used as coping methods to handle acute stressors in your daily life.

VOICE OF STRESS 8.1

Twenty-Nine-Year-Old Female Graduate Student

Sometimes I feel like my world is out of control. There is just so much to do. Being a graduate student, a wife, mother, and caretaker for my mother is too much. I don't remember the last time I did something just for me. I haven't even had a haircut in over a year! There are not enough hours in the day to get everything done.

Sometimes I fantasize about just waking up, getting in the car, and driving off. Maybe I could get a job at a resort in the Caribbean? I could be a tour guide in Europe! Sometimes these fantasies are what keep me going! They are entertaining to say the least.

I simply see no real way out. My marriage is not perfect, but I have no choice but to stay; I have no income of my own. My child is too young to do anything for himself. My mother is disabled. We have no family around who could help out. I feel trapped.

Luckily I have a great sense of humor and tend not to take things too seriously (although you'd never guess that with what I'm telling you now). I also make good use of my day planner and write everything down. I listen to comedy stations when driving and entertain myself with my imagination. Who knows, maybe someday I'll crack, but for now I'm just here doing the best I can.

Three Common Elements of Relaxation Techniques

The variety of methods presented all have several features in common. Here I will discuss three common elements.

Element 1: The Mind–Body Connection

It has long been known that the body and mind are intricately connected. Following in the tradition of ancient thinkers like Plato, the seventeenth-century philosopher René Descartes tried to treat mental and physical activity as dichotomous, belonging to related but separate systems. More recent formulations (Mate, 2003) have described a link between mind and body that is so closely related that it is virtually impossible to distinguish cause–effect influences. It is an artificial distinction that they are somehow separate entities. After all, the brain is an integral part of the body—the control center, so to speak—as well as the location of most senses. That is one reason why a new field has emerged, called **psychoneuroimmunoendocrinology**, which encompasses contributions from all the sciences that examine health from different vantage points.

It doesn't take much of a stretch to realize the ways that a healthy, well-disciplined mind facilitates a healthy body, just as strong physical conditioning serves as a sound basis for a healthy mind: each supports the other. This is a key feature of any attempt to moderate or control stress.

The use of particular images, visualizations, memories, or thoughts can help to sustain physical performance and endurance, whether in competitive sports or everyday life. When you are subjected to a stressful situation—say someone yelling at you in a disrespectful way—your particular responses, both internal and external, depend on the way that your mind reacts. Picture the abusing person as a clown who is out of control and, rather than feeling threatened by the situation, you are only slightly annoyed and perhaps even amused. You don't take the situation personally but instead interpret the behavior as a manifestation of the person's own lack of self-control. Likewise, if you choose to use some sort of "grounding" mental activity such as meditative deep breathing, you could respond to the situation with a certain equanimity.

Element 2: Altered States of Consciousness

All mentally or spiritually based relaxation techniques have the potential for eliciting **altered states of consciousness**: nonpsychotic states that have a particular content, form, or quality that is significantly different from ordinary states of consciousness. They can be induced by particular drugs, but they can also be attained solely through your own power of imagination and self-discipline. You may have experienced altered states in a number of ways. An orgasm qualifies, as does being high on drugs or alcohol. But so does the "runner's high" that you can experience through the endorphin rush that accompanies endurance sports that last longer than half an hour or so. Ecstatic religious experiences, mystical states, meditation, yoga, visions, dreams, and out-of-body experiences are other examples.

Charles Tart has studied altered states of consciousness for more than a quarter of a century (Tart, 1972a, 1972b, 1972c). Such conditions can be understood as changes in the **four dimensions of consciousness** (Baruss, 2003). These four dimensions of consciousness (all evident in "Voice of Stress Management 8.1") include:

1. the registration of information and acting on it in a goal-directed manner;
2. the explicit knowledge of your situation, mental states, and actions;
3. the stream of thoughts, feelings, and sensations that you have for yourself;
4. the sense of existence of the subject of mental acts.

VOICE OF STRESS MANAGEMENT 8.1

A Man in His Fifties Looking Back on the Most Transformative Period in His Life

While sitting in that church, completely alone, I began to feel this enormous love. As the heat grew in my spine, the love escalated as well. I began to weep and shake for the first time in my life. I began to feel tremors in my hands and my entire body. Then the heat got so hot it started to slowly climb, creeping gradually up my spinal column. As it rose, I felt more and more passion and connection to all things. I was completely absorbed in what was happening to me, but I wasn't thinking or analyzing, just fully experiencing.

All I know is that this whole thing started for me at dusk, and it was getting toward dawn when I finally found the power to get up and walk out of there. Every time I lifted up my head, the heat started radiating all over again, so I tried to keep myself looking down as much as possible, that next day, and for weeks afterward.

Unquestionably, it is the most mysterious thing that ever happened to me, but also the most important. It leveled me to the ground. Even though I was only 19 at the time, it changed my life in every way possible. It first set me on the path on which I have followed ever since.

You can appreciate that when you are dreaming, meditating, or otherwise immersed in an altered state, you are experiencing something qualitatively different from so-called "ordinary" reality. Your senses are heightened. You become aware of feelings, thoughts, and images that are usually not accessible. Often you feel that you have been completely transported into another dimension, one in which you may feel greater clarity or peace.

Martindale (1981) identified three pronounced common features associated with these altered states of consciousness. The first feature is a suspended critical judgment in the cognitive processes. For example, under hypnosis a person will believe what is suggested by the hypnotist without erecting any defenses. Once you start to make sense of what is going on, then the experience may come to an end. If you lose yourself totally watching the sunset, the surf, or a fire, you can reach an altered state, but once you start to comment internally on what is going on ("Isn't it interesting what is happening to me now?"), it is far more difficult to remain in that state.

The second feature of an altered state of consciousness is associated with changes in perceptions of yourself and often the world you live in. For example, under the **flow experience** some people perceive time to slow down or accelerate (Csikszentmihalyi, 1988). Flow represents the experience when you are so totally immersed in an activity (playing a video game, an athletic sport, even washing the dishes) that you lose all track of time, place, and even your sense of self.

The third feature is that normal control over behaviors is diminished to the point that you are less capable of judging the appropriateness of

Altered states of consciousness, or non-ordinary reality, may be initiated through focused concentration in a particular activity in which you totally lose yourself. It is as if you cease to be a separate being, and become immersed in the experience.

certain actions. The clearest example of this occurs when someone is under the influence of alcohol or other drugs.

How does this relate to the subject of better managing stress? One object of many relaxation methods is to help you attain an altered state of consciousness such that you stop worrying about anything else in your life except what you are currently doing, whether that is deep breathing, exercising, or engaging in any flow activity. Relaxation often accompanies the ability to let go of all other concerns and focus only on the present moment (Hanh, 1999).

FOR REFLECTION 8.1

One of the most difficult challenges in your hectic, overscheduled life is to stop focusing on the past, which you can't do anything to change, or the future, which has not yet occurred. Granted, there is some useful function to planning for the future and anticipating problems you might face, but not to the point that such thoughts interfere with your ability to appreciate the here and now.

If you kept track of how much of your life you spend actually thinking about, and being fully engaged in, what you are doing in the present moment, what percentage would that be? This means only the time you are totally immersed in the here and now, not dwelling on what has already occurred, or fantasizing about what might occur.

We'd guess you'd be quite fortunate if you could live in the present moment even half the time. If you doubt this, put the book down for a moment. See if you can spend a single minute, or even only 30 seconds, thinking about absolutely nothing except your own breathing. See if you can clear your mind of everything else except the full concentration on each of your breaths.

It can take years of practice to accomplish this, so let's try another experiment. Pay attention throughout a single 24-hour period of time to how often you are distracted or diverted from whatever you are doing in the present. This includes driving and walking time in which you are lost in a reverie, reliving something that has occurred, engaged in fantasy, or planning what you are going to do. It involves all the times you are listening to someone but not really paying attention because you are somewhere else in your head. It means all the time that you are working, studying, resting, or playing but you are distracted by something else that occupies your mind.

Managing stress, to a large extent, involves being able to tune out, temporarily, all that troubles you so that you can replenish energy and renew your spirit.

Another reason that altered states figure so prominently in our discussion is that certain relaxation techniques introduced in this chapter are aimed at attaining altered states of consciousness—autogenic states, creative states, flow states, and states that are drastically different from the stressed conditions in your normal daily routines. Still another reason is to understand that certain techniques of relaxation may provoke altered states that, initially, make you feel more anxious or provoke unpleasant thoughts. Like most things in life that are worth doing, relaxation methods take time, patience, practice, and self-discipline. For those who are used to distracting themselves with music, computers, television, and other diversions, it can be challenging to spend time truly *with* yourself. It is therefore important for you to know what to expect.

The final and most important reason is that in the altered state resulting from relaxation procedures, you're capable of more rapid and intense healing, growth, learning, and performance. Under such an enhanced perceptual mode, dominated by the right hemisphere of the brain, you are even potentially more intuitive and creative, more receptive to new experiences, and less critical of yourself and others.

FOR REFLECTION 8.2

Getting into Flow States

"Flow" is described as that state of altered consciousness where you are totally immersed in the present—when you lose a sense of time, and even of yourself, operating at effortless concentration and peak performance. This can occur during sports activities, during pleasurable times, or in any other instance when you are lost in the moment.

Describe some recent times when you have had flow experiences.

What would you like to do to create more flow in your life?

Element 3: Enhanced Internal Locus of Control

You will recall from Chapter 5 that *locus of control* refers to your beliefs about how much control you have over your life situations. Externally controlled individuals feel powerless, tending to blame others, bad luck, or extraneous factors for their troubles. Internally controlled individuals feel greater responsibility for what they experience. Ideally, they don't so much blame themselves for what goes wrong as examine their role in the situation, and then they can make adjustments to avoid a similar circumstance in the future. You feel less stressed, and more peaceful, when you feel you are in control of your life. This is also associated with higher optimism, self-esteem, and ability to tolerate pain, ambiguity, and stress.

FOR REFLECTION 8.3

Change each of the following statements from externally based language to internally based language. You learned some of these principles in Chapter 6.

1. It's not my fault.

2. The cold weather just gets me down.

3. The guy just drives me crazy.

4. I'm just not good at this. I've never been good at this.

5. It was just bad luck that things worked out this way.

Possible answers are at the end of the chapter.

Conversely, when you feel that forces outside your control impinge on your life, you will feel a greater sense of helplessness and even depression. After all, what can you do about changing luck, your body type, or other such variables when they are beyond your control?

Most relaxation techniques are internally driven activities, meaning that you decide when, where, and how these techniques or procedures are applied. It is within your power to apply one or more of these techniques, and thereby exert more control in your life—not only over stress, but any unpleasant circumstance.

Guided Imagery

Everyone holds on to particular memories or images that provide consistent feelings of peace and safety. Right now, think of some memory that comes to mind—a scene in which you felt a sense of security and tranquility. This is the place where you go first when you feel under stress or feel threatened.

VOICE OF STRESS MANAGEMENT 8.2

A Male College Student in His Twenties

When I was a kid and feeling upset about something, I'd go climb this tree in the woods behind my house. Not too long ago I tried to go back and find the tree, and even though it's been years since I last climbed it, I was amazed that it wasn't nearly as tall as I remembered it. I'm sure it's even grown a lot since those days but it still looked pretty small. Anyway, I remembered it as towering. I felt totally safe up there. It's like nothing could get me. And I'd sit up there on a branch, and dangle my feet over, and just hug the trunk.

Sometimes, when I'm really upset about something, I still picture myself in that tree. I've never told anyone this before because I know it sounds weird. But when somebody is mean to me, or something bad happens, I still feel like that scared little kid. And I just picture myself up in the tree where nobody can reach me.

Imagery refers to the thought process of creating, or recreating, scenes, objects, or events and their emotional reactions by involving all the senses. In hypnosis, a common part of the procedure is to ask the subject to think of a particular scene, event, or object that is especially comforting. This usually involves some memory from the past associated with feeling completely safe and secure. Once the subject has that particular visual image in mind, she may be asked to "hold" it as a means of reaching a deeper state of relaxation.

Guided imagery is the conscious use of the imagination to create positive images in order to bring about healthful changes in both the body and the mind. It can be self-guided or guided by an external source (CD, DVD, or person). Although it has been called **visualization**, guided imagery involves far more than just the visual sense; it often employs other senses such as the use of music or a person's voice. The object is to use this method in order to stimulate the body's immune system, fight disease, and improve overall health.

Many seriously ill cancer patients have used this technique to imagine the destruction of their disease or disorder (Rossman, 2003; Simonton, Matthews-Simonton, & Creighton, 1992; Trakhtenberg, 2008). They are taught to picture themselves mobilizing an army of white blood cells attacking the invading cancer cells, devouring them before they can do more damage. They might also be helped to use additional visualization to imagine the body healing itself. While there is limited empirical research evidence that this technique actually reverses the disease, a number of cancer survivors do report that it played a significant role in their recovery. Such imagery methods have been shown to promote relaxation and to accelerate the speed of recovery (Durham & Frost-Hartzer, 1994; Fanning, 1992; Iveleva & Orlick, 1991).

Since ancient times, people have been using imagery. Aristotle believed that imagery was the basis for thought, and Einstein thought that imagination, which uses imagery, is more powerful than knowledge because it facilitates creative processes. Imagery has been used to promote self-development and psychological change, relaxation, distraction from stressors, and healing (Payne, 2003). In addition, imagery can be used for enhancing skill learning and achieving peak performance.

FOR REFLECTION 8.4

A Walk on the Beach (a Guided Imagery Experience)

Make yourself comfortable. You may want to sit or lie down wearing loose-fitting clothing and adjusting your position so you can relax.

Begin to let go of tension and relax your body. Scan your whole body for any spot that is tense. Bring your attention to this area. Allow the tension to gradually ease. Imagine the tension melting away with each breath. A sense of relaxation spreads to all over your body.

Take a few deep breaths. With each breath, you breathe IN relaxation and breathe OUT tension and fatigue. Feel your body sinking more and more into deep relaxation.

On a warm and bright summer afternoon, you decide to take a walk on your favorite beach by yourself. The path leading to the ocean is surrounded by wild golden bushes. Everything along the path smells of sea and sun. Butterflies are flapping their wings above the goosefoot and the pollen stirred by the butterflies is visible in the afternoon sunshine. A salty ocean breeze is gently caressing your face. The late afternoon sun is warming your skin and is gilding the whole area with a spectacular hue of gold. The vast and endless blue sky is decorated with a few floating white clouds. You can hear the rustling of leaves of tall palm trees not far from the shores. In the distance seagulls are gliding over the ocean. Their cheeping noise often reaches your ears. Together with waves from the ocean, it forms a tranquilizing orchestra.

Arriving at the beach, you are pleased by the pure white and soft sand, as you have always been. The beach extends on both sides endlessly. A few beautiful shells like gems in the sand are shining. You decide to take off your shoes and walk barefooted. The grains of warm sand massage your bare feet. The sound of the waves washing up against the shore is peaceful and tranquilizing.

You keep walking along the shore. Once in a while, you bend down and pick up a few shining seashells.

As you walk further along the shore, you decide to stop for a rest. You sit down on a mound of pure white sand and gaze out at the sea, gazing peacefully at the rhythmic and cyclical motion of the waves rolling into shore. Everything is wonderful. This whole gorgeous coast, with its sand dunes, sandy beaches, piles of seaweed, palm trees, and seagulls, all belongs to you alone. You feel so peaceful. Free. And at one with everything around you. Time slows down to a halt.

Your mind begins to drift, being carried away by this intoxicating feeling of peace and tranquility ...

(pause)

Each wave breaks against the coast, rising slowly upward along the beach, leaving an area of white foam. Slowly the wave retreats back out to sea, only to be replaced by another wave that crashes against the shore ... working its way up the beach ... then slowly retreating back out to sea.

With each motion of the wave as it glides in and then out, you find yourself feeling more and more relaxed. The tranquility creates a sense of calmness, peace.

You forget about time. You don't know how much time has passed. You realize that the sun is lower and lower on the horizon. The sky is turning brilliant colors of red ... orange ... yellow ... while the sun sets, sinking down ... down into the horizon. You feel very relaxed and soothed. You continue to watch the sun as it descends.

The tranquilizing sound of the waves, the smell and taste of the sea and seaweed, the cries of the seagulls, the warmth of sunshine against your body – all of these sights, sounds, and smells leave you feeling very calm, refreshed, and relaxed.

Notice how deeply relaxed your mind and body feel right now ... Remind yourself that you can create these feelings on your own during your daily activities.

Remember that periodically during any day you may scan your body, discover any tension you are holding and then inhale relaxation and exhale the tension and tightness. Come back to this place as often as you like or create your own getaway. Relax–renew–recharge your mind and body.

When you are ready to wake up your body and your mind, and return to the present, give yourself a few moments to do so.

Return your awareness to your surroundings and notice the real environment you are in.

Let your muscles wake up by opening and closing your hands, shrugging your shoulders, and moving around a bit.

Keep with you the feeling of peace and calm you had while you were relaxing, as you open your eyes and sit quietly for a moment.

When you are awake and alert, you can return to your usual activities, knowing that you can return to this place in your mind whenever you want to relax.

Types of Guided Imagery

The various methods of using imagery have been divided into several categories.

FEELING STATE IMAGERY   Feeling state imagery can be used to elicit feelings of love, care, security, and happiness. For instance, when you recall a pleasant meeting with a dear friend in the past, or anticipate a social event, feelings of relaxation will often occur. The idea is that once a positive image occupies your mind, there is no room for negative feelings. This means that if you stick to a positive image whenever you can, you will feel better and less stressed.

You can try this right now. First, conjure up something going on in your life about which you feel a little anxious or stressed. Now, putting that image aside for a moment,

Athletes often use imagery to imagine the ball going into the hole or swishing through the basket, or see themselves breaking the tape at the finish line ahead of their opponents.

think about an incident that occurred not too long ago that brought you great pleasure. As long as you hold onto that more satisfying image, it is hard to clutter your mind with the more anxious one.

As one example, when I am feeling tired, I would close my eyes and fantasize going to a beautiful mountain resort with a pagoda on the top. I would slowly climb to the top of the hill and go to sit on a lovely mattress inside the pagoda facing the morning sunrise. Birds are chirping and the cool air caresses my face while I am savoring each second of the fresh air in the mountain. After five minutes of imagery, I will feel a sense of energy and light-heartedness.

END STATE IMAGERY Using end state imagery, you can create the ideal outcome or goal you desire to achieve. For example, you may imagine yourself being healthy, relaxed, confident, successful, and prosperous. Golf legend Jack Nicklaus used to visualize how the ball would roll into the hole before he putted it in. A salesperson might imagine the customer signing the check before the sales meeting even occurs.

Picture where *you* would like to be a few years from now and what you'd like to be doing. As vividly and clearly as possible, bring to mind this image of exactly what you are doing and where you are doing it. See yourself in your ideal job, doing what you would most love to do. The first step to making this happen is to imagine that it can really happen, if you set your mind to it.

PHYSIOLOGICAL IMAGERY This type of guided imagery, described earlier in the context of fighting off invading cancer cells, is designed to evoke healing processes of the body. For instance, a patient suffering from blocked arteries may imagine the coronary artery being gradually opened as plaque dissolves away. A cancer patient might use similar imagery to picture a tumor shrinking.

This sort of method does require a certain amount of accurate technical knowledge. For instance, to enhance your immune system, you may imagine the microbes being killed by T cells and swallowed by macrophages. If you suffer from asthma, you might imagine the mast cells being less reactive to neutral particles floating by.

Here are more examples of how imagery might be used with a variety of physical problems.

- *Bronchitis:* Picture the airways opening as you create more oxygen cells …

- *Chronic pain:* The nerve endings are being covered in a soft, cushiony coating that protect them from irritation …

- *Obesity:* Every time you take a bit of food it expands as it enters your body, filling you up …

- *High blood pressure:* Your heart is a drum and you are loosening and stretching the muscle so that it beats more slowly and softly …

Even if such methods do not demonstrably influence the physiological system, they do provide a person with a greater sense of control. Sometimes, in the face of chronic or life-threatening illnesses, a significant part of the battle is overcoming a sense of helplessness.

METAPHORIC IMAGERY   This type of imagery uses symbols to connect with the unconscious mind (Jung, 1963) and evokes healing from the core of your psyche. Each metaphor describes one thing in order to help the learner understand another thing. For instance, imagining a rose in bloom can suggest the power of healing and recovery.

Throughout human history, stories, proverbs, and fables have employed metaphoric images to convey powerful lessons of growth and transformation. In the classic children's story *The Velveteen Rabbit* (Williams, 1975, p. 17), a toy rabbit talks to a companion, the Skin Horse, about what it must be like to be made "real." The Skin Horse explains that the process of becoming real happens through love:

> "It takes a long time," explains the Skin Horse to the Velveteen Rabbit. "That's why it doesn't often happen to people who break easily, or have sharp edges, or have to be carefully kept. Generally, by the time you are real, most of your hair has been loved off, and your eyes drop out and you get loose in the joints and very shabby. But these things don't matter at all, because once you are real you can't be ugly, except to people who don't understand."

Whether or not children hearing this story would understand, their parents would realize that this metaphoric conversation between stuffed animals is really about how being real

---

FOR REFLECTION 8.5

Practice psychological rehearsal right now. Bring to mind someone with whom you have unfinished business. This could be someone who has treated you unfairly or disrespectfully, someone who has hurt you or ignored you, or otherwise caused you emotional pain. In the space below, draw a picture that captures the essence of this person as you experience him.

The second step is to get more in touch with exactly what you would like to say to this person that you have been holding back, or have not been able to communicate as effectively and clearly as you would like. Write below, as concisely and clearly as you can, the three most essential messages you wish to convey to this person.

The third and most critical part of this exercise is to now imagine yourself approaching this person and actually saying these things you've written above to him. Picture the *exact* circumstances under which this conversation would take place—where you are, how the meeting was arranged, what positions you are in, how you are expressing yourself, and how you are making adjustments to the person's defensiveness or denial.

The success in actually carrying through with this challenging task is *not* based on how the other person responds, which you can't control, but rather in the courage it takes for you to follow through on what you want to do. The imagery rehearsal helps to bolster your confidence and provide the internal fortitude needed to make this fantasy a reality.

occurs through intimacy and personal sharing. So it is with many metaphoric images that are used in—they are used to address complex issues.

PSYCHOLOGICAL IMAGERY "This type" of imagery targets a person's specific psychological issues by offering corrective emotional content. For example, for fear of rejection, imagine yourself being acknowledged and accepted by your friends and relatives. If you are a Type A personality, always in a rush, visualize yourself slowing down in your life and treating everyone you meet kindly and patiently.

SPIRITUAL IMAGERY This type of imagery brings forth a kind of being that transcends ordinary existence—an altered state of consciousness. You may imagine assistance coming from angels, saints, God, divine inspiration, or specific religious figures and symbols. You can also imagine being connected with all beings of nature. For example, in Tibetan medicine, creating a mental image of the healing god would improve the patient's chances of recovery, providing evidence that such methods can be useful in planting hope and empowering the patient, and perhaps even reversing the deterioration.

How to Perform a Therapeutic Imagery Session

Before any imagery session, a certain amount of planning is necessary. A session can be conducted by a trained stress management consultant who will read from a prepared script, or you may read your own script into an audio tape or burn it onto a CD, or listen to a commercially published recording.

A typical imagery session often involves four phases: (1) finding a comfortable and relaxed position, (2) closing your eyes and creating a relaxed state of body and mind, (3) following instructions to enter into the visualization experience, and (4) returning to a conscious state. Since individuals vary in their receptivity to the training effects, some will notice immediate benefits while others may take weeks before they feel significantly more relaxed. Just as in the case of other therapeutic and medical prescriptions, sometimes it takes several different methods before an optimal strategy is discovered.

How Does Guided Imagery Work?

There are several theories to explain how guided imagery might produce desired changes in the body, beginning with neurological and biochemical mechanisms. The brain does not appear to differentiate significantly between what is imagined versus what is real, which is why hallucinations can seem quite real to people suffering from psychotic disorders. Whether images emanate from the outside world and enter through the senses, or via created images, the brain appears to handle the information in the same way, and the body produces the same physiological responses. You can test this theory yourself by simply allowing yourself to imagine facing a stressful or terrifying situation and note how your blood pressure and pulse rate increase.

On a neurological level, nerve fibers are known to reach from the brain into the thymus gland, spleen, lymph nodes, and bone marrow, mediating the immune response from brain to body. In addition, you will recall how the brain produces chemicals that send messages to the body that mobilize certain reactive, protective responses. These chemicals transmit information from the hypothalamus to the pituitary, and then from the pituitary to the major hormone secreting glands of the body. Chemicals released by nerve cells transmit information to other nerve cells. Feelings, thoughts, and images can thus cause chemicals to be released and these chemicals can, in turn, cause feeling states as well as corresponding physiological changes through a kind of natural biofeedback loop.

Another explanation is derived from cognitive theory (presented in Chapter 6) and suggests that changing negative thought patterns leads to a reduction in autonomic nervous system arousal and a decrease in muscle tension, mood disturbances, and pain.

You will recall the ways that emotional responses can be dramatically changed just by changing your interpretations of those events.

Those who are familiar with the *Harry Potter* books may also recognize this method for dealing with fearful objects or individuals. In *Harry Potter and the Prisoner of Azkaban* (Rowling, 1999), Professor Lupin teaches his students to protect themselves against the terrifying *boggart* by using the "reddikulus spell." Since a shapeshifting boggart takes the form of whatever a person fears the most, the students are told to imagine an object of ridicule, such as a spider on roller skates, in order to deal with the stressful threat.

Another school of thought studying the effects of imagery on the experience of pain has postulated that its effect is due to cognitive distraction. This is based on the assumption that if there are competing stimuli, the brain filters out certain signals, such as pain, and attention becomes focused on other information, such as the guided imagery suggestions.

Generally speaking, guided imagery is safe and enjoyable for everyone, from children to the elderly. However, it should not take place of medical treatment nor should those who are suffering emotional disorders attempt it without professional supervision. Since imagery may create altered states of consciousness and allow you to connect with your deeper feelings, you may experience strong emotional reactions such as crying. When this happens, don't panic. Continue when your feelings subside. Again you may wish to consult a therapist to help you work through these feelings that have been evoked.

Autogenic Training

When you think of hypnosis, what most likely comes to mind is the image of someone on stage who is induced to cluck like a chicken after following the swinging of a watch on a chain. Or perhaps you think of someone who goes into a deep trance and regresses to childhood, or remembers repressed memories. While all of this has been done with hypnosis, the method is really just a form of focused concentration. It does *not* make you do anything you don't want to do and does not take away control; on the contrary, hypnosis actually increases your ability to control thoughts, feelings, and impulses at will.

A trance state is nothing more, or less, than intense concentration in which you are able to access abilities that might not otherwise be available to you. This is useful for a number of purposes—to increase creativity and problem solving, to cease an undesirable behavior, to improve self-esteem, to reduce chronic pain, or to reduce stress. After the method is learned, it can be initiated by one's own command; thus almost all hypnosis is self-induced.

Autogenic training (AT) is a kind of self-hypnosis that is often used as a relaxation technique. It was first described in 1932 by German psychiatrist and neurologist, Johannes Schultz (Davis, Eshelman, & McKay, 1988). The word "autogenic" comes from the Greek *autos*, meaning self, and *genous*, a suffix meaning produced by and reflecting the word *genesis*, or creation. Therefore, autogenic training can be thought of as a variant of self-suggestion.

In the early twentieth century, Schultz was greatly interested in the work of Oskar Vogt, a brain physiologist who worked at the Berlin Institute during the last decade of the nineteenth century. Vogt taught his patients auto-hypnosis in order to reduce fatigue, tension, and painful symptoms. Schultz wanted to achieve a similar outcome without relying on a hypnotist, by instructing patients to focus on specific body sensations. He found that people could create a kind of hypnotic trance just by thinking of heaviness and warmth in the extremities. In essence, AT was a combination of the auto-suggestions used by Vogt and yoga techniques.

PRINCIPLES OF AUTOGENIC TRAINING   AT is considerably more complex than some other relaxation techniques introduced in this book and is usually not mastered by simply reading a brief introduction. The primary purpose of this procedure is to reverse the "fight-or-flight" stress response and return you to the relaxation response as described by Benson (2000). To succeed in AT requires adhering to the following five principles:

1. *Non-stimulating setting.* The room should be quiet and the lighting dim. During the training, any distraction such as phones should be turned off.

2. *High motivation and ability for self-regulation.* In order to reap the fruits of AT, the learner must be patient and disciplined in going through weeks of training. Once learned from a professional, home practice is absolutely necessary.

3. *Passive concentration.* The effectiveness of this exercise comes from your ability to practice passive concentration on the feelings of heaviness and warmth in extremities and in the body for cardiac and respiratory regulation. By "passive concentration," I mean that you should remain alert to your experience without analyzing and judging it. During practice with an attitude of passive concentration, distracting thoughts may appear. Under these circumstances, the learner is encouraged to ignore them or gently coax them away without engaging them or being distressed that these thoughts have occurred.

4. *The repetition of certain scripted phrases.* These are used to induce relaxation based on the six autogenic "formulae" or "states" as follows:

   a. focus on heaviness in the arms and legs;
   b. focus on warmth in the arms and legs;
   c. focus on warmth and heaviness in the heart area;
   d. focus on breathing;
   e. focus on warmth in the abdomen;
   f. focus on coolness in the forehead.

   The first two formulae are often broken down to focus first on the dominant arm, followed by the other arm or the legs. For each formula one repeats a phrase, silently with closed eyes, such as "my arm feels heavy." Breathing is paced slowly and the phrase is repeated five to seven times before opening the eyes and stretching. A recommended practice session is three sets of five to seven repetitions with breaks, for a total time of about ten minutes. Practicing the technique twice daily is also recommended. Each individual formula should be practiced for about a week, or until

---

FOR REFLECTION 8.6

Autogenic Training

Find a comfortable position to sit or lie down. Autogenic relaxation is an effective relaxation technique that will allow you to relax your body and calm your mind. It is very important that you let the sensations of heaviness and warmth arise naturally without forcing it. Take a deep breath in, and hold this breath. Hold it ... hold it ... and now exhale. Let all the air go out slowly, and release all the tension. Let your worries and thoughts leave you as you breathe out.

Take another deep breath in. Hold it ... and then exhale slowly, allowing the tension to leave your body with your exhalation. Now breathe even more slowly and gently ... breathe in ... hold ... out ... Breathe in ... hold ... out ... Continue to breathe slowly and gently. Allow your breathing to relax you. The autogenic training consists of a series of exercises. Now turn your attention to your right arm. Repeat the following statements several times by yourself: "I feel relaxed and comfortable. My right arm is heavy." Continue to feel the heaviness in your right arm as if you are lying in the sunny meadow. Now turn your attention to your left arm. Repeat the following statements: "I feel relaxed and comfortable. My left arm is heavy." Continue to feel the heaviness in your left arm as if you are lying in the sunny meadow.

Now turn your attention to both your arms. Repeat the following statements: "I feel relaxed and comfortable. Both my arms are heavy." Imagine yourself lying on the warm and sunny meadow with your arms resting heavily on the comfortable and soft grass.

Now turn your attention to your right leg. Repeat the following statements: "I feel relaxed and comfortable. My right leg is heavy." Continue to feel the heaviness in your right leg as if you are lying in the sunny meadow. Now turn your attention to your left leg. Repeat the following statements: "I feel relaxed and comfortable. My left leg is heavy." Continue to feel the heaviness in your left leg as if you are lying in the sunny meadow.

Now turn your attention to both your legs. Repeat the following statements: "I feel relaxed and comfortable. Both my legs are heavy." Imagine yourself lying in the warm and sunny meadow with your legs resting heavily on the comfortable and soft grass. Now turn your attention to both your arms and legs. Repeat the following statements: "I feel relaxed and comfortable. Both my arms and legs are heavy." Continue to imagine yourself lying on the warm and sunny meadow with your arms and legs resting heavily on the comfortable and soft grass. Now turn your attention to your right hand. Repeat the following statements: "I feel relaxed and comfortable. My right arm is warm." Continue to feel the warmth in your right arm as if you are lying in the warm and sunny meadow. Now turn your attention to your left hand. Repeat the following statements: "I feel relaxed and comfortable. My left arm is warm." Continue to feel the warmth in your left arm as if you are lying in the sunny meadow. Now turn your attention to both your arms. Repeat the following statements: "I feel relaxed and comfortable. Both my arms are warm."

Note: Using the same pattern of sentences as shown above incorporate the following main sentences:

My right leg is warm.

My left leg is warm.

Both my legs are warm.

Both my arms and legs are warm.

Both my arms and legs are heavy and warm.

My heartbeat is calm and regular.

My breathing is calm.

My abdomen is warm.

My forehead is cool.

Imagine a cool breeze is caressing your forehead and you feel cool and comfortable.

Continue to feel the heaviness and warmth in your arms and legs, calmness in your breathing, strength in your heartbeat, and coolness on your forehead. You feel good. Just stay the way you are, relaxed, energized, filled with vibrant energy. I am going to count from one to five. At the count of five, you will open your eyes slowly and feel wide awake and alert.

1. .... becoming more awake and alert;
2. .... feeling your mind and body reawaken;
3. .... move your muscles a little;
4. .... almost completely awake now;
5. .... feeling full of energy and refreshed.

a satisfactory result is achieved. You would then move on to the next formula and practice it together with the previous ones. Once the technique has been mastered in practice sessions, it can be applied at will in situations of stress or difficulty.

5. *Attention to bodily sensations.* This principle is essential especially in more advanced learners. Only by maintaining mental contact with the named body part can the learner translate physical relaxation to mental relaxation. After completing the brief exercise For Reflection 8.5, note the way your body and dominant arm feel during and after the task.

Mindfulness and Mindfulness Meditation

Even though you already learned the concept of mindfulness in Chapter 4, it is always good to repeat some important ideas. Mindfulness describes a nonjudgmental and moment-to-moment awareness of bodily sensations, perceptions, emotions and thoughts (Grossman et al., 2004). It can also be thought of as our ability to pay close attention to what is happening to us with acceptance as the experience unfolds. Mindfulness is typically trained in mindfulness meditation practices, such as sitting meditation, walking meditation, standing meditation or mindful movements. The word "meditation" derived from the Latin word "meditari" means engagement in contemplation or deliberation. **Meditation** can be defined as a state of intense concentration and inner stillness, as well as a mental procedure to achieve this type of mental state. People practice meditation in order to find inner peace, obtain mental awareness, empty the mind, achieve enlightenment, and experience true reality (Payne, 2003).

Mindfulness practices originated in the East (from India, Nepal, Tibet, Japan, China) and have been used for more than 2,500 years, traditionally in religious practices. Mindfulness-based stress reduction strategies are now receiving increasing attention, not only for those who wish to prevent debilitating anxiety but also those who wish to treat serious illnesses such as cancer (Smith, Richardson, Hoffman, & Pilkington, 2005), chronic pain (Kabat-Zinn, 2003), and depression (Segal, Williams, & Teasdale, 2013). Such mindfulness techniques have even been shown to be effective in helping health professionals deal with the stress associated with their work (Shapiro, Astin, Bishop, & Cordova, 2005).

What are some characteristics of mindfulness meditation? Hölzel et al. (2011) surveyed a large number of studies on mindfulness meditation and extrapolated four components of how mindfulness meditation may work: (1) attention regulation, (2) body awareness, (3) emotion regulation (including reappraisal, exposure, extinction and reconsolidation), and (4) change in perspective on the self (see Table 8.1). The authors indicate that mindfulness practice comprises a process of enhanced self-regulation that can be differentiated into distinct but interrelated components.

Mindfulness-based stress management methods such as meditation include a broad range of strategies that have been applied to a variety of symptoms including asthma, heart disease, psoriasis, chronic pain, insomnia, and, as mentioned before, even cancer. Even with its increasing popularity, the research results supporting its effectiveness are mixed at best (Butler, 2006). Rather than a technique, it is best thought of as a "way of being" that points you in the direction of greater centeredness and presence in the moment. What this means is that it helps you to be more *awake*, more *alive*.

Meditation and mindfulness are thus:

- a way of *seeing*;
- a way of *feeling*;
- a way of *knowing*;
- a way of *loving*—both yourself and others.

There is nothing simpler than meditation, and nothing more difficult. "Meditation is not about trying to get anywhere else. It is about allowing yourself to be exactly where you

TABLE 8.1 Components of mindfulness meditation

Underlying Mechanisms	Exemplary Instructions
1.0 Attention regulation	Sustaining attention on the chosen object; whenever distracted, returning attention to the object
2.0 Body Awareness	Focus is usually an object of internal experience: Sensory experiences of breathing, emotions, pain, or other body sensations
3.1 Emotion regulation: Reappraisal	Approaching ongoing emotional reactions in a different way
3.2 Emotion regulation: Exposure, extinction, and reconsolidation	Exposing oneself to whatever is present in the field of awareness; letting oneself be affected by it; compassionate acceptance of what is happening and refraining from internal reactivity
4.0 Change in perspective on the self	Detachment from identification with a static sense of self

Source: Adapted from Hölzel et al. (2011)

are, and as you are, and for the world to be exactly as it is in this moment as well" (Kabat-Zinn, 2005, p. 61).

What makes this so challenging is the continual critical judgments you make of yourself and others. There is always chatter going on inside your head evaluating everything, comparing what is happening to something else, criticizing, blaming, scolding, whining, predicting, planning, plotting, ruminating, obsessing, craving, going on and on, escaping the *now*.

Try to stay here now. Close your eyes for a few moments and count to five. Slowly. Try not to think about anything except the numbers.

This is very difficult to do, isn't it?

Being mindful means sensitizing yourself to what is going on NOW. This moment stop reading further. Notice everything going on around you. Within you. What sounds do you hear? What colors, patterns, shapes are within view? What sensations are you aware of? Notice everything. Being mindful is being totally and completely aware. This is the essence of meditation, but also of living and experiencing life more fully.

One guy who was very skeptical about mediation and mindfulness-based stress reduction decided to try it as an experiment to help reduce his stress, since exercise alone wasn't doing the job. His breakthrough took place once he realized that meditation didn't have to take place sitting still—he could use the technique even when running.

"I bolted two miles up to a ridge," he said, "stopping to take in the autumn forest. I closed my eyes and found my breath. In, out. In, out … I can't stay how long it lasted —ten seconds? A minute?—and I can't say how it felt, because I didn't feel anything. I was just there. *Right there*. For the first time ever.

(Roberts, 2008, p. 68)

Types of Meditation

Popularization of meditation in the West has been made possible by two important phenomena. First, the Indian master Maharishi Mahesh Yogi started to teach a form of meditation called **transcendental meditation**. His teaching caught the attention of The Beatles during the 1960s. It quickly spread all over Britain, the United States, and elsewhere. Second, in 1975, Herbert Benson, a renowned American cardiologist, published his famous book *The Relaxation Response* (Benson, 2000), detailing the scientific benefits of meditation and simplifying the meditation practice, resulting in more people participating in this exercise. Motivational gurus such as Deepak Chopra and Wayne Dyer have contributed to the spread of meditation as a popular technique for stress reduction and achieving the union of mind, body, and spirit.

Meditation can be divided into two types, **restrictive** and **inclusive**. There are many forms within each type, although their goals are essentially the same. In restrictive forms of meditation, the practitioner focuses her consciousness on a single symbol, object, or thought in order to prevent all the other distracting thoughts from entering the conscious mind. Examples of restrictive meditation include transcendental meditation and visual meditation.

Inclusive meditation, on the other hand, involves opening the mind to all kinds of thoughts without getting bogged down in any one of them. It can be likened to an endless stream, flowing around a boulder in the middle without getting stuck or stagnant. Any thought is allowed to pop up and none is judged or engaged in order to determine its legitimacy or relevance. This meditation develops nonjudgmental or detachment thinking. The notion is that stress is the result of the mind creating all sorts of painful judgment. When the judgment is suspended, the pain also stops. Two examples of inclusive meditation are Zen meditation (Aitken, 1996; Kabat-Zinn, 1995) and mindfulness meditation (Bien & Bien, 2003; Hanh, 1999). The latter refers to focusing your concentration on a single object (e.g., a leaf) or task (e.g., breathing) in such a way that you are invited to become more "mindful" or aware of inner experience.

FOR REFLECTION 8.7

Breath-Focus Meditation

Find a comfortable position either lying down on your back, in a chair, or on a cushion on the floor. If you are in a sitting position, allow your back to be straight but not rigid. Allow your eyes to close gently. Bring your awareness to the present and notice what you have discovered. Is there any noise in the background? Scan through the body. Is it relaxed or tense? Do you notice any pain or discomfort? Do you notice any thoughts of judgment or worry? Release them as you breathe out. Pay attention to the sensations of your body breathing and focus your attention on the feel of the breath coming in and out. You may watch your breath by noticing the sensations of the air flowing through your nostrils or attending to the abdomen as it expands and contracts with each breath. When your mind wanders, notice, and gently guide attention back to the breath (over and over again). Practice for 5–30 minutes daily for lasting positive results.

TRANSCENDENTAL MEDITATION   In the late 1950s, an Indian monk named Maharishi Mahesh Yogi began to teach a form of transcendental meditation (TM) in the West. TM is based on the use of a **mantra**, or a verbal stimulus, consisting of short Sanskrit words or phrases, that can help the user reduce thought processes or patterns. Mantras are selected based on the learner's temperament and occupation. The simple technique purports to produce a restful alertness that transcends thinking to reach the source of thought, that is, the mind's own reservoir of energy and creativity.

Most of the research on the psychological and physiological effects of meditation has been conducted on TM. The plethora of evidence collected in support of TM as a stress reducer is weakened by some methodological problems. Herbert Benson, the American pioneer of research into relaxation responses, indicated in the 1960s that ritualistic techniques used in various Christian traditions, or even simple prayers repeated many times over, can be just as effective as TM in achieving the result of producing a relaxation response.

MINDFULNESS-BASED STRESS REDUCTION (MBSR)   MBSR is a highly structured program developed by Jon Kabat-Zinn (1990, 2003). It consists of three different techniques: (1) body scan, (2) sitting meditation, and (3) Hatha yoga. During the body scan, the participant is instructed to mentally go through the entire body gradually from feet to head, focusing and recognizing nonjudgmentally any sensation that may arise. Sitting meditation requires the participant to focus on the here and now, giving mindful attention to the breath, the rising and falling of the abdomen, any noise in the room, and so on. The mind is supposed to be in a state of nonjudgmental awareness with thoughts and feelings coming and going.

The participant is instructed to incorporate meditation into his/her daily activities. The program usually consists of interventions and homework for at least 45 minutes a day, six days a week for eight weeks. Researchers have found MBSR to be an effective therapy with no side-effects for patients to reduce stress and anxiety from chronic illness and for healthcare providers to improve their interactions with patients (Praissman, 2008). Practice of MBSR has been very effective in helping healthy people reduce stress (Chiesa & Serrett, 2009).

VISUAL MEDITATION   At the beginning of visual meditation, learners can gaze at a chosen object or symbol that has some personal meaning (see Table 8.2). Then they will close their eyes and "see" the object in their imagination.

Whereas in a mantra-based meditation you would close your eyes and repeat a word to yourself, in visual meditation you would select some object that is especially meaningful to you. It doesn't matter which object you choose, as long as it has some personal meaning for you. You can stare at this object as you concentrate on your breathing; a variation is to close your eyes and imagine a particular object.

WALKING MEDITATION   Yes, you really can meditate while you are walking! This is not intended, however, to get you where you want to go, and get your meditation session in at the same time. In fact, the intention is not to "go" anywhere at all (Hanh, 2005).

Just as the breath is the vehicle by which you enter into a mindful state of focused concentration in breathing meditation, here walking becomes a form of moving contemplation.

Take a break from the text for a moment and try taking just five steps, moving in slow motion. Concentrate on your breathing as you do this, as well as what it feels like to lift and place each foot as mindfully as you can. As your attention wanders away just bring it back to the task at hand. When distracting thoughts intrude, gently push them aside. For these five steps you are doing nothing else but walking.

Elements of Meditative Practice

There are hundreds, if not thousands, of meditation forms. In every monastery throughout India, Tibet,

Sitting meditation is an integral part of MBSR

TABLE 8.2 Meaningful objects used for visual meditation

Category	Description
Natural items	A flower, a candle flame, sunrise, sunset
Artistic items	Icons, spiritual pictures
Special words and symbols	Primal sounds, a crucifix, the yin/yang symbol, the wheel of life
Mandalas	Complex diagrams with a center, contained in a circle, and representing the unity of the personal and transpersonal
Yantras	Graphic representations of the energy pattern of one aspect of the divine

Nepal, Thailand, India, and other countries, there are unique methods that rely on different processes. There are still forms and moving forms such as tai chi. There are those that take years of practice to master, and others that you can learn in a few minutes—such as those I have introduced to you. Regardless of which method you may choose, there are certain features that they all have in common. Keep in mind that any meditative practice represents a commitment on your part to take a daily time-out in your life for contemplation. There is probably no other single thing you could do that could more easily reduce stress in your life.

A QUIET PLACE   The best environment for the practice of meditation is one that is comfortable, in which you can relax your muscles and quiet your mind. Find a quiet place with the minimum of distractions. This could be lying on the floor of an office, with the door shut. It could be sitting in your car. It could be somewhere outside in nature. The particular place is less important than its ability to shield you from interruptions. Once you become skilled in the practice, you will find that your location options increase with your newfound ability to concentrate and resist distractions. Skilled meditators can practice their relaxation strategy sitting in a busy airport, a bus, a library, or a park bench—almost anywhere in which they can go inside themselves for a few minutes.

A COMFORTABLE OR POISED POSTURE   The best attitude for meditation may itself be described as poised: alert yet also relaxed. The lotus position has been traditionally adopted as the "standard" meditation position, but in the West, more importance has been placed on comfort. Regardless, a major characteristic of recommended meditation postures is that the spine be kept straight. Experts believe that misalignments may feel uncomfortable in the beginning when assuming these postures. The spine is put back into a structurally sound line, and the weight of the body distributed around it in a balanced pattern in which gravity, not muscular tension, is the primary influence. It is possible, although it has not been conclusively proved, that this postural realignment affects the state of mind.

A sitting posture is better for meditation than lying down, since lying down is the normal sleep position and could easily lead to unconsciousness. If you are not a person who easily goes to sleep during the day, you may prefer to meditate in a semi-reclining position on a sofa or large armchair with the back of your head supported. In traditional meditation postures, however, the back is normally kept erect, though not rigidly upright. This is called *poised posture.*

AN OBJECT TO DWELL UPON   In Hindu yoga, the object of attention is often a mantra, usually a Sanskrit word or syllable. In Buddhism the focus for attention is often the meditator's own breathing. Both mantra meditation and awareness of breathing fulfill all the elements required for relaxed meditation.

Instructors in transcendental meditation make much of each person being given a mantra that suits his unique personality and nervous system, but there does not appear to be any scientific support for this. Any technique used with any sound, phrase, prayer, or mantra has been found to bring forth the same physiological changes noted during transcendental meditation.

There is much to be said for choosing either a neutral word or a meaningless sound for mantra meditation. Some people, however, like to use a word such as "peace" which has relaxing associations. This is fine provided the word does not set off associative thoughts. In this type of meditation the single thought-sound has the effect of quieting the mind; Maharishi Mahesh Yogi says that the thought-sound takes the meditator to the source of all thought. Studies of the brain-wave patterns of meditators indicate that the deepest relaxation occurs when thoughts are absent.

A PASSIVE ATTITUDE OR POISED AWARENESS   This last element of meditation for relaxation is said to be the most essential. It is sometimes called poised awareness or attention-awareness because relaxation and alertness are in perfect balance. There is nothing exotic about it: you were passively aware when you let go of tension in the muscles of your arms, legs, trunk, and face.

A passive attitude means that distractions from environmental sounds, physical sensations, and the inevitable intrusion into the mind of thoughts and images are viewed casually and detachedly. Let them come and go, of no more consequence than small clouds passing across an expanse of sky. But each time you become aware that your attention has slipped away from the mantra or the sensation of abdominal breathing, and you are engaging in a chain of logical thinking or developing interest in some sounds or other sensations, bring your attention and awareness back to the meditation object. It is simple, as long as you keep a relaxed attitude. Don't force, and don't cling. With practice, moments of great calm and deep restfulness during meditation will become more frequent.

Benefits of Meditation

Practitioners of meditation seek to achieve a state of ideal contemplation in which one is fully present, focused inward, and yet connected to all other living things. Whether undertaken for spiritual transcendence or stress reduction, meditation helps people to find greater clarity and serenity.

It has been a difficult challenge for researchers to measure the effects of meditation on stress reduction, largely because we are talking about an internal process that is often not clearly distinct from other states of rest, reverie, and relaxation. The traditional chief instrument for research is the electroencephalogram (EEG), which can measure moment-to-moment changes, but is also subject to noise. Thanks to the use of such advanced neuroimaging technologies such as positron emission tomography (PET), magnetic resonance imaging (MRI), and functional MRI (fMRI) neuroscientists can measure changes in brain function and brain structure as a result of mindfulness meditation. For instance, experienced meditating monks were studied in a laboratory by measuring their brain waves both during and after meditation (Davidson & Harrington, 2002; Lebow, 2005). It was found that the more meditation practice the subjects had, the more likely they were to have elevated gamma activity in the prefrontal cortex. In other words, accomplished meditators had higher brain function in the area of consciousness, *even when they weren't meditating.* Lazar and her colleagues (Lazar et al., 2005) found that long-term Western meditators had thicker anterior insulae, sensory cortices, and prefrontal cortices. These three areas were believed to be involved in integrating emotional and cognitive processes. Other researchers discovered that mindfulness meditation lowered resting-state amygdala activity (Way, Creswell, Eisenberger, & Lieberman, 2010) and reduced right amygdala volumes (Taren, Creswell, & Gianaros, 2013), which means that mindfulness meditation can reduce stress reactions (review the stress pathways in Chapter 2).

Meditation has been found to produce a number of benefits for regular practitioners (Benson, 2000; Delmonte, 1984; Kabat-Zinn, 1995, 2005) and even for professional helpers who assist others who are stressed (Shapiro, Astin, Bishop, & Cordova, 2005). While some of these findings are supported by empirical research, other results reported by devotees are subject to debate within the scientific community. There is a consensus among most advocates that meditation has resulted in:

- lowered stress levels;

- reduced high blood pressure;

- decreased metabolic rate (including heart rate);

- improved breathing efficiency;

- enhanced concentration;

- reduced depression;

- increased feelings of self-control;

- improved memory;

- improved immune system function;

- improved sleep;

- reduced chronic pain.

People who have been meditating on a regular basis for several years cannot imagine their lives without it. It becomes one of those non-negotiable structures in life that keep you sane and centered. It is not a matter of *whether* you will meditate, any more than you consider it an option to brush your teeth, or take a shower; it is one of those daily activities that just becomes part of who you are.

It is not difficult to *begin* meditative practice; the hard part is finding the commitment and self-discipline to stick with it over time. It is not all that difficult to find ten minutes per day to sit quietly and relax yourself, but an infinite number of excuses can still be made for why you forgot or didn't have time. The main impetus to continue meditation, and make it part of your daily life, is a major difference it can make in the way you feel. After you try meditation daily for a few weeks, if you notice yourself feeling less stressed and more focused, then you know that the payoff is worth the investment of time.

As I have mentioned, the object of meditation is not only to quiet the mind and reduce stress, but also to develop mindful attitudes that guide a more satisfying life (Corey, 2006; Kabat-Zinn, 1995, 2005). This includes the following "ways of being" that can develop over time.

- Live in the present moment as much as possible, rather than the past and future. Appreciate every waking moment as a gift.

- Avoid critical judgments about yourself and others. Accept the things that cannot be changed.

- Slow down the pace of life, valuing the process of what occurs rather than only the outcome.

- Trust your intuition as well as your logical thinking.

- Practice love and caring toward all people and all things.

You would recognize some of these principles as embedded in many Eastern and Western religious traditions as well. One difference, however, is that meditation does not usually focus on a higher power or complex rituals, but rather on the process of being fully present. This approach can be useful not only to distract yourself from suffering but actually to *embrace* the pain. In one such mindful approach, Hayes and Smith (2005) counsel people to simply observe their unpleasant sensations, not to challenge them or try to change them. According to them, pain becomes much more intense suffering when you make determined efforts to push it away. This attitude is consistent with much of Buddhist thought, which accepts discomfort as an inevitable part of a life. Stress is thus not a bad thing, nor does it have to interfere with happiness.

Seeking Serenity through the Spiritual Path

Once regarded as taboo in medicine, spiritual health has become a hot topic in mainstream media and has been studied in government-funded research in recent years. Many professionals, as well as their patients, have come to realize that health cannot be addressed solely by traditional medical technology alone. Many people report that their satisfaction in life arises not only from emotional and physical sources, but also from the spiritual realm (however that is individually defined and experienced).

VOICE OF STRESS MANAGEMENT 8.3

Twenty-Eight-Year-Old Educational Administrator

I find solace in my spirituality. I have found that when I am overly concerned with what is happening around me I become stressed out and paralyzed. When I take a breath and remember that there is a higher power and that I am but one grain of sand in this beautiful beach that is life, I relax. I stop, breathe, and focus on what is real. I know that life can sometimes distract me from what is most important.

I meditate on how beautiful and powerful nature is. I step outside and breathe. I watch a hummingbird or listen to the rain. I have not always been like this. There used to be times that I would do something self-destructive, like drink too much, or overeat. But my new outlook on life and getting in touch with my spirituality has changed that for me. I am accepting. Everyone is unique and I am not to judge others. It is for me to accept what is and to make the best of who I am and what I have. It took some time, but I have come to love my life.

"Spirituality" is a broad term that represents a unique quality of the individual that is associated with one's faith in a supernatural being, a search for meaning, a sense of connection with others, and a transcendence of self (Benson, 1997; Delgado, 2005). Awareness of spirituality is often associated with religion or belief in supernatural powers, but it may also occur in a secular context or one associated with Nature, insight, or greater awareness. Religion is a narrower concept represented by devotion to the beliefs and practices of established, organized rituals and is associated with a system of beliefs centered around the concept of a supernatural being or force (Tuck, Alleyne, & Thinganjana, 2006). In the following discussion, the use of the term "spirituality" includes the practice of religion. In a series of interviews with notable spiritual leaders and healers such as Arun Gandhi, Thomas Moore, Neale Walsh, and Michael Lerner, it was found that transcendent spiritual experiences take a variety of forms that can include being visited by the voice of God, surviving a near-death experience, recovering from trauma, feeling touched by love, fighting against injustice, or seeing oneself and the world more clearly (Kottler & Carlson, 2006).

Being spiritual contains those elements associated with inner qualities related to the soul and heart of the person, like the meaning and purpose of life, compassion, forgivingness, and love. It involves living an integral life in which your values and beliefs are integrated into the daily activities of work, relationships, recreation, and rest. The practice of spirituality is often accompanied by certain actions on the outside as well; for instance, meditation, daily prayer, fighting against oppression, and working on behalf of charitable causes. Spirituality is not just something you espouse but a way of life that pervades every aspect of your being.

After an extensive review of published studies on the relationship between religion/spirituality and mental health, Koenig (2009) concludes that "healthy normative" religious beliefs and spiritual practices are associated with better coping with stress and less depression, suicide, anxiety, and substance abuse. He also points out that "in the emotionally vulnerable, religious beliefs and doctrines may reinforce neurotic tendencies, enhance fears or guilt, and restrict life rather than enhance it" (p. 289).

Why is practice of religion and spirituality so beneficial as a coping strategy for those who suffer from tremendous levels of stress? Religious beliefs provide a sense of meaning and purpose during difficult life circumstances that assists with psychological integration; they usually promote a positive world view that is optimistic and hopeful; they provide role models in sacred writings that facilitate acceptance of suffering; they give people a sense of indirect control over circumstances, reducing the need for personal control; and they offer a community of support, both human and divine, to help reduce isolation and loneliness. Unlike many other coping resources, religion is available to anyone at anytime, regardless of financial, social, physical, or mental circumstances.

FOR REFLECTION 8.8

Your Spiritual Life

Many studies report on ways that people find comfort and relief from stress through their communion with a Higher Power, their association with a religious community, the power of prayer, or from their individual spiritual beliefs. Think of an instance recently in which you drew on some aspect of your spiritual life to provide support during a time of trouble. What do you see as the most important elements of this experience?

The Power of Prayer

All of the world's major religions have at their heart a code of morality with some fairly universal values related to practicing love, honesty, kindness, and "right" behavior. Spiritual traditions are intended to ground you in a purposeful life, one that has greater meaning. Almost every formal religion includes ritualized incantations to a higher power. Ordinarily, you might think of this as taking one of three forms. The first are the prescribed hymns you read in hymnals or prayers you might repeat in a church, synagogue, temple, or mosque. The second are the sort of ritualized sayings that you might repeat to yourself at bedtime or other times. Third are the sorts of prayers in which you ask for guidance or help from God or a higher power. But prayer can take many other forms as well.

Roughly half of Americans report that they pray every day in some form (Sheler, 2004). In a survey of what people pray about (Szegedy-Maszak, 2004), the responses are as varied as can be imagined. People pray for a cure to a terminal disease. They pray for wealth and job promotions, as well as for inspiration, strength, or wisdom. They ask for relief from depression and anxiety. They offer blessings of gratitude. They pray for world peace, or the end of violence. And they pray for serenity in lives that are over-scheduled and overstressed.

Whether in Christianity, Islam, Judaism, Hinduism, Buddhism, or any of the other formal religions, prayer evolved more than 5,000 years ago as a way to make connections with the beyond and recruit assistance from the unknown spirits to aid in the success of the hunt for food (Spoto, 2004). It has since taken forms in most religious traditions that give adoration to a higher power, offer thanks for past, present, or future benefits, request favors, or seek to prevent disasters (Zaleski & Zaleski, 2005). In the context of stress prevention and management, I am discussing prayer mostly in the context of the comfort it offers during times of difficulty.

The research on the effects of prayer is inconclusive. Billions of people on this planet would testify passionately that their prayer rituals bring them not only what they ask for, but also peace of mind. They claim to be in better health and feel greater life satisfaction as a result of their prayers. They report feeling a closer connection, not only to a higher power, but also to others around them. They feel less alone and isolated. They feel the support and love of a supreme being who loves and accepts them no matter how imperfect they might be. In the face of uncertainty, of trials and tribulations, they feel added strength knowing that they have a spiritual power at their side.

Yet, in spite of overwhelming anecdotal evidence, there is no concrete scientific support that true believers who pray frequently are healthier and live longer than atheists and agnostics who never pray. Nevertheless, even if no measurable effects can be consistently substantiated, it is enough that some people experience subjective benefits: as with so many things in life, if you believe an activity helps you, then it is worthwhile to continue it.

For some, prayer is about forgiveness, about letting go of negative energy and unresolved issues. You learned in earlier chapters about the toxic effects of holding on to anger and letting it fester inside. Practicing forgiveness means doing what you can to surrender all bitterness, resentment, hostility, humiliation, and residual anger. It *doesn't* mean letting people walk all over you, nor does it mean *forgetting* how you were treated unjustly; rather it involves making a conscious decision to abandon your own ongoing suffering (Lewis & Adler, 2004).

When the late John Paul II was shot in an assassination attempt by Mehmet Ali Agca, the Pope visited the man in prison and spent half an hour with him. He did this not only to relieve any lingering animosity he might have felt toward his assassin, but also to bring Agca some peace. He thus offered his blessing and presented the prisoner with a silver rosary as a symbol of his forgiveness.

This might strike you as going well beyond the call of duty—to actually forgive the person who tried to kill you—but it represents behavior that is not only generous but also self-restorative. This might be easy to say but extremely difficult to go against the natural tendency to seek revenge and retribution (Hallowell, 2004).

FOR REFLECTION 8.9

Regardless of religious background and spiritual beliefs, most people believe in a higher power. For you, that could be God, the Holy Spirit, Buddha, Allah, Yahweh, Jehovah, Elohim, Zeus, Vishwa, or it could be Nature, the universe, love, or whatever.

Write your own prayer of forgiveness. This should not be one that was already created for you, or one that you have read before. It should be something very personal that you create to speak directly to the core of your spiritual beliefs.

Think of a time recently in which you believe someone wronged you or harmed you, through either intention or neglect. This should be someone against whom you have harbored resentment and anger for some time. You have not been able to let this incident go, and it continues to invade your awareness at times when your guard is down.

Let's pretend that you are prepared to offer a prayer of forgiveness. You are tired of holding on to your anger, of feeling like a victim, and you want to ask for help to surrender your ongoing animosity.

Write a prayer of forgiveness in which you are able to let go of what happened, to feel compassion and understanding for the other person(s), and to move on in such a way that you no longer hold on to your negative feelings. I recognize that this task is extremely difficult, but that does not mean to say that you can't do it if you so choose. *That* is the power of prayer.

A prayer of forgiveness

SUMMARY

Psychological and spiritual methods of stress management and prevention have at their core a sense of personal power in which an individual can moderate negative emotional effects through various uses of the disciplined mind. All of the strategies described in this chapter make it possible to reduce significantly the tension that results from daily conflict and pressures. In particular, mindfulness meditation practice is associated with reduced stress, reduced depression, and alleviation of chronic pain. However, they all require some degree of ongoing commitment and daily practice in order to work well over time.

QUESTIONS FOR REVIEW

1. Explain how the mind and body are connected. Describe how this principle affects the practice of relaxation techniques.
2. Discuss the concept of altered states of consciousness. Identify three common characteristics of such states.
3. What is the relationship between relaxation techniques and altered states of consciousness?
4. Define guided imagery. Explain the six types of guided imagery.
5. Discuss why imagery is effective.
6. Give a history of autogenic training and then describe the six formulas of the technique.
7. Explain how mindfulness meditation can be used to help you relax and become more creative and peaceful. Discuss why meditation is effective when properly employed.
8. Differentiate between restrictive meditation and inclusive meditation by emphasizing the function of each.
9. Describe some functional and structural changes in the brain induced by mindfulness meditation practice.
10. Describe the difference between religion and spirituality. Discuss the role of religion and spirituality in stress management.

SELECTED ANSWERS

Answer to FOR REFLECTION 8.3

1. *It's not my fault.* Regardless of where the fault lies, I wonder what I can do to change it.
2. *The cold weather just gets me down.* I let myself feel discouraged by the weather.
3. *The guy just drives me crazy.* I really upset myself over what that guy sometimes does and says.
4. *I'm just not good at this. I've never been good at this.* I've struggled with this sometimes in the past but I could improve if I chose to devote the time and energy to it.
5. *It was just bad luck that things worked out this way.* I make my own luck through planning, practice, and perseverance.

Note: There are many possible ways to change these statements to make them internally based. The key aspect of the method is to accept as much responsibility as possible, avoid blaming others or external forces, and to frame statements in terms of possibilities for the future.

REVIEW ACTIVITY

Review Activity 8.1: The "Child Within" Guided Imagery Exercise (adapted from Branden, 1986)

Find a photograph of yourself taken when you were a three- to six-year-old child. Look at the picture carefully and get a clear image of what you looked like at that age. Choose a quiet spot where you won't be disturbed for the next 15 to 20 minutes. Slowly close your eyes, take several deep breaths, and say "relax" on each exhalation.

Begin to create the following scenario in your mind. First, visualize the home where you lived as a child between the ages of three and six. What was your favorite spot? Perhaps your home had a front porch, a balcony, a tree in the yard, or a nearby park where you used to go to sit. Now imagine yourself, at your present age, returning to that spot. Waiting for you in the distance is a young child. As you walk closer and closer, you discover that that child is *you*, at a much younger age. The child looks up and recognizes you as an adult. What are you feeling right now? Whatever you feel, it is safe to continue. Mentally picture yourself sitting down and facing the child. Start a conversation, as slowly as you can, answering these two questions: (1) What does the child say or ask? (2) What do you say or ask? Imagine a full conversation.

Reassure the child that you know he/she did the best he/she could, that he/she survived, that you still and always will love him/her, and that you will never leave him/her. Actually picture this situation, hear yourself saying the words, let yourself feel what's going on. Picture yourself holding and hugging yourself as a child. Allow the child to respond or not, as he/she chooses; be gentle and patient. Tell the child that you will always be available for conversation, whenever he/she desires. Ask the child if he/she would be willing to do the same for you. Then, say goodbye for now.

After this exercise, write down in the following space your feelings and thoughts.

REFERENCES AND RESOURCES

Aitken, R. (1996). *Encouraging words: Zen Buddhist teachings for Western students.* New York, NY: Pantheon.

Baruss, I. (2003). *Alterations of consciousness: An empirical analysis for social scientists.* Washington, DC: American Psychological Association.

Benson, H. (1997). *Timeless healing.* New York, NY: Simon & Schuster.

Benson, H. (2000). *The relaxation response* (2nd ed.). New York, NY: Perennial.

Bien, T., & Bien, B. (2003). *Finding the center within: The healing way of mindfulness meditation.* New York, NY: Wiley.

Branden, N. (1986). *The psychology of high self-esteem* (audio). Niles, IL: Nightingale-Conant.

Butler, C. K. (2004, December 27). Learn to meditate. *U.S. News and World Report,* pp. 38–39.

Butler, K. (2006). Being there. *Psychotherapy Networker,* January/February, 61–64.

Carrington, P. (1977). *Freedom in meditation.* New York, NY: Doubleday.

Chiesa, A., & Serrett, A. (2009). Mindfulness-based stress reduction for stress management in healthy people: A review and meta-analysis. *Journal of Alternative and Complementary Medicine, 15*(5), 593–600.

Corey, G. (2006). *I never knew I had a choice* (8th ed.). Belmont, CA: Thomson.

Csikszentmihalyi, M. (1988). The flow experience and its significance for human psychology. In M. Csikszentmihalyi, & I. S. Csikszentmihalyi (Eds.), *Optimal experience: Psychological studies of flow in consciousness* (pp. 15–35). Cambridge, UK: Cambridge University Press.

Davidson, R. J., & Harrington, A. (Eds.) (2002). *Visions of compassion: Western scientists and Tibetan Buddhists examine human nature.* New York, NY: Oxford University Press.

Davis, M., Eshelman, E. R., and McKay, M. (1988). *The relaxation and stress reduction workbook* (3rd ed). Oakland, CA: New Harbinger.

Delgado, C. (2005). A discussion of the concept of spirituality. *Nursing Science Quarterly, 118*(2), 157–162.

Delmonte, M. (1984). Physiological responses during meditation and rest. *Biofeedback and Self-Regulation, 9*(2), 181–200.

Durham, E., & Frost-Hartzer, P. (1994). Relaxation therapy for children and families. *Maternal Child Nursing, 19*(4), 222–225.

Ellis, A. (1987). *The practice of rational emotive therapy.* New York, NY: Springer.

Ellis, A. (2001). *Overcoming destructive beliefs, feelings, and behaviors: New directions for rational emotive behavior therapy.* Amherst, NY: Prometheus.

Ellis, A. (2004). *Rational emotive behavior therapy: It works for me—it can work for you.* Amherst, NY: Prometheus.

Fanning, P. (1992). *Visualization for treating cancer.* Oakland, CA: New Harbinger.

Grossman P., Niemann, L., Schmidt S, & Walach, H. (2004). Mindfulness-based stress reduction and health benefits. A metaanalysis. *Journal of Psychosomatic Research, 57,* 35–43.

Hallowell, E. M. (2004). *Dare to forgive.* Deerfield Beach, FL: Health Communications.

Hanh, T. N. (1999). *The miracle of mindfulness.* Boston, MA: Beacon Press.

Hanh, T. N. (2005). *The long road turns to joy: A guide to walking meditation* (rev. ed.). New York, NY: Unified Buddhist Church.

Hayes, S. C., & Smith, S. (2005). *Get out of your mind and into your life.* Oakland, CA: New Harbinger.

Hölzel, B. K., Lazar, S. W., Gard, T., Schuman-Olivier, Z., Vago, D. R., & Ott, U. (2011). How does mindfulness meditation work? Proposing mechanisms of action from a conceptual and neural perspective. *Perspectives on Psychological Science, 6*(6), 537–559.

Howard, V. (1981). *Psycho-pictography: The new way to use the miracle power of your mind.* West Nyack, NY: Parker.

Iveleva, L., & Orlick, T. (1991). Mental links to enhanced healing: An exploratory study. *Sport Psychologist, 5,* 25–40.

Jacobson, E. (1929). *Progressive relaxation.* Chicago, IL: University of Chicago Press.

Jung, C. G. (1963). *Memories, dreams, reflections.* New York, NY: Vintage.

Kabat-Zinn, J. (1990). *Full catastrophe living: Using the wisdom of your body and mind to face stress, pain and illness.* New York, NY: Dell.

Kabat-Zinn, J. (1995). *Wherever you go, there you are: Mindfulness meditation in everyday life.* New York, NY: Hyperion.

Kabat-Zinn, J. (2003). Mindfulness-based stress reduction (MBSR). *Constructivism in the Human Sciences, 8,* 73–107.

Kabat-Zinn, J. (2005). *Coming to our senses: Healing ourselves and the world through mindfulness.* New York, NY: Hyperion.

Kalb, C. (2004, September 27). Buddha lessons. *Newsweek,* p. 48.

Koenig, H. G. (2009). Research on religion, spirituality, and mental health: A review. *Canadian Journal of Psychiatry, 54*(5), 283–291.

Kottler, J. A., & Carlson, J. (2006). *When the spirit moved me.* Atascadero, CA: Impact.

Lazar, S., Kerr, C., Wasserman, R., Gray, J., Greve, D., et al. (2005). Meditation experience is associated with increased cortical thickness. *Neuroreport, 16*(17), 1893–1897.

Lebow, J. (2005). Mindfulness goes mainstream. *Psychotherapy Networker*, September/October, 91–92.

Lewis, J., & Adler, J. (2004, October 4). Forgive and let live: Revenge is sweet, but letting go of anger at those who wronged you is a smart route to good health. *Newsweek*, p. 54.

Martindale, C. (1981). *Cognition and consciousness.* Homewood, IL: Dorsey Press.

Mate, G. (2003). *When the body says no: Understanding the stress–disease connection.* New York, NY: Alfred Knopf.

McCullough, M. E., Hoyt, W. T., Larson, D. B., Koenig, H. G., & Thoresen, C. (2000). Religious involvement and mortality: A meta-analytic review. *Health Psychology, 19,* 211–222.

Miller, W. R., & Thoresen, C. E. (2003). Spirituality, religion, and health: An emerging research field. *American Psychologist, 58,* 24–35.

Naparstek, B. (1995). *Staying well with guided imagery.* New York, NY: Warner Books.

Noonan, D. (2004, September 27). Altered states. *Newsweek*, pp. 76–77.

Oxman, T. E., Freeman, D. H., & Manheimer, E. D. (1995). Lack of social participation or religious strength and comfort as risk factors for death after cardiac surgery in the elderly. *Psychosomatic Medicine, 57,* 5–15.

Payne, R. A. (2003). *Relaxation techniques: A practical handbook for the health care professional.* Edinburgh, UK: Churchill Livingstone.

Praissman, S. (2008). Mindfulness-based stress reduction: A literature review and clinician's guide. *Journal of the American Academy of Nurse Practitioners, 20*(4), 212–216.

Roberts, M. (2008). Running to stand still. *Outside*, January, 68.

Rossman, M. L. (2003). *Fighting cancer from within.* New York, NY: Owl Books.

Rowling, J. K. (1999). *Harry Potter and the prisoner of Azkaban.* New York, NY: Arthur A. Levine.

Sadigh, M. R. (1991). Hemi-Sync and insight-oriented psychotherapy. *Hemi-Sync Journal, IX*(2), 1–2.

Schultz, J. H., & Luthe, W. (1959). *Autogenic training: A psychophysiologic approach in psychotherapy.* New York, NY: Grune & Stratton.

Segal, Z., Williams, J., & Teasdale, J. (2013). *Mindfulness based cognitive therapy for depression: A new approach to preventing relapse* (2nd ed.). London, UK: Guilford Press.

Shapiro, S. L., Astin, J. A., Bishop, S. R., & Cordova, M. (2005). Mindfulness-based stress reduction for health care professionals: Results from a randomized trial. *International Journal of Stress Management, 12*(2), 164–176.

Sheler, J. L. (2004, December 20). The power of prayer. *U.S. News and World Report*, pp. 51–54.

Simonton, C. O., Matthews-Simonton, S., & Creighton, J. L. (1992). *Getting well again.* New York, NY: Bantam Books.

Smith, J. E., Richardson, J., Hoffman, C., & Pilkington, K. (2005). Mindfulness-based stress reduction as supportive therapy in cancer care: Systematic review. *Journal of Advanced Nursing, 52*(3), 315–327.

Spoto, D. (2004). *In silence: Why we pray.* New York, NY: Viking.

Szegedy-Maszak, M. (2004, December 20). How we talk to God. *U.S. News and World Report*, pp. 55–60.

Taren, A. A., Creswell, J. D., & Gianaros, P. J. (2013). Dispositional mindfulness co-varies with smaller amygdala and caudate volumes in community adults. *PLoS ONE, 8*(5), Article e64574. Retrieved on October 30, 2015 from http://www.plosone.org/article/info%3Adoi%2F10.1371%2Fjournal.pone.0064574.

Tart, C. T. (Ed.). (1972a). *Altered states of consciousness* (2nd ed.). Garden City, NY: Anchor.

Tart, C. T. (1972b). Introduction. In C. T. Tart (Ed.), *Altered states of consciousness* (pp. 1–6). Garden City, NY: Anchor.

Tart, C. T. (1972c). *States of consciousness.* New York, NY: E. P. Dutton.

Trakhtenberg, E. C. (2008). The effects of guided imagery on the immune system: A critical review. *International Journal of Neuroscience, 118,* 839–855.

Tuck, I., Alleyne, R., & Thinganjana, W. (2006). Spirituality and stress management in healthy adults. *Journal of Holistic Nursing, 24,* 245–253.

USA Today/Gallup Poll (2010, May 1–2). *Religion.* Retrieved on June 21, 2010 from www.pollingreport.com/religion.htm.

Way, B. M., Creswell, J. D., Eisenberger, N. I., & Lieberman, M. D. (2010). Dispositional mindfulness and depressive symptomatology: Correlations with limbic and self-referential neural activity during rest. *Emotion, 10,* 12–24.

Williams, M. (1975). *The velveteen rabbit.* New York, NY: Doubleday.

Zaleski, P., & Zaleski, C. (2005). *Prayer: A history.* Boston, MA: Houghton Mifflin.

9
Physical Methods for Stress Reduction

In the previous chapter I introduced you to stress management strategies that operate within the psychological or spiritual domain. The strategies in this chapter work at a physical level. The division is not quite as clear as it sounds, since many of the psychological techniques described earlier promote physical changes, just as those described here have strong psychological effects as well. In fact, many of the techniques in this chapter, such as yoga and tai chi, can also be called mind–body exercises since they attempt to unify the body, mind, and spirit.

If the techniques introduced in Chapter 8 are designed to achieve the goal of stress reduction and inner peace from the inside out, then the techniques in this chapter tend to achieve the same goals from outside in. What this means is that rather than thinking about certain ideas or images in order to reduce stress, you have to *do* something that requires **physical activity**.

Throughout this book I have sometimes made artificial distinctions between physical and psychological phenomena even though most scholars and writers believe them to be inseparable. This mind–body connectivity suggests that any emotional reaction you might have also contains neurochemical components. Similarly, wherever thought

KEY QUESTIONS IN THE CHAPTER

- How is physical fitness related to stress? What are the components of physical fitness?
- What are the principles for prescribing exercise for cardiovascular fitness?
- What does research say about the benefits of physical exercise?
- What are the differences between physical activity different from physical exercise?
- What is progressive muscle relaxation? How do you perform a progressive muscle relaxation?
- Why is it that breathing becomes shallow and irregular under stress?
- What is the connection between breathing and relaxation?
- What are the common elements of yoga and tai chi?
- What is the yin–yang theory?

goes, chemical and hormone reactions follow. When you examine an emotion—fear, for example—reducing the stress associated with it involves psychological feelings such as calmness as well as physical responses such as relaxed muscles. This leads, inevitably, to the realization that the best stress prevention and management strategies include both psychological *and* physical features. Learning deep breathing methods is excellent, for instance, in controlling sudden stress reactions to a threatening situation, but these are even more effective when accompanied by cognitive self-talk.

Another artificial dichotomy is often raised with respect to methods that originate from Eastern cultures such as China, India, Nepal, and Japan (i.e., tai chi, yoga, meditation) versus those that were developed primarily in Western countries (cognitive restructuring, **physical exercise**). Certainly the Eastern and Western world views are different in the ways they conceptualize disease, stress, and healing.

Western medicine tends to view the body as a mechanical system that is hard-wired and includes pumps and levers, while Chinese medicine views the body as a series of energy centers, dividing the body into meridians and energy lines that can be balanced with the right kinds of physical activity and psychological relaxation. Today more and more areas of health care are embracing a **holistic approach** to treating and preventing diseases (Fontaine, 2005).

The Cost of Progress

One reason for the increased stress in modern life is the reduced physical activity resulting from a more sedentary lifestyle in which we spend endless hours sitting in a car, behind a desk, in front of a computer, or watching television. Our bodies were designed to run at a high pace to keep them tuned and in peak condition; an absence of such regular exercise can be highly detrimental. It has been estimated that 10% of all deaths in the US are attributable to a lack of regular exercise and poor fitness levels (Casey & Benson, 2004).

As you may recall from Chapter 2, physical manifestations of stress are an inherent part of the fight-or-flight reaction. No doubt one reason for this is that our ancestors were confronted with primarily physical stressors that required combat, flight, and other movements. Whether a stressor is a physical threat or a psychological fear, your body still wants to respond with physical movement. It doesn't matter whether you go for a recreational jog or flee from a predator: it just craves physical exercise as a way to metabolize the stress.

VOICE OF STRESS 9.1

College Professor in His Forties

My job has changed so much since I first began teaching. A number of years ago, before we used desk computers all day, I used to have to walk across campus to the computer complex in order to have data run. Now I barely have to turn my chair. I used to spend a lot more time actually talking to students, sitting face to face to talk about issues. Almost all our communications these days are via email. When a student does come in to talk to me, I feel a bit annoyed because I have so much work to catch up on the computer. As fast as I can respond to email there is more coming in, sometimes over 100 in a day. I used to have to worry only about responding to messages on my office phone but now people can reach me 24/7 on my cell phone or mobile device.

The other day I had a question for a colleague in the office next door. I could have easily gotten up and walked over to his office to talk to him. I could have even probably just yelled through the wall. But instead I sent him an email. We hardly talk anymore. We hardly move out of our chairs. We're even teaching some classes via distance learning so we don't even have to walk to class. I don't know where all this is going to end but it frightens me.

The nature of stressors has changed significantly to those that are more emotionally based, yet our physiology has not evolved sufficiently to handle this shift. One reason for this is that whereas it takes only a few generations or less to alter human lifestyle (a single decade in the case of mobile devices) it takes tens of thousands of years in most cases for the body to make similar accommodations.

The fruits of technological innovation have resulted in far more convenient and efficient forms of communication and transportation that enable us to get from one place to another without having to exert much energy. Nowadays you can pick up the phone or send a text to a friend or relative across town in a matter of seconds, whereas 100 years ago it would have taken a day's journey on foot or horseback. This saves time but does not provide as many opportunities to stay in shape, to work off excess energy, or to have time for contemplation.

Benefits of Physical Exercise and Activity

Approximately one-third of Americans are significantly overweight and two-thirds don't exercise regularly (Gupta, 2008). This pattern of sloth for most adults began in their first year of college, when new demands on time resulted in much less physical exercise than occurred a year earlier. Even more telling is that during important life transitions, people tend to ignore old rules and develop new ones. Since college is the first major life transition for many people, it also provides a good excuse not to exercise—one of many that sabotage self-discipline (Gyurcsik, Spink, Bray, Chad, & Kwan, 2006).

The research is unequivocal: people who are physically fit are better able to handle stress. And college students who exercise regularly enjoy better health and psychological adjustment than do their peers who are less active (Bray & Kwan, 2006; Kim & McKenzie, 2014) and they report fewer symptoms of stress and better coping (Edward, 2006). Engaging in regular, sustained exercise—the kind that stimulates the cardiovascular system as well as maintaining muscle tone—produces a number of proven benefits (Blumenthal et al., 1999; Donaghy & Mutrie, 1999; Finlayson, 1997; King, Oman, Brassington, Bliwise, & Haskell, 1997; Scully, Kremer, Meade, Graham, & Dudgeon, 1998; Stains, 2007). People who exercise regularly have a higher sense of well-being and less stress in their lives than those who do not (Ensel, 2004). In particular, exercise helps to engender positive emotions (e.g., vigor, optimism), increase energy, and decrease negative emotions (e.g., anxiety, tension, tiredness and anger) (Puetz, 2006; Thaylor, 1987; Woo et al., 2009). They also enjoy a number of other benefits (see Table 9.1).

Given all these wonderful results such as prolonging life, improving health, and reducing stress, you might wonder why everyone doesn't engage in regular physical exercise. The answer is that is can be hard to maintain a regular schedule. Aerobic exercises (those that get your heart rate pumping and keep it at 80% of maximal intensity) involve a certain amount of pain and discomfort. You can easily check this out for yourself any time you see a runner or bicyclist on the side of the road—they usually look pretty grim. It is true that a vigorous workout, whether bicycling, running, swimming, or dancing, does involve discomfort, even if it can also produce a "high" once endorphins kick in. But those who are just beginning an exercise program for purposes of stress reduction will find that even starting with ten minutes of walking each day can make a difference.

Exercise and Stress Reduction

In addition to the physical benefits that accrue to regular exercisers, it has also been well established that working out regularly significantly improves your mental health (Ensel, 2004; Plante & Rodin, 1990; Scully, Kremer,

Table 9.1 What regular exercise will do for you

- Control weight
- Improve sleep
- Stabilize moods
- Improve cardiovascular functioning
- Reduce depression and anxiety
- Improve endurance and stamina
- Increase pain tolerance
- Improve body image
- Increase self-confidence
- Reduce high blood pressure and cholesterol levels
- Increase life expectancy
- Improve mental focus and concentration
- Provide periods of solitude for reflective thought
- Improve sex (yes, really!)

Meade, Graham, & Dudgeon, 1998). There are several explanations to account for this positive effect.

In the **biological adaptations hypothesis**, it is theorized that increased physical functioning and more efficient metabolism improve all the systems of the body including those that regulate mood (Jackson, Morrow, Hill, & Dishman, 2004). These adaptations include increases in body warming, brain blood flow, and endorphins; a more efficient regulation of pituitary–adrenal stress hormones; and changes in the autonomic nervous system, brain noradrenaline, and brain serotonin. These exercise-induced biochemical changes generate reduced arousal and enhanced mood, which may be accompanied by enhanced recovery time from stress and more healthy behaviors such as healthy eating habits during stressful times (Gerber & Pühse, 2009).

Another useful explanation, called the **psychosocial hypothesis** (Desharnais et al., 1993; Ekeland, Heian, & Hagen, 2005; Fox, 2000), proposes that exercise alters the *perceptions* that people have about themselves and their abilities. Once you become adept at tolerating the discomfort, as well as demonstrating the self-discipline involved in dedicating yourself to the activity, this can improve your confidence in a host of other areas. This enhanced self-confidence and self-esteem will have a positive influence on your ability to manage stress and thus maintain good health.

Regular exercisers report higher self-esteem than those who do not work out. They feel a greater sense of self-control and confidence (Jackson et al., 2004) as well as reduced anxiety in daily life (Morgan, 1985).

The good news is that it doesn't take a lot of exercise to make a difference in your life, especially in terms of stress control. In a series of studies on the effects of jogging or brisk walking on depression, it was found that regular exercise can sometimes work as effectively as antidepressant drugs (Servan-Schreiber, 2004). Furthermore, those who had begun walking or running were much more likely to sustain the improvement over those who had been taking drugs alone. Just 20 minutes per day, three times per week, produces significant results. Given increased concerns for weight control, and the need for regular rituals that can be incorporated into your life, it is better yet to include some exercise routine that you can maintain every day. It doesn't seem to matter which exercise you choose; the important thing is to make exercise a regular habit—a structure that is non-negotiable.

Kinds of Physical Activity and Exercise

Whether exercise is structured within a group activity like an aerobics or dance class, or maintained on your own, it is perhaps the single most effective stress management strategy, which also provides a number of health benefits. The main problem, however, is that people do not maintain their commitment over time.

Sometimes we use **physical activity** and physical exercise interchangeably in this text, but they are different concepts. According to the American College of Sports Medicine (ACSM) position stand paper on fitness guidelines (Garber et al., 2011), physical activity refers to any bodily movement involving contractions of skeletal muscles above resting levels. Examples of physical activity include housework, gardening, walking, and climbing stairs. Physical exercise, on the other hand, describes more structured and planned physical activity for the sake of improving health-related or performance-related **physical fitness**.

The best forms of exercise that garner much health benefits are those that maximize cardiorespiratory fitness, muscle strength and endurance, and flexibility. They allow you to function well over sustained periods of time (at least 20 minutes), to supply bursts of energy when needed, and to maintain a degree of flexibility to deal with whatever task may arise.

Exercise varies according to the type of energy production processes. **Aerobic exercise** refers to repetitive exercise done over a prolonged period of time, such as walking, running, and swimming. **Anaerobic exercises** are those in which the oxygen demands of muscles are so high that they rely on an internal metabolic process for oxygen, resulting in lactic acid buildup.

Short bursts of "all-out" activities such as sprinting or weight lifting are anaerobic, meaning that the lungs cannot physically take in all the oxygen required to sustain the level of performance. Activities such as baseball or tennis that last from 90 seconds to four-minute spurts are said to use a combination of aerobic (from the Latin *aero*, with oxygen, meaning that it burns oxygen and fat) and anaerobic (without oxygen, such as weight lifting) (Prentice, 1994). It is generally agreed that aerobic activities should be practiced regularly and moderately for the purpose of enhancing cardiovascular fitness and reducing stress. Ideally, a combination of the two types will maintain maximum fitness in terms of cardiovascular health, strength, and stress control.

Once you've decided to start an exercise program to improve your aerobic fitness, it is a good idea to get a physical checkup to make sure that you are not at risk for an injury. When someone has been sedentary for a long time, it can be dangerous to suddenly begin a vigorous change in lifestyle. That is one reason why progress should be incremental.

There are some basic guidelines to follow in order to reap maximum benefit from any exercise program (Garber et al., 2011):

1. *Type of exercise.* Choose a regular, purposeful exercise that involves major muscle groups such as walking, jogging, running, hiking, cycling, dancing, or swimming. You should pick an activity that appeals to you in terms of its movements and one that you can engage in on a regular basis without feeling bored or stale. Ideally it should be something that is fun for you.

2. *Exercise frequency.* Research indicates that three (vigorous) to five days (moderate exercise) per week is an optimal frequency (although daily is better yet). It is best to commit yourself to work out at the same time of day each session, and to program these time slots into your schedule just as you would with any important appointment.

3. *Exercise duration.* It is recommended that 30 to 60 minutes per day be spent on moderate to vigorous exercise. How much time you work out depends, in part, on the intensity of the workout. A spinning class (cycling on exercise bikes in a group) is a much more vigorous workout than riding your bike alone at a leisurely pace. Likewise, 45 minutes of brisk walking may be the equivalent of 25 minutes of moderate running.

4. *Exercise intensity.* Exercise intensity seems to be the most important factor. Most people may benefit from aerobic activities when intensity reaches at least 50% to 70% of their maximum output of cardiac functioning. In other words, it is important to push yourself in order to escape routines to which your body may have already become accustomed. It isn't so important to add more workouts each week, but rather to increase their intensity so that you burn more calories and energy (Hobson, 2005).

When you work out at a sufficient intensity, time, and frequency, your fitness level starts to rise and you will experience more energy and alertness, in addition to better conditioning. Once your body adjusts to the stabilized levels, it is best to increase one of the variables to further improve fitness levels. You can do this by working out more often, at a higher level, or for a longer period of time. You may also wish to include several different workout activities in your regimen to keep it interesting and protect against injuries from overuse of particular muscles. Some people do aerobic activity every other day, alternating with some form of weight training or recreational sport. What you do, and how often you do it, will depend on your degree of motivation, the level of fitness you wish to attain, your available time, and just how much stress you need to work off.

People's needs and interests vary, so it is important to match the preferred activity to your particular style. Some people can run on a treadmill for an hour without feeling bored; others need a variety of scenery. Some people enjoy working out in a fitness facility while others like to be in the outdoors. It is up to you to discover the level of challenge, comfort, and risk that you want in order to remain committed to a physical exercise program over time.

VOICE OF STRESS MANAGEMENT 9.1

Twenty-Three-Year-Old Female Student

There have been many stressful situations in my life. My husband is in the military and was headed for his second tour to Iraq. Knowing that he was going to be in a very dangerous area and not being able to call him to see how he was doing was very stressful for me. The worst thoughts would run through my mind when I didn't hear from him for a couple of days. Besides worrying if I would ever see my husband again, I had to study for finals. I had so much on my mind that I would break out in tears at least twice a day.

There would be days that I didn't want to get out of bed, because I knew that if I fell back asleep I wouldn't have to think about anything and when I woke up I would be one day closer to having my husband back home. My friends tried to cheer me up and take me out to get my mind off of things, but nothing really seemed to work. If anything it just made things worse; I always thought about how much more fun I would have if my husband were with me.

It took a while but I finally figured something out to get my mind off everything for a short time: running. I started running every night, and that was the only time throughout the day that my mind felt clear and my heart didn't ache. So for about five months straight I would run almost every night. It may have been only one mile, sometimes longer, but in that span of time I actually felt good. My husband has been home for a month now and we run together almost every night. The bad memories of running alone are gone and only good memories are being created now.

Aron Ralston is an example of someone on the far end of the risk continuum. He found himself easily bored by any activity that takes place indoors. He loves the outdoors, especially to be walking or climbing in the mountains. Just as much as the physical exercise, he feels driven to challenge and test himself. In fact, he set himself the goal to be the first person to climb all 59 of Colorado's 14,000 foot peaks—alone—in the winter! While there were a few others before him who managed to ascend all the mountains along with partners, in the usual summer climbing season, nobody else had managed to accomplish his stated goal, which was partially motivated by reducing stress in his life as an engineer who was feeling burned out. More and more often he found himself escaping into the mountains as a way to deal with the pressures at work.

Ralston's story is one of the most miraculous cases of courage and stamina ever recorded. It was during a "recreational" climb between his peak ascents that he found himself trapped in an isolated canyon with his arm pinned underneath a boulder that had dislodged on top of him. After spending a week dying of thirst, hunger, and exposure, he finally decided to amputate his own arm with a pocket knife (after first breaking the bones) and then try to hike out on his own for help.

Ralston eventually was rescued and recovered, but then resumed his mission to climb the remaining 14,000 foot peaks using a prosthetic limb, still alone in the winter. Why on earth would he ever do such a thing? Ralston does not suggest that anyone follow in his footsteps and take up solo mountaineering (especially after losing an arm). He explains:

But we all bring risk into our lives through our choices about how we make a living, how we drive, how we party, and how we eat: It's far riskier to be a McFood-pounding smoker than to climb solo. If it seems that I fill my days with moments that cause my heart to bound, my breath to rush, that's because those are the times I feel most alive.

(Ralston, 2006, p. 130)

Ralston seeks not only to improve his fitness by devoting himself to climbing but also to invigorate a life that felt meaningless and empty at times. Although I talk about ways to improve your own physical stamina, endurance, and strength, there are many psychological benefits that accompany this physical development.

Principles for Improving Fitness Levels

Physical fitness is defined as "[a set of] measurable health and skill-related attributes" that include cardiorespiratory fitness, muscular strength and endurance, body composition and flexibility, balance, agility, reaction time and power (Caspersen et al., 1985). Once you have started an exercise program and sustained it for a period of time, there are a number of things you can do to improve the quality of your workouts and the results you obtain:

1. *Progressive resistance.* In order to improve your strength, endurance, and fitness, you have to progressively increase the frequency, intensity, and time of your workouts. A simple way to stimulate your body is to try different activities. If you normally walk on the treadmill, try riding a bike to use different muscles. If you've been doing biceps curls with dumbbells, change to a barbell.

2. *Specificity.* Your training should be specific to your goals. For example, if you're trying to improve your racing times, you should focus on speed workouts. If your main goal is health, fitness, and weight loss, you should focus on total body strength, cardiovascular activity, and a healthy diet. Make sure your training matches your goals.

3. *Reversibility.* No fitness training produces permanent benefits. The cliché "use it or lose it" is mostly true, although the rate of loss depends on the previous intensity, frequency, and duration of workouts.

4. *Accumulation.* To benefit from aerobic activity, you don't have to work continuously in a workout for the target duration. What is important is the total number of minutes you have accumulated. For instance, congratulate yourself if you have done three ten-minute workouts during the day at 60% of your maximum cardiac output.

In order to prevent injuries and get maximum results from your exercise investment, a session should begin with a warm-up consisting of low-intensity exercise for a few minutes, followed by stretching, and then more vigorous workouts. A warm-up helps prevent potential injuries by preparing the body to work more efficiently. Likewise, it is a good idea to end each workout with some type of cool-down or stretching that gradually reduces heart rate, breathing, and core temperature. This has the added benefits of preventing blood pooling in your legs, removing lactic acid from muscles, reducing adrenaline in your system, and diminishing muscle stiffness and soreness.

It is most important to tailor the exercise program to your particular interests, needs, and schedule. It is senseless to begin a program that you are not prepared to maintain for the rest of your life. It is also critical that the form of exercise you choose is one that you actually enjoy; otherwise it will become just another dreaded obligation in your life that creates more stress.

Among all the ideas and techniques for stress reduction presented in this text, improving your level of physical fitness through exercise is probably the one that is most easily accessible and will produce the most immediate results. It doesn't require doing anything dramatically different from what you are already doing—just doing more of it at a more vigorous pace. Engaging in a regular exercise routine not only will get your body in shape, improving your body image and functioning levels, but will help to calm you down. You will sleep better, feel more relaxed throughout the day, and whatever is nagging at you can be kept at bay if you truly concentrate on what you are doing.

Principles for maintaining healthy exercise are:

1. *Start with a schedule that is realistic for you.* Make a commitment that you can stick with no matter what and have no excuse for not meeting your goal.
2. *Build exercise into your daily or weekly life.* Allocate a certain time block that is sacred and non-negotiable. This can be during mornings, the lunch hour, or after work, but it must be time that you don't trade away for other tasks that you might think are more important. *Nothing* is more important than taking care of your body and reducing stress.
3. *Monitor your progress over time.* One of the ways to reward and reinforce your continued commitment to exercise is to note the changes that take place in your body, weight, and sense of well-being.
4. *Build variety into your routines.* Prevent boredom by varying the exercise choices you make. Combine weight lifting, running, walking, swimming, bicycling, or aerobics with other options that could include martial arts, skiing, basketball, tennis, dancing, surfing, or tai chi.
5. *Make it social.* Find partners with whom you can work out with on a regular or occasional basis. It really helps to have a support system.
6. *Fit exercise into your daily routines and errands.* Take the stairs whenever you can. Park further away than normal so you can walk. Go dancing for entertainment. Play recreational sports that burn calories. Walk or ride your bike for simple errands.

Doing *any* form of exercise, in *any* manner, is better than nothing at all. However, if you spend the time while walking or working out obsessing about what is most bothersome, reliving past suffering, or planning all the things you have to do during the day, you might only be making things worse. It is not just the physical activity that makes exercise effective as a stress reducer; what you are doing inside your head during the activity is also critical. If you find yourself getting upset with your performance (which wouldn't be that surprising if you are doing the same thing in other areas of your life) then practice lightening things up, avoiding "keeping score" and otherwise making the activity more competitive than stress-reducing.

Monitor what you are feeling and thinking during the times you are exercising. If you catch yourself thinking about stressful events about the past or future, you have several choices.

The first option is to do nothing, which is self-defeating. In this case your time could be spent making things worse rather than better, especially if you are ruminating about things that make you crazy—reliving fights you've had, rehearsing all the things you wish you had said to someone, taking inventory of injustices you've suffered, and working yourself up over tasks that lie ahead. In this instance you could end up even more stressed than before you began the exercise.

The other options can be found in the methods you have already learned for counteracting stress-inducing thinking, such as cognitive restructuring to challenge irrational ideas and meditation for gently pushing aside undesirable or distracting thoughts. There are several ways that you can accomplish this end. Champion athletes have a different outlook than low-performing amateurs. Rather than escaping from the pain, they choose to constantly monitor what is going on in their bodies. They focus on their breathing, carefully observe their posture and body position, and make certain they are following proper technique that they have rehearsed to make sure they are operating at peak efficiency. They are using not only every possible source of physical activity but also mental energy. There is no room in their heads to think about anything else.

Increasing your fitness through exercise involves improving not only performance and conditioning but also your mental acuity. In order to reduce the stress in your life,

FOR REFLECTION 9.1

Current situation: What exercise are you currently doing on a regular basis?

Activities

Frequency

Duration

Future goals: What are you willing to commit yourself to do in the next two weeks to increase the level of your fitness and reduce your stress? Write down *exactly* what you are absolutely prepared to do, how often, with no possible excuses for failure to keep your promise.

If you are not currently exercising at all, then plan for a minimum workout that you know you can complete, even if it is just walking ten minutes per day, three days per week. At the beginning level it doesn't matter what you do, or how often, as long as you stick with your plan.

If you are currently exercising on a regular basis, write down what you intend to do in the next two weeks to improve the level of workout.

Week 1
What I will do

How often I will do it (which days and times)

Week 2
What I will do for continued improvement

How often

you must use the exercise time in the most fully functioning way possible. Distracting and self-defeating thoughts can also be managed by increasing the physical challenges. One way to stop the anxious thoughts is to stoke up what you are doing by increasing the pace, the difficulty, or the complexity.

A final word of caution: anything that can be done in moderation can also be taken to an extreme. College students, in particular, can be prone to a form of "exercise bulimia" in which they work out for hours each day in a misguided attempt to lose weight. Such behavior can lead to stress bone fractures, early osteoporosis, and is classified as an eating disorder because of the same compulsive behavior that results from a distorted body image. Almost half of college students know somebody with this problem (National Eating Disorders Association, 2006).

Progressive Muscle Relaxation

Progressive muscle relaxation (PMR) is a physical relaxation technique in which an individual learns to achieve the goal of stress reduction by becoming aware of tensions in various muscle groups, and then relaxing them one at a time throughout the body. It was Dr. Edmund Jacobson who developed PMR to treat many ailments of his patients more than 50 years ago (Davis, Eshelman, & McKay, 1988). In his original book *Progressive Relaxation*, published in 1929, he stated that failure to release the neuromuscular tension in the body is related to various somatic, neurological, and psychiatric disorders. For the first time, there was scientific evidence that tension and anxiety may cause disease and relaxation-based therapies could offer relief and treatment for many patients' health problems.

The PMR technique was based on scientific studies of muscular tension. The technique encompasses three major principles. First, muscular tension and deep muscle relaxation repel each other; the former contributes to illness and the latter brings forth healing. Second, in order to control tension and achieve body relaxation, individuals are encouraged to identify degrees of muscular tension by tensing and relaxing various muscle groups. Third, PMR allows individuals to actively participate in their own treatment and well-being.

PMR Technique

Before you start the training, you need to find a quiet room where you are not likely to be disturbed. The temperature should be just right for you. Assume a comfortable position. Even though a prone position is more effective, a sitting position has some advantages too, especially when the floor may be too cold or hard. It is helpful to work with a partner who has a soothing voice. He or she may offer instructions during the session, or you may listen to a prerecorded audio CD. A prerequisite in training for this relaxation technique is for you to become more aware of the unnecessary tension in your body, wherever it may be (Luskin & Pelletier, 2005).

The procedure requires you to alternately tense and relax each of the major muscle groups of the body, one at a time, with the objective of becoming aware of the different degrees of tension with the intention of reducing it.

Begin by sitting up straight in your chair with your spine vertical, as if you are sitting at attention in your best possible posture. Relax your shoulders with your hands resting comfortably in your lap. Now take a few deep breaths.

As you take in a deep breath, clench your left fist as tightly as possible and notice the tension as it accumulates from the fist to the hand to the forearm. Then you will be asked to relax the fist and pay special attention to the difference between tensed and relaxed states. The procedure will be repeated with the right hand, moving up the arms, shoulders, neck, face, back, chest, and so on. Normally, it takes about 20 minutes to tense and relax all these muscle groups. However, at times you don't have 20 minutes to practice. Here are two short versions to achieve effective results when you practice them often.

VERSION I   Tense every muscle in your body, and hold yourself that way for as long as you can, at least to the count of ten. Clench your hands, your teeth, tighten your stomach, shoulders, thigh and calf muscles, and even your sphincter muscle—every muscle in your body that you can identify and contract. Keep your eyes and face and lips clenched as well, and stay that way as long as you hold your breath.

After the count of ten, begin to exhale slowly. As you do so, unwind and let *all* your muscles relax. Keep your posture reasonably straight, with your back supporting you, but allow your shoulders to collapse as well. Just sit for a moment and observe what it feels like for your body to be relaxed as compared with maximum tension.

VERSION II   Scan your body for tension spots. Once you identify the area that needs to be relaxed, tense the muscle group and then relax it while focusing on the sensations of the relaxed muscle. You may notice the warmth and tingling in the relaxed muscle group. Use imagination to spread this sense of relaxation to all parts of the body.

The main idea is that in order to relax, you first have to become more aware of when you are tense, especially when you hold that stress in your muscles. This is the essence of progressive muscle relaxation, although there are many varieties that you can practice, such as the partner exercise highlighted in For Reflection 9.2. The main goal is to reduce psychological pressure and stress by bringing down the levels of tension you hold in your body.

VOICE OF STRESS MANAGEMENT 9.2

Twenty-Four-Year-Old Female Student

One of the most helpful things about therapy was learning how to relax. I was there for what my therapist called OCD [obsessive compulsive disorder]. I do still have a few of my old tendencies, but I am much better at dealing with the anxiety I feel when I can't do something I really want to do. Seeing a fingerprint on a glass, on anything, still freaks me out! But the whole muscle relaxation thing my therapist walked me through was awesome! She started off by having me close my eyes and tense up my entire body, every muscle, even my face! Slowly, little by little, I was instructed to relax a muscle, or an area of my body. After practicing this for a while, I really learned how to recognize cues from my body. I could tell when I was getting tense. When my shoulders and neck would start to scrunch up I would take control and relax them. I now know how to get a handle on my body. It just took a bit of practice.

I get nervous about a lot of little things, like a jacket left hanging over a chair (it should be in the closet!). When things really get me tensed up, I either sit or lie down and practice tensing and releasing my muscles. It's a great way to get my mind off of my irrational thinking and get my body to relax. It also really helps me when I am going to sleep. I have trouble getting to sleep, I just keep thinking about dust mites floating through the air and into my nasal passages, infecting me! Bedtime is no picnic. Now, the whole relaxation thing is like a routine thing for me. After a couple of times I'm sleeping like a baby. It's crazy how something so simple can help so much.

Since Jacobson's original observations, the idea of reducing psychological stress through muscle relaxation has received much attention and has been adapted into a number of well-researched relaxation methods. For example, early behaviorists such as Joseph Wolpe (Wolpe, 1973; Wolpe & Wolpe, 1988) used progressive muscle relaxation as part of **desensitization training** for people with phobias or chronic fears. The main idea was first to help the person enter a completely relaxed condition, using an exercise such as the one described in For Reflection 9.2. Beginning with the lower extremities and working all the way through every muscle group in the body, the afflicted person would systematically tense and relax each muscle group. Calming images might also be employed to reduce all anxiety. Then and only then would the person be exposed to the mildest possible version of the fear, progressively increasing the stimuli until the person could handle more challenging fears.

For instance, in the case of someone afraid of flying, the person might first be shown a film of graceful birds in flight. With the slightest indication of anxiety, muscle relaxation would be reintroduced to bring the tension to manageable levels. Subsequent steps, over a period of several sessions, would gradually introduce progressively more direct manifestations of flight, until such time as the person could watch a movie of flights without apprehension. Eventually, these muscle relaxation methods would be internalized to the point that they would be used during an actual flight: each time the person felt the slightest discomfort, she would go through the progressive muscle relaxation. This is often an effective strategy.

Clinical Benefits and Cautions

PMR has been found to help reduce stress and anxiety among college students (Dolbier & Rush, 2012), improve quality of life and decrease anxiety and depression among arterial hypertension patients (Li et al., 2015), and reduce depression of multiple sclerosis patients (Safi, 2015). In addition to dealing with chronic fears, phobias, and apprehensions, PMR has been used for a variety of stress-related physical disorders such as teeth clenching (bruxism), temporomandibular joint disorder (TMJ) (a more chronic, severe form of jaw clenching), chronic back pain, tension headaches, insomnia, hypertension, and a multitude of neurological disorders and muscular complaints (Orne & Whitehouse, 2000). Biofeedback methods, which use machines to provide direct data on physiological responses, also assist people to assess the effectiveness of their relaxation exercises. Electromyograms (EMGs) are used to measure muscle tension, galvanic skin response measures electrical current during tension sweating, and electroencephalograms (EEGs) measure brain wave activity. In each case, participants learn to exert more control over their physiological responses to stress by relaxing their muscles and modifying other reactions. The feedback they receive from the machines allows them to make adjustments to get closer to their desired goals.

Even though PMR benefits those with hypertension and tension headache, it should be pointed out that application of this technique may also contribute to the lowering of blood pressure and exacerbate tension. It is suggested that certain contractions may be adjusted to avoid excessive tension buildup in practice.

Muscle relaxation methods need not be employed solely in a formal, structured session requiring solitude and a prone position. While this is preferred if you want to help yourself relax before sleep or to handle a particularly vexing situation, you can also use abbreviated versions in the actual situations in which you feel the stress building—while embroiled in a conflict, sitting in the dentist's chair, or stuck in heavy traffic.

Breathing

As you read these words, you are inhaling and exhaling, all without conscious intention; your autonomic nervous system is on the job. If you are relaxed, your breathing is regular, slow, deep, and rhythmic. Yet when you are stressed, it is a different picture altogether—your breathing becomes ragged, hurried, shallow, perhaps even panicky.

Being called on in class when you don't feel prepared is one of many stressful situations that require skills for stress reduction to allow you to lower your anxiety level and think clearly. Muscle relaxation and breathing techniques are particularly well suited to these situations because of their brief and immediate results—if you have practiced the skills ahead of time.

What happens when you're stressed? For one thing you learned earlier that under perceived emergency conditions breathing becomes rapid and shallow to produce as much oxygen as possible as quickly as possible for fight-or-flight responses. The same condition occurs during workouts or vigorous exercise—heart rate and breathing cycles speed up, going for quantity rather than quality inhalations.

It would make sense that during the opposite of stress—relaxation—the goal would be to breathe as deeply and slowly as possible. In fact, this is exactly the tranquilizing purpose of learning to breathe in ways that use your whole diaphragm, called **diaphragmatic breathing**.

The quality of your breathing can affect your health and vitality. Your breathing is also directly connected with the way you feel. Feeling calm and relaxed, you breathe deeply and fully. When you are stressed, your breathing becomes shallow, rapid, less able to provide needed oxygen and energy (Lewis, 2004). Deep breathing, on the other hand, revitalizes your body and brings about relaxation and calmness. It plays an important role in neutralizing the deleterious effects of stress and tension you experience in daily life (Kabat-Zinn, 2005).

FOR REFLECTION 9.2

It is best to find a partner who can read these instructions to you, and then you can do the same for him. It is important to read the directions in a slow, hypnotic voice, giving the person time to follow.

First, make yourself as comfortable as possible, preferably lying down somewhere. If this is not possible, then sit in your chair with both feet resting on the ground and resting as naturally as you can.

[Partner begins reading]

Close your eyes. For just a minute or two, concentrate on your breathing. Breathe deeply and slowly, taking each breath in from your nose and exhaling very, very slowly through your mouth with your lips slightly parted.
[Wait one minute while partner breathes]
Good. Now as you continue breathing slowly and deeply, feel your chest enlarge and your shoulders rise as you breathe in. Hold the breath for just a second, and then slowly let the breath escape, thinking the word "relax" as you feel the breath leave your body.
    Take several more deep breaths until you can feel this warm feeling of relaxation spread throughout your body.

[Wait for partner to breathe a few more times]

I want you to imagine that you are lying on a beach very similar to the one in the photograph. You are alone without any disturbances. You are just lying there, peacefully, concentrating on your breathing. You hear the sound of the waves in the background. You feel the warmth of the sun. You are just resting there peacefully, concentrating on your breathing, and thinking the word "relax."
[Remember to continue to read this slowly and hypnotically in a soothing voice]
As your chest continues to expand, and relax, expand and relax . . .
[Read this so that it is coordinated with the person's chest actually rising and falling]
. . . I want you to concentrate on all the tiny muscles in your chest and picture them relaxing . . . unwinding . . . loosening . . . stretching. Picture all the muscles in your upper chest relaxing with each breath you take.
    Remember to keep breathing deeply and slowly, thinking the word "relax" each time you exhale. Good.
    Now, notice this warm feeling of relaxation spreading from your chest into your shoulders. Concentrate with all your energy on the muscles in your upper chest and shoulders loosening, stretching. Feel all the tension draining away as you lie [or sit] in this peaceful place. This feeling of relaxation is spreading from your shoulders into your neck.

Depending on the time you have available, continue these instructions, moving through every part of the body. Ask the person to imagine the stretching, loosening, relaxing taking place in the lower shoulders, the arms and the hands, the neck, in all the muscles around the face, in the back of the neck, the back, moving down the spine into the legs, tops and bottoms, and finally into the feet.

Take your time and help your partner move through every muscle group in the body. Help the person to visualize all the tension draining away, all the stress just melting from the warmth of the sun. Remind the person to concentrate on breathing, on thinking the word "relax" with each exhale.

After each muscle is systematically relaxed, instruct the person to just float for a while and enjoy the feeling of total relaxation, continuing to concentrate on breathing.

To bring the person back to reality, count back slowly from 10 to 1, telling the person that he can feel alertness returning between the numbers.

FOR REFLECTION 9.3

Imagine you are sitting in class, nervous about being called on by the instructor. You don't feel prepared for the discussion and your gut tells you that it is your turn to be selected for ritual humiliation (that's what it feels like anyway). You are certain that you will make an absolute fool of yourself as a stuttering idiot. Everyone will laugh at you. The instructor will realize how stupid you really are. You'll probably get so worked up you won't even be able to open your mouth. Such are the exaggerated fantasies that are going through your head as you see the instructor looking around the room to pick the next student.

You duck your head but know that this is futile; it will only draw more attention to you. You remember what you learned about cognitive interventions and so try a little self-talk to keep things in perspective. You ask yourself what is the worst that can happen? You remind yourself that you will probably not die if you are chosen. But this isn't working for you—either because you are so nervous you can't concentrate or you never learned the method well enough to apply it in crisis situations like this one.

It's time to bring out your secret weapon—for emergencies only. Muscle relaxation can be used during stress crises, but only if you have practiced and rehearsed ahead of time. In this instance you take a few deep breaths, close your eyes for just a moment so you don't appear as if you are sleeping, and then say to yourself:

Okay. Relax my shoulders. Lower them. Feel the tightness in my neck. Picture the muscles unwinding. Relaxing. Another breath. Chest loosening. Stretching. I can breathe again. One more breath. Good. Ready.

You open your eyes with a half-smile. Sure enough, the instructor is staring directly at you and you know the worst has happened—you're about to be called on. But now it doesn't feel like such a big deal. You are feeling calmer and can think straight. Even though you aren't as well prepared as you would prefer, you can now respond in a more intelligent way.

Stressful situations like this one can be brought under control—as they are occurring—but only if you practice ahead of time the skills you will need during crises.

FOR REFLECTION 9.4

Take a few deep breaths, paying attention to what happens in your body. Notice in particular how your inhalations affect your shoulders, chest, and stomach.

During these deep breaths, do your shoulders rise? If so, this is evidence of muscular tension. Try breathing again, but this time with your shoulders and neck relaxed.

You probably noticed your chest expanding each time you took a breath. What happens to your stomach during this process? Does it move in? This actually makes breathing less effective during so-called chest breathing. It means that rather than using your diaphragm to properly ventilate your lungs, you are using your chest muscles, which is less effective than diaphragmatic breathing.

Try taking a few more breaths, but this time relax your shoulders so they don't rise as much and try to breathe from your chest rather than your stomach. This is not easy to do, is it?

At this time, you may wonder why breathing is so connected with relaxation, or lack thereof. In fact, many different kinds of breathing methods have been used to promote relaxation such as slow breathing, deep breathing, and abdominal breathing. Our breathing is closely connected with the autonomic nervous system, which influences the level of arousal and activation. The breathing pattern that goes hand in hand with the sympathetic branch of the autonomic nervous system is often rapid and shallow. On the other hand, when the parasympathetic branch is activated, the respiration is slow and deep. Therefore, deep, gentle, and slow breathing tends to promote parasympathetic activity, and in turn, relaxation (Loehr & Migdow, 1999; Sudsuang, Chentanez, & Veluvan, 1991). Likewise, one of the clearest signs that stress has been reduced is when your breathing returns to a slow, deep, and regular rhythm (Luskin & Pelletier, 2005).

The implications of this are profound because it means that during times of stress, you will notice that you are breathing rapidly but with shallow inhalations. This is consistent with what you learned about physiological changes that take place during perceived crises—the body attempts to pump more oxygen into the system for anticipated energy during a battle or flight. But if you can consciously and deliberately slow down your breathing to a more relaxed, deep, and efficient pace, you will notice corresponding changes in your mood.

VOICE OF STRESS MANAGEMENT 9.3

Twenty-Two-Year-Old Female Student

Sometimes I have so much going on in one day that I'm not able to take a breath. At work I deal with a lot of people, trying to help them as much as possible, but there's not enough time. I need to take a break but I can't do that either or I'll fall further behind. Plus I've got papers to write and exams to study for.

I've been trying to eat better and keep myself energized for class but I've found that what works best for me because it's quickest is to practice breathing techniques. I can do them any time of day, wherever I am—in the car, at work, at school. I just take some deep breaths to calm myself down. It helps me to slow down and seems to give me more energy.

When I'm on my way home from work or school I practice deep breathing while driving so I can relax easier. By the time I pull up in front of my house I don't feel so overburdened any more.

The Process of Breathing

The process of breathing involves drawing air into and out of the lungs. Besides food and water, this is the main pathway by which you supply your body with the source of all energy so it is particularly important that the system operates at peak efficiency. If starved of oxygen, all the organs and other systems in the body will suffer.

The lungs are enclosed in a sort of cage bounded below by the diaphragm and at the sides by the chest wall. Inhalation is caused by the increase in the volume of the thoracic cavity. Such an increase causes the air pressure in the cavity to drop below atmospheric pressure and air to be drawn into the lungs. The contraction of the ribcage's muscles, which causes the cage to move up and out, and the contraction of the diaphragm affect the increased volume of the thoracic cavity. All of this works in concert to help you take a breath.

By contrast, exhalation is a passive process caused by the decrease in the thoracic cavity's volume. The relaxation of the ribcage's muscles and the diaphragm into their resting positions causes the air pressure in the lungs to rise above atmospheric pressure, forcing the air out of the lungs.

If breathing is such a natural and automatic process, what is there to discuss about how to do it better?

As you have learned, chronic stress affects almost every system of the body, including respiration, which is increased during periods of perceived crisis. In one sense, people who are anxious or stressed all the time have "forgotten" how to breathe correctly.

Just as stress can affect the quality of your breathing, so changing the way you breathe can reduce stress and focus the mind (Fontaine, 2005; Kabat-Zinn, 2005; Payne, 2003; Sheally, 1996; Sudsuang et al., 1991). That is one reason why breathing is such an integral part of yoga and meditation techniques.

The correct way to breathe is when your stomach gently moves up and down as you breathe in and out. This is due to the fact that the diaphragm presses down on contents of your stomach during inspiration, causing it to bulge out. A newborn child breathes with the abdomen. As the child gets older, breathing becomes partially intercostal (chest breathing). During adult life most of us breathe only through the chest. Abdominal breathing (maximal use of the diaphragm) is almost forgotten.

PRACTICE BELLY BREATHING

During any time when you feel unduly anxious or stressed, even when you have difficulty sleeping, try the following exercise to breathe deeply from your belly instead of shallowly from your chest. It is important to practice this technique regularly when you are calm, in order to apply it correctly in circumstances when you are under pressure.

1. Get in a comfortable position, either lying down or sitting up straight with good posture.
2. Take a deep breath while imagining that your stomach is a large balloon that you are trying to slowly fill with as much air as you can. Place your hands on your belly, with your fingers barely touching, while you do this so you can feel the balloon slowly inflate.
3. Watch your hands rise as you inhale, and your fingertips separate. This gives you solid feedback about the depth of your inhalation.
4. Slowly and gradually exhale, deflating the balloon in your stomach. Observe your hands moving inwards, the fingertips once again making contact. Make sure your stomach remains relaxed throughout the process.
5. Repeat the belly breathing several times, continuing to watch your hands move in and out as evidence of your deep breathing.

(Source: Adapted from Luskin & Pelletier 2005)

Once you have practiced the basic breathing techniques that have been introduced, you will find innumerable ways to adapt them to various stressful situations you might face. Called on in class and you don't feel prepared? Close your eyes and take a deep, intentional breath until you find the nervousness abates. Late for an appointment and feel yourself getting flustered? Whether you are walking or driving, still in motion, you can calm the jitters through deep breathing. Trouble falling asleep? Someone getting on your case? Upset over a disappointment? Any of these situations can be managed with the simple breathing technique to restore equanimity and balance.

Among all the techniques and suggestions that I have offered in this book, there is none more basic and more useful than breathing exercises that you can practice every day. Taking ten, even five minutes, once or twice each day, to focus on your breathing helps not only to reduce stress but also to become more focused on the here and now—to become more mindful. As you have learned, this is very, very difficult to do. As in other forms of meditation described in the previous chapter, the mind constantly wanders with what Buddhists call "monkey chatter." One beginner to breathing mediation exercises describes his inner dialogue:

Oh, I am doing meditation, how relaxing, oops, I shouldn't be thinking so much, my knee hurts, wait, just focus on the breath, is that a woman in front of me or a guy with long, pretty hair anyway, wonder what's for lunch, hey, wait, count your breath, one, two three, four, did I turn off my car lights?

(Moore, 1997, pp. 11–12)

Just as with any skill, the more you practice breathing "mindfully" the easier it gets to concentrate and lose yourself in the process. Your brain stops racing. Your thoughts slow down. Time flows by in a different rhythm in which nothing else exists except what you are doing in that moment—simply breathing.

What is the benefit of committing yourself to do one more thing during the day? Surely you don't want to add more stress to your already overburdened life by making a promise to yourself to take time out for breathing exercises. How are you ever to fit all these new stress reduction exercises—meditation, yoga, self-talk, exercise, and so on— with all the other things you can't keep up with?

The answer to these reasonable questions is that there is absolutely nothing more important in your life than breathing well. It is something that takes place every moment, without your awareness, so taken for granted that it may seem absurd that you should practice it more. But I am talking about breathing in a different way than you have ever done before. I am inviting you to use mindful breathing as the primary vehicle by which you can relax yourself at will. No matter where you are—in an argument, on stage, in the car, crowded on a bus, taking an exam, under a tight deadline—you can always release the tension and pressure by simply taking your time to breathe—to breathe slowly, consciously, mindfully, allowing the breath to still your mind and the ceaseless distracting and annoying chatter.

Yoga

Yoga is an ancient system of exercise that originated in India. It combines yoga postures, relaxation, breathing, and meditation techniques with psychological, moral, and ethical principles. The meaning of yoga comes from a Sanskrit word which means "join" or "creating union." Therefore, yoga is founded on the philosophical concept that our lives are an energetic combination of body, mind, and spirit. Likewise, the three main elements in yoga are exercise, breathing, and meditation. Regular daily practice of all three parts of yoga produces a clear, bright mind, and a strong, capable body. These benefits influence your day-to-day lives with increased ability to deal with challenges of all kinds.

Background on Yoga

Yoga has been practiced for thousands of years in the East. In India, yoga is a way of life that offers physical and mental exercises for achieving self-realization and spiritual enlightenment. In the West, yoga has been treated mainly as a fitness method aimed at stress reduction and illness prevention (Fontaine, 2005).

The popularization of yoga is due to an Indian sage by the name of Patanjali who wrote the *Yoga Sutra*, the first text that helped to shape and define the practice of yoga. Yoga was first introduced to America by Swami Vivekananda in the 1890s. In the 1960s, the Maharishi Mahesh Yogi created transcendental meditation and further spread the influence of yoga.

There are many styles of yoga ranging from the gentle, such as **hatha**, to the more vigorous like

Practitioners of yoga are able to demonstrate remarkable feats of endurance, flexibility, discipline, and skill. There have been documented reports of yogis who have been able to reduce their resting pulse rates to just a few beats per minute and who can remain in a posture for hours at a time without movement.

Men and women practicing yoga meditation led by a teacher.

astanga. Some forms of yoga have a strong spiritual dimension—an emphasis that is just as important as learning and practicing the various postures. Devotees are encouraged to practice love for all living things.

Fundamental Concepts of Yoga

Yoga is a powerful exercise system for healing that is based on several philosophical and scientific principles. An impressive body of research has demonstrated that regular yoga practice can reduce anxiety and depression by changing brain chemistry, alleviate symptoms of stress, and decrease anger and aggression. This is in addition to physiological benefits in reducing pain and insomnia as well as improving breathing.

Yoga is unusual in its emphasis on physical, emotional, and spiritual components. It seeks to achieve the following goals:

1. *Relaxation and tension release.* Yoga practice aims at releasing the tension in the muscles and putting the whole body at rest. This results in a revitalized nervous system, inner peace, and heightened energy.

2. *Postures.* Yoga postures are designed to help release tension and cleanse the body of toxins. Using proper postures you may systematically stretch and tone the muscles and ligaments, improve the flexibility of the spine and joints, and enhance blood circulation.

3. *Breathing.* As breath is considered the source of all life, yoga students increase their breath control to improve the health and the function of both body and mind.

VOICE OF STRESS MANAGEMENT 9.4

30-Year-Old Female Office Administrator and Student

When I started taking hatha yoga I wasn't quite sure it was for me. It seemed a little too complicated, like I would have to take years of classes to learn. The wonderful thing was that I felt great after the first class. Now, five years later I'm a regular.

I remember the very first night of class. I was stressed out, and not just from my day, but the traffic I encountered trying to get to the first class on time had me tense and sweaty before I even got there. When we got started, all of my worries disappeared. It took a little while for the tension to recede, but after the warm-up and a few stretches I felt free. The poses, or "asana" as Yogis call them, were hard to master at first, but the instructor always had modifications for those of us not ready, or in shape enough, to perform. At the end of the class the instructor had us lie down on our backs and close our eyes. She turned down the lights and guided us on a journey to a faraway place. Soon I found myself in a hammock on a beach in Jamaica, swaying in the wind and hearing nothing but the ocean breeze. I was hooked!

Now, every morning I wake up and perform the asana, Surya Namaskar (sun salutation). This sequence is designed to open my heart to the sun. It begins and ends with my hands pressed together touching my heart. I was taught that this is symbolic of the mantra that only the heart can know the truth.

Each posture is always accompanied and guided by breathing fully, deeply, and rhythmically.

4. *Self-control.* As a philosophy, yoga encourages moderation in all things. Practitioners are encouraged to apply the self-discipline of the exercises to other aspects of their lives.

5. *Focused concentration.* The practice of yoga requires complete concentration. It represents a kind of physical meditation in which you focus all your attention on breathing and clearing the mind.

6. *Inner peace.* The ultimate goal of yoga practice is the union of the body, mind, and spirit and the realization of one's true nature. This is the highest level of meditation wherein the individual has realized the true nature of his or her self.

Tai Chi

Tai chi, also known as tai chi chuan, is a traditional Chinese exercise system that combines martial arts movements with qi circulation, breathing, and stretching exercises. Tai chi was developed in China over 300 years ago; its theoretical basis dates back more than 3000 years (Liang, 1977; Liao, 1990). There is a legend that tai chi was created by Master Chang San Feng, who was inspired by his observation of a combat between a snake and a bird. The bird attacked the snake. At each pass, the bird fiercely pecked and clawed at the snake; however, the reptile, through suppleness and coiling of his body, was able to ward off the attacks and launch strikes of his own. The bird in his turn circled and used his wings to beat the snake aside when he struck. The creation of tai chi started a branch of martial arts that deemphasized overly vigorous movements that rely too heavily on physical strength.

Tai chi embodies the peak of organized movements and the ultimate in protection of self. It is a technique of harmonious postures and movements with its continuous flow, one evolving from another. Tai chi is a perfect example of mind–body exercise, because it symbolizes mental and physical coordination. A healthy body can facilitate the functioning of a skillful and adroit mind, while a strong and clear spirit is the driving force of motion. The body is the form; the mind is the spirit. Mental "motion" is present with every physical action. No wonder tai chi is often called a "moving meditation."

Foundations of Tai Chi

The essence of tai chi is to achieve balance of energy, or **qi** (pronounced "chi"). It is designed to blend mental and physical training into one complete exercise package (White & White, 1992).

According to tai chi philosophy, all of life is composed of, and has been set in motion by, the constant interplay of two vital energies, **yin** (the passive) and **yang** (the active). Every element of life exists in complementary interaction with the other. Tai chi is thus the practice of this duality (motion versus stillness) in a harmonious relationship.

Extensive research has been conducted to investigate its benefits for the body and mind. Convincing evidence suggests that tai chi promotes psychological well-being by reducing stress, anxiety, and depression (Chi, Jordan-Marsh, Guo, Xie, & Bai, 2013; Sandlund & Norlander, 2000; Wang et al., 2010; Wang et al., 2014). Additionally, tai chi has generated beneficial effects for balance and gait in the elderly (Gillespie et al., 2012; Leung, Chan, Tsang, Tsang, & Jones, 2011; Lin, Hwang, Wang, Chang, & Wolf, 2006; Wolf, Barnhart, Ellison, & Coogler, 1997), cardiovascular rehabilitation (Park et al., 2009), pain management (Lam & Horstman, 2002), and quality sleep (Li et al., 2005), aerobic capacity (Taylor-Piliae & Froelicher, 2004). Studies have also demonstrated its effectiveness for respiratory and gastrointestinal disorders (LoBuono & Pinkowish, 1999), and many other chronic conditions (see Li, Yuan, & Zhang, 2014 for a review).

Principles of Tai Chi Movement

Tai chi can be understood as a choreographed series of movements just like a martial arts form. There are several distinctive differences, however, that rely on the following principles (Metzger & Zhou, 1996).

- *Relaxation.* Attempts are made to apply just enough strength for every movement or task, thereby conserving energy and maintaining stamina. Tai chi movements should be light, agile, steady, rounded, and centrally balanced.

- *Slowness.* The movements are performed slowly and quietly. Slow motion requires mental control which helps to block out competing thoughts and distractions, allowing the mind an escape from daily routines.

FOR REFLECTION 9.5

Making a Public Commitment

Among the various stress management and prevention strategies presented in this and the previous chapters (tai chi, yoga, deep breathing, etc.), pick at least one that especially appeals to you. This should be an activity that you would like to practice regularly for the rest of your life.

Making a commitment to yourself is one thing, but doing so in front of witnesses significantly increases the probability that you will follow through. Declare to members of your family, and to your closest friends, that you intend to begin a new regimen designed to reduce the stress in your life.

Write down what you will do, how often you will do it, and the consequences if you fail to follow through. Sign your name in front of a witness.

What I will do:

How often I will do it:

How I will reward myself when I meet my stated goals:

What the consequences will be if I do not follow through:

I, _____, do solemnly swear that I will commit myself to complete the goals described previously.

Witness: _____

- *Separating yin and yang.* The performer must be aware of many paradoxes and opposites during performance, alternating motion with rest, expansion with contraction, inhalation with exhalation, rising and sinking. These are intended as metaphors for the complexities we face in life.

- *Circularity.* All tai chi movements are circular, spiral, or rounded. Small circles are embedded within larger circles. Again this is seen as a parallel to life.

- *Continuity.* All tai chi movements are connected in flowing motion, one spurring on the next movement. The end of one posture or step signals the beginning of the next one.

- *Harmony.* The harmony of mind and body leads to harmony of movement. Good performance is accompanied by a concurrence of intended, felt, and experienced movements with their actual performance.

Metaphorical Lessons of Tai Chi

I was first exposed to tai chi while a child growing up in China. I remember walking to school each day and seeing the park filled with hundreds of people all moving together as one unified organism. It struck me as so beautiful that I vowed that one day I would learn what they were doing. I have been practicing tai chi every day since then. These are some of the lessons I have learned.

- *Lesson 1: Root like an oak, bend like a willow, and move like a stream.* When performing tai chi, an experienced practitioner keeps his feet firmly rooted on the ground without locking knees. In dealing with daily stressors, it is important to remain grounded in solid values, principles, and ethics, yet flexible in your approaches to solve problems and achieve goals of peace of mind and success.

- *Lesson 2: A needle hidden in the cotton.* The more relaxed and softer the practice is, the faster the internal strength will build up. In work and life, I feel that I am most effective when I am soft-spoken, gracious, and polite (cotton) while still holding to my principles (needle). Compassion, sympathy, tears, and hugs are soft, but they can melt the hard and cold ice in human hearts. This lesson is especially useful in human relationships.

- *Lesson 3: Slow and sure brings best results.* I have a friend who is a great tai chi practitioner from Hong Kong. He told me that the more he practices tai chi, the slower he becomes. When asked why this is so he explained that slowness is good for developing the vital energy within the body.

- *Lesson 4: To move forward, it is important first to step back.* In tai chi performance, you may often notice that to move forward, the performer steps back, pivoting on the heel to make the transition as smooth as possible. This lesson states that a setback, a temporary defeat, or a heartbreak may serve you in the long run. Nothing is permanent. When you fail, that is temporary. When you succeed, that is also temporary.

In the abbreviated tai chi form, David Chen shows some of the basic positions that you can practice in a three-minute stress reduction technique (see photos overleaf).

As with any of the methods described in these chapters, unless you practice them regularly and diligently you will quickly forget the sequence of training. Tai chi is learned as a chain of movements in which each position leads to the next one. Yet if you don't continue the practice, the chain can easily become broken.

Step 1: Commencing form

Step 2: Repulse monkey

Step 3: Brush knee and twist

Step 4: Flashing arms

Step 5: Striking with both fists

Step 6: Crossing arms

Step 7: Resting

SUMMARY

This chapter covers several physical methods for relaxation. These can be used for prevention as well as for treatment. Most of them are safe and appropriate for people of all ages and fitness levels. All these techniques offer you approaches for releasing pent-up emotional and physical energy that might be harmful without a proper outlet. The most important technique is regular physical exercise because it is easy to start and implement. The only requirements are your sense of urgency and discipline to follow certain instructions. Once you start with a simple exercise program and taste the fruit of your discipline, you will be on your way to learn and add more sophisticated methods of relaxation such as yoga or tai chi.

Most of the techniques presented in this chapter require many months of instruction and dedicated practice in order to learn the rudimentary principles and forms. You could spend years, if not your whole life, trying to master the intricacies of yoga, tai chi, and the other methods. Among all the various options for stress reduction that have been introduced to you in this chapter and the preceding one, I hope that one will attract your interest enough for you to pursue it further. There are plenty of opportunities within your community to find instruction if you want to take your interest to the next level.

QUESTIONS FOR REVIEW

1. Identify psychological and physiological benefits of exercise as evidenced in controlled research studies.
2. Differentiate aerobic exercise and anaerobic exercise.
3. Describe the differences between physical activity and physical exercise.
4. What is physical fitness? Describe the five components of fitness.
5. Discuss the four guidelines in prescribing exercise for improving cardiovascular fitness.
6. Explore how you may start a comprehensive exercise program based on the principles of fitness.
7. What is progressive muscle relaxation? What is the mechanism of this method?
8. Describe the relationship between breathing and your stress level.
9. Define yoga. Describe the six principles of yoga.
10. Identify psychological and physiological benefits of yoga practice.
11. What is tai chi? Explain how the yin–yang theory may help you understand the challenges in your life.
12. What conditions can benefit from practice of tai chi?

REVIEW ACTIVITIES

Review Activity 9.1: Talk to People about Their Exercise Routines
Introducing the idea that you are doing a school project is always a good excuse to meet new people. Identify several acquaintances, fellow students (from other classes), or even strangers who exercise on a regular basis. Interview them about the benefits they enjoy from this commitment and what is most important to them about this aspect of their life. Focus in particular on how they remain dedicated to a regular exercise schedule in spite of all the distractions and excuses that are possible.

Write down your notes of what interested and impressed you the most and would be useful in your efforts to increase your own commitment to exercise.

Review Activity 9.2: Extraordinary Feats of Commitment to Physical Exercise
This chapter makes a strong case for the importance of maintaining regular physical exercise for reducing, preventing, and managing stress. Many individuals (including the authors of this text) are "addicted" to exercise as a means to control tension, burn off excess energy, aid sleep, remain at peak performance, and satisfy the urge for adventure. One example is the story of Aron Ralston in the chapter. As you recall, he was a mountain climber who was trapped in a canyon for several days, pinned under a rock, and then had to amputate his own arm with a pocket knife in order to survive. Once rescued and recovered, he continued his pursuit of mountain climbing and other outdoor activities, even with a prosthetic arm. So, here is the question to consider: What do you believe leads people to take such risks, even to the point of jeopardizing their lives, when they push themselves beyond their limits?

Think of something you did that may have appeared reckless to others but made perfect sense to you at the time. Over time, how have you learned to balance safety concerns with a hunger for pushing yourself to new levels of mastery?

REFERENCES AND RESOURCES

Alexander, F. M. (1932). *The use of the self.* New York, NY: Dutton.

Arroll, B., & Beaglehole, R. (1992). Does physical activity lower blood pressure? A critical review of the clinical trials. *Journal of Clinical Epidemiology, 45,* 439–447.

Blumenthal, J. A., Babyak, M. A., Moore, K. A., Craighead, W. E., Herman, S., Khatri, P., et al. (1999). Effects of exercise training on older patients with major depression. *Archives of Internal Medicine, 159,* 2349–2356.

Bray, S. R., & Kwan, M. (2006). Physical activity is associated with better health and psychological well-being during transition to university life. *Journal of American College Health, 55,* 77–82.

Casey, A., & Benson, H. (2004). *Mind your heart: A mind–body approach to stress management, exercise, and nutrition for heart health.* New York, NY: Free Press.

Caspersen, C. J., Powell, K. E., & Christenson, G. M. (1985). Physical activity, exercise, and physical fitness: Definitions and distinctions for health-related research. *Public Health Reports, 100*(2), 126–31.

Chi, I., Jordon-Marsh, M., Guo, M., Xie, B., & Bai, Z. (2013). Tai chi and reduction of depressive symptoms for older adults: a meta-analysis of randomized trials. *Geriatrics & Gerontology International, 13,* 3e12.

Davis, M., Eshelman, E. R., and McKay, M. (1988). *The relaxation and stress reduction workbook* (3rd ed). Oakland, CA: New Harbinger.

Desharnais, R., Jobin, J., Côté, C., Lévesque, L., & Godin, G. (1993). Aerobic exercise and the placebo effect: A controlled study. *Psychosomatic Medicine, 55,* 149–154.

Dolbier, C., & Rush, T. (2012). Efficacy of abbreviated progressive muscle relaxation in a high-stress college sample. *International Journal of Stress Management, 19*(1), 48–68.

Donaghy, M. E., & Mutrie, N. (1999). Is exercise beneficial in the treatment and rehabilitation of the problem drinker? A critical review. *Physical Therapy Reviews, 4,* 153–166.

Edward, S. (2006) Physical exercise and psychological well-being. *South African Journal of Psychology, 36,* 357–373.

Ekeland, E., Heian, F., & Hagen, K. B. (2005). Can exercise improve self-esteem in children and young people? A systematic review of randomised controlled trials. *British Journal of Sports Medicine, 39,* 792–798.

Ensel, W. M. (2004). Physical fitness and the stress process. *Journal of Community Psychology, 32*(1), 81–101.

Finlayson, J. M. (1997). The role of exercise in rehabilitation after uncomplicated myocardial infarction. *Physiotherapy, 83*(10), 519–524.

Fontaine, K. L. (2005). *Complementary & alternative therapies* (2nd ed.). Upper Saddle River, NJ: Pearson/Prentice Hall.

Fox, K. E. (2000). Self-esteem, self-perceptions and exercise. *International Journal of Sport Psychology, 31*, 228–240.

Garber, C., Blissmer, B., Deschenes, M., Franklin, B., Lamonte, M., et al. (2011). Quantity and quality of exercise for developing and maintaining cardiorespiratory, musculoskeletal, and neuromotor fitness in apparently healthy adults: Guidance for prescribing exercise. *Medicine and Science in Sports and Exercise, 43*(7), 1,334–1,359.

Gerber, M., & Pühse, U. (2009). Do exercise and fitness protect against stress-induced health complaints? A review of the literature. *Scandinavian Journal of Public Health, 37*, 801–819.

Gillespie, L. D., Robertson, M. C., Gillespie, W. J., Sherrington, C., Gates, S., Clemson, L. M., et al. (2012, September 12). Interventions for preventing falls in older people living in the community. *Cochrane Database of Systematic Reviews, 9*, CD007146.

Gupta, S. (2008). 'Paging Dr. Gupta' blog. http://edition.cnn.com/HEALTH/blogs/paging.dr.gupta.

Gyurcsik, N. C., Spink, K. S., Bray, S. R., Chad, K., & Kwan, M. (2006). An ecologically based examination of barriers to physical activity in students from grade seven through first-year university. *Journal of Adolescent Health, 38*, 704–711.

Hobson, K. (2005, December 27). A little more pedaling pays off. *U.S. News and World Report*, p. 55.

Jackson, A. W., Morrow, J. R., Jr., Hill, D. W., & Dishman, R. K. (2004). *Physical activity for health and fitness*. Champaign, IL: Human Kinetics.

Kabat-Zinn, J. (2005). *Coming to our senses*. New York, NY: Hyperion.

Kim, J., & McKenzie, L. (2014). The impacts of physical exercise on stress coping and well-being in university students in the context of leisure. *Health, 6*(19), 2,570–2,580.

King, N. J., Oman, R. F., Brassington, C. S., Bliwise, D. L., & Haskell, W. L. (1997). Moderate intensity exercise and self-rated quality of sleep in older adults: A randomized controlled trial. *Journal of the American Medical Association, 277*(1), 32–37.

Lam, P., & Horstman, J. (2002). *Overcoming arthritis*. Melbourne, Australia: Dorling Kindersley.

Leung, D. P., Chan, C. K., Tsang, H. W., Tsang, W. W., & Jones, A. Y. (2011). Tai chi as an intervention to improve balance and reduce falls in older adults: A systematic and meta-analytical review. *Alternative Therapies in Health and Medicine, 17*, 40e48.

Lewis, D. (2004). *Free your breath, free your life*. Boston, MA: Shambhala.

Li, F., Harmer, P., Fisher, K. J., McAuley, E., Chaumeton, N., Eckstrom, E., et al. (2005). Tai chi and fall reductions in older adults: A randomized controlled trial. *Journals of Gerontology Series A: Biological Sciences and Medical Sciences, 60*(2), 87–94.

Li, Y., Wang, R., Tang, J., Chen, C., Tan, L., et al. (2015). Progressive muscle relaxation improves anxiety and depression of pulmonary arterial hypertension patients. *Evidence-based Complementary and Alternative Medicine, 2015*, 1–8.

Li, G., Yuan, H., & Zhang, W. (2014). Effects of tai chi on health related quality of life in patients with chronic conditions: A systematic review of randomized controlled trials. *Complementary Therapies in Medicine, 22*(4), 743–755.

Liang, T. T. (1977). *T'ai chi ch'uan for health and self-defense: Philosophy and practice*. New York, NY: Vintage.

Liao, W. (1990). *T'ai chi classics*. Boston, MA: Shambhala.

Lin, M., Hwang, H., Wang, Y., Chang, S., & Wolf, S. (2006). Community-based tai chi and its effect on injurious falls, balance, gait, and fear of falling in older people. *Physical Therapy, 86*, 1189–1201.

LoBuono, C., & Pinkowish, M. D. (1999). Moderate exercise, tai chi improve BP in older adults. *Patient Care, 33*, 230.

Loehr, J. E., & Migdow, J. A. (1999). *Breathe in, breathe out*. New York, NY: Time-Life Books.

Luskin, F., & Pelletier, K. R. (2005). *Stress free for good*. San Francisco, CA: HarperCollins.

Metzger, W., & Zhou, P. (1996). *Tai chi ch'uan & qigong: Techniques & training*. New York, NY: Sterling.

Moore, D. W. (1997). *The accidental Buddhist*. New York, NY: Broadway.

Morgan, W. P. (1985). Affective beneficence of vigorous physical activity. *Medicine and Science in Sports and Exercise, 17*, 94–100.

National Eating Disorders Association (2006). *National Eating Disorders Association announces results of eating disorders poll on college campuses around the nation*. Seattle, WA: NEDA.

Orne, M. T., & Whitehouse, W. G. (2000). Relaxation techniques. In G. F. Fink (Ed.), *Encyclopedia of stress* (Vol. 3, pp. 341–348). San Diego, CA: Academic.

Park, I. S., Song, R., Oh, K. O., So, H. Y., Kim, D. S., Kim, J. I., et al. (2009). Managing cardiovascular risks with tai chi in people with coronary artery disease. *Journal of Advanced Nursing, 66*(2), 282–292.

Payne, R. A. (2003). *Relaxation techniques: A practical handbook for the health care professional* (2nd ed.). Edinburgh, UK: Churchill Livingstone.

Plante, T. G., & Rodin J. (1990). Physical fitness and enhanced psychological aspects. *Current Psychology, 9*, 1–20.

Prentice, W. (1994). *Fitness for college & life*. St Louis, MO: Mosby.

Puetz, T. W. (2006). Physical activity and feelings of energy and fatigue: Epidemiological evidence. *Sports Medicine, 36*(9), 767–780.

Ralston, A. (2006). My summit problem. *Outside*, April. http://outsideonline.com/outside/features/200604/aron—1.html

Safi, S. (2015). A fresh look at the potential mechanisms of progressive muscle relaxation therapy on depression in female patients with multiple sclerosis. *Iranian Journal of Psychiatry and Behavioral Sciences, 9*(1), e340.

Sandlund, E. S., & Norlander, T. (2000). The effects of tai chi chuan relaxation and exercise on stress responses and well-being: An overview of research. *International Journal of Stress Management, 7*, 139–149.

Scully, D., Kremer, J., Meade, M. M., Graham, R., & Dudgeon, K. (1998). Physical exercise and psychological well-being: A critical review. *British Journal of Sports Medicine, 32*(2), 111–120.

Servan-Schreiber, D. (2004). Run for your life. *Psychotherapy Networker*, July/August, 47–51.

Sheally, C. N. (Ed.) (1996). *The complete guide to alternative medicine: An illustrated encyclopedia of natural healing*. New York, NY: Barnes & Noble.

Stains, L. (2007). High anxiety. *Men's Journal*, September, 77–80.

Sudsuang, R., Chentanez, V., & Veluvan, K. (1991). Effect of Buddhist meditation on serum cortisol and total protein levels, blood pressure, pulse rate, lung volume and reaction time. *Physiology and Behavior, 50*, 543–548.

Taylor-Piliae, R. E., & Froelicher, E. S. (2004). Effectiveness of tai chi exercise in improving aerobic capacity: A meta-analysis. *Journal of Cardiovascular Nursing, 19*(1), 48–57.

Thaylor, S. E. (1987). Energy, tiredness, and effects of sugar snack versus moderate exercise. *Journal of Personality and Social Psychology, 52*, 119–125.

Wang, C., Bannuru, R., Ramel, J., Kupelnick, B., Scott, T., & Schmid, C. H. (2010). Tai chi on psychological well-being: Systematic review and meta-analysis. *BMC Complementary and Alternative Medicine, 10*, 23.

Wang, F., Lee, E., Wu, T., Benson, H., Fricchione, G., et al. (2014). The effects of tai chi on depression, anxiety, and psychological well-being: A systematic review and meta-analysis. *International Journal of Behavioral Medicine, 21*(4), 605–617.

White, P., & White, R. (1992). Soft fist fitness: With concentrated purpose, tai chi offers a balanced blend of mental and physical training. *American Fitness, 2*, 46–47.

Wolf, S., Barnhart, H., Ellison, G., Coogler, C., & Atlanta FICSIT Group (1997). The effect of tai chi quan and computerized balance training on postural stability in older subjects. *Physical Therapy, 77*, 371–381.

Wolpe, J. (1973). *The practice of behavior therapy*. New York, NY: Pergamon Press.

Wolpe, J., & Wolpe, D. (1988). *Life without fear*. Oakland, CA: New Harbinger.

Woo, M., Kim, S., Kim, J., Petruzzello, S. J., & Hatfield, B. D. (2009) Examining the exercise–effect dose–response relationship: Does duration influence frontal EEG asymmetry? *International Journal of Psychophysiology, 72*, 166–172.

10

Preparing for the Future College and Occupational Stress

There are some unique challenges facing college students today, regardless of your economic status, living situation, major, career plans, and social group. In addition to the stress you feel on a daily basis to read assignments, complete your studies, prepare for exams, write papers, and get to classes on time, there are also pressures from family, friends, and classmates to meet additional obligations. Then, for the majority of students who are also working part-time or even full-time jobs, there are difficulties in balancing responsibilities and commitments at work versus those at school.

Although considerable stress is related to managing daily tasks in the present, there are also anxieties connected to future plans. Ever since you can remember you were likely pestered by grown-ups with the annoying question: What do you want to be when you grow up? It was never enough to simply say you wanted to be a good person; you had to come up with a specific occupation, probably one that fitted the particular ideals of your family culture. Whatever you answered—astronaut, neurosurgeon, president, or police officer—there was an unsettled feeling that you were supposed to decide your future, once and for all, before you even had a chance to find out what was involved.

KEY QUESTIONS IN THE CHAPTER

- What are the major stressors for college students?
- Why do nontraditional students face special challenges, and what are they?
- What are effective study habits that reduce stress and improve performance?
- What are the areas of greatest stress and risk for college students?
- What are the sources of occupational stress?
- Compare the three theories of occupational stress.
- What are the three levels of intervention for occupational stress?
- What is burnout and how can you prevent it?

Now that you are a college student, there is an assumption on the part of some family members and friends that you have finally made your decision and know what you want to do with the rest of your life. What can be particularly absurd is that most of the people who are jumping to that conclusion hardly know what *they* want to do in the next years.

VOICE OF STRESS 10.1

Twenty-Two-Year-Old Female College Student

I faced stress in all three big areas—classes, my parents, and my social life. I had school and a part-time job on campus. Working and going to school part-time was a bit rough but somehow I managed. Eventually my schoolwork began to fall behind because I had to work to pay my bills that were accumulating month by month. Before I knew it, my cell-phone service was cancelled. There were times when I had to decide to pay one bill and leave the other one for the following month. I had not even gone to visit my family once. I did somewhat miss them, but then I would remember the issues I had to go through when I was home. Finally, a time came where I was in extreme debt. I didn't have enough funds to pay my bills. The collection agencies were harassing me on a daily basis. I tried searching for a full-time job, but I couldn't find a position with flexible hours, so I was stuck with my minimum-wage, part-time job.

After work and classes, I would go back to my apartment to study. I started to become so lonely. I barely had any food in my apartment. I wanted to ask for a loan from my parents, but then I knew they would complain and nag me to death about moving back in with my aunt, since they were against my living on my own from the beginning. I borrowed money from my roommate but now I couldn't pay it back when I said I would. There was no one that I could really turn to except my family. Every night I used to cry myself to sleep; my pillow used to be wet in the morning. I just couldn't see any way out until, finally, I had to ask my family for help. It was pride that got in the way.

You may take some comfort in knowing that the average college student changes her major three to four times prior to graduation. Keep in mind that this is an average—so for every education, engineering, nursing, or pre-med student who started school with that major and stuck with it all the way through, there is another student who might have changed fields six or seven times! Even if you are one of the rare individuals who came to college knowing *exactly* what you wanted to do—and have stuck to that plan—you still have to face the competitive challenges of succeeding well enough to obtain your preferred job.

I hardly have to remind you that your "job" of being a college student is still among the most stressful occupations imaginable. You may have time to think, to read, to socialize, to party, to participate in sports or clubs, to attend concerts, plays, or sporting events, but that does not detract from the unrelenting pressures you face from teachers, friends, and family, not to mention your own ambitions for the future.

The Nature of College Stress

College is a period of time marked by transitions, change, and new experiences, especially for young college students who have just left behind a familiar environment and entered a new one. How quickly you make adjustments to this new lifestyle will determine your quality of life. You have to take on more responsibilities, relate to different kinds of people, and manage emotions and finances.

Some stressors alone don't cause much difficulty; it is the *interaction* among them that can produce a compounded effect. You have an exam in a few days but have plenty of time to prepare for it: no big deal. But add to the situation that a close relationship has ended, your hours at work just increased, you have three other classes to keep up with, and your car broke down—then you are close to the breaking point.

Academics

The first and most obvious source of stress for college students arises from academic pursuits. Each year, there are 250,000 college students who cannot be absorbed by the job market (Kennedy, 2007) and this has only become more challenging in recent years. Such limited opportunities produce competition in which you must perform better than your peers, distinguishing yourself with the highest possible grades and achievements. This competitive atmosphere is exacerbated by pressing dead-lines, ever-present examinations, and a lack of time to do the kind of job you would prefer. No wonder that academic exams have been associated with suppression of the immune system, leading to increased physiological difficulties (Kiecolt-Glaser et al., 1986).

Related academic stressors include excessive homework, unclear assignments, and uncomfortable classrooms. There are also challenges associated with the sometimes competitive, divisive atmosphere during some classes that require active participation. It is not uncommon that students feel criticized, judged, or marginalized because they express opinions that may differ from what the instructor or others think is best.

Finances

The costs of college tuition have been steadily rising by as much as 10% each year, including some of the largest increases in the past 30 years. An education at a top-tier private university can cost as much as $250,000 and a public education about half as much. In terms of the ratio of cost to benefit, this sort of price tag creates a lot of ambiva-lent feelings about whether the amount of time, money, and energy is actually worth investing, especially during tough economic times and budget cuts: students are paying more than ever before for college with less help available.

If parents pay for tuition, it means that they need to make some sacrifices at home, such as longer hours at work, adding a second job, taking a second mortgage, or borrow-ing from relatives. When students are responsible for their own college costs, they have to juggle with a full load of academic course work and a part-time or full-time job. Most students resort to financial aid and loans, which means long-term financial challenges in the future.

The situation is made far more difficult because few people ever receive systematic training in financial management and budgeting. Many students, for the first time in their lives, are trying to take care of their own bills, often unsuccessfully: the average college student carries a credit card debt of thousands of dollars. With scholarships more competitive and loans more difficult to secure, financial stress is becoming more of an obstacle than ever before.

Social and Intimate Relationships

Some of the most rewarding educational experiences in college do not take place in the classroom but through social encounters. We could make the case that while the informa-tion and knowledge that are imparted in formal learning environments are important, so too are the informal learning experiences that take place in cafes, bars, clubs, dormitories, the student union, during breaks and other gatherings. It is one thing to listen to a lecture or participate in a seminar discussion in class that is guided by an instructor, but quite another to personalize the learning afterward through informal conversations and critical discussions with trusted friends.

If you asked a group of adults who have been out of college for more than ten years to reflect on their educational experiences and tell you what stood out as most significant to them, rarely would they mention anything that occurred in the classroom (see Voice of the Authors 10.1). It is more likely that they would identify ways they grew and learned

---

VOICE OF THE AUTHORS 10.1

When I (Jeffrey) think back to my college years, I remember some amazing experiences I had in my classes, particularly dramatic demonstrations that had unexpected results—something that surprised me. But most of the rest has faded over time although I presume I have incorporated the best stuff into my knowledge base and reasoning skills.

This is what I do remember from my college years, in no particular order . . . Staying up late at night playing cards, learning lessons in probability, strategy, cooperation, and sleep deprivation . . . Feeling part of a group, a tribe, of likeminded people who shared my view of the world . . . Learning that I could be smart by reading lots of books . . . Grieving for weeks on end when the relationship with my girlfriend ended . . . Getting glowing feedback on a paper I wrote and realizing for the first time I could write . . . Realizing I didn't need my parents anymore to get along in the world . . . Realizing that what matters most in life is not only what you know, but who you know . . . Accepting that although I was troubled and wounded I could find a place for myself as a productive professional . . . Making a few friendships that lasted several decades . . . Volunteering to work on a research study in my spare time and learning how science works . . . Learning to love university life so much that I never wanted to leave—and never did.

---

as a result of interactions and conversations that took place one-on-one with instructors, during social gatherings, and in other encounters where they had the opportunity to apply what they learned in class. The content of this text is the raw material for making potentially major and significant growth and learning in your life, but only if you have opportunities to apply what you learned. This means talking to friends, family, and classmates about ideas that stimulate or provoke you. It means actively integrating concepts into your own value system and practicing the strategies in your everyday encounters—with yourself and others.

The amount of time you actually spend in the classroom represents just a fraction of your waking moments compared to the time you spend doing other things. The preparation and reading you do for classes add to the power of that learning but that still leaves the majority of your hours devoted to other social, work, and leisure activities.

College is about not just educating your intellect but also developing social skills, emotional maturity, a sense of justice and moral clarity, spiritual growth, physical competence, and interpersonal skills; basically a greater sense of who you are and what you have to offer the

Although romantic relationships are among the most satisfying and important aspects of college life, they can also become a source of ongoing stress as a couple negotiates differences in their interests, goals, values, attitudes, sexual preferences, and family and cultural backgrounds. Such disagreements are not only expected but a normal part of partnerships.

world. During the years that you embark on this journey, you will enter a number of relationships with faculty, fellow students, and coworkers, and form other friendships. You will experiment with many new behaviors, some of which may be self-defeating and others self-enhancing. You will become involved in romantic and perhaps sexual relationships. At times you will struggle with loneliness and feelings of isolation.

Depending on culture and context, sexual experimentation may be viewed as an antidote to loneliness, as well as a search for connection. When taken to an extreme, it can carry some negative consequences. Promiscuity, obsessive internet sex, or treating sex as conquests can carry consequences such as guilt and anxiety, sexually transmitted disease (even computer viruses), unintended pregnancies and abortions, and sticky emotional entanglements that lead to lingering conflict and stress. What may begin as a temporary escape from boredom or anxiety can evolve into a far more complex set of problems.

Choice of a Career

As I have mentioned, and a number of career theories support, it is not usually the case that occupations are chosen once and then become entrenched throughout a lifetime. You may know people who have been satisfied in one career throughout their lives—perhaps in the military, law, education, construction, or a self-employed business, to mention a few—but for most people the choice is constantly reassessed as new opportunities arise, as new talents come to the forefront, and as you hunger for new challenges. We'd like to think that it takes some pressure off of you to understand that whatever you decide right now or decided last year is neither permanent nor irrevocable. As you receive additional education and training, gain experience and receive supervision, meet new people and encounter new experiences, you will likely evolve in your aspirations and dreams, as well as your ambitions.

FOR REFLECTION 10.1

When you were a kid, what did you want to do when you grew up?

In high school, how did your career aspirations change as you learned more about the world of work, as well as your abilities and limitations?

When you started college as a first-semester freshman, what was your anticipated major and career plan?

What is your latest, best plan for what you intend to do and how you will do it?

Where do you see yourself in ten years from now, in terms of your career plans?

Even making an initial career choice is no easy matter. There are so many possibilities. How do you know if you've made the "right" decision? And no matter what you settle on there are always doubts and uncertainties, always other paths you could have taken.

It may surprise you to learn that which direction you head probably makes less of a difference than you think. There is no single best occupation for you or for anyone, but rather a broad range of possibilities that might meet your needs, interests, and abilities. Interest inventories are designed to help you sort out what you value most and how these interests are related to specific careers. There are skilled career counselors on your college campus who can assist you with these instruments or can help you begin or continue your decision process. Keep in mind, however, that this is an ongoing journey that will continue throughout your lifetime.

Being a Nontraditional Student

Whereas once upon a time there was a thing called a "traditional" student—an 18-year-old freshman who had just graduated high school, living away from home in a residence hall for the first time—nowadays the majority of students are "nontraditional," meaning that they manifest extreme diversity in age and background. Many, if not most, students today are older (often in their twenties and thirties or even past 60). More than ever before, college students represent diversity in ethnicity, religion, socioeconomic status, age, gender, sexual orientation, and every other variable imaginable.

Nontraditional students are often defined as those who are over the age of 25, have a job while going to college, have children, and depend on themselves for tuition, among other criteria (Brock, 2010). One third of American undergraduate students enrolled in 2011 were considered nontraditional students and this population was expected to increase (Markle, 2015). With job opportunities scarcer, adult studentship is becoming increasingly common for those hoping to wait out a limited job market and retrench for another career. Even though some research indicates that these more mature students have some advantages over younger ones because they may have already experienced success in life experiences, they may have a greater number of roles that may cause conflicts and stress in experiencing success and well-being (Giancola, Grawitch, & Borchert, 2009; Home, 1997; Johnson & Robson, 1999).

VOICE OF STRESS 10.2

Female Student in Her Thirties

It's been years since I've been in school. I used to be a good student, but that was so long ago I've forgotten most of what I learned. I sit in my classes and see some of these kids, most of whom just ignore me, and I feel invisible, like I don't belong. They look at me like I'm their parent or something which only makes me feel more like some kind of alien. I wish they'd accept me, or at least treat me like I'm equal, but instead—I don't know—it feels like I don't belong.

I've got enough to deal with right now. I'm a single mom. My kids are in school but they aren't crazy about the idea that I'm not totally available for them. My own parents give me crap too—like I'm crazy for doing this while trying to raise my kids and earn a living. But I never had a chance to go to school when I was younger. I got married when I was 17, just out of high school. Then I had the children, so there was never any time for me to consider what I wanted to do.

I listen in on the conversations of these young people and listen to the things they worry about—remember I'm invisible. I envy them. I wish I had started school when I was their age. Now I've got all this other stuff to worry about, plus my school work. Plus I have to do it all alone.

The common stressors for the nontraditional students include the following:

As college campuses become more diverse in the percentage of minorities and older students who attend, such supposedly "nontraditional" students face additional challenges balancing multiple roles and facing prejudices.

- *Fears and self-doubts.* Nontraditional students, no matter how experienced they are in multiple situations, may feel a fear of failure (see Voice of Stress 10.3). Stress and anxiety occur because they have to get used to an unfamiliar environment and deal with fellow students whom they may perceive as different. However, it is this diversity of backgrounds that makes the college learning environment so rich and interesting. Where else can so many people—new immigrants, international students, people from farms and cities, from every imaginable background—get together to share their experiences and work together cooperatively?

- *Conflicting loyalties.* Coexistence of family responsibilities with the demands of academia can create additional challenges and barriers to academic success, especially for female students (Anderson & Miezitis, 1999; Giancola, Grawitch, & Borchert, 2009). Adult students often have lived long enough to have encumbrances such as a job, a spouse, children, and financial concerns outside of college that must be managed in addition to the demands of college coursework and study.

- *Preexisting stress factors.* For some nontraditional students, a life-altering event may have been a motivating factor in the decision to return to school. The loss of a job, divorce, the death of a spouse, and career limitations due to lack of education are common reasons adults return to school. Given these circumstances, many adult students may be managing high levels of stress before becoming a student.

Being a Minority College Student

There is little doubt that being different, in any manner, creates special challenges for students. Whether the student is physically disabled, a member of a minority religion, race, socioeconomic status, ethnicity, sexual orientation, gender, or nationality, there are additional hurdles to overcome. What constitutes a minority depends on the particular region of the college campus. In some parts of the world, the college environment may be relatively homogeneous with respect to native language or ethnicity or religion. In other areas, diversity may be the norm. Nevertheless, on any college campus there are always students who are marginalized based on their appearance, manner, language, or background. Minority status stress occurs when an individual's coping resources are insufficient to deal with perceived and/or actual threat from the majority group. In addition to everything else I have described, they must also face additional stressors:

- *Prejudice and discrimination.* Being singled out for ridicule or ostracism not only damages one's self-esteem and emotional stability, but also affects academic performance and satisfaction with college life. Racial discrimination and prejudice directed against minority college students have been associated with poor academic performance (Parker & Jones, 1999) and increased depression symptoms and anxiety (Lopez, 2005; Wei, Heppner, Ku, & Liao, 2010).

- *Language problems.* International students and new immigrants not only must contend with the same academic challenges as other students but must do so in another language. Just imagine what it is like to attend classes when you can't understand much of what the teacher is saying or you have to use a dictionary to translate dozens of words on every page of the readings.

- *Culture shock.* It is often the case that curricula are set up consistent with the conventions of the mainstream culture. Students who have immigrated to North America with their parents are not used to the ways that instructors deliver the material or communicate with them.

- *Lack of resources.* Many minority students come from low socioeconomic status families, and therefore lack financial resources.

- *Parental pressure.* As first-generation college students, minority students may face strong pressures from their families to conform to their expectations, often in direct conflict with the values that may be imparted from their peers.

VOICE OF STRESS 10.3

Twenty-Two-Year-Old Female International Student

I am not a native English speaker. My first year in college was a nightmare. Stress came from everywhere, such as overcoming anxiety from tests, writing term papers, and most of all, learning the proper way of using the English language. My four years of college life have gone by so quickly, but I can still feel the burdens on my shoulders. I have to say this stress has lowered my ability to learn. I feel intimidated whenever I have to talk in front of the entire class or take an essay exam. Although this stress lowered my ability to learn, it has never stopped my will to learn. I was determined that I was going to do well no matter what it took and how hard I had to work. I know I had to work harder than others but eventually I developed good friends here. More than anything it was making English-speaking friends that helped me to fit in and improve my language. I learned a lot in school but I also learned a lot about this country.

Developing Effective Study Habits

Whether you are taking a single stress management class or have a full semester's load, it is likely that school work is one source of stress in your life, especially if you don't feel like your study efforts are as organized and efficient as they could be. This is not simply a matter of managing time effectively (see Chapter 7) but also involves specific strategies and skills that maximize learning retention or help you to produce quality products.

You have probably already learned the lesson that there is not necessarily a clear correlation between how much you learn in a class and the grade you receive at the end of the semester. There may have been times when you received an A, but can't remember much of anything from the experience. There were probably other times when your head practically exploded with new insights and information, yet the actual grade you earned didn't come close to reflecting this achievement. Of course, in an ideal world, you would always get exactly what you deserve—no more and no less.

Whether your goal is to reduce stress related to school work, to increase your retention of information and mastery of skills, or to improve your grades in classes, there are certain strategies that have consistently proved most helpful. The first thing to understand is that some misconceptions might be getting in your way. School achievement, at least as measured by grade performance, is not so much related to intelligence, or even to devoting maximum time to studying, but rather is the result of applying particular skills that allow a person to study effectively and efficiently.

There are courses and workshops devoted to study skills, as well as excellent resources you might consult (Burns & Sinfield, 2003; Rose & Nicholl, 1997; McWhorter, 2006). In order to best target your efforts, it is important to have some sense of where you need most improvement. Answer the following questions to help clarify the issues:

1. Do you spend frantic time cramming or preparing the night before an exam or paper is due?

2. Do you become easily distracted or bored when you are studying, unable to concentrate for sustained periods of time?

3. When you are in class do you tend to daydream, fall asleep, or fail to pay attention?

4. When you take notes in class do you find that they are not focused on the most important points?

5. Do you find that you can't easily remember material that you read in chapters or learned in class?

6. Even though you might be well prepared, or know the material, do you find that you still don't do well on exams?

7. When you take tests do you feel so anxious that it is hard for you to concentrate?

8. When assigned to write a paper, do you find it difficult to organize your thoughts and structure the assignment to best represent what you have to say?

From these questions, you can see that some of them have to do with stress (6, 7), concentration and motivation (2, 3, 4, 7), time management (1, 8), or poor skills (4, 6, 8). Depending on the particular challenges you face, efforts can be made to improve your areas of weakness. In many cases it is a matter not just of spending more time, but of doing so more systematically.

Study Habits for Improved Performance

There are a number of essential habits that can be incorporated into your studying behavior. These are designed not only to help you work better but also to reduce stress that can be sabotaging your ability to concentrate.

Habit 1: Identify Clear Goals and Intentions

Having definite long-term and short-term goals is a prerequisite to academic achievement. No one achieves excellence accidentally. Great success always comes as a result of careful planning and organization. For instance, the following two students articulate widely different goals for their education.

Ellen intends to go to law school upon graduation so it feels to her like grades are a matter of life and death. She devotes considerable time and energy to her studies because she is well aware of how competitive it is to reach her goal. The consequences of getting a C on any assignment seem so dire to her that it is absolutely unacceptable. She has no problem with motivation whatsoever; rather, she struggles with the stress and pressure she puts on herself to achieve the highest possible levels.

Trent isn't exactly sure what he wants to do when he graduates. Most likely he will keep working for the company where he is presently employed in sales. He sees no immediate benefit to performing at the highest level so he doesn't devote as much time and energy to his studies as he could. Not surprisingly, his learning and grades reflect his ambivalence about being in school in the first place.

While it is perfectly normal to be confused about what you want to do with your life, and it is equally common to have a flexible agenda, you must have compelling reasons for doing well in your classes. You may not aspire to go to medical, law, or business school, but you should have some goals. These goals may not necessarily be as closely connected to the grades you achieve as to the knowledge and skills you develop to do what you want in the future.

Habit 2: Make it Easy to Work

Even with clear goals and the best of intentions, it may still be difficult to work well if you are faced with distractions. Although certain individuals appear to be able to study reasonably well with the television or music on, with friends coming by, with the phone ringing and email beeping, generally this is not an ideal environment for maximum concentration and retention of material. One hour studying in such a cacophony of auditory, visual, and sensory distractions is probably the equivalent of studying for only 15 minutes in a more focused environment in which you devote all your energy and attention to the task at hand. In most circumstances, learning takes place when most of your senses are completely engaged in the task. It isn't enough to read a chapter like this unless you are *actively* engaged with the material on multiple levels—not just intellectually, but also emotionally and physically. So, if you are reading these words while you are doing other things, there is far less likelihood that you will retain the material.

- *Create an attractive study environment.* Start a policy of studying only in a certain room, or part of a room. Make that space as comfortable as possible, furnishing it with everything you might require. Remove anything that might become distracting or is not directly relevant to what you are doing. Try to keep the space well organized. You may say that this is not your style, but unless you are planning to be an artist, most work settings will require you to function in this organized manner. In some cases, supervisors will make judgments about you based not only on the work that you produce but also on the style in which you do it.

- *Make a list of important tasks beforehand.* You may have heard the saying, "out of sight, out of mind." This refers to the phenomenon that you forget to do a certain task if you don't see it, hear it, and touch it. By writing down what you plan to do the next day, and putting the list in a conspicuous place, you will be more likely to follow through. There is just no excuse to "forget" to do your homework or assignment, unless your behavior is saying that it is not important to you.

- *Keep affirming the benefits of learning.* On a daily or weekly basis, it is challenging to keep a focus on studying when there is no immediate payoff. You may be required to take certain classes that seem irrelevant or boring. You may be forced to do assignments that seem to have no direct relationship to anything you are remotely interested in. Yet if you keep the big picture in mind, it can

---

FOR REFLECTION 10.2

Changing the Way You Study

What changes can you make in terms of the way you study in order to improve the quality and quantity of work you do? Write some ideas down here.

In addition to the ideas listed above, consider the following adjustments: creating a special, private work space; reducing distractions that get in the way of sustained concentration; and keeping an ongoing inventory of tasks that need to be completed by certain dates.

give you the resolve to study a subject that is not immediately compelling. This is part of the challenge involved in a college education—you are asked to learn about new subjects to broaden your perspective, even if you sometimes have difficulty finding the enthusiasm needed.

Habit 3: Make Learning Fun

Studying is difficult when it seems like dreaded work to be avoided. You may feel it takes every ounce of energy to force yourself to open a book, review your notes, or write a paper. As soon as you even think about beginning the task you can immediately feel yourself yawning and losing interest. You can complain about how boring/irrelevant/confusing/difficult a particular class might be but you still have to do the work, and do it at the highest possible level, if you want to achieve your goals in other areas. It is part of college life, just as it is in the world of work, that sometimes you have to do things that you would prefer not to do. Still, there are ways you can make learning any subject more engaging and fun:

- *Adopt a preferred way of absorbing information.* Even though people can be differentiated in terms of their learning preferences, some preferring visual, auditory, or hands-on modes, the most effective way to learn is an active approach in which multisensory experiences are engaged. For example, you may take notes (kinesthetic) while you listen to the teacher (auditory). Then you reorganize your notes into a learning map (visual).

- *Give yourself breaks.* Research shows that short periods of study time can be more effective than those that drag on endlessly. Reward yourself for 30 minutes of uninterrupted study with something you really enjoy—listen to one favorite song, do some stretching exercises, practice yoga or tai chi, make a brief phone

---

FOR REFLECTION 10.3

Rewarding Yourself

Think of a class assignment, reading, project, or task that you are putting off *right now*. Make a schedule for the next week of what exactly you will do, and when you will do it. For instance, if you figure the task requires three hours of work, then allocate one and a half hours to each of two days (or nights). Describe the task below.

Think of a mini-reward you can give yourself after each study session of 30 to 45 minutes of solid work. This should be some treat that will not occupy more than a few minutes. Describe what this will be below.

What is a reward you can give yourself for completing the task in its entirety and with excellent quality? This should be something that motivates you, yet something reasonably healthy. List some possibilities below.

call. Limit the interlude to five or ten minutes so you can devote the next half hour to continued work.

- *Break a large project into manageable chunks.* Writing a term paper, or studying for a final exam, can be a daunting task. It can feel overwhelming to organize a whole semester's worth of material. It is usually best to subdivide the task into manageable units. If you are writing a paper, for instance, start with just making a list of the key points that you want to include. If studying for a final exam, organize the material into units that make it more accessible.

- *Reward yourself when you've completed a project.* Not every study task requires a reward, especially when you are learning about things that you really want to know—this becomes its own reward. But in cases where you have been struggling to remain focused, plan a desirable but healthy reward for yourself when you complete the task. Positive rewards can be watching a great movie, dining in a good restaurant, or buying yourself a nice shirt.

Habit 4: Maximize Your Resources

When you come to a college or university, you are not on your own. Make use of what's available to you—faculty, staff, peers, and resources. First, get to know your professor in person and introduce yourself before or after one of your classes. Make a note of office hours, email address, and phone number. Ask the instructor to help you to focus or prioritize your efforts. After each exam, set up an appointment to go over difficult questions with your instructor. If you have difficulty writing papers, submit a first draft to get initial reactions before you turn in the final draft.

Organize or join study groups of like-minded peers. Make sure that these groups include people who are serious about their studies so it doesn't end up being pure social time, which can actually make things worse in terms of your school performance.

Avail yourself of other services on campus that include the counseling center, learning center, librarians, technology experts, staff in student affairs, and your academic advisor. There are many support staff on campus precisely to help you do better in your work—*if* you ask for help.

VOICE OF STRESS MANAGEMENT 10.1

Twenty-Year-Old Male Human Services Major

I've always said I have a terrible memory. It's one of the legends in my family. They say I can't even remember my own name. I get teased for it a lot, I guess to the point that I totally believed it myself. When I am meeting new groups of people I start to panic right away because I just know that as soon as everyone introduces themselves I won't remember any of their names. Then, because I don't know what to call anyone, I don't say anything at all. I just sit quietly until someone talks to me.

It was mentioned in one of my human services classes about how limiting people's self-perceptions are. I didn't understand the theory all that well but the basic idea is that people construct their own realities. For me, that means that I've always thought of myself as having a terrible memory. But then I realized that maybe I could change that self-perception. So at the beginning of the semester I was totally determined that I was going to learn everyone's name in the class. I kept a notebook in which I wrote down features of each person next to their names, stuff like how they dress or talk, their hair color, or mannerisms. Then I studied my list just like I would my class notes so that when I came to class I was about the only one who could call everyone by name. Pretty amazing, huh? I realized, then and there, that maybe I didn't have a bad memory after all.

Habit 5: Improve Your Memory

This is a skill that will serve you well not only with regard to your academic career but beyond. While there may be individual differences in a person's capacity for remembering certain kinds of information (visual images, data sets, vocabulary, conceptual ideas), anyone can improve their memory with training and learning skills.

There are courses you can take, and resources you can consult (Hermann, Raybeck, & Gruneberg, 2002; Mason & Kohn, 2001) to increase your ability to remember things important to you, whether that is people's names, lists of words, anatomical terms, or conceptual differences. The most important factor in such a task is motivation—you would be amazed what you can do when you really want to.

Most techniques to improve memory involve making information more relevant and meaningful to you, by using your imagination and creativity to create meaning where none appears to exist. **Mnemonic devices** in which the first letter of a code word refers to the terms to be recalled work well in this regard. They enable you to make connections

---

FOR REFLECTION 10.4

Inventing a Mnemonic Device

In Chapter 2 you learned about the major systems of the body and how each is affected by stress. Let's say you were given an essay question in which you were expected to discuss how each of the nine physiological systems is affected by stress. In order to complete this task, the first thing you'd need to be able to do is to name the systems. To review, they are:

1. nervous
2. endocrine
3. circulatory
4. respiratory
5. immune
6. skeletal
7. muscular
8. digestive
9. reproductive.

Invent a mnemonic device to remember these systems. You can do this in several ways, such as:

- inventing an *acronym* in which each letter of a word stands for the first letter of one of the systems (CIA = Central Intelligence Agency);
- an *acrostic* in which the first letter of each word in a sentence stands for the system (Every Good Boy Does Fine = the notes of the treble clef in music);
- a *grouping* in which you organize the systems according to some common variable (for instance, nervous, endocrine, and immune could be grouped, or muscular and skeletal);
- a *visualization* used to imagine a clear, vivid picture that holds each of the features to be recalled: you actually picture the body of someone you know, or your own body, and then link each of the systems to the various parts;
- *rhymes* used to make up a poem or saying, like the children's rhyme to learn the alphabet.

In the space below, use a mnemonic device of your choice to help you remember the nine major systems of the body.

between lists and easy-to-remember terms. For instance, "A. C. Helms" is used by physics students to remember the various forms of energy: **a**tomic, **c**hemical, **h**eat, **e**lectrical, **m**echanical, **l**ight, and **s**ound. The best memory tricks are those that you make up yourself that have some humorous or personal connection to your experience.

Other ways to improve your memory include the following:

- Organize and reorganize the information you have learned in a way that is easy for your memory to file and retrieve.

- Review what you have learned within 24 hours after initial exposure to the material. Cramming for an exam the night before is not nearly as effective in promoting memory retention as spending several days engaged in meaningful, purposive work.

- Employ appropriate analogies to help you remember new material by relating something obscure and esoteric to something familiar. For instance, you may compare your brain's short-term and long-term memory to the RAM and hard drive of your computer.

- Visualize what you learn. Visualization is an active mental reproduction of what we have experienced, read, or want to see in the future. It reinforces your memory.

- Seek to understand before you commit what you learn to memory. If you can explain a concept in your own words and share it with a peer or friend, this information is more likely to be recalled.

- Take regular breaks. You tend to best remember the beginning and end of what you learn. By taking more breaks, the mind will have more beginnings and endings related to the material you learn.

- Engage all your senses as much as possible, not just sight but also hearing, touch, and even taste.

Habit 6: Demonstrate What You've Learned

Stress and anxiety often interfere with a complete demonstration of what you know. In order to prevent unnecessary test anxiety from getting in the way of successful performance, take the following steps:

- Read the syllabus and class notes regarding the upcoming exam and then make an appointment with your instructor one or two weeks before the exam to clarify the material.

- Convert study materials to outlines, flash cards, or a few key study pages. Record the study material so that you can listen to it over and over in the car or at home.

- Join a study group and quiz each other. Make sure that the material on which you base your answers is reliable and accurate.

- Testing is often associated with extra study time and stress. Pay special attention to balancing your diet.

- Get plenty of rest the night before a test.

- Practice relaxation techniques daily in addition to at least thirty minutes of an aerobic activity such as walking or jogging.

- On the day of the exam, get to the classroom early so you can sit where you want.

- Budget your time in order to finish the test. Show as much work as possible to get partial credit. Never leave a question blank.

- Read the question thoroughly and underline certain key words. Don't jump to quick conclusions before reading the last word of a sentence.

- If you have time, review your answers. Don't change an answer unless you are sure your second answer is correct.

- Use encouraging self-talk and have a positive attitude toward the test.

- Reward yourself after the test for completing it and don't dwell on possible mistakes.

- Practice deep breathing, meditation, and other techniques you have learned to keep yourself calm and focused.

Occupational Stress

Rather than being separate from college stress, pressures and anxieties related to work are simply an extension of the "job" of being a student. In the worlds of both work and academic life there are considerable pressures to perform. There are sometimes overwhelming time commitments, deadlines to meet, competition to prove yourself, not to mention interpersonal struggles with coworkers with whom you must find consensus.

It has been said that work is something that you *have* to do—as opposed to play, which is something that you *want* to do. Yet for many people work is far more than an obligation to earn money; it is what gives life meaning. One reason why you may be obtaining a college education is so you have more choices in the kinds of work you can do, not to mention the opportunity to put more of your abilities to use. Your work gives meaning to your life, affects your self-worth, connects you with other people socially, and most importantly provides you with an income for making a living. It is true that work occupies a central place in most people's lives. Since work is so important to you, the conditions in the workplace affect your health and well-being.

As a consequence of rapid globalization of the economy and constant social, economic, and technological changes, the workplace is more and more associated with increased psychological and emotional stress that may cause illness and decline in mental and physical well-being. Stress has also been blamed for the deterioration of performance efficiency on the part of both managers and subordinates in organizations. When performance efficiency suffers, the quality of the overall organizational environment and productivity deteriorate. Furthermore, the effect of stress on one employee has a ripple effect of promoting stress, anxiety, and depression within the person's family (Crossfield, Kinman, & Jones, 2005). This means that if a parent or someone close to you is undergoing severe stress at work, it can also significantly affect your well-being.

Occupational stress is a very complex phenomenon. As you may recall from Chapter 1, the definition of stress involves stressors, stress responses, and the mediating variables between these two factors. Thus, we can define occupational stress as the harmful physical and emotional responses that occur when the requirements of the job

---

VOICE OF STRESS 10.4

Twenty-Six-Year-Old Female Service Representative
In my new job, the computer routes the calls and they never stop. I even have to schedule my bathroom breaks. All I hear the whole day are complaints from unhappy customers. I try to be helpful and sympathetic, but I can't promise anything without getting my boss's approval. Most of the time I'm caught between what the customer wants and company policy. I'm not sure who I'm supposed to keep happy. The other reps are so uptight and tense they don't even talk to one another. We all go to our own little cubicles and stay there until quitting time. To make matters worse, my mother's health is deteriorating. If only I could use some of my sick time to look after her. No wonder I'm in here with migraine headaches and high blood pressure. A lot of the reps are seeing the employee assistance counselor and taking stress management classes, which seems to help. But sooner or later, someone will have to make some changes in the way the place is run.

do not match the capabilities, resources, or needs of the worker (National Institute for Occupational Safety and Health, 1999). It is also recognized that this imbalance between demand and capability to cope varies dynamically with many conditions including social support, perceptual management, and personal style interventions such as exercise and regular practice of relaxation.

It probably does not surprise you to find that work can make people sick. This is especially the case with those who work in high-pressure jobs, log excessive hours, are engaged in conflict with peers, or cannot complete assigned tasks in the allotted time. It has also been found that if you have a demanding job, one with little control over what you do and how you do it, and with colleagues and supervisors who are not supportive, you can easily experience major stress symptoms (Cheng, Yawachi, Coakley, Schwartz, & Colditz, 2000; Stranks, 2005). It might surprise you to learn that researchers who surveyed 21,000 women about the physical symptoms they experienced related to stress discovered that the solution to resolving the symptoms was *not* found merely in changing the way they work but in changing the work conditions. Specifically, this means reducing workload (number of class credits, number of work hours, number of tasks), as well as increasing the support you get from others and the control you feel over your work environment (Madison, 2000).

Symptoms of Occupational Stress

There are many different signs and symptoms that can indicate when you are having difficulty coping with the level of stress in your job (Stranks, 2005). Table 10.1 presents detailed symptoms.

Sources of Occupational Stress

In the workplace, stress can be derived from variables interacting with one another, making it difficult to identify exactly the reasons behind an episode. These variables have been classified in six categories (Cartwright & Cooper, 1997; Cooper & Marshall, 1976): (1) factors intrinsic to the job itself, (2) role in the organization, (3) career development, (4) relationships at work, (5) organizational structure and climate, and (6) work–family interface.

1. *Factors intrinsic to the job itself.* Stress results from the specific characteristics of the job such as excessive workload, inadequate resource support, pace of work, meaningfulness of work, lack of autonomy, erratic hours of work, or

TABLE 10.1 Job-related stress symptoms

Physical symptoms	Psychological symptoms
Headaches, back pain, grinding teeth, clenched jaws, chest pain, shortness of breath, pounding heart, high blood pressure, muscle aches, indigestion, constipation or diarrhea, increased perspiration, fatigue, insomnia, frequent illness	Anxiety, irritability, sadness, defensiveness, anger, mood swings, hypersensitivity, apathy, depression, slowed thinking or racing thoughts; feelings of helplessness, hopelessness, or of being trapped
Behavioral symptoms	**Job symptoms**
Overeating or loss of appetite, impatience, short temper, procrastination, increased use of alcohol or drugs, increased smoking, withdrawal or isolation from others, neglect of responsibility, poor job performance, poor personal hygiene, change in religious practices, change in close family relationships	Accidents, lower productivity, lower efficiency, lower quality of work, increased absenteeism, increased mistakes in work

isolation at the workplace (Murphy, 1996). Environmental factors such as temperature variations, noise, vibrations, and lighting may significantly affect individual stress (Cooper, 1987). Rapid changes in technology for which workers are unprepared bring about mental and physical strain.

2. *Roles in the organization.* A role is associated with the behaviors and demands expected of someone in a particular position. The individual's stress often results when her work role and responsibilities have not been clearly defined (Cooper, Dewe, & O'Driscoll, 2001).

3. *Career development.* Job insecurity and lack of opportunity for growth, advancement, or promotion can all pose psychological strain within an organization. In today's global economy, fears about downsizing and layoffs are universal among employees, especially among middle-level managers whose jobs are often the first to go. Employees are also interested in working for an organization where they perceive more room for growth and development (Jewell, 1998).

4. *Relationships at work.* Another source of occupational stress relates to interpersonal demands. Employees are expected to develop working relationships with other people in the organization including supervisors, coworkers, and subordinates. However, negative interpersonal relationships and lack of support from colleagues and supervisors are related to excessive stress for many workers.

5. *Organizational structure/climate.* Leadership style of managers and supervisors is often a source of stress for their employees. Role demands are external to the tasks associated with a job. This particular type of stress typically develops as a result of flawed organizational structures, ineffective organizational development, the inability of an individual to successfully pursue achievement goals within an organization, or some combination of these.

6. *Home–work interface.* This issue deals with how you manage the conflicts between the roles and responsibilities at your job and off the job. This conflict is created by the finite resources at your command, including a scarcity of time, energy, and money. Virtually everyone has some family/home responsibilities that sometimes interfere with work obligations, and vice versa: finding a balance is the most difficult challenge (Peeters, Montgomery, Bakker, & Schaufeli, 2005). How to manage home–work interface directly influences job and life satisfaction (De Simone et al., 2014).

Reducing Stress on the Job

As you have no doubt noticed, some work environments are dysfunctional. Within organizations, or even noticeable in some classrooms, are norms that lead to uncivil, disrespectful behavior. Sometimes this results from an oppressive atmosphere in which it doesn't feel safe to express yourself; other times such dysfunction can emerge because there is a marked lack of structure. Think of classes you've had that were either too strict or too permissive and chaotic: the same factors operate within any organizational structure.

It may not be within your power to promote organizational change, but it is often worthwhile to at least offer feedback to those who are in control. This could involve speaking to a supervisor, or in the case of dysfunctional classrooms, talking to the instructor (see Voice of Stress Management 10.2). Usually it is better to present such feedback in a way that is not perceived as threatening, critical, or disrespectful. It is also useful to provide specific examples and come across as constructive and helpful. Whereas this is always a first choice for trying to change a toxic system, you may also have to accept the reality that it is not within your power to make a difference on your own. A second option is to try to create your own cocoon of like-minded, supportive peers who share your values. This is, in fact, exactly what you try to do in classes that are unduly challenging, boring, or otherwise frustrating—you create a support system of peers to try to get your needs met.

In job situations in which there is extreme organizational dysfunction, often the result of poor leadership or toxic relationships, it may be necessary to find other employment. Although this may not be an easy option, you have learned how chronic exposure to abuse often leads to a number of physical and psychological problems, some of which can cause permanent damage.

In situations in which it is not practical or possible to leave the stressful work environment, the next option is to do what you can to alter the way in which you work. This can mean changing hours or shifts, reducing workload, transferring to another area, or developing new skills. It also means applying the skills of cognitive restructuring (Chapter 6) to interpret things differently. Compare, for example, the ways that two different employees think to themselves about the identical stressful situation in which their supervisor screamed at them for not meeting a deadline.

VOICE OF STRESS MANAGEMENT 10.2

Twenty-Year-Old Science Major

I had to take this required class; there was no way around it. Everyone knew that the instructor who always taught the class was really bad but it's like we didn't have a choice. I don't know if he never read his student evaluations or what, but he never changed. I decided, at one point, that I'd had enough. The class was just such a waste of time and money it was driving me crazy. I knew I could get an A in the class just by following his stupid rules but I wasn't learning anything.

Even if I couldn't do anything to help myself I figured I had to try to do something to help the next generation of students. So, based on what we'd all observed and been talking about all semester, I wrote a list of five things that I thought would make the class better, things like not lecturing for more than a half hour at a time, or not letting people ask distracting questions that go on and on forever. I scheduled an appointment with him and tried to tell him in the nicest possible way what I thought would make the class better. He seemed grateful that I took the time to do this. Honestly, I don't think it changed a whole lot about the class but I felt so much better that at least I tried to change things. That's the thing: I felt less powerless.

Employee 1:

> *I hate this. I hate this. I hate this. I can't stand being here. I can't believe I take this crap day after day. It's so unfair. This guy drives me crazy. He never appreciates anything I do and berates me for the mistakes that he makes. He never even asked us if we could meet this deadline then he blames us for his stupidity. I hate this damn job. I can't stand being here. It just makes me sick.*

Employee 2:

> *This guy has definitely got a problem. Interesting how he keeps blaming others for his own shortsightedness. I don't much care for his abusive attitude but I realize he has got a definite problem. This really isn't about me, about what I've done, or not done; it's about him. I need to make plans to get out of this department, out from underneath his wrath, but in the meantime I just need to take a deep breath and remind myself that while I can't control his outbursts, I sure can control the way I react internally.*

You will notice in the first employee's reactions all the signposts of irrational thinking—the insistence that life should be fair, the awfulizing and exaggerating that this was terrible rather than only annoying, the surrender of control ("This guy drives me crazy"). In the thinking of the second employee you will notice how he minimizes the damage by keeping things in perspective. He doesn't much like the situation but neither is he willing to give it much weight. Sure, his boss is a jerk: there's not much he can do about that for now. But he can keep himself calm and refuse to personalize the encounter.

Everything you have already learned in this book—deep breathing exercises, use of imagery, exercise, problem solving, relaxation strategies, lifestyle changes, and conflict resolution (in Chapter 12) are designed to work as well for work environments as they are for any other setting.

Burnout: A Special Form of Occupational Stress

When stress becomes insidious and chronic, a condition known as **burnout** can develop in which your energy becomes depleted and you can't seem to muster enough motivation to do much about it, or even take reasonable care of yourself (Maslach, Leiter, & Schaufeli, 2008; Spickard, Gabbe, & Christensen, 2002; Smith, Richardson, Hoffman, & Pilkington, 2005). It has several recognizable features that may become familiar to you at some point in your life (Leiter & Maslach, 2005; Maslach, Jackson, & Leiter, 1996):

1. *Exhaustion.* Your energy is gone. You can't seem to catch up on sleep, or there is no amount of sleep that seems to replenish you. You feel overwhelmed and can't find the resources to continue what you are doing. At times you ask yourself why you should even bother.

2. *Pessimism and cynicism.* The lack of energy and motivation can be accompanied by a negative attitude in which you feel frustrated, discouraged, and hopeless. Nothing seems to matter much to you now: customers always bugging you, your boss a threat to your psyche, and even greeting your colleagues an extra hassle. You find yourself counting the hours until the day is over and the number of days until the weekend. You consider what you do meaningless and feel impatient with anyone who dares challenge you.

3. *Feelings of failure.* Given the negative attitude you carry during burnout, it also makes sense that you feel a certain amount of despair. There is no sense in trying to make anything better, you reason, because it is all hopeless anyway. There's no way out.

Burnout is most likely to occur during circumstances in which there is an incompatibility between the requirements of the job and your abilities and resources, when there is an imbalance and lack of control (Joshi, 2005). It is often the result of (1) too much work with too little time to accomplish the tasks, (2) too much effort without discernible rewards for the investment of time and energy, (3) perceived injustice or unfairness in the workplace, and (4) conflicts with coworkers, supervisors, or the dominant values of the environment (Leiter & Maslach, 2005). It is not so much a condition of individual disruption as the result of a work environment that is not responsive to human needs (Maslach, 2005). A recent study published in the *Journal of Clinical Psychology* shows that burnout and depression overlap (Bianchi, Schonfeld, & Laurent, 2015), implying that burnout is a kind of depression.

There are a number of ways that you can cope with this condition of burnout, the most obvious being to change *where* you work or *how* you work. That is one reason why many people go back to school—to retrain for another job that has more of the qualities that are desired, providing greater satisfaction, higher morale, and more support. Predictions have been made that for the future it will be crucial to remain adaptable to changing times and technological innovations (Friedman, 2005).

Even if you can't change your particular job because of limited opportunities, there are still some things you can do to alter your personal work environment (Thornton, 2005):

•   *When you face too many unrealistic demands:* reduce the hours and workload; provide more time for recovery between jobs; and negotiate with yourself and your supervisor to increase effectiveness by better matching the demands to the time available and your ability.

VOICE OF STRESS MANAGEMENT 10.3

Thirty-Eight-Year-Old Male Commercial Real Estate Agent

I'm at the top of my game. I've worked my butt off and I wouldn't have it any other way. I spent the first ten years working 16-hour days, seven days per week. Now, I'm at about 12 to 14 hours per day but at least I sometimes take a day off. My wife complains that I'm not around enough for her and the kids. I remind her that this is what she signed on for. She knew when we met how it was going to be.

Commercial real estate is a tough game, and being a top earner, I have got to put in the time. Yeah, I did put on a few pounds in the last few years and I've got a few health problems. I drink way too much coffee during the day and too much beer at night. I'm losing my hair but I drive a brand new Porsche and can afford the best education for my children.

There is just no way I can ever stop what I'm doing. I love the thrill of my work. I just can't slow down. I will do this until I die. Let's just hope that isn't any time soon.

- *When you feel powerless and lack control:* meet with your supervisor to express your concerns; change your own way of functioning so that you feel more control over what you are doing.

- *When you don't feel appreciated or appropriately rewarded:* there are many ways that you can feel compensated for the work you do. Certainly money is important, but so are opportunities for growth, learning, and feedback.

- *When you don't feel sufficient support:* examine what you are doing to isolate yourself; make more of an effort to reach out to coworkers; plan to work as part of a team; and initiate social activities at work.

Still, there are limits to what you can do if you find yourself in a dead-end situation in which the stress is unremitting and the burnout feels intractable. Sometimes the signs and symptoms of the condition—especially boredom and stress—are clear indications that it is time to move on and make necessary changes in what you do, and how you do it.

Each of the stress reduction strategies described in this chapter and elsewhere will provide you with some relief. But they cannot take care of the larger, systemic problems in your life if you don't address the bigger picture. You can make great strides in changing your diet, initiating a regular exercise program, starting yoga or tai chi, but these things will only help you to maintain the status quo if you are miserable doing what you are doing in the first place. Sometimes burnout is your body's drastic way of getting your attention and telling you that it's time to do something else.

SUMMARY

This chapter examines the nature of college stress and occupational stress. Most of today's college students have to juggle the combined pressures of school work, job demands, and peer and family influences at an early age. The myriad factors simultaneously acting on a young college student just entering society can often be overwhelming. A student, be it a young freshman, a returning nontraditional student, or a minority student, has to deal with many challenges on a college campus. These challenges include adjusting to a new lifestyle, academic pressure, housing arrangements, parental pressure, social pressure, sex and intimate relationships, freedom and responsibilities in lifestyle behaviors, and choice of a career. Since pursuit of academic goals is paramount at college, you are also provided with information on how to study more effectively by developing good habits.

Occupational stress is closely related to college stress in that it is affected by the stress within the organization. It is derived from factors intrinsic to the job itself, your role in the organization, career development, relationships at work, organizational structure and climate, and work–family interface. Over time, chronic occupational stress may develop into a serious work-related depression called burnout. Unless you can set limits on the pressures you handle, take care of your body through proper nutrition and sleep, develop effective skills for keeping up with work, incorporate forms of stress relief into your routines, and extricate yourself from unhealthy relationships, any intervention attempts are going to be less successful than you desire.

QUESTIONS FOR REVIEW

1. Identify and discuss the major stressors for a college student.
2. What are some possible relationships between academic pressure, job demands, and social pressure? Use your personal story to illustrate your points of view.
3. Discuss some effective study habits that have enabled you to succeed in college studies. Share them with your class.
4. Define occupational stress. Identify and discuss the six sources of occupational stress.
5. Describe the three levels of interventions for combating occupational stress.
6. Define burnout and describe three recognizable features of it. Also, list a few strategies to prevent burnout.

REVIEW ACTIVITY

Review Activity 10.1: Career Planning
Interview several adults of different ages and stages in life about their career journeys, including how they ended up where they are now. Ask them about how they started out, where they are now, and where they see themselves headed next. One lesson you may learn from this is that career choices are always fluid and evolving.

Write down what you see yourself doing five, ten, and twenty years from now. Keep this entry in a safe place so that in the future you can compare what happened to what you planned.

REFERENCES AND RESOURCES

Anderson, B., & Miezitis, S. (1999). Stress and life satisfaction in mature female graduate students. *Initiatives, 5*, 33–43.

Bianchi, R., Schonfeld, I., & Laurent, E. (2015). Burnout-depression overlap: A review. *Clinical Psychology Review, 36*, 28–41.

Brock, T. (2010). Young adults and higher education: Barriers and breakthroughs to success. *The Future of Children, 20*(1), 109–132.

Burns, T., & Sinfield, S. (2003). *Essential study skills: The complete guide to success at university.* Thousand Oaks, CA: Sage.

Cartwright, S., & Cooper, C. (1997). *Managing workplace stress.* Thousand Oaks, CA: Sage.

Cheng, Y., Yawachi, I., Coakley, E., Schwartz, J., & Colditz, G. (2000). The association between psychosocial work characteristics and health functioning in American women. *British Journal of Medicine, 320,* 1,432–1,436.

Cooper, C. L. (1987). The experience and management of stress: Job and organizational determinants. In A. W. Riley, & S. J. Zaccaro (Eds.), *Occupational stress and organizational effectiveness* (pp. 53–69). New York, NY: Praeger.

Cooper, C. L., Dewe, P. J., & O'Driscoll, M. P. (2001). *Organizational stress: A review and critique of theory, research, and applications.* Thousand Oaks, CA: Sage.

Cooper, C., & Marshall, J. (1976). Occupational sources of stress: A review of the literature relating to coronary heart disease and mental ill health. *Journal of Occupational Psychology, 49,* 11–28.

Crossfield, S., Kinman, G., & Jones, F. (2005). Crossover of occupational stress in dual-career couples. *Community Work and Family, 8*(2), 211–232.

De Simone, S., Lampis, J., Lasio, D., Serri, F., Cicotto, G., et al. (2014). Influences of work–family interface on job and life satisfaction. *Applied Research in Quality of Life, 9*(4), 831–861.

Friedman, T. L. (2005). *The world is flat: A brief history of the twenty-first century.* New York, NY: Farrar, Straus and Giroux.

Giancola, J. K., Grawitch, M. J., & Borchert, D. (2009). Dealing with the stress of college students: A model of adult students. *Adult Education Quarterly, 59*(3), 246–263.

Gilberg, K. R. (1993, April). Open communications provide key to good employee relations. *Supervision, 54*(4).

Gottman, J. (1999). *The marriage clinic: A scientifically based marital therapy.* New York, NY: Norton.

Hermann, D., Raybeck, D., & Gruneberg, M. (2002). *Improving memory and study skills: Advances in theory and practice.* Ashland, OH: Hogrefe & Huber.

Home, A. (1997). Learning the hard way: Role strain, stress, role demands, and support in multiple-role women students. *Journal of Social Work Education, 33,* 335–347.

Jewell, L. (1998). *Contemporary industrial/organizational psychology* (3rd ed.). Pacific Grove, CA: Brooks/Cole.

Johnson, S., & Robson, C. (1999). Threatened identities: The experiences of women in transition to programs of professional higher education. *Journal of Community and Applied Social Psychology, 9,* 273–288.

Joshi, V. (2005). *Stress: From burnout to balance.* Thousand Oaks, CA: Sage.

Kadison, R. D., & Digeronimo, T. F. (2004). *College of the overwhelmed: The campus mental health crisis and what to do about it.* San Francisco, CA: Jossey-Bass.

Kennedy, D. (2007). *How to ace your way through college and still have a life.* Broomfield, CO: Wellness Research Publishing.

Kiecolt-Glaser, J. K., Glaser, R., Strain, E. C., Stout, J. C., Tarr, K. L., Holliday, J. E., et al. (1986). Modulation of cellular immunity in medical students. *Journal of Behavioral Medicine, 9,* 5–21.

Leiter, M. P., & Maslach, C. (2005). *Banishing burnout: Six strategies for improving your relationship with work.* San Francisco, CA: Jossey-Bass.

Lopez, J. D. (2005). Race-related stress and sociocultural orientation among Latino students during their transition into a predominantly White highly selective institution. *Journal of Hispanic Higher Education, 4,* 354–365.

Madison, D. (2000). Can your job make you sick? *Psychology Today,* Nov./Dec.

Markle, G. (2015). Factors influencing persistence among nontraditional university students. *Adult Education Quarterly, 65*(3), 267–285.

Maslach, C. (2005). Understanding burnout: Work and family issues. In D. F. Halpern, & S. Elaine (Eds.), *Work–family balance to work–family interaction: Changing the metaphor* (pp. 99–114). Mahwah, NJ: Lawrence Erlbaum Associates.

Maslach, C., Jackson, S., & Leiter, M. (1996). *Maslach burnout inventory manual* (3rd ed.). Palo Alto, CA: Consulting Psychologists Press.

Maslach, C., Leiter, M. P., & Schaufeli, W. B. (2008). Measuring burnout. In C. L. Cooper, & S. Cartwright (Eds.), *The Oxford handbook of organizational well-being* (pp. 86–108). Oxford, UK: Oxford University Press.

Mason, D. J., & Kohn, M. K. (2001). *The memory workbook: Breakthrough techniques to exercise your brain and improve your memory.* Oakland, CA: New Harbinger.

McWhorter, K. (2006). *College reading and study skills.* New York, NY: Longman.

Murphy, L. R. (1996). Stress management in work settings: A critical review of health effects. *American Journal of Health Promotion, 11*, 112–135.

National Institute for Occupational Safety and Health (1999). *Stress ... at work.* Retrieved on December 28, 2005 from www.cdc.gov/niosh/docs/99-101.

Padula, M. A. (1994). Reentry women: A literature review with recommendations for counseling and research. *Journal of Counseling and Development, 73*, 10–16.

Parker, M. N., & Jones, R. T. (1999). Minority status stress: Effect on the psychological and academic functioning of African American students. *Journal of Gender, Culture, and Health, 4*(1), 61–82.

Peeters, M. C., Montgomery, A., Bakker, A., & Schaufeli, W. (2005). Balancing work and home: How job and home demands are related to burnout. *International Journal of Stress Management, 12*(1), 43–61.

Rose, C., & Nicholl, M. J. (1997). *Accelerated learning for the 21st century.* New York, NY: Dell.

Scott, C., Burns, A., & Cooney, G. (1996). Reasons for discontinuing study: The case of mature age female students with children. *Higher Education, 31*, 233–253.

Seaman, B. (2005). *Binge: Campus life in an age of disconnection and excess.* New York, NY: Wiley.

Shelton, J. N., Yip, T., Eccles, J. S., Chatman, C. M., Fuligni, A. J., & Wong, C. (2005). Ethnic identity as a buffer of psychological adjustment to stress. In G. Downey, J. S. Eccles, & C. M. Chatman (Eds.), *Navigating the future: Social identity, coping, and life tasks* (pp. 96–112). New York, NY: Russell Sage Foundation.

Smith, J., Richardson, J., Hoffman, C., & Pilkington, K. (2005). Mindfulness-based stress reduction as supportive therapy in cancer care: A systematic review. *Journal of Advanced Nursing, 2*(3), 315–327.

Spickard, A., Gabbe, S., & Christensen, J. (2002). Mid-career burnout in generalist and specialist physicians. *Journal of the American Medical Association, 288*, 1,447–1,450.

Stranks, J. (2005). *Stress at work: Management and prevention.* New York, NY: Butterworth/Heinemann.

Thornton, J. (2005). Worked over? *Men's Health*, March, 108–113.

Wei, M., Heppner, P. P., Ku, T., & Liao, K. Y. (2010). Racial discrimination stress, coping, and depressive symptoms among Asian Americans: A moderation analysis. *Asian American Journal of Psychology, 1*(2), 136–150.

11

Care of the Self
Nutrition and Other Lifestyle Issues

Lifestyle refers to the particular attitudes and values you hold as they are reflected in the choices you make and the ways you behave. Stress can be manifested in a number of these dimensions related to your work, sleep, and finances, as well as personal habits such as drinking, smoking, and the use of prescription or illicit drugs. Stress is also embedded in the ways you are treated by others, not just within relationships (covered in the next chapter) but also in extreme cases of psychological abuse and harassment.

More than any other chapter in the book, this chapter exposes you to different factors that can either be the cause of problems or the effects of choices you have made. Many of these personal decisions regarding how you manage your life can be reassigned in such a way as to minimize or even prevent additional stressors in the future.

KEY QUESTIONS IN THE CHAPTER

- What are the dimensions of a lifestyle?
- How are the dimensions of lifestyle related to your stress experience?
- What are ways that technological intrusions can cause more stress?
- What are the major problems with the typical Western diet?
- What is the connection between stress and nutrition?
- How do you assess your weight problems?
- What are the main food groups suggested by MyPlate for creating your meals?
- What is the connection between nutrition and mental and physical health?
- What are the most effective strategies for stopping smoking or excessive drinking?
- How is stress affected by the quality and quantity of sleep?
- What is the connection between your financial situation and stress?

Portrait of a Lifestyle

Monica is a person on the run. If she were an acquaintance or classmate of yours, you would notice a couple of things about her right away. First, she is a whirlwind of energy—she thinks fast, talks fast, and is almost always ready to move on to the next thing. She is always a little late, out of breath, and apologetic. Although she is fun to be around, there is something about her that makes you feel a little jittery.

You might be inclined to label her as a Type A personality since she manifests some of the usual characteristics such as appearing hurried and harried. A closer examination of your new friend, however, would reveal that she is not a particularly ambitious person, just someone who always seems to be behind schedule. Also, she does not exhibit the typical pattern of manipulation, ruthlessness, and drive that is associated with Type A patterns. Whether Monica's behavior is the result of poor organization, lousy planning, or just inefficiency, you aren't sure. But one thing you do know—her life seems out of control.

After getting to know Monica a little better, you note that she always seems behind in her classes—late with assignments and cramming for tests the night before an exam. She is sleep-deprived, which she attempts to manage by smoking cigarettes and drinking cappuccinos with an extra shot of espresso. She seems to survive nutritionally on the snack machines that are strategically placed throughout the campus.

One of the reasons that Monica doesn't sleep well at night, besides the excessive caffeine and nicotine consumption, is that she has a tough job. It is not the actual workload that gets to her as much as the pressure she feels from some of her coworkers. Her boss has a terrible temper that he is not afraid to display at the slightest provocation. Another guy at work keeps harassing her and won't leave her alone. She would love to quit the job and do something else, but she is so far in debt that she can't risk losing a paycheck.

Generally, by the time Monica leaves work and gets to class, she is so flustered she can barely concentrate. During weekends she does her best to calm down by going out drinking with friends, but when Monday rolls around she already feels depleted and burned out.

There are a number of possible causes you might identify that appear to be the source of Monica's stress problems. Although the way she is treated at work, apparently one major area of tension, is not her choice, she has made her own choices about the ways she deals with the pressure. Her sleep and eating habits, dependence on stimulants (caffeine and nicotine) and depressants (alcohol), time management, study skills, and financial decisions all contribute to a chronically stressful lifestyle that is out of control. There doesn't seem to be any one thing that she can do to break this vicious cycle. She even enrolled in a stress management class but then dropped it after she found it too depressing learning about everything she was doing to her body. Sometimes, she figured, denial is a savior.

You may actually know someone like Monica, a person whose lifestyle only sabotages any attempt to make more healthy adjustments. You may also recognize a part of yourself in some aspect of her predicament. There is little doubt that the quality of life is determined, to some extent, by the ability to prevent and manage stress in daily activities and events, a situation that Monica feels helpless to change. Since many stressful events occur on a daily basis, a closer examination of your routines and habits may reveal some hidden sources of difficulty.

Assessing Lifestyle Dimensions

Most people who drive know the importance of regular automobile maintenance like changing the oil and filter, rotating tires, and getting a tune-up. Yet only a small minority of people realize the importance of giving themselves regular health maintenance.

You have already learned enough about the subject to realize that the best way to manage stress is to prevent it from getting out of control in the first place. More than anything else, such efforts are controlled by your lifestyle, meaning the characteristic ways in which you conduct your daily life. This includes all of your personal habits, usual behaviors, and the choices you make with regard to basic functioning such as sleep, nutrition, and safety. A healthy lifestyle is one in which you have adequate knowledge, skills, and attitudes to allow you to protect and take care of yourself to prevent illness, minimize stress to your system, and engage in optimal functioning. These lifestyle factors can be examined in several areas related to your physical conditioning, personal habits, relationships, and satisfaction.

FOR REFLECTION 11.1

Check Yourself: A Wellness Inventory

Put a check beside *each* statement that applies to you. Your score may range from zero to five checks in each category.

1. Alcohol use
- ___ I drink two or fewer alcoholic drinks a day.
- ___ In the past year, I have not driven an automobile after having more than two drinks.
- ___ When I'm under stress, I do not drink more.
- ___ I do not do things when I'm drinking that I later regret.
- ___ I have not experienced any problem because of my drinking in the past.

2. Tobacco use
- ___ I have never smoked cigarettes.
- ___ I haven't smoked cigarettes in the past year.
- ___ I do not use any form of tobacco (pipes, cigars, chewing tobacco).
- ___ I smoke only low-tar and low-nicotine cigarettes.
- ___ I smoke fewer than a dozen cigarettes per day.

3. Blood pressure
- ___ I have had my blood pressure checked within the past six months.
- ___ I have never had high blood pressure.
- ___ I do not currently have high blood pressure.
- ___ I make a conscious effort to avoid salt in my diet.
- ___ There is no history of high blood pressure in my family.

4. Weight/Body composition
- ___ According to height and weight charts, I am in the average range.
- ___ I have not been on a weight reduction diet in the past year.
- ___ There is no place on my body that I can pinch an inch of fat.
- ___ I am satisfied with the way my body looks.
- ___ My family, friends, or doctor have not urged me to lose weight.

5. Physical fitness
- ___ I do some form of vigorous exercise for at least thirty minutes three times a week or more.
- ___ My resting pulse is sixty beats a minute or less.
- ___ I don't get fatigued easily while doing physical work.
- ___ I engage in some recreational sport such as tennis or swimming on a weekly basis.
- ___ I would say that my level of physical fitness is higher than most of the people in my age group.

6. Stress/Anxiety level
- ___ I find it easy to relax.
- ___ I am able to cope with stressful events as well as or better than most people.
- ___ I do not have trouble falling asleep or waking up.
- ___ I rarely feel tense or anxious.
- ___ I have no trouble completing tasks I have started.

→

7. *Car safety*
- ___ I always use seat belts when I drive.
- ___ I always use seat belts when I am a passenger.
- ___ I have not had an automobile accident in the past three years.
- ___ I have not had a speeding ticket or other moving violation in the past three years.
- ___ I never ride with a driver who has had more than two drinks.

8. *Relationships*
- ___ I am currently living with a spouse or partner.
- ___ I have a lot of close friends.
- ___ I am able to share my feelings with my partner or other family members.
- ___ I am not involved in a major conflict with a family member, coworker, or friend.
- ___ When I have a problem, I have people I can talk to.

9. *Rest/Sleep*
- ___ I almost always get between seven and nine hours of sleep each night.
- ___ I wake up few, if any, times during the night.
- ___ I feel rested and ready to go most of the time when I get up in the morning.
- ___ Most days, I have a lot of energy.
- ___ Even though I sometimes have a chance, I rarely take naps during the day.

10. *Life satisfaction*
- ___ If I had my life to live over, I wouldn't make all that many changes.
- ___ I've accomplished many of the things that I've set out to do in my life.
- ___ I can't think of an area in my life that really disappoints me.
- ___ I am generally a happy person.
- ___ Compared with the people I know, I feel I've done well in my life.

Scoring

Record the number of checks (from zero to five) for each area. Then add up the numbers to determine your score.

Area	*Subscore*
Alcohol use	___
Tobacco use	___
Weight/Body fat	___
Physical fitness	___
Stress/Anxiety level	___
Car safety	___
Relationships	___
Rest/Sleep	___
Life satisfaction	___

Interpreting your score:
- 40–50: Healthier than average lifestyle
- 25–39: Average lifestyle
- 0–24: Below average: need for improvement
- A score of less than 3 in any of the ten areas: need for improvement in that area

(Source: Adapted from Pruitt & Stein, 2004)

Technological Intrusions

While reviewing aspects of lifestyle that contribute to increased stress it is important to also mention the impact of various technological devices in our lives. There once was a time, just a few years ago, when people would actually give one another their full attention. Nowadays, with cell phones, Blackberries, iPhones, iPads, computers, Facebook,

Twitter, music and videoplayers, streaming video, global positioning units, earbuds, and other mobile devices (and soon implants!), it is rare that we are ever fully present. We are bombarded by emails, text messages, tweets, and phone calls every waking minute of the day. This sort of gadget abuse leads to all kinds of distractions and multitasking, making it virtually impossible to just sit back and relax. In one poll (CNN, 2010) 25% of young people say they don't mind being interrupted by an electronic message when they are on the toilet and one in ten wouldn't mind answering a message while having sex!

These communication and entertainment devices are wonderful sources of fun and pleasure—if they are managed within reasonable limits. How often have you seen groups of friends or family members all sitting around *talking to someone else* on their hand-held device? How often have you noticed yourself having an intense conversation with someone that is suddenly interrupted by a phone call or text message? How often have you found yourself talking to someone who is important to you, all the while you are simultaneously texting, emailing, or otherwise splitting your attention toward another person or task?

The cumulative result of all this stimulation and opportunities is that there is almost never downtime. You are almost always accessible. Even more stressful is that it is becoming more and more difficult to just enjoy what you're doing in any given moment because you are also likely doing something else at the same time.

Just as it takes a certain amount of self-discipline to maintain a healthy diet, an exercise program, or self-improvement strategy, so too must you show restraint to limit the ways that gadget abuse can compromise your tranquility. In particular it is a good idea to set some rules for yourself in terms of when and how you will incorporate technology into (or banish it from) your life. This means: (1) giving people you care about your full attention without interruptions, (2) turning off your phone or device at times when you wish to maintain full appreciation of what you are doing, (3) avoiding reading emails, texts, or other potentially arousing stimulation right before you go to bed, (4) and taking time for yourself without external intrusions.

Diet, Nutrition, and Stress

What you eat affects not only the condition of your body but also the thoughts you generate, your moods, the quality of your performance (e.g., tests and giving a speech), as well as your mental health (Karren, Hafen, Smith, & Frandsen, 2006). Not only does what you eat affect your mood, but there is also a close connection between chronic stress and the craving for comfort foods that have nothing to do with your appetite but rather serve as a form of self-medication for excessive pressure. Roughly half of people surveyed admit that that they overindulge when under stress (Harris Interactive, 2002). One reason for this is that when your system is flooded with triggered chemical reactions in response to stress, it is far more difficult to tell when you are still hungry—you keep eating because your body mistakenly thinks you require more energy supplies (Childre & Rozman, 2005; Rosch & Clark, 2001).

Even though the relationship between stress and diet is complex, some useful principles are derived from the existing body of knowledge. I are going to discuss some research findings regarding diet, nutrition, and stress, and offer suggestions for coping with stress and warding off diseases.

Eating and Weight Problems Nationwide and on College Campuses

Incredibly, six out of ten Americans are considered overweight and almost one-third qualify as obese (Flegal, Carroll, Ogden, & Johnson, 2002; Ogden et al., 2014). This is the result of not just eating habits but also the ways that people use food to help cope with the stress in their lives (Dallman, Pecoraro, & La Fleur, 2005). As a screening tool

College campuses sometimes offer limited and poor options for healthy eating. Looking at this photo, what would be the best and worst choices you could make for a snack?

for weight issues, you can use **body mass index** (BMI), which is your weight in kilograms divided by the square of height in meters. An alternative to BMI is the waist-to-hip ratio. A high BMI can be an indicator of high body fatness. You can easily calculate these numbers by going online. Your weight is considered normal if your BMI falls between 18.5 and 24.9. You will be considered overweight if your BMI is between 25 and 29.9. Anything equal to or above 30 is considered obese. For the waist-to-hip ratio, your goal is to reach for less than .95 if you are male and less than .85 if you are female. According to the USDA, the average American diet includes too much unhealthy animal fats, additives, preservatives, and processed foods, and too little fresh fruits and vegetables.

If eating problems are universal all over the continent, college campuses are hardly immune from the temptations. While many students in college complain about eating too much junk food, not exercising enough, and consequently becoming overweight and feeling sluggish, another segment of the college population suffers from more serious eating problems including anorexia nervosa, bulimia nervosa, and binge eating (see Chapter 4 for more details).

The challenge to control weight and binge eating in the face of chronic stress is made all the more difficult by our culture. As people spend more and more time sitting in front of their computer and television screens, they are becoming less active and burning off fewer calories. The stress begins to accumulate, continuing a vicious cycle in which you crave more treats but spend less energy working them off.

One critical habit in controlling weight and eating healthfully is being able to distinguish between **physical** and **emotional hunger**. How do you know the difference between the two?

FOR REFLECTION 11.2

How *can* you tell the difference between when you are truly hungry—that is, have a physiological need for nutrition to keep your energy going—versus an emotional hunger to ward off stress? What are the comfort foods that you crave most during times when you feel anxious or depressed?

During emotional hunger, ignited by stress, the craving for food develops suddenly rather than as a gradual gnawing. You feel a distinct urge for a particular food, especially one that is high in fat or sugar. This is not about taking care of your nutritional needs but rather a kind of self-soothing after feeling sad, depressed, lonely, anxious, or bored. The urge comes about during unexpected periods that are not associated with the usual meal times but rather with negative emotional states. Finally, instead of feeling satisfied after eating, you feel guilt and shame. This is a self-perpetuating cycle in which the bad feelings are now worse, sometimes leading to the next binge. In one study, for example, people who were stressed ate five times the number of M&M chocolate candies than those who were relaxed. One reason may be because of the temporary boost in serotonin levels that occurs after a sugar infusion, a feeling of well-being that doesn't last long (Campbell, 2006).

This behavior is difficult to stop because it works—in the short run. For the few minutes you are stuffing your face with pizza, potato chips, ice cream, or chocolate, you are only aware of feeding and trying to satisfy your emotional hunger. But ten minutes later, remorse and regret kick in.

How do you break this cycle of choosing (and it is a choice) to cope with stress with food? By exercising the self-control to apply the other alternatives you have learned—exercise or go for a walk, practice meditation or deep breathing, reach out to a friend, do something productive, journal about your negative feelings, anything that helps you to burn off the negative energy in a healthy way.

The Stress and Eating Cycle

Stress changes not only what you crave to eat, but also the way you eat. Recall what happens during chronic stress when the fight-or-flight switch is permanently turned on. Cortisol production is in overdrive. Hormones are circulating throughout the body, mobilizing for what is perceived as a permanent state of emergency. In this way, energy reserves are run down and the metabolic system becomes depleted. Under such circumstances, you need to replenish your energy, and you need to do it quickly, with foods that can be converted into energy right away. What sort of foods would replenish energy most quickly?

If you guessed calorie-rich, fat-laden treats, you are correct. During times of ongoing stress, the body sends a signal that says, "Feed me! I need fuel! And I need it quick!" Although that is not the only reason why people eat junk food during times of stress, it is one source of such cravings.

Once you stuff yourself with sufficient quantities of cake, pizza, nachos, candy, or greasy burgers, you might feel a surge of energy, for these foods will calm your emotions through temporarily increasing sugar and serotonin levels in the brain. Unfortunately, the effects won't last very long. Two or three hours later, your insulin level will reach its peak in order to bring down the sugar levels (see Figure 11.1). Since insulin prevents the body from using stored fat for energy, when the level remains high, the body will store fat. On average, a person can store about 300 to 400 grams of carbohydrates and about 90 grams of carbohydrates in the liver. The stored carbohydrates are called glycogen, a form of glucose that can be released from the liver and muscles upon request from the brain at the moment of stress. However, when these stores of energy are filled, the body starts to convert any extra carbohydrates into fat that will be stored in fatty tissue. This stress-induced eating cycle helps explain why obese people find it difficult to lose weight when they are under pressure; they are caught in a vicious cycle that becomes self-perpetuating. When the fat cells are full leaving no more space for storing surplus nutrients,

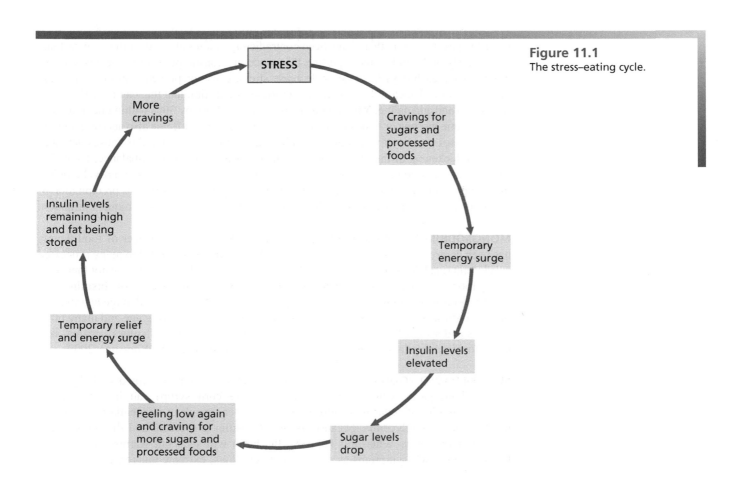

Figure 11.1
The stress–eating cycle.

another health issue will happen known as **insulin resistance** or **Type 2 diabetes** that causes hyperglycemia, which, in turn, results in cardiovascular damage and **metabolic syndrome** (Sapolsky, 2004).

Foods that Can Exacerbate Stress

Your ability to eat healthfully first involves being able to distinguish between physical and emotional hunger, as described earlier. Second, it is important to know which foods actually make things worse for you. This information is not enough to make a difference on its own. After all, before I launched into this section you probably already had a good idea of which foods are better for you than others and yet this knowledge does not necessarily change your eating behavior. Nevertheless, even if you persist in eating unhealthily, you should be fully aware of what you are doing to yourself.

VOICE OF THE AUTHOR 11.1

When I first came to America I didn't have the knowledge and financial resources to eat well. I used to buy loads of Coca-Cola, cheap beef and pork, and potato chips. My favorite foods included French fries, Whoppers, and Dr Pepper. I skipped breakfast most of the time and ate huge amounts of fatty foods close to bedtime (because I worked in a Chinese restaurant). It didn't take long for me to start to feel queasy in my stomach. It was years later that I learned that I had developed a disease called gastroesophageal acid reflux. At that time, I didn't know that several cans of cola might have made me feel good for only a short while and I ended up feeling much worse later.

Caffeine

Over the past few years there have been contradictory studies about the effects of caffeine on the body and mind, some reporting that moderate consumption (a few colas, cups of coffee or tea each day) increase or decrease stress, cause or prevent cancer, and so on. What is clear is that caffeine is a central nervous system stimulant that can raise the levels of cortisol and adrenaline. Your blood cortisol level will rise by 30% within one hour after you consume just one or two cups of coffee (Colbert, 2005). Caffeine also acts as a diuretic that increases the rate at which the body eliminates fluid. Over time, this causes dehydration and thickening of the blood, digestive disorders and metabolic imbalance. Excessive caffeine consumption is also to blame for many stress-related disorders and psychological disturbances, including anxiety states, depression and psychosis as well as precipitation of a fast pulse, insomnia, nervousness, headache, irritability, diarrhea, and frequent urination.

MONOSODIUM GLUTAMATE (MSG)   The use of MSG as an enhancer of food flavors has been controversial. It is commonly used in Asian cuisine and added to many processed snacks and salad dressings. The reason that people may feel tired and hungry not long after eating foods that contain MSG is that it stimulates the pancreas to release more **insulin**. This, in turn, leads to a drop in blood sugar (Blaylock, 1997). MSG is related to the aggravation of premenstrual syndrome symptoms in some women of childbearing age and many other diseases and symptoms including headaches, dizziness, balance difficulties, asthma, skin rash, flushing, palpitations, and so on (Schwartz, 1988; Williams & Woessner, 2009).

SUGAR-LOADED FOODS   Foods that contain refined sugar or refined carbohydrates (white flour, pasta, white rice, and high-fructose corn syrup) can increase stress. Consuming a lot of sugar in a short period of time can result in a potentially hazardous health issue, hypoglycemia, because too much insulin is secreted and the blood sugar level drops too low. When this happens, the brain will send out warning signals that translate into such symptoms as carbohydrate cravings, extreme hunger, mood swings, and fatigue (Colbert, 2005). Consequently, the person will reach for something sweet or high in processed carbohydrates to quench the cravings. Meanwhile, the brain will signal the adrenal glands to secrete cortisol which will, in turn, cause the release of glycogen from the liver and muscles. Protein starts to break down into amino acids to be converted to sugar. The result is that blood sugar levels rise again. Now more insulin will pour into the bloodstream to cause a plunge in blood sugar levels. Even if you don't follow all the physiology, you can conclude that particular foods such as sugar, caffeine, and MSG have powerful negative effects that increase stress.

Warding Off Stress through Proper Nutrition

Having proper nutrition is probably the most effective step to prevent and manage stress brought about by life's challenges. Nutrients are substances that the body needs to regulate bodily functions, promote growth, repair body tissues, and obtain energy. Even though the body needs many kinds of nutrients, six are essential nutrients, because these six kinds of nutrients cannot be synthesized from other nutrients and must be supplied through proper diet. Carbohydrates, fats, and proteins provide the fuel for daily activities. Vitamins and minerals are needed to regulate the body's normal functions. Water is the most important and neglected nutrient, simply because every living organism needs it for basic functions.

CARBOHYDRATES   After reading the previous section about the dangers of too much refined sugars, you may want to avoid carbohydrates altogether. Yet not all carbohydrates are created equal. You need a sufficient quantity of good carbohydrates to be healthy. Carbohydrates contain all the vitamins (except B12) and minerals your body needs for optimal functioning. They also contain fiber, which assists digestion and strengthens intestines in addition to helping with weight control, heart disease, **diabetes**, cancer, and intestinal diseases. Best sources of carbohydrates are whole plant foods that include whole grains and fresh fruits and vegetables.

To determine which kinds of carbohydrates are good for you, you need to look at how quickly they are broken down into their component simple sugars. The speed at which the breakdown takes place determines how much sugar actually enters your bloodstream. High-glycemic carbohydrates can be rapidly converted into sugar and lead to an insulin spike. Examples include starches and most processed grains (white breads, processed pastas, white rice), starchy vegetables (potatoes and corn), and dried fruits. Large amounts of medium glycemic foods (bananas, sweet potatoes) also cause elevated insulin levels. Ideally, the best nutritional strategy is to avoid high glycemic foods and concentrate on those that are converted into sugar at a slower speed. Such foods stress the body's insulin-making machinery less, and so help prevent type 2 diabetes (Ludwig, 2002).

FOR REFLECTION 11.3

Which of the foods below would you guess are high glycemic (spike insulin levels in the bloodstream because of their fast sugar breakdown) versus low glycemic (those that break down gradually and provide more nutrient value)? Indicate H for high glycemic and L for low glycemic foods.

____ Watermelon	____ Gatorade®
____ Lentils	____ Skim milk
____ Ice cream	____ French fries
____ Corn flakes	____ Baked potato
____ All-Bran® cereal	____ Yogurt
____ Soybeans	____ Cheerios® cereal
____ White bread	____ Plain bagel
____ Pumpernickel bread	____ Orange
____ Chickpeas	____ Apple

Answers are at the end of the chapter.

FATS   Fats are a major source of energy, even though they are not the first source. They also perform many other functions, including controlling gene formation, cell membrane construction, transporting fat-soluble vitamins, improving metabolism, and regulating the immune system. In fact, more than 60% of the dry brain weight is fat (Colbert, 2005).

Just as not all carbohydrates are the same, fats vary tremendously in terms of their relationship to your health. In making a distinction between unhealthy and healthy fats, the former are **saturated** and **trans fatty acids** that raise low-density lipoproteins (LDL) and reduce high-density lipoproteins (HDL). This can lead to clogged arteries and cardiovascular diseases. These are also known as animal fats and consist of butter, cream, cheese, and whole milk. They are solid at room temperature and contain bad cholesterol. HDL cholesterol is often called the good cholesterol because it can be transported by other organs back to the liver for elimination, while LDL cholesterol can offload its cargo of cholesterol in bad places, such as on the lining of arteries. There are also a few vegetable saturated fats to watch for such as palm oil and coconut oil that are found in many processed and snack foods, as well as French fries.

Another group of fats are unsaturated fats and they are liquid at room temperature and contain essential fatty acids. Among these unsaturated fats, omega 3 and omega 6 fatty acids are "good" fats and they are essential because our bodies cannot make them and they are necessary for good health; however, intake of omega 3 and omega 6 fatty acids should be in a balanced ratio. The optimal ratio is supposed to be 4:1, but in the past 150 years, the ratio of omega-6 to omega-3 fats has increased from 1:1 to 10:1 or 20:1 (Hyman, 2009). Our diet has too much omega 6 disrupting the balance, which makes us more susceptible to disease (e.g., Okuyama et al., 2007). Choosing food high in omega 3 fatty acids can restore proper balance. Fish, especially fatty fish such as salmon and tuna, are excellent sources of omega 3 fatty acids. Benefits of omega 3 are improved lipid profile reducing cardiovascular risk, improved diabetes outcome, improved neurotransmission stimulation improving depression, reduced suicide and hostility, and improved memory function.

PROTEINS   Proteins, composed of amino acids, form muscles and bones as well as parts of blood, enzymes, hormones, and cell membranes. Since they are essential for growth and restoration, choose forms of protein that do not have unhealthy fat. This means eating lean meats that have been carefully trimmed of visible fat, eating poultry without the skin, and avoiding fried foods whenever possible. Avoid processed meats such as hot dogs, sausages, and bacon. In addition to meat, protein can also be found in nuts, skim milk, and other foods.

A major connection between proteins and stress is that the quality and quantity of proteins you consume affect the neurotransmitters in the brain. Embedded inside the membranes of cells, neurotransmitters are made from primarily eight essential amino acids that must be supplied from our diet. The level of neurotransmitters is directly related to our health. Depression is associated with low levels of serotonin and norepinephrine. Attention deficit hyperactivity disorder (ADHD) patients are deficient in dopamine. People who experience excessive anxiety are low in gamma-aminobutyric acid (GABA), and Alzheimer's disease is related to low levels of acetylcholine. What causes deficiencies in these key neurotransmitters? To answer this question, I need another book, but researchers have found that stress is often implicated (Hyman, 2009).

Another link between stress and protein is that some common sources of protein such as beef, pork, lamb, and shrimp contain large amounts of arachidonic acid that may be converted in the body into various kinds of inflammation-causing compounds known as eicosanoids (Boyce, 2008).

VITAMINS   Thirteen vitamins are essential to health. If food is the fuel that runs a car, then vitamins are like the oil that keeps the engine running smoothly. Four are fat-soluble (A, D, E, and K), and nine are water-soluble (C and eight B-complex vitamins: thiamine, riboflavin, niacin, B6, folate, B12, biotin, and pantothenic acid). Ideally, vitamins should come from the foods you eat; however, they are often destroyed by the ways we store, cook, and process food.

Vitamins serve to unleash energy stored in carbohydrates, proteins, and fats. They are critical in producing red blood cells and in maintaining the nervous, skeletal, and immune systems. Unfortunately, stress tends to deplete B-complex vitamins and vitamin C so efforts have to be made to keep them in balance through supplements and careful nutrition. The B group vitamins are important for ensuring that the nervous and immune systems are able to function effectively. Vitamin C will provide the immune and nervous systems with a boost during stress. Severe deficiencies in vitamins such as folate, B6, and B12 are associated with depression, mood disorders, dementia, ADHD, and autism (Hyman, 2009).

MINERALS   Minerals are inorganic elements required in small amounts to help regulate body functions, aid growth in maintenance of body tissues, and act as catalysts for energy release. There are about seventeen essential minerals including calcium, phosphorus, magnesium, sodium, potassium, and chloride. Most multivitamin tablets contain mineral supplements. They can also be found in many vegetables, skim milk, and lean meats. However, due to overfarming and the typical poor diet, many Americans are deficient in these essential minerals. Deficiency in magnesium is implicated in such health problems as depression, ADHD, chronic fatigue, and asthma (Hyman, 2009). Zinc deficiency is related to eating disorders and selenium shortage may cause mood disorders.

Using MyPlate to Design a Balanced Diet

MyPlate (see Figure 11.2) was launched in June 2011 to replace MyPyramid by the United States Department of Agriculture (USDA) Center for Nutrition Policy and Promotion (CNPP). MyPlate is a change to "relatively" simple image that portrays a plate cut into four quadrants: one each for fruits, vegetables, grains, and proteins with a smaller plate representing dairy on the right top corner. This icon essentially represents the 2015–2020 **Dietary Guidelines for Americans (DGA)** (see Table 11.1). MyPlate replaces MyPyramid and serves as a more straightforward reminder for making healthiest choices among major food groups. MyPlate is part of a multimodal communication strategy that includes the MyPlate website with the SuperTracker tool to personalize food plans, consumer educational materials and e-tools, social media engagement, and a partnership initiative to help coordinate and disseminate consistent messages of the DGA. MyPlate gives consumers more freedom and responsibilities to choose healthy foods based on the DGA, which are reviewed and updated by law every five years.

There is some good diet advice presented by health scientists from Harvard who created Harvard's Healthy Eating Plate to clarify and augment MyPlate (Healthy eating plate, 2011):

- Eat more fruits and vegetables in more variety.

- Half of every meal should consist of fruits and vegetables.

- For carbs, eat whole-grain variety.

- For protein, choose fish, fowl, beans, and nuts over red meat.

TABLE 11.1 USDA 2015–2020 Dietary Guidelines for Americans: General guidelines and key recommendations for the general population

The Guidelines
1. **Follow a healthy eating pattern across the lifespan.** All food and beverage choices matter. Choose a healthy eating pattern at an appropriate calorie level to help achieve and maintain a healthy body weight, support nutrient adequacy, and reduce the risk of chronic disease.

2. **Focus on variety, nutrient density, and amount.** To meet nutrient needs within calorie limits, choose a variety of nutrient-dense foods across and within all food groups in recommended amounts.

3. **Limit calories from added sugars and saturated fats and reduce sodium intake.** Consume an eating pattern low in added sugars, saturated fats, and sodium. Cut back on foods and beverages higher in these components to amounts that fit within healthy eating patterns.

4. **Shift to healthier food and beverage choices.** Choose nutrient-dense foods and beverages across and within all food groups in place of less healthy choices. Consider cultural and personal preferences to make these shifts easier to accomplish and maintain.

5. **Support healthy eating patterns for all.** Everyone has a role in helping to create and support healthy eating patterns in multiple settings nationwide, from home to school to work to communities.

Key Recommendations

The *Dietary Guidelines'* Key Recommendations for healthy eating patterns should be applied in their entirety, given the interconnected relationship that each dietary component can have with others.

Consume a healthy eating pattern that accounts for all foods and beverages within an appropriate calorie level.

A healthy eating pattern includes:

- A variety of vegetables from all of the subgroups—dark green, red and orange, legumes (beans and peas), starchy, and other
- Fruits, especially whole fruits
- Grains, at least half of which are whole grains
- Fat-free or low-fat dairy, including milk, yogurt, cheese, and/or fortified soy beverages
- A variety of protein foods, including seafood, lean meats and poultry, eggs, legumes (beans and peas), and nuts, seeds, and soy products
- Oils

A healthy eating pattern limits:

- Saturated fats and *trans* fats, added sugars, and sodium

Key Recommendations that are quantitative are provided for several components of the diet that should be limited. These components are of particular public health concern in the United States, and the specified limits can help individuals achieve healthy eating patterns within calorie limits:

- Consume less than 10 percent of calories per day from added sugars
- Consume less than 10 percent of calories per day from saturated fats
- Consume less than 2,300 milligrams (mg) per day of sodium
- If alcohol is consumed, it should be consumed in moderation—up to one drink per day for women and up to two drinks per day for men—and only by adults of legal drinking age.
- In tandem with the recommendations above, Americans of all ages—children, adolescents, adults, and older adults—should meet the *Physical Activity Guidelines for Americans* to help promote health and reduce the risk of chronic disease. Americans should aim to achieve and maintain a healthy body weight. The relationship between diet and physical activity contributes to calorie balance and managing body weight. As such, the *Dietary Guidelines* includes a Key Recommendation to
- Meet the *Physical Activity Guidelines for Americans*.

Source: Reproduced from U.S. Department of Health and Human Services and U.S. Department of Agriculture (December, 2015). 2015–2020 Dietary Guidelines for Americans. 8th Edition. Available at http://health.gov/dietaryguidelines/2015/guidelines/.

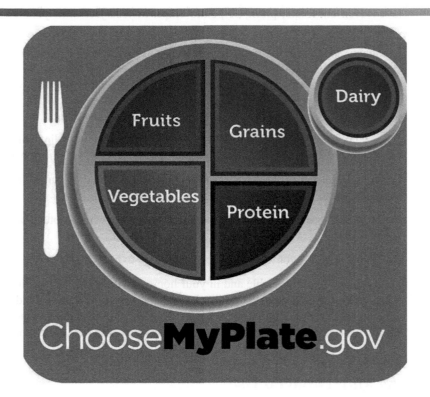

Figure 11.2
MyPlate. An iconic representation of the 2015–2020 Dietary Guidelines for Americans.
Source: Courtesy of USDA

- Use healthy oils (e.g., canola and olive) in place of solid fats (e.g., butter and lard).

- Consume no more than one or servings of dairy for protein and calcium.

- Drink water, tea, or coffee and avoid sugar-added beverages altogether.

Eating Healthfully: A Summary of Suggestions

You've reviewed some important principles regarding diet and nutrition. Below are some guidelines that include three principles: *what* to eat, *when* to eat, and *how* to eat.

- Eat a good breakfast every day. Many students skip breakfast, eat a small lunch, then have a large dinner in the evening. This pattern of eating is often a recipe for stress, diabetes, and obesity.

- For those who want to lose weight: Each evening before you go to bed, write down on a sheet of paper *everything* that you think you *might* eat the next day. Plan for snacks. Put anything you want on the list. You aren't allowed to eat anything that isn't on your list. This cuts out all impulsive indulgence. It also requires you to be thoughtful about what you put in your mouth.

- Stay away from fast-food restaurants that offer choices high in fat and sodium. If you must eat at such an establishment, then make informed food choices that include salads with low-fat, low-calorie dressings, and vegetables. Be warned that some fast-food salads with high-fat dressings might actually have more fat and calories than a hamburger.

- Reduce consumption of sugar-saturated sodas and alcoholic beverages, and drink more water and diluted juices.

- Don't go on any diet that you aren't prepared to stay on for the rest of your life. That means you shouldn't ban yourself from eating the foods you really love—even chocolate, pizza, or potato chips. Instead just limit yourself to a small quantity.

- Eat slowly and mindfully. Pay attention to what you eat and how you eat. Enjoy every mouthful. Actually taste and savor everything that enters your mouth. Rest the fork or spoon between mouthfuls, then take another bite—slowly. Eat as many fresh vegetables and fruits as you can. Whenever possible, replace snacks that are high in sugar and fat with those low in sugar and fat.

- When you eat, don't do anything else at the same time, such as reading, talking on the phone, or watching television. Instead, really concentrate on the experience.

- Create an environment to enjoy your meals more by including fun rituals such as lighting candles.

- Eat a balanced variety of foods including carbohydrates, fats, protein, and fiber in each meal.

- Do not eat anything for three hours before you go to bed.

- Keep healthy foods available and in your home. If your downfall is things like potato chips or ice cream, then don't keep them around. If during the day you are tempted to indulge in unhealthy snacks that are readily available, then keep a piece of fruit, carrot sticks, or a low-fat granola bar with you at all times.

Smoking and Tobacco Use

As you have no doubt heard before, smoking is the number one preventable health problem, killing half a million people each year (Hobson, 2005). About 18 percent of U.S. adults smoke (Centers for Disease Control and Prevention, 2009). Even if you don't use tobacco yourself, you may have observed people who tend to light up during times of stress, as well as when they are bored. In one sense, smoking is a form of self-medication for stress, even though it brings considerable side-effects and health hazards.

Despite the fact that there is so much knowledge about the harm that smoking can cause, it remains an indomitable habit for millions of people in the world. When asked why they use tobacco, smokers often cite the following reasons: reduction of negative emotions, weight control, increased mental alertness, enhanced positive affect, and habit (Gilbert & McClernon, 2000).

Research also indicates that people smoke for such reasons as heredity, parental role models, adolescent experimentation and rebellion, limited education, aggressive marketing, and addiction (Hales, 2002). It is also part of social behavior, giving you something to do to occupy yourself when bored, and contributing to an image of being "cool" as represented in the media.

Why Is Smoking So Harmful?

You already know that smoking causes lung cancer, but it also contributes to stroke, heart disease, arthritis, blindness, and a variety of other ailments (USDHHS, 2014). The instant stress relief afforded by cigarette smoking makes smoking a difficult habit to avoid or eliminate. A vicious cycle is initiated the moment someone picks up a cigarette. Research has shown that nicotine addiction begins after only a few days of use (Kassel, Stroud, & Paronis, 2003). Once you're addicted to it, any time you want to cease, you tend to feel stressed because quitting requires another adjustment of chemicals in the body. When a person is already stressed, tobacco smoking will worsen the condition. For instance, nicotine stimulates the adrenal glands to produce adrenaline that in turn increases blood pressure, raises the heart rate by 15 to 20 beats per minute, and constricts blood vessels. As if this is not frightening enough, smoking has been associated with heart disease, strokes, lung cancer, bronchitis, gum disease, miscarriages, infertility, and premature aging of skin.

Because nicotine is highly addictive and present in low concentrations in a legal and accessible product, many people fall prey to it before they even realize its potential damage to their health. Smoking tobacco is not only highly addictive but is also constantly being romanticized in the media as a way to remain cool, calm, and collected. In fact, it is a temporary stress reducer even though it has major long-term side-effects.

How to Stop Smoking

There are generally several strategies that are considered most helpful in ceasing tobacco use. It is critical to have a structured plan that includes what you are going to do according to a schedule. Seeing a counselor is often helpful in this regard, because a professional can help with motivation and viable treatment plans. If you try to quit on your own, or you are helping someone else to do so, here are a few other tips that are important:

1. *Get rid of cues that provoke smoking urges.* Remove all ashtrays from sight, as well as matches and lighters. If you tend to smoke in a particular location at home, don't sit there anymore; change chairs and the seating arrangement so you break the associations you have. At least until you are stabilized, avoid hanging out with others who smoke.

2. *Use an aid.* There are a number of products on the market—nicotine patches, gum, nasal sprays—that help you to quit slowly without painful withdrawal effects.

3. *Commit yourself to the mission with all your heart.* Make public declarations to friends and family about when you are going to stop. Announce to the world, and to yourself, that you are about to become an ex-smoker. This makes it harder for you to change your mind.

4. *Don't give up if at first you don't succeed.* Smoking and tobacco use are drug addictions that are constantly being sold by the media and entertainment industries. It takes more than willpower to become free of this unhealthy habit; it takes sustained commitment over a long period of time.

Responsible Use of Alcohol

Like tobacco, alcohol is often used as a form of self-medication for stress, in addition to its use as a "social lubricant." Moderate use of alcohol, in itself, is not a health problem — some research indicates that it can even improve health in small doses—but it all depends on when and how it is consumed (Roizen & Oz, 2005). Compare someone who has a glass of wine or beer with a meal each day to someone who drinks himself into oblivion several nights each week. Or contrast the person who has a few drinks with friends once or twice on weekends versus someone who consumes a bottle of wine or six-pack of beer almost every night.

You may have observed the ways that alcohol can be a highly dangerous, addictive drug that destroys people's lives. Too much of it can produce problems including impairment of the immune system and liver cirrhosis. Because inhibitions are also suppressed, people engage in risky, destructive, or inappropriate behavior that can be seriously harmful to themselves and others.

The most common reason people report drinking alcohol is for relaxation and unwinding. It is reported by some to reduce boredom and inhibitions, and to boost confidence in social situations, but in one form or another, anxiety and depression are at the core of excessive, chronic indulgence (Seaman, 2005). Stressful life events such as divorce and unemployment are highly correlated with the consumption of alcohol (Taylor & Pilati, 2000). This is also often true for relationship conflicts, stress of studying for exams, and financial pressures associated with college life.

Individuals may be very different in terms of onset of consumption patterns. More than half of the American population, about 64%, are regular users of alcohol; among college students, 44% report occasional binge drinking in which they fall into a drunken stupor (Hales, 2002).

FOR REFLECTION 11.4

Do *You* Have a Drinking Problem?

If you answer "yes" to three or more of the following questions, consider yourself dependent on alcohol.
- Do you have a strong desire or compulsion to drink despite your knowledge of the dangers of excessive drinking?
- Do you have trouble controlling the amount of alcohol you consume and when you consume it?
- Do you experience withdrawal symptoms when you stop drinking?
- Have you noticed that you need increased amounts of alcohol to achieve the effects you could obtain with lower amounts previously?
- Do you ever drive when you have been drinking?
- Is someone in your family concerned about your drinking?
- Have you ever been absent from work or lost a job because of drinking?
- Have you noticed any evidence of negative impact of alcohol on your physical and psychological health?

Dealing with Alcohol Abuse

For most college students, alcohol use is part of their weekly, if not daily, lifestyle. If you admit that you are experiencing negative consequences from your drinking, such as bad behavior, lowered school performance, or physical symptoms such as blackouts, there are constructive steps that you can take to address the problem. In many cases, chronic alcoholism or alcohol dependence are brought to your attention by friends and family who have concern for your welfare.

Like any form of substance abuse, it is extremely difficult to bring alcohol abuse under control. There are hereditary issues that predispose certain people to excessive drinking and physiological components of addiction. There are also social pressures from friends, not to mention interpersonal conflicts that lead to drowning your troubles. Finally, there are many emotional pressures and lifestyle stressors that make drinking alcohol an attractive coping strategy in the short term. As with marijuana, stimulants, and other recreational drugs, continued use of these substances as a stress coping method creates additional problems such as dependence, addiction, erratic behavior, and myriad health problems.

Although I offer some helpful suggestions for dealing with alcohol abuse, in many cases you may need to seek professional help in the form of substance abuse counseling or a 12-step program such as Alcoholics Anonymous. The track record for ceasing or curtailing addictions to alcohol (or anything else for that matter) on your own is grim. I'm not saying that you can't do it—just that it is very difficult. Here are some helpful suggestions:

1. *Have the courage to acknowledge that you have a problem.* Honesty is the first step towards resolution of the problem.

2. *Make a definite decision to change the way you use alcohol.* Be determined to take responsibility for how much you drink and when you drink in order to cut down the total amount of alcohol you consume.

3. *Record how much you drink and when you start to drink.* Awareness often precedes changes. Knowing your patterns of alcohol usage allows you to avoid certain stimuli that lead to drinking and to be aware of certain emotions you

need to manage. Also, being aware of your patterns of consumption gives you some power to break those patterns. For instance, if you tend to drink while watching a football game, next time, deliberately choose an alternative nonalcoholic beverage.

4. *Take active steps to resolve your mental conflicts or worries.* Alcohol can only help you delay dealing with certain problems. The only solution is to have the courage to face the problems and solve them or forget about them.

5. *Learn to use more healthy relaxation methods for managing stress.* I don't dispute that alcohol is an effective stress manager, because it is—but it also has many undesirable side-effects. Throughout this text you have been exposed to a variety of alternative strategies that will provide the same relief without negative consequences.

6. *Develop a personal strategy to manage alcohol consumption.* No matter how many methods exist to manage alcohol consumption, the best one is the one that works for you. The only way to find out is to learn and practice. If one method doesn't work, don't give up right away. Persist for a while and then try another method until it works for you.

7. *Seek help.* If you think you are dependent on alcohol or abusing alcohol, I recommend that you see a health professional, either your doctor or someone from your campus counseling services. Seeing your doctor will offer two immediate benefits. First, he/she will tell you what help and support are available and how to get them. Second, he/she will help treat certain dangerous withdrawal symptoms if you have been drinking for a long time.

Sleep

You might be surprised to find sleep mentioned as a stress intervention technique, but it is actually the most important thing you can do, along with diet, to keep yourself in balance. Sleep disruption is one of the first and most notable signs that stress levels have become overloaded in your life. It becomes a vicious cycle because chronic sleep problems only make the stress harder to deal with, which creates more stress, and so on.

Recently researchers have identified sleep as an important factor in the stress–health connection. McEwen (2006) has proposed that sleep deprivation can be considered as an additional contributor to allostatic load. For one thing, when you don't get enough sleep, the levels of your glucocorticoids go up (Sapolsky, 2004). As you recall from Chapter 2, glucocorticoids are stress hormones and too much of cortisol can wreak havoc on your health. Benham (2010) recognizes that sleep is not only a factor in psychosocial stress but also an important intervention process. Figure 11.3 shows the stress–health model that indicates a reciprocal relationship between sleep and psychological stress, and the effects of psychological stress and poor sleep on allostatic load.

As our world becomes more connected through technology, a "nonstop global economy where night never falls" has developed and sleep is increasingly seen as an annoyance that gets in the way of "precious time that might better be spent producing, circulating, buying, and selling" (Wylie, 2008, p. 26). This is only going to become more challenging by the time you graduate. Already many people check their messages before they even brush their teeth in the morning and do so as their last act before turning out the lights. Although in college such behavior is primarily related to social interactions which are fun, it sets a precedent you might very well follow into your career to improve so-called productivity while significantly increasing stress and disrupting sleep.

Whereas taking a nap may help you catch up, it can make falling asleep at night more challenging. What is critical is that you get enough sleep in order to function at peak levels during the day. The actual amount of sleep required varies between individuals and also depends on age. Generally, most people need seven to nine hours each night.

FIGURE 11.3
The stress–health model (Benham, 2010).

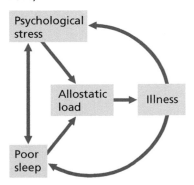

Stress often manifests itself in disrupted sleep patterns—difficulty falling asleep or frequent awakenings. Sleep can also be disrupted by excessive alcohol or caffeine consumption, indigestion, and physical problems, but is most often the result of excessive worry and chronic tension. The estimated three-quarters of adults who are sleep-deprived sacrifice quality for quantity in their work. Getting less than seven to eight hours per night, every night, puts you at risk for impaired concentration, memory, and problem solving, as well as moodiness and stress.

No matter the ideal number of hours that your body and mind require, if you are like most people, you are not getting enough sleep.

A National Sleep Foundation (2005) poll showed that a large majority of individuals (75%) report having had at least one symptom of a sleep problem for a few nights a week within the past year. In addition, sleep problems afflict nearly half of employed adults and two-thirds have trouble getting through the day as a result (Jacobs, 2005). One reason for the widespread sleep problem is that Americans spend more hours working each week than any other industrialized country in the world.

So, what's the big deal if you are not getting enough sleep on a regular basis? As long as you can function reasonably well, doesn't this allow you to get more done? Let's take a look at some basic facts about sleep and then examine the toll sleep deprivation can exact on your health. You probably know that sleep helps our body repair damaged tissues, build bone and muscle, and strengthen the immune system. In particular, sleep helps the brain restore energy. The human brain, although making up only 3% of the body weight, consumes 20%–25% of your body energy. There are different stages of sleep. When you first slide into sleep, you **have slow-wave sleep** followed by a shorter period of **rapid eye movement (REM) sleep**, and then the cycle starts over again. Dreams typically happen during REM sleep when your primary sensory cortex becomes quiet and your secondary sensory cortex becomes active, meaning that your brain is processing the events that occurred during the previous day (Sapolsky, 2004). Sleep is particularly useful to your cognitive functioning because memory consolidation happens during sleep whether it is during slow-wave or REM sleep (Genzel et al., 2014).

In the short run, this might seem like the case but actually inadequate sleep interferes with your ability to concentrate, especially affecting complex tasks such as studying. It weakens your immune system, elevates cortisol levels, accelerates aging, interferes with growth, impairs memory, reduces sex drive, and contributes to a greater susceptibility to diseases such as diabetes and Cushing's syndrome, a hormonal disorder.

If you are not sleeping well on a regular basis, more than a few nights per week over a period of several months, you must consider that stress is taking a toll on your ability to recover and replenish your energy. Over a prolonged period of time, the damage can become irreversible. In addition, sleep deprivation affects the mind's functioning just as much as the body's. In studies done to examine what happens for those who consistently get less than the recommended eight hours per night on average, researchers found that even if people reported feeling okay, their performance in memory, problem-solving, and concentration tasks declined significantly (Song, 2006). It may appear that you can catch up with your work by stealing an extra couple of hours of bedtime, bolstered by caffeine, but the extra time does not produce the kind of mental sharpness that is often needed for quality productivity.

What Helps You to Sleep Better?

There are several things you can do to better regulate your sleep:

- *Identify how much sleep you need in order to function optimally.* It is recommended that you note when you wake up naturally on a weekend day, without using an alarm.

- *Establish a regular sleep schedule.* Whenever possible, go to bed at the same time every night and wake up without using an alarm clock at the same time every morning, including weekends. Establish routines before going to sleep that condition your body to slow down and become drowsy.

- *Create a comfortable environment.* As much as possible, darken your room and keep it cool. Keep the clock turned away from your view. Invest in a pillow, sheets, and coverings that help you feel most comfortable.

- *Control your thoughts.* If you lie awake worrying about what happened during the day, or what you are going to do the next day, get up and write down your thoughts so as to put them out of mind until you can do something constructive about them.

- *Avoid excessive stimulation before bed.* It is generally not a good idea to get yourself worked up by exercising too close to bedtime, watching overstimulating movies, playing video games, checking messages, or surfing the net—all activities that can get you thinking about things just at a time when you should be slowing down the part of your brain involved in such activities.

- *Prepare your body.* Minimize caffeine intake after noon, and alcohol consumption. Include some form of regular exercise (even walking) as part of your daily schedule.

- *Take a warm bath.* Relax in the bathtub or shower. This form of "hydrotherapy" can help soak away stress. Taking hot baths soothe aches and strains, both mental and physical, providing warmth, buoyancy, and a relaxed spirit.

- *Use relaxation exercises.* In earlier chapters you learned methods of deep breathing, meditation, visual imagery, and others that help you to calm yourself.

- *Don't get in bed until you are sleepy.* If after 20 minutes of trying to fall asleep you find yourself tossing and turning, get up and read a little, watch television, or do a little homework. Then try again.

- *If all else fails …* If after trying every strategy you still can't sleep, just relax and enjoy this extra time that you are conscious and alive. After all, when you die you are going to be asleep for a *very* long time.

Managing Your Finances

While eating and sleeping patterns have a definite impact on the way that stress is experienced and managed, another significant lifestyle issue is money. Students often cite financial difficulties as the major stressor while studying in college. Some studies have found that credit card debt actually increases the health risk of college students as they are more prone to engage in risk-taking behavior, follow poor diets, and engage in sedentary behavior (Nelson, Lust, Story, & Ehlinger, 2008).

Almost by definition, a student lives a life of restricted resources. From ancient times students were expected to live in poverty, devoting themselves completely to their studies while eschewing material possessions. Although you may enjoy certain comforts and live well above the poverty line, it is still likely that you are experiencing some financial challenges to maintain a reasonable lifestyle.

Financial management is one of those life skills that most people have to learn through trial and error—mostly the latter. The premise is deceptively simple: spend less money than you earn. Unfortunately, since many people in North America live month to month, use credit cards to defer payments, and borrow as much as they can to upgrade their lifestyles, this does not present the best model for college students who are following in these footsteps. The average American household now has 12 to 13 credit cards in its possession, with an average outstanding balance of over $9,000, paying interest at over 18% (Chatzky, 2005).

FOR REFLECTION 11.5

Track Your Spending Patterns

Directions: For a period of one month, starting today, keep track of all the purchases you make. This includes not only objects you buy—necessities and luxuries—but also splurges for meals and social activities.

After you have accumulated your list, go through the items one at a time and ask yourself in retrospect, with strict objectivity, which of these purchases you wish you could cancel. Which ones represented an impulsive decision? Circle those items on your list.

Add up the cost of all those unnecessary purchases.

Consider what it would feel like to have saved that amount of money this month, which could have been applied to existing debt, or saved for something *really* important.

Examine and write a summary of your purchases. Is what you eat conducive to handling much stress and improving health? Look at the frequency and amount of food you eat.

Apart from the pressure to work harder, and earn more money to pay accumulated bills, financial problems create additional stressors in terms of the toll they take on your psyche. Sleep and appetite loss or increase, addictions, and self-destructive behavior can all be ignited by worrying excessively about money issues. In couple relationships as well (covered in Chapter 12), arguments about money are among the most common ongoing conflicts, along with fights about sex and children.

Like many of the issues covered in this chapter, it would help to take a whole course on managing your finances. However, there is little time for such an "indulgence" with all the other things you are trying to control. I will boil down the essentials to several basic principles to keep in mind. Some of these points may seem rather obvious, but you would be amazed at how few people actually follow this advice.

Spend Less than You Earn and Save the Rest

In our culture of instant gratification, companies market the idea that you can have whatever you most desire, right now, no waiting—on credit. Visa and MasterCard beseech you to order their "passports to freedom," meaning that you can give in to any whim or indulgence and worry about paying for it later. The fact that you are seeking a college education says you understand the importance that investing in your future can have on future earnings and security. So many people feel stuck in dead-end jobs and stressful lifestyles because they feel they don't have the freedom to make different choices. By keeping debt low, and savings high, you will always have the prerogative to make different choices if you should ever feel dissatisfied with what you are doing. This strategy, of living within one's means, is one of the distinguishing factors of those who achieved wealth from humble beginnings (Stanley & Danko, 1996).

Start Investing Early

Whether you decide to put discretionary funds in real estate, the stock market, savings bonds, or graduate education, money invested today can pay huge dividends a decade or two from now. Of course, you can make bad investments as easily as good ones, so get some training or advice from experts who can guide you.

Keep Your Credit Clean

Pay your bills and taxes first. Do everything to build up your credit. When your credit is high, it is easier to get loans from banks and strengthen your financial future. Lapses in paying your bills and missed payments will follow you for the rest of your life on credit reports that seem to have no statute of limitations.

Avoid Credit Card Interest

One reason why credit card companies are so eager to give you their services for minimal fees is that they make their profits, in part, from customers who fail to pay off their balances and are stuck with exorbitant interest, sometimes exceeding 16%. Once you start making partial or even minimal payments on your balance, you are essentially saying by your behavior that you are living beyond your means. As just one example, if the average family has a credit card debt of $7,200 and pays 2% of the balance each month, it would literally take a lifetime to pay it off (52 years actually), ending up with $20,000 in interest. Yet by paying off 2% more each month, the balance would be cleared in 14 years with "only" $4,000 in interest. The moral of the story: If you insist on using a credit card instead of a debit card, pay off the balance each month or you can drown in the interest (Chatzky, 2005).

VOICE OF THE AUTHOR 11.2

I remember buying my first TV in America on a Sears credit card. I was so excited to finally own this device that was so rare back in my country. I was preparing for my wife's arrival from China and I wanted to show her how well I was doing in my adjustment to this lifestyle. Naturally, as a student I didn't have any savings. I was doing everything I could just to earn enough money to feed myself and pay for tuition. Yet I was amazed that I could take home a brand new television just by signing my name on a piece of paper and giving them a $10 down payment. As I walked out of the store proudly carrying the box, I kept looking over my shoulder thinking they would change their minds.

Unfortunately, my excitement did not last very long once the bills started to arrive. It took me over a year to pay off the debt and it still bothers me today that I wasted so much money on interest; if only I could have been patient enough to wait until I saved enough money. But I wanted to impress my wife with how well I was doing. Ever since that time I learned my lesson and make a point to pay off my credit card balance every month.

Buy What You Need Instead of What You Want

I don't dispute the reality that life's enjoyment comes, in part, from indulgences and luxuries. It is so exciting to get a new car, a new outfit, or even a new pair of shoes. What is the use of working hard if you don't have resources to occasionally reward yourself? The operative word in the preceding sentence is "occasionally," meaning that it is important to distinguish between things that you absolutely have to have, versus those that represent a whim that you will later regret.

SUMMARY

Lifestyle issues have a way of being both the cause and the effect of stressors. Any attempt to change one aspect of your behavior influences and is influenced by other things. There is a systemic effect in which stress creates sleep problems, which then impair your ability to concentrate, which leads you to make poor decisions, which you then might attempt to manage through self-medication, which exacerbates stress, and so on.

The example of Monica, a fictitious new acquaintance, represents someone displaying significant lifestyle dysfunction in a number of areas. In fact, she exhibited stress problems in almost every one of the categories covered in this chapter—at work, in her study skills, sleep, eating, drinking, smoking, and finances. Although I examined various stress problems as individual factors, they are actually part of an overall package that constitutes your lifestyle. There is no doubt that you have to juggle a host of challenges on a daily basis, keeping up with responsibilities, being involved in social activities, managing finances, and taking care of yourself as best you can.

Unless you can set limits on the pressures you handle, take care of your body through proper nutrition and sleep, develop effective skills for keeping up with work, incorporate forms of stress relief into your routines, and extricate yourself from unhealthy relationships, any intervention attempts are going to be less successful than you desire. Lifestyle issues reflect your personal values, the choices you make, and the ways that you conduct yourself from day to day.

QUESTIONS FOR REVIEW

1. Identify the components of a healthy lifestyle. Summarize what healthy behavior entails.
2. Describe how the dimensions of lifestyle are related to your stress experience.
3. Identify the major problems with the typical American diet.
4. Discuss how stress influences the way you eat, and what and how you eat influence your stress experience.
5. Discuss the recommendations of MyPlate and how you plan to change your diet based on these suggestions.
6. What are the best nutrients and foods that can be used in the battle against stress?
7. Summarize the reasons why people smoke. Explore the connection between stress coping and smoking.
8. What are the most effective strategies for stopping excessive drinking and smoking?
9. What are some strategies for coping with alcohol abuse?
10. How is stress affected by the quality and quantity of sleep?
11. Describe why financial management is essential to living a low-stress life.

SELECTED ANSWERS

Answers to FOR REFLECTION 11.3
H for high glycemic and L for low glycemic foods.

H: Watermelon	H: Gatorade	L: Soybeans	H: Cheerios cereal
L: Lentils	L: Skim milk	H: White bread	H: Plain bagel
H: Ice cream	H: French fries	L: Pumpernickel bread	L: Orange
H: Corn flakes	H: Baked potato	L: Chickpeas	L: Apple
L: All-bran cereal	L: Yogurt		

REVIEW ACTIVITIES

Review Activity 11.1: Making Lifestyle Changes
Among all the subjects covered in the chapter related to diet, alcohol and drug use, sleeping habits, finances, and other lifestyle issues, what are some specific areas that contribute most to your stress levels?

Review Activity 11.2: Watch Your Dietary Patterns
Directions: Analyze your dietary pattern for a week by using the following table. Examine it and write a summary of it. Is what you eat conducive to handling much stress and improving health? Look at the frequency and amount of food you eat.

	Breakfast	Midmorning snack	Lunch	Mid-afternoon snack	Dinner	Late-night snack
Day 1						
Day 2						
Day 3						
Day 4						
Day 5						
Day 6						
Day 7						

REFERENCES AND RESOURCES

Benham, G. (2010). Sleep: An important factor in stress health models. *Stress and Health, 26,* 204–214.
Blaylock, R. (1997). *Excitotoxins: The taste that kills.* Santa Fe, NM: Health Press.

Boyce, J. A. (2008). Eicosanoids in asthma, allergic inflammation, and host defense. *Current Molecular Medicine, 8*, 335–349.

Campbell, A. (2006, June). The comfort-food zone. *Men's Health*, p. 56.

Centers for Disease Control and Prevention (2009). State-specific secondhand smoke exposure and current cigarette smoking among adults—United States, 2008, *MMWR, 58*(44), 1,232–1,235.

Chatzky, J. (2005, December 16). Trimming your debt. *Time*.

Childre, D., & Rozman, D. (2005). *Transforming stress*. Oakland, CA: New Harbinger.

CNN (2010). *Texting during sex? Some say it's OK*. Retrieved on August 15, 2010 from http://scitech.blogs.cnn.com.

Colbert, D. (2005). *Stress less*. Lake Mary, FL: Siloam.

Dallman, M. F., Pecoraro, N. C., & La Fleur, S. E. (2005). Chronic stress and comfort foods: Self-medication and abdominal obesity. *Brain, Behavior, and Immunity, 19*(4), 275–280.

Flegal, K. M., Carroll, M. D., Ogden, C. L., & Johnson, C. L. (2002). Prevalence and trends in obesity among U.S. adults. *Journal of the American Medical Association, 288*(14), 1,723–1,727.

Genzel, L., Kroes, M. C. W., Dresler, M., & Battaglia, F. P. (2014). Light sleep versus slow wave sleep in memory consolidation: A question of global versus local processes? *Trends in Neurosciences, 37*, 10–19.

Gilbert, D. G., & McClernon, F. J. (2000). Smoking and stress. In G. F. Fink (Ed.), *Encyclopedia of stress* (Vol. 3, pp. 458–466). San Diego, CA: Academic Press.

Greeno, C. G., & Wing, R. R. (1994). Stress-induced eating. *Psychological Bulletin, 115*, 444–464.

Hagan, M. M., Chandler, P. C., Wauford, P. K., Rybak, R. J., & Oswald, K. D. (2003). The role of palatable food and hunger as trigger factors in an animal model of stress induced binge eating. *International Journal of Eating Disorders, 34*, 183–197.

Hales, D. (2002). *An invitation to health* (brief 2nd ed.). Belmont, CA: Wadsworth.

Harris Interactive (2002). *Tension tracker 2002: Report of findings*. Fort Washington, PA: McNeil Consumer.

Healthy eating plate dishes out sound diet advice: More specific than MyPlate, it pinpoints the healthiest food choices. (2011). Healthy eating plate dishes out sound diet advice: More specific than MyPlate, it pinpoints the healthiest food choices. (2011). *Harvard Heart Letter: From Harvard Medical School, 22*(4), 6.

Heatherton, T. F., & Baumeister, R. F. (1991). Binge-eating as escape from self-awareness. *Psychological Bulletin, 110*, 86–108.

Helmering, D. W., & Hales, D. (2005). *Think thin, be thin: 101 psychological ways to lose weight*. New York, NY: Broadway Books.

Hobson, K. (2005, December 27). Quit smoking. *U.S. News and World Report*, p. 74.

Hyman, M. (2009). *The UltraMind solution: The simple way to defeat depression, overcome anxiety, and sharpen your mind*. New York, NY: Scribner.

Jacobs, G. D. (2005). The National Sleep Foundation's 2005 Poll. Available at http://www.talkaboutsleep.com/sleep-disorders/2005/04/insomnia-nsf-poll.htm.

James, L., & Nahl, D. (2000). *Road rage and aggressive driving: Steering clear of highway warfare*. Amherst, NY: Prometheus Books.

James, L., & Nahl, D. (2002). Dealing with stress and pressure in the vehicle taxonomy of driving behavior: Affective, cognitive, sensorimotor. In J. P. Rothe (Ed.), *Driving lessons—Exploring systems that make traffic safer*. Edmonton, Canada: University of Alberta Press.

Karren, K. J., Hafen, B. Q., Smith, N. L., & Frandsen, K. J. (2006). *Mind body health: The effects of attitudes, emotions, and relationships*. San Francisco, CA: Benjamin-Cummings.

Kassel, J. D., Stroud, L. R., & Paronis, C. A. (2003) Smoking, stress, and negative affect: Correlation, causation, and context across stages of smoking. *Psychological Bulletin, 129*, 270–304.

Larson, J., & Rodriguez, C. (1999). *Road rage to road-wise: A simple step-by-step program to help you understand and curb road rage in yourself and others*. New York, NY: Forge.

Ludwig, D. S. (2002). The glycemic index: Physiological mechanisms relating to obesity, diabetes, and cardiovascular disease. *Journal of the American Medical Association, 287*, 2,414–2,423.

McEwen, B. S. (2006). Sleep deprivation as a neurobiologic and physiologic stressor: Allostasis and allostatic load. *Metabolism: Clinical and Experimental, 55*(10), S20–S23.

National Sleep Foundation (2005). *2005 Sleep in America Poll summary findings*. Retrieved on December 25, 2005 from www.sleepfoundation.org.

Nelson, M. C., Lust, K., Story, M., & Ehlinger, E. (2008). Credit card debt, stress, and key health risk behaviors among college students. *American Journal of Health Promotion, 22*(6), 400–407.

Ogden, C. L., Carroll, M. D., Kit, B. K., et al. (2014). Prevalence of childhood and adult obesity in the United States, 2011–2014. *Journal of the American Medical Association, 311*(8), 806–814.

Okuyama, H., Ichikawa, Y., Sun, Y., Hamazaki, T., & Lands, W. E. M. (2007). ω3 fatty acids effectively prevent coronary heart disease and other late-onset diseases: The excessive linoleic acid syndrome. *World Review of Nutritional Dietetics*, *96*, 83–103.

Pruitt, B. E., & Stein, J. J. (2004). *Decisions for healthy living*. San Francisco, CA: Pearson/Benjamin Cummings.

Roizen, M. F., & Oz, M. C. (2005). *You: The owner's manual: An insider's guide to the body that will make you healthier and younger*. New York, NY: HarperCollins.

Rosch, P., & Clark, C. (2001). *De-stress, weigh less*. New York, NY: St Martin's Press.

Sapolsky, R. M. (2004). *Why zebras don't get ulcers* (3rd ed.). New York, NY: Henry Holt.

Schuckit, M. A. (1998). Biological, psychological and environmental predictors of the alcoholism risk: A longitudinal study. *Journal of Studies on Alcohol*, *59*, 485–494.

Schwartz, G. R. (1988). *In bad taste: The MSG syndrome*. Santa Fe, NM: Health Press.

Seaman, B. (2005). *Binge: Campus life in an age of disconnection and excess*. New York, NY: Wiley.

Song, S. (2006, January 16). Sleeping your way to the top. *Time*.

Stanley, T. J., & Danko, W. D. (1996). *The millionaire next door: The surprising secrets of America's wealthy*. Marietta, GA: Longstreet Press.

Szuba, M. P., Kloss, J. D., & Dinges, D. F. (2003). *Insomnia: Principles and management*. New York, NY: Cambridge University Press.

Taylor, A. N., & Pilati, M. L. (2000). Alcohol, alcoholism and stress: A psychobiological perspective. In G. Fink (Ed.), *Encyclopedia of stress* (Vol. 1, pp. 131–136). San Diego, CA: Academic.

USDA Health and Human Services (2010). Dietary Guidelines for Americans, 2010 (7th Ed.). Washington, DC: US Government Printing Office, US Department of Health and Human Services (2014). The health consequences of smoking –50 years of progress: A report of the Surgeon General. Retrieved on November 1, 2015 from http://www.surgeongeneral.gov/library/reports/50-years-of-progress/exec-summary.pdf.

USDA Health and Human Services (2015). *ChooseMyPlate.gov. Let's eat for the health of it*. Retrieved on October 23 2015 from http://www.choosemyplate.gov/food-groups/downloads/MyPlate/DG2010Brochure.pdf.

Valencia, M. E., Weil, E. J., Nelson, R. G., Esparza, J., Schulz, L. O., Ravussin, E., et al. (2005). Impact of lifestyle on prevalence of kidney disease in Pima Indians in Mexico and the United States. *Kidney International*, *68*, S141.

Wardle, J. (2000). Diet and stress, non-psychiatric. In G. Fink (Ed.), *Encyclopedia of stress* (Vol. 1, pp. 694–699). San Diego, CA: Academic.

Willet, W. (2001). *Eat, drink, and be healthy: The Harvard Medical School guide to healthy eating*. New York, NY: Free Press.

Williams, A. N., & Woessner, K. M. (2009). Monosodium glutamate "allergy": Menace or myth? *Clinical & Experimental Allergy*, *39*, 640–646.

Wylie, M. S. (2008). Sleepless in America. *Psychotherapy Networker*, March/April, 24–31.

12

Stress and Conflict in Relationships

You live in a world of relationships. At work, at home, at school, in social and civic gatherings, even during the course of daily business, you deal with people all day long. Such relationships are the source of much satisfaction—they provide love, intimacy, support, stimulation, and the feeling of being part of a "tribe." Yet relationships can also be the scourge of your life and one of the biggest sources of stress.

KEY QUESTIONS IN THE CHAPTER

- How are stress and relationship problems related to one another?
- What are some barriers to effective interpersonal communication and resolving personal conflicts?
- What does it mean to say that all conflicts involve interactive processes?
- Is it important to assign blame and responsibility for a relationship conflict before a solution can be found?
- What are the effects of abuse and sexual harassment on victims and bystanders?
- What steps can you take to prevent being a victim of violence?
- What are the key functions of conflict in terms of the benefits they might provide?
- What are some ways to resolve interpersonal stress in your life?
- What are some of the key principles in dealing with people who appear difficult?
- What are the best predictors for divorce?
- What are some of the most useful communication skills for improving relationships?
- How is mindfulness related to effective interpersonal communication?
- What are the four mindfulness communication skills?

When you can't sleep at night, tossing and turning with worry, anger, or resentment, what are you most often thinking about? It often has something to do with a relationship that has gone wrong. When you are depressed or anxious, when you feel misunderstood or neglected, the stress most often emanates from relationship conflicts. In one study of stress hormone levels among newlyweds it was found that those who were experiencing conflict had elevated norepinephrine and epinephrine as a result of the interpersonal stress (Kiecolt-Glaser, Bane, Glaser, & Malarkey, 2003). Another study investigated the stress levels of college students and found that the quality of relationships with friends, family members, parents, and romantic partners was a significant factor (Darling, McWey, Howard, & Olmstead, 2007).

Whatever conflicts you may be currently experiencing represent not just a single disagreement but part of an ongoing pattern of relationship difficulties that you have experienced throughout your life. It is highly likely that whatever you are struggling with now is familiar to you from previous interpersonal difficulties.

This chapter introduces you to the background and skills needed to make sense of the relationship problems that you encounter, especially those that create unwanted stress in your life. You will find out how to develop new ways of relating to others, new methods for dealing with people you perceive as difficult, and innovative strategies for diffusing conflicts that plague you.

Effects of Conflict on Your Body and Mind

You learned earlier (in Chapter 10) that stress in the workplace and school can literally make you sick. Such pressures result not only from trying to meet deadlines, manage overburdened workloads, and perform under adverse circumstances, but also from the strains of relationship problems.

It will probably not surprise you to learn that conflicts at home also have a significant impact on stress, increasing blood pressure and cortisol levels. In studies of couples, for instance, it was found that mutually supportive relationships could actually moderate the negative effects of hurtful relationships at work and elsewhere; likewise, conflicted relationships at home increase blood pressure, cortisol levels, and overactivate the endocrine system (Kiecolt-Glaser et al., 2003). This is even more the case with women, who tend to be more emotionally aroused and responsive than men. Women are the ones who most often manifest the overt symptoms of stress in a relationship and they are far more likely to be the ones who reach out for help.

VOICE OF STRESS MANAGEMENT 12.1

Nineteen-Year-Old Female Sophomore

I had a hard time adjusting from high school to college. The work was much harder than I was used to. I had a boyfriend for the first time. That was nice but it meant that now I was dividing my time between classes, studying, working out, and spending time with my boyfriend.

It wasn't any one thing but more a combination of everything piled up. Then things started to get more intense with my boyfriend and that affected my school work. I hadn't realized how stressed I really was until I noticed that I was losing my hair. I got so worried that I went to see a doctor. She reassured me that it wasn't anything physical, but I needed to reduce the pressure I was under.

I had to make some decisions about priorities because I was just trying to do too much and I couldn't deal with the strain. I figured that the main problem was the stuff with my boyfriend, the separations we had, the difficulties communicating. Once we both made a commitment to work on things together and talk more regularly it was like all the pressure was gone. Now I have a full head of hair!

Problem relationships have negative impacts on the body and mind. During those times when you are actively engaged in arguments, or reliving conflicts and grudges, stress disrupts not only your peace of mind but also your sleep. Whereas that may not be particularly surprising to you, consider that relationship conflicts get passed on from one generation to the next—issues and struggles that your parents and grandparents faced can easily become entrenched in your own interactional patterns, all without your awareness (Bowen, 1985; Klever, 2005).

Functions of Conflict

It may not have occurred to you to think about conflict in this way, but like almost everything else in life, behaviors tend to persist when they serve some useful function. With respect to ongoing relationship problems, one question to consider is what useful purpose might the conflict be serving? In other words, what are the *constructive* functions of conflict? In spite of the accompanying misery associated with arguments and overt hostility, what good might it be doing for you?

Getting Your Attention

One way to look at relationship conflicts, and why they persist even after your best efforts to address them, is that they are trying to get your attention to look at some underlying issues that you may have been ignoring. Drew and Dom had been involved in an ongoing dispute for months. They were both on the soccer team, both valuable members of a successful season, yet at each other's throats. This not only was a problem for the two of them, but created tension for everyone else, most of all the coach. Every attempt at mediation seemed doomed to fail.

Drew and Dom were both negatively impacted as a result of their fighting. Not only did their performance on the field suffer, but they each lost sleep, spent time ruminating over perceived slights, and avoided one another whenever possible. The conflict was clearly disruptive to their lives and spoiled what would have otherwise been an enjoyable season.

A sports team, like any other human system, is composed of complex dynamics and processes, some of which operate beneath the surface. While at first glance it might appear as if Drew and Dom "owned" this problem, in reality they were only one facet of a larger issue that affected not only the behavior of the soccer team but also the larger university community.

Drew was originally from Bosnia, as were several other members of the team who came over during the same immigration wave. Dom was Latino, another large constituency within the campus community. Lately there had been tensions between the two groups, not just on the soccer team but elsewhere in student government, editorials in the student newspaper, and in the residence halls.

In their own way, Dom and Drew were designated combatants who were part of a larger battle. They might have imagined that their dispute was some personality problem between them, but it was actually part of something much larger than both of them. As long as the two of them remained in conflict, however painful it might be for

Poor health and mortality are caused not only by physical factors such as smoking, cholesterol, obesity, and inactivity, but also by interpersonal conflicts with friends, family, or coworkers.

them, it was bringing attention to an important issue of cultural strife that needed to be addressed.

When you are similarly involved in a conflict that is a source of tremendous stress in your life, and the impasse seems difficult to work through, ask yourself what underlying issue this might be bringing to your attention. People may seem to fight over rather inane, inconsequential things, but they are really in dispute about important issues that remain hidden. The challenging—and critical—task is to figure out what those might be.

Power and Control

More often than not, interpersonal conflicts revolve around power and control. Someone wants to control you in a way that you resent, or another person feels that you are trying to over-control him. Such disagreements may arise in the first place to bring your attention to some negotiation that needs to take place around how power can be distributed more equitably.

Zach and Lisa had been together for over three years when they decided to split up. Although Lisa was the one to initiate the ending of their relationship, Zach was just as relieved to move on. Although they had loved one another, and enjoyed many good times—even anticipating marriage someday—the relationship had turned sour to the point that they were now actively hostile toward one another.

You might ask yourself why so many divorces and separations end up in such vicious disputes in which the previous partners end up hating one another so much. It does help people to resolve their ambivalence, as well as to create distance during a difficult time of transition. It is also a kind of leveling and renegotiation of control and power issues.

FOR REFLECTION 12.1

The idea that conflict can have positive functions is often a useful one because it helps you to sort out that even with the stressful side-effects it is helping you to look at issues that you might otherwise ignore. When you think about some disagreement that is going on in your life right now, consider what this dispute might actually be doing that could ultimately be helpful to you.

Throughout their relationship, Lisa had continuously deferred to Zach with regard to most decisions in their daily life. He was happy to take charge, felt that he was competent to do so, and so they settled into a pattern in which he exhibited more power and control. Although Lisa acted as if she was content with this, in truth she felt marginalized, disrespected, and sometimes ignored. Her resentment festered to the point that finally she just announced one day that she wanted out of the relationship. They had been arguing for many months prior to this final split.

If Zach and Lisa had paid attention to the underlying meaning of their escalating arguments they might have resolved their conflict and renegotiated a new kind of relationship in which power and decision making were shared more equally. Unfortunately, chronic neglect and building resentments led them to a point of no return.

When embroiled in a dispute with someone over time, ask yourself whether whatever you are fighting about is really about issues of power and control. Knowing this doesn't necessarily lead to a solution to the problem, but it is a good starting point for you to address what is really going on rather than the surface issues.

Conflict Regulates Distance

In spite of what people may say to the contrary, intimacy is often a frightening prospect. This was certainly the case between Bradley and his father Nicholas, who had been fighting for years. They could barely be civil together, either in person or on the phone, which made family gatherings tense for everyone present.

During the early years of their relationship, up until the time Bradley entered high school, they enjoyed a close father–son relationship that revolved around sports. Yet once Bradley yearned to know his father better, to talk about more personal matters, Nicholas would either withdraw or scold the young man to mind his own business. A few years later, when Nicholas tried to bridge the gap between them by inviting Bradley to share more about his life, it was the son's turn to start a fight between them. In subsequent years, it became almost a dance between them in which each took turns starting a fight as a means to push the other way. They were so afraid of being close to each other that this was how they learned to relate to each other.

Whether between father and son, siblings, or lovers, conflict can become a way that people push each other away to a perceived safe distance. It can serve a highly self-protective function that helps some people to maintain a sense of control when they feel vulnerable.

Conflict Promotes Reflection and Growth

Whether you like it or not, conflicts force you to take time out and think about matters in your life, some of which you might prefer to avoid. Conflict is a time of reassessment. It is a period when you ask yourself what went wrong, what you did, or what could you have done differently.

VOICE OF STRESS MANAGEMENT 12.2

Twenty-Six-Year-Old Female Graduate Student

I was involved in this small seminar class in which we were expected to share personal things about our lives. It seemed like people were mostly beating around the bush, not being really honest about stuff, you know, talking about safe things. I was feeling impatient and, yes, frustrated. Maybe even bored. So I said to the other students—most of whom I didn't know that well anyway—that nobody was really being honest with one another. Maybe I came on a little strong. I don't know.

First one person said to me that she thought I was aloof, that I was the one who was hiding and not being honest. I really took offense by that but tried not to show it. When another person said basically the same thing, and then another, and another, I really felt ganged up on. After all, they were judging me and criticizing me.

When I left that class I didn't want to come back again. I didn't feel safe. But it was too late to drop the class so I didn't have a choice. I was determined, though, that I wasn't going to say anything anymore. And it really started to bother me.

Eventually I realized that what was going on in that class was familiar in some ways. I had sort of set the whole thing up. First I challenged everybody to be more honest. Essentially I told them that they were being shallow and superficial. Then when they tried to be more honest—with me—I felt attacked. I gotta tell you, this really hurt me a lot. I stewed about it for a long time. But then I realized some things about myself that were pretty tough.

Naturally, you will try to assign blame. It is almost always someone else's fault. But eventually, even when in the throes of denial, you will have to admit that you share some culpability for whatever happened. In fact, it is a virtual certainty that any conflict is always a shared responsibility. No matter how it may seem to you, no matter how much temptation you might feel to blame others or external circumstances, you also played a role in the deteriorating situation. Furthermore, this isn't the first time something like this has happened. This is part of an ongoing pattern in your life.

Unless you are prepared to examine your role in the conflict, and your contributions to starting or maintaining the disagreement, there is virtually no opportunity to prevent similar situations in the future. Since you can rarely do anything to change anyone else's behavior—this is hardly within your power—often the first place to try to reduce stress is by looking inward rather than outward. Instead of complaining about what the other person is doing to you, or focusing on how you feel like a victim of maltreatment and injustice, it is often preferable and empowering to think about your own behavior in the situation.

FOR REFLECTION 12.2

Looking Inward rather than Outward

Think about an argument, fight, or conflict you are involved in with someone else in your life. This could be one you identified earlier, or one that comes to mind in which you are especially aware that you have been feeling victimized and have been blaming the other person for almost all the trouble.

Now, this may be difficult, but temporarily put aside your tendency to focus on what the other person is doing, or not doing, and instead focus on yourself.

What was *your* role in initiating or maintaining this conflict?

What are you doing, or failing to do, that is making this conflict worse than it needs to be?

What could you do differently in the future to avoid getting involved in similar struggles?

Barriers to Resolving Relationship Conflicts

Before you can hope to work through stressful relationships, you will need to understand what is getting in the way for you: 1) that you may have unrealistic expectations for others, 2) that you might be over-personalizing what is going on, 3) that you, and the other person, might be deriving benefits from the struggle (power, distraction, stimulation), 4) that the current conflict is a reenactment of previous ones, 5) that certain people get to you again and again because of vulnerable issues that have never been resolved. There are other reasons as well, notably that you may lack skills for mediating conflicts (what this chapter is for) or that you have certain misunderstandings and beliefs that may be getting in your way.

Before we get into the skills that will prove helpful to you, let's first clear up some of the myths and misunderstandings about conflict:

- Conflicts are not always what they seem. Look beneath the surface during an ongoing argument and ask yourself what is really happening? What are you really fighting about?

- *Conflicts are about the past as well as the present.* Resentments build over time so that by the time a flare-up occurs there is a long history of stored-up hurts.

- *Conflicts are about the past as well as the present.* Resentments build over time so that by the time a flare-up occurs there is a long history of stored-up hurts.

- *Conflicts involve "invisible" participants.* Often fights involve other persons who are not present but continue to haunt the interactions. Some of these people are from your past, some are lurking elsewhere.

- *Most problems can't be resolved.* It is a myth that every problem has a simple, single solution. Conflicts also revolve around complex issues in which a complete resolution is highly unlikely.

- *There are distinct benefits to being in conflict.* These are the benefits I discussed earlier—the sense of power that someone feels, or the distraction that conflict plays, or its entertainment value.

- *People often want to be heard, not fixed.* It is often more important to let a person know that you hear him or her, and understand what is being conveyed, rather than necessarily fixing things.

- *Techniques are less important than relationships.* You may be hungry for simple strategies that will make everything better but the best approach is one that builds trust in the relationship.

One significant barrier to resolving relationship difficulties occurs when you keep trying to defend yourself, to assign blame, and to fix fault by determining who is most responsible for the problem. First of all, it is virtually impossible to definitively figure out who is at fault. Secondly, even if you could, what good does that do in terms of making things better?

It is often helpful to learn from mistakes and failures, to receive feedback on the impact of behaviors, and to make corrections based on negative outcomes. However, here I am speaking about the fixation that many people have to blame others, or circumstances, for what went wrong. Not only does this not make the situation any better, but even if you are successful in getting the other person, or yourself, to admit that you were mainly at fault, what good does *that* do?

Notice how often that you, and others, attempt to make excuses for what goes wrong (see the "List of Excuses"). In order to resolve the relationship problems you have, you're first going to have to move beyond placing blame. If it is your fault, then you are only going to feel guilty and ashamed. If you are successful in convincing the other person that he or she is at fault, then you do so at the risk of increasing the resentment. It is far more helpful to assume in almost every situation that: 1) *everyone is to blame*, meaning there is shared responsibility for any interpersonal conflict, and 2) *nobody is to blame*, meaning that, ultimately, fault-finding is not useful.

A list of common excuses includes:

I didn't do it.	I couldn't help it.
It was just dumb luck.	I didn't mean it.
I wasn't even there.	Don't look at me-- she did it.
She asked for it.	Yes, but …
I didn't mean to do it.	Anyone would have done it.
It wasn't my fault.	He was asking for it.
I was just kidding.	I wasn't really trying.
It was meant to be that way.	I didn't know the rules.
It wasn't a big deal.	Nobody told me.
I had no choice.	It runs in my family

Working through Relationship Conflicts

Interpersonal conflicts, with their accompanying stress, are the result not of situations you find yourself in but rather the way you handle them. Your particular conflict management style is what determines the outcome, in terms of both a resolution and the feelings that go with it. Among college students, a negative attitude has been found most often to create problems and create stress. This behavior is characterized by a condescending attitude, blaming others for what is wrong, avoiding eye contact, and appearing annoyed (Furr & Funder, 1998). In other words, it is your own disposition and attitude toward conflict that determines how well you deal with it.

As has been suggested in the previous discussion, in order to reduce the stress in your life that results from conflicted relationships, you are going to have to focus on your behavior far more than that of others. As much as you would love to refashion others according to your mold, it is not within your power to do so. The good news, however, is that you can make major changes in the ways you respond to conflict to reduce significantly the emotional distress. Even if you can't get others to change the ways they behave, you can minimize the effects you experience. This is especially important with extreme cases of abuse.

Dealing with Emotional or Interpersonal Abuse

Once conflicts escalate out of control, or include someone who is disrespectful of others' rights, abuse can result. Sexual harassment, in particular, has become increasingly common on college campuses, involving an unfair use of influence, power, or authority by one person over another. It also shows a lack of respect in which someone is treated as an object rather than as a person.

Sexual harassment on the college campus includes offers of good grades, extra help and attention, or the promise of employment in exchange for sexual favors. It can also involve making sexually suggestive remarks and using inappropriate language in a class, as well as repeated suggestive looks. Even in subtle forms, sexual harassment creates confusion because the normal boundary between professional or social roles and personal relationships becomes blurred.

Examples of sexual harassment can include the following:

- A fellow student, instructor, supervisor, or coworker hugs or otherwise touches you in an inappropriate way.

- Your supervisor or instructor offers you some privilege or favor in return for your sexual attention, perhaps threatening reprisal if you refuse.

- An instructor, or someone else in a position of power, makes repeated sexual comments, or asks you questions of a sexual nature that make you feel uncomfortable.

- Another student or staff member persistently asks you out despite your answer of "no," follows you, corners you in a classroom or in an office, and will not leave you alone.

- Your supervisor or instructor persistently uses crude, sexually oriented language that you find offensive, demeaning, and inappropriate in a job-related context.

Whether on the college campus, in the workplace, or in any other environment, sexual harassment affects victims in many ways, often creating stress that may not be noticeable to others. Victims may feel powerless to stop the situation. They often fear retaliation, for example, with grades or recommendations. They fear that their complaints will not be taken seriously, or that they will be perceived as causing trouble. In some cases, they may blame themselves for bringing the situation on themselves. There are

VOICE OF STRESS MANAGEMENT 12.3

Twenty-Three-Year-Old Female College Student

The teacher, I'll call him Mr. X, was well liked and even revered by some of the high school "nerds." I didn't really belong in the class; I was more of a hippie who happened to excel academically. I was from a poor part of town but I was still a straight A student. I thought taking advanced placement classes would really give me an edge in college, and the honors classes had been a bore. Mr. X took an immediate interest in me. The first day he asked to see me after school. He made it clear, while putting his hand on my knee, that it would be very difficult to do well in his class without his personal tutelage. I thought he was joking at first but he made it clear that he was not. This scared the crap out of me.

After some thought I went to talk with my guidance counselor who informed me that my allegations were most likely off base and that if I knew what was good for me I would take advantage of Mr. X's knowledge. I began to think that maybe I was crazy. After giving me a D on a paper, which I knew was an A paper, Mr. X requested my coming to see him after class again. He stated that he had heard about my speaking with my guidance counselor and that there might have been a misunderstanding. He shut the door to the classroom and approached me, putting both of his hands on my shoulders, and preceded to massage me while he explained to me that he could do a lot for my future. He leaned over and began whispering in my ear, so I jumped up and said that I had a ride waiting for me. I didn't know what to do! I was terrified.

I tried to mention the incident to my dad, with whom I lived, but he told me that I was just making it up to get out of working. I felt so helpless and numb. I think that put me over the edge. In fact, I dropped out of my AP history class too. It was like I just didn't have it in me anymore. It took me a while to "wake up" out of my daze and eventually I graduated and went on to the university. I still get anxious when any male professor asks to see me after class, or with whom I have to meet alone. I guess that is something I'll get over in time but sometimes I wonder.

tremendous feelings of shame and humiliation that lead to fears that they will be accused of responsibility for the problem.

- Victims often blame themselves, and fear that others will also blame them, even though it is the harassing person's authority or influence that has been misused.

- Victims often change academic plans. They drop courses, change majors, drop out of school, change residence, avoid advisors, or neglect academic commitments or responsibilities in order to avoid an offending person.

- Victims often have physical symptoms of stress, such as stomach problems or headaches. They can also become depressed, moody, or irritable without knowing why.

- Victims often suffer lower self-esteem, self-respect, and self-confidence.

- Victims are often confused about what is happening or what could be done about it.

The trauma from being bullied, sexually harassed, or physically or psychologically abused can last a lifetime. Such abusive behavior often persists because bystanders refuse to intervene or get involved. We all have a moral responsibility to protect the rights of others when it is within our power to do so.

Dealing with Sexual Harassment

In many cases, the people who are engaging in sexual harassment do not realize what they are doing. Such individuals use denial or excuses to justify behavior that may be offensive or hurtful to others, then write it off as others being too sensitive.

Ignoring harassment or abuse, either as a victim or bystander, is most likely *not* going to make it stop; in some cases, the offender may take this as an invitation to continue the behavior. Instead, there are several things that you can do:

- *Tell someone.* Discuss the behavior with a friend, professor, classmate, counselor, or appropriate university personnel. You may find that you are not alone in your experience, and you can get help in planning an appropriate way to deal with it.

- *Keep a record.* Make notes of specific behaviors and comments, times and dates, your responses, and any witnesses.

- *Seek advice and support to resolve the issue.* If direct assertion does not stop the behavior, initiate formal proceedings of censure.

- *Allow yourself to get angry.* Use the energy of your anger to help you focus and take action.

- *Take action.* Confront the person. Let the harasser know that you will not tolerate this behavior, that a line has been crossed.

FOR REFLECTION 12.3

Fighting against Abuse

There is almost always a witness to harassment and abuse. If you are honest with yourself, you would admit to having observed, sometime in the past, someone treated with disrespect—whether this involves sexual harassment, physical intimidation, or psychological abuse. Such behavior continues because it is not challenged. Yet you may often fear for your own psychological or physical safety and so tell yourself it is best to ignore it.

Make a commitment to standing up against all forms of human disrespect by taking action instead of being a passive bystander. In a classic case that occurred a few decades ago, Kitty Genovese was stabbed to death in front of 38 witnesses who watched from their windows. They heard her screaming, "I'm dying," over and over again as she slowly bled to death over the course of a half hour. When the bystanders were interviewed afterwards, their excuse for not intervening was, "It's none of my business."

When someone is being treated disrespectfully, is harassed, abused, or assaulted, it is *everyone's* business.

Date Rape

According to the US Department of Justice, a woman is sexually assaulted in the United States every two minutes. One in four women are raped in their lifetime but less than 10% ever report the assaults because of shame and fear of reprisal (Seaman, 2005). Although it is rarely reported, it should be mentioned that men are victims of rape as well. Half of all sexual assaults are committed by men who have been drinking. A total of 72% of college women who were raped were intoxicated at the time of the attack. Over 97,000 students between ages 18–24 suffer alcohol-related sexual assault or acquaintance rape each year (Mohler-Kuo et al., 2004).

Most women are more in danger of being raped by a man they know or date than by a stranger. These people may be friends, acquaintances, someone on a date, or even within an existing romantic relationship. Date or acquaintance rape means being forced or pressured into having sex by someone you know—against your will, without your consent. Few people believe that it could happen to them, but studies at colleges indicate that between 10% to 25% of women report they were raped by men they knew.

Date rape can occur for several reasons, as follows:

- *Miscommunication.* Miscommunication is related to the double standard about appropriate sexual behavior for men and women. For instance, it is culturally accepted that "nice women" are expected to say "no" to sex and that "real men" don't take no for an answer. This double standard, mixed with differences in gender roles, can make it challenging to communicate clearly.

- *Drug or alcohol abuse.* In college, date rape is most common at parties or in situations where one or both people involved were drinking. After a few too many drinks, it can sometimes be difficult to distinguish between what you should be doing versus what you are doing. In addition, an increase in the use of drugs such as Rohypnol ("roofies") has been correlated to the increase of date rapes. These drugs lead to sedation, blackouts, and memory loss.

- *Rape myths and attitudes.* Some attitudes and beliefs contribute to a culture that tolerates sexual violence. For example, certain men carry a stereotype of women as being weak or incapable of speaking for themselves. This can lead to a lack of respect for a woman's wishes with regard to sex. Victim-blaming places some or all of the responsibility for sexual violence on the victim, rather than the perpetrator. The victim's actions may have been unwise, but they do not excuse or justify sexual violence.

Sexual assault such as date or acquaintance rape can result in severe emotional reactions. The first reaction is confusion about what has happened and what to do next, since date rape is often believed to be in a gray area. Victims also feel degraded and sometimes blame themselves for what has happened. Furthermore, the victim may fear that the offender will return, and thus become frightened of all members of the offender's sex.

After the initial shock has worn off, people may experience a variety of other emotions from anger over what has occurred to depression, feelings of helplessness, guilt, and self-reproach about incidents that led to the assault. In other cases, the person may feel dirty or damaged, numb, or fearful. Such trauma can lead a person to feel like everything has changed, interfering with school work and all other relationships. Needless to say, trust issues in future relationships can become compromised.

Preventing Assaults

Verbal, physical, and sexual abuse are hardly limited to college campuses. In the workplace as well, covered in the following sections, both men and women will be confronted with situations in which it is necessary to stand up for themselves. With respect to sexual assaults, the subject of our preceding discussion, there are several steps you can take to keep yourself out of threatening situations, most of which involve common sense. Although applied here to sexual threats, many of the principles can be applied to other situations.

- *Find out more about your date before you go out.* If you don't know someone well, meet in a public place. Don't go to the person's house or go back to yours. Consider going out with a group of couples. Don't go anywhere you can be vulnerable.

- *Be assertive in setting limits for relationships.* Be clear and consistent in these communications, avoiding double messages. Engage in open discussions about these limits and eliminate any chance for misinterpretation.

- *Defend your limits.* Once the limits are set, you need to enforce them without equivocation. This is sometimes difficult because you may, in fact, feel ambivalent about wanting a physical relationship but having doubts about these desires. You are entitled to feel this way and also entitled to change your mind once you reach a point where you no longer feel comfortable.

- *Be prepared for a strong reaction to your limit setting.* Most date rapes involve men and women who conform to traditional, rigid sex roles, so it is important to examine sexism in order to prevent rape. Avoid stereotypes such as "being assertive is unfeminine" that prevent you from expressing yourself. You have the right to protect yourself.

- *Be careful of alcohol and drugs.* Alcohol and drugs decrease your inhibitions and make you vulnerable to be taken advantage of. They also reduce the inhibitions of the people you are with, putting you in a more vulnerable position, making it more difficult to get out of the situation.

- *Trust your instincts.* If you think something is wrong, or you feel uneasy, end the date. You can always explore the reasons for the feeling later in a safe place. Your instincts are much better in these circumstances than your rational reasoning.

- *Call the police.* Many acquaintance rapes go unreported. Victims often feel that their peers will blame them, not believe them, or their social status will be affected. Others do not want their attacker, who may have been a friend, to get in trouble or they do not want their family to find out. All of the reasons for not reporting have merit and validity but all victims must also be aware that a criminal who gets away with a crime once will very likely repeat it. A stand must be taken by someone in order for a sexual predator to be stopped.

VOICE OF STRESS 12.1

Thirty-Year-Old Female Nursing Student

I grew up in a remote part of India in a place where everyone knew everyone else. When I was 13, a friend of the family—I called him "Uncle"— assaulted me in bed. He raped me. At first I told no one about this. I was so ashamed. It would bring such shame on my family. Then one day I told my mother what happened and she sent me away. In my culture, it is believed that it is always the girl's fault. I must have done something to bring this on. For a long time I believed this.

I still have bad dreams about this thing that happened. I not only lost my childhood, but my whole family. Even today, with my husband, it is difficult for me to have sex. I do not enjoy it because I keep picturing my uncle and what he did to me. My husband does not understand why I am the way I am, but I am afraid to tell him or he will feel my shame.

Improving Your Relationship Skills

Most conflicts result from a situation in which one or both parties feel like they have not been heard or understood. Divorces take months to resolve, and tens of thousands of dollars, not because the combatants care that much about how the possessions are divided but because they feel anger and resentment that have not been worked through.

The single most important thing that you can do to prevent conflicts from escalating in the first place is to improve your listening and responding skills. You will be amazed at the difference such training can make not only in working through disagreements when they arise, but in improving the quality of *all* your relationships.

Most of the time people do not listen to one another. When you try to listen to others, or pretend to do so, it is often with divided attention. Notice how often you are involved in a conversation with someone important to you, but you are juggling other tasks at the same time—making a note, grooming yourself, talking on the phone, waving to someone, thinking about what you will do next. How often are you actually totally immersed in a conversation, focusing all your attention on what the other person is saying?

Most people don't know how to communicate well in relationships; even if they do have the necessary skills, they are often unwilling to devote the energy and commitment that is required. It takes a lot of work to remain fully present with someone and to give full attention to a conversation. If you've ever wondered why people would pay large sums of money to a therapist for someone to listen to their troubles, one reason is that you can so rarely find even a dear friend or family member who is willing to listen uncritically and respond compassionately with total interest.

FOR REFLECTION 12.4

Observing Yourself in Conversation

Pay attention to some of your conversations during a typical day. Notice how often you are talking to someone while doing something else at the same time. Notice how often your attention wanders. Monitor carefully how judgmental you are about what the other person is saying. When you speak, observe how often you interrupt someone before he is done.

You may find it even more disturbing to notice how rarely anyone gives you undivided attention Watch the nonverbal behavior of people as they talk to you throughout the day. If you are perceptive and attentive, you will observe the disturbing revelation that most of the time people are simply not listening to you.

Practice Mindfulness in Communication

As discussed in Chapters 4 and 8, mindfulness is both a trait as well as an attentional state that can be cultivated in an individual. It represents the ability to pay purposeful and nonjudgmental attention to the present moment with acceptance (Kabat-Zinn, 1990). Practicing mindfulness in communication requires gentle acceptance of oneself, first of all, which then permits honest, nonjudgmental, and accurate observations of what takes place both outside and inside oneself. It has been mentioned earlier that some barriers exist that interfere with effective communication, including: 1) humans' tendencies to operate on an autopilot, 2) resorting to reflexive and habitual patterns of behavior, 3) misinterpreting others based on limited experience and perspective, and 4) imposition of one's assumptions and expectation on oneself and others. Mindfulness traditions recommend four important skills that can be adopted for effective communication and conflict resolution (Dimidjian & Linehan, 2003; Hudson et al., 2011): 1) mindful observation, 2) acting with awareness, 3) acting without judgment, and 4) mindful description. Mindful observation refers to attending to internal and external phenomena such as thoughts, emotions, bodily sensations, and external sounds. Acting with awareness is immersing oneself in what is going on with undivided attention. Accepting without judgement refers to the process of treating one's experiences dispassionately without evaluation. Finally, mindful description refers to the immediate, non-judgmental labeling of observations without conceptual analysis. It is important to point out that practicing mindfulness in communication does not equate endorsing what is happening. Rather, when you are fully aware and present, you will have more options to choose from instead of being overwhelmed by your emotional reactivity or blinded by perceptual biases (Goldstein, 1993). Mindfulness can be cultivated in communication as shown in a study by Huston and his colleagues (Huston et al., 2011) who demonstrated that mindful communication training increased positive reappraisal among the participants suggesting that mindfulness training is a potent mechanism to reduce negative emotional reactivity and enhance mental health.

VOICE OF THE AUTHOR 12.1

I have benefited greatly from mindfulness meditation almost on a daily basis. One of the benefits is that it enables me to improve my relationships with my wife and my children. I have noticed, to my amazement, that I often catch myself and refrain from saying things that I would later regret. I am much less judgmental and listen with more attention to what is being said to me. For instance, one day, I came back from work and went to greet my younger son Andrew in his room doing homework. He talked to me in an unpleasantly groggy tone which I immediately interpreted as being disrespectful. However, I noticed his red eyes and recalled that he had not slept much the night before in order to prepare for one major exam, so I stopped my urge to reprimand him. After asking him how his day had been, I gave him a hug and said that I loved him, and then went back to my routine. That day was quite special to me because I practiced mindfulness in my communication with my son.

Listening with Focused Attention

For professional therapists, or for those who just want to improve the quality of all their relationships, the most important adjustment takes place within your own heart and mind. Before you ever open your mouth to begin a conversation, there are certain internal attitudes that are crucial to careful listening as well as mutual understanding.

Similar to what you might do in meditation, the first step to good listening is to clear your mind of all distractions. This means putting aside all the other things going on in your life: all the swirling *mélange* of thoughts, all the plans for the future, all the action going on around and within you. Just as you would in meditation, you might begin by taking a deep breath as a reminder to stay focused on the present, to give full and complete attention to the person you are with.

You will notice the immediate difference such focused concentration can make in your relationships. Every time you notice your attention drifting, bring your full energy back. This takes dedication and commitment. We are all so used to listening with half-attention, listening from a position of self-indulgence, or with ongoing criticism and judgment, that it becomes difficult to not do so without major effort and sustained commitment.

What is the payoff in doing so? Why would you choose to invest energy in such an enterprise? The biggest reason is that you will hear and notice things that have been invisible previously, making you extraordinarily sensitive. Second, the other person will know that you are really listening—that you care enough to give so much of yourself.

FOR PRACTICE 12.1

Deep Listening

Most of the For Practice exercises in this chapter require working with a partner.

Your partner should speak to you for about two minutes. During that time, you are not going to say or do a thing—on the outside. Instead, your only job is to give this person your full and complete attention.

Start by taking a deep cleansing breath as you would in meditation and yoga. Clear your mind of all distractions. During the time your partner is speaking, concentrate intently on what he is saying. Don't worry about making sense of the communication at this time. Your only task is to practice listening with undivided attention.

After the two minutes is up, ask your partner what this was like for him.

Switch roles to give your partner the chance to practice the skill of deep listening.

Nonverbal Cues

Once you have adopted an internal attitude that is quiet, serene, noncritical, and focused, the next step is to convey nonverbally to the other person that you are truly listening. This is communicated not by telling someone, "I hear you," but by demonstrating it through your behavior.

How do you know someone is listening to you? They are making eye contact. They also communicate with their body posture, their facial expressions, their head nods, and even subtle gestures that they are tracking what you have to say.

What does such attentive nonverbal behavior look like?

The person is facing you fully, not turned away in such a manner as to convey divided attention. The posture should be natural rather than stilted, communicating with every fiber of your body, "I am really listening to you with every part of me."

It is difficult to overestimate the power of nonverbal attending skills to communicate that you are truly listening to another person. So many conflicts can be talked through, or avoided altogether, if both parties feel they are being heard noncritically and understood with compassion and empathy.

This may sound easy but is actually very difficult. When students are first learning how to become therapists, they might spend several weeks just practicing their nonverbal **attending** skills. These are the special listening behaviors that demonstrate focused concentration and interest. Trainees watch videos of themselves noticing how often they appear bored or distracted. They literally practice how to sit, facing the other person, leaning forward, communicating interest but without seeming too intrusive.

Again, if you watch other people in normal conversation you will notice how often their body language communicates disinterest, boredom, distraction, or just plain indifference. How do you think that feels to the other person, to be talking to someone and know that they don't care to even pretend to listen?

How to Listen

While you are attending carefully to the other person, showing by your nonverbal behavior that you are intently interested, you are trying to make sense of what you are hearing.

FOR PRACTICE 12.2

Nonverbal Attending

With a partner, position yourselves in chairs at a comfortable distance.

Start with a deep cleansing breath, just as you did before, and clear your mind of all distractions.

While your partner speaks to you for two minutes, you are going to do everything within your power to convey, nonverbally, that you are intently interested in what she is saying. During this particular exercise you cannot speak (except with verbal encouragers) but you can use your body, your face, your gestures and facial expressions, and head nods, to let the person know you are listening and following what is being said.

Smile, frown, or show concern on your face as appropriate. Make good eye contact that is natural rather than intense staring. Nod your head as much as you can. You can also use minimal verbal encouragers such as "uh huh," "yes," and "I see" to let the person know you are listening carefully.

After the time is up, ask your partner how this felt.

Reverse roles to give your partner the opportunity to do the same.

All communications carry a **surface message**, one that is concrete and obvious, and a **deep message**, one that conveys the underlying meaning.

If a student approaches a professor and says, "Excuse me, but is this stuff about surface and deep messages going to be on the test?" there are several ways that the teacher could respond:

"Yes, this is going to be on the test."

"No, this is not going to be on the test."

"I don't know if it is going to be on the test but you'd better study it anyway."

Each of these three statements responds to the surface message in the communication. The student asked a direct question and got a direct answer. But what if the student was not really asking a question but making a statement of feeling? What if the student didn't want a direct answer but an acknowledgment? What would it sound like if the professor decided to ignore the surface message and respond to the possibly deeper one?

"You sound like you're confused about the difference between the two concepts and you're nervous about how you're going to do on the exam."

It is entirely possible, of course, that the student was really asking a simple question. For illustrative purposes, however, let's imagine that he really was communicating stress in the form of a surface question.

If you are practicing the attending and listening skills you just learned, then you are hearing nuances in the communication that might not be immediately obvious. Essentially, you are asking yourself the question: What is the person really saying to me in this moment? In other words, you are attempting to decode the deeper meaning of the message in order to promote better understanding of the other person's experience. This is what builds greater intimacy and avoids prolonged conflict.

In the exercise to decode surface messages, if you paid attention to what the person was really trying to say beneath the surface you may have surmised that the little boy in the first example was not only asking a question but also communicating fear and apprehension. In the second example, the person was saying that she didn't mind if someone borrowed her homework, but she really did mind and felt resentful and put upon. In the third example, the person acted like it wasn't important whether he got a ride or not, but it was actually very important. And finally, in the fourth example, the person seemed to say that she was indifferent and didn't care about what they did, but she was saying in her own quiet way that she did have a preference.

Perhaps you devised other possible meanings from these brief statements taken out of context. There are no actual correct answers here; this is only intended to sensitize you to the decoding process so that you ask yourself what a person might really be saying. If conflicts arise over seemingly insignificant things, it is because the bigger issues get ignored.

Responding Reflectively

If you have been listening carefully, then you have some notion of what the other person might be trying to say to you—or perhaps, digging even deeper, what is being experienced inside. The next task is to respond to the person by communicating not only that you heard what was said but that you truly understand.

FOR PRACTICE 12.3

Decoding Surface Messages

Decode each of the statements below by writing in its possible deeper meanings. What might this person really be trying to communicate in terms of underlying feelings?

1. A little boy crossing the street with his mother: "Mommy, does that doggie bite?"

2. "Sure, you can borrow my homework. I guess I don't mind."

3. "I was just wondering if you could give me a ride to work? It's no big deal, really. I can take a bus or something if you're too busy."

4. "If you really want to, I guess we could do that. I mean, it doesn't really matter that much. Well, it does, and it doesn't, if you know what I mean."

In the dialogue below, notice the way the three different people speak to someone who is upset. Respondent A is defensive and B is so uncomfortable that she ignores what is being said. Only C actually seems to understand what is being communicated and responds in such a way that she acknowledges this.

*   *You never reciprocate in our relationship. I invite you to do things all the time but you never invite me to do anything.*

*   A: "That's not true. You exaggerate. You don't always invite me to do things."

*   B: "If you say so, but what do you want to do now?"

*   C: "You feel like our relationship is unequal, that you invest more in it than I do, and you feel resentful towards me because of it."

What stands out most about how Person C chose to respond?

This is called **reflection of feeling** and it involves three steps: 1) listening carefully to what is being said, 2) decoding the deep meaning of the message, and 3) reflecting back what was heard by focusing on the underlying feelings.

This response style of careful listening and reflection is the best tool therapists have, being virtually guaranteed to diffuse conflicts and build more trust in relationships. In this mode, the listener functions as a mirror, reflecting back what was heard. This can be done by homing in on *what* is said, through **reflection of content** – paraphrasing the feeling implied in the statement.

Reflections accomplish several things simultaneously:

1. They keep you from explaining or defending yourself: "You're upset with me right now."

2. They let the person know that they've been heard and understood: "It's not just that you are mad with me about this situation, but you've been feeling this way for some time."

3. They encourage deeper, more intimate exploration: "When you say that our relationship is frustrating for you, you seem to be saying that you wish it was different. You wish we might restructure things in such a way that it felt more equal to you."

4. They keep the conversation going, even when you don't know what else to say.

5. They empower the other person to work things out on her own, or in collaboration with you, instead of trying to offer a quick fix.

6. Even when they are not perfectly on target or accurate, reflections still encourage deeper level exploration:

   • Person 1: "You're really feeling sad about that."
   • Person 2: "No, not so much sad as disappointed."

When people are talking to someone who is troubled, they often try to fix the problem by giving advice. Giving such advice may make you feel better but rarely helps the other

---

VOICE OF STRESS MANAGEMENT 12.4

Twenty-Four-Year-Old Male

The stress in my relationship has caused me to not only to gain weight, but also to lose sight of who I want to be. When we first met I thought Michael was the perfect catch—ambitious, talented, intelligent, hard working. I was attracted to him, in part, because he was stable. Well, since I had taken a year off of school and was waiting tables, I pretty much made myself available to him when his schedule permitted. I would accompany him to his weekend job and help out, run errands and pick up lunch. A few months into it I realized that my entire identity began to revolve around his needs and what he was doing. I totally lost myself. His stress became my stress.

Once I started voicing my discontent, the fighting began. For ten months he had a devoted slave and when I finally declared my needs all hell broke loose. I found myself unable to control my anger and would just yell and throw things. Eventually I realized that I deserve the same time and quality of care as I had been giving to Michael. For that to happen, though, it means I would have to ask for help and attention. It was hard for me to do that, but once I told Michael what I wanted, he immediately agreed. That opened new lines of communication between us and made the relationship that much better.

FOR PRACTICE 12.4

Reflecting Content and Feelings

With a partner you are now going to put everything together that you've learned so far. To review, that means you will begin with your usual cleansing breath to clear your mind. You are going to practice nonverbal attending in order to communicate your interest, including good eye contact and appropriate head nods. In addition, you should use minimal verbal encouragers.

While listening carefully, you will be decoding the messages you hear and then responding using only reflections of content and feeling.

Your partner should talk about something in her life that she feels stressed about so you have some genuine material to work with. After you have completed a few minutes of conversation, reverse roles.

Discuss what this exercise was like for you and give one another feedback on what you liked most, as well as suggestions for improvement.

---

person; often it does the exact opposite. Moreover, people rarely listen to advice. It is not as if you are going to tell someone something they've never thought of and then, all of a sudden, a light bulb is going to go on, they will see the light, and immediately they will act on whatever you say. It just doesn't happen.

Putting it All Together

Let's take a look at how a conversation might proceed in which two people have been involved in a dispute, but one of them decided to practice some listening and responding skills to diffuse the hostility.

Magda and Fran had been close friends for over a year. Even though they came from different backgrounds, they started hanging out together because of mutual interests. Eventually they became inseparable, planning even to take some of the same classes together and going out socially a few nights per week.

The problem began after Magda met a guy she liked and this became a source of tension between them. Fran felt that Magda was no longer as committed to their friendship; sometimes she didn't even seem interested in getting together much anymore. As far as Magda was concerned, this was not really the case. She didn't even like the guy that much, and certainly didn't want to risk losing Fran as a friend. In spite of Magda's efforts to explain this to Fran, her friend had begun to withdraw and wouldn't return her calls. When Magda came to class one day, Fran deliberately arrived late so she could sit on her own. This wounded Magda even more deeply. Over the course of the previous weeks, she had been extremely upset about the breach in their friendship. The stress was now interfering with her ability to concentrate on her studies and was affecting her ability to sleep at night.

Magda had never enjoyed such a close friendship before, one with total trust, so she was especially wounded when this one fell apart. She was determined that after class she would sit down with Fran and have a talk about things. She knew that they both had a break before afternoon classes since this was a time when they would usually go to lunch. She resolved that during this conversation she would practice the new listening and responding skills she had been learning.

MAGDA: Hey Fran, wait up. (*Magda runs to catch up with Fran who seems intent on escaping as quickly as possible*)

FRAN: What? I gotta go. I'm kinda in a hurry.

MAGDA: This won't take long, Fran. I just wonder if we could chat for a few minutes. I'll walk you wherever you are going. *(Notice that Magda responds calmly and does not snap back—which a part of her wants to do)*

FRAN: Fine. What's this about?

MAGDA: You seem upset about something and I just wanted to hear more about what is going on. *(A gentle invitation to talk)*

FRAN: I'm surprised you even care.

MAGDA: You're angry with me about something and I'd like to know more. *(She does not take the bait and attack back, or defend herself. Instead she simply reflects the underlying feeling)*

FRAN: You know what's going on so why do you pretend you don't? You don't even care about me and you're just talking to me now so you don't feel guilty.

MAGDA: Your feelings are really hurt because I've done something to offend you. *(Again, she doesn't defend herself. She doesn't explain anything. She just keeps reflecting back what she senses Fran is feeling—which is hurt and anger.)*

FRAN: Look, you've been spending all that time with what's-his-name. You know that. I know that. So now you don't need me anymore. End of story.

MAGDA: You think that I've been spending so much time with Gary that I don't value our friendship any more. You think that I don't care about you. *(Note that this is a reflection of content—a paraphrase—in which she feeds back what she heard. It isn't necessary to always reflect feelings. Also notice that this is made as a statement rather than a question, which would have the inflection raised at the end of the sentence. Reflections carry more weight if they are offered as statements rather than questions. If a statement is not accurate, the person will let you know.)*

FRAN: Well, you don't. You don't call much anymore. You don't invite me to do things. You don't seem interested in me now that you have someone else in your life.

MAGDA: You think I've just written you off because I was dating someone. I can tell that you are really hurt by this. *(This took remarkable restraint on Magda's part because so much of what Fran said is exaggerated or inaccurate. In truth, she hasn't seen much of Gary; she has called Fran several times but Fran doesn't return the calls, and Fran is the one who withdrew. But Magda doesn't bring any of this up, which would only inflame things.)*

In this conversation you can see that Magda is taking a much different position than what might ordinarily be expected. It is not only what she is doing—listening and reflecting the feelings of her wounded friend—that is significant, but what she is *not* doing. Magda is not defending herself. She is not explaining her side. She is not making excuses. She is not attacking Fran for pouting and acting like a hurt child, no matter how much she might want to say it. Since her only agenda is to patch things up with her friend, resolve the conflict between them, and move on, she is carefully keeping the focus on communicating understanding.

Will these simple skills alone be enough to make things better? Probably not. After all, Magda does have the right to communicate her own feelings of frustration and hurt as well, and to be heard and understood in turn. If this does not occur, then she may have second thoughts about whether she even wants to continue this friendship.

While this brief introduction to relationship skills may get you started, it will help if you study more about the ways you can improve your interpersonal skills, not only to reduce stress and diffuse conflicts in your life but simply to improve intimacy. Even the simplest skills can have a huge impact. For example, in studies of predictors of divorce (Gottman, 2002; Gottman & Silver, 2000) it was found that when husbands fail to respond to their wives' overtures for some type of interaction ("I'm busy now" or "I wasn't listening"), divorce results 82% of the time. All it takes to make a huge difference is simply your commitment and willingness to be a more patient listener and active responder.

Expressing Yourself

So far, we've been examining skills that are designed to help others feel heard and understood. Yet conflicts arise not only because of poor listening but also because you have not been clear about your own feelings. In the previous example, the conflict between Magda and Fran occurred not only because Fran did not feel heard, but also because Magda did not express her own feelings.

There are a few additional skills to add to your repertoire in this regard, which help you to be clearer about your own reactions.

An **"I" message** is one in which you use the pronoun "I" to own and express your thoughts and feelings. You do so by simply stating what you are feeling or thinking. It is a kind of assertive response that is designed to accept responsibility for what you are experiencing, but without attacking or negating what the other person might be feeling. You are just letting the person know what is going on with you.

Whenever possible, it is beneficial to convert "you" statements (which are accusatory) to "I" statements (in which you "own" the problem). Note the difference in the examples below:

"You" Statements	"I" Statements
You are really pissing me off right now.	I feel angry right now in response to what just happened.
Do you have a problem right now? I notice that you keep interrupting.	I have a problem right now with the interruptions.
Maybe you would like to clean this up since you made the mess.	I feel upset when I come home to a big mess.
You seem to have some kind of problem with me, don't you?	I am having a problem with you and wonder if you might help me with my problem?

You will notice that in the "I" statements, the person is accepting responsibility for her own feelings. She is "owning" the problem, admitting that she is the one who is unhappy with things. In doing so she is also communicating her feelings in a way that is clear and assertive, but hardly aggressive. In the last example, notice how instead of attacking the other person ("*You* have a problem with me"), she completely owns the situation as her own difficulty ("*I* am the one having the problem. Can you help me with *my* problem?").

In addition to the assertive examples previously presented, "I" messages can be used to show approval and validation when someone demonstrates love and caring. For example: "I feel loved when you get the children's breakfast ready and let me sleep another ten minutes," or "I really appreciate it when you are so thoughtful to bring me this coffee."

Nothing diffuses conflicts more, especially when you are in the midst of an argument, than to take a step back, stop accusing the other person with "yous" and instead start owning your own reactions to what is going on. Telling someone you have a problem with something they are doing or saying doesn't necessarily mean they will care, much less respond the way you prefer. It is a preferred strategy, assuming the other person will be motivated to help you work on *your* problem. If that doesn't work, there are other options to use.

Strategies for Managing Conflict

So far we have been operating under the assumption that most conflicts can be resolved by communicating better listening and understanding skills, coupled with clearer assertions of your own needs. Notwithstanding the usefulness of these strategies, there are certain situations and individuals for which they will not work. This can be for a number of reasons already mentioned, as follows:

1. Individuals are emotionally disturbed and unable to behave in a civil, respectful manner.

2. They have a kind of personality disorder (narcissistic, sociopathic, borderline, hysterical) in which they are unable (or unwilling) to take other people's needs and feelings into consideration.

3. They enjoy being in conflict for a number of reasons—as a distraction, for entertainment, as a demonstration of power, as stimulation, or simply to make everyone else in the world as miserable as they are.

In each of these cases, these are difficult people that are challenging for almost everyone to be around. In such situations, the skills previously introduced are not going to work well. You are going to have to be far more creative.

Stay Flexible

By definition, a so-called difficult person is someone who does not respond to ordinary strategies. This means you are going to have to try something else, something different from what you usually do in such circumstances. If pleading does not work, then stop doing that. If using "I" messages is all but ignored, then abandon that tactic as well. If reflecting feelings only encourages the person to be more emotionally abusive, stop that behavior. It is critical that you observe carefully the impact of what you are doing on the other person, note the effects, and make adjustments.

Tit for Tat

In a landmark study of the ways that people cooperate during stressful conflict situations, Axelrod (1984) devised a game called **prisoner's dilemma** in which participants had to figure out the best way to "win" without sacrificing their own best interests. The intent of this exercise was to study the ways that people might handle conflicts in political, economic, or social situations in which they had to choose between cooperation versus competition with an opponent.

The scenario is as follows: imagine being questioned by the police for a crime that you are suspected to have committed with an accomplice. The authorities have no compelling evidence to prove that you were involved in the crime even though they have strong suspicions.

The police are interrogating you isolated from your partner, hoping to get one of you to implicate the other. They have promised you that if you confess but provide testimony against your partner, you will go free but he will be imprisoned. If, on the other hand, you refuse to cooperate but your partner implicates you, then he goes free but you don't. If you both confess, then you both go to jail but for a shorter time. Here are the possibilities:

1. You implicate your partner and he remains silent: You win and go free.

2. You remain silent and your partner implicates you: You lose and go to jail for five years.

3. You each implicate the other: You both lose and go to jail for three years each.

4. You both refuse to cooperate: Both of you win and go free.

You can see that the best strategy is not one of conflict but of cooperation in which you both trust your partner. But if your partner betrays you after the first round of the game, what do you do during subsequent rounds?

The strategy that proved to be most effective in this "war game" was to do what your opponent last did. Called **tit for tat**, you start out with a trusting, cooperative spirit, but if the other person does not respond in a similar manner, then you do not let yourself be betrayed a second time. Likewise in any conflict situation it is best to begin from a position of trust and openness. But if you are betrayed—if you can't trust the other person to behave in a civil, respectful manner—then you would be foolish to keep setting yourself up to be clobbered.

FOR REFLECTION 12.5

Reframing Conflict

Recalling to mind the various functions of conflict that were covered earlier in the chapter, think of a time in your life in which you experienced a huge growth spurt as a result of a conflict you faced. For some period of time there may have been a certain amount of stress, inconvenience, perhaps emotional turmoil. But looking back, regardless of how the situation turned out, what benefits did you accrue as a result of what happened?

Now that you think back on the situation, how would you reframe the conflict differently than you did at the time?

This may sound like a rather adversarial posture, especially with regard to the ideas already discussed that emphasize mutual caring and respect. However, when you have to deal with someone who plays by a whole different set of rules than yours, give back exactly what you get. This is not advocating vengeance or retribution, which only get in the way of forgiveness, but rather of cautious, sensible self-protection. If someone betrays your trust, don't trust that person again. If someone resorts to underhanded behavior, expect that it will continue in the future. If someone says one thing but does another, don't believe that this will change. If it does change, be pleasantly surprised.

Reframe Conflict

One of the major predictors of divorce in a marriage is not necessarily the presence of conflict but its avoidance (Fincham, 2003; Gottman & Gottman, 2006). In several manuals written specially for couples, it is recommended that couples do not ignore or deny their problems, but remain engaged with one another. It isn't conflict itself that is necessarily stressful but rather how it is conducted.

One way to look at conflict is that it represents a form of constructive disagreement. It is from such diverse points of view that innovations are possible (Fisher-Yoshida, 2005). But this only takes place when partners are respectful and caring in their communications, remaining calm and relatively stress-free.

In previous chapters, I covered that the way you look at a situation is often what determines whether it is stressful or not. If you see a particular conflict as being extremely painful, rather than a minor annoyance, it will feel much more disruptive to your life. Likewise, if you choose to view an argument as merely a difference of opinion, then you will be far more likely to take it in your stride. If you value the potentially positive outcomes of honorable disputes, then you will find some long-term gain in the relatively short-term pain. It makes the temporary discomfort worthwhile to tolerate and work through.

Repeat Mantras

In the chapter on meditation you learned that a mantra is a repetitive sound, phrase, or word that focuses the mind and soothes the spirit. There are certain mantras, or soothing phrases, that work well in conflict situations as well, especially during the critical moments when you are feeling most out of control.

Here are a few useful mantras:

- *Take a deep breath*. This is a reminder to just calm down. Take a deep breath. Relax. Count to ten, slowly.

- *In 100 years*. In 100 years who is going to care about what happened? Who is going to care? This is a reminder that what may seem like such a catastrophe right now will seem meaningless over the course of time. Remember the things that seemed so upsetting to you a few years ago but now seem almost laughable.

- *This will make me stronger*. Remind yourself that it is from facing adversity that you are most likely to grow. What does not kill you will indeed make you stronger, *if* you learn from the experience.

- *This isn't about me*. Remind yourself that you may be over-personalizing what is going on. Perhaps it isn't really about you, but represents some issue of the other person.

- *He's doing the best he can*. If this person knew how to do something other than what he is doing he'd probably do it. He is coping as best as he can in a situation that feels threatening to him.

- *What am I missing*? Often conflicts result from some cultural misunderstanding in which one or both of you is interpreting the other person's behavior according to your own standards.

Practice Assertiveness

Earlier I presented "I" messages as one form of assertive behavior, but there are many others. Assertiveness training is a program that is designed to help people who are ordinarily either overly passive or excessively aggressive to better get their needs met by standing up for their rights without trampling those of anyone else (Alberti & Emmons, 2008). You do this, in part, by learning to say no—firmly, decisively, and respectfully. It is about framing confrontation in a positive, constructive, sensitive manner that sets limits but does so in a way that does not escalate the difficulties.

You might think that the opposite of being assertive is being passive, and that is true to a certain extent, but another form is being overly aggressive. In this case a person is so concerned with standing up for her own rights, and getting her own needs met, that she does it at the expense of others' welfare. If you didn't check many of the items in the reflective exercise, it could mean you are effective as an assertive individual who stands up for your rights. It could also mean that you are overly aggressive to the point that you elicit a lot of resentment in others. Being assertive is a midpoint between being passive and being aggressive.

The first skill that is employed in assertive behavior is a similar kind of attentive listening to that described earlier. By nonverbally and verbally communicating to others that you are carefully tracking what they are saying, that you are understanding their messages and can prove it by reflecting back what you hear, you are establishing a non-adversarial position. The use of "I" messages also conveys that you are willing to "own" your feelings and thoughts but also makes it clear that you have clear limits about what you are willing to tolerate. In addition to what you've already learned, additional assertiveness skills include the following:

- *Set rules.* It is important to enforce clear boundaries about what you will permit and what you will not. Let others know in firm language that you will not tolerate abuse, neglect, or disrespect in any form. Make sure to enforce the rules consistently if you expect to be taken seriously.

- *Say no.* Sometimes people walk all over you because they can, or because they don't really know what it is that you want. It is up to you to say clearly and firmly what you are willing to do, and what you are not.

- *Ask for what you want.* You can't expect that people will give you what you want unless you are prepared to ask for it, sometimes repeatedly.

- *Convey assurance.* Even if you do not feel completely confident it is important to communicate a degree of power in your words—that you really mean what you say. One question at the back of everyone else's mind is: "I heard what you said. But what do you *really* mean by that?"

- *Don't explain.* You are under no obligation to explain or justify yourself; it is enough that you don't want to do something. Everyone has the right to decline.

FOR REFLECTION 12.6

Are You Assertive?

Check those of the following issues that challenge you the most:
- ____ I find it hard to say no to people who want something from me without feeling guilty.
- ____ I don't often stand up for myself, or speak up, even when someone is taking advantage of me.
- ____ I try to avoid confrontation at all costs.
- ____ I let myself be intimidated by certain people and situations, especially those with bad tempers and loud voices.
- ____ When someone disrespects me in some way I usually just keep my mouth shut.
- ____ When someone attacks me in some way I usually just let it go, hoping that things will work out on their own.
- ____ I do favors for people even when I don't want to because I don't want them to feel disappointed.
- ____ I usually will not ask for what I really want because I don't want to be a burden on others.
- ____ I often feel that I am treated unfairly but I don't speak up.
- ____ I find it hard to keep eye contact with people when I am speaking with them.
- ____ When people do annoying things around me, I don't usually tell them to stop.

VOICE OF STRESS MANAGEMENT 12.5

Twenty-Five-Year Old Female Graduate Student

When I came to this country I was just 14 and very eager to fit in. My parents had divorced and my mother thought there would be more opportunities for us in America versus staying in Mexico. I remember feeling torn. I loved my life in Mexico, but I knew that America had so much to offer. At first I was confused. How do I fit in? What do I wear? How do I make new friends? I was an excellent student in Mexico, but when I tried to enroll in advanced algebra and a physics class, I was denied. My mother and I were told that I was not ready for those types of classes and I should start in basic math and focus on ESL [English as a Second Language] classes. I was totally stressed out. I was in a new country, away from the majority of my family, had no friends, did not speak the language, and wasn't even able to challenge myself academically due to the school's stereotypes toward Latinos. I was shocked that in this land of opportunity I was being denied my right to excel academically. I just wanted to go back home.

At first I took what they said and was the good little student. After about a semester of boredom and frustration I decided I needed to speak up. First I went to talk with my guidance counselor who was no help at all. Then I met with the assistant principal who told me to wait until the following year. Finally I convinced the principal to allow me to take the math and science tests to prove my abilities. My scores were off of the chart and I was allowed to enroll in advanced algebra and physics. I was the only freshman in both. Looking back I remember it being more stressful feeling like I was being put down and demeaned than standing up for myself and getting into some really tough classes that I knew I could handle. Looking back I can see that my determination and assertiveness led me to speak up for myself.

- *Dispute your guilt.* Some people will try to guilt you into compliance. You have a right to stand up for yourself without berating yourself or feeling regretful afterwards.

- *Countermanipulation.* People will try unfair means to dominate or control you. Expect such behavior—and counter it by recognizing what is going on and refusing to participate.

Another effective method for assertive communication is the DESC (describe, express, specify, and consequences) method, a simple structured approach to practice assertiveness (Hall, 2015). You may adapt the following example to your own situation:

- *Describe.* Describe the behavior/situation completely and objectively by focusing on the facts and avoiding attacking any person. "We agreed that you would wash dishes and I take care of the cooking, yet you seldom washed the dishes occasionally in the last few weeks."

- *Express.* Express your feelings and thoughts about the situation/behavior. "As a result, I felt exhausted after having to do both cooking and washing."

- *Specify.* Specify what behavior/outcome you would prefer to see. "I would like to see you keep our original agreement and do the dishes."

- *Consequences.* Specify the consequences (both positive and negative). "If we can stick to our original agreement, we will be happy and I will not be exhausted and irritable."

Even if you can't change anyone else's behavior, there is an immediate sense of empowerment and stress reduction in feeling like you have choices in the ways you are treated. In some cases you may not have any other choice except to protect yourself in other ways.

FOR PRACTICE 12.5

Assertiveness Skills

Team up with a partner who will ask you to do something that you would prefer not to do. Your partner is going to be persistent, and not take no for an answer, so you are going to have to progressively assert yourself in such a way that you make it clearer that you will not comply with the request. Be careful not to go so far that you become aggressive or disrespectful. Concentrate instead on being consistent and firm, as in the sample dialogue below:

"I want you to go with me."

"I would prefer not."

"Oh, come on. It's no big deal."

"No thanks."

"You don't really mean it. I know you want to go."

"Perhaps you didn't hear me, but I really don't want to go."

"I think you do. And I think you really have to do this."

"Please listen clearly, because I don't think you are hearing me: I don't wish to go. I really don't like feeling pressured by you, nor do I like that you are not listening to me."

Exit the Conflict

You have learned that many conflicts cannot be easily resolved. Sometimes you just have to accept that, at least for now, the best you can hope for is to extricate yourself from an argument with minimal damage either to yourself or the other person.

As mentioned earlier, John Gottman (2002; Gottman & Gottman, 2006) has studied successful love relationships, as well as those that are fraught with pain and destined to fail. Based on observing the way couples communicate, even for just a few minutes, he can predict with 90% accuracy whether or not the relationship is going to last. He has developed the most troubling warning signs of relationship failure. After studying videotapes of interactions between spouses he found that he could easily predict and anticipate future problems based on four "relationship killers":

1. criticism and verbal attacks;

2. contempt, name calling, and mockery;

3. defensiveness and blaming;

4. stonewalling, withdrawal, passivity.

It turns out that arguing itself is not necessarily indicative of a bad relationship or one that is doomed. Sometimes people communicate with one another in a more argumentative style. It isn't the heated conversations that are the problem, but rather how they take place, especially when they involve attacking the other person personally or showing signs of disgust for the other person.

In his research, Gottman discovered that one crucial skill in successful marriages is knowing how to end the argument or conflict and to move on, even when it isn't fully resolved. Solid relationships are characterized by both partners being willing and able to let go of a disagreement. This can be done in several ways, as follows:

- *Changing the topic to something that is safer and less emotional:* "Okay, so let's agree to disagree about that. So, where do you want to go for dinner?"

- *Taking a time-out:* "We don't seem to be getting anywhere with this. Why don't we take a break for a little while and talk about it again a little later?"

- *Emphasizing mutual ownership of the problem:* "Look, this isn't just my problem, and it's not yours either; it's both of ours. We are in this together."

- *Backing down:* "You may very well be right. You certainly feel strongly about this. So I don't mind deferring to you on this."

- *Using humor:* "We sound like little kids, don't we? It feels like we are fighting in a sandbox for who gets to play with what toys."

- *Reflecting feelings:* "I can see that you are really upset with me over this and feel frustrated because I am not responding the way you had hoped."

- *Focusing on the positive:* "Okay, we might not be able to agree on this but generally I think that we are together on most of the other things."

Each of the strategies for reducing relationship stress emphasizes things that you can do, either internally or interpersonally, to promote greater understandings. Nevertheless, there will be times when no matter what you can do, or how you do it, you won't seem to make much headway. This may occur not necessarily as a result of the other person being difficult, or you employing an ineffective strategy, but rather because the problem is so intractable or complex that it requires some form of mediation.

You must be willing to ask for help from an outside source or professional when conflicts appear hopeless and you have tried everything within reason. Professional mediators and therapists are experts at helping people to work through their struggles in ways that focus not only on conflict resolution but also on relationship issues. There may be times when you have to admit—to yourself and your adversary or partner—that you are both losing sleep and increasing stress as a result of the ongoing feud. You must find some way to put the conflict behind you even if that involves recruiting or hiring a specialist.

SUMMARY

Relationships represent the best in life, and also the most gut-wrenching. You lose more sleep, and experience more stress, over conflicts with others than practically any other facet of your life. The best way to handle relationship conflicts involves a series of skills that prevent finger-pointing and defensiveness. It is important to express yourself honestly but also to be sensitive to what others are feeling. It is critical that you learn to be a better, more active listener, one who can make sense of what people are really saying to you and then respond reflectively in ways that soothe rather than aggravate the other person. This does not mean that you are being either condescending or deferential, but that you are helping others to feel more understood.

If you are interested in learning more about relationship skills and conflict resolution for reducing stress, you can attend classes in counseling or human services, find workshops on the subject, or even consult books on the subject that go into greater depth. You will find resources available that teach interpersonal skills for use in every imaginable field and context, including those that specialize in helping college students become more effective leaders.

Reflective listening skills are used to help others feel understood. They are good companions to assertive skills and "I" messages that help you to express your own positions and yet do so in a way in which you accept responsibility for your share of the problem. Remember that you can't really make anyone else change their behavior but it is within your power to change the ways you respond to them.

Even with the best of training and most diligent practice you are still going to encounter people who are difficult to be around and may even thrive on conflict. In such circumstances you must protect yourself by setting limits, enforcing boundaries, and if necessary extricating yourself from chronically stressful relationships that are not good for you.

QUESTIONS FOR REVIEW

1. Describe barriers to resolving personal conflicts and myths and misunderstandings about conflict.
2. Explain what positive functions conflict might serve in people's lives.
3. Describe why it is more effective to use "I" statements rather than "you" statements when working through a conflict.
4. How would you "reframe" a feud between two students who continually compete with each other in ways that create dysfunctional stress for both of them?
5. Discuss the effects of abuse and sexual harassment on victims and bystanders.
6. Describe steps you can take to prevent being a victim of violence.
7. Explain why it is detrimental to blame others for the conflicts and stress that you encounter.
8. Describe possible reasons why someone might be perceived as "difficult."
9. Explain how mindfulness is related to effective interpersonal communication? Identify the four mindful communication skills discussed in the chapter.
10. Discuss what it means to listen actively and respond reflectively.
11. Describe the DESC method in resolving a personal conflict.

REVIEW ACTIVITIES

Review Activity 12.1: A Stressful Relationship
Interpersonal conflicts are an ongoing source of stress in your life. Think of the one relationship that has been most troubling to you in recent times—the one that repeatedly leads to disappointment, frustration, and misunderstanding. As best you can, describe below what it is about this relationship that is so difficult for you.

Describe specifically all the ways this ongoing conflict increases stress in your life. List as many symptoms and negative consequences as you can.

This next step is challenging but also potentially enlightening: What are the possible "benefits" or secondary gains that you might be enjoying as a result of this ongoing conflict? Think about the ways you might be keeping someone at a distance, protecting yourself, enjoying attention or self-pity, expressing control, or similar side-effects. If you get stuck, refer back to the part of the chapter that talks about the "functions" of conflict.

REFERENCES AND RESOURCES

Alberti, R. E., & Emmons, M. L. (2008). *Your perfect right: Assertiveness and equality in your life and relationships* (9th ed.). Atascadero, CA: Impact.

Axelrod, R. (1984). *The evolution of cooperation.* New York, NY: Basic Books.

Bowen, M. (1985). *Family therapy in clinical practice.* Lanham, MD: Rowman & Littlefield.

Darling, C. A., McWey, L. M., Howard, S. N., & Olmstead, S. B. (2007). College student stress: The influence of interpersonal relationships on sense of coherence. *Stress and Health, 23,* 215–229.

Dimidjian, S., & Linehan, M. M. (2003). Defining an agenda for future research on the clinical application of mindfulness practice. *Clinical Psychology: Science and Practice, 10,* 166–171.

Evans, D. R., Hearn, M. T., Uhlemann, M., & Ivey, A. (2003). *Essential interviewing: A programmed approach to effective communication* (5th ed.). Belmont, CA: Wadsworth.

Fincham, F. D. (2003). Marital conflict: Correlates, structure, and context. *Current Directions in Psychological Science, 12*(1), 23–27.

Fisher-Yoshida, B. (2005). Reframing conflict: Intercultural conflict as potential transformation. *Journal of Intercultural Communication, 8,* 1–16.

Folger, J. P., Poole, M. S., & Stutman, R. K. (2004). *Working through conflict.* Boston, MA: Allyn and Bacon.

Friedman, R. A., Tidd, S. T., Currall, S. C., & Tsai, J. C. (2000). What goes around comes around: The impact of personal conflict style on work conflict and stress. *International Journal of Conflict Management, 11*(1), 32–55.

Furr, R. M., & Funder, D. C. (1998). A multimodal analysis of personal negativity. *Journal of Personality and Social Psychology, 74,* 1,580–1,591.

Goldstein, J. (1993). *Insight meditation: The practice of freedom.* Boston, MA: Shambhala Publications.

Gottman, J. M. (2002). *The relationship cure: A 5-step guide to strengthening your marriage, family, and friendships.* Three Rivers, MI: Three Rivers Press.

Gottman, J. M., & Gottman, J. (2006). *Ten lessons to transform your marriage.* New York, NY: Three Rivers Press.

Gottman, J. M., & Silver, N. (2000). *The seven principles for making marriage work.* Three Rivers, MI: Three Rivers Press.

Grenyer, B. S. (2002). *Mastering relationship conflicts.* Washington, DC: American Psychological Association Press.

Hall, B. (2015). *Communicate assertively–Getting your message through!* Retrieved on September 30, 2015 from http://www.tsbi.com.au/wp-content/uploads/2013/04/Communicate-assertively-%E2%80%93-Getting-your-message-through.pdf.

Hanh, T. N. (2001). *Anger: Wisdom for cooling the flames.* New York, NY: Riverhead.

Huston, D., Garland, E., & Farb, N. (2011). Mechanisms of mindfulness in communication training. *Journal of Applied Communication Research, 39*(4), 406–421.

Kabat-Zinn, J. (1990). *Full catastrophe living.* New York, NY: Delacorte.

Kiecolt-Glaser, J. (1999). Stress, personal relationships, and immune function: Health implications. *Brain, Behavior, Immunity, 13,* 61–72.

Kiecolt-Glaser, J. K., Bane, C., Glaser, R., & Malarkey, W. B. (2003). Love, marriage, and divorce: Newlyweds' stress hormones foreshadow relationship changes. *Journal of Consulting and Clinical Psychology, 71,* 176–188.

Kiecolt-Glaser, J., Newton, T., Cacioppo, J., MacCallum, R., Glaser, R., & Malarkey, W. (1996). Marital conflict and endocrine function. Are men really more physiologically affected than woman? *Journal of Consulting and Clinical Psychology, 64,* 324–332.

Klever, P. (2005). Multigenerational stress and nuclear family functioning. *Contemporary Family Therapy, 27*(2), 233–250.

Komives, S. R., Lucas, N., & McMahon, T. R. (1998). *Exploring leadership: For college students who want to make a difference.* San Francisco, CA: Jossey-Bass.

Kottler, J. A. (1994). *Beyond blame: A new way of resolving conflicts in relationships.* San Francisco, CA: Jossey-Bass.

Kottler, J. A. (2002). *Students how drive you crazy: Succeeding with resistant, unmotivated, and otherwise difficult young people.* Thousand Oaks, CA: Corwin Press.

Kottler, J. A., & Brew, L. (2003). *One life at a time: Helping skills and interventions.* New York, NY: Routledge.

Mischel, W., & Shoda, Y. (1998). Reconciling processing dynamics and personality dispositions. *Annual Review of Psychology, 49*, 229–258.

Mohler-Kuo, M., Dowdall, G., Koss, M., & Wechsler, H. (2004). Correlates of rape while intoxicated in a national sample of college women. *Journal of Studies on Alcohol, 65*(1), 37–45.

Pachter, B., & Magee, S. (2001). *The power of positive confrontation.* New York, NY: Marlowe.

Seaman, B. (2005). *Binge.* Hoboken, NJ: Wiley.

Strategies of Synthesis and Prevention

13

Resilience and Stress

This chapter describes many of the adaptive functions of stress, particularly with regard to how you can go far beyond merely managing the challenges in life and use adversity as a means to improve your quality of life. This process involves learning to develop greater resilience and flexibility, as well as learning to process perceived failures and disappointments in more constructive ways. It involves adopting particular attitudes and cognitive strategies that were presented earlier in the book and using them to approach adversity more effectively. Finally, you will learn to prepare and "inoculate" yourself better against future challenges you will face. These include becoming resilient not only with respect to dealing with stress, but in every other aspect of life that requires flexibility and adaptability.

KEY QUESTIONS IN THE CHAPTER

- What is resilience?

- Why is resilience an important topic to study in stress management?

- Why are some people more capable of handling life's challenges and setbacks than others?

- Why do some people resort to drugs, alcohol, and excessive eating when they encounter stress while others exercise, watch their diet, and meditate? What's wrong with the statements, "It's not fair," "It's all my fault," and "This is terrible"?

- What is posttraumatic growth?

- What are protective factors?

- What is the hardiness theory?

- How is toughening related to resilience?

- What is learned optimism? How does it affect resilience?

- What is the effect of enhancing emotional intelligence on resilience?

- What is sense of coherence? How is it related to resilience?

- How can you improve resilience when confronted with stress?

- What is cognitive flexibility? How is it related to resilience?

The ability to perform at the highest levels, whether in acting, sports, public speaking, social situations, or the workplace, depends on far more than good luck, inborn abilities, or even stress management skills—it also results from personal qualities such as flexibility, resilience, and hardiness. Similarly, those who are most likely to recover from adverse situations are those who are prepared to respond in particular ways. There are even situations where people who are subjected to trauma, catastrophic illness, and other tragedies end up stronger afterwards as a result of how they processed the experience.

Resilience and Stress

Resilience is the ability to adapt well when confronted with adversity, trauma, and inordinate levels of stress in life. It represents the best in flexibility in that strengths and resources usually held in reserve may be tapped under circumstances requiring extraordinary effort or unusual challenges. Resilience can also be understood as the skills, attributes, and abilities that enable individuals to adapt to hardships, difficulties, and challenges (Alvord & Grados, 2005). It is what allows some people to choose positive attitudes when confronted with life difficulties, as well as to move beyond disappointments to make the best of situations (Childre & Rozman, 2005). It is also a concept that is confusing, complex, and ambiguous, because it is so difficult to pin down what qualifies as resilience as opposed to adaptability or even self-deception and denial (Kaplan, 2005). If someone tells you, for example, that a recent tragedy is "God's will," or "It'll work out for the best," or "This helped me grow," is this a positive, resilient attitude or representative of delusions? It could be either or both.

Although so much of our attention throughout this course has been centered on the negative aspects of stress and how it tears us apart physically, emotionally, socially, and spiritually, there are also positive benefits reported from those who experience "stress-related growth." As just one example that may surprise you, imagine the effects of having your leg or arm amputated. Surely nothing beneficial could possibly result from such a catastrophic loss? Yet it has been found that the majority of such individuals report that they gained something positive from this experience, some even finding that it helped them to reevaluate and reorient their lives towards increased growth and satisfaction (Oaksford, Frude, & Cuddihy, 2005). This is true resilience.

Although some attributes are biologically determined, resilience skills can be strengthened as well as learned. This means that your success in dealing with challenging situations in the future is determined by not only the stress management and prevention skills you have learned and practiced, but also your capacity to adapt to these situations with a certain equanimity and resourcefulness (Hawkley et al., 2005). This could include times when, initially, you may have felt crushed by disappointment, or faced debilitating personal challenges that resulted from health problems, financial hardship, death of a loved one, or interpersonal conflict. Somehow, perhaps even surprising yourself, you rose to the occasion and managed to make the best of a lousy situation. In some cases you might even have flourished, demonstrating that you learned from the experience and grew stronger.

Resilience resides in everyone, but some people can draw on their internal resources better than others, especially during the most vulnerable of times. This reserved power enables you to function at a reasonably high level, given the circumstances, and then return to a previous state of normalcy and stability. Recovery from stress is mostly a matter of self-determination; that is, the ability to stop ruminating about things outside your control and to take constructive, persistent action, even in the face of obstacles along the way (Beckmann & Kellmann, 2004).

Imagine, for example, that two students both received disappointing grades on a school assignment. One student decided to drop the class, convinced that he could never master the material; the other student treated the feedback as evidence that he needed to work that much harder in the future. This motivated him to work harder not only in that one class, but in other areas of his life as well.

VOICE OF STRESS MANAGEMENT 13.1

Nineteen-Year-Old Male College Freshman

Four years ago, I immigrated to the United States with my parents. Since English is not my native tongue, I had to spend extra time studying the language while catching up with my peer students in every other subject. What made the situation more challenging was that my parents constantly fought in bitter arguments. Several times, police had to be summoned to stop the fight. On Christmas two years ago, police had to take away my mom because she was throwing things and threatened my dad's life. Soon after that, they divorced. My mom went back to my native country and my dad stayed behind to take care of me.

I love my dad and think of him as my hero. He works hard to support me and I didn't let him down. During the last four years, I worked very hard. I never took a vacation during the summer and spent a lot of time studying. I took several high school Advanced Placement classes in computer science, mathematics, and biology and excelled in them in addition to winning several awards at international computer competitions. Not long ago, I was admitted into the University of California at Berkeley. My dream is to own my own computer firm when I finish my studies.

Resilience in Adulthood and Later Life

In Chapter 3, you learned that stress often accompanies the transitions from one stage of development to the next. In adulthood, people are confronted with many challenges that may include working through unresolved issues from childhood, negotiating love relationships and friendships, renegotiating relationships with parents and siblings, raising children, financial issues, health problems, career advancement, and unforeseen crises. Yet many individuals are able to maintain or even enhance their well-being as they deal with these various challenges of life (Ryff & Singer, 2003).

Recent research has suggested that positive changes may occur after life crises such as bereavement, illness, major accidents, chronic disability, and abuse. This response is often referred to as *posttraumatic growth* (Ryff & Singer, 2003; Tedeschi & Calhoun, 2004). Trauma, such as that experienced by victims of natural disasters, sometimes serves as a springboard for growth and development (Calhoun & Tedeschi, 2006; Peterson, Park, Pole, D'Andrea, & Seligman, 2008). There is even evidence that some veterans of battlefields report tremendous growth rather than trauma as a result of their life-threatening experiences (Feder et al., 2008). The following changes may occur:

- new perceptions of oneself (feeling stronger and more self-assured);

- gains in recognizing and appreciating one's own vulnerability;

- change in relationships with others (closer family ties and more appreciation of significant others in life);

- changed philosophy of life (taking things easier, greater spirituality).

Posttraumatic growth is a universal phenomenon that occurs across various cultures (Weiss & Berger, 2010), in different occupations (Shaw, Joseph, & Linley, 2005), and among people of different genders and personalities. In addition, life stress can provide a context from which you may develop enhanced coping skills, self-esteem, self-confidence, and self-knowledge (Aldwin & Sutton, 1998). Posttraumatic growth has been linked to spirituality and heightened mindfulness (Askay & Magyar-Russell, 2009; Chopko & Schwartz, 2009) that allow those in adversity to experience increased well-being. Even though posttraumatic growth is quite common, it does not happen to everybody and its manifestation is moderated by culture and individual factors. I will discuss certain factors that will promote posttraumatic growth later in this chapter.

For Reflection 13.1

Here are two different ways that a student might respond to receiving a disappointing grade on an assignment:

- *Defeatist attitude*: (1) "I can't believe I completely blew this assignment"; (2) "This is just about the worst thing that ever happened to me"; (3) "I'll never be able to do well in this stupid class"; (4) "This kind of thing always happens to me"; (5) "It's not fair, anyway, that the teacher made us study this stuff without warning us about what was going to be covered"; (6) "I might as well just give up"; (7) "This proves that I don't have what it takes to succeed".

- *Resilient attitude*: Well, this is unexpected and disappointing. I thought I'd prepared well for this assignment, but apparently I missed something significant. I wonder what that could be? I did poorly on this assignment but I have done well on others in situations similar to this. I wonder what this means. I could let this be discouraging but I'd prefer to figure out what I can learn from this to improve how I do on the next assignment. If anything, this really gets my attention so I'll prepare better, and differently, next time. I need to look at what some of my weak areas are so that I can strengthen them in the future, not only for assignments in this class, but other challenges I will face. In some ways, I'm grateful that now I have the opportunity to work on some things that will make me better prepared.

For Analysis

In the self-talk of the defeatist attitude, what manifestations of irrational thinking do you recognize? These represent evidence of distortion, exaggeration, overgeneralization, and awfulizing.

Note the following questions for consideration:

1. Did she really completely blow the whole assignment, that is, fail in every dimension?
2. Is this the worst thing that ever happened to her?
3. Where is the evidence that this one disappointing performance signals that improvement will never be possible?
4. By telling herself that she will "never improve," how does that contribute to a defeatist attitude?
5. What is the consequence of telling herself that things are not fair?
6. How is giving up a choice she is making rather than a circumstance she finds herself in?
7. How does her performance in this episode "prove" anything? All this does is provide feedback that can be employed in a number of ways that could result in discouragement—or renewed commitment to do better.

The first example demonstrates a defeatist attitude while the second one shows a high level of functional adaptability—making the best of a difficult situation. Using the cognitive restructuring methods introduced in Chapter 6, the second student chooses to think in more positive, self-enhancing ways about circumstances that are now over. She can't do much about what already happened, but rather than berating herself, she resiliently makes the best out of the circumstances, attempting to learn from what happened so that she can do better next time. Whether in academics, sports, the workplace, or the social arena, such a resilient approach to life allows you to treat disappointments and stressors as opportunities for growth. The key question that can be asked is, what can I learn from this that will help me do better next time?

In the context of stress management, we may say that resilience represents your ability to mobilize your resources in those circumstances when you need them the most. You are able to maintain a level of optimism and hope, even during those times when you may feel most tempted to give in to despair. You are able to let the past go while you honor what happened and try to find something meaningful and personally useful in the situation. Most importantly, rather than allow yourself to feel immobilized and dispirited, you draw on your internal strengths, as well as the support of loved ones, to move forward as much as possible.

There are certain times in life when stress is inevitable, when there is little you can do to prevent those situations that will test and challenge you. Almost no one is going to maintain a resting heart rate while being yelled at by a supervisor, rushing to meet a deadline, or performing in front of an audience. Yet the key question is what can be done to build resilience so that you can draw on internal strengths when you need them the most. How can you teach yourself even to thrive under pressure, like many world-class athletes and stage performers?

Factors Underlying Human Resilience

Why certain individuals are resilient in the face of stress is an important question. Resilience represents a person's ability to recover from some stressful life event and restore previous levels of functioning in such a way that there is some immunity against similar situations in the future. If, for instance, you feel rejected by someone you approach, a resilient response is one that would not only allow you to process the disappointment, but also permit you to face similar risks in the future without feeling incapacitated.

Substantial research has been conducted on responses to disaster and other stressors. In one large-scale review of over 300 completed studies, Miller and Segerstrom (2004) concluded that in some cases the immune system can actually be *strengthened* as a result of facing adversity. It is true that what does not kill you may make you stronger—depending on how the experience is processed.

Protective Factors

What are the factors that prevent certain people from developing maladaptive behaviors and enable them to thrive in defiance of their adverse circumstances? Researchers (Calhoun & Tedeschi, 2006; Garmezy, 1985; Rutter, 1987) have been looking for those variables that can buffer against, and moderate, the impact of stress and traumas in life.

Researchers have been interested in studying both children and adults to see who survives after being subjected to disadvantaged environments. One predictor is temperament: those who hold optimistic, positive attitudes are more likely to make the best of their situation. Those with pessimistic temperaments will lose hope, complain a lot, and feel helpless to do anything constructive. Often they will develop the most severe symptoms of posttraumatic stress (Nutt, 2006).

For Reflection 13.2

Before I supply you with a list of the most important variables that predict resilience among those who are facing life crises, what do *you* think they would be? What do you believe would lead some people to be most vulnerable and others to demonstrate resilience?

Base your hypotheses on your own experiences, as well as those you have observed in others who have either fallen apart or risen to the occasion.

A second universal feature that predicts greater resilience is a solid support system. If there is strong family cohesion, close friendships, emotionally stable parenting, and counsel and leadership from elders in the community, then adjustment to adversity proceeds more smoothly.

A third factor has to do with socioeconomic status, which is also associated with educational level. If you have financial resources and economic opportunities, it is a lot easier to deal with adversity. This is illustrated clearly in the reactions that victims of tsunamis, hurricanes, and earthquakes experienced: those without transportation, savings, and alternative housing options remained destitute while those who were upper middle class were able to more easily recover.

One other factor that seems to increase resilience and help people to recover quickly from stress is involvement in leisure activities that serve as positive diversions and "time-outs" from pressure (Iwasaki, Mactavish, & Mackay, 2005). If you have recreational interests or hobbies that occupy your time in pleasurable ways, this can act as a buffer against pressure.

The Hardy Personality

People behave differently in almost everything they do, most notably when they are under tremendous pressure. You may have noticed this phenomenon in the radically different ways that people respond to the same challenge. When faced with a natural disaster, for instance, some people slip into depression and give up; others rebuild with enthusiasm for the future. We have seen in earlier chapters how cognitive activity influences one's viewpoint, but according to hardiness theory, so too do certain personalities.

Kobasa, Maddi, and Kahn (1982) studied business executives and managers who had to deal with the threat of losing their jobs during a period of economic downsizing. They discovered that stressful events—the death of a spouse, a job transfer, or being passed over for promotion—didn't affect everyone in the same way. They singled out a group of people whom they called hardy personalities. These are people who could put themselves together and continue to perform at superior levels, regardless of the adversity they faced. The researchers concluded that what differentiated the hardy personalities from the overstressed executives was *three Cs: commitment, challenge,* and *control.* In other words, they responded by viewing their situations as challenges to be faced.

In the first C, *commitment,* hardy individuals feel a sense of devotion to a mission and underlying purpose in life. They feel less stress, in part, because they view setbacks as minor obstacles to be overcome on the journey toward some larger goal. This relates to the second C, *challenge,* as well. Hardy personalities fully expect to encounter difficulties along the path; when they are inevitably encountered, it feels like it is all part of the experience. Most things in life that are really worth doing involve dealing with challenges along the way. If you want to spend time in a pristine wilderness area, enjoying total solitude and nature at its best, often the only way to get there is to backpack long miles over a mountain pass. Hard work, but usually worth it.

The third C, *control,* refers not to controlling others but controlling oneself. This is similar to what Seligman (2002) talks about as "temperance" or self-discipline. It is what leads you to exercise every day and subject yourself to temporary discomfort for some greater benefit to your body and spirit. As described in Chapter 5, it is also what has been referred to as an *internal locus of control*: rather than feeling victimized by external circumstances, hardy people feel like they are in charge of their lives, and believe they have more control over what happens to them, if not how they choose to respond.

Those who are able to practice the three Cs feel a greater sense of control. They deal with stress better because they find ways to turn the situations to some advantage. The executives who experienced the most stress were those who believed that they were helpless in their circumstances. They thought they were victims of fate, bad luck, a lousy economy, God's will, a mean supervisor, or many other external factors that they could not possibly control. They "enjoyed" the excuse that it was not their fault, that someone else was to blame for their predicament, but they paid a high price for this external attribution of blame. It may feel good to blame your mother, poor genes, an economic downturn, unfair competition, bad weather, a traffic jam, or the dog eating your homework for whatever ails you, but blaming others only emphasizes that you are more helpless. This creates more stress in the long run.

Recent findings have revealed that hardiness enhances resiliency in a wide range of stressful circumstances (da Silva et al., 2014; Maddi, 2002), including the following life situations:

- nurses who regularly confront death and dying in hospice settings;

- business travelers who experience culture shock in their work overseas;

- immigrants who arrive in the United States.

FOR REFLECTION 13.3

Think of a time recently when things did not work out as you had hoped. You may have gotten a poor grade on an assignment, or felt rejected by a friend, or lost out on an opportunity that is important to you. Briefly describe the situation below.

Recall your immediate explanation for this predicament. Write down what reasons and excuses you supplied to account for this disappointment. List, in particular, those explanations that represent externalized blame, that is, someone or something else's fault for what happened. As you do this, note how much you felt like a victim of circumstances beyond your control.

Based on what you now understand about the power implicit in an internalized locus of control, wherein you take responsibility for the outcome and your role in what happened, describe the situation differently whereby you "own" aspects of your behavior that might have contributed to the negative outcome.

Hardiness enhances resiliency in response to the ongoing demands and pressures of everyday life. For example, a firefighter observes how some of his peers spend all their free time between emergencies "griping about every little thing" and how much stress they feel on the job. Yet he takes a different, far more resilient position: "Stress is like electricity. It's a powerful force that only wants to get something accomplished and be on its way. You can either let the force bounce around inside you, tearing you up as it looks for an outlet, or you can try to complete the circuit and get some things done before the charge goes to ground and leaves you in peace" (Unger, 2010). This firefighter has chosen an attitude that helps him feel more in control.

The Toughening Factor

If you've ever heard a coach tell her players that facing tortuous conditioning exercises will toughen them up for competition, then you've had a taste of the toughening factor, which proposes controlled levels of incremental stress as a means to improve capacity for dealing with life's challenges (Dienstbier, 1989, 1991). This is a model where practice dealing with anticipated obstacles can better prepare you for high-level performance. This applies not only to athletic contests but also mental ones. Most of the test preparation courses for admission to schools are based on the idea of simulating the test conditions as much as possible. Whether training pilots, army personnel, soccer players, debaters, or chess players, instructors subject apprentices to incrementally more difficult situations.

Sometimes one of the most difficult aspects of parenting, teaching, or coaching is allowing people to make their own mistakes so they can learn from the experience. According to toughening theory, this helps to immunize against future stressors.

This theory is a departure from the traditional stress theory that suggests that heightened physiological arousal is a sign of distress and may lead to psychosomatic diseases. Based on earlier research and his own work, Richard Dienstbier developed a theory of toughness. The essence of the concept is that controlled levels of physical or mental stress promote a physical toughening characterized by an increased arousal capability, which, in turn, will lead to more positive appraisals of the stressor and thereby more effective coping mechanisms. Simply put, conditioning pays off in the end.

Research evidence indicates that children and animals growing up under stimulating and enriched environments (availability of physical activity and intellectual pursuits) are more capable of dealing with adult challenges. Toughening experiences are important because they alter neurohormonal processes that underlie successful coping behavior. Individuals exposed to controlled stimulation experience lower overall base rates of autonomic nervous system activity than those who are not exposed. The former are relaxed and will not be caught off guard when given unexpected situations in life in comparison to those who have never been toughened. Compared to unexposed individuals, toughened individuals react to novel stressors with a more rapid onset of neurohormonal processes that sharpen focus of attention and increase self-awareness necessary for successful coping. At the same time, toughened individuals experience delayed onset of neurohormonal processes that tend to decrease performance and bring about negative effects to the body. After the stressor stops, it takes less time for the toughened individuals to return to baseline levels than the non-toughened people.

Applied to the perspective of parenting or teaching, it is best *not* to overprotect children from any and every stressor they will face but to allow them to handle reasonably controlled situations in such a way that they can improve their abilities over time. This is the rationale behind most effective instructional coaching that occurs in schools: children are exposed to increasingly more difficult challenges that prepare them for the future.

The key evidence that supports the toughness factor is the finding that toughened and non-toughened individuals differ in how they appraise the stressor in two phases (Dienstbier, 1989; Thomas, Adler, Whittels, Enne, & Johannes, 2004). During the initial appraisal phase, both types of person may conclude that the event is stressful. However, those who have become toughened are able to access increased energy and resources that allow them to reevaluate the situation during the second (reassessment) phase. Whereas initially they may have seen the situation as a potential threat, once they realize that it is within their potential capability they recast the assessment as a challenge. This enhances their mental coping resources, as well as physiological reactions.

The toughening theory suggests that physiological toughness underlies mental toughness. It implies that our physiology is adaptable under controlled levels of external stress. Without experiencing external stress, individuals will pay a price of suffering more from more paralyzing stressors. Like an inoculation against mumps or hepatitis B, we need to get exposed to reasonable levels of challenges throughout our entire life.

Learned Optimism

Earlier in his career, before formalizing the positive psychology movement, Seligman (1991) was known for his theories of learned helplessness and learned optimism. These are two sides of the same issue that basically say that people feel helpless or empowered, depending on the point of view they have learned to apply in stressful situations.

Using *three Ps—permanence*, *pervasiveness*, and *personalization*—as criteria, Seligman differentiates between optimists and pessimists in terms of attributional style. Based on this theory, when a setback occurs, there are three basic differences in the reactions of optimists and pessimists. The first difference, permanence, is that the optimist sees a setback as temporary, while the pessimist sees it as permanent. The optimist sees an unfortunate event, such as the breakup of a relationship, as a temporary event, something that is limited in time and that has no real impact on the future. The pessimist sees this event as permanent, as part of life and destiny.

The second difference, pervasiveness, between the optimist and the pessimist is that the optimist sees difficulties as specific, while the pessimist sees them as pervasive. This means that when things go wrong for the optimist, he looks at the event as an isolated incident largely disconnected from other things that are going on in his life, while the pessimist sees it as part of a pattern.

The third difference between optimists and pessimists, personalization, is that optimists see events as external while pessimists interpret them as far more personal. When things go wrong, the optimist will tend to see the setback as resulting from many factors, some of which are not within one's control. If the optimist is cut off in traffic, for example, instead of getting angry or upset he will simply downgrade the importance of the event by saying something like, "Oh, well, I guess that person is just having a bad day." The pessimist, on the other hand, has a tendency to take everything personally and react as if he was subjected to a personal assault.

The optimistic personality hardly buries his or her head in the sand, pretending that everything is glorious in the face of progressive deterioration. In fact such an individual is far more relaxed, aware, and capable of interpreting events more realistically and less emotionally than is someone who is consistently pessimistic. As a result, this person exerts a far greater sense of control and influence over his environment, and is far less likely to be angry, upset, or distracted. In some studies it has even been discovered that those with a more optimistic disposition, as opposed to those who worry incessantly, tend to live longer (Vaillant, 2002).

FOR REFLECTION 13.4

Have you ever wondered why some people on the road become so enraged and out of control if another car cuts in front of them or gets too close to their rear bumper? I am not talking about deliberate acts of aggression, but rather the usual situation where you might have unknowingly gotten too close to another car. Before you know it, the person in the other car is honking at you, showing you a middle finger, and screaming so loud that you can see the cords in his neck standing out. If you're not careful, you can easily get sucked into the vortex of anger and respond in kind.

What you are seeing is evidence of the pessimistic, personalized style within Seligman's model. The person is likely saying something to himself or his passengers along the lines of, "How dare that sonofabitch do this to me! I've taken enough crap from people today, and by God, I won't allow you to treat me this way!"

The next time you catch yourself reacting in an extreme or exaggerated way in response to a minor annoyance of daily life, ask yourself to what extent you are over-personalizing the situation.

Emotional Resilience

The concept of emotional intelligence broadened the notion that IQ is something measured by tests. Gardner (1983) proposed a **theory of multiple intelligences**, each of which capitalized on different strengths. Later he developed a similar theory of multiple forms of creativity (Gardner, 1993) such as those manifested in different ways by geniuses such as Sigmund Freud (scholastic), Albert Einstein (logical), Pablo Picasso (spatial), Igor Stravinsky (musical), T. S. Eliot (linguistic), Martha Graham (bodily), and Mahatma Gandhi (political).

Based on questionnaires, interviews, and studies of historical figures, Gardner discovered that most people are specialists in areas in which they excel. Freud was brilliant as a writer and scientist but clueless in the areas of spatial or musical creativity. Martha Graham, the innovative dancer and choreographer, could do wonders with her body but struggled mightily with anything that involved logical–mathematical reasoning. Albert Einstein was the exact opposite—he could manipulate numbers with complete fluency but had little control over his body or personal domain.

Another form of intelligence, related to one's thoughts and feelings, was added to the list by Peter Salovey and John Mayer (1990) and later popularized by Daniel Goleman (1995). Proponents of the emotional intelligence theory argue that traditional measures of intelligence, as measured by the Stanford Binet and Wechsler Scales, and other IQ tests, are far too narrow and restrictive, failing to value more people-oriented abilities. You probably know people who are considered quite brilliant but who can't manage a coherent conversation. They may have academic intelligence but very little in the way of social and emotional intelligence or "street smarts."

Emotional intelligence (EI) is constructed of several domains that have been generalized to a wide variety of contexts (Ciarrochi, 2005; Matthews, Zeidner, & Roberts, 2006). These include the following:

1. *Self-awareness*: the ability to identify and recognize your emotions as they are occurring. This also includes being aware of the relationship between thoughts, feelings, and actions.

2. *Expressing feelings*: this includes the skills of accurately and effectively communicating feelings in ways they are likely to be heard and understood.

3. *Reading others*: empathy involves the ability to walk in other people's shoes and know what they must be feeling. This allows you to look at things from multiple perspectives, and to feel compassion for others who might operate from different perspectives.

4. *Motivating action*: it is not enough to become aware of feelings in yourself or others; you must be willing to respond appropriately based on this knowledge.

5. *Managing relationships*: this involves responding effectively to feelings when they arise and resolving interpersonal conflicts.

Individuals who possess a high degree of EI tend to be effective in leadership positions. They are often sensitive and charismatic people who are able to perceive and express emotions accurately and adaptively. They have the ability to understand emotions in themselves and others, using this knowledge to facilitate healthy relationships. Furthermore, they are able to manage emotions in such a way that they enhance communication without getting out of control (Salovey & Pizarro, 2003). Research evidence indicates that people scoring high in one or more of these measurable abilities produce more desirable results at work and play. They are less likely to abuse drugs and alcohol, they earn better grades in school, and function more effectively within the interpersonal world. They show greater resilience and flexibility and are less inclined to experience disruptive stress.

Sense of Coherence

The conceptualization of Aaron Antonovsky (1979, 1987) about individuals' recovery from adversity known as "sense of coherence" is probably the most unifying explanation for the power of resilience. The sense of coherence concept emerged as a derivative from Antonovsky's idea about the human potential for health and well-being. It is composed of three elements: (1) comprehensibility (ability to grasp cognitively constantly changing life events and predict their future course), (2) meaningfulness (life makes sense emotionally, problems are seen as challenges rather than burdens), and (3) manageability (ability to take advantage of available resources to handle life events).

According to Antonovsky (1979), an individual's sense of coherence strength is determined by their level of general resistant resources. These resources include physical (e.g. strong immune system and genetic make-up), artefactual (e.g., money, clothing, food, power), cognitive (e.g. intelligence, education, adaptive strategies for coping), emotional (e.g., emotional intelligence), social (e.g., support from friends and/or family), and/or macrosocial (e.g., culture and shared belief systems). The sense of coherence concept has led to the publication of more than 500 studies and serves as an explanation for why some people stay well despite stressful situations (Eriksson & Lindstrom, 2005, 2006). A key factor in the sense of coherence concept is that individuals' ability to bounce back from stressful events is related to how they interpret the event (see Chapter 6). How you interpret a particular life event is more important than the event itself. People who develop interpretative patterns of coping and attempt to modify the present situation positively may find it easier to overcome psychological traumas. On the other hand, pessimistic patterns of thinking such as self-pity, abandonment, self-victimization, and self-depreciation may intensify the negative emotions related to a traumatic memory and exacerbate psychological suffering (Peres et al., 2005). Research has also indicated that individuals' sense of coherence strength promotes effective coping with stressors in the rehabilitation/recovery process (Feigin & Sapir, 2005), moderates the effects of traumatic experiences (van der Hal-van Raalte, 2009), improves the quality of life for family members of the mentally ill (Suresky, Zauszniewski, & Bekhet, 2008), and reduces occupational stress (Kinman, 2008).

Abraham Lincoln's road to the White House: Failed in business 1831. Defeated for Legislature in 1832. Second failure in business in 1833. Suffered nervous breakdown in 1836. Defeated for Speaker in 1838. Defeated for Elector in 1840. Defeated for Congress in 1843. Defeated for Congress in 1848. Defeated for Senate in 1855. Defeated for Vice President in 1856. Defeated for Senate in 1858. Elected President in 1860.

Strategies for Developing Resilience

Resilience and its accompanying traits of hardiness, toughness, and emotional intelligence are essential for dealing with stressful situations effectively. Unless you are

FOR REFLECTION 13.5

Think of a time when you were working with single-minded determination toward an important goal. This could have been in a sporting event, at work, or in school. It is likely that you suffered some roadblocks and setbacks along the way. What did you do to overcome your discouragement? Share your favored strategies with classmates.

flexible enough to deal with challenges, rebound from setbacks, and recover from inevitable failures, there is little chance of improving personal effectiveness, much less ever reaching a higher potential. It also helps to have some diversions in your life that can provide "time-outs" from the stress associated with modern life (Iwasaki, Mactavish, & Mackay, 2005).

Learning from Failures

Although most people try to avoid failure at all cost—who in their right mind would *choose* to fail at something?—making mistakes and experiencing setbacks actually produce learning, resilience, and growth that would not be possible any other way. While studying how psychotherapists deal with disappointments and setbacks with their clients, it was found that such experiences were potentially among the most useful critical incidents in a professional's career (Kottler & Blau, 1989; Kottler & Carlson, 2003). This is true for people in any line of work. There are several benefits that can accrue to those who are open to such experiences.

FAILURE PROMOTES REFLECTION   You spend more time thinking about things that don't work out than those that went well. Under the best circumstances, negative outcomes represent feedback to you that something you tried did not work the way you hoped. This is valuable information, if you reflect on what happened and what you might do differently next time.

FAILURE STIMULATES CHANGE   When things don't work out the way you expected, a posture of resilience would lead you to change the way you operate in some significant way. If, for instance, you studied for an exam using a particular method, and scored lower than expected, you would not do the same thing next time but would adopt another strategy that might work better for you. Failure teaches you to be more flexible and resourceful.

FAILURE INCREASES RESOLVE   Unless you allow disappointments to be discouraging, you can use them to motivate you to work harder next time. If you examine the lives of famous historical figures, inevitably you will discover that their eventual accomplishments were preceded by consistent failures. Abraham Lincoln failed in several attempts to seek political office.

FOR REFLECTION 13.6

Consider a time when you experienced an extremely stressful setback. You felt like a failure or made a painful mistake. Write out below what you learned from that experience that helped you thereafter.

In small groups, share your story of what happened and what you learned from it. Save a few minutes at the end of your conversation to look for common themes that emerged in your stories.

FAILURE TEACHES HUMILITY   Failure is an experience that forces you to consider your own limits. No matter how hard you try, no matter how much you prepare and practice, you are still going to fail some of the time at whatever you do. Peak performance, not to mention life satisfaction, directly results from two paradoxical factors. The first is to have high expectations for yourself that lead you to reach for goals that may, at first, seem out of reach. The second is to forgive yourself if, and when, you fall short.

Processing Failures Effectively

One way to redefine failure is that your performance does not match your expectations. There are two basic ways to alter this equation. First is to improve your behavior, which is not often feasible. Second is to change your expectations. I don't mean that you must necessarily lower them, but that you alter them to be more realistic in matching your current abilities and resources with the demands of the situation.

There are a number of other questions you might ask yourself in order to process experiences that feel like failures to you.

- *What are the signs that what you are doing isn't working?* Take inventory of strategies that are not producing the results you hope for. Stop doing those things and try something else instead.

- *What "payoffs" are being celebrated as a result of the failure?* In earlier chapters you learned about the "secondary gains" that people enjoy as a result of messing up. For instance, it is a way to get others to do the work, have an excuse for being lazy, control and manipulate others, lower expectations for your behavior in the future, or sabotage things on your own terms.

- *Has the problem been defined in such a way that it cannot be resolved?* Failure is as much a label as a set of circumstances. Losing three pounds in a week can be termed a failure if you unrealistically set your sights on losing five.

- *Where was the turning point when things started slipping downward?* Constant monitoring of how things are going allows you to make a determination as to what went wrong, and what you can do to reverse the slide.

- *What can you learn from this to help you grow?* Failure provides you with an opportunity to assess your weaknesses for purposes of improving your functioning in the future.

Dealing with failure is one kind of resilience, a response to stress and adversity that provides valuable feedback for future encounters with similar situations. There are several other strategies for increasing resilience to review. Each of these can help you become more flexible in the ways you respond to challenges you face.

Practice the Principle of Giving Up and Letting Go

At birth, an infant will grasp an object involuntarily once it is inserted into its palm. It takes another 13 months to let it go voluntarily. Holding on to something steady will bring stability, but holding on to something treacherous and shaky brings danger. An airplane dumps extra fuel in case of an accident or emergency. A stressed-out person needs to let go of an unachievable goal or unrealistic plan.

One way that resilience is developed is by lightening your load. It is hard to be flexible, fluid, and adaptable when you are so weighed down with responsibilities and commitments that options seem few. Giving up has its role in the process of developing resilience. Without giving up plans that didn't work, new plans can't be implemented. Without letting go of outdated ideas, you will not have the time or energy to generate new ones.

When Andrew was queried as to why he was having difficulty completing many of the tasks that he had begun, he could do nothing but shrug. In truth, he was as puzzled as any of his family, friends, and coworkers as to why he was having so much trouble staying on top of things. He was generally a highly responsible person, prone to following through on his commitments. But now, for reasons he didn't understand, he found himself constantly rushing around trying to stay on top of things. Moreover, the harder he tried to catch up, the further behind he seemed to be falling.

Andrew decided to take inventory of his daily life and write down all the commitments he had made during the preceding month. This is a sample of what his list looked like:

1. Search for a more affordable apartment closer to his family.

2. Complete a research paper for one of his classes.

3. Help his younger sister build bookshelves for her room.

4. Put in extra hours of overtime each week to save money for a new car.

5. Make selections for his fantasy baseball team.

6. Learn new software to manage the overflowing inbox in his email account.

7. Study for an upcoming exam.

8. Practice karate forms for taekwondo.

9. Spend time with his grandmother to help her around the house.

You can see that Andrew is literally all over the place, running from one thing to another, without much consideration for each task's relative importance in his life. Once he saw the unrealistic number of simultaneous tasks he was trying to complete, he realized the absurdity of his situation: no wonder he was so stressed! Any former reserves of energy were sucked up by the endless treadmill that was his life. He wanted to do all these things but he realized that it was not possible. His solution: to cut loose a few things that were less of a priority. He also needed to start saying no to future demands on his time until he could catch up.

Let Go of the Material World

We can be controlled and enslaved by things to which we are attached. Nowhere is this more the case than with the material world. You may covet certain things—a nice car, a home, a leather jacket, a plane ticket, a watch, a pair of shoes. It would be wonderful to have all of the things you want, but it is not going to happen. Over time, things start to own you, rather than the other way around. In fact, one of the greatest sources of stress in people's lives, throughout their lifetime, is managing their flow of money: most people spend more than they have. For the first time since the Great Depression when statistics started being compiled, Americans have their lowest savings rate in history, spending 1% more income than they have available. Moreover, the average amount of debt that households owe on their credit cards is over $9,000 (Lazarus, 2005).

You have heard the saying that "money doesn't buy happiness." Unfortunately, few people actually believe this, or if they do, hardly anyone acts on this realization. People buy lottery tickets hoping for that one shot at wealth that they believe will bring them eternal happiness. Others work 50, 60, or 80 hours per week, hoping to earn enough money to buy the things they want. Then they work even longer hours trying to pay for them.

No matter what your income level, whatever money you have isn't quite enough. Even those people who are obscenely rich—millionaires and billionaires—are not significantly happier than the average person. Similarly, students in Calcutta, India, living in abject poverty, are no less satisfied with their lives than you are. In his book on what makes people happy, Seligman (2002) cites research that shows that, regardless of how much money one makes, people who value material things tend to be much less happy than those who value other things such as relationships and creativity. But it seems like no matter how much people hear this or believe it, it doesn't seem to change anyone's behavior.

I am not implying that it isn't fun to have discretionary income to buy the things that you want. But those who become inordinately attached to things end up condemning themselves to a life of dissatisfaction: what they have, whatever they own, will never be enough. They will actually have fewer degrees of freedom in the choices they make, and the ways they respond to situations, because of reluctance and fears of losing what they already have.

Letting go of attachments does not mean giving up the things in life you enjoy most. Rather, it means examining your degree of commitment to owning things that may or may not improve the quality of your life. Often just a few weeks, or months, after you finally manage to obtain the prized object that you want so much, it loses its luster and has use only in its functional value in keeping you warm, telling the time, or transporting you from place to place.

FOR REFLECTION 13.7

Think of a time in your childhood when you coveted a particular possession with complete devotion. You thought you absolutely had to have this thing or life wouldn't be worth living. This could have been a particular toy, an article of clothing, a bike, or something else that you wanted so badly you actually dreamed about it. You begged your parents to buy it for you. You prayed to God, or Santa Claus, that it would finally become yours.

Remember, now, how it felt to finally get this treasured thing. Recall how excited you were, how it felt like the happiest day of your life.

How long did the effects last? How long did it take before that prized thing became just another of the many things that you owned? Ultimately, how much did having this thing change your life?

Consider that the things you covet now are considerably more expensive than that those you wanted when you were a kid. Think about what it is in your life right now that you want the most. Think about the ways you plot and plan to get this thing once you manage to secure the funds.

What do you think will be different once you finally own this thing, compared with when you were a child?

Let Go of the Past

Another of the detriments to resilience, and sources of stress in people's lives, is dwelling on the past, especially over things that can't be changed.

In many ways, you allow the past to rule your life in the present. So many of the attitudes, scripts, and beliefs that you carry around within you were shaped by past experiences. There are hundreds of voices within you, hiding in the deeper recesses of your mind, telling you what is possible, what you are allowed to do, and what is beyond your reach.

- "You're shy."

- "You know you don't have the patience for that."

- "You've never been good at math."

- "That's wrong. You're not supposed to be thinking about that."

- "That person will never go out with you."

- "You deserve what happened to you. It's all your fault."

- "You're ugly."

- "You're stupid."

- "You made a mistake and now you have to pay for it."
- "You know you can't do that."

Many of those voices from the past, instilled in you by parents, teachers, friends, and previous failures, limit your ability to respond effectively to situations in the present. Resilience is compromised when the choices available to you seem limited.

In order to let go of past experiences and self-defeating voices that restrict your ability to act in optimal ways, you first have to become aware of the extent to which they are operating inside you. If you aren't aware that you actually have other alternatives, then you won't know you could behave any other way.

People sometimes spend years in therapy trying to overcome the past. They become aware of how previous events currently rule their lives, looking at their families and how certain behavioral patterns became established early in life. They identify early traumas that may have become repressed, or pushed out of conscious awareness as a defense against further stress. Most of all, they look at self-defeating ways they are behaving in the present and identify how these represent recurrent themes from the past.

It isn't necessary to spend years or even months in therapy in order to free yourself of the past (though it often helps). It does help if you begin looking at the characteristic ways you respond to situations in your life and try to determine exactly how these patterns got established.

In order to pull yourself out of a difficult situation, it is important to first figure out what you are already doing that is not working, *and then to stop doing that*. It may not be altogether clear what will fix the problem, or resolve the difficulty, but it is fairly certain what will *not* work. You must free yourself from the past in order to capitalize on maximum options in the present and future.

Let Go of Dysfunctional Beliefs

In a peaceful and murmuring stream, a rock stands in the middle with water gently passing around it. Water is the softest thing in the world, but also the most powerful. Water would never fight with an obstructing rock, or any other obstacle for that matter. It just yields and goes around it, eventually wearing it down and pulverizing it into sand. Novelist Tom Robbins once claimed that water invented humans as a way to transport itself from one place to another.

Human beings become indignant, furious, enraged, and jittery whenever things happen in a way that is different from what they anticipate or expect. Letting go of dysfunctional beliefs is not unlike surrendering obsessions with owning things; it means really looking at the impact of your choices.

In previous chapters I have talked about some of the dysfunctional beliefs and irrational interpretations that tend to increase stress levels and reduce resilience. To review, some of them are as follows:

1. If I don't get what I want I will be miserable.
2. People should believe what I do, and act the ways I would, and when they don't there is something wrong with them.
3. I really can control other people's behavior and make them act as I prefer.
4. I can predict the future and control future events by worrying about them ahead of time.
5. If I try hard enough, and avoid taking risks, I can protect myself from being hurt.
6. It is terrible when things don't go my way.
7. It's not fair that I didn't get what I deserve.

FOR PRACTICE 13.1

Challenge Dysfunctional Beliefs

In the list of internal statements just listed, there is compelling evidence that each belief represents an exaggeration, distortion, or misinterpretation of reality. Earlier in the book, you learned ways to counteract such dysfunctional beliefs by substituting alternative, more clear-headed statements that accurately reflect reality. For each of the statements, substitute what you could say to yourself instead that would likely produce a more resilient, positive frame of mind.

1.

2.

3.

4.

5.

6.

7.

Sample answers are at the end of the chapter.

We gain lightness of heart and peace of mind whenever we decide to let go of our attachment to how others should treat us, or think of us. In fact, more people pay attention to what they are going to eat for lunch than what they plan to do for their life. Many people fail to take initiatives to realize their dreams because they are afraid of what others may think of them. Some people never ask someone they love out for a date because they are afraid of the potential rejection. A dysfunctional belief can be as harmful as a real rock standing in the middle of the road leading to our destiny. We must let go of the thought that people have to approve of actions before we can act.

Boost Your Hardy Perception of Life

As you have learned throughout this book, stress is *not* a response to what happens to you; rather it is your interpretation of what has happened to you. Depending on how you choose to view the situation, and how you decide to think about the matter, you will feel varying degrees of stress and other accompanying emotional reactions. While I am not advocating that you should ever delude yourself, or minimize the impact of an event, I am suggesting that you can take a more optimistic perspective if you so choose.

This perception of the world must be based on a collection of sound principles, which can be called a *hardy perception of life*. First, you must accept the reality that life will never be free from stressors as long as you live. You will repeatedly encounter all kinds of problems and challenges, many of which will test you in unforeseen ways. Depending on how you respond to these situations, you can become toughened by them, developing the sort of resilience that allows you to not only bounce back, but grow beyond where you were.

Second, you must accept that change is inevitable. The pace of life will be faster and probably more unpredictable in the future. Instead of fighting against change, you can deal with life's problems more effectively when you expect to deal with such adjustments in the future. This involves preparing for the possible consequences of your actions, including planning for various scenarios you might face, and rehearsing backup plans for things that might develop in unforeseen ways.

Third, you should try to keep things in perspective. There is good and bad in everything you experience. Resilience means recognizing that even in the middle of painful events, there is awareness that growth and learning are taking place. There is also the realization that no matter how difficult and trying the challenge, it too shall pass.

Embrace Paradoxical Traits

To develop resilience, flexibility, and adaptability requires that you be willing to incorporate seemingly contradictory qualities and concepts into strategies for coping with stress (Pearsall, 2003). Just as you have agonist and antagonist muscles in your body, you possess mental traits that seem to oppose each other, but in reality facilitate one other. For instance, it is common and healthy to be serious and playful, trusting and cautious, liberal and conservative. A person can be rigid in sticking to his core values but flexible in dealing with the nitty-gritty details of the process of life. A resilient person realizes that the fastest way to reach a goal is take a slow approach with insurance and certainty. A resilient person appreciates the growth and lessons in hardships and failures, the lesson of "no pain, no gain." A resilient person feels blessed by the harsh criticisms of her enemies and often cautions herself when showered with praise. The following paradoxes have specific implications for building resilience:

1. *The process of building resilience is often a long process.* The pathway to resilience is paved with bumps, regressions, and dead ends. The only way to succeed is to have the determination to hang tough when things become difficult. The hope of gaining quick-fix resilience is mere illusion.

2. *Resilient people come in many shapes and sizes.* Some resilient people are gregarious and assertive, while others are not.

3. *Building resilience does not require that you be adaptable to every circumstance and challenge you face.* There are times when everyone feels lost, confused, and insecure. Recognize that no matter how hard you try, or how much you prepare, you are still going to encounter situations when you feel in way over your head. This is inevitable and part of being alive.

4. *The process of building resilience is invisible.* It is an inner battle that happens during times and places where no one pays attention. It does not always receive recognition and become glorified. Unlike winning an athletic competition followed by trophies and prizes, resilience represents subtle, incremental growth.

At the time things are happening, it is difficult to determine their long-term effects. Sometimes what seems like a disaster can turn out to have been a gift in that it stimulated growth in new directions. Likewise, what may appear to have been good fortune may eventually turn out to have been the beginning of misery. This has certainly been the case with lottery prize winners, many of whom ended up with ruined lives after collecting their millions of dollars (Seligman, 2002).

According to a Chinese folktale, there once lived a wise old man who lost his horse when it ran away. When people came to comfort him for his loss, the old man shrugged and told them it might not be a bad thing. Sure enough, his horse returned a few days later, accompanied by a beautiful white mare. Friends and neighbors came by to rejoice in his good fortune, but the old man only shook his head, and said, "This may not be a good thing."

A few days later, the old man's son was riding the mare and was thrown from the horse, breaking his leg. Again, the old man refrained from judgment as to whether this mishap was necessarily a bad thing. This proved to be prudent when his son's injury prevented him from going to war, perhaps saving his life.

Like many Chinese parables, this one's message is subtle yet also clear: what may appear to be bad could turn out to be good fortune, and what may seem fortunate can turn out to be your undoing. The paradoxical thinking embedded in this Chinese folktale represents a type of **cognitive flexibility** which can be defined as the mental ability to switch between thinking about different concepts and view the same situation from multiple perspectives simultaneously (see Ritter et al., 2012). For instance, you may recall in Chapter 5 that how an individual explains things is associated with stress reactions, also known as explanatory style. David Fresco and associates have demonstrated in their studies that college students tended to be more resilient to stressful events if they possessed more flexibility in explaining what happened to them (Fresco, Rytwinski, & Craighead, 2007).

Develop Higher Levels of Emotional Intelligence

As mentioned earlier, emotional intelligence consists of several abilities: perceiving emotions in oneself and others, using emotions to facilitate thought, understanding emotions, and managing emotions. Satisfaction in life, not to mention relatively low stress and high productivity, is correlated with intrapersonal and interpersonal effectiveness. This means your skills in dealing with your own emotions, as well as those of others.

1. *Develop empathy for others.* Your ability to perceive emotions in yourself and others permits you to interact effectively in a social setting. Practice imagining what it is like to be someone else, especially someone with whom you feel little connection.

2. *Cultivate healthy self-esteem.* People with higher self-regard (realistic confidence) are more willing to accept themselves as they are, not as they wish to be; at the same time, they are also willing to accept others. Adolescents with high self-esteem cope with stress by using strategies that focus on solving problems, whereas adolescents with low self-esteem cope with stress using emotion-based passive strategies (Dumont & Provost, 1999). Self-esteem can be improved when you learn to manage stress, become better organized, and achieve self-set goals on a daily basis.

3. *Learn the skills of communicating clearly, openly, diplomatically, and assertively.* A high level of emotional intelligence is characterized by your ability to express feelings honestly. You will build your resilience when you can experience and express anger, love, dislike, appreciation, and sadness openly and honestly, yet are capable of suppressing these feelings when circumstances don't allow (emotional management).

4. *Take advantage of positive emotions for promoting health and cognitive processes.* Positive emotions such as love and gratitude build resilience and enhance your well-being (McCraty & Children, 2004). By identifying positive emotions and knowing their functions, you can more effectively tap their power for promoting health and well-being.

5. *Recognize positive attributes that are part of who you are.* Dyer (2001) suggests that when we concentrate on the negative thoughts and emotions, negativity will expand. However, when we dwell on positive thoughts and emotions, they will also expand.

6. *Learn the skills of giving and receiving compliments.* Sincere compliments will raise the self-esteem of the giver and the recipient while insincere compliments will backfire.

7. *Develop knowledge of the patterns, stages, triggers, and traps of anger.* Realize how anger escalates and can hurt yourself and others.

8. *Develop responsibility for your own actions and accept their consequences.* Before you take any action, ask yourself what will be its potential consequences. The clearer you are about the future consequence of your action, the more judicious your decisions will be and the better the consequences will be in the future.

Strengthen the Biological Factor of Resilience

Resilience is linked to strong physiological composition. Often we overemphasize the importance of the psychological aspects of resilience and ignore the daily maintenance of the body, like physical exercise, sufficient sleep, a healthy sex life, and a balanced diet. We often hear the cliché that a chain breaks at its weakest link. Prolonged distress can result from one of the weakest physiological factors. That is why keeping your body in peak physical condition is so important for preparing you to deal with any challenges you might face. Deuster and Silverman (2013) examined the accumulated evidence over the years and concluded that physical fitness serves as a pathway to resilience and "physical fitness blunts stress reactivity, confers physiologic and psychological benefits, serves as a buffer against stress, and can protect against stress-related disorders and chronic illness" (p. 5).

Flach (1988) observed in his book on resilience that people with overactive or underactive thyroid function usually have difficulty managing stress successfully until the physical condition is diagnosed and corrected. He also cited a case where a patient,

Table 13.1 Physiological basis of impaired resilience

Physiological condition		Possible links to impaired resilience
1.	Insomnia or lack of sleep	Irritability, anxiety, impatience
2.	Endocrine gland disorders	Mental depressions and unrelenting fatigue
3.	Heart rhythm disturbance	Neurosis like symptoms, anxiety, vomiting
4.	Brain tumor	Mental depression symptoms
5.	Allergy to food	Dizziness, anxiety, and depression
6.	Gastroesophageal reflux disease (GERD) and gastritis	Anxiety and depression
7.	Poor visual perception systems	Psychiatric diagnoses from bipolar affective disorder to schizophrenia
8.	Viral diseases such as hepatitis	Depression-like symptoms
9.	Use of oral contraceptives	Migraine headaches and depression
10.	Nutritional deficiencies	A variety of psychological problems ranging from unrelenting fatigue to anxiety to depression
11.	Blood disorders	Depression

who had been in psychiatric treatment for a decade, was a given a second chance of life when the real cause of her mental problems was identified: poor visual perception. An early collapse of her visual perceptual systems contributed to her prolonged stress and later psychiatric conditions.

There are many other physiological factors that impact resilience, either positively or negatively (see Table 13.1). Together, these conditions present a compelling motive for doing all you can to increase resilience not only by working inside your mind, but also by working to get your body in optimal shape.

S U M M A R Y

In this chapter on resilience, you have learned about the ways that people can not only manage stress in their lives, but thrive as a result of their exposure to challenges. Resilience represents a kind of adaptability that allows one to recover from adversity, and in some circumstances, to even go beyond previous functioning levels. Viewed from this perspective, stress can be seen as much as an impetus for growth as an assault on your peace of mind.

FIGURE 11.1 The *wei ji* character.

Like many Chinese characters, *wei ji* has several meanings, depending on context (Figure 13.1). It means risk or danger or crisis, but also opportunity. The Chinese treat any situation, including a stressful one, as potentially dangerous—or a blessing. Much depends on your attitude, and your ability to respond to the challenge with maximum resilience and resources at your disposal. Highly resilient individuals are able to learn from mistakes, failures, disappointments, and even trauma and tragedy, and develop new abilities and confidence for the future.

The positive psychology movement has been instrumental in directing research and theory building toward a strength-based model that focuses on what is going right in our lives instead of what is going poorly. In addition, you have learned how developing hardiness, toughness, and emotional intelligence helps to inoculate you against future dangers or opportunities that you will inevitably encounter.

Q U E S T I O N S   F O R   R E V I E W

1. Discuss the adaptive functions of stress and how they can enhance performance in a variety of areas.
2. Define resilience and explain how it is related to stress.
3. Identify the psychological elements of a resilient person.
4. Describe the hardiness theory and the toughening theory.
5. Explain the concept of emotional intelligence, including its main features.
6. Describe what can be learned from mistakes and failures.
7. Discuss how to develop mental toughness and a hardy personality.
8. Define sense of coherence and explain how it is associated with one's resilience.

S E L E C T E D   A N S W E R S

Answer to For Practice 13.1

1. If I don't get what I want, I will be miserable. *Rather than feeling miserable about this setback I will only feel disappointed.*

2. People should believe what I do, and act the ways I would, and when they don't, there is something wrong with them. *People are entitled to think, and act, any way they want, even if I don't like it. That doesn't make them bad, or wrong, or misguided – simply different from me.*

3. I really can control other people's behavior and make them act as I prefer. *I have no power to make anyone do anything that he doesn't want to do, just as I am not a victim of other people's desires to control me.*

4. I can predict the future and control future events by worrying about them ahead of time. *The only thing that I can truly control is how I behave in the present. Worrying about things that may, or may not, occur will not magically affect the eventual outcome. Planning may help, but worrying will not.*

5. If I try hard enough, and avoid taking risks, I can protect myself from being hurt. *Preparation can improve my chances of avoiding disappointments but will not insulate me from future failures. Avoiding risks may keep me safer but will also prevent me from reaching my most cherished goals.*

6. It is terrible when things don't go my way. *"Awful" means the worst thing that could ever happen to me. It may be disappointing, or slightly upsetting, when I don't get what I want, but hardly a catastrophe.*

7. It's not fair that I didn't get what I deserve. *The world is not fair, and there is very little in life to which I am actually entitled.*

REVIEW ACTIVITIES

Review Activity 13.1: Recovering from Trauma

Think of a time when you faced an extremely difficult situation in your life. This could have been the death of a loved one, losing a job or friendship, failing at something important to you, experiencing trauma early in life, dealing with hardships, or overcoming some form of adversity. Describe how you originally felt when this situation first occurred.

What did you do to help yourself recover? Analyze how you were able to demonstrate a degree of resilience in order to go on with your life in such a way that you now feel stronger as a result of what you lived through.

Review Activity 13.2: Reflection on the Positive

Thinking back on the last week, list as many times as you can remember in which you dealt effectively with stressful events, situations, and challenges:

1.

2.

3.

4.

5.

6.

REFERENCES AND RESOURCES

Aldwin, C. M., & Sutton, K. J. (1998). A developmental perspective on posttraumatic growth. In R. G. Tedeschi, C. L. Park, & L. G. Calhoun (Eds.), *Posttraumatic growth: Positive changes in the aftermath of crisis* (pp. 43–64). Mahwah, NJ: Lawrence Erlbaum Associates.

Alvord, M. K., & Grados, J. J. (2005). Enhancing resilience in children: A proactive approach. *Professional Psychology: Research and Practice, 36,* 238–245.

Antonovsky, A. (1979). *Health, stress, and coping: New perspectives on mental and physical well-being.* San Francisco, CA: Jossey-Bass.

Antonovsky, A. (1987). *Unravelling the mystery of health: How people manage stress and stay well.* San Francisco, CA: Jossey-Bass.

Askay, S. W., & Magyar-Russell, G. (2009). Post-traumatic growth and spirituality in burn recovery. *International Journal of Psychiatry, 21,* 570–579.

Beckmann, J., & Kellmann, M. (2004). Self-regulation and recovery: Approaching an understanding of the process of recovery from stress. *Psychological Reports, 95*(3), 1,135–1,153.

Calhoun, L. G., & Tedeschi, R. G. (2006). *Handbook of posttraumatic growth: Research and practice.* Mahwah, NJ: Lawrence Erlbaum Associates.

Childre, D., & Rozman, D. (2005). *Transforming stress: The heartmath solution for relieving worry, fatigue, and tension.* Oakland, CA: New Harbinger.

Chopko, B. A., & Schwartz, R. C. (2009). The relation between mindfulness and posttraumatic growth: A study of first responders to trauma-inducing incidents. *Journal of Mental Health Counseling, 31,* 363–376.

Ciarrochi, J. (2005). *Emotional intelligence in everyday life* (2nd ed.). New York, NY: Psychology Press.

da Silva, R., Goulart, C., Lopes, L., Serrano, P., Costa, A., et al. (2014). Hardy personality and burnout syndrome among nursing students in three Brazilian universities—an analytic study. *BMC Nursing, 13*(1), 9.

De Shazer, S. (1985). *Key to solutions in brief therapy.* New York, NY: Norton.

Deuster, P., & Silverman, M. (2013). Physical fitness: A pathway to health and resilience. *U.S. Army Medical Department Journal,* October–December, 24–35.

Dienstbier, R. A. (1989). Arousal and physiological toughness: Implications for mental and physical health. *Psychological Review, 96,* 84–100.

Dienstbier, R. A. (1991). Behavioral correlates of sympathoadrenal reactivity: The toughness model. *Medicine and Science in Sports and Exercise, 23,* 846–852.

Dumont, M., & Provost, M. A. (1999). Resilience in adolescents: Protective role of social support, coping strategies, self-esteem, and social activities on experience of stress and depression. *Journal of Youth and Adolescence, 28,* 343–363.

Dyer, W. W. (2001). *You'll see it when you believe it: The way to your personal transformation.* New York, NY: Perennial Currents.

Eriksson, M., & Lindstrom, B. (2005). Validity of Antonovsky's sense of coherence scale: A systematic review. *Journal of Epidemiology & Community Health, 59,* 460–466.

Eriksson, M., & Lindstrom, B. (2006). Antonovsky's sense of coherence scale and the relation with health: A systematic review. *Journal of Epidemiology & Community Health, 60,* 376–381.

Feder, A., Southwick, S. M., Goetz, R. R., Wang, Y., Alonso, A., Smith, B. W., et al. (2008). Posttraumatic growth in former Vietnam prisoners of war. *Psychiatry, 71,* 359–370.

Feigin, R., & Sapir, A. (2005). The relationship between sense of coherence and attribution of responsibility for problems and their solutions, and cessation of substance abuse. *Journal of Psychoactive Drugs, 37,* 63–74.

Flach, F. (1988). *Resilience: Discovering a new strength at times of stress.* New York, NY: Fawcett Columbine.

Fresco, D., Rytwinski, N., & Craighead, L. (2007). Explanatory flexibility and negative life events interact to predict depression symptoms. *Journal of Social and Clinical Psychology, 26*(5), 595–608.

Gardner, H. (1983). *Frames of mind: The theory of multiple intelligences.* New York, NY: Basic Books.

Gardner, H. (1993). *Creating minds.* New York, NY: Basic Books.

Garmezy, N. (1985). Stress-resistant children: The search for protective factors. In J. Stevens (Ed.), *Recent research in developmental psychopathology* (pp. 213–233). Oxford, UK: Pergamon.

Garmezy, N., Masten, A. S., & Tellegen, A. (1984). The study of stress and competence in children: A building block for developmental psychopathology. *Child Development, 55,* 97–111.

Goleman, D. (1995). *Emotional intelligence: Why it can matter more than IQ.* New York, NY: Bantam.

Hawkley, L. C., Berntson, G. G., Engeland, C. G., Marucha, P. T., Masi, C. M., & Cacioppo, J. T. (2005). Stress, aging, and resilience: Can accrued wear and tear be slowed? *Canadian Psychology, 46*(3), 115–125.

Iwasaki, Y., Mactavish, J., & Mackay, K. (2005). Building on strengths and resilience: Leisure as a stress survival strategy. *British Journal of Guidance and Counselling, 33*(1), 81–100.

Kaplan, H. B. (2005). Understanding the concept of resilience. In S. Goldstein, & R. Brooks (Eds.), *Handbook of resilience in children* (pp. 39–47). New York, NY: Kluwer.

Kinman, G. (2008). Work stressors, health and sense of coherence in UK academic employees. *Educational Psychology, 28*(7), 823–835.

Kling, K. C., Ryff, C. D., & Essex, M. J. (1997). Adaptive changes in the self-concept during a life transition. *Personality and Social Psychology Bulletin, 23*, 989–998.

Kling, K. C., Seltzer, M. M., & Ryff, C. D. (1997). Distinctive late life challenges: Implications for coping and well-being. *Psychology and aging, 12*, 288–295.

Kobasa, S. C. (1979). Stressful life events, personality, and health: An inquiry into hardiness. *Journal of Personality and Social Psychology, 37*, 1–11.

Kobasa, S. C., Maddi, S., & Kahn, S. (1982). Hardiness and health: A prospective study. *Journal of Personality and Social Psychology, 42*, 168–177.

Kottler, J. A. (1994). *Beyond blame: A new way of resolving conflicts in relationships.* San Francisco, CA: Jossey-Bass.

Kottler, J. A., & Blau, D. (1989). *The imperfect therapist: Learning from failure in psychotherapy.* San Francisco, CA: Jossey-Bass.

Kottler, J. A., & Carlson, J. (2003). *Bad therapy: Master therapists share their worst failures.* New York, NY: Brunner-Routledge.

Lazarus, D. (2005, November 25). This way, consumers all, to the cash register. *San Francisco Chronicle.*

Maddi, S. R. (2002). The story of hardiness: Twenty years of theorizing, research, and practice. *Consulting Psychology Journal, 54*, 173–185.

Matthews, G., Zeidner, M., & Roberts, R. D. (2006). *Science of emotional intelligence: Knowns and unknowns.* New York, NY: Oxford University Press.

McCraty, R., & Children, D. (2004). The grateful heart: The psychophysiology of appreciation. In R. A. Emmons & M. E. McCullough (Eds.), *The psychology of gratitude* (pp. 231–255). New York, NY: Oxford University Press.

Miller, S. C., & Segerstrom, G. E. (2004). Psychological stress and the human immune system: A meta-analytic study of 30 years of inquiry. *Psychological Bulletin, 130*(4), 601–630.

Nutt, D. J. (2006). *Posttraumatic stress disorder: Diagnosis, management, and treatment* (2nd ed.). New York, NY: Taylor & Francis.

Oaksford, K., Frude, N., & Cuddihy, R. (2005). Positive coping and stress-related psychological growth following lower limb amputation. *Rehabilitation Psychology, 50*(3), 266–277.

Pearsall, P. (2003). *The Beethoven factor: The new positive psychology of hardiness, happiness, healing, and hope.* Charlottesville, VA: Hampton Roads.

Peres, J. F. P., Mercante, J. P. P., & Nasello, A. G. (2005). Psychological dynamics affecting traumatic memories: Implications in psychotherapy. *Psychology and Psychotherapy: Theory, Research and Practice, 78*, 431–447.

Peterson, C., Park, N., Pole, N., D'Andrea, W., & Seligman, M. (2008). Strengths of character and posttraumatic growth. *Journal of Traumatic Stress, 21*(2), 214–217.

Ritter, S., Damian, R., Simonton, D., Baaren, R., Derks, J., et al. (2012). Diversifying experiences enhance cognitive flexibility. *Journal of Experimental Social Psychology, 48*(4), 961–964.

Rutter, M. (1987). Psychosocial resilience and protective mechanisms. *American Journal of Orthopsychiatry, 57*, 316–331.

Ryff, C. D., & Singer, B. (2003). Flourishing under fire: Resilience as a prototype of challenged thriving. In C. L. M. Keyes & J. Haidt (Eds.), *Flourishing: Positive psychology and the life well-lived* (pp. 15–36). Washington, DC: American Psychological Association.

Salovey, P., & Mayer, J. D. (1990). Emotional intelligence. *Imagination, Cognition, and Personality, 9*, 185–211.

Salovey, P., & Pizarro, D. A. (2003). The value of emotional intelligence. In R. J. Sternberg, J. Lautrey, & T. I. Lubart (Eds.), *Models of intelligence: International perspectives* (pp. 263–278). Washington, DC: American Psychological Association.

Seligman, M. (1991). *Learned optimism.* New York, NY: Knopf.

Seligman, M. (2002). *Authentic happiness: Using the new positive psychology to realize your potential for lasting fulfillment.* New York, NY: Simon & Schuster.

Shaw, A., Joseph, S., & Linley, P. A. (2005). Religion, spirituality, and posttraumatic growth: A systematic review. *Mental Health, Religion & Culture, 8*, 1–11.

Suresky, J., Zauszniewski, J. A., & Bekhet, A. K. (2008). Sense of coherence and quality of life in women family members of the seriously mentally ill. *Issues in Mental Health Nursing, 29*, 265–278.

Tedeschi, R. G., & Calhoun, L. G. (2004). Posttraumatic growth: A new perspective on psychotraumatology. *Psychiatric Times, 21*(4), 58–60.

Thomas, J. L., Adler, A. B., Whittels, P., Enne, R., & Johannes, B. (2004). Comparing elite soldiers' perceptions of psychological and physical demands during military training. *Military Medicine, 169*, 526–530.

Unger, Z. (2010). Fight stress like a fireman. *Men's Health*. Retrieved on July 10, 2010 from www.menshealth.com.

Vaillant, G. (2002). *Aging well*. New York, NY: Little, Brown.

van der Hal-van Raalte, E. A. M. (2009). Sense of coherence moderates late effects of early childhood Holocaust exposure. *Journal of Clinical Psychology, 64*(12), 1,352–1,367.

Weiss, T., & Berger, R. (2010). *Posttraumatic growth and culturally competent practice: Lessons learned from around the globe*. Hoboken, NJ: Wiley.

14

Optimal Functioning and Lasting Changes

Much of the material related to stress focuses on when you are operating at your worst: those times when you feel a loss of control, initiative, or peace. Yet many of the strategies and skills you learned throughout this course are useful not only when recovering from adversity, but also to enhance your performance in every dimension: in physical or mental fitness, emotional experiences, the spiritual world, or relationships. In other words, much of what you learned can be employed not only to fix what is wrong, but to enhance what is going right. Stress often represents a hormonal surge in your body to provide extra strength, heightened perception, and peak performance during times when you need them most. When you can feel your hands

KEY QUESTIONS IN THE CHAPTER

- What are the distinguishing features of positive psychology?
- How is positive psychology related to managing and preventing stress?
- What are signature strengths?
- How can you identify your signature strengths?
- What are well-being and mental health? What are the main dimensions of mental health and well-being?
- What are the determinants of happiness and subjective well-being?
- What is the connection between human strengths and well-being?
- What are the strategies for producing peak performance?
- What are the elements of a proactive approach to managing and preventing stress?
- What are the characteristics of flow experiences and what are the conditions that produce these experiences?
- Why has the subject of lasting change often been ignored?
- What sabotages lasting change?
- What can you do to inoculate yourself against stress in the future to prevent relapses?

shaking, your heart racing, and your mouth dry, that's adrenaline kicking in to help get you through a (perceived) challenging situation.

This chapter focuses on your strengths rather than your weaknesses. It is intended to take you way beyond merely managing or preventing stress and examines how you can create a more fulfilled life and facilitate optimal functioning in every area important to you. Relatively speaking, only a small percentage of the time do you actually become aware that you are stressed; most often you are either coping reasonably well or simply not thinking about how you are doing at all. With that in mind, I ask you to consider what is going *right* with your life rather than what is going *wrong*. This places a strong emphasis on optimal rather than dysfunctional functioning—an approach that can increase your personal effectiveness in a variety of areas. It also helps you to incorporate the new skills you have learned throughout the semester to make the changes last.

A Proactive Approach to Stress Management and Prevention

Abraham Maslow was among the first theorists to explore what is right with people instead of what is wrong with them. As you may know from first-hand experience, much of psychology is devoted to labeling human experience in terms of problems. Maslow, however, was curious about what we can learn from those individuals who are at the top of the mental health scale instead of those who are struggling at the bottom. He decided to identify people—college students as well as historical figures—who appeared to be the most well adjusted and fully functioning, what he called *self-actualized*. Although plagued by their own demons in some ways, people such as Abraham Lincoln, Franklin Roosevelt, and Amelia Earhart have much to teach us in terms of how they overcame adversity, managed their stress, and went on to accomplish important feats. This led Maslow to develop a list of those qualities that are most common among self-actualized people—those who are operating at optimal levels (see For Reflection 14.1). These were people who were resilient, who could adapt to changing circumstances and face life's challenges while demonstrating resourcefulness and internal fortitude.

FOR REFLECTION 14.1

Think of some people you know who are the most emotionally healthy, fully functioning, and personally happy among anyone you have ever spent time with. Describe below the personal characteristics that you believe may be most responsible for their self-actualized behavior.

After you have completed your list, compare it to the list of characteristics Maslow discovered, based on his research (answers at the end of the chapter).

Championed by Martin Seligman (2002, 2003, 2011; Seligman, Rashid, & Parks, 2006; Seligman, Steen, Park, & Peterson, 2005), Mihaly Csikszentmihalyi (Seligman & Csikszentmihalyi, 2000), Paul Pearsall (2003), and others (Linley & Joseph, 2004; Snyder & Lopez, 2005), **positive psychology** studies positive experiences, positive character traits, and the institutions that help cultivate them (Seligman, 2011). The movement focuses on identifiable human strengths such as courage, optimism, and hope that can serve as buffers against stress-related problems. It seeks to identify and bolster a person's resources that are available instead of diagnosing problems, failures, and limitations. In other words, a positive approach to life and its challenges significantly reduces stress, or at least makes it easier to tolerate. "Optimists are often healthier because they actively engage in life, not because of a miracle happy juice that pessimists lack" (Neimark, 2007, p. 91). This doesn't mean merely wishing for things you want, nor blind optimism in which you hope for the best possible outcome, but rather a kind of "realistic optimism" in which you hope for a good outcome but also work hard to make that happen; if it doesn't, you reassess and try something else.

The traditional approach to stress management has been one of reactions to events. It is conceived as similar to extinguishing a fire after it ignites, or even rages out of control. Stress management strategies are portrayed as the fire-fighters, always on call, ready to respond to emergencies. The goal is to become as prepared as you can to deal with what adversity you might face.

This traditional model is based on certain assumptions that emphasize the person as a responder to situations that arise. In addition, there are several other implicit ideas, as follows.

FOR REFLECTION 14.2

Think of a situation going on in your life right now that is disturbing or upsetting in some way. This could be a problem in school, at home, in a relationship, at work, or elsewhere—it should be something that occupies a lot of your time and energy.

Note below the things you have been complaining about most—to others, as well as to yourself. These are all the things that feel like they have been going wrong lately.

Using a positive psychology approach, instead of bringing undue attention to what is most upsetting and stressful about this problem situation in your life, list below several things that are going relatively, or even extraordinarily well.

Note how this more balanced inventory feels empowering, not to mention being a more accurate and realistic portrayal of your life. No matter how bad things *seem* to be going at any given moment in time, there are also elements that demonstrate your resourcefulness and strength.

- The term "stress management" has been used to address symptoms rather than underlying causes.

- The benefits of stress management are usually short-lasting. There is little or no emphasis on prevention of recurring problems.

- Exercise, meditation, biofeedback, and other techniques require considerable time and discipline, which many people lack.

- Like other symptom-oriented approaches (such as addiction to cigarettes, alcohol, drugs, food), the more you rely on stress management techniques, the more you become dependent on them.

The proactive, positive psychology approach does not renounce the traditional stress coping model. Rather it incorporates the techniques and methods into a more comprehensive approach that looks at not only problems that need to be addressed but also strengths and resources that can be developed to prevent difficulties in the future. It also seeks to address the natural human interest, if not need, to seek pleasure, stimulation, excitement, and relief of suffering by pursuing more healthful options than escape into self-destructive or addictive behaviors (Milkman & Sunderwirth, 2010). This involves accessing and creating more natural "highs" such as those that can be obtained through physical exercise, spiritual fulfillment, productivity and creative accomplishments, relationship intimacy, and altered states of consciousness achieved through mindfulness activities such as yoga, meditation, and deep breathing.

Identification of Human Strengths

The essence of human intelligence can be captured in the ability to create self-defined goals and then to adapt, shape, and select environments that capitalize on one's strengths to achieve those objectives (Sternberg, 2003). Since one of the main missions of positive psychology is to identify and promote human strengths and virtues, it is important to have a clear idea of what they are.

Human strengths are those cognitive, emotional, and social characteristics that are necessary for life success (Fernández-Ballesteros, 2003). They have several distinguishing features such as their stability across different situations and their adaptability to changing situations (Seligman, 2003). Whether you are at school, home, or work, you can still exhibit a degree of patience or compassion or flexibility.

Typically, your strengths are exhibited in the form of virtues, which are, in turn, representative of underlying character strengths (see Table 14.1). In each case, such strengths provide a sense of grounding in the world. They not only immunize you against stress but also lead you toward optimal functioning—not only on behalf of your own interest but for the welfare of others.

TABLE 14.1 Six virtues and 24 character strengths

Wisdom	Creativity, curiosity, open-mindedness, love of learning, creativity
Courage	Authenticity, bravery, persistence, zest
Humanity	Kindness, love, social intelligence
Justice	Fairness, leadership, teamwork
Temperance	Forgiveness, modesty, prudence, self-regulation
Transcendence	Gratitude, hope, humor, religiousness

Source: Peterson & Seligman (2004)

Cultures provide role models and parables that illustrate valued strengths that may be real (Martin Luther King and integrity), apocryphal (George Washington and honesty), or explicitly mythic (Luke Skywalker in *Star Wars*). News reports and media are constantly searching for new examples of idealized strengths, especially with regard to demonstrations of courage that inspire others.

What Are Your Signature Strengths?

Signature strengths are those prominent character strengths you possess that can be easily identified. One of the premises of positive psychology is that trying to overcome your weaknesses is not particularly effective since it does not lead you to achieve excellence. Instead, it is recommended that you concentrate on developing your signature strengths—those that are characteristic of you and that represent what you do best.

How do you know what your signature strengths are? Take a brief strengths test developed by Seligman and colleagues (see For Reflection 14.3). After you complete the test, rank them from high to low. Seligman (2002) defines signature strengths as those an individual "self-consciously owns, celebrates, and (if he or she can arrange life successfully) exercises every day in work, love, play, and parenting" (p. 160).

FOR REFLECTION 14.3: TEST YOUR OWN SIGNATURE STRENGTHS (SOURCE: ADAPTED FROM SELIGMAN, 2002, WWW.AUTHENTICHAPPINESS.SAS.UPENN.EDU)

Answer the following questions about how you have acted in the actual situations described below during the past month (four weeks) (Not applicable = 0; Never/rarely = 1; Occasionally = 2; Half the time = 3; Usually = 4; Always = 5).

1. How frequently did you show CREATIVITY or INGENUITY in novel or innovative situations?
2. How frequently did you show CURIOSITY or INTEREST in new or different situations?
3. How frequently did you show CRITICAL THINKING, OPEN-MINDEDNESS, or GOOD JUDGMENT in situations requiring complex decision making?
4. How frequently did you show LOVE OF LEARNING in situations requiring new information or skills?
5. How frequently did you show PERSPECTIVE or WISDOM when you offered advice to another person?
6. How frequently did you show BRAVERY or COURAGE when faced with fear?
7. How frequently did you show PERSEVERANCE, PERSISTENCE, DILIGENCE, or INDUSTRIOUSNESS when dealing with a difficult and time-consuming task?
8. How frequently did you show HONESTY or AUTHENTICITY when it was possible for you to lie about who you are or what had happened?
9. How frequently did you show ZEST or ENTHUSIASM?
10. How frequently did you express your LOVE or ATTACHMENT to others (friends, family members)?
11. How frequently did you show KINDNESS or GENEROSITY to others?
12. How frequently did you show SOCIAL INTELLIGENCE or SOCIAL SKILLS when you needed to view a situation from someone else's perspective?
13. How frequently did you show TEAMWORK when other people needed your help or loyalty?
14. How frequently did you show FAIRNESS when you had power or influence over two or more other people?
15. How frequently did you show LEADERSHIP when the group you were in needed direction?
16. How frequently did you show FORGIVENESS or MERCY when you were hurt by someone else?
17. How frequently did you show MODESTY or HUMILITY?
18. How frequently did you show PRUDENCE, DISCRETION, or CAUTION when you were tempted to do something you might regret later?
19. How frequently did you show SELF-CONTROL or SELF-REGULATION in these situations?

20. How frequently did you show APPRECIATION OF BEAUTY AND EXCELLENCE or AWE?
21. How frequently did you show GRATITUDE or THANKFULNESS when you received help from another person?
22. How frequently did you show HOPE or OPTIMISM in the face of adversity?
23. How frequently did you show PLAYFULNESS or HUMOR?
24. How frequently did you show RELIGIOUSNESS or SPIRITUALITY?

In addition to filling out this questionnaire, one way to identify signature strengths is to ask people who are close to you, especially those whom you trust, to be truthful and frank. Conduct interviews with at least five friends and family members who have observed you in a variety of situations over a long period of time. Ask them what they believe your primary strengths are. Prompt them to supply examples of the traits they select.

Serena, for example, doesn't think of herself as excelling in much of anything. She is an average student, and always has been. She has never been especially athletic, even feeling somewhat uncoordinated. She is awkward in many social situations; although she has a few close friends, she would never describe herself as popular. Across the board she would describe herself as "average" in appearance and ability. She has tried her whole life to blend in.

It was not only difficult but uncomfortable for Serena to examine her strengths. As a woman from an Asian culture, it was considered unseemly and immodest in her family to bring undue attention to herself. She is the youngest child with four older brothers, so her early life was characterized by trying to avoid attention.

At first, Serena couldn't think of any special talent or ability she might have. However, once it was pointed out to her that she was unusually skilled at blending in to any social situation, she began to think of this as the first of many examples of her adaptability and flexibility. No matter where she finds herself, with whatever group of people, in almost any situation, Serena can fit in. She never complains. She is endlessly patient. She is hardly ever critical of others. And she is highly valued by friends because of her consistency and easy-going nature.

Serena has had some difficulties with being passive, overly compliant, and unwilling to stand up for herself in some situations. As long as she focused on her weaknesses, she felt increasingly hopeless and frustrated. It was by recognizing and valuing her signature strengths that she realized that she did have some special talents that served her well and could even further immunize her against stressful situations in the future.

Achieving Well-being and Mental Health

Mental health is not merely the absence of mental illness (Keyes, 2005). Mentally healthy adults display effective mental function, fulfilling relationships, productive activities, and the ability to adapt to change and cope with adversity. There are two important concepts of mental health: *flourishing* and *languishing*. *Flourishing* describes a state of being characterized by positive emotions toward life and successful psychological and social functioning. In other words, flourishing represents those who are truly mentally healthy, yet only 17% of adults between ages 25 and 74 fit the criteria (Keyes, 2003). *Languishing* describes a state between flourishing and a major depression in which the individual shows few positive emotions toward life and has difficulty functioning effectively. Such a person may be getting most of the tasks in life completed, but without passion or joy.

It is not enough to stave off stress in order to achieve a sense of well-being and optimal functioning. That is like saying that the definition of pleasure is an absence of pain. While this may be true for someone who has experienced chronic, debilitating agony for a considerable period of time, there is more to life than merely coping with discomfort.

Psychological health is often described not only by the absence of symptoms and psychopathology but also by the presence of several virtues such as those described in Table 14.1 (Carr, 2004; Ryff & Singer, 2003). The **well-being therapy** (WBT) (Fava, 1999; Fava & Ruini, 2003) based on the multidimensional model of psychological well-being (Ryff & Singer, 1998) aims at developing self-acceptance, personal growth, meaning in life, environmental mastery, and social well-being and can be used for treating patients with affective disorders in conjunction with drug therapy or psychotherapy. I will describe the characteristics of the WBT.

SELF-ACCEPTANCE   This involves high regard for yourself—as a person—in spite of your limitations, mistakes, and failures. It means an honest assessment of both your strengths and weaknesses, working to improve the latter but forgiving lapses that are less than what you had hoped. It requires having compassion and understanding not only for others but also for yourself.

FOR REFLECTION 14.4

Think of a time recently in which you feel like you made a major gaffe or mistake, one that had ongoing negative consequences. Jot down what happened below.

It is a given that you wished that this had never happened. It is also inevitable that as a human being, no matter how hard you try, you will do and say things that are awkward, stupid, insensitive, or otherwise imperfect. So this was one of those times in which you acted in a way that was somehow inappropriate even though it may have been hard to know that at the time.

Even though you may regret the incident, or wish you had done or said something differently, what does this experience say about you *as a person*?

It says nothing. Even though you may *do* things that occasionally appear rude, unkind, ignorant, or offensive, this does not mean that you are a rude, unkind, stupid, or offensive person. It just means that you made a mistake. Period. Of course if you keep making the same mistake repeatedly then it is time to look at behaviors requiring some type of change.

Self-acceptance involves honestly examining your own behavior critically for the purposes of improving yourself in the future. But, most important, even though you might judge your behavior as less than adequate, this does not mean you judge yourself. You take yourself off probation no matter what you do, no matter how many times you perform less than perfectly.

People who flourish, as opposed to those who languish, are willing to accept themselves as human, with all their flaws and limitations. This does not mean that you can't work to improve them, just that critically judging yourself (or others) only contributes to further difficulties.

In one study of how prominent psychotherapists deal with their failures, it was found that those who most flourished in their work had two distinctive qualities (Kottler &

Carlson, 2002). First of all, they *owned* their failures, meaning that they readily accepted their imperfections and mistakes rather than denying them or pretending that everything was always going well. When asked to describe his most memorable failure, one well-known psychiatrist responded, "Do you want one today, or yesterday?" It was his philosophy that you can't perform at the highest level unless you are taking risks and making mistakes. He went on to describe a patient that he had seen in front of an audience of 300 colleagues. He made some sort of blunder that caused the patient to get up in anger and storm off the stage, never to be seen again. The audience was so stunned by his perceived insensitivity that they, too, got up indignantly and left. When he was asked how he could have possibly have recovered from such a humiliating public gaffe, the psychiatrist just shrugged it off, saying you win a few and you lose a few. This shows the second feature of self-acceptance—forgiveness.

PERSONAL GROWTH   A second feature of well-being, related to self-acceptance, is striving for self-actualization: developing your abilities to the highest levels that are possible. Ironically, for this to occur, you have to display not only commitment, motivation, and drive, but also the kind of forgiveness described earlier. Most world-class athletes, for instance, push themselves to do things that previously had been unimaginable but they also know how to let go of past failures so they can move on to the next challenge at an even higher level.

Picture what it must be like to be a hitter in baseball, or a quarterback in football, or a forward in hockey or soccer—most of the times your efforts to score will fail. In baseball, almost all hitters fail two-thirds of the time! Yet if they are going to flourish, they have to learn from their mistakes, to forgive the lapses, and move forward to the next level.

All students are required, as a function of their "job description," to be embarking on a journey of personal growth. It comes with the territory that you are constantly reading, studying, wrestling with new ideas, and learning new skills, all of which contribute not only to preparing you for the workplace, but also to developing yourself as a person.

Apart from the work demanded by your instructors, or required as part of course assignments, what are you doing to improve yourself in the areas that matter the most? This could be related to your emotional development, your relationships, your spirituality, or your physical or mental fitness. What distinguishes people who flourish from those who languish is this commitment to growth in every dimension that matters most to each individual.

FINDING MEANING   What gives your life purpose? What are you on this planet to do before you die? What meaning do you attach to your existence? These are some of the questions that many people wrestle with while trying to clarify the underlying reasons for their being.

You have learned previously that it is not events themselves that determine whether people experience stress, frustration, anger, or any other emotion; rather it is their personal interpretation of these situations. So it is with respect to any aspect of life. People who have achieved a state of well-being and optimal functioning have a clear sense not only of where they are going, but also of why it is important to go there. Likewise, people who are resilient and recover relatively quickly from adversity are also able to find some meaning in their experiences. Even when subjected to horrifying experiences, they sometimes find a way to grow from the challenges they faced, but only if they can find meaning in them (see Voice of Stress Management 14.1).

ENVIRONMENTAL MASTERY   Fully functioning individuals are able to actively manage the environments within which they operate. This means being able to get your needs met, assuming that you know what they are. Beyond Maslow's basic needs such as food, shelter, and safety, there are also needs for love, support, stimulation, growth, and learning. This includes satisfying relationships with peers and family.

SOCIAL WELL-BEING   Satisfaction in life, especially during the stage of early adulthood in the college years, is ruled by the quality of social interactions. You will recall from

VOICE OF STRESS MANAGEMENT 14.1

Thirty-Three-Year-Old Graduate Student and Counselor in a Women's Shelter

I had been abused as a child, in a lot of ways. This is still difficult for me to talk about but I can say this about what happened—my parents must have had a lot of problems of their own so I must have been not a very high priority. I didn't get much food to eat and so I had to find stuff on my own, sometimes looking through garbage cans on my way to school. When I was bad—and I never really did anything that was that out of line—my mother would lock me in the basement—she'd tie me to a pole with a bowl of water and some bread—like a dog. There were beatings but I don't remember those too well. What I do remember were the "uncles" that my mother brought to my bed. I must have been—I don't know—14 or 15 when it started—when she brought these men to have sex with me for money. It was soon after that I ran away and never went home again.

You'd think that after things like that there is no way that anyone like me could recover. You'd think I'd end up a prostitute or in jail or something. But, I don't know, in some ways, those things from my childhood made me stronger. Sure, I've had a hard life, and it took me a long time to get to this point, but I think that will only make me a better counselor. I think I'm a better parent to my own children now because of what I suffered as a child. And I think I'm a better person too.

What made the difference, you want to know? How come I'm not so screwed up? I don't know [laughs]. I think it's because I wanted to figure out why people act the way they do. I wanted to figure out how my parents could have been so neglectful and abusive. Most of all, I wanted to stop this from happening with other children.

Chapter 3 some of the developmental tasks during your twenties and thirties—(1) to enjoy an intimate love relationship that may lead to a life partner, (2) to locate a peer group of like-minded people who share your values and interests, (3) to renegotiate adult relationships with parents and siblings, (4) to find a career that is personally, professionally, and economically fulfilling, and (5) to settle into a community where you can function as a cooperative and useful citizen. Many of these tasks are social in nature and involve getting along well with others.

Well-being is integrally connected not just to *self*-reliance but also to *other*-reliance. Ask yourself how satisfied you are with the relationships in your life. If there is something missing in terms of the quantity of friendships, or their quality in terms of intimacy and trust, then you are not going to feel as satisfied and stress-resilient as you would if you felt the loving support of family and loved ones. A

Whereas a certain amount of self-reliance and autonomy is important to feel in control of your life, social well-being means being able to surround yourself with friends, peers, and loved ones whom you can trust and enjoy support, respect, and stimulation.

recent study shows that service and volunteering activities in the community enhance college students' well-being (Bowman, Brandenberger, Lapsley, Hill, & Quaranto, 2010).

Determinants of Happiness

Happiness is a complex term to define and study scientifically. For some time, researchers have been interested in investigating what contributes most to life satisfaction and happiness, and it was not until recently that psychologists began to study it scientifically. They have looked at both causal factors—those that directly contribute to well-being—and mediating variables that play a more indirect role. Some of what has been found may surprise you. For instance, in his study of what leads to happiness, Seligman (2002) noted that neither health nor wealth played as important a role as you might expect (as mentioned in the previous chapter). It is certainly not much fun to be sick or poor, but apart from extremes in economic deprivation or terminal illness, these conditions are not that significant in predicting happiness. Specifically, Seligman found the following:

1. Money isn't that important, except for extreme situations. He observed that people in China or India who have a fraction of the wealth of those in Japan or North America are just as happy and satisfied with life.

2. People who are wealthy are not significantly happier than those of average income. For someone in the upper income bracket, purchasing a new Mercedes or Porsche brings them no more pleasure than a struggling student who buys a used Kia. People who win the lottery most often find that the millions of dollars they gain only make their lives more complex and stressful rather than more satisfying. It is also interesting that when people attempt to reduce stress by "shopping therapy," the effects rarely last longer than a few days.

3. Physical health is not necessarily correlated with well-bing. Even when people experience catastrophic illness or accidents, they tend to recover psychologically within months and return to the point they were before the incident. The vast majority of quadriplegics (84%) believe their lives to be average or above average in satisfaction.

4. Physical attractiveness does bring certain advantages, just as physical size does, but attractive people are no more happy and satisfied with life than are those who are not particularly attractive. So-called "genetic celebrities," meaning those who exhibit extraordinary beauty or physical prowess, are provided with more opportunities but that does not mean that these result in greater life satisfaction. We may envy movie stars, models, or athletes for their greater resources and options, but these still don't make them any more content with life than the rest of us.

5. Your educational level, race, gender, age, and geographical location also do not predict how happy you are. You might expect that people in sunny California would be happier than those in North Dakota, but that is not the case. Likewise, Caucasians are not happier than ethnic minorities, even among those in lower socioeconomic conditions.

Many people dream of the time when they will have more income, a nicer car, a bigger house, and more expensive clothes. Yet with more wealth comes greater responsibility and stress. A number of studies have shown fairly conclusively that rich people are not any happier than those with moderate income; in many ways, they are even more stressed and unhappy trying to figure out how to hold onto what they've got (Kahneman et al., 2006).

FOR REFLECTION 14.5

Evaluate How Happy You Are in a Few Moments!

Instructions
For each of the following statements or questions, please select the number from the scale that you think is most appropriate in describing you. Reverse code the fourth item (i.e., turn a 7 into a 1, a 6 into a 2, a 5 into a 3, a 3 into a 5, a 2 into a 6, and a 1 into a 7) (see Lyubomirsky & Lepper, 1999).

1. In general, I consider myself:

Not a very happy person 1 2 3 4 5 6 7 A very happy person

2. Compared with most of my peers, I consider myself:

Less happy 1 2 3 4 5 6 7 More happy

3. Some people are generally very happy. They enjoy life regardless of what is going on, getting the most out of everything. To what extent does this characterization describe you?

Not at all 1 2 3 4 5 6 7 A great deal

4. Some people are generally not very happy. Although they are not depressed, they never seem as happy as they might be. To what extent does this characterization describe you?

Not at all 1 2 3 4 5 6 7 A great deal

Scoring
Average the four numbers you selected to get your score. The higher the number the happier you are. The average happiness score runs from about 4.5 to 5.5.

Others believe that once they lose weight or have plastic surgery, they will finally feel some sort of peace and self-satisfaction. Still others anticipate that when their health improves, when they graduate from college, when they get older, or when they move to a new location, they will finally achieve happiness. However, research shows that none of these matter very much. It is no fun to be sick or poor or unemployed, but except for these extreme conditions, happiness is not significantly influenced by most of these factors.

So what does make a difference in predicting happiness and well-being? I have mentioned previously how important your attitude is in approaching life, especially one that is characterized by optimism, positive feelings, and flexibility. Also noteworthy and consistent with what has been presented before is that friends, relationships, and social ties are key predictors of well-being (Camfield & Skevington, 2008). People who are married (or who have life partners) are happier than those who are single (Myers, 1999). Experiencing love and emotional support provides a number of benefits that immunize you against stress and related problems that diminish your life satisfaction (Ornish, 1998). Being involved in satisfying recreational activities is also positively correlated with happiness, especially physical and leisure activities that help manage stress (Argyle, 2003; Sarafino, 2002). Religious and spiritual involvement generally has positive effects, as does altruistic involvement—making a difference in the community through volunteer efforts (Kottler & Marriner, 2009; Rietschlin, 1998). Happiness-enhancing strategies are summarized in Table 14.2.

In summary, what was mentioned in the previous paragraph can be nicely encapsulated by the three components of happiness proposed by Seligman (2002): (1) positive emotion (optimism, leisure), (2) meaning (e.g., spirituality and religiosity), and (3) engagement (e.g., flow, productivity, growth). I will further elaborate on the connection between flow and happiness and optimal functioning.

FOR REFLECTION 14.6

Week-by-Week Summary Description of Group Positive Psychotherapy Exercises Session Description (adapted from Seligman, Rashid, & Parks, 2006)

1. Using Your Strengths: Identify your top five strengths, and think of ways to use those strengths more in your daily life.
2. Three Good Things/Blessings: Each evening, write down three good things that happened and why you think they happened.
3. Obituary/Biography: Imagine that you have passed away after living a productive and satisfying life. What would you want your obituary to say? Write a one–two-page essay summarizing what you would like to be remembered for the most.
4. Gratitude Visit: Think of someone to whom you are very grateful, but who you have never properly thanked. Write a letter to them describing your gratitude, and read the letter to that person by phone or in person.
5. Active/Constructive Responding: An active-constructive response is one where you react in a visibly positive and enthusiastic way to good news from someone else. At least once a day, respond actively and constructively to someone you know.
6. Savoring: Once a day, take the time to enjoy something that you usually hurry through (examples: eating a meal, taking a shower, walking to class). When it's over, write down what you did, how you did it differently, and how it felt compared to when you rush through it.

Flow and Optimal Human Functioning

One of the most satisfying experiences of life is called "flow" (introduced in Chapter 8). Its original investigator, Mihaly Csikszentmihalyi, called flow the optimal experience of life (1975, 1990, 1997). It is that experience you have when you totally lose yourself in an activity, when all sense of time, of space, even the sense of your self disappears. During flow states you have potential to function at your absolute peak level. Imagine trying to do well playing tennis, or giving a speech, or having sex—much less enjoying the experience—if the whole time you were consumed with thoughts assessing how you were doing and whether you were doing it well. It is when you totally lose yourself in the experience, when it seems effortless, when you are just flowing along, that you often surprise yourself with your own potential.

While still a student himself, Csikszentmihalyi noticed a difference between his friends who played on the hockey team and those who played on the soccer team. Hockey was a prestige sport at his college so it was no wonder that guys vied to play on the team, but why would other friends choose to play soccer when nobody even showed up to watch their games? The answer was related to intrinsic motivation. From there, Csikszentmihalyi next began studying people in other professions and activities—surgeons, rock climbers, and dancers, to mention a few—who similarly engaged in their chosen passion because of some internal devotion to their craft. From talking to them, he noticed how one word kept cropping up again and again to describe the ways they would so totally immerse themselves in their activities that they would virtually disappear. He recalled one interview, in particular, with a surgeon who had been conducting a complex procedure when there was an earthquake that forced the evacuation of the hospital. Everyone fled, everyone, that is, except the surgeon, who kept operating totally oblivious to the chaos going on around him. The ceiling had collapsed in places and he never noticed!

Flow can thus be described as a state when people are engaged in something to the degree of forgetting time, fatigue, and everything else except the activity itself (Csikszentmihalyi, Abuhamdeh, & Nakamura, 2005). When you are immersed in a flow state, you feel a sense of control but without consciously thinking about it. Your critical mind is disengaged. You have no sense of time, no awareness of what you are doing—it is as if you are functioning on a different plane.

Flow can occur not only during competitive performances but also during everyday activities that you take for granted. Flow occurs when you are washing the dishes, when you are watching a fire or clouds float by, when you are listening to music or making love. Any time you are totally immersed in a task—with your whole being—you are flowing. It is under such conditions that you are able not only to perform at peak capacity but also to maximally enjoy the experience.

Flow is most likely to occur when you can find a balance between boredom and anxiety. If the activity induces too much stress in you, such as when you are competing against someone you think is better than you are or completing a task that feels beyond your capability, then you will feel too inhibited to flow. Likewise, if the task is not challenging enough for you, boredom will ensue. Flow takes place when there is a perfect match between your skill level and the demands of the job. That is why in the game of golf there is a built-in "handicap" that allows each person to adjust the score according to experience and skill levels; this makes the game equally challenging for everyone.

In order to experience more flow in life, and subsequently less stress and greater optimal functioning, it is necessary to practice what you have already learned about mindfulness and meditation. Rather than doing so in a passive, sitting state, however, the goal is to incorporate this sort of focused concentration in almost anything that you do. Whether you are involved in a conversation, going for a walk, sitting on the porch, writing a paper, giving a massage, playing a sport, eating a cracker, or completing any task, your goal is to totally focus on what you are doing in such a way that you become what you are doing.

If this sounds a little elusive, consider the flow experiences you have already experienced this week, if not today. Recall a time recently in which you lost yourself totally in what you were doing. There was no conscious awareness of what you are doing—just the intrinsic pleasure of doing it. Rather than there being an absence of attention there was actually total attention.

Toward Peak Performance: From Stress to Success

You are constantly being evaluated, or evaluating yourself. There are tests to get into school, tests during school, tests to get out of school. There are exams to get a driver's license, assessments of your physical skills, and competitions in every working environment and playing field. In your spare time, when other people aren't measuring your performance in some area, you tend to do it yourself to see how you stack up against others. You can't resist a glance when passing a mirror, which is just another kind of test to see if you look good enough. Are you normal? Are you better than average? Our culture is filled with performance assessments to see how you rate compared with others.

Peak performance can be measured in terms of how a given person's behavior stands out against others, but it can also be assessed according to how well it compares with that person's unique potential. This is what is called *personal best* in sports. It doesn't matter how well you do compared with others but that you far exceed your own expectations and what you ever thought was possible.

A lot of research has been completed on peak performance, that is, what has allowed athletes such as golfer Tiger Woods, basketball player LeBron James, or triple women's

TABLE 14.2 Strategies for enhancing happiness

Domain	Strategy
Relationships	• Find a romantic partner • Communicate kindly and clearly; forgive faults • Maintain contact with your extended family • Maintain a few close friends • Cooperate with acquaintances • Engage in religious or spiritual practices
Environment	• Secure reasonable physical and financial safety and comfort • Avoid consumerism and materialism that have temporary effects • Periodically enjoy fine weather • Live in a stimulating environment, based on your values
Physical state	• Eat healthily • Maintain good health • Engage in regular physical exercise
Productivity	• Use skills that are intrinsically pleasing for tasks that are challenging • Achieve success and approval at work that is interesting and challenging • Work toward a coherent set of goals • Volunteer to make a difference in your community
Recreation	• Rest, relax, and take holidays in moderation • Do cooperative recreational activities with groups of friends • Diversify your life with multiple interests • Make leisure activities a priority • Experiment with new and exciting options
Distressing emotions	• Avoid distressing situations when possible • Focus on the positive as much as you can • Keep an optimistic, upbeat attitude in which you expect success • Challenge perfectionistic thinking and unrealistic expectations • Take constructive risks outside of your comfort zone • Use the coping strategies to counteract mild stress before it gets out of control • Practice compassion and empathy toward others • Learn to be more self-accepting and less self-critical • Dispute irrational thoughts that lead to upsetting feelings

Source: Adapted from Carr (2004)

world champion swimmer Luo Xuoejuan to excel beyond the competition. Peak performance refers to superior functioning exceeding expectations or past behavior. Whether applied to the Olympics, the world stage, or any situation in which you excel at a level that had previously seemed impossible, there are certain attitudes that are often present at the time (Loehr, 1986). Peak performance is linked to several internal states such as calmness, absence of anxiety, optimism, alertness, self-confidence, and effortlessness.

Peak performance is achieved by following several strategies that are employed by superstars in any field, whether athletics, business, or science.

Strategic Planning

Strategic planning is about spending your energy and time doing what you are most capable of doing with greatest satisfaction. Peak performance occurs when people create a vision of their goal that is so compelling that they will devote total commitment to achieving it. By taking the time to plan thoroughly before acting, you will greatly increase the likelihood that you will achieve your personal goals.

Research in sports psychology consistently indicates that goal setting greatly influences subsequent results, especially when those objectives are clear and challenging, yet realistic. Visualization and the use of mental imagery are techniques often employed by high performers.

Once you set clear goals, you should make a step-by-step plan to carry them out. In Chapter 7, you learned about the 80/20 rule which suggests that 20% of what you do often accounts for 80% of your achievement. In other words, when you use your time strategically in the most valued activities, you will get more done and still have time for recreation and relaxation. On the contrary, your hard work on the wrong projects will yield little fruitage. Your actions in implementing the goals will bring feedback that can be integrated into future performances. Improvement is far more likely when you find ways to either modify goals or improve efficiency.

Self-Initiatives

Every action taken to improve yourself creates momentum for future actions. Only by becoming action-oriented can you expect to achieve the results you desire. It is one thing to think about what you'd like to accomplish, another to talk about it, and quite another to actually do something about it. Everyone has dreams about the great things they would like to do: it is not usually stress that prevents the realization of these goals, but rather inertia—a lack of sustained commitment to follow through.

People often become discouraged easily. They try something, it doesn't work out, so they give up. Yet once you start moving forward, even in tiny steps, you are in a position to make necessary corrections. Ronstadt (1988) has proposed a **corridor principle** based on his study of business students and other entrepreneurs. This principle suggests that the major underlying reason for the success of many entrepreneurs is that they mustered enough courage and resources to launch their businesses. He observed that many students had more than sufficient knowledge, skills, and resources, yet they never succeeded in starting up their own business because of a lack of courage and initiative; they were afraid to take risks.

Mental Conditioning

Sport psychologists have noted that world-class athletes who do well under stressful conditions have learned to talk to themselves in particular ways during the competitions. Even under normal circumstances most people have conversations with themselves inside their heads at the rate of about 500 words per minute. Athletic trainer Trevor Moawad notes that such personal chatter can doom someone who is under pressure if they don't control it (Park, 2006). Picture all the "down time" a tennis player spends between points, or a basketball player before shooting a free throw, or a golfer before a putt. Athletic skills are one thing that leads to peak performance, but just as important is mental conditioning that keeps your internal voice encouraging and supportive.

Contrast the difference in self-talk between these two students who are both feeling nervous prior to giving a class presentation that represents a significant component of their final grade:

> I hope I'm ready. If I blow this, I'm in deep trouble. My whole grade depends on getting at least a B+ on this stupid assignment. I've never been good at this sort of thing. It's not fair that so much depends on how I do. Maybe if I screw up I can ask if I can do some extra credit or something. God, this is going to be awful but here goes …

> Okay. Deep breath. This is going to go fine. I'm ready. I'm ready. Done all I've can. Nothing else to do. Just follow the outline. Do what I've rehearsed. Over and over and over. Never been more ready. I'm good at this. They'll love me.

These two samples illustrate how important it is to interrupt the flow of negative thinking that might occur during pressure situations. All you have learned in previous chapters about controlling your breathing, practicing meditative states, talking to yourself in constructive, healthy ways, comes into play prior to, and during, an actual performance that requires your highest functioning. It is important to rehearse not only what you are planning to do on the outside in terms of your behavior, but also what you say to yourself on the inside.

It is also important to be honest with yourself about your capabilities, that is, not to demand things that may be beyond reasonable expectations (a standing ovation or world record). While boosting your confidence through internal chatter can lead to higher performance, it is also critical that you demonstrate forgiveness of any lapses or mistakes. Slumps in any activity or sport tend to linger when a person fails to make needed adjustments that are based on an honest assessment of what went wrong.

Rehearse under Stress

When athletes or speakers choke under pressure, it is not because they didn't have the training, preparation, and skills to perform at peak levels. You can practice for an exam or a musical recital 100 times and still fall apart during the performance, largely because the practice didn't take place under simulated conditions. Pro golfers miss putts, musicians play wrong notes, skaters fall during competitions, and students panic during exams, not because they weren't sufficiently prepared but because they didn't rehearse under stressful situations with all the distractions that are usually present during the actual test (Beilock & Carr, 2001).

If you want to improve your ability to perform well during an exam, it may not be best after all to study for it under perfectly silent, insulated conditions, considering that you will be asked to perform when in the presence of many others, with all the accompanying distractions and pressure. Similarly, if you were going to perform in a musical recital, deliver a speech, or run a race, it is best to do so under conditions that most closely parallel the actual performance.

Scenario Planning

The purpose of stress management is not to eliminate stress, but rather to control it so that it doesn't disrupt peak performance. **Stress inoculation** involves gradually desensitizing yourself to the stressors you fear the most in such a way that they begin to lose their power to upset you. The idea is to gradually and repeatedly immunize yourself against those situations you find most disturbing and inhibiting (see Voice of Stress Management 14.2).

Most stress inoculation strategies involve three distinct phases (Meichenbaum, 1985). First, you educate yourself as much as you can about what to expect; this alleviates some of the apprehension. If you were going to the dermatologist to have a suspicious mole examined you might first do research on the signs of skin cancer. More commonly, if you were traveling to an unfamiliar area you would first plot and plan out your route.

Second is the rehearsal phase where you practice dealing with the situation you fear most. Sometimes this practice takes place internally when you rehearse in your head what you want to say and how you want to proceed. Even better is to practice through roleplaying in which you actually rehearse the scenario under simulated conditions.

Flynn, for example, was really nervous about talking to his instructor about a grade on an assignment. He had made a lot of progress in combating paralyzing anxiety that led him to become passive and withdrawn. Once he received the poor grade, his initial reaction was to give up as he had done throughout his life. By practicing the skills he had learned, he was determined to talk with the instructor but he was terrified he would fall apart. Flynn recruited his roommate to pretend to be the teacher so he could try out what he wanted to say. After practicing the conversation a few times, as well as incorporating some suggestions from his friend, Flynn felt better prepared to face the situation.

Finally, in the last phase you implement the plan. This means that you repeatedly subject yourself to the stimulus that has elicited such trepidation in the past—you force yourself to deal with the circumstances that you have been avoiding. In the previous

VOICE OF STRESS MANAGEMENT 14.2

Student in Her Twenties

I haven't been involved in a relationship—at least a decent one—in some time. I'm tired of being single and on my own and was thinking a lot about how much I'd like to meet someone. I don't care for those online dating services; there's something about them that doesn't feel right. But I still wasn't meeting anyone and I got tired of waiting for guys to approach me. I always wanted to be able to make something happen myself but in my family we learned that girls just weren't supposed to do that sort of thing. Regardless of the reason, I just couldn't make myself go up to anyone who I liked.

With the encouragement of a girlfriend in a support group I went to, I started out just trying to make eye contact with a few guys I passed. I pictured what I would do, just glance up at someone and smile, and walk on. I thought it would be so hard but it really wasn't. Then, after I got comfortable with doing that, I tried staring a little longer and giving a bigger smile, sometimes even saying hi. Finally, one night I actually worked up the nerve to approach a guy who'd been in one of my classes. I'd noticed him for months but I didn't think I'd ever have the courage to do anything about it. Who knew? Anyway, things didn't work out with him but it gave me the confidence to approach anyone who looks interesting to me.

example, Flynn realized that he had to stay conditioned and "in shape" to handle confrontations in the future, so he deliberately looked for situations in which he could assert himself.

During scenario planning, you anticipate what might happen, what could go wrong, and almost every contingency that could arise, and plan according to how you might respond or deal with the situation. This kind of preparation is empowering in that it gives you potential control over stressful predicaments in which you may previously have felt helpless.

For example, Fredo was invited to give a speech at a student organization gathering, something he had never done before. Although he tried to avoid the situation because the prospect of speaking in front of such a large group seemed terrifying, he was pressured into doing it because of his special expertise.

Fredo was losing a lot of sleep over this upcoming event, until he began to take some control by doing thorough preparation. He wasn't that worried about what he would say but was concerned that the technology would go wrong during his slides—his whole program was linked to illustrations and photos. What if the projector bulb burned out? What if the computer and projector weren't compatible? What if his file was corrupted and wouldn't run? The list of possible disasters ran on and on in his head.

Fredo decided to protect himself, initially, by preparing an alternative set of slides on transparencies. Even if the computer and projector didn't work, he would still have a plan. Second, he made arrangements to visit the room where he would be speaking ahead of time so he could familiarize himself with the setting. He planned many other scenarios as well—his friends would say compulsively and excessively—but he gained confidence and reduced his stress by feeling like he was in control of the situation. There was almost nothing imaginable that could occur, short of an earthquake, for which he would have been unprepared.

Perseverance, Perseverance, Perseverance

The ability to persist in the face of adversity probably accounts for most human miracles. People want instant gratification. They want what they want, they want it now, and they don't want to have to work for it. That is why so many people flock to get-rich-quick schemes, faddish diets, self-help books that promise instant cures, casinos and lotteries, and other devices that advertise getting a lot for almost nothing in return.

People flock to products or programs that promise instant results with almost no effort. This is especially the case with regard to stress reduction—looking for a pill, an easy technique, or simple solution that will produce relief and satisfaction.

Mastery of anything in life takes time and considerable effort. Mastery is exemplified by Michelangelo working flat on his back for seven years, on unstable scaffolding, painting *The Creation of Adam* and *The Last Judgment* that adorn the ceiling of the Sistine Chapel; by Ernest Hemingway completely rewriting *The Old Man and the Sea* 38 times before he was satisfied; and by Thomas Edison failing 10,000 times before finding the right filament for the electric light bulb. Mastery is when you stick with a task or challenge that is extremely hard until you meet your standard of excellence.

Making Changes Last

As we approach the end of this semester, and this textbook, the most important question is: what will stick with you over time? What new knowledge and skills will remain a part of your habitual patterns for years to come? How will you incorporate what you learned into a daily part of your life to manage and prevent stress in the future?

Unfortunately, research shows that most initial self-improvement efforts don't last. The majority of people who make New Year's resolutions to reduce stress in their lives give up within a few months (Prochaska, Norcross, & DiClemente, 1995). Among those trying to stop addictions to alcohol, drugs, or other self-destructive behavior, up to 80% of people in treatment programs end up relapsing (Laws, 1999). Even among those who enter psychotherapy to deal with ongoing stress difficulties, whereas 80% to 90% make solid progress during and immediately after the sessions, almost half will eventually relapse (Kottler, 2001). In addition, apparently the reason why there are over 20,000 self-help books on the market is that they don't usually work for very long, causing readers to be on the hunt for other quick cures (Pearsall, 2005).

Why should things be any different with what you have learned in *this* course and text?

While making changes that last a lifetime is challenging, it is not impossible—*if* you take certain steps to avoid the usual mistakes that people make, especially those who are unprepared. There is some good news: among those who make lifestyle changes to reduce stress and improve quality of life, three-quarters are *eventually* successful, even if this takes more than a half dozen attempts (Butler, 2005).

The key to making constructive changes in your own life, whether related to reducing stress or initiating any other significant improvement, is to understand the nature of the ways your behavior is self-regulated. This means that in addition to becoming influenced by events, people, and stressors around you, there is within your control the potential to make adjustments that can prevent relapses and failures. In fact, most stress-related disorders and problems, ranging from addictions to excessive spending, can be traced to a lack of self-control or self-regulation (Baumeister, Heatherton, & Tice, 1994).

What Sabotages Lasting Change

You may have already experienced the phenomenon of learning certain things for a particular class, or test, but soon afterwards forgetting the material. Schools and other institutions routinely assess performance immediately after content is learned, but do very little in the way of follow-up to determine how much of it stays with you over time.

FOR REFLECTION 14.7

Think of a change you made in your life, one that seemed very important to you at the time, but for some reason the results did not endure.

Think of another instance in which you initiated a change that you have managed to stick with over time, in spite of distractions, obstacles, and setbacks.

What strikes you as the difference between these two change efforts, one that lasted and one that did not?

There are several reasons why so little attention has been devoted to studying lasting change. First, the news is usually depressing. Pick out a course you had your first term in college: how well would you do if you had to take a test on that material right now? Second, there is little consensus about how to define a failure. How do you know if you are experiencing a temporary setback rather than a complete relapse? It is often difficult to view what constitutes success versus failure. People may not report accurately what is actually going on in their lives, because they are in denial, lying, or don't see clearly what is happening. Therapists are often frustrated in their work because clients will say that things are going well, when they really are not; or they will say that things are going miserably when they are actually improving quite significantly. To complicate matters further, the client will report one perception of change, family members will see another, and the therapist may see something quite different.

Perhaps the most compelling reason why so little is understood about lasting change is that it is the nature of the world, in terms of both physical and human processes, to remain in a constant state of flux. Things are always evolving and rarely staying the same. Yet it is still difficult to see these developments except retrospectively, after a considerable period of time.

As you will note in For Reflection 14.7, there are many reasons why changes don't seem to last very long, and why once you initiate some sort of constructive program you often end up failing.

FOR REFECTION 14.8

Undermining Changes

Think about what has most often sabotaged your efforts to make changes last— not your attempts to initiate the changes in the first place, but your efforts to maintain them.

Among all of the techniques and strategies of stress management presented in this text, think of one or two that you began some time ago with the best intentions to continue for the rest of your life (or at least to get you through the next year or two). You thought to yourself: "Gee, this sounds intriguing. I really need something like this in my life. I'll give this a try."

It is now several weeks or months later, and you are no longer following through on this change you started. It didn't last. What went wrong? In other words, what sabotaged your effort to continue your commitment?

For each of the following common factors that sabotage lasting change, note below how they applied to your situation:

- *Unrealistic goals.* You set objectives for yourself that were not reasonable or attainable, thus setting yourself up for discouragement and failure.

- *Developmental readiness.* You rushed things and forced yourself to make a commitment to do something before you were really ready.

- *Personality traits.* You didn't seem to have the motivation, the hardiness, or perseverance to keep going because at times you got distracted, forgot, or didn't have the energy.

- *Lack of coping skills.* Once you began the effort you realized at some point that you were not well enough equipped to deal with the obstacles and challenges along the way. This could occur because you were missing other necessary coping skills (time management, problem solving, assertiveness).

- *Secondary gains.* Remember the idea that sometimes you fail because you "enjoy" the benefits? What were the advantages to you of failure? Think in terms of being able to avoid responsibility and blame others—or things outside of your control.

- *Lack of support.* You weren't reinforced and supported in your efforts by friends and family. In some cases, they may have even sabotaged your efforts.

- *Negative moods.* If you find yourself becoming unduly depressed or discouraged by the progress you made, or didn't see immediate results, you may have lost motivation and initiative to keep going.

Social Support System

You have learned how stress can be contagious. When you spend time around people with frantic lifestyles, or who engage in unhealthy behavior, it is difficult to resist the temptation to follow their examples. Likewise, when you function in an environment that reinforces self-destructive behavior, it is hard to break away to practice healthier options.

Whatever changes you have decided to make as a result of your study of stress management and prevention, those behaviors will not persist unless you surround yourself with others who hold similar values and are equally committed to making healthy, stress-free choices. This can be a challenge with respect to your family because you can't choose your parents, siblings, and other relatives, some of whom may aggravate you or try to sabotage your work; for better and for worse, your family is a part of your life, although you can set certain limits and also minimize unhealthy interactions. Your friends and peer group are another matter.

In order to maintain constructive changes, you will have to make an honest assessment of who in your world is most supportive of your efforts, as well as those who seem most threatened. It is a common experience that whenever anyone makes significant lifestyle changes, it almost always involves some degree of negotiation and adjustment with friends and family: you should expect this and not be surprised if you encounter some resistance.

If prior to your self-improvement program you were into a life of sloth and self-indulgence, it is likely you hung out with people who shared your interest in self-neglect. You will not necessarily end these relationships (although you may experience some distance), but you will probably make connections with new friends and peers who share values that are now more consistent with your own (see For Reflection 14.8).

It is critical that you surround yourself with others you trust, not only those who support constructive changes, but also those whom you can talk to about things that are bothering you and feel safe doing so. Talking about difficult challenges you are facing goes a long way in helping you reduce the stress you might be feeling (Barry, Hudley, Kelly, & Cho, 2009).

FOR REFLECTION 14.9

Make a list below of the people with whom you share the closest trust and intimacy. This may include friends, family, classmates, and coworkers.

Next to each of their names, write down what you have in common with that person, as well as a few notes about your shared values.

Put a star (*) next to the names of those who you believe will be most supportive of your efforts to initiate and maintain desired changes in your life.

Put a question mark (?) next to the names of those who you think may feel threatened by, or unhappy with, the adjustments you intend to make.

Suggestions for a Positive Stress Management and Prevention Program

Based on what you have learned about positive psychology, optimal functioning, and making changes last, you may feel intrigued enough to want to apply the concepts to enhance your own signature strengths. Already you have been introduced to the counter-idea that one can think about stress in terms not only of its presence but also of its absence—to focus on the times when you demonstrate tranquility and control.

Here are several suggestions as to how you might apply these concepts to prevent and manage undue stress in your life.

1. *Accept the fact that stress is an inevitable part of life and decide to respond to it positively.* No matter what you do, and how hard you try, there will be failures, heartbreaks, and disappointments in your life. The only thing you can control is how you respond to these challenges. This begins with the reconceptualization of disappointments and stressors as challenges for you to face that can potentially help you grow more resourceful and flexible in the future. That which is not within your power to change (the weather, other people's behavior) can be

accepted, or at least acknowledged as relatively stable factors. Instead you can concentrate on changing states of stress to eustress, the sort of positive arousal that actually enhances performance.

2. *Prevent stress by studying your usual patterns of vulnerability.* Based on this knowledge, take preemptive measures to stop stress before it does any major damage to your health. As you may recall from Chapter 1, stress is composed of a four-stage process that includes a *stressor*, then your *perception* of what you are facing, a *response* to that situation, and subsequent *consequences*. Before each stage in this process, you have certain choices that allow you to respond in a particular way. You can, for instance, change your perception of the situation, or alter your usual response to a more measured alternative. It is within your power, even if it sometimes doesn't feel that way, to reduce the power of any perceived threat. This is most easily accomplished when you have a number of stress management options in your repertoire. When you can identify the types of stressors that cause you the most difficulty, then you can better prepare a different set of responses to deal with them.

3. *Find out what you love to do and plunge into it.* One of the greatest sources of stress is being stuck in a job or classes you don't like or that you feel are over your head. When you enjoy what you are doing, time seems to pass faster. Too much leisure time can leave room for doubts and worries. It is a matter of finding a calling, something that speaks to you in such a way that you totally immerse yourself in the activity.

4. *Turn stress into energy for success.* Stress presents a paradoxical façade in that its initial negative energy can provide opportunities for constructive action. So many great achievements in science, the arts, athletics, and other fields occurred precisely because the innovator was under significant pressure—and rose to the occasion. Stress is one price you pay for performing at your highest level.

5. *Become more mindful about ways you can enjoy the present instead of ruminating about the past or worrying about the future.* Piet and Hougaard (2011) completed a meta-analysis suggesting that mindfulness-based cognitive therapy is an effective intervention for relapse prevention in patients with recurrent major depression disorder. There are several ways you can practice mindfulness every day, even every hour.

- *Remember to breathe.* Take a cleansing breath as often as possible to clear your mind and center yourself. There is probably no other single technique or skill that works quite as well to reduce stress. Practice breath-focus meditation (see Chapter 8) for 15 minutes a day.
- *Stretch your body.* Roll your shoulders. Touch your toes. Loosen your back. Open your mouth wide. Do something, anything, to eliminate the tension you feel.
- *Take a break from technology.* Turn off your phone. Disconnect yourself from the computer. Spend at least an hour a day in which you deliberately focus only on what you are doing, with no distractions or interruptions.
- *Do one thing at a time.* Reduce stress by forcing a clearer focus on one task that is important to you, whether this is talking to a friend, reading an assignment, or taking a walk.
- *Give or ask for a hug.* I mean this literally but also as a symbol of expressing and receiving affection from those you care about most. Physical touch and hugs actually are helpful in reducing stress and improving performance. Some studies have shown that team athletes who touch each other more (pats on the back, high fives, celebratory hugs) perform better than those who avoid such contact.

VOICE OF STRESS MANAGEMENT 14.3

Thirty-Six-Year-Old Female

My life was a complete fiasco until my 36th birthday. I had had two unsuccessful marriages and was dating someone I was considering marrying. I was struggling financially because I was raising my three-year-old son all by myself and going to college part-time. My health was failing—even my teeth were becoming loose. My stress level went through the roof. I tried to handle the situation by taking yoga and eating healthy foods. These disciplines made me feel a little better, but they didn't eliminate my problems. Deep inside, I was filled with anger and fear. I did not have any confidence in my future, and I had my doubts about this impending marriage. I thought it was doomed as another failure.

The real turning point came when I realized how I had become a passive victim in my own life. I consulted books that talked about how you can't get what you really want in life until you change the underlying structures. It's not about problem solving or mastering a few techniques but about unleashing our own creativity. This helped me to understand myself better and my patterns of when and how I get in trouble. With the help of a therapist at this point, I realized the role of my childhood in shaping my views, my deepest fears, and my desires. I sat down and wrote my goals for my health and financial future. From then on, my life has changed dramatically and permanently, for I realized that I used to be a passive recipient of what life handed to me and I am now the creator of my circumstances. Every day, I am working toward my desired goals, feeling in control and confident.

Ask for Help if You Can't Manage on Your Own

There is a difference between so-called "normal stress," the kind that is part of daily living and the usual adjustments associated with college life, and mental disorders that require medical or psychological intervention. In Chapter 4 you learned about the phobias, panic disorder, anxiety disorder, obsessive-compulsive disorder, posttraumatic stress disorder, depressive disorders, eating disorders, and other self-destructive behaviors that represent underlying emotional problems or mental illness. The prevalence of these psychological disorders seems to be growing on college campuses, with 40% of women reporting problems with eating disorders at some time and half of all students experiencing severe depression (Kadison & DiGeronimo, 2005). Suicide is the third largest cause of death among high-school and college-age students, most of whom do not seek help prior to killing themselves (Marano, 2004).

Such extreme stress-related difficulties will often not improve without some professional intervention, whether in the form of prescriptive medication, psychotherapy, inpatient treatment, or a combination of these options.

How do you know if you are—or a friend or family member is—struggling to the point that it is time to seek help? Consider the following warning signs:

- sleep and eating patterns seriously disrupted for at least two weeks;

- significant weight loss or gain within a three-month period;

- symptoms continuing for more than six months without significant improvement;

- concentration, memory, and daily functioning impaired;

- lethargy and lack of energy;

- work and school performance affected;

- feelings of helplessness and hopelessness;

VOICE OF STRESS MANAGEMENT 14.4

Twenty-Five-Year-Old Female Graduate Student

I was having these anxiety attacks a while back, when I was an undergraduate. I tried breathing exercises and taking walks, but they just didn't go away. My life was stressful and I was overwhelmed with work, school, and just trying to survive. I went to see a counselor, but we could never agree on a good time to meet. I started feeling better, though, and figured that just making some small changes like the breathing and walking had helped. Maybe I felt better because I had actually tried to talk to someone. Whatever it was, it seemed to work for a little while. I was still stressed, but was not having actual anxiety attacks. Then when I got into graduate school, things seemed to get worse.

I tried more breathing exercises, walking more, even talking to my friends about it. That stuff didn't work for me this time. I decided that it was time to try counseling again. This time I found a therapist who could see me in the evenings when I had time. At first nothing seemed to change, but soon I found that I had all this stuff (a lot of parental resentment) all pushed down inside of me. After getting it out and using some new techniques . . . journaling, some behavior modification . . . I felt better! This time the anxiety really didn't come back. I think that getting out all of that pent-up anger really helped. I was also taught to be flexible in my approach to problem solving and to accept that if one thing doesn't work, or stops working, there are always other options and that it was okay.

- chronic thoughts of doom and gloom that don't respond to cognitive restructuring;
- relationship conflicts that are becoming consistently worse;
- use of illicit drugs or alcohol making things worse;
- auditory or visual hallucinations;
- thoughts of suicide.

At most university campuses, a minimum of 10% of the student population will visit the counseling center during any given year (Marano, 2004). Students most often report problems related to anxiety and depression, as well as relationship problems with family, roommates, instructors, and boyfriends/girlfriends. It's a time when many students grapple with issues related to independence, identity, and values. They also frequently struggle with the various stressors that are part of student life, many of which can overload your ability to juggle multiple responsibilities.

Being a student on most college campuses affords you distinct benefits that you would not otherwise have access to—not only are counseling services completely private and confidential, but they are prepaid with the student fees that are part of your registration. Regardless of whether you need help with study skills; becoming more assertive; dealing with roommate, relationship, or family conflicts; dealing with depression; overcoming addictions; coping with stress; finding greater meaning to your life—counseling can give you support, guidance, and direction that you might not be able to find on your own.

There are several sources of help available to you if you find that you cannot handle things on your own, or if you feel that it would be helpful to speak with an impartial professional who can help you sort things out. The first thing you can do is to join a support group, whether it is offered on campus or in your community. Because stress is such a common problem in contemporary life, there are stress management groups to help you to practice many of the things you have learned in this course in a context of ongoing support. It also helps to do some more reading about stress on your own, particularly

---

FOR REFLECTION 14.10

Self-Assessment Comparison

In the first chapter you were asked to complete this self-assessment exercise. Now that you are on the verge of completing the course and text, go through the activity again to identify the top five stressors in your life, describe how you have coped with them, and rank your effectiveness of coping. After you finish the exercise, go back to Chapter 1 to see what changes have occurred since last time.

Stressors in my life	Coping strategies	Ranking: 1 = least effective; 5 = most effective
1.		
2.		
3.		
4.		
5.		

---

books that describe in greater detail specific exercises that you can learn and practice on your own (for example, see Davis, Eshelman, & McKay, 2008; Forsyth & Eifert, 2007; McKay, David, & Fanning, 2007; Stahl & Goldstein, 2010).

Another option you have is to seek a medical consultation if the symptoms have some biological basis. In this case, you may be asked to take a physical exam, get some tests completed, and then perhaps take medication to help control the symptoms. An additional possibility is to consult with a psychotherapist who can assist you in addressing some of the underlying problems that are getting in your way. In some cases, a physician and therapist may work collaboratively to help you.

A Review of Things You Learned

The stress management and prevention strategies you have learned in this book can be organized according to the symptoms manifested, as follows:

1. *Physical arousal.* These are the fight-or-flight responses felt in your body such as muscle tension, jittery nerves, stomach aches or headaches, and feeling faint.

2. *Mental anguish.* These are the disturbing thoughts that represent exaggerations, dread, obsessions, and ruminations.

3. *Emotional reactions.* These include fears, worries, apprehension, anger, frustration, anxiety, and depression.

Table 14.3 summarizes the strategies you have learned according to the appropriate symptoms (Wehrenberg, 2005). Many of the methods operate on multiple dimensions at the same time, affecting the physical, cognitive, and emotional realms.

Table 14.3 A summary of stress management and prevention strategies

Physical arousal	Nutrition
	Meditation
	Exercise
	Sleep
	Autogenic training
	Tai chi
	Yoga
	Muscle relaxation
	Breathing
Mental anguish	Cognitive restructuring
	Creating meaning
	Reframing
	Self-talk
	Study skills
	Thought stopping
	Time management
	Psychotherapy
	Journaling
Emotional reactions	Imagery
	Anger control
	Prayer
	Trauma recovery
	Medication
	Assertiveness training
	Conflict resolution

FOR REFLECTION 14.11

Looking Back

As you look back on all the things that you have reflected on and written about in this class and text, what stands out for you as being most significant?

A Final Summary And Some Honest, Realistic Parting Messages

After you read a book, take a class, or even consult with a therapist, you may find yourself mobilized to make some positive changes to improve your life. In reality, a new habit, a new way of living, takes a *lot* of effort and self-regulation before it becomes a part of who you are and what you do. In this chapter, you have learned the importance of setting goals for change, monitoring feedback, and making adjustments once relapses occur.

To create lasting change, it is important to know what factors will most likely sabotage your efforts so that you may anticipate and plan for them. In addition to improving your self-regulatory skills, establishing a strong social support system is a key factor that predicts continued progress. When all else fails, or simply when you want the assistance of a trained professional, it is a good idea to consult with a therapist who specializes in stress-related problems.

Although this book—and this class—are drawing to a close, this is really the beginning for you, not the end. Throughout the semester you learned many concepts and skills that can literally change your life in many ways that not only reduce the stress but also enhance satisfaction and joy. Like so many exercise programs or diets you have begun, as well as promises you have made, the initial effort can only be sustained with ongoing commitment. So far, the going has been relatively easy considering you have had the structure of regular assignments, required class sessions, and programmed activities. At times you may have resented this structure because you had other things you'd rather do, or other places you'd rather be, but ultimately it was this structure that made it easier for you to learn the material and skills in the course.

Now the really hard part begins. Without the structure of needing to attend classes, an instructor to help you be accountable for your behavior and to complete your assignments, a peer group to share your experiences, or the threat of external evaluation to keep you focused on the work, there is a great temptation to let yourself slide. Will everything you have learned slowly fade into oblivion? Will you "forget" the valuable lessons that seemed so important when you made the promise to apply them? Within a few months from now will it seem like this course never occurred?

In order to make these—or *any*—changes last *you* are the one who has to decide just how important it is to keep stress under control in your life. Such a task is not easy, nor is the prognosis all that optimistic—unless you take steps to plan for setbacks ahead of time and follow through on those things that you now say are so important.

ONE FINAL REFLECTIVE ACTIVITY

To complete this exercise you will need to bring a stamped, self-addressed envelope to class with a sheet of paper sealed inside that includes the following resolution.

Make a commitment, in writing, about what you intend to do and follow through with in the coming year. Declare *exactly* what you will do to reduce stress in your life and improve the quality of your life. Be as specific as you can in listing your plans, what you will do, how you will do it, and what you will do in those instances when you "forget." It is also important that you be realistic about what you can follow through with given your lifestyle, your history, your time commitments, and your goals.

Sign and date your declaration at the end. Put the paper in a sealed envelope and bring it to class. You will either give the envelope to your instructor or exchange it with a peer, who will mail it to you one year from today. Throughout the next year, there will be times when your energy will flag, when you drift from your intentions, and when you will find excuses as to why it no longer matters. That's fine: it is *your* life. But when that envelope comes in the mail, remember that once, one year earlier, you thought it was extremely important that you take better charge of your life.

I wish you all the very best in your journey!

QUESTIONS FOR REVIEW

1. Discuss the essence of a proactive approach to stress management and prevention based on the science of positive psychology.
2. Discuss how human strengths are connected with well-being.
3. What makes people happy and satisfied? List all possible causes and describe them briefly.
4. Describe the domains of human well-being and optimal functioning in terms of their significance to understanding human strengths and promoting mental health. Explain why psychologists call these components the symptoms of well-being.
5. Discuss different ways to enhance happiness. Share with each other in small groups your personal experiences in these areas.
6. Define flow experience and explain what are the conditions that lead to flow. Discuss the connection between flow and happiness.
7. Define peak performance.
8. Describe ways to achieve peak performance in your work and life.
9. Summarize the ways you can manage and prevent stress by taking a proactive approach.
10. List and explain the reasons why the subject of lasting change has often been ignored.
11. How can you build a support system to support the changes you have made, and intend to make in the future?
12. Summarize all the steps you need to take to create lasting change.

SELECTED ANSWERS

Answer to For Reflection 14.1

- clear, logical, rational thinking that allows people to see reality with minimal distortion;
- high degree of self-acceptance and absence of self-critical attitude, plus the ability to examine their own behavior critically and honestly;
- involved in loving, intimate, and healthy relationships that are supportive;
- independence, autonomy, and resourcefulness to be able to take care of one's own needs (within a particular cultural context);
- ability to be spontaneous and playful, even during potentially stressful circumstances;
- plays well with others and can function well as part of a team to complete tasks;
- empathy and caring toward others, regardless of individual and cultural differences;
- resist peer pressure and acculturation but able to feel a part of their culture;
- constructive risk-taking and openness to new experiences and embracing change;
- high sense of moral duty and responsibility that leads them to engage in selfless, altruistic behavior;
- creativity in their work, their relationships, and every facet of their lives;
- enjoyment of solitude and time alone without feeling lonely;
- sense of humor that allows them to see the absurdity of some aspects of life;
- appreciation for their own and others' limitations, but able to focus on strengths.

REVIEW ACTIVITY

Review Activity 14.1: Recovering from Relapses

It is not only probable but inevitable that you will experience relapses in your attempts to incorporate stress prevention and management skills into your normal pattern. Old habits are difficult to break. You will "forget" what you learned and slip back into familiar routines. People in your life will feel threatened by the changes you are making, even trying to sabotage them at times. During times of stress, when you are under maximum pressure, you may regress. Temptations will continue to challenge you. Rather than feeling afraid of the relapses and backslides you may (and will) experience, remember how you learned to "reframe" them as temporary learning experiences. The most important part of what you learned in this class is not what you do that works well for you, but rather how you respond to disappointment, discouragement, and *initial* failures.

While you have been enrolled in this course you have already encountered times when you fell backward. Describe one such relapse in which you resorted to old, maladaptive patterns, recognized what you were doing, and then made the adjustments it took to get back on track.

Remember in the coming months and years that it is no big deal to have a *temporary* relapse, *if* you recognize what is going on and motivate yourself to apply what you have learned.

REFERENCES AND RESOURCES

Argyle, M. (2003). Causes and correlates of happiness. In D. Kahneman, E. Diener, & N. Schwarz (Eds.), *Well-being: The foundations of hedonic psychology.* New York, NY: Russell Sage Foundation Press.

Barry, L. M., Hudley, C., Kelly, M., & Cho, S. (2009). Differences in self-reported disclosure of college experiences by first-generation college student status. *Adolescence, 44*(173), 56–68.

Baumeister, R. F., Heatherton, T. F., & Tice, D. M. (1994). *Losing control: How and why people fail at self-regulation.* San Diego, CA: Academic.

Baumeister, R. F., & Vohs, K. D. (2004). *Handbook of self-regulation: Research, theory, and applications.* New York, NY: Guilford.

Beilock, S. L., & Carr, T. H. (2001). On the fragility of skilled performance: What governs choking under pressure. *Journal of Experimental Psychology: General, 130*(4), 701–725.

Bowman, N., Brandenberger, J., Lapsley, D., Hill, P., & Quaranto, J. (2010). Serving in college, flourishing in adulthood: Does community engagement during the college years predict adult well-being? *Applied Psychology: Health and Well-Being, 2,* 14–34.

Butler, C. K. (2005, December 27). 50 ways to fix your life. *U.S. News and World Report,* pp. 30–32.

Camfield, L., & Skevington, S. M. (2008). On subjective well-being and quality of life. *Journal of Health Psychology, 13,* 764–775.

Carr, A. (2004). *Positive psychology: The science of happiness and human strengths.* New York, NY: Brunner-Routledge.

Csikzentimihalyi, M. (1975). *Beyond boredom and anxiety: The experience of play.* San Francisco, CA: Jossey-Bass.

Csikzentimihalyi, M. (1990). *Flow: The psychology of optimal experience.* New York, NY: Harper & Row.

Csikszentmihalyi, M. (1997). *Finding flow: The psychology of engagement with everyday life.* New York, NY: Basic Books.

Csikszentmihalyi, M., Abuhamdeh, S., & Nakamura, J. (2005). Flow. In A. J. Elliott, & C. S. Dweck (Eds.), *Handbook of competence and motivation* (pp. 598–608). New York, NY: The Guilford Press.

Davis, M., Eshelman, E. R., & McKay, M. (2008). *The relaxation and stress reduction workbook* (6th ed.). Oakland, CA: New Harbinger.

Fava, G. (1999). Well-being therapy: Conceptual and technical issues. *Psychotherapy and Psychosomatics, 68,* 171–179.

Fava, G. A., & Ruini, C. (2003). Development and characteristics of a well-being enhancing psychotherapeutic strategy: Well-being therapy. *Journal of Behavior Therapy and Experimental Psychiatry, 34,* 45–63.

Fernández-Ballesteros, R. (2003). Light and dark in the psychology of human strengths: The example of psychologerontology. In L. G. Aspinwall, & U. M. Staudinger (Eds.), *A psychology of human strengths: Fundamental questions for a positive psychology* (pp. 131–147). Washington, DC: American Psychological Association.

Fitzsimons, G. M., & Bargh, J. A. (2004). Automatic self-regulation. In R. F. Baumeister, & K. D. Vohs (Eds.), *Handbook of self-regulation: Research, theory, and applications* (pp. 151–170). New York, NY: Guilford Press.

Forsyth, J. P., & Eifert, G. H. (2007). *The mindfulness and acceptance workbook for anxiety.* Oakland, CA: New Harbinger.

Fraser, K. (1991). *Bad trips.* New York, NY: Vintage Books.

Ingersoll, R. E., & Rak, C. F. (2006). *Psychopharmacology for helping professionals.* Belmont, CA: Thomson.

Kabat-Zinn, J. (2005). *Coming to our senses: Healing ourselves and the world through mindfulness.* New York, NY: Hyperion.

Kadison, R., & DiGeronimo, T. F. (2005). *College of the overwhelmed: The campus mental health crisis and what to do about it.* San Francisco, CA: Jossey-Bass.

Kahneman, D., Krueger, A. B., Schkade, D., Schwartz, N., & Stone, A. A. (2006). Would you be happier if you were richer? A focusing illusion. *Science, 312,* 1908–1910.

Keyes, C. L. M. (2003). Complete mental health: An agenda for the 21st century. In C. L. M. Keyes & J. Haidt (Eds.), *Flourishing: Positive psychology and the life well-lived* (pp. 293–312). Washington, DC: American Psychological Association.

Keyes, C. L. M. (2005). Mental illness and/or mental health? Investigating axioms of the complete state model of health. *Journal of Consulting and Clinical Psychology, 73,* 539–548.

Kottler, J. A. (1997). *Travel that can change your life.* San Francisco, CA: Jossey-Bass.

Kottler, J. A. (2001). *Making changes last.* New York, NY: Routledge.

Kottler, J. A., & Carlson, J. (2002). *Bad therapy: Master therapists share their worst failures.* New York, NY: Brunner-Routledge.

Kottler, J. A., & Marriner, M. (2009). *Changing people's lives while transforming your own: Paths to social justice and global human rights.* New York, NY: Wiley.

Kunzmann, U., & Baltes, P. B. (2003). Wisdom-related knowledge: Affective, motivational, and interpersonal correlates. *Personality and Social Psychology Bulletin, 29,* 1104–1119.

Laws, D. R. (1999). Relapse prevention: The state of the art. *Journal of Interpersonal Violence, 14,* 285–302.

Linley, P. A., & Joseph, S. (2004). *Positive psychology in practice.* New York, NY: Wiley.

Loehr, J. E. (1986). *Mental toughness training for sports: Achieving athletic excellence.* Lexington, MA: Stephen Greene Press.

Lyubomirsky, S., & Lepper, H. (1999). A measure of subjective happiness: Preliminary reliability and construct validation. *Social Indicators Research, 46,* 137–155.

Marano, H. E. (2004). Up against the ivy wall in 2004. *Psychology Today.* Retrieved from http://psychologytoday.com/articles/200405/against-the-ivy-wall-in-2004.

Marlatt, G. A., & Donovan, D. M. (Eds.) (2005). *Relapse prevention* (2nd ed.). New York, NY: Guilford.

McKay, M., David, M., & Fanning, P. (2007). *Thoughts and feelings: Taking control of your moods and life.* Oakland, CA: New Harbinger.

McQuaid, J. R., & Carmona, P. E. (2004). *Peaceful mind: Using mindfulness and cognitive behavioral psychology to overcome depression.* Oakland, CA: New Harbinger.

Meichenbaum, D. (1985). *Stress inoculation training.* New York, NY: Pergamon.

Metcalf, J., & Mischel, W. (1999). A hot/cool system analysis of delay of gratification: Dynamics of willpower. *Psychological Review, 106,* 3–19.

Milkman, H. B., & Sunderwirth, S. G. (2010). *Craving for ecstasy and natural highs.* Thousand Oaks, CA: Sage.

Myers, D. (1999). Close relationships and quality of life. In D. Kahneman, & E. Diener (Eds.), *Well-being: The foundations of hedonic psychology* (pp. 374–391). New York, NY: Russell Sage Foundation.

Neimark, J. (2007). The optimism revolution. *Psychology Today,* May/June, pp. 88–92.

Ornish, D. (1998). *Love and survival.* New York, NY: HarperCollins.

Park, A. (2006, January 16). Getting and staying in the zone. *Time,* pp. 102–103.

Pearsall, P. (2003). *The Beethoven factor: The new positive psychology of hardiness, happiness, healing, and hope.* Charlottesville, VA: Hampton Roads.

Pearsall, P. (2005). *The last self-help book you'll ever need.* New York, NY: Perseus.

Peterson, C., & Seligman, M. E. P. (2004). *Character strengths and virtues.* New York, NY: Oxford University Press.

Piet, J., & Hougaard, E. (2011). The effect of mindfulness-based cognitive therapy for prevention of relapse in recurrent major depressive disorder: A systematic review and meta-analysis. *Clinical Psychology Review, 31*(6), 1,032–1,040.

Prochaska, J. O., Norcross, J. C., & DiClemente, C. (1995). *Changing for good.* New York, NY: Avon Books.

Restak, R. (2004). *Poe's heart and the mountain climber: Exploring the effect of anxiety on our brains and our culture.* New York, NY: Harmony.

Rietschlin, J. (1998). Voluntary association membership and psychological distress. *Journal of Health and Social Behavior, 39,* 348–355.

Ronstadt, R. (1988). The corridor principle. *Journal of Business Venturing, 3,* 31–40.

Ryff, C. D., & Singer, B. (1998). Human health: New directions for the next millennium. *Psychological Inquiry, 9,* 69–85.

Ryff, C. D., & Singer, B. (2003). Flourishing under fire: Resilience as a prototype of challenged thriving. In C. L. M. Keyes & J. Haidt (Eds.), *Flourishing: Positive psychology and the life well-lived* (pp. 15–36). Washington, DC: American Psychological Association.

Sarafino, E. (2002). *Health psychology* (4th ed.). New York, NY: Wiley.

Segal, Z. V., Williams, J. M. G., & Tisdale, J. D. (2001). *Mindfulness-based cognitive therapy for depression: A new approach to preventing relapse.* New York, NY: Guilford.

Seligman, M. E. P. (2002). *Authentic happiness: Using the new positive psychology to realize your potential for lasting fulfillment.* New York, NY: Free Press.

Seligman, M. E. P. (2003). Foreword: The past and future of positive psychology. In C. L. M. Keyes & J. Haidt (Eds.), *Flourishing: Positive psychology and the life well-lived* (pp. xi–xx). Washington, DC: American Psychological Association.

Seligman, M. E. P. (2011). *Flourish: A visionary new understanding of happiness and well-being.* New York, NY: Free Press.

Seligman, M. E., & Csikszentmihalyi, M. (2000). Positive psychology: An introduction. *American Psychologist, 55*(1), 5–14.

Seligman, M. E., Rashid, T., & Parks, A. C. (2006). Positive psychotherapy. *American Psychologist, 61,* 774–788.

Seligman, M. E. P., Steen, T. A., Park, N., & Peterson, C. (2005). Positive psychology progress: Empirical validation of interventions. *American Psychologist, 60,* 410–421.

Snyder, C. R., & Lopez, S. (Eds.) (2005). *Handbook of positive psychology.* New York, NY: Oxford University Press.

Stahl, B., & Goldstein, E. (2010). *A mindfulness-based stress reduction workbook.* Oakland, CA: New Harbinger.

Sternberg, R. J. (2003). Driven to despair: Why we need to redefine the concept and measurement of intelligence. In L. G. Aspinwall & U. M. Staudinger (Eds.), *A psychology of human strengths: Fundamental questions for a positive psychology* (pp. 319–329). Washington, DC: American Psychological Association.

Wehrenberg, M. (2005). 10 best-ever anxiety management techniques. *Psychotherapy Networker,* September/October, 47–70.

Zimmerman, B. J., & Kitsantas, A. (1997). Developmental phases in self-regulation: Shifting from process to outcome self-regulatory goals. *Journal of Educational Psychology, 89,* 29–36.

Glossary

ABC theory of emotions. A psychotherapy theory that plots, logically and sequentially, the mechanisms by which people become upset and how they might change the negative feelings through certain thinking patterns that are deemed more rational and reality-based.

Absolute demands. An irrational belief that the world is supposed to grant the individual's any wish.

Absolute judgments. Overgeneralizations about oneself or others based on limited information or insufficient evidence.

Abstract reasoning. Patterns of mental operations marked by children's increasing ability to use logical thought processes typical in the last of Piaget's four major cognitive development stages.

Acculturation stress. The cultural and psychological changes that result from continuous contact between two or more groups.

ACTH. An abbreviation for adrenocorticotropic hormone, which regulates the activity of the adrenal cortex and is released by the anterior portion of the pituitary.

Activating event (A). The first stage in the ABC theory of emotions, which describes a situation that most people believe is *causing* the stressful difficulty.

Adrenal gland. The endocrine glands on top of each kidney that secrete stress hormones including the catecholamines and cortisol.

Adrenaline. Same as epinephrine.

Aerobic exercise. Physical activity performed at moderate levels of intensity for extended periods of time in which the body is supplied with sufficient oxygen.

Ageism. A pervasive negative view about advancing age, stereotyping older persons as debilitated, inadequate, dependent.

Allostasis. The process by which bodily functions change in response to environmental or mental challenges.

Allostatic load. The excessive and prolonged environmental and mental challenges that lead to wear and tear on the body.

Altered states of consciousness. Non-psychotic states that have a particular content, form, or quality to them that is significantly different from ordinary states of consciousness.

Amygdala. Part of the limbic system that is central in regulating emotion and fear responses.

Anaerobic exercise. Physical activity in its initial stage, or of short duration, in which the demand for oxygen in the body exceeds the supply.

Angst. Extreme anxiety about existence.

Anorexia nervosa. A medical condition primarily affecting adolescent girls, involving a loss of 15–25% of ideal body weight and subsequent refusal or inability to eat normally.

Arteriosclerosis. The hardening and narrowing of artery walls due to cholesterol buildup and calcium deposits.

Astanga. A style of yoga that is a physically demanding practice targeted at focusing the mind and body.

Attending. Special listening behaviors that demonstrate focused concentration and interest.

Attributional style. The habitual way of explaining the causes of good and bad events along three dimensions: internal, stable, and global.

Autogenic training. A relaxation technique that involves self-induced sensations of heaviness, warmth, and tingling in the limbs.

Autoimmune diseases. Diseases that occur when an overactive immune system attacks the body.

Autonomic nervous system. The self-governing part of the nervous system containing nerves that control smooth muscle, cardiac muscle, and glands; motor portion of the visceral or involuntary nervous system.

Awfulizing. A set of irrational beliefs in which an individual thinks he/she has suffered the worst tragedy imaginable.

Battle fatigue.   The chronic stress response that results from prolonged exposure to combat.

Behaviorism.   A psychological approach that places an emphasis on taking constructive action rather than simply developing insight as in psychoanalysis.

Binge eating disorder.   A maladaptive behavior in which the person eats a large amount of food in one sitting, often as a form of self-punishment or self-medication for stress.

Biological adaptations hypothesis.   A theoretical view accounting for the benefits of exercise for stress reduction, which states that increased physical functioning and more efficient metabolism improve all the systems of the body including those that regulate mood—such as increases in body warming, brain blood flow, and endorphins.

Bracing.   Unnecessary muscular contractions.

Brainstorming.   A strategy of problem solving with the aim of generating as many potential solutions as possible without regard to their practicality.

Bulimia.   Binge eating followed by purging through vomiting or laxatives as a result of over-concern over body shape and weight.

Burnout.   A physical and psychological condition caused by chronic stress, characterized by exhaustion, diminished interest, and feelings of failure, usually in the work setting.

Cardiovascular system.   The system that delivers oxygen, hormones, nutrients, and white blood cells throughout the body by circulating blood.

Catastrophizing.   The tendency to imagine the worst scenario.

Catharsis.   Expression of pent-up feelings or emotional discharge of tension.

Central nervous system.   The largest part of the nervous system, including the brain and the spinal cord.

Circulatory system.   See *cardiovascular system*.

Classical conditioning.   A pattern of learning discovered by Ivan Pavlov in which a neutral stimulus (bell) paired with an unconditioned stimulus (food) develops a learned or conditioned response (salivation).

Codependency.   One form of learned helplessness embedded in relationships in which the spouses, partners, parents, children, and friends of people with addictive behaviors allow or enable their loved ones to continue their self-destructive behaviors.

Cognitive appraisal.   The part of the transactional model related to cognitively assessing the demands of the situation as well as one's resources for coping with those demands.

Cognitive behavioral therapy (CBT).   A brief psychotherapeutic approach aimed at changing thinking.

Cognitive flexibility.   Mental ability to switch between thinking about different concepts and view the same situation from multiple perspectives simultaneously.

Cognitive restructuring.   A therapeutic process of helping individuals identify self-defeating and negative thoughts, beliefs, or images and present them with more empowering and positive alternatives.

Concern.   Attention given to circumstances in which you might make intelligent plans.

Corridor principle.   A business theory proposed by Ronstadt suggesting that the major underlying reason for the success of many entrepreneurs is that they mustered enough courage and resources to launch their businesses in the first place.

Cortisol.   A corticosteroid hormone produced by the adrenal cortex that is involved in the response to stress.

CRF.   An abbreviation for corticotrophin-releasing factor, a hormone produced by the anterior part of the hypothalamus to trigger the release of ACTH.

Deep message.   The underlying meaning in communication.

Defense mechanisms.   An array of evolved behavioral responses to perceived threats or physical intimidations.

Denial.   A defensive behavior characterized by pretending that something hurtful never occurred, such as when a child acts as if his parents never divorced.

Desensitization training.   A method of psychotherapy used to help the client to reduce anxiety for certain situations by means of repeatedly exposing the individual to a situation.

Developmental tasks.   Specific challenges that are supposed to arise at a particular stage in life.

Diabetes.   (Sapolsky) Type 1 diabetes (a.k.a. juvenile diabetes) is an autoimmune disorder in which the pancreas is unable to secrete insulin. Type 2 diabetes (a.k.a. adult-onset diabetes) is a disorder caused by obesity in which the cells of the body are resistant to the effects of insulin.

Diaphragmatic breathing.   Deep breathing that uses the whole diaphragm, expanding the belly as well as the chest.

Dichotomous thinking.   Irrational reasoning where one forces things into absolute categories.

Digestive system.   Consists of organs that process food sources, converting them into usable energy.

Displacement.   A defensive behavior marked by converting felt anger away from one source (a parent or sibling) and toward another (a doll or toy).

Disputing irrational beliefs (D).   The fourth stage in the ABC theory of emotions where the individual is challenging some of the assumptions to determine the extent of exaggeration or distortion.

Distress.   A kind of stress experience that harms and debilitates the body and mind.

Dopamine.   A neurotransmitter in various brain structures released by dopamine neurons.

Dynamical systems theory (DST).   The interpretation of reality including psychological, physiological, and natural phenomena in terms of self-organizing and coevolving patterns of relationships among the elements in the systems rather than in terms of static and isolated factors.

Ego.   One of the three divisions of the mind in psychoanalytical theory that acts as the negotiator and mediator of the conflicting forces of the id and the superego, constantly attempting to find compromises that allow the individual to pursue pleasure without doing harm to the self and others.

Emergence.   The appearance of new properties that have not existed before as a result of self-organization.

Emotional consequences (C).   The third stage in the ABC theory of emotions, which describes negative feelings as a result of faulty perception of the activating event such as fear, anger, and insecurity.

Emotional hunger. Stress-triggered craving for food especially high in fat or sugar.

Emotional intelligence. The ability to read and respond sensitively to interpersonal situations, as well as to manage feelings effectively.

Emotional intelligence theory. A theory proposing that emotional intelligence is a major type of intelligence that comprises five basic qualities: the ability to recognize one's own emotions, the competence to manage these emotions, self-motivation, accurate recognition of emotions in others, and the capacity to handle relationships.

Endocrine system. Comprises endocrine glands that produce hormones and empty them into the bloodstream to influence physiological functions.

Endogenous depression. A severe form of depression that is mostly biologically based.

Enteric nervous system. Part of the nervous system that directly controls the gastrointestinal system.

Epinephrine. One of the two catecholamines (the other being norepinephrine) secreted by the adrenal medulla resulting in immediate physical preparation for the fight-or-flight response.

Eustress. A kind of stress experience that is potentially good for promoting health and peak performance.

Existential philosophy. A philosophy that emphasizes the uniqueness and isolation of the individual experience in a hostile or indifferent universe, regards human existence as unexplainable, and stresses freedom of choice and responsibility for the consequences of one's acts (*American Heritage Dictionary*).

Explanatory style. A person's idiosyncratic way of explaining personal historical events.

External locus of control. A belief that outside forces determine a person's life and that an individual is at the mercy of his or her environment.

Externalized language. A style of interpretation that blames outside factors for the trouble.

Family life cycle. A sociological term referring to the stages through which typical families progress.

Fetal origins of adult disease (FOAD). An emerging theory in medicine that posits that events during early development have a profound impact on one's risk for development of future adult disease.

Fight-or-flight reaction. The body's reaction to a stressor characterized by increased heart rate, blood pressure, and serum cholesterol.

Flow experience. A positive experience that occurs when an individual is totally immersed in an activity to the extent of losing all track of time, place, and even the sense of self.

Four dimensions of consciousness. Four dimensions of consciousness according to Baruss: (a) the registration of information and acting on it in a goal-directed manner, (b) the explicit knowledge of your situation, mental states, and actions, (c) the stream of thoughts, feelings, and sensations that you have for yourself, and (d) the sense of existence of the subject of mental acts.

General adaptation syndrome (GAS). A pattern of physiological responses, consisting of three phases (alarm, resistance, and exhaustion), to a psychological or physiological stressor.

Glucocorticoids. The adrenal cortex hormones that affect metabolism of fats and carbohydrates.

Guided imagery. Conscious use of the imagination to create positive images in order to bring about healthful changes in both the body and the mind.

Hardiness theory. A theoretical framework positing that three cognitive appraisal processes (i.e., commitment, challenge, and control) serve to buffer the deleterious effects of stressful life situations.

Hardy personalities. Individuals who can put themselves together and continue to perform at superior levels, regardless of the adversity they face.

Hatha. A style of yoga that emphasizes physical balance.

Hippocampus. A cortical structure lying in the medial region of the temporal lobe that plays an important role in memory, spatial navigation, and stress termination.

Holistic approach. A concept of stress management and prevention based on the premise that stress involves physical, emotional, mental, and spiritual components and that well-being occurs when all the four components function as a harmonious unit.

Homeostasis. Balanced environment in the body that is internally regulated.

Hormone. Hormone is an organic chemical substance produced and secreted by a specific organ or tissue and carried through blood circulation to affect some aspect of metabolism.

HPA axis. An abbreviated form for hypothalamic–pituitary–adrenal axis, a chemical pathway starting with the release of corticotropin-releasing factor (CRF) from the hypothalamus causing a series of chemical reactions to prepare the body for the fight-or-flight response.

Hyperstress. An excessive level of stress that overloads the system.

Hypertension. A technical term for increased arterial blood pressure above the normal range in a particular age group.

Hypochondriac. A person with an exaggerated fear of disease.

Hypostress. An insufficient level of stress to keep the body tuned and ready for action.

Hypothalamus. A part of the diencephalon that processes emotions and activates the fight-or-flight response.

"I" message. A verbal message in which the individual uses the pronoun "I" to own and express his or her thoughts and feelings assertively without attacking or negating what the other person might be feeling.

Id. One of the three divisions of one's personality in psychoanalytic theory that consists of instinctual drives for selfish pleasure.

Imagery. Thought process of creating, or recreating, scenes, objects or events and their emotional reactions by involving all the senses.

Immune system. The system that provides defense against foreign invaders.

Incessant worrying. A chronic and persistent focus on things that can go wrong, on disasters that may befall you, and on even minor disruptions in your routine that may require greater flexibility and adaption.

Inclusive meditation. A form of meditation that involves opening the mind to all kinds of thoughts without getting bogged down in any one of them.

Insulin.   A hormone secreted from the pancreas when blood glucose levels rise to promote the storage of glucose throughout the body.

Internal environment.   Bernard's metaphor of how stored energy is concentrated to provide motion and energy.

Internal locus of control.   A belief that an individual can direct self-behavior to achieve desired goals.

Internalized language.   A style of interpretation that focuses on the self as the source of the problem.

Irrational beliefs (B).   The second stage in the ABC theory of emotions, comprising negative and distorted thoughts based on false evidence.

Learned helplessness.   The way in which humans and animals act when exposed to unavoidable situations that are harmful, disdainful, or painful with the effect that learning will be prevented or retarded in subsequent situations where escape or avoidance is possible.

Learned optimism.   A consistent pattern of viewing aversive events as unstable, specific, and (to a lesser degree) external.

Libido.   The energy of the sexual instinct in all its expressions; based on Freud.

Limbic system.   A region of the brain between the neocortex and the brainstem, which regulates emotions and controls certain forms of memory.

Long-term stress.   A stress episode that occurs when the system is turned on at high volume and remains that way even when the initial danger has passed.

Looking for exceptions.   Part of the strategic therapy that examines when the problem is absent and how the client feels about it.

Low frustration tolerance.   A mental attribute that results in agony and agitation over temporary setbacks or inconveniences.

Mantra.   A syllable, word, or phrase that is repeated audibly or silently for the purpose of concentration in meditation.

Meditation.   A state of intense concentration and inner stillness; a mental procedure to achieve this type of mental state.

Metabolic syndrome.   A constellation of symptoms including hypertension, obesity, hyperglycemia, and insulin resistance.

Mindfulness.   A state of clear objective awareness of what is going on at the moment.

Mindfulness-based stress reduction (MBSR).   An effective stress relief program developed by Jon Kabat-Zinn. Consists of three different techniques: (1) body scan, (2) sitting meditation, and (3) Hatha yoga.

Mindsets.   Implicit theories people hold about their traits such as intelligence and personality that have significant impact on the quality of their lives.

Mineralocorticoids.   Adrenal cortical steroid hormones that regulate mineral metabolism and fluid balance.

Mnemonic devices.   Techniques or methods used to assist memory that involve forming a link or association between the new information to be remembered and information previously acquired.

Musculoskeletal system.   Makes up the framework of the body and allows us to move when our muscles contract.

MyPlate.   Current USDA food guide that identifies five food groups and their meal proportions including fruits, vegetable, grains, protein, and dairy and whose simple image reminds Americans to build a healthy plate at meal times.

Musterbation.   An irrational belief where the individual holds a rigid line of thinking without considering alternatives.

Negative problem orientation.   A pessimistic mind state assumed by those who approach situations with a degree of passivity and trepidation.

Nervous system.   Collective name for all of the neurons in the body.

Neustress.   A kind of harmless stress.

Norepinephrine.   A catecholamine secreted by the adrenal medulla to produce immediate physical readiness to stress, including increased heart rate and blood pressure.

Operant conditioning.   A process in which behavioral change can be produced by means of rewarding desired behavior or punishing undesired behavior.

Oral stage.   Freud's first stage of psychosexual development, lasting from birth to approximately eight months of age. This stage is characterized by preoccupation with the immediate gratification of desires primarily accomplished through the mouth, such as sucking and biting.

Panic disorder.   An insidious and severe form of anxiety in which a person suddenly feels a rush of dread, fear, and terror, often without warning.

Parasympathetic nervous system.   Part of the autonomic nervous system that calms the body and reduces energy expenditure.

Perceptual and cognitive barriers.   Ways in which a person interprets and evaluates a situation that may hinder the resolution of a problem.

Peripheral nervous system.   The part of the nervous system that lies outside the brain and the spinal cord and contains many sensory and motor pathways as well as ganglia that regulate various organ systems.

Personalization.   A way of behaving in which individuals exaggerate their belief that events in the world apply only to them; their sense of being special.

Phobias.   Excessive, unrealistic, uncontrollable fears of and anxious reactions to specific situations or stimuli.

Physical activity.   Any bodily movement involving contractions of skeletal muscles above resting levels.

Physical exercise.   Structured and planned physical activity for the sake of maintaining/improving physical fitness.

Physical fitness.   A set of measurable health and skill-related attributes that include cardiorespiratory fitness, muscular strength and endurance, body composition and flexibility, balance, agility, reaction time and power.

Physical hunger.   A compelling need for food which is characterized by such physical symptoms as gurgling stomach, lightheadedness, shaky hands, and wobbly legs.

Pituitary gland.   The endocrine gland under the hypothalamus that secretes hormones that control other glands.

Positive problem orientation.   The optimistic mind state assumed by individuals who believe that daily problems are not only normal and may even be beneficial but, given sufficient time and effort, can be reasonably resolved.

Positive psychology.   An emerging new science that studies positive experiences, positive character traits, and the institutions that help cultivate them.

Posttraumatic stress disorder.   Psychiatric disorder that can result from experiencing or witnessing trauma such as combat, rape, accidents, or terrorism.

Prefrontal lobe.   The area in the brain located at the front of each cerebral hemisphere.

Primary appraisal.   One aspect of the cognitive appraisal wherein the individual estimates the degree to which a particular situation is a threat to his/her personal goal attainment.

Prisoner's dilemma.   A game used in social-psychological studies in which participants must choose between competition and cooperation.

Progressive muscle relaxation.   A physical relaxation technique in which the practitioner contracts and relaxes muscle groups throughout the body.

Psychoneuroimmunoendocrinology.   The study of the relation of the nervous system, immune system, endocrine system, and psychological factors.

Psychoneuroimmunology.   The study of the interactions between the immune system, the nervous system, and behavior.

Psychosocial hypothesis.   An explanation of exercise benefits suggesting that exercise alters the perceptions people have about themselves and their abilities.

Puberty.   A normal growth process that begins in early adolescence, lasts two to four years, and leads to sexual and physical maturity.

Qi.   A fundamental concept of traditional Chinese culture that is believed to be part of everything that exists, as in "life force" or "spiritual energy."

Quantity principle.   A concept in problem solving suggesting that the more ideas that are generated, the more likely a reasonable solution will be found.

Rapid Eye Movement (REM) Sleep.   A stage of sleep characterized by rapid conjugate eye movements and dreaming in which some areas of the brain produce higher levels of brain function than normal waking hours.

Rational emotive behavior therapy (REBT).   A brief psychotherapeutic treatment that relies on persuasion and reason.

Rationalization.   A defensive behavior characterized by justifying yourself or exonerating yourself of guilt in situations in which your behavior does not match your stated intentions.

Reflection of content.   A therapist's response to a client's comment in which the therapist paraphrases the feeling implied in the statement.

Reflection of feeling.   A therapist's response to a client's comment in which the therapist attempts to indicate both an understanding of what the client is saying and how the client feels.

Reframing.   A technique of redefining problems so as to make them more amenable to resolutions.

Regression.   A defensive mechanism where an individual resorts to an earlier or less mature pattern of coping behaviors under stress.

Relaxation response.   The physiological state achieved when one is relaxed.

Repressed memories.   Traumatic memories or recollections of trauma that are psychological pushed into the unconscious.

Repression.   An unconscious process of blocking out disturbing thoughts.

Repressive personalities.   People who feel particularly vulnerable to life's stressors and try to organize their lives in such a way as to prevent or minimize things that might upset their fragile world.

Reproductive system.   Structures of the body dedicated to the production of offspring.

Resilience.   The ability to adapt well when confronted with adversity, trauma, and inordinate amounts of stress in life.

Respiratory system.   The system that provides oxygen and nourishment to the body's cells.

Response.   Overt or covert reaction of the body or any part of the body as the result of being stimulated.

Response–stimulus learning.   A learning process in which the result of a behavioral change is rewarded and therefore reinforced.

Restrictive meditation.   A form of meditation wherein the practitioner focuses his or her consciousness on a single symbol, object, or thought to prevent all the other distracting thoughts from entering the conscious mind.

Saturated fatty acids.   Fats that consist of triglycerides containing only saturated fatty acid. These fats are solid at room temperature.

Secondary appraisal.   One aspect of the cognitive appraisal wherein the individual estimates the degree to which he/she has the resources to cope with the demands posed by a situation.

Secondary gains.   Hidden but self-reinforcing payoffs that make it difficult to change a maladaptive behavior.

Self-defeating thoughts.   Ideas or beliefs that often produce negative emotions and behaviors.

Self-efficacy.   This is a person's belief in his or her ability to produce a desired result or action.

Self-organization.   A process in which the internal organization of an open and dynamic system changes automatically without being guided or managed by an external script.

Self-talk.   Internal dialogue with oneself that may be negative or positive.

Sense of coherence.   Recognition by a person considered resilient and well-adjusted of being part of society, of having control over one's own destiny, and knowing who he or she is. A global orientation of confidence that life is meaningful, and of being capable of meeting worthwhile challenge.

Short-term stress.   A stress episode that is activated by a sudden threat or danger and is terminated shortly.

Signature strengths.   Prominent character strengths individuals possess that can be easily identified.

Skin.   Occupies about 3,000 square inches of body surface and consists of the epidermis and dermis. Some major functions of the skin are protection, sensory reception, and Vitamin D synthesis.

Slow-wave sleep.   A stage of deep sleep characterized by slow, synchronous delta waves, helpful to restoration of energy and elimination of feelings of fatigue.

Social problem solving. A process of solving problems in the real world and finding effective coping responses for problematic life situations.

Socioeconomic status (SES). An aggregate measure as well as a hierarchical grouping of people based on education, occupation, wealth, and place of residence.

Somatic nervous system. The branch of the vertebrate peripheral nervous system that carries voluntary motor commands to the skeletal muscles of the torso and limbs.

Somatization. Manifestation of stress in the form of physical complaints.

Stimulus. Any event or situation, internal or external, real or imaginary, that elicits a response from the organism.

Stimulus–response learning. A learning process in which a behavioral change is reinforced by a stimulus.

Stress. A psychological and physiological reaction to a perceived threat that requires some action or resolution operating on cognitive, behavioral, and biological levels and results in significant negative health effects when sustained.

Stress hormone. A hormone, such as cortisol, that is activated by stress.

Stress inoculation. The process of gradually desensitizing a person to the stressors feared the most in such a way that they begin to lose their power to upset the person.

Stressors. External events (conflicts, disasters, challenges, traumas) as well as internal events (worries, fears, irrational beliefs) that result in perceived pressure.

Superego. The ethical component of one's personality, representing the conscience of the individual based on internalized societal standards, personal standards of moral right and wrong, including his or her aims and aspirations.

Surface message. The meaning of a communicated statement that is concrete and obvious.

Sympathetic nervous system. Part of the autonomic nervous system that increases the bodily metabolism and increases energy expenditure.

Systematic desensitization. A process of reducing anxiety by first imagining or encountering an anxiety-provoking stimulus in a progressive manner.

Tai chi. A traditional Chinese exercise system that combines martial arts movements with qi circulation, breathing, and stretching exercises.

Tend-and-befriend. An alternative theory to explain how females cope with stress; proposes that when females are under stressful conditions they seek social contact and support from others.

Thalamus. A part of the diencephalon through which all of the sensory systems project in order to reach the neocortex, the so-called "sensory relay center."

Theory of multiple intelligences. A theory proposed by H. Gardner who identified seven types of intelligence: spatial, logical-mathematical, linguistic-verbal, bodily-kinesthetic, musical, interpersonal, and intrapersonal.

Thought journal. A method of self-monitoring in which the individual records a stress situation, his/her feelings associated with the situation, and the interpretations about the situation.

Thought-stopping. A simple Western technique employed for people stuck in obsessive thinking patterns by using a rubber band worn on a wrist.

Thyroid gland. The endocrine gland in the neck that secretes the hormone thyroxin.

Time management. A process of optimizing the use of time for the purpose of achieving one's worthwhile goals.

Tit for tat. The most effective strategy in the prisoner's dilemma game in which one starts out with a trusting, cooperative spirit, but if the other person does not respond in a similar manner, then one won't let oneself be betrayed a second time.

Toughening factor. A theory that proposes using controlled levels of incremental stress as a means to improve capacity for dealing with life's challenges.

Toxic thoughts. Negative thoughts that prevent individuals from achieving peace of mind and cause unnecessary physiological arousal.

Trans fatty acids. A type of unsaturated fat formed as a side-effect of hydrogenation of plant oils and also found in dairy and meat products; believed to be linked to chronic health conditions.

Transactional model of stress. A psychological model that suggests that stress occurs when (a) an individual experiences a challenging life situation, (b) the person appraises the demand of the situation and his/her resources to deal with the demands, and (c) a strategy for coping is initiated.

Transcendental meditation. A technique for achieving a transcendental state of consciousness through the use of a Sanskrit word as an object of intense concentration.

Type A. A personality pattern that predisposes individuals to coronary heart disease and is characterized by hostility, aggression, and competitiveness.

Variety principle. A concept in problem solving that encourages people to think of a wide range of possible solutions across various strategies or classes of approaches instead of focusing on only one or two narrow ideas.

Visualization. An ability to create or the process of creating a visual image in the mind; often used as a technique of motivation.

Well-being therapy (WBT). A therapeutic approach with the purpose of building self-acceptance, personal growth, meaning in life, environmental mastery, and social well-being and can be used for treating patients with affective disorders in conjunction with drug therapy or psychotherapy.

Workaholism. An addiction to overwork that interferes with other aspects of life.

Worry. Persistent attention to matters that are actually beyond what you can manage on your own.

Yin and yang. The two complementary and opposing forces based on Chinese Taoist philosophy, with *yin* representing negative, passive, and feminine and *yang* standing for positive, active, and masculine.

Yoga. A set of relaxation exercises based on a school of Hindu philosophy designed to seek union of the mind, body, and spirit.

Index

Note: f = figure; t = table; **boldfaced** page numbers denote definitions